Quaternary Coastlines
and Marine Archaeology

Quaternary Coastlines and Marine Archaeology:

Towards the prehistory of land bridges and continental shelves

Edited by

P. M. MASTERS *Scripps Institution of Oceanography, La Jolla, USA*

N. C. FLEMMING *Institute of Oceanographic Sciences, Godalming, UK*

1983

 ACADEMIC PRESS

A Subsidiary of Harcourt Brace Jovanovich, Publishers

London   New York
Paris   San Diego   San Francisco
São Paulo   Sydney   Tokyo   Toronto

ACADEMIC PRESS INC. (LONDON) LTD.
24/28 Oval Road
London NW1

United States Edition published by
ACADEMIC PRESS INC.
111 Fifth Avenue
New York, New York 10003

British Library Cataloguing in Publication Data
Quaternary coastlines and marine archaeology.
   1. Geology, Stratigraphic—Quaternary—Congresses
   2. Man—Migrations—Congresses
   I. Masters, P.M.   II. Flemming, N.C.
   304.8   GF101

   ISBN 0-12-479250-2

Printed in Great Britain

CONTRIBUTORS TO THIS VOLUME
AND PARTICIPANTS IN THE SYMPOSIUM

An asterisk indicates contributor. An asterisk in brackets indicates that the contributor or second author did not attend the Symposium.

ADOVASIO, J.M.(*) University of Pittsburgh, Pittsburgh, PA 15261, USA.

AXFORD, L. MICHAEL Department of Anthropology, Mesa College, 7250 Mesa College Drive, San Diego, CA 92111, USA.

BADA, J.* Scripps Institution of Oceanography, A-012, La Jolla, CA 92093, USA.

BAILEY, G.N.* Faculty of Archaeology and Anthropology, Cambridge University, Downing Street, Cambridge CB2 3DZ, England.

BARHAM, A.J.(*) Department of Geography, University College, Gower Street, London WC1, England.

BELKNAP, D.F.(*) Department of Marine Science, University of South Florida, 830 First Street South, St Petersburg, FL 33701, USA.

BERGER, R.* Institute of Geophysics, Radiocarbon Laboratory, UCLA, Los Angeles, CA 96024, USA.

BIRDSELL, J.* Emeritus Professor of Oceanography, University of California Los Angeles, Los Angeles, CA 90024, USA.

BLOOM, A. Department of Geological Sciences, Kimball Hall, Cornell University, Ithaca, NY 14850, USA.

BOEHM, T. 3708 Watseka Avenue, Los Angeles, CA 90034, USA.

BRYAN, A.L. Department of Anthropology, University of Alberta, Edmonton, Canada T6G 2H4.

BUDINGER, F.E. Calico Early Man Site, P.O. Box 535, Yermo, CA 92398, USA.

BULL, C.S. 1094 Cudahy Place, Suite 204, San Diego, CA 92110, USA.

CARTER, G.F. Department of Geography, Texas A & M University, College Station, TX 77843, USA.

CHAFFIN-LOHSE, M. Department of Anthropology, Rice University, Houston, TX 77001, USA.

CURRAY, J. Scripps Institution of Oceanography, La Jolla, CA 92093, USA.

DIKOV, N.N.(*) NE Interdisciplinary Research Institute, Academy of Sciences, 16 Portovaya, Magadan 685013, USSR.

FAIRBRIDGE, R.W. Department of Geology, Schermerhorn Hall, Columbia University, New York, NY 10027, USA.

FLEMMING, N.C.* Institute of Oceanographic Sciences, Wormley, Godalming, Surrey, England.

FLOYD, R.J. 217 Thibodeany Drive, Lafayette, LA 70503, USA.

GAYMAN, W. P.O. Box 7246, San Diego, CA 92107, USA.

GEDDES, D.(*) E.H.E.S.S. Centre d'Anthropologie des Soc. Rurales, 56 Rue du Taur, 31000 Toulouse, France.

GIFFORD, J.* Department of Geography and Archaeometry, University of Minnesota, Duluth, MN 55812, USA.

GREBMEIER, J.M. Department of Oceanography, University of Washington, Seattle, WA 98195, USA.

HARRIS, D.R.* Department of Human Environment, Institute of Archaeology, University of London, 31-34 Gordon Square, London WC1, England.

HOPKINS, D.M.* US Geological Survey, Menlo Park, CA 94025, USA.

INMAN, D.L.* Scripps Institution of Oceanography, A-009, La Jolla, CA 92093, USA.

IRVING, W.N. Department of Anthropology, University of Toronto, Ontario, Canada.

JOHNSON, D.* Geography Department, University of Illinois, Urbana, IL 61801, USA.

JONES, E.M. 4266 Ridgeway, Los Alamos, NM 87545, USA.

JONES, R. Department of Prehistory, Research School of Pacific Studies, Australian National University, P.O. Box 4, Canberra, ACT, 2600 Australia.

KAYAN, I. (*) Department of Geology, 101 Penny Hall, University of Delaware, Newark, DE 19811, USA.

KELLY, K. Scripps Institution of Oceanography, La Jolla, CA 92093, USA.

KRAFT, J.C.* Department of Geology, 101 Penny Hall, University of Delaware, Newark, DE 19811, USA.

LARSSON, L.(*) Institute for Archaeology, University of Lund, 223 50 Lund, Sweden.

LAUTRIDOU, J.P.(*) Centre de Geomorphologie du CNRS, rue des Tilleuls, 14000 Caen, France.

MacGREGOR-HANIFAN, J. Pacific OCS Office, Bureau of Land Management, 1340 W. 6th Street, Los Angeles, CA 90017, USA.

MARCUS, L.F.* Department of Biology, Queen's College, City University of New York, Flushing. NY 11367, USA.

MASTERS, P.M.* Marine Archaeology A-012, Scripps Institution of Oceanography, La Jolla, CA 92093, USA.

McCASLIN, D. Department of History, Marine Science Institute, UC Santa Barbara, Santa Barbara, CA 93106, USA.

McMANUS, D.* Department of Oceanography, University of Washington, Seattle, WA 98195, USA.

MEIGHAN, C.* Department of Anthropology, University of California Los Angeles, CA 90024, USA.

MOORE, D. Scripps Institution of Oceanography, La Jolla, CA 92093, USA.

MORZADEC-KERFOURN, M.T.(*) Institut de Géologie et Equipe du CNRS Anthropologie, 35042 Rennes Cedex, France.

NEWMAN, W.S.* Department of Earth and Environmental Sciences, Queen's College, City University of New York, Flushing, NY 11367, USA.

NORWOOD, R. Recon, 1094 Cudahy Place, No 204, San Diego, CA 92110, USA.

ORZECH, J.K. Scripps Institution of Oceanography, A-008, La Jolla, CA 92093, USA.

PARDI, R.R. Radiocarbon Laboratory, City University of New York, Flushing, NY 11367, USA.

PARKER, C.J. California State University Long Beach, 9872 Leite Drive, Huntingdon Beach, CA 92646, USA.

PRIGENT, D.* Service Archéologie, Département Maine-et-Loire, 106 rue de Frémur, 4900 Angers, France.

RABAN, A.* Department for History of Maritime Civilisations, University of Haifa, Mount Carmel, Haifa, Israel.

REEVES, B.O.K.ˣ Department of archaeology, University of Calgary, 2500 University Drive NW, Calgary, Alberta, Canada.

RONEN, A.* University of Haifa, Mount Carmel, Haifa, Israel.

RUPPE, R. Department of Anthropology, Arizona State University, Tempe. AZ 85287, USA.

SMITH, D.D. 8384 Sugarman Drive, La Jolla, CA 92037, USA.

SOMERVILLE, R.C.J. Scripps Institution of Oceanography, La Jolla, CA 92093, USA.

SORDINAS, A.(*) Department of Anthropology, Memphis State University, Memphis, TN 38152, USA.

STEWART, J. Scripps Institution of Oceanography, La Jolla, CA 92093, USA.

STRIGHT, M. US Department of the Interior, New Orleans Outer Continental Shelf Office, Hale Boggs Federal Building, Suite 841, 500 Camp Street, New Orleans, LA 70130, USA.

TINDALE, N.B.* 2314 Harvard Street, Palo Alto, CA 94306, USA.

TUOHY, D.R. Nevada State Museum, Capital Complex, Carson City, NV 89710, USA.

TYSON, R. San Diego Museum of Man, San Diego, CA, USA.

VAN ANDEL, T.H. Department of Geology, Stanford University, Stanford, CA 94305, USA.
WATTERS, D.R. Marine Policy and the Ocean Management Program, Woods Hole Oceanographic Institution, Woods Hole, MA 02543, USA.
WILLIAMS, S.J. Coastal Engineering Research Center, Kingman Building, Fort Belvoir, VA 22060, USA.
WRESCHNER, E. (*) University of Haifa, Mount Carmel, Haifa, Israel.

PREFACE

The papers in this volume were presented at a Symposium held 26-29 October 1981 at Scripps Institution of Oceanography. The purpose of the Symposium was to bring together scholars of oceanography, archaeology, geology and anthropology to examine intensively the factors determining human movements on the continental shelves during glacial low sea levels, and the submarine data on Quaternary migration bridges between continents and between continents and islands. The Symposium was sponsored by the Quaternary Shorelines Commission of the International Union for Quaternary Research, and the Scientific Committee of the World Confederation of Underwater Activities, and was funded by Scripps Institution of Oceanography.

Recent advances in climatology, oceanography, plate tectonics and estimates of global sea level changes provide a basis for approximate reconstruction of palaeocoastlines and land bridges. The coastal and nearshore conditions at times of low sea level influence human activities in the littoral zone as well as the potential ease of sea crossings over critical straits and channels. However, at present the resolution of the data in time and space is seldom sufficient to make accurate reconstructions of coastal environments. Uncertainties of eustatic sea level, vertical tectonic movements, the timing of erosion and deposition, and climatic data can introduce errors. Nevertheless, it is possible to make general models of the land bridges and submerged shorelines, whilst detailed site investigations in certain areas have provided data which enable the models to be checked, improved, or rejected.

The fact that the continental shelves were exposed to subaerial conditions and coastal processes during periods of glacial low sea level has been known since the beginning of the twentieth century. Archaeological evidence from dredged tools and examination of coastal caves demonstrated the certainty of human activities on the continental shelves, and these observations were published in the 1920s and 1930s with reference to the North Sea and the

Mediterranean coasts of France and Italy. It was apparent that the glacial low sea levels provided the maximum development of land bridges for human and faunal crossings between Asia and Australia, and from Siberia to the Americas, as well as to offshore islands such as Britain, Cyprus, Ceylon, the Caribbean archipelago, and Japan.

The inevitability of human activities and population movements on the continental shelves during periods of low sea level creates the central questions of our Symposium. The first questions concern the migration of human groups into previously uninhabited continents and islands: the timing, the routes, the stimuli, and the technologies required to make the journeys. The second is the origin and persistence of coastal zone economies. Are the known marine-oriented economies of the Holocene archaeological record solely phenomena of the last phase of the Flandrian transgression? or are they, like the Paleolithic-Mesolithic-Neolithic transition in Europe, representative of a much older, more continuous tradition, evidence of which is now lost to sight on the continental shelves? Related to both of the preceding questions is the larger unknown: what was happening environmentally on the shelves during the glacial periods and during the transgressions? What were the subaerial and climatic characteristics of the exposed shelves? What plant and animal communities existed on them? How did these communities and, presumably, the associated human populations adapt to fluctuating sea levels, subaerial space, and climates during the Quaternary? Were there periods when the shelves were wholly inhospitable to plant and animal life? Did the changing conditions of the shelves and land bridges stimulate population movements, even the crossing of sea straits and channels?

Until the last decade it would have been impractical to seek field evidence for the solution of these problems. The population density on the exposed continental shelf was certainly low, though not necessarily lower than that on the adjacent continents, and the relics left by prehistoric cultures would be scanty and insubstantial. Marine transgression, the risk of erosion, or burial under sand or mud would further reduce the chances of discovering cultural materials. Even if the artifacts of Palaeolithic or Neolithic cultures did survive on the sea floor, how could one possibly find them, survey them, or excavate them? The area to be searched, the smallness of the target, and the detailed scrutiny necessary seem to preclude a start on the grounds of cost, effort, and the probability of failure.

The invention in the 1940s of the self-contained underwater breathing apparatus (SCUBA) has made possible detailed exploration of the shallow, nearshore areas of the continental shelves for scientific, commercial, and recreational purposes. Marine technology laboratories have engineered sophisticated equipment for visualizing the deep shelf and features beneath the sea floor. In addition, a range of small mechanical and electronic devices have been developed to permit reasonably accurate position fixing, search patterns, data recording, and communications. Thus, the technological capability exists for carrying out field work on the continental shelves. Nevertheless, the initial task of searching for and finding submerged terrestrial sites will remain of monumental difficulty unless an economic search strategy can be developed.

During the 1960s and 1970s marine archaeology was popularized by reports of the excavation of Spanish treasure ships and Greek and Roman cargo ships carrying thousands of amphorae. Less well publicized were the activities of diving arachaeologists who discovered and surveyed several hundred submerged or partially submerged Greek and Roman harbours and coastal towns on the shores of the Mediterranean. The popular interest in marine archaeology, combined with the enormous number of people diving, resulted in the gradual recognition of older and older submerged occupation sites. Most of the original finds were by chance, but informed amateurs sometimes reported their finds to local museums or universities, and the surveys and excavations became more systematic and professional. Some discoveries, such as that of the Bronze Age material in the Lagoon of Thau, France, and the Bronze Age town off the coast of the island of Pavlo Petri, Greece, were made as the result of deliberate and carefully planned searches.

Although the total number of known prehistoric submarine sites more than 4000 years old is still small, they have been charted in a wide variety of submerged settings around the world. The papers in this volume attempt to take stock of the situation in 1981-82. The convenors of the present Symposium start with the thesis that it is now possible to draw tentative conclusions about the potential for survival of prehistoric sites following marine trangression and to propose effective methods for search and discovery. The present body of knowledge and experience, known until now to small groups of people scattered throughout many countries, is sufficient to comprise a new, coherent field of scientific endeavour: the prehistory of the continental shelves.

The plan of this volume is first to lay a foundation from the physical sciences of coastal oceanography, geology, and climatology. Specifically oriented to questions of submerged sites, the papers of Section 1 review and synthesize knowledge of sea level chronology, coastal forms, and dynamics of nearshore waves, currents and sediments. A background for the following section is developed by the summary of previously reported underwater lithic and Bronze Age sites, and their circumstances of preservation.

Section 2 deals with unpublished or little known field studies of prehistoric sites now submerged on nearshore shelves. One of the most significant achievements of the Symposium and this volume is the documentation of sites dating from the early to mid-Holocene and surviving on the submerged shelves. Field reports come from the Atlantic coast of France, a strait between Denmark and Sweden, the southern California coast, and coasts throughout the Mediterranean. The variety of preservational environments and types of sites provide the beginnings of a systematic understanding of site location on the shelves.

The land bridges as migration corridors of the late Quaternary are discussed in Sections 3 and 4. Beringia, its plant/animal relations, its climate, its final sequence of transgression, and its potential human entrants are examined in Section 3. Also in this section is a discussion of the faunal migrations across late Quaternary water gaps onto the California borderland islands. The other major human migrational movement of the Upper Pleistocene, the populating of Greater Australia, is addressed in Section 4. One of the possible routes, that through Torres Strait, is treated in detail. The earliest potential immigrants and the spatial, temporal distribution of coastal shell midden sites are also examined.

In the final chapter, the editors have synthesized a prospectus of what comes next in this new field of marine archaeology. Many concepts arose in the paper presentations and in the subsequent open discussions which are incorporated into this chapter: the evaluation of worthwhile effort in continental shelf archaeology, the effective use of sea level data, a synopsis of submerged site information, what influences site survival, the prediction of sites on the deeper shelves, the ecology and physiography of palaeocoastlines. Finally, we have tried to estimate the most fruitful paths for future research involving the prehistory of the continental shelves.

March 1983   Patricia M. Masters
                                              Nicholas C. Flemming

CONTENTS

SECTION 4: AUSTRALIA AND THE OLD WORLD

APPLICATION OF COASTAL DYNAMICS TO THE RECONSTRUCTION OF PALEOCOASTLINES IN THE VICINITY OF LA JOLLA, CALIFORNIA

Douglas L. Inman

Center for Coastal Studies
Scripps Institution of Oceanography
University of California
La Jolla, California 92093, USA

ABSTRACT

Paleocoastlines and Holocene environments coinciding with human habitation are reconstructed for the coastal area near La Jolla, California. The reconstruction considers worldwide geologic phenomena of importance to this coastal area, but is based primarily on the application of principles of coastal dynamics to the known geology of the area. It is shown that the type and amount of sediment brought to the coast is controlled by sea level changes through their effect on stream erosion and transport capacity. Valley cutting and transport of coarse material are enhanced by sea level lowering. Rapid sea level rise transforms stream-cut valleys into deep embayments that trap stream-supplied sediment and limit the sediment in the littoral cell to that contained within the small coastal segments between embayments. Along mountainous coasts this is a time of terrace formation, rocky coastlines, and cobble beaches. Sand beaches develop during sea level still-stands following the filling of embayments and the extension of the littoral cell to include the sediment supplied by streams.

Although man undoubtedly inhabited and migrated along coasts during times of sea level changes, the probability of recovery of evidence of habitation is markedly increased for those times of still-stand when coastal terraces attained their maximum stability.

QUATERNARY COASTLINES
ISBN 0 12 479250 2

INTRODUCTION

There are two approaches to reconstructing the past: geological exploration and the application of first principles to the chronology of past events. Both approaches are necessary; one to show what events took place, i.e. the chronological/stratigraphical record, the other to interpret that record. The reconstruction of paleocoastlines requires an extrapolation back in time from a present known location and coastal environment. This reverse extrapolation involves the application of our understanding of the physics of coastal processes and of geomorphology to conditions of previous tectonics, sea level, and climate.

However, in detail, the past was never like the present. This is because an element of Markovian memory applies to geologic processes such that the present always depends in part upon previous events and conditions. The continuing movements of the earth's plates and continents gradually modify the position of land and water on time scales of millennia and longer. The present relatively long still-stand in sea level has produced coastlines that are unique in this millennium and probably for the entire Pleistocene Epoch. The sea level has been relatively high during the past 3 to 6 thousand years, accentuating the broad shelves carved into the continental platform during this and previous high stands. As a consequence, stream valleys cut at lower sea level are filling, streams near the coast are "at grade", and coastlines typically have long continuous beaches of sand.

There have been a number of studies of paleocoastlines and marshes (e.g. Gofseyeff, 1953; Gould and McFarland, 1959; Curray *et al.*, 1969; van Andel *et al.*, 1980) A classic among these is that of Alfred Redfield (1965) who reconstructed the development of Barnstable Estuary on Cape Cod, Massachusetts, from the beginning of spit formation about 4,000 years B.P. Redfield's reconstruction is based on a chronology of C-14 dates of peat and a stratigraphy obtained from the horizontal depth sequence of layered high and intertidal marsh peats as relative sea level in that area rose from -6m 4,000 years B.P. to its present level (Redfield and Rubin, 1962).

The intent of this study is to reconstruct the Holocene environments coinciding with human habitation along the coastline near La Jolla, California (see Masters, this volume). The following reconstruction of paleocoastlines is based on the application of basic principles of coastal dynamics to the known geology of the region. The procedure will be to outline worldwide geologic phenomena important to the region, establish principles of coastal dynamics applicable to this area, and then to briefly describe the local geology and geomorphology. With these in mind, a model for the paleocoastlines of the Linda Vista terrace (*ca.* 2 million years B.P); the Nestor terrace (ca. 125,000 years B.P.); the 10-fathom terrace (*ca.* 10,000 years B.P.); and, the mortar shoreline (*ca.* 6,000 years B.P.) will be described. The mortar terrace is the precursor of the present coastline which began when the sea level rise slowed to near its present rate.

WORLDWIDE GEOLOGIC SETTING

A number of worldwide phenomena have a fundamental bearing on the morphology of the world's coastlines. The most important of these are plate tectonics, climate, sea level, and the rheological response of the earth to changes in the distribution of masses of ice and water. The movement of oceanic plates and adjacent continental mass determines the type of coast and its exposure to waves and currents. While worldwide climate affects marine and terrestrial organisms and terrestrial erosion, its principal coastal impact is on sea level. Sea level determines the position of the coastline and the basic erosional datum for the continents. The earth's rheological responses, both elastic and viscous, to the shifting masses of ice and melt water further modifies the earth's geoid, producing additional regional and local relative changes in sea level.

Plate Tectonics

The recent development of a unifying global tectonic theory for the earth has provided a model for understanding worldwide tectonic processes that shape the ocean basins and the adjacent continents (e.g. Dietz, 1961; Elsasser, 1969; Bullard, 1969; Harrison and Bonatti, 1981). This tectonic theory assumes that the earth's crust is subdivided into a number of large plates and that the plates are in motion relative to one another. Some plates are oceanic in character and occupy the ocean basins; other plates are largely continental. Both types of plate are considered to be semi-rigid, elastic material riding on a viscous asthenosphere in the upper mantle of the earth (Anderson, 1975; Elsasser *et al.,* 1979; Sclater *et al.,* 1981).

Oceanic plate is created by the intrusion of molten ingenous material along spreading centers forming the mid-ocean ridges. This molten material from the mantle continues to rise and fill the cracks in the spreading center, where it solidifies and attaches itself to the moving oceanic plate (Fig. 1). The ocean floors resemble giant conveyor belts moving away from the mid-ocean ridges and towards the subduction zones, where oceanic plate is consumed as it plunges under the collision edges of continents and island arcs. This model of moving plates, with oceanic lithosphere generated at spreading centers and moving towards subduction zones, makes the understanding of young ocean basins relatively simple. In contrast, the collision edges of continents and island arcs are far more difficult to interpret.

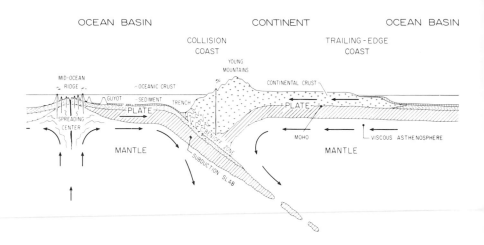

FIG. 1. *Schematic illustration of the formation of a collision coast and a trailing-edge coast. New crust is formed at the mid-ocean ridge, while crust is consumed in the subduction zone (Benioff Zone) where it plunges into the mantle. Arrows indicate direction of relative motion. Representative of section from the East Pacific Rise through South America at 35° South Latitude (from Inman and Nordstrom, 1971).*

The moving plates also have an effect on relative sea level. Coasts on the collision side of continents are mountainous and subject to tectonic uplift. Also, islands formed near the mid-ocean ridges tend to sink (about 1 cm per century) as the ocean plates move away from the relatively high mid-ocean ridges. The sinking is also associated with thermal contraction accompanying the cooling of hot oceanic crust as it spreads away from the ridges.

Since the large scale features of a coast are associated with its position relative to plate margins, plate tectonics provides a convenient basis for the first order classification of coasts, i.e., longshore dimensions of about 1,000 km (Inman and Nordstrom, 1971). Such a classification leads to the definition of three general tectonic types of coasts: 1) collision coasts, 2) trailing-edge coasts, and 3) marginal sea coasts.

Collision coasts are those that occur along a plate margin where the two plates are in collision or impinging upon each other (Fig. 1). Tectonically this is an area of crustal compression and consumption. These coasts are characterized by narrow continental shelves bordered by deep basins and ocean trenches. Submarine canyons cut across the narrow shelves and enter deep water. The shore is often rugged and backed by irregular sea cliffs and coastal mountain ranges; earthquakes and volcanism are common. The sea cliffs and mountains often contain elevated sea terraces representing former relations between the level of the sea and the land.   The western coasts of South and Central America are typical examples of collision coasts.

Trailing-edge coasts occur on the "trailing-edge" of a land mass that faces a spreading center, and are thus situated upon the stable portion of the plate and move with the plate. The eastern coasts of North and South America are examples of trailing-edge coasts (Fig. 1).   These coasts typically have broad continental shelves or passive margins, that slope into deeper water without a bordering trench.   The coastal plain is also typically wide and low-lying and usually contains lagoons and barrier islands as on the east coasts of the Americas.

Marginal sea coasts are those that develop along the shores of seas enclosed by continents and island arcs.   These coasts do not usually occur along plate margins since the spreading centers are commonly in ocean basins, while the collision edges of plates face oceans.   These coasts are typically bordered by wide shelves and shallow seas with irregular shorelines.   The coastal plains of marginal sea coasts vary in width and frequently the coast is bordered by hills and low mountains. Rivers entering the sea along marginal sea coasts often develop extensive deltas because of the reduced intensity of wave action associated with small water areas.   Typical marginal sea coasts border the South and East China Seas, the Sea of Okhotsk, and the Gulf of Mexico.

It is noted that Southern California is no longer a collision coast because the spreading center has passed the Southern California coastline and is now in the Gulf of California.   The Gulf of California spreading center is joined to the Gorda spreading center (off Eureka, California) by the San Andreas transform fault.   Yet because of the Markovian nature of geological processes, the California coast still retains most of the attributes of a collision coast - narrow shelves cut by submarine canyons, offshore residual trench, coastal mountains, and uplifted coastal terraces - all remnants from its previous tectonic history as a collision coast.

Paleoclimate and Sea Level Change

The earth's climate has varied throughout its history.   The Pleistocene Epoch (past 1-2 million years) is characterized by cycles of alternate cold and warm periods producing glacial and interglacial stages. The cyclic nature of the fluctuating climate is clearly shown by the temperature fluctuations interpreted from the changing oxygen isotope content of pelagic foraminifera from deep sea cores shown in Fig. 2.   The basic chronology for deep sea cores was established from residual magnetism in the cores which clearly show the Brunhes/Matuyama boundary of the last geomagnetic reversal 700,000 years B.P. (Shackelton and Opdyke, 1973).   Revelle (1981) points out that this composite curve of paleotemperatures shows three remarkable features: (i) the occurrence of peaks and troughs at more or less regular intervals of almost 100,000 years; (ii) the sawtooth pattern of gradual temperature drop to the most pronounced glacial events followed by a rapid warming to the maximum interglacial temperature; and (iii) the nearly equal values of temperature maxima and minima over the period of 750,000 years. The last glacial stage known as the Wisconsinan had a maximum about 18,000 years B.P. Since that time climate has warmed causing glaciers to melt and sea level to rise in what is generally known as the Flandrian transgression. We are currently in an interglacial stage and at or near a climatic optimum.

Sea Level Changes. The large volumes of water from melting glaciers caused a general worldwide sea level rise commonly referred to as "eustatic" or "true" sea level rise. Originally eustatic sea level changes were thought to be essentially uniform for all temperate latitudes well removed from the glacial rebound known to occur in areas where thick sheets of ice developed. Thus we know that the magnitude of the eustatic sea level fluctuations during the past 200,000 years ranged from about 150 meters below the present to about 10 meters above. If all of the ice presently on earth were to melt, it would raise sea level about 78 meters above present level (Barry, 1981).

We now know that the so-called eustatic sea level rise is not uniform everywhere because the earth responds as a viscoelastic medium to both the released stress of unloading due to ice-sheet melting, as well as to the applied stress of the meltwater as it fills oceans and covers continental shelves. Thus in detail, the sea level curves differ, depending upon their location and their relative proximity to the ice sheets. Details of relative sea level curves for all areas known at the time are shown in an "atlas of sea-level curves" compiled by Bloom (1977).

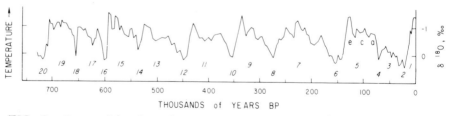

FIG. 2. *Generalized paleotemperature curve based on oxygen isotope content of pelagic foraminifera from deep sea cores (after Emiliani and Rona, 1969; Broecker and Ku, 1969; Emiliani and Shackleton, 1974; Emiliani, 1978; 1981; Chappell, 1981). Chronology from Shackleton and Opdyke (1973), and the sequence of interglacial (odd) and glacial (even) stages from Arrhenius (1952).*

Models of the earth's response to ice unloading and meltwaterloading have been constructed and show an encouraging similarity with measured sea level trends during the past 16,000 years for a wide variety of regions (Peltier, 1980; Clark *et al.*, 1978; Clark, 1980). These models assume that the earth can be treated as a viscoelastic solid whose total response to stress-strain forcing consists of an immediate elastic deformation plus a time dependent viscous flow (Peltier, 1974).

The model of Clark *et al.* is strictly rheological where the basic input is the assumed amount and rate of ice deloading and resulting meltwater loading. This model is a rational first approach. Its principal limitations are that it does not differentiate between the different portions of the earth's lithosphere as to rigidity, and neglects horizontal and vertical stresses associated with the earth's moving plates. Nor does it consider other possible climatic processes and factors that may be superimposed upon the uniform rate of ice-melt assumed in the model.

On the basis of the similarity of measured sea level curves, Bloom (1977) subdivides the earth into five arbitrary zones that generally have sea level curves with similar trends. It is interesting to note that the rheological model of Clark *et al.* (1978) gives similar geographic distributions. In fact, Clark *et al.'s* zones I-V corresponds to Bloom's zones A-E. In a gross sense, both works suggest that sea level curves can be grouped into three more general types based on the shapes of the curve:

Type 1 - areas of "net emergence" that include the glaciated coasts and those near them with submergence due to collapsing forebulge (zones A and parts of B of Bloom, 1977; zones I and parts of II of Clark *et al.*, 1978).

Type 2 - areas of "continuous submergence" that include temperate northern hemisphere coasts and much of the southern hemisphere (zone C with much of B and D, and parts of E; zone III, with much of II and IV and parts of V).

Type 3 - areas with "climatic optima" about 5,000 years B.P. These areas include parts of Brazil, Nigeria, New Zealand, Fiji Island, and possibly the South China coast.

Sea level curves for deglaciated areas (Type 1) show a net emergence due to the "glacial rebound" associated with the removal of the ice load. In areas where the ice load was removed, say 5,000 years ago, the curve may now show recent submergence due to the eustatic sea level rise. By far the most common set of sea level curves is that for continuous submergence (Type 2). These curves generally show a rapid rise in sea level of about 1 m per century from about 16,000 years B.P. to about 6,000 years B.P.

followed by a more gradual rise of about 10 cm per century from
6,000 years B.P. to the present. This type curve will be referred
to as a "generalized eustatic" sea level curve and is illustrated for
the past 18,000 years by the solid line in Fig. 3. This curve is
typical for the central and southern coasts of the United States,
Gulfs of Mexico and California, the Netherlands, the north of
France (Jelgersma, 1980), and southeastern Australia (Thom and
Chappell, 1975).

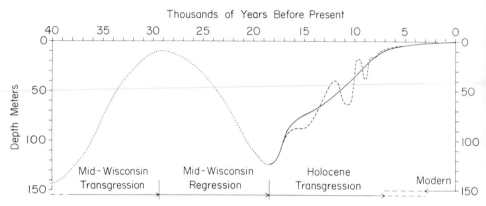

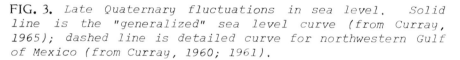

FIG. 3. *Late Quaternary fluctuations in sea level. Solid
line is the "generalized" sea level curve (from Curray,
1965); dashed line is detailed curve for northwestern Gulf
of Mexico (from Curray, 1960; 1961).*

Sea level curves having a climatic optimum in height about
5,000 years B.P. (Type 3) are similar to the "generalized eustatic"
curve in showing a rapid rise beginning about 16,000 years B.P.,
however they "overshoot" and the maximum sea-stand occurs at
5,000 years B.P. The type example for this curve is Receife,
Brazil (e.g. Fairbridge, 1976) but inspection of curves in Bloom's
(1977) atlas indicate it is not common on a worldwide basis. In an
extensive investigation of terraces in Micronesia, Curray *et al.*,
(1970) found elevated reefs on Guam, a tectonically active island,
but none in the Caroline and Marshall Islands which are stable. In
what follows, only the Type 2 sea level curve will be considered.

Plate tectonics and sea level change associated with glacial
cycles have influenced sea level curves along the California coast
in the area of our interest. Of specific interest here is the
possible correlation of the maxima of the astronomic variations
that occurred *ca.*10,000 years B.P. as described later with the
formation of the ten-fathom terrace. A number of sea level
curves show fluctuations and/or a stillstand of sea level at about
10 fathoms (18 m) below present about 10 thousand years ago
(Curray, 1960; 1961; 1965; Kenney, 1964; Nelson and Bray, 1970;

Nardin *et al.*, 1981). Inman and Veeh (1966) obtained a date ofabout 10,000 years B.P. for coral from a dead barrier reef at a depth of 10-fathoms off the island of Kauai, Hawaii, using both U/Th-230 and C-14 (Fig. 4). A stillstand and slight lowering of sea level followed by a rapid sea level rise seems to be the only explanation for this extensive, drowned, dead coral platform. The lowering killed the coral and the subsequent sea level rise was too rapid for new coral growth to become established on the dead reef platform. New coral heads that have grown under present conditions are broken off and removed by the occasional 15 m-high North Pacific swell that breaks along this coast.

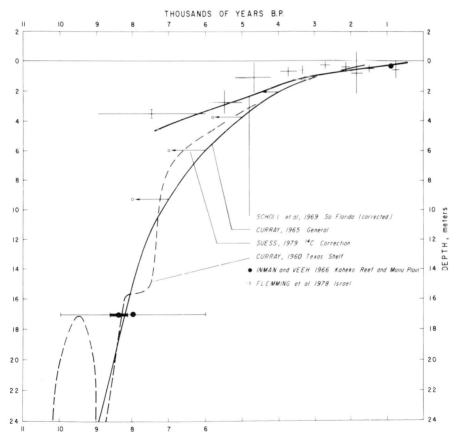

FIG. 4. *Sea level curves during the last 10,000 years for areas of continuous submergence, Type 2. The dashed curve (Curray, 1960) is assumed to apply to the coast of La Jolla, California. Arrows from the general curve (Curray, 1965) give correction from C-14 age to tree-ring age (Suess, 1979).*

The location and chronology of submarine glacial moraines along West Greenland and in Davis Strait between Greenland and Baffin Island show a definite pause in the retreat of the Greenland ice sheet between 10,200 and 11,000 years B.P. followed by a markedly increased retreat rate from 9,500 to 6,500 years B.P. (Ten Brink and Weidick, 1974). Taken together, the evidence is for a relatively rapid rise in sea level (a meter/century and more) from 16,000 to about 6,000, punctuated by a brief stillstand at about 10,000 years B.P. at which time the 10-fathom terrace was cut. Subsequent to about 6,000 years B.P. the rise has been much slower at a mean rate of about 10 cm/century (e.g. Emery, 1980). This biphasic concept of sea level rise most closely resembles the older "eustatic" sea level curves (e.g. Shepard, 1963; Curray, 1965).

Neglecting tectonic uplift, the sea level curve that best fits the Southern California region is shown by a dashed line in Fig. 4. This curve is supported locally by the data of Nardin et al. (1981) for the Santa Monica, California, shelf and by that of Curray (1969) for the Gulf of California. The generalized curve of Curray (1965) shown by the solid line is representative of the California coast and other areas of "generalized eustatic" submergence around the world (e.g. Jelgersma, 1980; Scholl and Stuiver, 1967).

In passing, it should be noted that tide gauge records show that sea level is still rising on a worldwide (eustatic) basis at a rate of about 10 cm/century (Rossiter, 1967; Hicks and Crosby, 1974; Hicks, 1981). This continuing rise in sea level increases sea cliff erosion and produces a gradual retreat of beaches on a worldwide scale.

PRINCIPLES OF COASTAL DYNAMICS

The coastal dynamics of primary interest here are: the action of waves in eroding and terracing the land and in transporting sediment along the coast; the tractive forces of streams in eroding, transporting, and depositing sediments; the effect of changing sea level on valley cutting and filling; and finally, the influence of tides and streams in the maintanance and filling of coastal lagoons. The cumulative effect and interaction of these coastal dynamic factors are considered in the context of the sources and sinks of sediment and their balance in a littoral cell.

Waves and Currents

Waves and currents that they generate are the single most important factor in the erosion, transportation, and deposition of nearshore sediments. Waves erode sea-cliffs and cut terraces. When sediment is available, they are effective in moving material along the bottom and in placing it in suspension for weaker currents to transport.

PLATE 1. *(a) Wave notch in alluvium sea cliffs south of Scripps Institution of Oceanography, La Jolla, California. (b) Collapse of the cliff following storms of January 1953.*

12   D.L. Inman

Wave-cut Terraces. In the absence of beaches, the direct force of the breaking waves erodes cliffs and the country rock the waves break upon. The rising and lowering sea levels during the Pleistocene epoch caused the seas to transgress and regress across the land eroding and depositing material as they went. Erosion is most pronounced during relative stillstands or pauses in the transgressive/regressive cycles. The signature for the sea's presence at a relative stillstand is usually in the form of a wave-cut terrace on gently sloping terrain, backed by sea cliffs when the stillstand has been long (as at present) or the terrain is steep.

Active cliff erosion still occurs during severe winter wave conditions at La Jolla Shores Beach, California, as shown by comparison of Plate 1a, b, taken before the area was protected by sea walls. The wave-cut terrace associated with the sea cliff in Plate 1 is shown in cross-section in Fig. 5. The decrease to one degree in slope of the wave-cut terrace, beginning about 200 meters seaward of the sea-cliff and at a terrace depth of 4 to 5 meters below mean sea level, probably represents the terracing that began about 6,000 years B.P. at the beginning of the slow (10-15 cm/century) rise to present sea level.

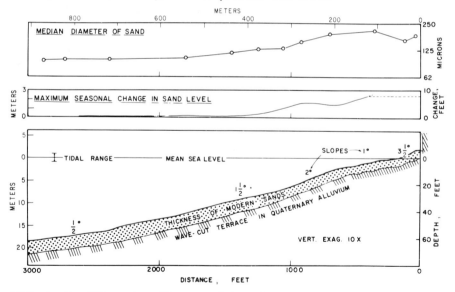

FIG. 5. *Profile of a fine sand beach at La Jolla, California, showing the median sand size, the maximum seasonal change in the level of the sand associated with winter and summer waves, and the thickness of the modern nearshore sand over the wave-cut terrace. The recent slow rise in sea level that began 6,000 years B.P. produced the gently sloping terrace beginning 200 m seaward of the cliff (from Inman and Bagnold, 1963).*

Formation of Beaches. Wherever there are waves and an adequate supply of sand or coarser material, beaches form. Even man-made fills and structures are effectively eroded and reformed by the waves. The initial and most characteristic event in the formation of a new beach from a heterogenous sediment is the sorting out of the material, with coarse material remaining on the beach and fine material being carried away. Concurrent with the sorting action, the material is rearranged, some being piled high above the water level by the run-up of the waves to form the beach berm, some moved back and forth by the swash to form the beach face, some carried back down the face to form the terrace characteristic of beach surf zones. In a relatively short time, the beach assumes a profile which is in equilibrium with the forces generating it as shown by the beach profile of modern sands over the wave-cut terrace in Fig. 5.

Longshore Transport. When waves approach at an angle to the shoreline they transport sand and cobbles along the beach. This longshore transport results from the combined effect of the breaking waves which place sand in motion and the presence of a longshore current in the surf zone which moves the sand along the beach. Theory and field measurements of waves and the resulting longshore transport of sand, show that the sand transport is directly proportional to the energy flux of the waves and the angle the breaking wave makes with the shoreline. It has been shown that the longshore transport of sediment along a sandy coast can be estimated if the budget of wave energy (that is, the wave climate) is known (e.g. Inman *et al.*, 1980). The relation for the prediction of sand transport would also apply to the transport of larger particles such as cobbles. But they would travel at a much slower rate because the stress required to move gravel or cobbles increases in direct proportion to the diameter of the particle.

STREAM PROCESSES

The flow in a river is driven by the force of gravity acting on its fluid mass. The fluid therefore has a potential energy given by the product of this driving force and the fluid's height above some datum such as sea level. The general concept is that this potential energy is converted to kinetic energy when the fluid moves down the slope, and the friction associated with the down slope motion produces a boundary layer between the bed and the moving fluid that transmits energy and momentum between fluid and bed. If we assume "steady state energetics," there will be a balance between energy supplied to the system (by converting potential to kinetic energy) and energy lost from the system by friction, so that the rate of working (energy flux) is constant (see Fig. 6).

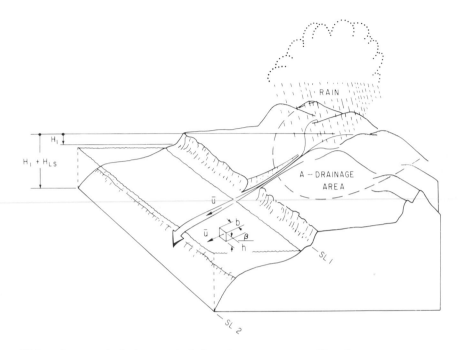

FIG. 6. *Definition sketch for stream flowing across the continental shelf during lowered sea level. Refer to text and Table 1 for definition of symbols.*

If the flow is more or less steady, then it is apparent that the force of gravity exerts a steady driving force that must be balanced by the drag that the fluid exerts on its bed. Since the river is in motion, the product of its mean velocity $\bar{u}$ with the bottom drag τ_0 constitutes an energy flux that is exerted on unit area of the bed, so that

(1) $$\omega = \tau_0 \bar{u}$$

Now the fluid possesses a potential energy per unit volume attributable to its height H above some datum such as sea level (Fig. 6). This potential energy per unit volume is given by $\rho g h$ where ρ is the fluid density and g is the acceleration of gravity. The potential energy of the fluid over unit area of its bed therefore becomes,

(2) $$E_\rho = \rho g h . H$$

where h is the depth of the river. Since the river flows down hill at the constant velocity $\bar{u}$, it loses potential energy at the constant rate $\bar{u}[\frac{\partial}{\partial x} \rho g h H]$, which becomes

(3) $\rho g h \frac{dH}{dx}. \ \bar{u} = (\rho g h \tan \beta) \ \bar{u} = \tau_0 \bar{u} = \omega$

where, in the absence of any other source of dissipative work, the bottom drag, which is a force per unit area of the bed, must be

(4) $\tau_0 = \rho g h \tan \beta$

From boundary layer theory it can be shown that the bottom drag also has the familiar form,

(5) $\tau_0 = c_f \ \rho \bar{u}^2$

where c_f is a dimensionless drag coefficient (e.g. Inman, 1963).

Therefore, the total available supply of energy to unit area of the bed is clearly the time rate of liberation of potential energy, in the form of kinetic energy. This kinetic energy in turn is dissipated in drag over the stream bed and in the transport of sediment. The mean stream velocity $\bar{u}$ can be obtained by equating relations 4,5, which gives

(6) $\bar{u} = [\ gh \tan \beta/c_f]^{\frac{1}{2}}$

where the resistance coefficient c_f varies from about 0.005 to 0.1 for natural streams (e.g. Graf, 1971).

Sediment Transport. Both theory and laboratory experiments show that the criterion for the onset of grain motion is given by

(7) $D_t = \tau_t / \ [(\rho_s - \rho) \ g \theta_t]$

where D_t is the diameter of a sediment particle that is just moved by a bottom stress τ_t, ρ_s and ρ are the densities of the solid and fluid respectively, and s is the threshold value of the Shields criterion, a dimensionless number that varies from about 0.04 to 0.06 for quartz grains in water. Streams carry sediment by rolling and dragging it along the bed (bed load) and by turbulent suspension above the bed (suspended load). Bagnold (1963, 1966) derived relations for the transport rate of sediment in streams which gives the immersed weight transport rate of sediment as proportional to the work done on unit area of bed, which in turn is equal to the energy flux of relation (3). In their simplest forms

TABLE 1

Dependance of flow and sediment transport on the local depth h, and slope β of the stream, and upon the total available potential energy per unit of rainfall A•H, over area A at height H above sea level. Other symbols are defined in text and Fig.6.

	Relation (per unit area, width)	Dependence					Total Available Energy
		ω	τ_0	$\bar{u}$	h	β	A•H
Potential Energy	$E_p = \rho g h H$			H	h		⟵————————⟶
Stream Velocity	$\bar{u} = [\,gh\,\tan\beta/c_f\,]^{\frac{1}{2}}$				$h^{0.5}$	$\beta^{0.5}$	
Bottom Stress	$\tau_0 = \rho g h\,\tan\beta = c_f\,\rho\bar{u}$			$\bar{u}^2$	h	β	
Largest Size Moved	$D_t \curvearrowright \tau_0$		τ_0	$\bar{u}^2$	h	β	
Work Done on Bed	$\omega = \tau_0\,\bar{u}$		τ_0	$\bar{u}^3$	$h^{1.5}$	$\beta^{1.5}$	
Bedload Transport	$i_b = K_b\,\omega$	ω	τ_0	$\bar{u}^3$	$h^{1.5}$	$\beta^{1.5}$	
Suspended Load Transport	$i_s = K_s\,\omega$	ω					
Eddy Viscosity	$\varepsilon \curvearrowright \bar{u}$			$\bar{u}$	$h^{0.5}$	$\beta^{0.5}$	

the relations for bedload and suspended load transport respectively are given as

(8a)
$$i_b = K_b \, \omega$$

and

(8b)
$$i_s = K_s \, \omega$$

where i is the immersed weight transport rate per unit width of stream, $\omega = \tau_0 \, \bar{u}$ is the energy flux per unit area of stream bed defined by relation (3), and the K's are dimensionless coefficients of efficiency. For fully developed bed load transport K_b has a value of about 0.3. The efficiency coefficient for suspended sediment K_s is more complicated and depends upon the settling velocity of the sediment, and the velocity and turbulence (eddy viscosity) of the stream. These dependencies of K_s are discussed in detail by Bagnold (1966). The eddy viscosity $\hat{\epsilon}$ that suspends sediment increases with increasing stream velocity $\bar{u}$, so that a larger suspended load is to be expected in a faster flow (refer to Table 1). Further, since the suspended load is generally much finer than the bed load in a stream.

Bagnold (1980), using data from flumes (Williams, 1970) and from natural rivers (e.g. Emmett, 1980) shows that the total load transport rate ($i_b + i_s$) near the bed varies as $\omega^{1.5}$ The modern conditions in five Southern California rivers, the Ventura, Santa Clara, Santa Margarita, San Luis Rey, and the San Diego Rivers, Brownlee and Taylor (1981) find that the instantaneous suspended load is proportional to the water discharge (velocity x cross-sectional area) raised to the 1.75 power.

From the above discussion, summarized in Table 1, it is apparent that the velocity of a stream increases both as the square root of its depth and slope of its bed ($h^{0.5} \, \beta^{0.5}$). The stress τ_0 of the stream on its bed increases directly with depth and slope and as the square of its velocity ($\bar{u}^2, h, \beta$). The maximum size of the material the stream can transport is proportional to the stress ($D_t \backsim \tau_0$) and therefore also increases as a function of ($\bar{u}^2, h, \beta$). The amount of material transported as bed load by a stream increases as the product of the stress and velocity ($\omega = \tau_0 \bar{u}$) and therefore varies as a function of ($\omega_0, \bar{u}^3, h^{1.5}, \beta^{1.5}$). Suspended load, because of its dependance on turbulence and eddy viscosity varies as lower powers of $\bar{u}$, h, and β. Thus in the final analysis, the transport of cobbles is critically dependent upon steep, fast flowing streams, while suspended, fine sediment can occur in slower, more gently sloping flows.

Valley Cutting. The energy for eroding and transporting sediments by stream action is supplied by rainfall on the inland area (Fig. 6). Thus the energy available from a given amount of rainfall is directly proportional to: (i) the elevation H of the land above sea level; and, (ii) the area A of the drainage basin. It follows, that streams with larger, higher water sheds (drainage areas) will erode and transport more sediment. Thus a lowering of sea level increases the relative height of the drainage area above sea level and increases the potential for the stream to erode a valley across the area previously covered by the sea (Fig. 6).

This concept can now be extended to a fluctuating sea level. Suppose, as shown in Fig. 7, that sea level changes from a high stillstand (t_1) to a low stillstand (t_2, t_3) and then rises rapidly to near its former level (t_4) and then more slowly to its former level $(t_5 = t_1)$. Since it is assumed that the stillstand leading to time t_1 was of long duration, the streams would have eroded the valley floor to near sea level. During major floods the stream would deposit a sand delta that would become a source sand and a part of the longshore transport system as waves erode the delta (Fig. 7, t_1). Thus if the waves have sufficient intensity, the delta would be intermittent as is the case along the present coast of Southern California.

When sea level falls, the stream will begin to cut a valley into the exposed shelf (t_2), and finally to incise a deeper valley into its former flood plain (t_3). The stream erosion will begin where the slope β is steepest and gradually extend both up and down stream. Initially because of the steep slopes the stream will transport coarser material, such as cobbles. The longshore transport by waves as sea level lowers will cause the cobbles to cover more or less evenly the exposed shelf. Finally, if sea level remains at a low stand for sufficient time, the stream will cut a channel which has an average slope less than the initial maximum slopes, and the sediment load will decrease in size (compare t_2 with t_3).

When sea level rises, particularly if the rise is rapid, the newly incised valleys will become bays and the streams will deposit their loads at the inland edge of the bays (t_4). During the entire time between t_3 and t_4 streams ceased to be a source of sediment for the outer coastal area, as all of their sediment load was deposited at the heads of the bays. This means that in the presence of a significant longshore transport demand by wave action, sand which is easily and rapidly transported along the coast would have been transported out of the area, leaving only cobbles and coarse material which are more resistant to longshore transport. Further, while many streams may be contributory sources to the coastal longshore transport regime during times t_1, t_2 and t_3; the sediment sources from time t_3 to t_4 are limited to shelf areas between streams, and to cliff erosion. Thus stage t_4 becomes a time of cobble beaches, with the ocean waves working and concentrating cobbles whose source was stream transport during the previous lowering of sea level. Before waves concentrate cobbles into a protective beach, waves will break directly on sea cliffs, causing relatively rapid coastal retreat.

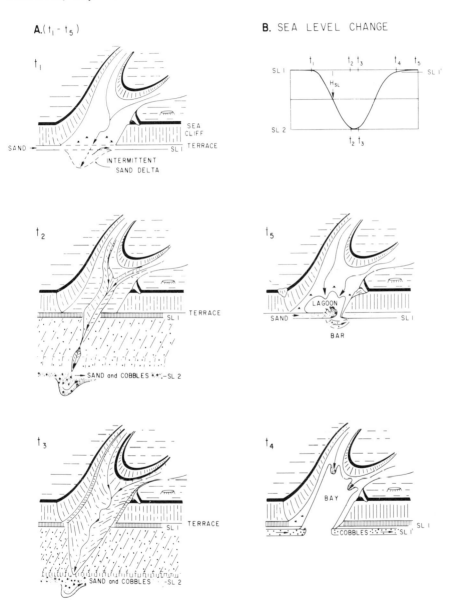

FIG. 7. (a) Schematic diagram for valley cutting during lowered sea level, and bay-trapping of sediment during sea level rise. (b) Assumed sea level curve for times t_1-t_5

Finally, as sea level gradually rises from t_4 to t_5, waves will cause spits to close off the bays forming tidal lagoons as in t_5. The streams will gradually fill in the tidal lagoons, causing the coast to return to a situation similar to that shown in t_1, and the cycle will be complete.

The analogy between the above discussion, aided by the schematic drawing of valley cutting and filling (Fig. 7), and the glacial and interglacial sea levels of the past 40,000 years (Fig. 3) should be apparent. However, if the paleotemperature curves are realistic guides (Fig. 2); the sea level fluctuations were less symmetrical and uniform. That is, sea level fell in a series of oscillations and over a relatively long time, while the rise in sea level was more rapid. This would have accentuated valley cutting because of the longer interval of depressed sea level, and subsequent occurrance of deep embayments following the rapid sea level rise. This indeed seems to be the case in our Southern California study area, as most valleys are now filled to sea level and above with stream sands, gravels and cobbles extending to depths of 60 meters and more below sea level (Ellis and Lee, 1919).

Littoral Cells and the Budget of Sediment

Application of the principle of conservation of mass to the sediments in the coastal zone has proven to be a very useful tool in evaluating the relative importance of the various possible sources of sediment and agents of transport. The procedure, sometimes referred to as the budget of sediments, consists of assessing the sedimentary contributions (credits) and losses (debits) and equating these to the net gain or loss (balance) of sediments in a given coastal segment. Studies of the sediment budget show that coasts can be divided into a series of discrete sedimentation compartments called "littoral cells." Each cell contains a complete cycle of littoral transportation and sedimentation including sources, transport paths and rates, and sediment sinks (Inman and Chamberlain, 1960; Inman and Frautschy, 1965; Inman, 1973).

Along the Southern California coast, the principal sources of sediment for each littoral cell were the rivers, which periodically supplied large quantities of sandy material to the coast. The sand is transported along the coast by waves and currents until the "river of sand" is intercepted by a submarine canyon, which diverts and channels the flow of sand into the adjacent submarine basins and depressions (Fig. 8). Each littoral cell begins with a stretch of rocky coast where the supply of sand is limited. In a down coast direction, determined by the prevailing waves, the beaches gradually become wider and the coastline straightens where the streams supply a sufficient amount of sand. Submarine canyons terminate the littoral cell by capturing the supply of sand, thus causing the next littoral cell to begin with a rocky coast devoid of beaches, etc.

The concept of littoral cells and their sedimentary budget applies to all coasts; the budgets differing principally in the nature of the sources and sinks for the sediment. Along coasts having large estuaries such as the East and Gulf coasts and portions of the Oregon coast, the river sand is trapped in the estuaries and cannot reach the open coast (Emery, 1968; Hoyt and Henry, 1971). For these coasts the sediment source is from erosion of sea cliffs and shelf sediments deposited at a lower stand of the sea, while the sinks are sand deposits that tend to close and fill the estuaries as in t_4 and t_5 of Fig.7.

The relative importance of streams v. cliff erosion as a source of sediment for the littoral cell depends upon the coastal topography, type of country rock, climate, and the rate at which material is transported away by waves. A copious beach is a very effective deterrant against cliff erosion. Thus other things being equal, there is an inverse relationship between the sediment contributions of streams and cliff erosion. If streams with moderate topographic relief flow into the ocean at the coastline, they are usually more important sources of sediment than are sea cliffs.

The apparent inconsistency between the episodic nature of the supply of coarse sediment by rivers and the concept of a littoral "river of sand" that moves frequently and with some regularity along the coast, is resolved when the proper time scales are considered. Similarly, in computing sediment budgets, the usefulness of a mean annual sediment supply and a mean annual longshore transport rate is also resolved when averaged over the appropriate time scales. The "annual mean" situation may never occur because the dynamics of the wave-induced littoral systems are more frequent than annual, while the occurrance of major coarse sediment supply by rivers is usually less frequent. The annual rates simply represent a middle ground between the longshore transport rates on beaches, which are individually calculated in mass or volume per second, and that of deposition at river mouths which is usually in volume per flood. As a rate, the latter may be more descriptively stated in terms of decades or centuries.

The concept of a budget of sediment that has differing spatial and temporal scales in supply, transport rates, and sinks, is placed in proper perspective when considered in terms of the "littoral cell". Spatially, a littoral cell includes a complete cycle of littoral transportation and deposition including all sources, transport paths and rates, and sediment sinks (e.g. Inman and Frautschy, 1965). Temporally, the budget of sediment for a littoral cell must be averaged over sufficiently long time spans to be meaningful in terms of episodic events within the cell as well as fluctuations and trends in sediment amounts in sources, paths, and sinks.

The occurrence and magnitude of river floods that bring sediment to the coast, and the changes in magnitude and trend of the littoral forcing functions (waves and winds) that transport the sediments along the coast, are both integrally related to changes in climate; as are local and regional changes in sea level. Thus the budget of sediment for a given littoral cell may be quite different from one decade, century or millennium to another, making the budget of sediments that is of interest to coastal dynamicists, planners and engineers quite different in time span, magnitude, and to some extent in the kind of source, transport path, and sink, than would be of interest to geomorphologists and archaeologists.

Sediment Yield. Climate is an important factor in determining the amount (yield) and size of sediment brought to the coast by streams. The sediment yield is influenced by vegetation, temperature, rainfall characteristics, and the topography and size of the drainage basin. The sediment yield in temperate latitudes for moderate size drainage basins (1,000 to 10,000 km^2) with moderate relief (500 to 1,500m) is about 100 to 250 tons per km^2 per year. An upper limit for a yield of coastal rivers of 3,000 tons km^{-2} yr^{-2} was found for the Eel River in Northern California (Brown and Ritter, 1971).

Surprisingly, the contribution of sand by streams in arid countries is quite high. This is because arid weathering is physical rather than chemical and thus produces sand-size material. It also inhibits the growth of vegetation that would protect the land from erosion. Therefore, in arid climates, the occasional flash floods transport large volumes of sand. The maximum sediment yield occurs from drainage basins where the mean annual precipitation is about 30 centimeters per year (Schumm, 1963). Thus Southern California which now is semi-arid produces a greater yield of sand-size material than it did formerly when the climate was wetter.

Oceanside Littoral Cell. The present Oceanside Littoral Cell extends along the coast for 84 km from the rocky headland at Dana Point to the heads of Scripps Submarine Canyon off La Jolla, California (Fig. 8). The cell has a land area of 6,300 km^2 and interior elevations generally averaging about 700 m, with maximum elevations along the granitic Peninsular Range of 1,991 m at Hot Springs Mountain and 1,871 m on Palomar Mountain. A more detailed description of the cell and its transport rates and paths is given in Inman (1976).

The cell contains a number of drainage basins, including from north to south: San Juan Creek (440 km^2); Santa Margarita River (1,930 km^2); San Luis Rey River (1,450 km^2); San Dieguito River (896 km^2); and Los Penasquitos drainage area (537 km^2). All of these have streams that are intermittent, but can carry large

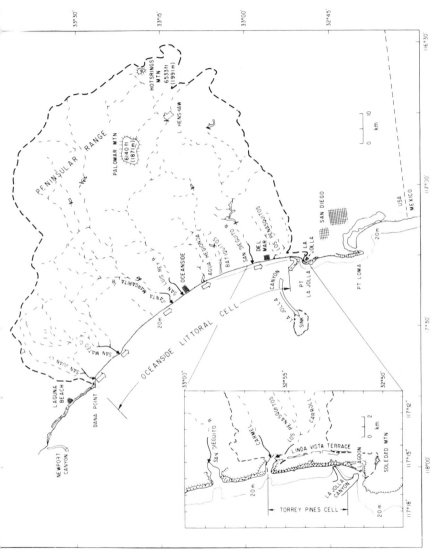

FIG. 8. The present Oceanside Littoral Cell and its upland drainage area before the streams were dammed. Sand was transported to the sea by streams, along the coast by waves, and down Scripps-La Jolla Submarine Canyon by currents. Inset shows the much smaller Torrey Pines Cell that existed ca 6,000 years B.P. when present stream valleys were embayments.

quantities of sedimentary material during floods. Estimate of the natural sediment yield from stream run off is complicated by the numerous dams built during the mid 1900s for water supply and flood control. The decrease in drainage area is shown in Fig. 8 by the dams which effectively block the transport of sediments to the ocean. From Equations (3), (4), and (8) it is observed that the transport rate is related to the stream power which is proportional to the cube of the stream velocity. Thus the decreased area of the drainage basins makes it difficult to measure what the natural contribution would have been.

The estimation of the stream contribution under pre-dam conditions can be approached in several ways. Estimates of the sediment yield can be based on the drainage basin area, considering the climate, terrain and type of country rock. The procedure for calculating sediment yield and the value for various types of drainage basins is discussed by a number of authors (e.g. Langbein and Schumm, 1958; Schumm, 1963; Garrels and Mackenzie, 1971; Inman, 1973, Table 24-3). This procedure requires that the percentage of solid particulate material vs. dissolved material in the weathering process be known, as well as the erosion rates which are functions of climate, topography and type of country rock. Generally this procedure is best suited to gross estimates over long periods of time rather than short periods such as years and decades. Nevertheless, using this approach and an estimate of 100 m^3 km^{-2} yr^{-1} yield of sand would give a total natural yield of 630,000 m^3 yr^{-1} for the entire land area of the Oceanside cell.

An alternate procedure is to determine the instantaneous sediment discharge rates at existing stream gauging stations, and sum these values over time. This would give estimates for the suspended load discharge of sediment by streams under present conditions. The instantaneous transport must be corrected for bed load, and the sum of the suspended and bed loads becomes the total load discharge rate for the stream (e.g. Colby and Hembree, 1955; Colby, 1963). The contribution of sediment from areas behind dams and for areas without gauging stations can then be estimated by considering the similarity of the areas, in terms of terrain and country rock, to those with gauging stations. Additionally, the rate of entrapment of sediment in dams can be determined by repeated survey, and the sediment yield for the drainage area behind the dam estimated.

Estimates of the instantaneous discharge rate were made from stream velocity and suspended sediment measurement at gauging stations on three of the drainage basins in the Oceanside littoral cell - Santa Margarita, San Luis Rey, and the San Dieguito Rivers (Brownlie and Taylor, 1981). Excluding the drainage area behind dams, their calculations give a yield from stream discharge of 64 m^3 km^{-2} yr^{-1}. On the other hand, accumulation rates of sediment behind the dam on Lake Henshaw, which is on the San Luis Rey River, give an annual yield of 490 m^3 km^{-2} yr^{-1} for the 531 km^2 area behind the dam. When extrapolated to the area of Oceanside cell, the stream discharge method and the dam entrapment method give total annual sediment yields of 403,000 m^3 and 3,090,000 m^3 respectively, differing by an order of magnitude. However, taking their average and assuming one-half is sand and coarser, the total discharge to the coast under natural pre-dam conditions is 870,000 m^3 of sand. Inman (1976) estimated the annual yield of sand to be 520,000 m^3 under natural conditions and 240,000 m^3 under present dammed conditions.

Wave energy and direction have been measured at various locations and times in the nearshore waters of this cell. These include a continuous series of measurements off Torrey Pines Beach in 1973 and 1974 (Pawka et al., 1976) and during the winter months of 1977 and 1978 (Inman et al., 1980). The wave measurements (e.g. Pawka et al., 1976; Inman et al., 1980) and entrapment of sand behind coastal structures show that the net transport of sand is to the south along the entire Oceanside littoral cell.

The sand is deposited in the head of Scripps Submarine Canyon where it periodically moves down the canyon into deeper water and is lost from the cell. The sand is transported down canyon by turbidity currents generated by shelf seiche during storms (Inman et al., 1976). The weight of suspended sand in the up and down canyon currents associated with the seiching (standing edge waves) leads to sustained down-canyon currents. Once started, the turbidity currents continue until the sand is all removed from the canyon head and adjacent shelf. Turbidity currents cannot occur in the absence of an abundant supply of sand, which, under the influence of gravity, is their driving force.

Chamberlain (1964) measured the rate of loss of sand deposited in the heads of Scripps Submarine Canyon by repeated survey of the sand fill in the canyon heads, which are cut into the hard sandstone country rock. From 1948 to 1960 sand deposited in the canyon head was lost into deeper water at the rate of 172,000 m^3 per year. This series of observations provides the only direct measurements of sand loss from the Oceanside littoral cell. They represent a lower limit for the actual loss, because they do not include the sand that was later shown to be lost from the adjacent shelf by the aspiration associated with strong turbidity currents (Inman et al., 1976). Thus Chamberlain's measurements probably represent only part of what must have been a total annual loss of more than 200,000 m^3 per year.

The measurements of sand loss in Scripps Canyon were made during the time when dams were limiting the sediment supply to the coast (i.e. 1948-1960), and therefore larger amounts probably were lost under pre-dam conditions. The occurrence of a sand turbidity current requires that a storm of sufficient intensity occur when an appropriate supply of sand is available. In the 1948-1960 observations it was determined that the sand loss occurred as a single event each year associated with the first intense storm. Since many storms may occur annually, this mechanism appears to have the capacity to remove as much sand as the littoral cell provides.

In summary, it appears that under natural, pre-dam conditions the yield of sediment from the drainage basins to the coast was about 1,000,000 m³ per year, of which about one-half was sand. The fine material is removed in suspension by waves and currents and deposited in the outer shelves, canyons and basins. The sand fraction was transported as beach sand along the coast and eventually lost down Scripps Submarine Canyon.

In general a plentiful supply of sand to the beaches prevented erosion of sea cliffs by waves. Therefore the recent pre-dam natural condition was probably one of a minimal cliff erosion by waves, although occasional cliff erosion during periods of intense storms has always been a characteristic of this and other collision coasts.

Paleo-Littoral Cells. The characteristics of the present Oceanside cell are the result of the relatively long sea level still-stand during the past three to four millennia, and are not necessarily like the littoral cells of previous times. For example, the small rocky Torrey Pines Littoral Cell (Fig. 8, inset) and its shoreline of cobbles that occurred *ca.* 6,000 years B.P. is in marked contrast with the large, sandy Oceanside cell of the present. It seems likely that similarly contrasting littoral cells have occurred in the past during similar phases of the sea level cycle. For example, terraces occurring in the past during high still-stands, such as the Linda Vista (*ca.* 2 million years B.P.) probably were also associated with large sandy littoral cells. On the other hand, terraces cut just after a rapid sea level rise probably were rocky and associated with small littoral cells as was the case for the Mortar shoreline formed in the Torrey Pines littoral cell *ca.* 6,000 years B.P. (Fig. 8, inset).

The development of a large sandy littoral cell from a series of small rocky cells follows a progressive sequence related to the distance between embayments and the contribution of sediment from the streams entering the embayments. Generally speaking, the larger the area of the drainage basin the sooner the stream will fill the embayments and bring sediment directly to the coast. The size of the drainage basins in the Oceanside cell decrease towards the south: the Santa Margarita River (1,930 km²), the San Luis Rey River (1,450 km²), the San Dieguito River (896 km²), and finally Los Penasquitos drainage area (537 km²). Thus the sandy beaches began in the north and progressed south. It is interesting to note that the largest tidal lagoons today are those fed by very small drainage areas such as Buena Vista Lagoon (drainage area 101 km²) and Batiquitos Lagoon (246 km²). The longshore transport of sand has closed these lagoons, except when they are opened by heavy rainfall or acts of man.

LOCAL GEOLOGY AND THE INTERPRETATION OF PALEOCOASTLINES

The Torrey Pines-La Jolla coastal area, is relatively simple in general outline. The northern, Torrey Pines block consists of a narrow continental shelf backed by a 90 meter high wave cut cliff, which is cut into nearly horizontal Eocene sandstones and siltstones. The cliff is capped by the resistant reddish sediments of the Linda Vista Terrace, which is composed of the basal sandstones and conglomerates of a former Plio-Pleistocene sea floor. The terrace rises gently to the east forming a coastal plain 10 to 20 km wide. The sediment of the coastal plain overlies and abuts the uplifted granitic complex of the coastal Peninsular Range (Hanna, 1926; Inman, 1953; Kennedy and Peterson, 1975).

The continental shelf off Torrey Pines is approximately 3 to 4 km wide and slopes at 1 in 50 to 1 in 100 out to the break in shelf at a depth of about 100 meters. The shelf is cut into Eocene sediments and is overlain by a 1 to 4 meter thick layer of sand (Moore, 1960; Kennedy and Moore, 1971). During severe winter storms the beach sand is occasionally cut away and the waves actively erode the sea cliffs.

The southern part of the area has been folded, faulted, and uplifted, exposing resistant sandstones of Late Cretaceous age that now protrude seaward as the headland of Point La Jolla (Fig. 9). Movement along the Rose Canyon fault, which uplifted Soledad Mountain and formed Point La Jolla, also created a structural weakness along which the La Jolla Submarine Canyon has been incised. The contrast between the Torrey Pines block with its relatively horizontal Eocene formations and wave-cut terraces and the tilted and uplifted Soledad Mountain block is shown in Fig. 9. There has been a gradual rather uniform tectonic uplift of the Torrey Pines block of about 5 to 10 cm per millennium since the Linda Vista Terrace was formed 2 million years ago. In contrast, portions of the Linda Vista Terrace are found on top of Soledad Mountain at an elevation of 250 m, and the terraces have been tilted and uplifted at rates of 12 to 45 cm per millennium (Table 2). The trend is for a more rapid rate of uplift for the younger terraces (Kern, 1977).

Linda Vista Terrace

The Linda Vista Terrace was cut into the underlying Eocene sediments by a Plio-Pleistocene sea that formed the prominent 10 to 20 km wide coastal plain upon which most of the City of San Diego is built. It was first described and named by Ellis (Ellis and Lee, 1919, p. 27 pl. 7) and portions of it surveyed in greater detail by Hanna (1926). The terrace material is predominantly reddish-brown sandstone with a basal conglomerate, cemented with ferruginous mostly hematitic material that forms a resistant cap rock over the more friable coastal Eocene sediments. The abrasion platform of the terrace rises from about 90m along the coastal sea cliffs to 150m where it abuts the igneous rocks of the Peninsular Range.

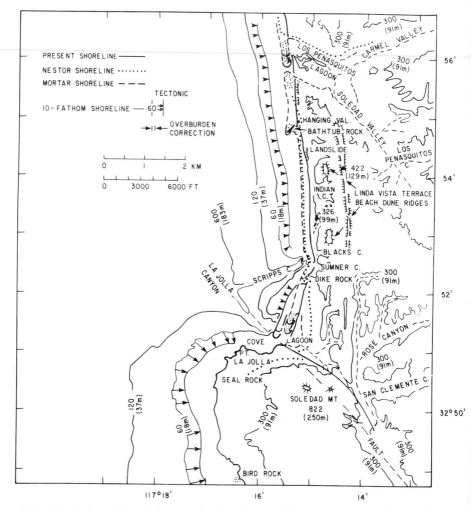

FIG. 9. *Paleoshorelines of the La Jolla area superimposed on the present topography.*

TABLE 2

*Present elevations and inferred rates of tectonic uplift
for the Linda Vista and Nestor Terraces.*

Terrace: Assumed Age	Torrey Pines Block	Soledad Mountain
Linda Vista: 2 million years		
Present elevation beach-dune ridge	150 m (a)	250 m (b)
Uplift rate if formed at MSL	7.5 cm/10³yr	12.5 cm/10³yr
Uplift rate if formed at MSL + 78 m	3.6 cm/10³yr	8.6 cm/10³yr
Nestor: 120,000 years		
Present elevation	20 m	60 m (c)
Uplift rate if formed at MSL + 6 m	11.7 cm/10³yr	45 cm/10³yr

(a)   earliest and most eastern beach-dune ridge
(b)   highest portion of Soledad Mountain
*(c)   highest elevation on Soledad Mountain reported by
        Kern (1977)*

The westwardly sloping Linda Vista Terrace is broken by four or five north-south trending ridges that rise about 25m above the terrace deposits. The seaward two extend along the coast for over 50 km, as far north as Oceanside. These represent old beach-dune ridges created during the recession of a former sea (Figs 9, 10).

The upper portions of the beach-dune ridges are characterized by spheroidal, reddish sandstone concretions about 0.5 to 1.5 cm in diameter. These have been studied by Emery (1950) and by Ritter (1964) who concluded that they formed around nuclei by the precipitation of iron oxide weathered from the heavy minerals in the sands of the ridges. In the lower portion of the ridges, Ritter (1964, p. 42, Fig. 15) found beach laminations that extended for "tens of feet" and sloped at 4 to 8 degrees. These laminations are caused by shear sorting as the swash moves sand on the beach face (Inman et al., 1966, p. 801). Their thickness, continuity, and low slope are diagnostic features for beach deposits (Inman, 1953, Fig. 13). Similar structures are found in the Nestor terrace (Plate 3a).

The Linda Vista Terrace is assumed to be about 2 million years old. G. Kennedy (1973) describes a molluscan fauna from the formation that is not known for the late Pleistocene, suggesting an early Pleistocene to late Pliocene age. Karrow and Bada (1980) find molluscan shell to be beyond the range of dating by amino acid racemization and conclude an age for the formation "of at least 1 million years".

The extensive wave-cut platform of the Linda Vista Terrace, with its many long beach-dune ridges, indicates a high stand of sea for a much longer period than has been usually associated with the Pleistocene interglacials (e.g. Fig. 2). Also, the copious quantity of sand in the long beach-dune ridge system clearly indicates a large littoral cell with a high yield of sandy sediment.

This terrace was deposited before the present extensive drainage system was developed, and before the faulting and uplifting of Soledad Mountain upon which portions of the seaward beach-dune ridge are found. However, the eastward trend of the ridges south of Soledad Mountain and east of Mission Bay suggest that the Mission Bay depression existed as a depression in this sea, and that the Soledad uplift was just beginning (e.g. Hanna, 1926; Emery, 1950; Ritter, 1964). The elevation of the sea that formed the Linda Vista is not known, but the differential of 150 m in elevation between the seaward beach ridge and Soledad Mountain gives a minimum rate of tectonic uplift of the mountain of 7 cm per millennium. If the highest inland ridge was formed at present sea level, then the Torrey Pines block has uplifted at a rate of about 8 cm per millennium and the Soledad block at a rate of about 12 cm per millennium. Since eustatic sea level could not have been more than 78 m above present (Barry, 1981), the minimum rate of tectonic uplift must be at least 4 to 9 cm per millennium respectively for the two blocks (Table 2).

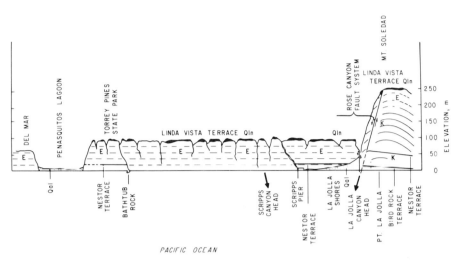

FIG.10. *Schematic section from Del Mar to Soledad Mountain showing formations and elevation of terraces. Formations: Qal - Quaternary alluvium, Qln - Lindavista Formation, E - Eocene sediments, K - Cretaceous sediments. Terraces from Kern (1977), Hanna (1926), and the author (vicinity of La Jolla Shores).*

Nestor Terrace

The Nestor abrasion platform is the most prominent late Pleistocene terrace observed along the coast of Point Loma, La Jolla, and intermittently in the Torrey Pines sea cliffs. It is generally about 20 m above present sea level, except along the Soledad Mountain block where it is as high as 60 m (Kern, 1977). Hanna (1926), who called it the La Jolla Terrace, observes that both San Dieguito and Los Penasquitos valleys were present at the time of formation of the Nestor terrace as remnants of that high sea stand are found as far as 8 km and 3 km inland respectively in the two valleys.

The widest extent of the Nestor abrasion platform and its sandy deposits occurs in the La Jolla Shores area. It occupies a triangular area extending inland from the coast near the La Jolla Beach and Tennis Club for 1.2 km along the Rose Canyon Fault, and then northward for 2.3 km to an apex just north of the ocean pier of the Scripps Institution of Oceanography (Figs 9, 10). Before seawalls were built, the lower portions of the terrace sands could be seen outcropping along the sea cliffs near the institution. The author followed the inland extent of the terrace by observing its outcrops in the excavations for house foundations during the 1950s as the area developed. Valley fill covered it to a thickness of

PLATE 2. *Nestor terrace outcrop at Torrey Pines Park.*
(a) Looking north along Torrey Pines cliffs to the Hanging
Valley site of Nestor Terrace, indicated by "N".
(b) "Bathtub Rock", (B) is a resistant cemented sandstone
that extends underwater where it is terraced at 4 to
5 meters and has mortar artifacts (see Masters, this volume,
Plate 3a). The Nestor terrace outcrops on the right above
the Eocene cliffs (E). See Figures 9 and 10 for locations.

about 3 to 4 m along the sea cliffs (e.g. Plate 1), and gradually decreased inland to elevations of about 20 meters where the terrace occasionally outcropped at the surface. A 20 m high contour line would approximately delineate the area underlain by the Nestor terrace.

Elsewhere in the Torrey Pines block, the Nestor terrace is intermittently found at about 20 m above sea level. The best studied area is that at Hanging Valley in Torrey Pines Park (Plates 2, 3) where it has been dated (Masters and Bada, 1977; 1979), its molluscan fauna analysed (Valentine, 1960), and its beach deposits described (Inman, 1972). The terrace has a maximum elevation of about 60 m on Soledad Mountain just south of the Rose Canyon Fault (Kern, 1977). Valentine (1960, Fig. 2) describes the development of the Nestor terrace, and its gradual narrowing and in places disappearance as the present sea cliff erodes. At one time a two-stepped sea cliff probably existed along most of the Torrey Pines cliffs. However, it is doubtful that the platform for the Nestor Terrace ever extended more than about one-half kilometer seaward of its present position.

Uranium-series analysis of fossil corals from Nestor terrace outcrops along the west side of Point Loma gave an age of 120,000 ± 10,000 years B.P. (Ku and Kern, 1974), establishing its association with the interglacial oxygen isotope substage 5e (Fig. 2). Using the Point Loma site as a calibration for the rate constant for amino acid racemization, Masters and Bada (1977; 1979) obtained dates from molluscs shells from the Nestor terrace at Los Penasquitos valley of 120,000 years B.P.; at Hanging Valley Torrey Pines cliff (Plates 2a, 3b) of 110,000 years B.P.; at Tourmaline Canyon, Pacific Beach, of 130,000 years B.P.; and, at the Scripps Institution of Oceanography (Karrow and Bada, 1980) of 120,000 years B.P.

Terraces with ages of 120,000 to 130,000 years B.P., coinciding with the age of substage 5e, have been observed on a worldwide basis and in all oceans. Generally, sea level is thought to have been about 6 m higher at that time than it is today (e.g. Veeh, 1966; Broecker et al., 1968; Veeh and Chappell, 1970; Ku et al., 1974; Kern, 1977; Chappell, 1981; Cronin et al., 1981).

The Nestor shoreline, although extensively notched into the older formations, represents an interglacial stillstand in sea level of much shorter duration than that occurring during Linda Vista times. The maximum width of about 1 km for its abrasion platform is in marked contrast to the over 20 km width of the Linda Vista terrace. Further, we know that during a portion of that time San Dieguito and Penasquitos valleys were embayments, limiting the size of the littoral cells. It would appear that the Nestor shoreline was more irregular than the present shoreline and consisted of embayments and cobble beaches in its earlier stages, and of large sandy crescent beaches (as at Hanging Valley and La

PLATE 3. *The Nestor terrace outcrop in Hanging Valley, Torrey Pines Park (a) Sampling wave-formed beach laminations, (b) sampling shells for amino acid dating. Refer to Figures 9, 10 and Plate 2 for location.*

Jolla Shores) during its latter stages.

The uniform, 20 m high level of the Nestor terrace in the Torrey Pines block indicates a uniform tectonic uplift. Assuming that the terrace was formed when sea level was about 6 m above present gives a tectonic uplift rate for the Torrey Pines block of about 12 cm per millennium. In contrast, Soledad Mountain has risen at a

TABLE 3

Radiocarbon dates from shelf and head of La Jolla Submarine Canyon.

Identification Number	Date yrs BP	Depth below MSL (meters)	Material	Location and Comment	Submitted by
LJ-GAP-53	12,000 ± 1000	38	oak limb	Wall at canyon head; part of accumulated drift wood in lagoonal clay layer exposed by submarine erosion	R.F. Dill
GX-738	12,800 ± 320	38	drift wood	as above	R.F. Dill
I-2105	13,200 ± 200	38	drift wood	as above	R.F.Dill
LJ-607	8,270 ± 500	23	fibrous root	Wall at canyon head; deposited between clay layers (lagoon?)	R.F. Dill
I-2152	5,390 ± 100	11.6	Pismo clam shell	Outcrop of shallow shelf sands in canyon head (?); description from LJ-GAP-53	R.F. Dill
LJ-208	4,230 ± 200	2	peat	Shelf between ancient cobble beach and present shoreline.	R.W. Thompson

rate of 45 cm per millennium since the formation of the Nestor terrace (Table 2).

Ten-Fathom Terrace

A wave-cut platform at about ten-fathoms (18 m) is a very common feature of the world's continental shelves (e.g. Emery, 1960, p. 35; Stanley and Swift, 1968; Stanley, 1970). Sea level was most recently at that level about 10,000 years B.P. (Fig. 4; Inman and Veeh, 1966), but sea level was also about this level at other interglacial times, for example substages 5a and c of Fig. 2. In the La Jolla area, Kern (1977) attributes the Bird Rock Terrace to an interglacial at 80,000 years B.P. that occurred 14 m below present sea level, and is now uplifted above present sea level by the Mount Soledad anticline and Rose Canyon fault (Fig.10).

There is good evidence that barrier beaches and lagoons formed near the head of La Jolla Submarine Canyon at various times during the Flandrian transgression. A series of radiocarbon dates from material exposed on the shallow shelf and from the eroding wall of the head of the submarine canyon give a consistant sequence for beach and lagoon occurrence beginning ca. 13,000 years B.P. at a depth of 38 m (Table 3). The sand covered rim at the canyon head occurs at depths of 11 to 15 m, and the exposed seaward facing wall of the canyon head consists of beds of clay, cobbles and occasionally sand. Because clay beds have a tendency to slump, recorded depths of samples may be greater than actual in situ depths.

It is thought that the fibrous root (LJ-607, Table 3) was deposited in a lagoon behind a cobble barrier beach of the ten-fathom terrace as shown in Fig. 9. Erosion of the head of the canyon has now progressed landward of the ancient barrier, exposing the lagoonal clays that formed behind the barrier. The date of 8,270 + 500 (LJ-607) for the fibrous root is contemporaneous with the radiocarbon date of 8,370 ± 50 (LJ-753) obtained by Inman and Veeh (1966) for the ten-fathom terrace on Kauai, Hawaii. The tree-ring correction for radiocarbon dates of this age gives a date about 1,000 years older (Suess, 1979), (see also Berger, this volume), so that the ten-fathom terrace is assumed to be ca. 9,000 or 10,000 years B.P.

The position of a terrace that would have formed at a depth of 18 m, about 10,000 years B.P. is shown in Fig. 9 where the length of arrow gives the correction from the existing 60 foot curve for thickness of overburden and for tectonic uplift. The sediments of the ten-fathom terrace are exposed (?) at depths of 18 m on the relatively broad shelf off Mission Bay between Point La Jolla and Point Loma. The sediment is a coarse (310 μm), reddish, oxidized quartz sand. Coring shows that clays of the "Mission Bay" of ten-fathom terrace times are found about 2 m beneath the sand (Dill, 1958).

While the outer shelves in the La Jolla area have been extensively studied (e.g. Moore, 1960; 1963), very little sub-bottom profile data has been taken in depths that are now less than 18 m where the ten-fathom terrace would be expected to occur. However, the broad Santa Monica shelf near Los Angeles, California, contains an extensive partially buried terrace at depths of about 20 m. This terrace consists of lagoonal muds and basal transgressive deposits whose molluscan fauna have been radiocarbon dated as 9,420 ± 1,120 and 10,165 ± 630 years B.P. respectively (Nardin et al., 1981).

Mortar Shoreline (ca. 6,000 years B.P.)

Sea level rose very rapidly between 8,000 and 6,000 years B.P. (radiocarbon age), at a rate of 50 to 100 cm per century (Fig. 4). This was followed, beginning about 6,000 years B.P., with a much more gradual rise of 10 to 15 cm per century to its present level. There was little terracing by waves during the period of rapid rise, but with the decrease in the rate of sea level rise (ca. 6,000 years B.P.) the waves began to cut a terrace and continue cutting to this day. The nascent terrace can be observed at a depth of 4 to 5 m about 200 m seaward of the sea-cliff in Fig. 5. Since sand of that time was trapped in the valley-embayments (Fig. 7, t_4) the waves concentrated coarse material into cobble beaches that were transported along the coast forming a cobble spit and an ancient lagoon at the head of La Jolla Submarine Canyon. The terrace and cobble beach are referred to here as the Mortar Shoreline because of the prehistoric artifacts associated with it (see Masters, this volume).

At that time the present Los Penasquitos Lagoon was a bay, and the Mortar Shoreline was part of a much smaller littoral cell extending for 7 km along the coast from Penasquitos to the ancient lagoon at La Jolla. The total drainage area for this small cell was 550 km², only slightly larger than the present drainage basin of Los Penasquitos Creek. We will refer to this small ancestral cell as the Torrey Pines Littoral Cell (Fig. 8, inset).

The Torrey Pines cell had a coastline length and drainage area less than one-tenth that of the present Oceanside cell. The reduced sediment yield from streams was deposited at the head of Los Penasquitos bay, and only that from small gullies got directly to the coast. This was a period of cliff erosion by waves, and the formation of rocky, cobbly beaches (Fig. 5; Plate 1). Sea level had slowed from its previous rapid rise (Fig. 4), permitting waves to begin to concentrate cobbles and form cobble beaches for the first time since the brief still stand of about 10,000 years B.P.

The longshore transport of material along the southern California coast was probably generally to the south as it is now. It was only to the south in the southern part of Torrey Pines cell because of the protection from Point La Jolla. Cobbles and coarse material were concentrated and retained on the beach, and then transported along the coast and south around the head of Scripps Submarine Canyon. The canyon acts as an inverse filter; only the coarsest material is by-passed around it. Sand and fine material were deposited in the canyon and lost from the system. Even today the finest sand is lost in the canyon, and the shelf and nearshore sediment south of the canyon are coarser than that to the north (Inman, 1953, Figs 24, 25).

The waves formed a cobble spit fronting a small tidal lagoon where the present La Jolla Beach and Tennis Club stands. The lagoon had an area of about 0.3 km² and was kept open by tidal currents. This size lagoon under present tidal conditions would maintain an entrance channel with a cross-sectional area below mean sea level of 70 m² (e.g. Inman and Frautschy, 1965, Fig. 8). The remnant cobbles of the beach are now found in 3 to 4 meters depth (Fig. 9), and the ancient lagoon still existed as a low area in old photographs (e.g. Moriarty, 1964, Fig. 24.4) and is now the site of the duck pond for the club.

Paleoclimate analyses appear to confirm the above model for the Mortar Shoreline with its small rocky littoral cell and cobble beaches. Artifacts found in the cobbles of the Mortar terrace are thought to be associated with the La Jollan culture known to occupy this coastal area *ca*. 8,500 to 3,000 years B.P. (Masters, this volume). La Jollan shell middens are common along the coast and provide good radiocarbon chronology. A midden site near the sea cliffs just north of Scripps Institution of Oceanography dates from 7,370 ± 100 (LJ-109) to 5,460 ± 100 (LJ-110) years B.P. and one at the north end of Torrey Pines Mesa dates to 3,700 ± 200 years B.P. (LJ-19). An analysis of food remains from the former site led C. L. Hubbs (Shumway *et al*, 1961, p. 113) to comment: "Thus we are confronted with good indications that, during the period from 7,300 years ago or earlier until at least 3,700 years ago, the shore north of La Jolla was considerably more rocky than at present with estuaries sufficiently deep and in sufficient contact with the sea to maintain, in baylike conditions, flourishing populations of Pecten and Chione. These conditions would be met by a rapidly rising sea level, during which the accumulation of shore sand would be kept low."

Climate during the Holocene has been interpreted from pollen analysis of a core from Santa Barbara Basin located about 250 km northwest of La Jolla (Heusser, 1978). This analysis showed that from 12,000 to 7,800 years B.P. upland coniferous communities were gradually succeeded in importance by oak and Artemisia, and subsequently (5,700 to 2,300 years B.P.) by chapparel and coastal sage scrub; inferring a change from wet, cool conditions to warmer, drier climate. This generally supports the climate assumed for the Mortar terrace and the associated change in rate of sea level rise. However, the chronology which is based on varve-sequence may not be accurate beyond a few millennia (A. Soutar, personal communication).

The relation of the artifacts at the Beach and Tennis Club site and the associated paleoshoreline and lagoon has been addressed by Moriarty (1964, p. 519). He attributes the ancient lagoon to a "low-lying sand spit behind which a shallow lagoon formed . . . Starting at a period of lowered sea level, the encroachment of the sea slowly reduced the face of the sand barrier overlain with midden material and caused a shoreward movement of the barrier." In contrast, the present study has the lagoon formed behind a cobble spit, which probably contained many of the original cobbles from which the mortars were made. The source of the cobbles was in part material transported to the sea by streams during the previous lowering of sea level, and transported along the beach by wave actions. However, most of the material used for artifacts was eroded from cliffs and transported only a short distance to its point of deposition as a cobble spit. Undoubtedly there was some sand, particularly after Los Penasquitos embayment filled. This sand probably accounts for the interlayering of sand and peat 2 m below MSL which Robert Thompson had dated as 4,230 ± 200 years B.P. (LJ-208), Table 3.

Also, Moriarty (1964, Fig. 24.3) shows the distribution of artifacts from this site extending continuously out to depths of 100 feet (30 m) with a modal depth of 20 to 30 feet (6 to 9 m). A discrete distribution from 3 to 5 m depth for artifacts from this site and other Mortar terrace sites is shown by Masters (this volume). The latter depth distribution is in good agreement with the model for this study which has the Mortar wave-cut terrace beginning at a depth of about 5 m (Fig. 8) with cobble beach berm deposits extending up to 2.5 m depth.

CONCLUSIONS

Man undoubtedly inhabited and migrated along coasts during times of sea level change. However, the probability of recovering evidence of habitation representative of times of rapid sea level change is not high. Still-stands in sea level, on the other hand, lead to a stability of terrace formation and coastal form that favors the concentration and permanency of cultural deposits.

During still-stands coastal terraces are most actively incised into the country rock, and their basal and subaerial deposits become stable physiographic features. Coastal lagoons and ecological zones are established, and become stabilized, supplying resources of interest to early peoples. The intensity or length of time people exploited these resources would be reflected in the depth of cultural deposit (see Bailey, this volume). As a consequence, the identification of shorelines associated with still-stands in sea level is the most logical first step in the process of locating areas of human activity on the shelf.

ACKNOWLEDGEMENTS

Most of the concepts that are summarized and applied here to the development of paleocoastlines are the cumulative results of long term support of basic coastal studies by the Office of Naval Research.

REFERENCES

Anderson, D.L. (1975). Accelerated plate tectonics. *Science* 187, 1077-79.

Arrhenius, G. (1952). Sediment cores from the east Pacific. *Swedish Deep-Sea Expedition 1947-1948*, Reports, 5, pt. 1, 91 pp.

Bagnold, R.A. (1963). Mechanics of marine sedimentation, pp. 507-528 in M.N. Hill (ed.) *The Sea*, Vol. 3: *The Earth Beneath the Sea*, Interscience Pub. New York, London, 963 pp.

Bagnold, R.A. (1966). An approach to the sediment transport problem from general physics, *U.S. Geological Survey, Professional Paper* 422-I, 37 pp.

Bagnold, R.A. (1980). An empirical correlation of bedload transport rates in flumes and natural rivers. *Proc. Royal Soc. London, Ser. A*, 372, 453-473.

Barry, R.G. (1981). Trends in snow and ice research. *EOS* 62, 46, p. 1139-44.

Bloom, A.J. (compiler) (1977). *Atlas of sea-level curves*, Internat. Geological Correlation Program, Project 61, IUGS, UNESCO, (Dept. Geol. Sci., Cornell Univ., Ithaca, New York 14853), *ca.* 100 pp.

Broecker, W.S. and Ku, T.L. (1969). Caribbean cores P6304-8 and P6304-9: New analysis of absolute chronology. *Science* 166, 405-6.

Broecker, W.S., Thurber, D.L., Goddard, J., Ku, T.L., Matthews, R.K., and Mesolella, K.J. (1968). Milankovitch hypothesis supported by precise dating of coral reefs and deep-sea sediments. *Science* 159, 197-200.

Brown, W.M. and Ritter, J.R. (1971). Sediment transport and turbidity in the Eel River basin, California, *U.S. Geological Survey*, Water-Supply Paper 1986, 70 pp.

Brownlie, W.R. and Taylor, B.D. (1981). Coastal sediment delivery by major rivers in Southern California, Part C of Sediment Management for Southern California Mountains, Coastal Plains and Shoreline, *California Inst. Technology*, Pasadena, EQL Report n. 17C, 314 pp.

Bullard, E. (1969). The origin of the oceans. *Scientific Amer.* 221 66-75. (Also reproduced, 1972, as p. 88-97 in J.T. Wilson (ed.) *Continents Adrift*, W.H. Freeman & Co., San Francisco, 172 pp.)

Carter, G.F. (1957). *Pleistocene Man at San Diego*, The Johns Hopkins Press, Baltimore, 400 pp.

Chamberlain, T.K. (1964). Mass transport of sediment in the heads of Scripps Submarine Canyon, California, pp. 42-64 in R.L. Miller (ed.) *Papers in Marine Geology*, Macmillan Co., New York, 531 pp.

Chappell, J. (1981). Relative and average sea level changes, and endo-, epi-, and exogenic processes on the earth, pp. 411-430 in I. Allison (ed.) *Sea Level, Ice, and Climatic Change*, International Assoc. Hydrological Science, 471 pp.

Clark, J.A. (1980). A numerical model of worldwide sea-level changes on a viscoelastic earth, pp. 525-534 in N.-A. Mörner (ed.) *Earth Rheology, Isostasy and Eustasy*, John Wiley & Sons, New York, 599 pp.

Clark, J.A., Farrell, W.E. and Peltier, W.R. (1978). Global changes in postglacial sea level: a numerical calculation. *Quaternary Research* 9, 265-287.

Colby, B.R. (1963). Fluvial sediments - a summary of source, transportation, deposition, and measurement of sediment discharge. *U.S. Geological Survey, Bull.* 1181-A, 47 pp.

Colby, B.R. and Hembree, C.H. (1955). Computations of total sediment discharge, Niobrara River near Cody, Nebraska, *U.S. Geological Survey, Water-Supply Paper* 1357, 187 pp.

Cronin, T.M., Szabo, B.J., Ager, T.A., Hazel, J.E., and Owens, J.P. (1981). Quaternary climates and sea levels of the U.S. Atlantic coastal plain. *Science* 211, 233-240.

Curray, J.R. (1960). Sediments and history of Holocene transgression, continental shelf, northwest Gulf of Mexico, pp. 221-266 in F.P. Shepard, F.B. Phleger, and Tj.H. van Andel (eds), *Recent Sediments, Northwest Gulf of Mexico, 1951-1958,* Amer. Assoc. Petroleum Geologists, Tulsa, Oklahoma, 394 pp.

Curray, J.R. (1961). Late Quaternary sea level: a discussion. *Geological Soc. Amer. Bull.* 72, 1707-12.

Curray, J.R. (1965). Late Quaternary history; continental shelves of the United States, pp. 723-735 in H.E. Wright, Jr. and D.G. Frey (eds) *The Quaternary of the United States,* Princeton Univ. Press, 922 pp.

Curray, J.R., Emmel, F.J., and Crampton, P.J.S. (1969). Holocene history of a strand plain, lagoonal coast, Nayarit, Mexico, pp. 63-100 in A. Ayala-Castanares and F.B. Phleger (eds) *Coastal Lagoons, a Symposium,* (Memoir of the Internat. Symp. on Coastal Lagoons, UNAM-UNESCO), Univ. Nacional Autonoma de Mexico, Mexico City, 686 pp.

Curray, J.R., Shepard, F.P., and Veeh, H.H. (1970). Late Quaternary sea-level studies in Micronesia: Carmarsel Expedition. *Geological Society of America, Bulletin* 81, 1865-1880.

Dietz, R.S. (1961). Continental and ocean basin evolution by spreading of the sea floor. *Nature* 190, 854-857.

Dill, R.F. (1958). Burial and scouring of ground mines on a sand bottom, *U.S. Navy Electronics Laboratory,* San Diego, California, Research Report 861, 32 pp.

Ellis, A.J., and Lee, C.H. (1919). Geology and ground waters of the western part of San Diego County, California, *U.S. Geological Survey, Water-Supply Paper* 446, 321 pp. + plates.

Elsasser, W.M. (1969). Convection and stress propagation in the upper mantle, pp. 223-246 in S. Runcorn (ed.) *The Application of Modern Physics to the Earth and Planetary Interiors,* John Wiley & Sons, London, 692 pp.

Elsasser, W.M., Olson, P. and Marsh, B.D. (1979). The depth of mantle convection. *Journal of Geophysical Research* 84, 147-155.

Emery, K.O. (1950). Ironstone concretions and beach ridges of San Diego County, California. *California Journal of Mines and Geology,* California Dept. Natural Resources, 46, 213-221.

Emery, K.O. (1960). *The Sea off Southern California,* John Wiley & Sons Inc, New York, 366 pp.

Emery, K.O. (1968). Relict sediments on the continental shelves of the world. *American Association of Petroleum Geologists, Bulletin* 52, 445-464.

Emery, K.O. (1980). Relative sea levels from tide-guage records. *Proc. National Academy of Sciences USA* 77, 6968-72.

Emiliani, C. (1978). The cause of the Ice Ages. *Earth and Planetary Science Letters* 37, 349-352.

Emiliani, C. (1981). A new global geology, pp. 1687-1728 in C. Emiliani (ed.) *The Sea,* Vol. 7: *The Oceanic Lithosphere,* John Wiley & Sons, New York, 1738 pp.

Emiliani, C., and Rona, E. (1969). Caribbean cores P6304-8 and P6304-9: new analyses of absolute chronology. A reply. *Science* 166, 1551-2.

Emiliani, C. and Shackleton, N.J. (1974). The Brunhes Epoch: Isotopic paleotemperatures and geochronology. *Science* 183, 511-14.

Emmett, W.W. (1980). A field calibration of the sediment trapping characteristics of the Helley-Smith bedload samples, *U.S. Geological Survey, Professional Paper* 1139, 44pp.

Fairbridge, R.W. (1976). Shellfish-eating preceramic Indians in coastal Brazil. *Science* 191, 353-359.

Flemming, N.C., Raban, A. and Goetschel, C. (1978). Tectonic and eustatic changes on the Mediterranean coast of Israel in the last 9,000 years, p. 33-93 in R.A. Yorke and J. Gamble (eds) *Progress in Underwater Science,* Vol. 3 Pentech Press, London, 279 pp.

Garrels, R.M. and MacKenzie, F.T. (1971). *Evolution of Sedimentary Rocks,* W.W. Norton & Co., Inc., New York, 397 pp.

Gofseyeff, S. (1953). Case history of Fire Island Inlet, N.Y., p. 272-305 in J.W. Johnson (ed.) *Third Conference on Coastal Engineering,* Council on Wave Research, Univ. of California, Berkeley, 343 pp.

Gould, H.R., and McFarlan Jr., E. (1959). Geologic history of the Chenier Plain, Southwestern Louisiana, *Gulf Coast Association of Geologists Society, Trans.* 9, 1-10, 3 pl.

44   D.L. Inman

Graff, W.H. (1971). *Hydraulics of sediment transport*, McGraw-Hill Book Co., New York, 513 pp.

Hanna, M.A. (1926). Geology of the La Jolla Quadrangle, California, University of California, Berkeley, *Bull. Dept. Geological Sciences* 16, 187-246.

Harrison, C.G.A., and Bonatti, E. (1981). The oceanic lithosphers, pp. 21-48 in C. Emiliani (ed.) *The Sea* Vol. 7: *The Oceanic Lithosphere*, John Wiley & Sons, New York, 1728 pp.

Heusser, L. (1978). Pollen in Santa Barbara Basin, California: a 12,000-yr record. *Geological Society of America, Bulletin* 89, 673-678.

Hicks, S.D. (1981). Long-period sea level variations for the United States through 1978. *Shore and Beach* 49, 26-29.

Hicks, S.D., and Crosby, J.E. (1974). Trends and variability of yearly mean sea level 1893-1972. *NOAA Technical Memo, NOS* 13, 14 pp.

Hoyt, J.H., and Henry Jr., V.S. (1971). Origin of capes and shoals along the southeastern coast of the United States. *Geological Society of America Bulletin* 82, 59-66.

Inman, D.L. (1953). Areal and seasonal variations in beach and nearshore sediments at La Jolla, California, *Beach Erosion Board*, Corps of Engineers, Technical Memo 39, 134 pp.

Inman, D.L. (1963). Sediments: physical properties and mechanics of sedimentation, pp. 101-151, Ch 5, in F.P. Shepard, *Submarine Geology* (2nd edition), Harper & Row, Publ., New York, 447 pp.

Inman, D.L. (1972). Geologic setting of Torrey Pines State Preserve, p. 72-81 in C.L. Hubbs and T. Whitaker (eds) (2nd edition) *Torrey Pines State Preserve*, The Torrey Pines Assoc., La Jolla, CA, 96 pp.

Inman, D.L. (1973). Shore processes. pp. 317-338 in R.C. Vetter (ed) *Oceanography: The Last Frontier*, Basic Books Inc., New York, 399 pp.

Inman, D.L. (1976). Summary report of man's impact on the California coastal zone, *State of California, Department of Navigation and Ocean Development*, Sacramento, California, 150 pp.

Inman, D.L., and Bagnold, R.A. (1963). Littoral processes, pp. 529-553 in M.N. Hill (ed.) *The Sea*, Vol. 3. *The Earth Beneath the Sea*, Interscience (John Wiley & Sons), New York, London, 963 pp.

Inman, D.L., and Chamberlain, T.K. (1960). Littoral sand budget along the southern Californa coast, *Report of the Twenty-First Int. Geological Cong.*, Copenhagen, v. of abstracts, p. 245-246.

Inman, D.L., Ewing, G.C., and Corlis, J.B. (1966). Coastal sand dunes of Guerrero Negro, Baja California, Mexico. *Geological Society of America, Bulletin* 77, 787-802.

Inman, D.L., and Frautschy, J.D. (1965). Littoral processes and the development of shorelines, pp. 511-553 in *Coastal Engineering*, (Santa Barbara Specialty Conf.), American Society of Civil Engineers, New York, 1006 pp.

Inman, D.L., and Norstrom, C.E. (1971). On the tectonic and morphologic classification of coasts. *Journal of Geology*, 79, 1-21.

Inman, D.L., Nordstrom, C.E., and Flick, R.E. (1976). Currents in submarine canyons: an air-sea-land interaction, pp. 275-310 in M. Van Dyke *et al.* (eds) *Annual Review of Fluid Mech.*, Vol. 8, 418 pp.

Inman, D.L. and Veeh, H.H. (1966). Dating the 10-fathom terrace off Hawaii. *American Geophysical Union, Trans.* 47, 125.

Inman, D.L., Zampol, J.A., White, T.E., Hanes, D.M., Waldorf, B.W. and Kastens, K.A. (1980). Field measurements of sand motion in the surf zone, *Proceedings of the 17th Coastal Engineering Conference*, American Society of Civil Engineers, New York, Vol. 2, pp. 1215-34.

Jelgersma, S. (1980). Late Cenozoic sea level changes in the Netherlands and adjacent North Sea Basin, pp. 435-447 in N.-A. Mörner (ed.) *Earth Rheology, Isostasy and Eustasy*, John Wiley & Sons, New York, 599 pp.

Karrow, P.F. and Bada, J.L. (1980). Amino acid racemization dating of Quaternary raised marine terraces in San Diego County, California. *Geology* 8, 200-204.

Kennedy, G.L. (1973). Early Pleistocene invertebrate faunule from the Lindavista Formation, San Diego, California. *San Diego Society of Natural History, Trans.* 17, 119-128.

Kennedy, M.P. and Moore, G.W. (1971). Stratigraphic relations of Upper Cretaceous and Eocene formations, San Diego Coastal Area, California. *American Association of Petroleum Geologists, Bulletin* 55, 709-722.

Kennedy, M.P. and Peterson, G.L. (1975). Geology of the San Diego Metropolitan Area, California: Del Mar, La Jolla, Point Loma, La Mesa, Poway and SW $^1/_4$ Escondido $7\,^1/_2$ minute quadrangles, *California Div. of Mines and Geology, Bulletin* 200, Sacramento, 56 pp. & pl.

Kenney, T.C. (1964). Sea-level movements and the geologic histories of the post-glacial marine soils at Boston, Nicolet, Ottawa, and Oslo. *Geotechnique* 14, 203-230.

Kern, J.P. (1977). Origin and history of upper Pleistocene marine terraces, San Diego, California. *Geological Society of America, Bulletin* 88, 1553-66.

Ku, T.-L., and Kern, J.P. (1974). Uranium-series age of the upper Pleistocene Nestor terrace, San Diego, California. *Geological Society of America, Bulletin* 85, 1713-16.

Ku, T.-L., Kimmel, M.A., Easton, W.H., and O'Neil, T.J. (1974). Eustatic sea level 120,000 years ago on Oahu, Hawaii. *Science* 183, 959-962.

Longbein, W.B., and Schumm, S.A. (1958). Yield of sediment in relation to mean annual precipitation. *American Geophysical Union, Trans.* 39, 1076-1084.

Masters, P.M. (this volume). Detection and assessment of prehistoric artifact sites off the coast of southern California.

Masters, P.M., and Bada, J.L. (1977). Racemization of isoleucine in fossil molluscs from indian middens and interglacial terraces in southern California. *Earth and Planetary Science Letters* 37, 173-183.

Masters, P.M., and Bada, J.L. (1979). Amino acid racemization dating of fossil shell from southern California. pp. 757-773 in R. Berger and H.E. Suess (eds), *Radiocarbon Dating* (Proc. Ninth Internat. Radiocarbon Conference), University of California Press, 787 pp.

Moore, D.G. (1960). Acoustic-reflection studies of the continental shelf and slope off Southern California. *Geological Society of America, Bulletin* 71, 1121-36.

Moore, D.G. (1963). Geological observations from the bathyscaph Trieste near the edge of the continental shelf off San Diego, California *Geological Society of America, Bulletin* 74, 1057-1062.

Moriarty, J.R. (1964). The use of oceanography in the solution of problems in a submarine archaeological site, pp. 511-522 in R.L. Miller (ed.) *Papers in Marine Geology: Shepard Commemorative Volume*, MacMillan, New York, 531 pp.

Nardin, T.R., Osborne, R.H., Bottjer, D.J. and Scheidemann, Jr., R.C. (1981). Holocene sea-level curves for Santa Monica Shelf, California continental borderland. *Science* 213, 331-333.

Nelson, H.F. and Bray, E.E. (1970). Stratigraphy and history of the Holocene sediments in the Sabine - High Island Area, Gulf of Mexico, pp. 48-77 in J.P. Morgan (ed.) *Deltaic Sedimentation Modern and Ancient*. Soc. Economic Paleontologists and Mineralogists, Special Publication No. 15, 312 pp.

Pawka, S., Inman, D.L., Lowe, R.L. and Holmes, L. (1976). Wave climate at Torrey Pines Beach, California, U.S. Army Corps of Engineers, *Coastal Engineering Research Center, Tech. Paper* No 76-5, 372 pp.

Peltier, W.R. (1974). The impulse response of a Maxwell earth. *Reviews Geophysics & Space Physics* 12, 649-699.

Peltier, W.R. (1980). Ice sheets, oceans, and the earth's shape, pp. 45-63 in N.-A. Morner (ed.) *Earth Rheology, Isostasy and Eustasy*, John Wiley & Sons, New York, 599 pp.

Redfield, A.C. (1965). Ontogeny of a salt marsh estuary. *Science* 147, 50-55.

Redfield, A.C., and Rubin, M. (1962). Age of salt marsh peat and its relation to recent changes in sea level at Barnstable, Massachusetts. *National Academy Science, Proc.* 48, 1728-35.

Revelle, R., (1981). Introduction, pp. 1-17 in C. Emiliani (ed.) *The Sea*, Vol. 7. *The Oceanic Lithosphere*, John Wiley and Sons, New York, 1738 pp.

Ritter, J.R. (1964). Beach-dune ridges of San Diego County, California *University of California, San Diego, M.S. Thesis in Oceanography*, 67 pp.

Rossiter, J.R. (1967). An analysis of annual sea level variations in European waters. *Geophysical Journal of the Royal Astronomical Society* 12, 259-299.

Schumm, S.A. (1963). The disparity between present rates of denudation and orogeny, *U.S. Geological Survey, Professional Paper,* 454H, 13 pp.

Sclater, J.G., Parsons, B. and Jaupart, C. (1981). Oceans and continents: similarities and differences in the mechanisms of heat loss. *Journal of Geophysical Research* 86, 535-552.

Scholl, D.W., Craighead, Sr., F.C. and Stuiver, M. (1969). Florida submergence curve revised: its relation to coastal sedimentation rates. *Science* 163, 562-564.

Scholl, D.W.,and Stuiver, M. (1967). Recent submergence of southern Florida: a comparison with adjacent coasts and other eustatic data. *Geological Society of America, Bulletin* 78, 437-454.

Shackleton, N.J., and Opdyke, N.D. (1973). Oxygen isotope and paleomagnetic stratigraphy of equatorial Pacific core V28-238: oxygen isotope temperature and ice volume on a 10^5 year and 10^6 year scale, *Quaternary Research* 3, 39-55.

Shepard, F.P. (1963). 35,000 years of sea level, pp. 1-10 in T. Clements (ed.) *Essays in Marine Geology,* University of Southern California Press, Los Angeles, 201 pp.

Shumway, G., Hubbs, C.L. and Moriarty, J.R. (1961). Scripps Estates Site, San Diego, California: a La Jolla site dated 5460 to 7370 years before the present. *Annals New York Academy of Science* 93, 37-132.

Stanley, D.J. (1970). The ten-fathom terrace on Bermuda: its significance as a datum for measuring crustal mobility and eustatic sea-level changes in the Atlantic. *Zeitschrift fur Geomorphologie (Berlin), Neue Folge* 14, 186-201.

Stanley, D.J. and Swift, D.J.P. (1968). Bermuda's reef-front platform: bathymetry and significance. *Marine Geology* 6, 479-500.

Suess, H.E. (1979). A calibration table for conventional radiocarbon dates, pp. 777-784 in R. Berger and H.E. Suess (eds) *Radiocarbon Dating,* University of California Press, Berkeley, Los Angeles, London. 787 pp.

Ten Brink, N.W. and Weidick, A. (1974). Greenland ice sheet history since the last glaciation. *Quaternary Research* **4**, 429-440.

Thom, B.G. and Chappell, J. (1975). Holocene sea levels relative to Australia. *Search* **6**, 90-93.

Valentine, J.A. (1960). Habitats and sources of Pleistocene mollusks at Torrey Pines Park, California. *Ecology* **41**, 161-165.

van Andel, T.H., Jacobson, T.W., Jolly, J.B., and Lianos, N. (1980). Late Quaternary history of the coastal zone near Franchthi Cave, southern Argolid, Greece. *Journal of Field Archaeology* **7**, 389-402.

Veeh, H.H. (1966). Th^{340}/U^{238} and U^{234}/U^{238} ages of Pleistocene high sea level stand. *Journal of Geophysical Research* **71**, 3379-3386.

Veeh, H.H., and Chappell, J. (1970). Astronomical theory of climate change: support from New Guinea. *Science* **167**, 862-865.

Williams, G.P. (1970). Flume width and water depth effects in sediment-transport experiments, *U.S. Geological Survey, Professional Paper* **562-H**, 37 pp.

SEA LEVELS AND TREE-RING CALIBRATED RADIOCARBON DATES

Rainer Berger

Institute of Geophysics and Planetary Physics,
Departments of Anthropology and Geography,
University of California, Los Angeles,
Los Angeles, California 90024, USA

ABSTRACT

It is now generally agreed that curves showing secular sea level changes in considerable detail apply only to their immediate geographic area of measurement. This, however, does not preclude generalized world-wide assessments. The regionality of sea level analyses is due to the effects of local tectonism and/or isostatic adjustments which in themselves are not always quantitatively understood so far. For maximum accuracy sea level estimates should be based upon terrestrial sample materials inasmuch as sea shells can have varying apparent ages of uncertain magnitude. Moreover, terrestrial sample ages need to be tree-ring calibrated for optimum veracity. These considerations apply specifically to regional sea level analyses, whereas the world-wide treatment remains largely unaffected due to the different scale of graphic presentation.

INTRODUCTION

Quantitative assessments of secular changes in sea levels have been based to a very large extent on radiocarbon dates derived from sea shells, wood and other sample materials. Since the advent of tree-ring calibrated radiocarbon dating (Suess, 1965), the question has arisen to what extent these revisions would affect the sea level curves postulated by such authors as Berger and Libby (1967); Bloom (1969); Curray (1965); Fairbridge (1961); Jelgersma (1961, 1966); Morrison (1976); Mörner (1969); Newmann (1969); Scholl *et al.*, (1969); Shepard (1963); and Suggate (1968). It is the purpose of this contribution to consider the radiocarbon calibration effect in some detail.

QUATERNARY COASTLINES
ISBN 0 12 479250 2

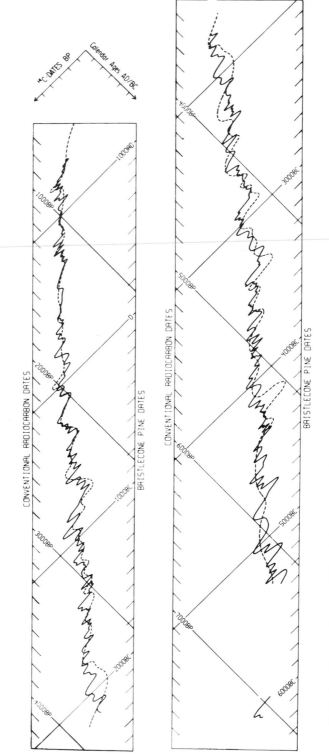

FIG. 1. Tree-ring calibration curve by Suess (1979) showing both short-term variations (wiggles) and long-term deviation (departure of calibration curve from horizontal).

TREE-RING CALIBRATED RADIOCARBON DATES

The change-over from Libby's (1952) solid radiocarbon measurement technique to proportional gas counting (DeVries, 1958) was largely due to the greater accuracy of the new approach. Typical statistical errors of $\pm$ 300 years were reduced to $\pm$ 50 years or so. As a consequence certain known-age samples no longer fitted perfectly on the ideal decay curve of radiocarbon but lay significantly outside. This prompted the suggestion that the production rate of radiocarbon was not uniform in time. It remained for the systematic exploration of these secular changes by Suess (1979) to show what the actual magnitude of the deviations from the theoretical ideal relationship was. In fact, the investigation of secular variations became an important subfield of radiocarbon studies in which many scientists, too numerous to mention here, became active. Their publications are found largely in the proceedings of the last three International Radiocarbon Conferences (1972, 1976, 1979). As to the cause of these variations, they are the result of modulations of the ^{14}C production rate characterized by both short and long term excursions from the theoretical mean.

Inspection of the Suess (1979) calibration curve (Fig.1) shows relatively short-lived deviations lasting about a century or so which have been called "Suess' Wiggles". They most likely are due to heliomagnetic field changes affecting the extent to which cosmic rays enter the earth's atmosphere. The essential correctness of these wiggles was established by dating medieval timbers of known age (Berger, 1970). Briefly stated, tree-ring calibrated radiocarbon dates of wood from known age buildings agree with their historical ages.

The long term variation on the order of several thousands of years is due to geomagnetic field changes which influences directly the production rate of radiocarbon (Bucha, 1967). This effect results in radiocarbon ages being too recent by maximally a thousand years. The long term variation also has been checked against the historical chronology of the Egyptian dynasties, the oldest and most reliable known. As a result, early dynastic samples of known age are far more accurately dated when tree-ring calibration is used (Berger, 1970).

During the 1981 International Radiocarbon Conference at Groningen, Heidelberg, La Jolla and Seattle radiocarbon calibrations were compared and found to be in virtual agreement. Indeed, all four calibrations were at most a few decades apart. Thus the veracity of tree-ring calibrated radiocarbon dating has been demonstrated for most of the last 7,000 years.

SEA LEVEL CURVES

Over the years a series of sea level curves have been published which are intended either for regional geographic or world-wide applications (Fig. 2). Especially for the Holocene there exists considerable disagreement about the fine structure of these curves. The reasons for such discrepancies appear to lie in differing tectonic activities in various regions of the world, the influence of isostatic compensation where applicable and the selection of samples, (Clark, Farrel & Peltier, 1978).

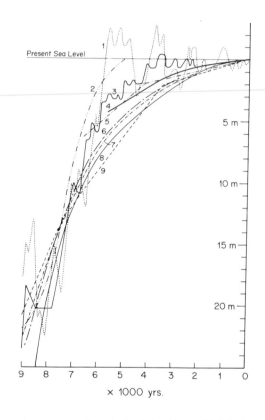

FIG. 2. *Sea level curves by 1-Fairbridge (1961), a synthesis; 2-Suggate (1967), New Zealand; 3-Mörner (1969), calculated; 4-Scholl et al. (1969), Florida; 5-Bloom (1969), Micronesia; 6-Curray (1965), average; 7-Shepard (1963), average; 8-Jelgersma (1961, 1966), Netherlands; 9-Newman (1969), Bermuda. Adapted from Mörner (1970).*

Inasmuch as tree-ring calibrated radiocarbon dating reaches as yet only to roughly 7,000 years ago, any discussion of using the method to date Late Pleistocene sea level stands is premature. There exist suitable tree remnants in the White Mountains of California in fluvial deposits of the Danube, as well as elsewhere which predate the Holocene (Ferguson, Becker, priv. comm). But so far no contiguous tree-ring master chronology is available. Moreover, radiocarbon dating by itself is limited to the last glacial period (Wisconsin or Würm), since dates greater than about 100,000 years are inherently impossible. This is caused, amongst other reasons, by the natural distribution of uranium in ppm levels throughout the world. Radioactive decay of that element constantly produces ultra-low levels of neutrons which interact with nitrogen to form radiocarbon (Berger, 1979a,b).

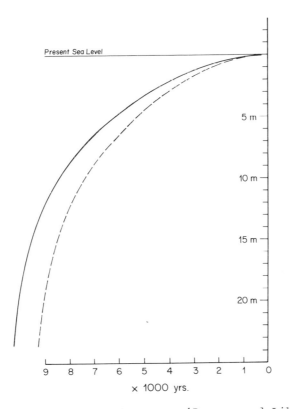

FIG. 3. *Sea level changes at Panama (Berger and Libby, 1967). The dashed line is based on non-calibrated radiocarbon dates (half-life 5568 ± 30 years) obtained from organic materials such as wood and peat. The solid curve is a tree-ring calibrated transformation using Suess (1979) calibration. The calibrated sea level curve falls off more slowly than the uncorrected curve. This scale makes the difference clearly visible, unlike correlations of the entire Pleistocene.*

It is important to realize that calibrated radiocarbon dating applies only to terrestrial materials such as wood, charcoal or bones. Shells are often subject to substantive apparent ages due to the mixture of old and new water masses which determine the initial radiocarbon content (Berger *et al.*, 1966). Hence, the systematic and calibrated variations in radiocarbon concentration in air or the terrestrial biosphere are obscured in the ocean. There does not exist at present a curve of secular ^{14}C variations in the ocean although a regional chronology might be deducible from annual growth rings in coral, somewhat similar to the tree-ring based chronologies however which are world-wide in scope. Since a considerable number of sea shell samples were used in the past to construct the sea level curves above, there remains as a result a measure of ambiguity in their accuracy.

Another important consideration involves the intended scale of resolution of quaternary eustatic oscillations, for example, that presented by Fairbridge (1961) (see Fig. 2). A one thousand year displacement, which does not significantly alter the pattern, is also the maximum deviation observed in calibrated radiocarbon dating. Consequently these Fairbridge curves are not likely to change in appearance with respect to corrections in time elapsed.

For comparison of the effect of tree-ring calibrated and non-calibrated radiocarbon dating, a sea level curve for Panama is included (Fig. 3; Berger and Libby, 1967). It is not detailed enough to show short term variations in sea level on the order of several centuries. However, it illustrates that earlier Holocene dates become progressively older when calibration is applied. Thus there is concomittantly observed a gradual displacement farther into the past of sea level-related events.

ANCIENT SEA LEVELS AND PREHISTORY

A thorough understanding of sea level conditions for a given geographic area is very important in all prehistoric studies involving both coastal and riverine environments as the following cases show. In each case improved precision of dates would improve the interpretation of events.

In this volume Johnson discusses the palaeogeography of the Channel Islands of California with their Pleistocene dwarf mammoth population and related events. As the ocean rose and fell in response to Pleistocene climatic changes the land mass of the islands, Santarosae, contracted or expanded (Orr, 1968). This permitted mammoths first to immigrate and later forced them into dwarfism, a process also recorded elsewhere in the world. At the same time the changes in sea level affected the settlement of the islands by man as the land area responded to the encroaching ocean after the last glacial maximum 18,000 years ago (Berger and Orr, 1966), and see also Johnson (this volume).

In another study Masters (this volume) presents an assessment of prehistoric artifact sites off the coast of southern California. A precise knowledge of the seastands along any given coast permits direct dating of sites discovered by underwater archaeological techniques provided that they are demonstrably related to the shoreline.   Equally transgressions of the ocean, especially in the European lowlands, can be a measure for the establishment of protective mounds such as the Dutch "Wierde" or North-German "Warft"-structures (Vander Hoeven and Berger, 1982).

Finally sea level variations and the birth of Egyptian civilization have been connected by Labeyrie (1979). During Pleistocene times the level of the Mediterranean was depressed just as the rest of the worlds oceans. Therefore the Nile had dug a deep canyon into lower Egypt that gradually silted up as both the level of the Mediterranean and consequently the Nile rose after 18,000 years ago. Some time after stabilization of the ocean and river levels, the Nile flood plain became essentially geomorphologically stable as well and permitted continued settlement by large numbers of people.   This sequence of events applies to a greater or lesser extent to all the major rivers of the world. In the Mediterranean the sea level stabilization coincides with the cultural transition from the Neolithic to the Bronze Age.   Some evidence for this scenario lies in (1) the dating of charred wood at 10,580 B.P., found at the depth of 50 m in a boring in the ancient Nile channel and (2) the establishment of the I Dynasty around 3,000 B.C. coincides with the end of the major ocean level adjustments of the Holocene.   The rise of sea level also created numerous natural inlets and harbours which encouraged seafaring during the Bronze Age, but many of these silted up over the course of the next 2,000 years.

REQUIREMENTS FOR THE FUTURE

Inasmuch as many of the sea level curves have been based in the past on marine and terrestrial radiocarbon samples, there is a need to reduce reliance on shell-based dates. Lake-plants may provide occasionally inviting dates, however; they are also unsuitable as Hakansson (1979) has shown.   Preferentially only terrestrial materials should be used.   This can be checked by determining $^{13}C/^{12}C$ isotope ratios which can often be decisive as to the origin and the suitability of the material in question.

Whenever dates of terrestrial origin are used whether from past or recent studies, they need to be tree-ring calibrated for optimum accuracy. Since tree-ring calibrations exist for only the Holocene, it must be understood that any late Pleistocene dates will also have to be calibrated when the necessary tree-ring master chronologies become available.   On the whole palaeomagnetic measurements suggest that the earth's magnetic field did not vary generally more than was observed during the Holocene (Bucha, priv. comm.), except for certain major excursions (Barbetti, 1980). If, therefore, calibrated dates are not off more than a thousand years, all dates with statistical errors in excess of 1,000 years may not need to be calibrated. At present the boundary lies at about 30,000 years as most radiocarbon dates of greater age have typical one sigma standard deviations of $\pm$ 1,000 years. It is not known at present to what extent radiocarbon dating with accelerators will be more precise. Yet it offers the promise of extending ^{14}C-based sea level curves much farther into the past.

On the shorter time scale of the Holocene, tree-ring calibration will make significant differences in sea level curves. The period of 10,000-5,000 years B.P. marks the terminal phase of rapid transgression during the Flandrian. The estimated rate of sea level rise over this time is 3 m per millennium. Adjustments up to 1,000 years in the dates clearly affect sea level chronologies when depth measurements are attaining accuracies of $\pm$ 0.5 m (Flemming, 1978). Thus, tree-ring calibrated radiocarbon dates on samples of terrestrial origin are the preferred methodology for constructing Holocene sea level curves. Increased accuracy of calibrated sea level curves promises useful chronologies for the archaeology of submerged sites of the Bronze Age and New World Archaic periods.

ACKNOWLEDGEMENT

This is publication No. 2276, Institute of Geophysics and Planetary Physics, University of California, Los Angeles, 90024.

REFERENCES

Barbetti, M. (1980). Geomagnetic strength over the last 50,000 years and changes in atmospheric ^{14}C concentration: emerging trends. *Radiocarbon* **22** (Stuiver, M., and Kra, R., eds). pp. 192-199.

Berger, R. (1970). The potential and limitations of radiocarbon dating in the Middle Ages: The radio chronologist's view. In *Scientific Methods in Medieval Archaeology* (Berger, R., ed.). University of California Press, Berkeley, Los Angeles, London, pp. 89-139.

Berger, R. (1979a). Radiocarbon dating with accelerators. *Journal Archaeological Science* **6**, 101-104.

Berger, R. (1979b). The advantages of a accelerator-based radiocarbon measurments in geophysical research. *Environmental International* **2**, 457-459.

Berger, R. and Libby, W.F. (1967). UCLA radiocarbon dates VI. *Radiocarbon* 9, 477-504.

Berger, R. and Orr, P.C. (1966). The fire on Santa Rosa Island, California II *Proceedings at the National Academy of Sciences (USA)* 56, 1678-1682.

Berger, R., Taylor, R.E. and Libby, W.F. (1966). Radiocarbon content of marine shells from the California and Mexican West Coast. *Science* 153, 864-866.

Bloom, A. (1969). Holocene submergence in Micronesia as the standard for eustatic sea level changes, Preprint of *Symposium on the evolution of shorelines and continental shelves during the Quaternary,* 4 and 5 September 1969, Unesco, Paris.

Bucha, V. (1967). Archaeomagnetic and palaeomagnetic study of the magnetic field of the earth in the past 600,000 years. *Nature* 213, 1005-1007.

Clark, J.A., Farrel, W.E. and Peltier, W.R. (1978). Global changes of post glacial sea level: a numerical calculation. *Quaternary Research* 9, 265-287.

Curray, J.R. (1965). Late Quaternary history, continental shelves of the Unites States. In *Quaternary of the United States* (Wright, H.E., and Frey, D.G., eds). Princeton Univ. Press, Princeton, N.J., pp. 723-735.

De Vries, H.L. (1958). Variation in concentration of radiocarbon with time and location on earth. *Koninkl. Nederland Akad. Wetenschap. Proc.* B61, 94-102.

Fairbridge, R.W. (1961). Eustatic changes in sea level. In *Physics and Chemistry of the Earth* (Ahrends, L.H., Press, F., Rankama, K. and Runcorn, S.K., eds). Pergamon Press, New York, London, Oxford, Paris, Vol.4, pp. 99-185.

Flemming, N.C. (1978). Holocene eustatic changes and coastal tectonics in the north-east Mediterranean: implications for models of crustal consumption. *Philosophical Transactions of the Royal Society London, Series A* 289, 405-458.

Hakansson, S. (1979). Radiocarbon activity in submerged plants from various south Swedish lakes. In *Radiocarbon Dating* (Berger, R. and Suess, H.E., eds). Univ. California Press, Berkeley, Los Angeles, London, pp. 433-443.

60 R. Berger

International Radiocarbon Conference, (1972). *Proceedings of the Eighth International Radiocarbon Dating Conference* (Rafter, T.A., and Grant-Taylor, T., eds). Royal Society of New Zealand, Wellington, New Zealand, Vol. I and II.

International Radiocarbon Conference, (1976). Proceedings in *Radiocarbon Dating* (Berger, R., and Suess, H.E., eds., Univ. California Press, Berkeley-Los Angeles-London, 1979, pp. 1-787.

International Radiocarbon Conference, (1979). Proceedings in *Radiocarbon* (Stuiver, M., and Kra, R., eds). Vol. 22, No. 2, pp. 1-562 and No. 3, pp 565-1016.

Jelgersma, S. (1961). Holocene sea level changes in the Netherlands *Mededeling Geol. Stichting, Series C* VI, No. 7, 1-101.

Jelgersma, S. (1966). Sea level changes during the last 10,000 years. Proceedings International Symposium "World climate from 8,000 to 0 B.C," Imperial College, London, 18 and 19 April 1966. *Royal Meteorological Society,* London, pp. 54-71.

Labeyrie, J. (1979). Sea level variations and the birth of the Egyptian civilization. In *Radiocarbon Dating* (Berger, R., and Suess, H.E., eds.) Univ. California Press, Berkeley, Los Angeles, London, pp. 32-36.

Libby, W.F. (1952). *Radiocarbon Dating.* Univ. Chicago Press, Chicago, pp. 1-175.

Mörner, N.-A. (1969). Eustatic and climate changes during the last 20,000 years. *Abstracts,* INQUA VIII Congress, Paris, p. 226.

Mörner, N.-A. (1970). Eustatic changes during the last 20,000 years and the method of separating the isostatic and sustatic factors in an uplifted area. *Contrib. Department of Geology, Univ. Western Ontario,* London, Canada, pp. 1-41.

Morrison, I.A. (1976). "Comparative stratigraphy and radiocarbon chronology of Holocene marine changes on the western seaboard of Europe. In *Geoarchaeology* (Davidson, D.A., and Shakeley, M.L., eds). Westview, Boulder, CO, pp. 159-174.

Newmann, A.C. (1969). Quaternary sea level data from Bermuda. *Abstracts,* INQUA VIII Congress, Paris, pp. 228-229.

Orr, P.C. (1968). *Prehistory of Santa Rosa Island.* Santa Barbara Museum of Natural History, Santa Barbara, CA, pp. 1-253.

Scholl, D.W., Craighead, F.C., and Stuiver, M. (1969). Florida submergence curve revised: Its relation to coastal sedimentation rates. *Science* <u>163,</u> 562-564.

Shepard, F.P. (1963). Thirty-five thousand years of sea level. In *Essays in marine geology in honor of K.O. Emery* (Clements, T., ed.). Univ. Southern California Press, Los Angeles, pp. 1-10.

Suess, H.E. (1965). Secular variations of the cosmic-ray-produced carbon-14 in the atmosphere and their interpretations. *Journal of Geophysical Research* <u>70</u> : 5937-5952.

Suess, H.E. (1979). A calibration table for conventional rdiocarbon dates. In *Radiocarbon Dating* (Berger, R., and Suess, H.E., eds). Univ. California Press, Berkeley-Los Angeles-London, pp. 776-784.

Suggate, R.P. (1968). Post-glacial sea level rise in the Christchurch metropolitan area, New Zealand. *Geol. en Mijnbouw* <u>47,</u> 291-297.

Vander Hoeven, P., and Berger, R. (1982). The settlement of the Northsea coast as deduced from archaeological and oceanographic techniques, Publications, Institute of Archaeology, University of California, Los Angeles.

HOMINID MIGRATIONS AND THE EUSTATIC SEA LEVEL PARADIGM: A CRITIQUE

Leslie F. Marcus and Walter S. Newman [1]

Department of Biology,
Queens College of the City University of New York,
Flushing, New York 11367, USA

[1]*Department of Earth and Environmental Sciences,*
Queens College of the City University of New York,
Flushing, New York 11367, USA: National Research
Council Resident Senior Research Associate, Goddard
Institute for Space Studies, National Aeronautics and Space
Administration, 2880 Broadway, New York, NY 10025, USA

ABSTRACT

Computer-assisted analyses and graphic reconstruction of sea levels over the past 13,000 years yield results so ambiguous as to invite further inquiry into the centrality of glacial eustasy when modeling hominid migration routes. Our date base includes 3,700 radiocarbon dates reported by numerous investigators throughout the world. The data frequency distribution mode peaks in mid-Holocene time and there is little data prior to 13,000 years ago. Excluding those areas which have experienced postglacial isostatic rebound, the vertical range of reported sea-level stand exceeds 50 meters at 10,000 years ago. The earth's rheological behaviour due to glacial-interglacial cycles superimposed on the complexities of plate tectonics prevents a simple assessment of landmass outlines in the antediluvian world. Furthermore, since our sea level indicators define the geoid at specific points in time, the shape of the earth (and therefore mass distribution), has changed significantly through time. We conclude that glacial eustasy alone provides a poor and probably fallacious basis upon which to model the migrations of hominid populations.

QUATERNARY COASTLINES
ISBN 0 12 479250 2

INTRODUCTION

The present global marine strandline is the location of organisms and material possessing a firm relationship to the local sea level datum. This includes autochthonous organic materials such as coral and basal peat as well as allochthonous items such as the remains of stranded marine mammals, driftwood and littoral archaeological sites. These strandline indicators presumably exhibited similar relationships throughout the late Quaternary Period and are measured relative to the local datum in time, by absolute date techniques, and elevation.

Consider the much-used concept of "eustatic sea level". "Eustatic" refers to worldwide changes in the level of the sea. During the Quaternary, these changes were largely in sympathy with varying glacier ice volume. The subject is of fundamental interest to both earth scientists and archaeologists because the level of the sea affects paleogeography, local and regional climate, and Man's food-gathering strategies. For both disciplines, the rhythm of sea level fluctuations would seem to provide a guide towards establishing and correlating regional stratigraphies.

Contemporary sea level aproximates a gravitational equipotential surface - the geoid. Since past isochronous marine surfaces must also have been gravitational equipotential surfaces these ancient sea levels describe the departure of the Palaeogeoid at a point in time and space with respect to the contemporary geoid (Mörner, 1976; Newman et al., 1980). Mass distribution has also changed appreciably since the last glacial maximum; consider the melting of ice sheets and the distribution of the resulting water throughout the world's oceans as well as the phenomenon of postglacial isostatic rebound. Thus paleogeodesy is still another factor that must be considered when investigating sea-level change.

The purpose of this paper is to once again demonstrate that Quaternary sea level fluctuations are the summation of eustasy, isostasy, neotectonics and geoidal displacements, all operating at varying rates so that it would be rather exceptional to find chronologically equivalent shorelines at identical levels over widely scattered areas. Although there is obviously a volumetric relationship between glacial ice and sea volume, and therefore sea level, it would be naive to reconstruct palaeo-coastlines by simply tracing specific isobaths for great distances under the sea. Coastal mobility has been ubiquitous during the Quaternary Period because of the effects of waxing and waning glaciers, isostasy, and the gravitational anomalies resulting from both surficial and deep-seated mass transfer. These factors, plus plate tectonics and intraplate neotectonics, considerably complicate the study of hominid migration routes.

Flemming (1969), used archaeological evidence to demonstrate that sea level changes in the western Mediterranean involved both eustasy and crustal movements. More recently, Brooks and others (1979), Colquhoun and others (1980) and Depratier and Howard (1980) utilized a mix of archaeology, stratigraphy, geomorphology, clay mineralogy, geochemistry, paleontology and radiocarbon dates all providing (at least for Georgia and South Carolina) persuasive evidence for a fluctuating Holocene sea level superimposed on a longer term marine transgression rate of less than one meter/millennium, a rate that presumably includes some neotectonic element. Clearly archaeology is making a major contribution to sea level studies.

Ruppé (1980) observes that the rise of sea level since 17,000 B.P. (years before present) has radically altered the outlines of the world's land masses and drowned the continental shelves, a vast area that has the potential of containing large numbers of archaeological sites. Over the past decade, Ruppé has been involved in the study of submarine archaeological sites off the west coast of Florida. A major frustration has been his inability to relate his littoral and estuarine sites to published sea level curves. Ruppé writes (*op. cit.*, p. 42):

> The lack of consistency in the various sets of dates will require additional research for clarification. The discrepancies are serious and must be resolved. On the basis of incomplete evidence several alternative explanations are possible: 1) The carbon date of the charcoal may be in error: 2) The peat dates may be wrong: 3) The underwater midden may represent redeposited material from the adjacent land site: 4) Current ideas about the magnitude of sea level rise may have to be revised: 5) The problem of sea level change is most difficult.

Ruppé has seized upon a fundamental geophysical dilemma under study by earth scientists. The sea level surface is constantly being distorted, not only by transient inhomogeneities in the solid earth (witness postglacial isostatic rebound), but also by winds, currents and tides. These oceanographic phenomena, coupled with glacial eustasy and neotectonics, constitute noise that has to be allowed for in the analysis of Holocene and older sea level data. Indeed, it is now obvious to earth scientists that no single sea level curve can adequately trace the course of sea level through time since there appears to be no objective way to unequivocally determine the absolute stability of either coastal segments of crustal plates. The very fact that the many sea level curves are incompatible requires that at least some, if not all of these curves include some element of tectonic or isostatic instability and/or oceanographic anomaly (Newman and Munsart, 1968; Clark, *et al.*, 1978).

This paper addresses the problem of processing sea-level date so as to produce a product that can be easily used by both the earth

```
LAT                (a)
90 +
   ^
75 +                    B  AFBA FFAI CCEC       CBAC
   ^                    BBJHEFRPTFZZCB BA      F GGBC                FFZZB    A   B AA
60 +                  B AADBDEA DDHECIOGZNE HF  A HZ   A  B CNGDDZ A      CP
   ^                    A NCAGBBFEAABGND UM        HE          ADA
       CQF GJ          DG    GLFACC  AA               BBGZSIPABA
       EZ        BABBCZ   ABN                        ACZZQ GZZF
45 +                C EEUZDJZ                         AZZX A
   ^       IC          ZZZZZ                          AVDCD
   ^       A            ZZZC                              B
30 +              G   F F FX  AR                      I  B   A ZC BD
   ^     E         C   H  OUO                            B
   ^     AG           G   KMH  E                          CA      A
15 +                       F D  A EA  P   G             Z  A       A
   ^                                                   AA ZA        C
   ^      D                                                A
 0 +      A   E                A                        KFDD A
   ^     AA  A  DA  H                            F                  A
   ^              A  A H             B          RF              A   C
-15 +                                           A
   ^                             B              AZT
-30 +                          B  AD                              AB   A   D
   ^                              A                               H
   ^                                                             BAFA
-45 +                                                    B
   ^                             B  D
   ^                             B
-60 +                                                                        A
   ^
   ^
-75 +
   ^
   ^
-90 +
     +----+----+----+----+----+----+----+----+----+----+----+----+
    -180 -150 -120  -90  -60  -30   0    30   60   90  120  150  180
                              LONG
```

FIG. 1. Geographic distribution of radiocarbon-dated sea level. A = one observation; B = two observations; etc. For dimensions of unit geographical cells, see text. Note the many areas lacking data.

(a) The data roughly outline the world's landmasses.

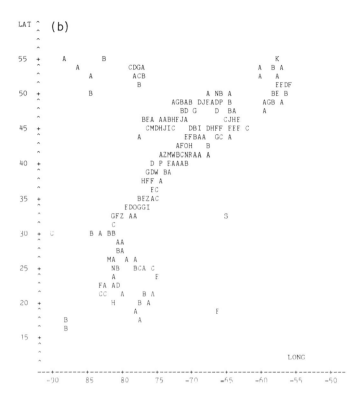

FIG. 1. (b) The distribution of data from eastern North America and Bermuda. Note that there is still little data from the Gulf Coast, much of the Florida Peninsula and the Labrador coast.

science and archaeological communities. We avoid the subject of sea level curve comparison by acknowledging that most local and even regional curves faithfully trace the level of the sea through time for a specific area. However, we suggest an alternative display method that is both easily understood and, at the same time, also opens up new avenues of inquiry.

MATERIALS AND METHODS

We believe that the bulk of reported radiocarbon-dated late Quaternary sea-level indicators accurately record the level of the sea at a point in time with respect to the contemporary local datum. We have assembled more than 3,700 radiocarbon dates purporting to measure the level of the sea back to 14,000 B.P. (years before present = 1950). Data stored in our computer bank include latitude, longitude, laboratory number, date and standard deviation, elevation with respect to the local datum, and the nature of the dated material. The sources of our data are the journal *Radiocarbon* (1959-1981), the literature on the subject, and the contributions of colleagues. These data are accepted as reported with no attempt to standardize as, e.g. using a single half-life for radiocarbon. We also use the reported local datum since a normalizing procedure might only serve to mask geoidal anomalies, i.e. departures from the "sea level geoid". Note also that contemporary geodetic datums are strictly provincial and are not tied into a universal levelling system. For example, the 1929 North America datum appears presently to be moving towards the mean low water mark at most United States' east coast marigraph (tidal) stations. In this paper, we compare relative changes in sea level from station to station.

Figures 1a and b display the geographical distribution of our data for the entire world as well as eastern North America. The data distribution roughly outlines land masses. The upper case letters indicate the number of observations available within each unit cell. The cell dimensions are 5.0 degrees of latitude by 3.3 degrees of longtitude for the world map (Fig. 1a) and 1.25 degrees of latitude by 0.625 degrees of longtitude for the east coast of North America (Fig. 1b). A=one observation; B=two observations, etc., within each cell. There are still little or no data for vast reaches of continental coastlines. Furthermore, the bulk of our data is concentrated in eastern North America, northwestern Europe and Japan. The former two areas were covered by glacial ice and suffered postglacial isostatic rebound and apparently crustal subsidence peripheral to those glaciated areas. The latter area is astride plate boundaries. Oceanic islands are generally poorly represented in our data bank.

Figures 2a and b are histograms displaying the distribution of our current data holdings through time. The world distribution peaks in mid-Holocene time while the eastern North America plot is bimodal reflecting the large fund of data obtained from isostatically uplifted areas which were formerly covered by glaciers.

Figures 3a and b are time-elevation plots of all the data we have recorded for the entire world and eastern North America respectively. The upper case letter convention is as noted previously; A=a single observation; B=two observations; etc. The unit cell width is 125 conventional radiocarbon years. The unit cell height changes at $\pm$ 10 meters. Between $\pm$ 10 meters, the unit cell height is 2 meters, while the height is 10 meters at elevation less than -10 meters or more than +10 meters. These plots show a clear separation into two fields prior to about 8,500 B.P. In almost all instances, the points near or above the present datum were collected from formerly glaciated areas - a manifestation of postglacial isostatic rebound. Prior to about 6,000 B.P., the generalised eustatic sea level curve lies below the modern datum - present sea level. On Fig. 3a (the world plot), these data show a reasonable concentration of data going back in time to a depth of about 40 meters at 10,500 B.P. However, even at this point in time the spread of data is fully 50 meters. For eastern North America (Fig. 3b), the display yields a similar story. We can follow a concentration of data back in time to a depth of about 30 meters at about 11,500 B.P. The spread of data at this point in time is about 50 meters. From these displays, we conclude that the achievement of a widely applicable eustatic sea level curve is improbable.

There is a well established method of displaying sea level data that avoids the limitations of the sea-level curve - the isobase map. An Isobase is a contour line that connects all areas of equal uplift or depression with respect to the contemporary datum. An isobase map is also a palaeogeoidal map. If the present sea level approximates the surface of the geoid, then an isobase map depicts the palaeogeoid or, more properly, the departure of an earlier geoidal surface with respect to the contemporary geoid. Sea level studies are in part exercises in palaeogeodesy. We use isobase maps in this study because these maps both avoid the frequent controversy associated with sea level curves and also provide a far better vehicle to display the available data in a four - dimensional format.

ISOBASE MAPS

Our data are stored in both the City University and GISS/NASA (Goddard Institute for Space Studies/National Aeronautics and Space Administration) computers. We have been using millennial (1,000-year) intervals in order to secure sufficient data to plot our maps and permit the effective resolution of the dates on the varying materials used for radiocarbon dating. Our programs utilize the NASA WOLFPLOT routines to draw isobase maps. The WOLFPLOT Plotting and Contouring Package is a FORTRAN subroutine using a Versatec electrostatic plotter. If the data are not regularly spaced, they must be gridded. The actual plotting uses a 4-point polynomial smoothing and averaging technique. The centers of the high and low points are established by fitting a Lagrande polynomial to a set of nine neighboring points. We have constructed two sets of maps: one set based on nearly 1,000 data entries portrays eastern North America while the other set based on more than 3,700 data points shows the entire world.

The data upon which these isobase maps are constructed are patchy in their distribution as demonstrated in Fig. 1. A few areas are well represented by data while much of the world yields little or no data. Because of the data distribution problem as well as

FREQUENCY BAR CHART

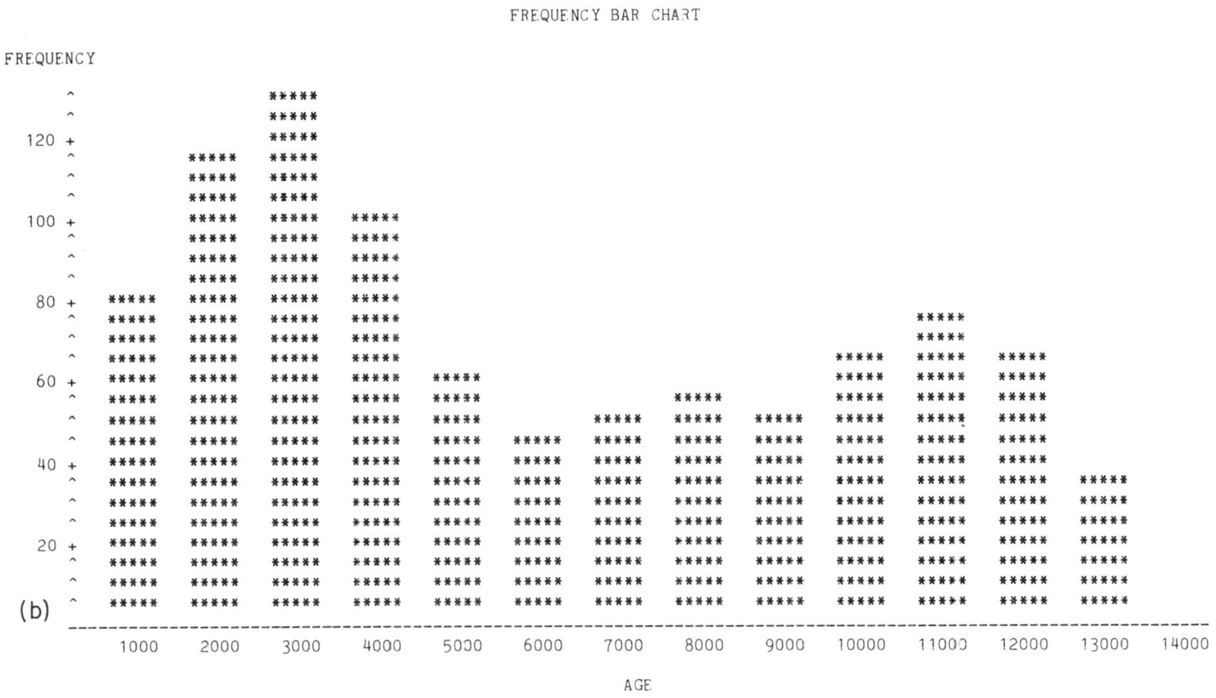

FIG. 2. *Histograms of radiocarbon-dated sea level data through time in 1,000-year intervals. (a) World-wide distribution. (b) Eastern North America and Bermuda.*

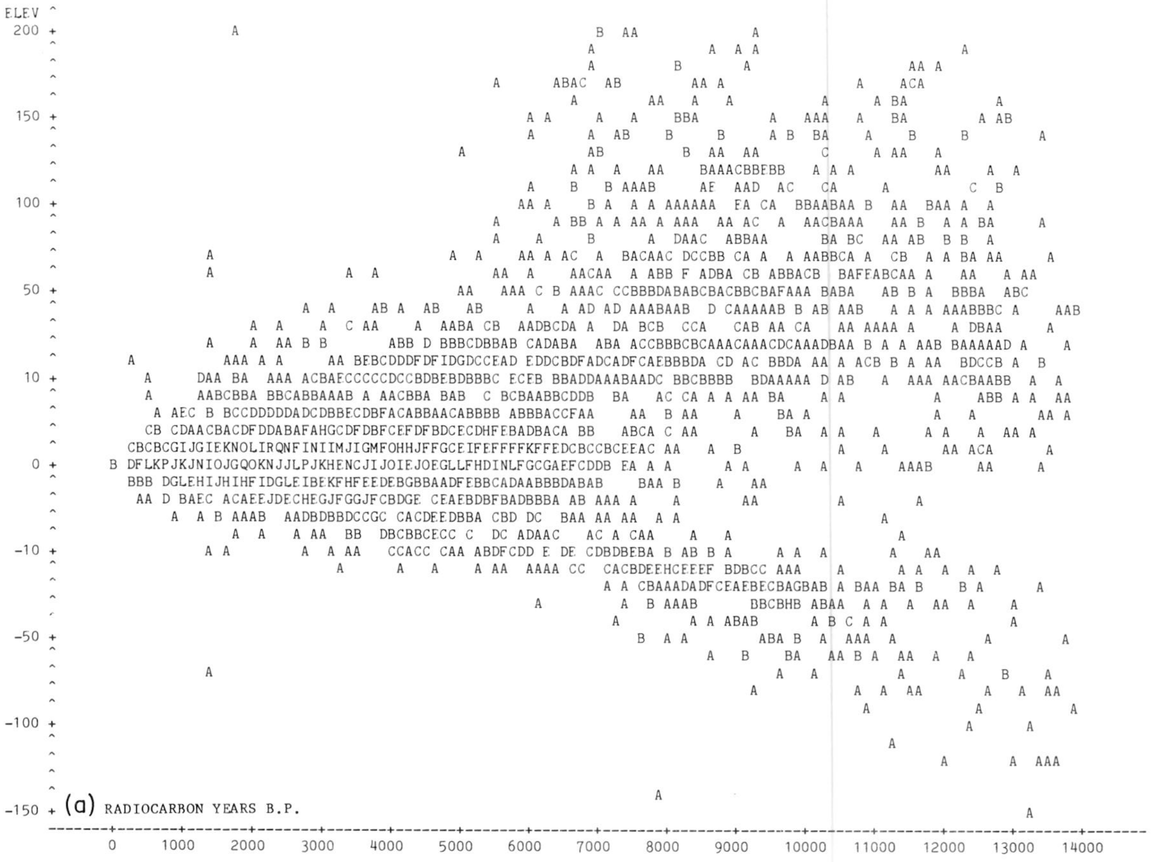

ELEV

200

150

100

50

10

0

-10

-50

-100

-150

(a) RADIOCARBON YEARS B.P.

0   1000   2000   3000   4000   5000   6000   7000   8000   9000   10000   11000   12000   13000   14000

ELEV

200 +

150 +

100 +

50 +

10 +

0 +

-10 +

-50 +

-100 +

-150 +

```
     0    1000  2000  3000  4000  5000  6000  7000  8000  9000  10000 11000 12000 13000 14000
```

RADIOCARBON YEARS B.P.

(b)

FIG. 3. Time vs. elevation distribution of radiocarbon-dated sea level. The bulk of the data comes from those areas which have undergone postglacial isostatic rebound. Presumably, the postglacial marine transgression is represented by the negative elevation data. Note that the range of data in this sector at any point in time prior to about 8,000 years ago exceeds 50 meters. A = one observation; B = two observations; etc. For dimensions of the unit cells, see text. (a) World date distribution. (b) Eastern North America and Bermuda distribution.

physical space limitations, the world map isobases were
constructed using a 5 x 5 degree grid as the smallest unit. All
values contained in a single five degree area (within the millennial
frame) were averaged in order to obtain a single value. The same
procedure was followed for eastern North America except that the
dimensions are 0.5 degrees. In those quads having more than one
entry, the averaging procedure tends to diminish extreme maxima
and minima values. Finally, the use of the grid pattern dictated
by scale considerations effectively masks evidence of vertical
fault movement and tight folding.

Our maps trace 17 contour lines: -40, -30, -20, -15, -10, -8, -6,
-4, -2, -1, 1, 2, 5, 10, 20, 50 and 100 meters.

The WOLFPLOT routine permits several options. Contour lines
may be open or closed; that is, the contour lines either terminate
or are directed to return to their point of origin. We arbitrarily
chose the latter course as easier to follow as well as aesthetically
more pleasing. For those areas of the world with little data, the
closed contour option does produce misleading hills and holes.
However, the open contour option produced ragged results. The
absence of contours indicates either the unavailability of data or
sea levels within one meter of the local datum. The routine also
permits extrapolation, or "filling". Units without elevations
adjacent to those with data are assigned the neighboring value.
Filling improves the readability of isobase maps. Another
procedure is "smoothing". This procedure uses a weighting
coefficient $0<C<1$. Each unit's elevation in turn is weighted by C
and adjacent units are weighted by (1-C) to produce a new
average elevation value. Smoothing tends to round the spacing
between contours at the expense of elevation. Maximum and
minimum elevations are stated as center signatures which express
both the sign and elevation at contour envelope maxima and
minima. Similar signatures are found when isobase surfaces meet
the contemporary datum.

The letter "H" and the symbol "+" indicate former sea level
elevated above the contemporary datum while the letter "L" and
the symbol "-" mark negative departures below the present datum.
The same signatures mark the positive and negative sides of our
imaginary zero contour lines.

Many combinations of contour elevations, filling, smoothing and
center specifications were tried. Not smoothing or filling, for
example, produces ragged peaks and holes. Over-filling or
smoothing obscures regional patterns. We chose to provide
maximum utility and readability. We are still experimenting with
the procedures, which obviously are not yet ideal. Finally, our
maps have no zero contour. Between the plus one and minus one
contours we have an amalgam of estimated error (0 ± 1) that
includes tides, datum uncertainty and operator error.

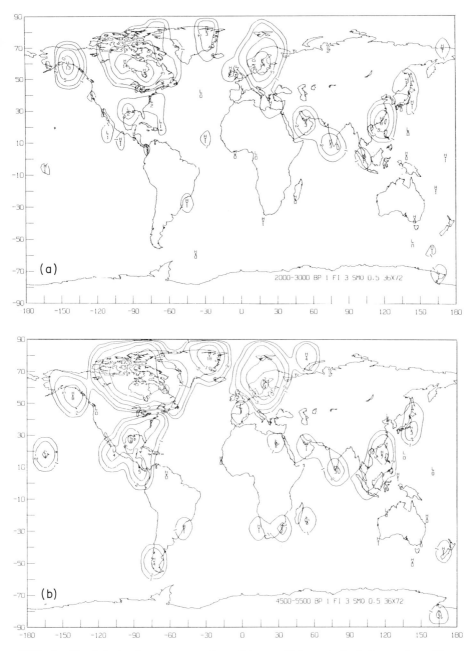

FIG. 4. *World isobase maps for five millennial intervals. The rationale and specifications are explained in the text. (a) 2,500 ± 500 B.P. (b) 5,000 ± 500 B.P. (c) 7,500 ± 500 B.P. (d) 10,000 ± 500 B.P. (e) 12,500 ± 500 B.P.*

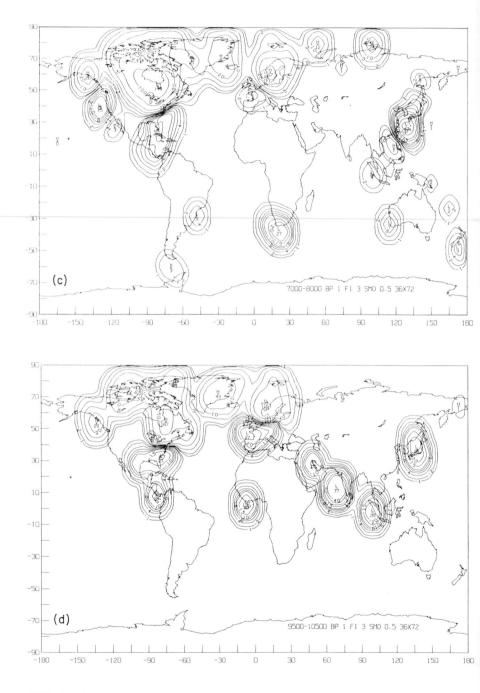

FIG. 4. *(continued)*

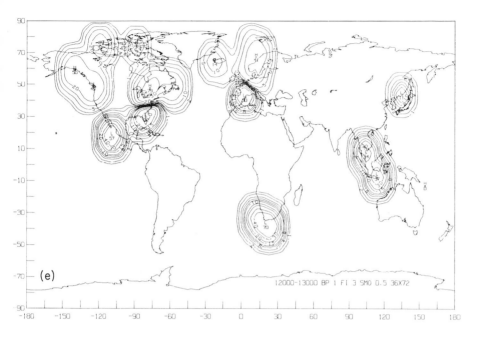

FIG. 4. *(continued)*.

WORLD ISOBASE MAPS

Figures 4a through 4e are five isobase maps for the millennial intervals 2,500, 5,000, 7,500, 10,000 and 12,500 + 500 B.P. The millennial time range, fill and smooth specifications, smoothing coefficient and array dimensions composing the map grid are noted in the lower right-hand corners of these maps. Areas of strong positive departure from the contemporary datum include those formerly glaciated areas centering around Hudson Bay and the Baltic Sea. Note that the earliest two of these world maps clearly show positive maximum values migrating from the edge of the then existing ice sheets towards their present high positions. Other persistent positive areas include island arc and plate boundaries such as southern Alaska, the west coast of Mexico, the South China Sea area including Formosa, and the Puget Sound area. The latter area's positive nature is primarily due to rebound following the demise of the Cordilleran Ice Complex. On the other hand, negative departures from the contemporary datum reflect, for the most part, the postglacial marine transgression of varying magnitude.

The negative minima represent a lower sea level for those areas where data exist. For example, Fig. 4d, 10,000 ± 500 B.P., grid values obtained going east from the Gulf of Panama are: -18, -23,

-31, -24, -18, -90, -31 and -28 meters. The full range is 72 meters although the median value lies between -24 and -28 meters. The minimal values for Fig. 4e, 12,500 ± 500 B.P., are -66, -37, -36, -76, -48, -39, and -13 meters for a range of 63 meters and a median value of -39 meters. What was the true level of the sea at 10,000 and 12,500 B.P.? It seems difficult to believe that these varying values will provide the answer.

The steep gradient that exists between the glaciated and marginal areas of northwestern Europe and northeastern North America are noteworthy. Are we seeing the effects of peripheral bulge subsidence, glacial sediment loading, or still some other phenomena affecting these passive continental margins? Clearly these world maps raise questions that require additional data and further study. Some of the patchiness or discontinuities on the maps reflect lack of data rather than actual discontinuities in our isobases. (e.g. compare Fig. 1a to Fig. 4). The data anisotropy therefore limits the utility of our maps for many coastal reaches. The lack of an adequate data base is a severe restraint on the testing of realistic models to explain these changes.

NORTH AMERICAN EAST COAST MAPS

Figs 5a through 5e are five isobase maps of the millennial intervals 2,500, 5,000, 7,500, 10,000 and 12,500 ± 500 B.P. The millennial time range, fill and smooth specifications, smoothing coefficient and cell array dimensions composing the map grid are noted in the lower right-hand corners of these maps. Formerly glaciated areas such as James Bay, Labrador, northern and western Newfoundland, and the St. Lawrence Valley demonstrate strong positive departures from the contemporary datum. The density of data for the east coast of the United States permits the 0.5 by 0.5 degree grid pattern to discern the contrasting transgression history of the northeast and southwestern segments of this coast. Holocene transgression rates for the embayed coast ranging from Pamlico Sound and Cape Hatteras northeast to Nova Scotia exceeds by a factor of two that of the coastal reach further to the southwest. However, Fig. 5e, for latest Wisconsinan time, finds the indicators of relative sea level about 70 meters below present sea level off Florida and South Carolina while further to the northeast, just south of Cape Cod, sea level indicators are only some 27 meters below present sea level. This in contrast with Fig. 5d, the beginning of Holocene time, which finds the sea level indicators southeast of Cape Cod more than twice as low as they appear to be off the southern coast.

Comparing the North American east coast data displays of both Figs 4 and 5 demonstrates the effect of data averaging within individual grid trapezoids. Fig. 5e (12,500 ± 500) B.P., finds sea level as much as 70 meters below the present datum while the

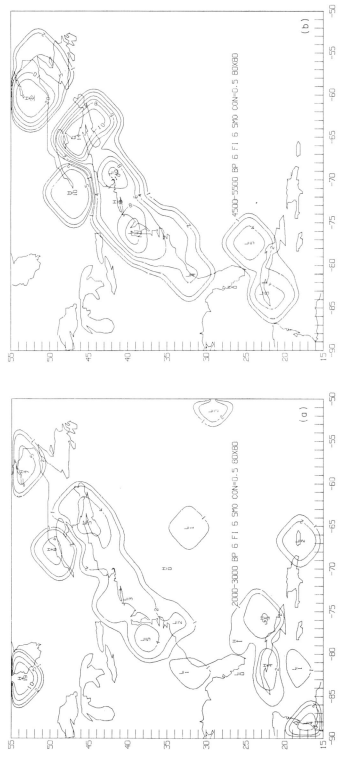

FIG. 5. *Isobase maps of eastern North America and Bermuda for five millennial intervals. The rationale and specifications are explained in the text. (a) 2,500 ± 500 B.P. The anomalous data at the extreme right margin of this map is a "bug" whose origin we have been unable to trace. (b) 5,000 ± 500 B.P. (c) 7,500 ± 500 B.P. (d) 10,000 ± 500 B.P. (e) 12,500 ± 500 B.P.*

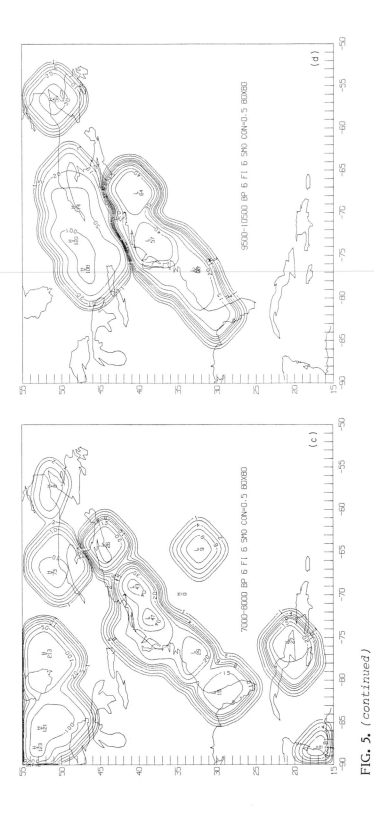

FIG. 5. (continued)

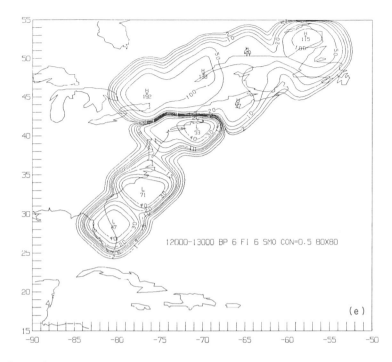

FIG. 5. *(continued)*

world map (Fig. 4e) for the same area and time interval records only 37 meters of sea level lowering. The world map obviously loses detail. Given the availability of data, regional maps are of greater accuracy and intrinsic value.

The maximum tilt of the earth's crust during Holocene time appears to have occurred at the contact zone between uplifted and downwarped areas in New England. This very sharp boundary shifts north as successively viewed on Figs 5e and 5d. A similar shift can be noted in the North Sea area on world maps Figs 4e and 4d. These boundary shift phenomena were noted by Newman and others (1971) who believed these shifts represented the migration of peripheral bulge subsidence towards the regional center of postglacial isostatic rebound.

DISCUSSION

Holocene sea level studies have demonstrated that various forms of crustal develeling diminish the possibility of determining a "eustatic" sea level curve. Extensive field data and thoretical explanations are reported in a large number of papers in the book edited by Mörner (1980). Few coastal areas have been immune from differential crustal warping. Archaeology supports the argument for develing. Examples of such archaeologic support are found in papers by Grant (Canadian Maritime Provinces), Black (Aleutian Islands), Faure (western Africa), and Sugio and his colleagues (Brazil) - all in the Mörner volume (*op. cit.*).

Concerning the migration of hominids into Australia and the New World, we have so far found remarkably few data suitable for our analysis. Beringia and the Indonesian Archipelago are virtual data deserts with respect to radiocarbon-dated late Quaternary sea level indicators. The proximity of formerly glaciated areas to Beringia and the plate boundary-island arc situation of Indonesia appear to ensure unusual and somewhat unpredictable land-sea relationships.

A major value of our study is that it enables a potential investigator to estimate the level of the sea with respect to the local datum for the past 12,000 years for those regions for which there are some data. For example, we estimate for the west Florida shelf (see Ruppé, 1980) that local relative sea level was within one meter of its present level 2,500 ± 500 B.P., between 4 and 5 meters below its present level 5000 ± 500 B.P., about -15 meters some 7,500 ± 500 B.P., near -20 meters 10,000 B.P., and about 35 meters below present sea level at 12,500 B.P.

Some may object that the last value is much too shallow. But, in fact we know remarkably little about the date and magnitude of the last sea level minimum. Though most investigators use a ballpark figure of about -100 meters at 18,000 B.P., documentation is sparse. The CLIMAP project members (1976) analyzing several classes of data suggest the sea level minimum was close to -85 meters. Blackwelder (1980) working along the east coast of the United States finds that sea level was at a rather constant -30 meters at 12,000 B.P. The late Wisconsinan sea level minimum should be synchronous with the maximum extent of northern hemisphere glaciers. Even this item is contentious for the known glacial maxima were clearly diachronous ranging from 21,000 to 14,000 Y.B.P. (Denton and Hughes, 1981; Peterson and other, 1979). Perhaps oxygen-isotope ratios can give us the date and magnitude of the last sea level minimum. However, Fairbanks and Matthews (1978) thoroughly discuss the oxygen-isotope sea level and estimate the last Wisconsinan lowering as about 100 ± 10 meters. Moreover, they amplify the error margin to as much as ± 20 meters in recognition of possible local temperature variation from one highstand of the sea to the next.

It seems we are a long way from quantitatively assessing the varying levels of the sea during late Quaternary times. The dynamics of the "Ice Ages" perturb the earth and its hydrosphere and atmosphere so that instabilities of all sorts are constantly causing changing relationships. We believe "eustatic" sea level is a casualty of, rather than a scientific touchstone for, the "Ice Ages". We close our argument by noting that Holocene crustal delevelling is of the same order of magnitude as Holocene sea level change. Therefore, archaeologists must look to local or regional sea level changes before projecting a tenable hypothesis concerning hominid migration routes.

SUMMARY AND CONCLUSIONS

1) The range of reported Holocene and latest Wisconsinan relative sea levels diverge back in time to a separation of at least several hundred meters at 12,000 B.P.

2) There are few reported data prior to 13,000 B.P. Indeed we are not certain of the level of the sea at the last glacial maximum - even if such an event can be defined in space and time.

3) Even the data points from below present sea level show a spread of more than 50 meters at 10,000 B.P.

4) Our data analyses suggest that the traces of any former sea level geoid have exhibited vertical displacement so that there cannot exist a stable datum from which to measure absolute "eustatic" fluctuations.

5) It follows that any model of hominid migration based on eustatic sea level change alone may well be fallacious since documented crustal delevelling is at least of the same order of magnitude as sea level fluctuations.

6) There is a need for more dated sea level indicators so that we can improve world isobase maps and produce regional ones for possible hominid migration routes.

ACKNOWLEDGEMENTS

We are grateful for the assistance and encouragement of J.T. Andrews (University of Colorado), D.L. Colquhoun (University of South Carolina), H. Faure (Laboratoire de Géologie du Quaternaire, Marseille), C. Hillaire-Marcel (University of Quebec at Montreal), P. Kaplin (Moscow State University), P. Pirezzoli (Laboratoire de Géomorphologie, de l'Ecole Pratique des Hautes Etudes, Montrouge), and F.W. Stapor, Jr., (Exxon Research and Production, Houston) all of whom supplied us with unpublished data. R.W. Fairbridge's (Columbia University) remarkable memory and fine library were the source of additional data. The project was supported by research grants from the Earth Science Division of the National Science Foundation and the Research Foundation of the City University of New York. Additional support came through a contract from the Earthquake Hazards Reduction Program of the U.S. Geological Survey. Most of the computer time was provided by the Goddard Institute for Space Studies of NASA while Newman was a National Research Council Resident Senior Research Associate. D. Soll provided continuing assistance and solace at the latter institution, J. Hansen, now Director at Goddard, arranged visiting scientist privleges for Marcus at both Goddard and the Jet Propulsion Laboratory in Pasadena. Dr. M. Rampino (GISS/NASA) and Professor Fairbridge reviewed and improved upon an earlier version of this paper.

REFERENCES

Blackwelder, B.W. (1980). Late Wisconsinan and Holocene tectonic stability of the United States mid-Atlantic coastal region. *Geology* **8**, 534-537.

Brooks, M.J., Colquhoun, D.J., Pardi, R.R., Newman, W.S. and Abbott, W.S. (1979). Preliminary archaeological and geological evidence for Holocene sea level fluctuations in the lower Cooper River valley, S.C. *The Florida Anthropologist* **32** (3), 85-103.

Clark, J.A., Farrell, J.E. and Peltier, W.R. (1978). Global changes in post-glacial sea level: a numerical calculation. *Quaternary Research* **9**, 265-287.

CLIMAP Project Members, (1976). The surface of the ice age Earth. *Science* **191**, 1131-1137.

Colquhoun, D.J., Brooks, M.J., Abbott, W.H., Stapor, F.W., Newman, W.S., and Pardi, R.R. (1980). Principles and problems in establishing a Holocene sea-level curve for South Carolina. In *Excursions in Southeastern Geology* (J.D. Howard, C.B. DePratter and R.W. Frey, eds.). Geological Society of America Guidebook **20**, 143-159.

Denton, G.H. and Hughes, T. (eds.) (1981). *The Last Great Ice Sheets*. Wiley, New York.

DePratter, C.N. and Howard, J.D. (1980). Indian occupation and geologic history of the Georgia coast, a 5,000-year summary. In *Excursions in Southeastern Geology* (J.D. Howard, C.N. DePratter and R.W. Frey, eds.) Geological Society of America Guidebook **20**, 1-65.

Fairbanks, R.G. and Matthews, R.K. (1978). The marine oxygen isotope record of Pleistocene coral, Barbados, West Indies. *Quaternary Research* 10, 181-193.

Flemming, N.C. (1969). Archaeological evidence of eustatic change of sea level and earth movements in the western Mediterranean during the last 2,000 years *Geological Society of America Special Paper* 109.

Mörner, N.A. (1976). Eustasy and geoid changes *Journal of Geology* 84, 123-151.

Mörner, N.A. (ed.) (1980). *Earth Rheology, Isostasy and Eustasy*. Wiley, New York.

Newman, W.S., Fairbridge, R.W. and March, S. (1971). Marginal subsidence of glaciated areas: United States, Baltic and North Seas. In *Etudes sur le Quaternaire dans le Monde*, Union Inter. l'Etude Quat. (M. Ters, ed.) 2, 795-801.

Newman, W.S., Marcus, L.F., Pardi, R.R., Paccione, J.A. and Tomacek, S.M. (1980). Eustasy and deformation of the geoid: 1,000-6,000 radiocarbon years B.P. In *Earth Rheology, Isostasy and Eustasy* (N.A. Mörner, ed.). Wiley, New York, pp. 555-567.

Newman, W.S., Marcus, L.F. and Pardi, R.R. (1981). Palaeogeodesy: late Quaternary geoidal configurations as determined by ancient sea levels. In *Sea Level, Ice, and Climatic Change*. (Allison, I. ed.). International Association of Hydrological Sciences Publication No. 131, Washington, D.C. pp. 263-275.

Newman, W.S. and Munsart, C.A. (1968). Holocene geology of the Wachapreague Lagoon, eastern shore peninsula, Virginia. *Marine Geology* 6, 811-105.

Peterson, G.M., Webb III, T., Kutzbach, J.E., van der Hammen, T., Wijmstra, T.A. and Street, R.A. (1979). The continental record of environmental conditions at 18,000 yr B.P.: an initial evaluation. *Quaternary Geology* 12, 47-82.

RADIOCARBON, (1958-1981). *American Journal of Science*. 1-23. New Haven.

Ruppé, R.J. (1980). The archaeology of drowned terrestrial sites: a preliminary report. In *Bureau of Historical Sites and Properties Bulletin No. 6*, Division of Archives, History and Records Management, Department of State, Tallahassee, Florida, 35-45.

POTENTIALS OF DISCOVERY OF HUMAN OCCUPATION SITES ON THE CONTINENTAL SHELVES AND NEARSHORE COASTAL ZONE

J.C. Kraft, D.F. Belknap[1] and I. Kayan[2]

*College of Arts and Science, Department of Geology,
101 Penny Hall, University of Delaware,
Newark, Delaware, 19711, U.S.A.*

[1]*Department of Marine Science, University of South Florida,
St. Petersburg, Florida 33701, USA.*

[2]*Üniversitesi Fizki Çoğrafya Fakültesi,
University of Ankara, Ankara, Turkey.*

ABSTRACT

It is no longer a question that man occupied the continental shelves of the world and the land bridges between continents during the middle and latter Quaternary period of geologic time. A wealth of data on land bridge migration in Beringia, and the southeast Asian mainland to Australia, for instance, have been widely dealt with in the literature. (see chapters in this volume by Flemming, Dikov, McManus *et al.*, and Barham and Harris). On the other hand, the identification of early man's sites on the continental shelves is another matter. Very few such sites are known to exist except in the immediate periphery of the present nearshore zone. These occupancy sites are evidenced by submerged cities and other occupancy sites from the past 5,000 years. Accordingly, the problem of identifying early man's sites on the submerged continental shelves of the world becomes, under present technologic conditions, a matter of luck or random search. Nevertheless, we can optimize those areas in which the search should be concentrated. The issue is made more complex by the many glacial and interglacial episodes of the Quaternary Period. Thus, we are faced with interglacial erosion and incised topography on the continental shelves, later infilled by sediments of the rising and transgressing shorelines and shelf sedimentation processes.   Taking the Holocene Epoch as an example, we know that the possibility of discovery of lmajor sites does exist. Palimpsests of recognizable coastal depositional environments similar to those of the present coastal zone have been discovered in various areas around the world, mainly by random dredging by fishermen.   This paper examines two extremes: 1) an area of active undergoing wave cut terrace erosion and the deposition of a thin veneer of Holocene Epoch sediment over the present and prior wave-cut terraces in the northern Aegean Sea; and 2) the Atlantic continental shelf off Delaware and southern New Jersey, an area of a subsiding geosyncline in which erosional and depositional processes are presently advancing landward and upward via erosion of the shoreface and relative sea-level rise over coastal environmental systems.   Study of the present coastal zone and its environments in each of these extreme examples can lead us to models that should be empirically useful.

INTRODUCTION

Study of human ancestors on the continental shelves and migrations via the land bridges between continents has been continuing for over a century.   Nevertheless, very few, if any, significant sites have been found on the continental shelves to date (see Flemming, this volume, for a review of human sites). One of the primary reasons is that the continental shelves are dynamic areas of sedimentation and erosion.   There tends to be both cataclysmic destructive elements as well as depositional elements that might preserve sites, both going on at the same time. Further, in the earlier part of the Holocene Epoch, beginning with the waning of the Wisconsin (Wurm) latest glaciation approximately 14,000 years ago, we know that man had spread throughout all of the continents of the world. We also know from the archaeological record that man occupied the coastal zone throughout at least the past 6,000 years for the specific purpose of utilizing its shellfish and finfish resources for food. It is most logical to assume that earlier man did the same thing, at least throughout the Holocene Epoch and probably in the Pleistocene Epoch as well.

Whitmore *et al.* (1967) and Edwards and Emery (1977) have listed some of the materials dredged up by fishermen on the outer Atlantic continental shelf of the United States.   These demonstrate with positive evidence that coastal environments similar to those of the present shorelines have migrated distances up to 150 km landward since early Holocene times; the evidence includes salt and fresh-water marsh peats and nearshore-estuarine molluscs such as *Crassostrea virginica* (the oyster) and *Mercenaria mercenaria* (the northern quahog). Because these earliest areas of the Holocene Epoch lie below the photic zone, methods and technology for discovery of these sites remain in a primitive state. We shall probably need to rely on hypothesis and chance to advance the study of these potentials in the near future. In the longer term, the more active geologic programs now on the continental shelves of the world conducted by the major oil companies should begin to provide abundant geophysical and sedimentological data regarding the thin Quaternary veneer on the world's continental shelves. However, to date, there appears to be no systematic approach by researchers in this field to collect this data, collate it, and form actual models of transgression and regression on the inner, middle, and outer shelves of the world. The problem is further complicated by the fact that the spudding-in of oil wells usually ignores the Quaternary veneer without sampling or geophysical recording. On the other hand, in many cases, for site stability reasons, cores have been taken in concentrated detail on the continental shelves and these should and could provide data necessary for our studies. Beyond that, the challenge to us is to examine the continental shelves from the point of view of rationalizing the optimal site areas of the migrating coastal environments into and up the estuarine river systems and putting our major research resources to the study of these areas in particular. Random studying of the shelves appears to be an impossible approach in terms of present technology and what we can expect for the next several decades.

DISCUSSION

Fig. 1 is a location map for the mid-Atlantic coast of the US. Shorelines, cross-section lines, and the location of the ancestral Delaware River valley are discussed later in the text. Fig. 2 is a location map for the Aegean coast. A discussion of evolution of the shelves in these two localities requires first an understanding of shoreline changes through time and the driving mechanism for that change: sea-level changes. The melting of the latest Wisconsin (Wurm) glacial ice resulted in a worldwide eustatic rise of sea level of at least 95 meters (Fairbridge, 1976) and possibly as much as 130 meters (Milliman and Emery, 1968). (see Inman, this volume). Radiocarbon dating of sea-level indicators, especially tidal-marsh peats, has resulted in several different views of worldwide sea-level change through the Holocene (for example, Shepard and Murray, 1967; Fairbridge, 1976). Belknap and Kraft (1977) have preferred the use of local relative sea-level curves, recognizing the unlikelihood of the formation of a single worldwide eustatic curve based on present status of the science. Fig. 3 shows two published local relative sea level curves: the Delaware coastal curve is after Belknap and Kraft (1977), from basal peats on the Delaware coast. The Delaware shelf curve, (Belknap and Kraft, 1981) and Milliman and Emery's (1968) curve based on a few

90   J.C. Kraft *et al.*

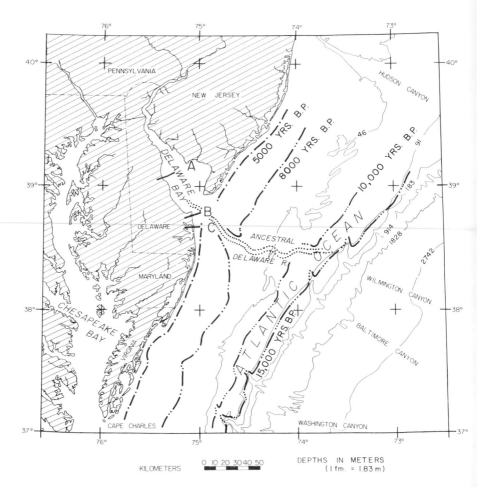

FIG. 1. *Index map to the mid-Atlantic United States. The locations given are for profiles A, B, and C described in the text and shown in Fig. 7. Shoreline positions are based on the sea-level curve of Belknap and Kraft (1977), adjusted for shelf-tilt by comparison to the Milliman and Emery (1968) curve. Position of the former course of the Delaware River valley is from Belknap et al. (1976), and Twichell et al. (1977).*

peats and oyster shells, are considerably lower than most other coastal curves, suggesting a tilt of the shelf of some 40 meters at the shelf break, due to hydroisostatic loading or tectonics (Belknap and Kraft, 1977). The history of sea-level change in Delaware has been a steady rise at a generally decreasing rate throughout the

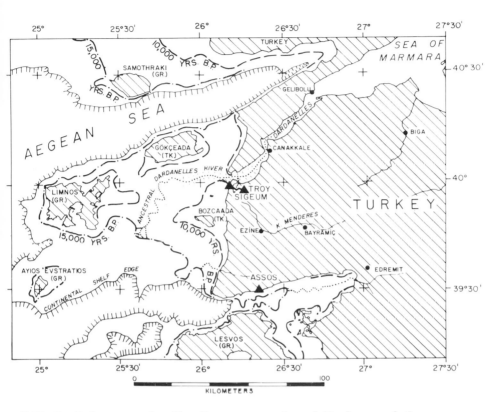

FIG. 2. *Index map to the Aegean coasts of Turkey and Greece. Important archaeological sites discussed in the text are shown as triangles; Turkish cities are shown as circles. The shoreline positions 15,000 and 10,000 years B.P. are based on Erol's sea level curve (Fig. 3), after Kraft (1980).*

past 15,000 years. The effect of this rise has been migration of the coast from near the shelf break to the present position. Shorelines at various times are shown in Fig. 1, based on estimates from the present bathymetry and the postulated shelf tilt. The position of the ancestral Delaware Shelf Valley is from high resolution seismic reflection profiles published by Belknap *et al.* (1976), Twichell *et al.* (1977), and Belknap and Kraft (1981). This river flowed to the shelf edge at the Wilmington Canyon during the sea-level minimum, and during shoreline retreat maintained a fluvial to estuarine character as it too retreated (Swift, 1973). The trace of the present shelf valley is well to the southwest of the ancestral thalweg, indicating a migration involving erosion of the southwest bank and deposition on the northeast, as is well demonstrated by prograding crossbeds in the seismic traces

(Belknap *et al.,* 1976). A researcher of archaeological remains would intuitively concentrate near this ancient river valley, as a desirable place for Indian occupancy. However, the history of erosion on the southwest and masive shelf sedimentation, up to 40 meters in thickness, on the northeast side, makes preservation and discovery potential of such sites very low. The character of the shorelines away from the estuary also changed with the rising sea level, as summarized by Belknap and Kraft (1981). Rapid migration due to rapid sea-level rise, and shallow depth of erosion may have enhanced preservation potential for sedimentary lithosomes and archaeological sites on the mid-shelf. This is the pattern that Edwards and Emery (1977) find, where dredged oysters and mammoth remains are concentrated in the mid-shelf. Erosion has reached deeper (at least 10 meters) on the inner shelf, so preservation potential is lower. Probability of discovery of an archaeological site will depend on specialized circumstances of pre-Holocene topography and rate of sea-level rise, discussed in detail in a following section.

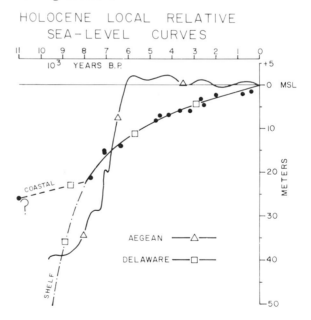

FIG. 3. *Local relative sea level curves for Delaware and the Aegean. The Delaware curve is constructed from basal peats in the coastal zone, after Belknap (1975), Kraft (1976), and Belknap and Kraft (1977). The Aegean curve is from marsh peats, wave cut notches, and pumice data (courtesy of O. Erol). Radiocarbon dates have been corrected to the 5730 year period half-life and the MASCA tree-ring correction to 7500 years BP.*

The second curve in Fig. 3 is a local relative sea-level curve from the eastern Aegean, courtesy of Prof. Oguz Erol (Kraft *et al.*, 1980). Local relative sea-level studies are extremely difficult owing to high tectonic activity in this area. This curve differs from the Delaware curve in being steeper before 6,000 years B.P., and reaching a gently fluctuating sea level near or above present since then. It is based on several radiocarbon dates in marshes, and on pumice radiometric data. The mildly fluctuating relative sea level since 6,000 years B.P. leads to profoundly different shoreline changes in the Aegean, specifically cycles of cliff retreat at faster and slower rates on exposed headlands. Prior to 6,000 years B.P. shoreline retreat across the continental shelf (Fig. 2) proceeded rapidly on the low-gradient plain occupied by the ancestral Dardanelles River, until sea cliffs were encountered. These cliffs were the remnants of former high sea-level shorelines of prior interglacials, which had cut terraces and scarps to their sea-level maxima. Absolute location of these features is unknown at present, until seismic reflection profiles for this portion of the world become available. The estimated shoreline positions of 15,000 and 10,000 years B.P. are shown in Fig. 2, based on Erol's Curve, after Kraft *et al.* (1980). The search for earlier man before 6,000 years B.P. on the continental shelf must be with the understanding of rapid sea-level rise relative to land and accordingly very high rates of coastal transgression. Whether or not the sedimentation rates accompanying this were fast or slow (thick or thin) are not known. However, based on the example of the Atlantic coast continental shelf, the rapidity of the transgression would suggest that this is an optimal area for study in that the time frame is short, the transgression is rapid, and the possibility of exposed areas of Holocene coastal sedimentary environments is great. After 6,000 years before present, with a fluctuating shoreline, conditions and techniques for searching for early man on the continental shelf of the north Aegean Sea change. We are faced with times of rapid transgression, short times of retreat of the coast or regression, transgression again, etc. The complexity of this type of erosion/deposition would create a very complex veneer over the wave cut terrace formed over the past 6,000 years. Therefore, our possibility of discovery of sites of occupancy by earlier man decrease until we get to Classical to early Helladic time (2,500 years before present to 5,000 years before present) when man's structures became those of fortified massive stone construction.

We know the Aegean Sea to be a very complex area of collision between several of the world's crustal plates (Flemming, 1978). It is tectonically extremely active. Nowhere is this more true than in the northern part of the Aegean Sea. We know a great deal about the morphology of the continental shelf south of Thrace (Greece) and the shelf south of European Turkey and the west of

Asia Minor. In the vicinity of the Biga Peninsula in the Troad at the mouth of the Dardanelles, we know the area to be seismically active and upwarping. Miocene marine sediments, for instance, crop out high above the deeply incised valley of the Dardanelles. Further, when sea level was lowered 100 meters, approximately at its maximum low in the latest Wisconsin (Würm) glaciation, a wide shelf became exposed to the south of Thrace, European Turkey, and the Biga Peninsula. Little is known about the Quaternary stratigraphy of this submarine shelf, let alone the Holocene stratigraphy or the geophysical form and shape of the various sedimentary environmental lithosomes and the many incised valleys that must have crossed this shelf area in latest Würm time. However, the Dardanelles have been studied and provide a direct example of pre-Holocene deeply incised topography of a river that flowed in the ancestral valley of the Dardanelles, across the continental shelf and into the Aegean Sea of 13,000 to 14,000 years ago. Presently we do not know the precise path of this river and its tributaries (at least it is not published to the authors' knowledge), but, on the other hand, we do know much about the Dardanelles and can conjecture the form of this valley system in pre-Holocene time across the shelf (Fig. 2). We further know that the Sea of Marmara to the north of the Dardanelles lies along the "greater Anatolian fault", is of great depth, far below any pre-Holocene incision of valleys, and tectonically active. Thus an inland sea lay in this area throughout the Quaternary time. The greater Anatolian fault does not follow the path of the Dardanelles but rather crosses the Gallipoli Peninsula and thence into the Aegean Sea. This was the pre-Wisconsin (Würm) pathway or marine connection between the Aegean Sea and the Black Sea. Studies of this system would be important to those interested in early man on the shelf south of Thrace and European Turkey before late Wisconsin (Würm) time. For some reason, probably tectonic and possibly fault related, the Holocene incision of stream valleys included the incision of the present Dardanelles valley leading southward accross the shelf and incision of the pre-Bosphorus valley northward into the Black Sea. With eventual rise of sea level to its present level, the present straits of the Dardanelles, Sea of Marmara, and Bosphorus were formed between the Aegean Sea and the Black Sea.

Returning to the shelf south of Thrace (Greece) and European Turkey, we can study the present morphology of the submerged shelf to form hypothetical models as to what occurred and optimize the areas of possible search for earlier man occupation sites. The most rational inital approach would be that of shallow seismic studies to delineate the stream systems which would have formed the leading edge of the transgression landward. On the other hand, this is an area of presently active wave-cut cliff retreat and, therefore, the form of an area of wave-cut terrace

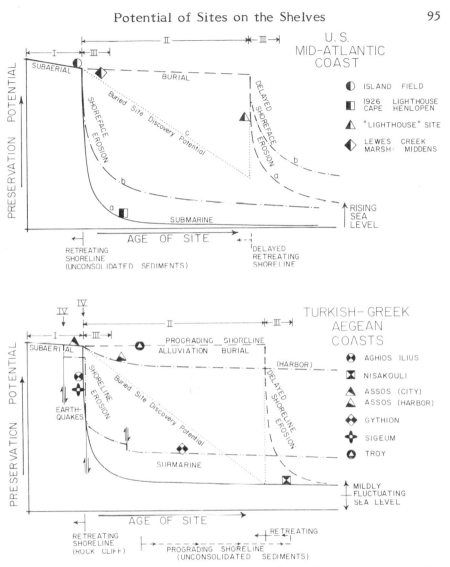

FIG. 4. *Conceptual time-line models of the preservation potential of coastal archaeological sites, comparing and contrasting the mid-Atlantic and Aegean coasts. The half-black shapes refer to specific archaeological sites discussed in the text. The horizontal axis represents relative age of a site, non-quantitatively. The vertical axis represents relative preservation potential of a site, or in some cases discovery potential. Position of the shoreline at the present time is shown on the horizontal axis. Roman numerals refer to phases in the history of a coastal site. Phase I is subaerial degradation. Phase II is burial. Phase III is shoreline erosion: IIIa*

Fig. 4 (cont)
representing   open   ocean   conditions,   IIIb   representing
estuarine   conditions.   Phase IV is tectonic movement, such
as dropping of a graben valley block.   The dotted lines
refer to discovery potential of a buried site only. Relative
sea-level change is indicated to the right.

and resultant depositional units of Holocene age might tend to
have covered many of the earlier human sites (particularly the
Holocene sites). Our model for this submerged land bridge-shelf
must therefore be formed only partly on fact and much on an
empirical basis.

Conceptual Models

Fig. 4 is a conceptual model of coastal archaeological sites in the
US mid-Atlantic coast contrasted with the Aegean coasts of
Greece and Turkey. The vertical axis represents the preservation
potential of an archaeological site. The horizontal axis is a
relative measure of the age of a site. For actual examples, this
axis will stretch or shrink depending on rate of shoreline
movement and original distance of the site from the shoreline. The
relative shoreline position at present is shown below. The
horizontal axis should not be misinterpreted as a strict linear,
quantitative measure of time. Similarly, the vertical axis is also
relative: architectural ruins of quarried stone from the Aegean
would be far more resistant to shoreline processes than Indian
middens of the mid-Atlantic coast, but conversely a midden or
mound is more resistant to earthquakes than a building. Thus the
relative preservation potentials are purely qualitative in nature.

On the mid-Atlantic coast, sites initially pass through a subaerial
degradation phase (I on Fig. 4) in which running water, frost, and
biological activity alter the site. Phase II is common for sites on
the landward side of marshes and lagoons, such as Island Field
(Fig. 9), which ultimately are buried by tidal marsh or lagoon muds
with continuing sea-level rise. Under these quiet environments
preservation is enhanced (dashed line). Probability of discovery,
however, falls as burial hides sites from view (dotted line). Phase
III is as the erosive shoreface passes the site. Degree of
preservation is dependent on the depth of scour, which reaches 10
meters on the Atlantic coast and 3 to 4 meters on the Delaware
Bay shore (Fig. 4, Cape Henlopen light house, 1926). Thus,
probability of destruction is dependent in part on whether a site is
intersected by a deeply-eroding oceanic shoreface (line a) or a
shallowly-eroding estuarine shoreface (line b). Either 5 or 10
meters depth of scour is sufficient to remove most Indian
archaeological sites on a flat plain. Delayed arrival of the

PLATE. 1. *The ruins of Aghios Ilios, a church ca.1,300-1,400 B.P. eroding high on the face of a rapidly receding cliff. In the back-ground is the dark island of Nisakouli, occupied in Helladic times approximately 3,100 to 3,700 years B.P. In both cases the sites will eventually be totally destroyed. Artifacts from the sites will be incorporated into the thin veneer of sediment covering the wave cut terrace of the transgressive coastline. Methone embayment, SW Peloponnese.*

shoreface, however, such as a valley floor or wall site which has subsequently been inundated by marsh or lagoonal mud, may allow preservation as the shoreface passes above it. The zone of erosion passes above the site because sea level has risen in the interim. Discovery potential (dotted line) jumps briefly for buried sites if they are re-exposed at the shoreface, but declines as rapidly as a non-buried site thereafter.

The lower half of Fig. 4 shows a similar evolution pattern for Aegean sites, with several notable differences. Most importantly, sea level has apparently fluctuated mildly since about 6,000 years B.P. in the Aegean (Fig. 3), so the assumption of constantly rising sea level made in Delaware is not valid. Also, shoreline erosion takes place as a cliff-retreat in most places. Localities originally on a cliff top, such as Sigeum in the Troad (*ca*. 2400 - 2000 years B.P.) and Nisakouli in southwestern Peloponnese (*ca*. 3100 - 3700 years B.P.), would be destroyed as a coherent site, although blocks of rock from their buildings would probably remain in the surf zone. Aghios Ilios in southwestern Peloponnese *ca*. 1400 years B.P. (Plate 1) is an example of a site currently in the process of this cliff-retreat erosional phase. A site which was originally a

PLATE 2. *The submerged harbor of the Classical-Roman city*
of Assos in the embayment at Edremit in Turkey. Remnants of
the harbor are submerged by relatively well preserved.
Should the transgression continue, they may be covered by a
thin veneer of sandy sediment.

harbor, however, would have a much better chance of
preservation, as it sinks or is buried by sediment. An example is
Assos, a Classical-Roman city in the embayment at Edremit in
Turkey, where the harbor is well preserved, but the lower city is
mostly destroyed (Plate 2). A process lacking in Delaware but
important in the Aegean is shown by the bouble dot-dashed line: a
site in a graben valley which has undergone earthquakes, dropping
it rapidly below sea level. An example is Gythion, a Classical city
in the Gulf of Laconia in the Peloponnese. This tectonic dropping
may avoid shoreline erosional processes, but probably causes
massive direct destruction by the earthquake itself. The burial
phase in the Aegean is mostly from alluviation at the mouths of
rivers. An example is Troy, as discussed by Kraft *et al.* (1980),
where major alluviation has caused progradation of the shoreline
15 km seaward in the past 9,000 years. Thus burying villages on
the alluvial plain up to 5 meters since Troy I, 5,000 years B.P.
Continued erosion into the future may eventually reach Troy,
placing it in the delayed shoreline erosion phase, but this may
require a wait until the next interglacial, some tens of thousands
of years hence.

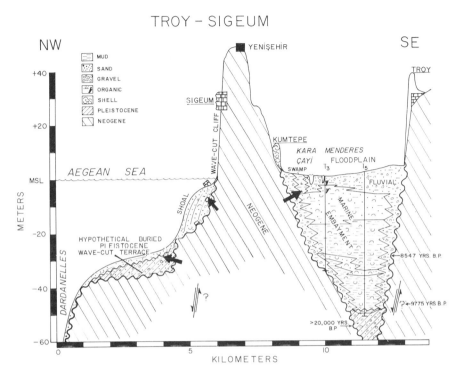

FIG. 5. *A geological profile - cross section from the Aegean Sea and the cliffs at Sigeum across the Scamander River valley to the tel or archaeological site at ancient Troy. Drill holes from Kraft et al. (1980). Location shown in Fig. 2.*

AEGEAN ARCHAEOLOGICAL SITES

The remnants of many submerged sites from Roman to early Helladic times can be expected to be discovered in the coming decades. A prime example is the problem of the location of ancient Sigeum of only 2,000 plus years before present, already mentioned.

Fig. 5 is a profile cross section from the shelf to the cliffs of Yenişehir and southeast to the site of ancient Troy, an example of man's occupancy of the continental shelf in an embayment in the Scamander (Kara Menderes) River valley which became flooded to its peak 7,000 years before present. Massive fortification structures were built beginning about 5,100 to 5,200 years before present (Kraft *et al.*, 1980). Ancient Troy (Plate 3) remains as an archaeological tel of occupancy from 5,000 years before present to 2,000 years before present. Ancient Sigeum is possibly totally eroded into the sea by wave cut cliff retreat or a small remnant of it may remain in place under the abandoned town site of Yenisehir with the majority of the city broken up and fallen into the sea (Plate 4). Kumtepe is a shell midden, of marine organisms, now at the edge of the wide alluvial plain. Beyond this, we know nothing about the occupancy of still earlier Holocene people on the continental shelf south of Thrace (Greece) and Turkey in the north Aegean Sea. The problem is made more complex by the fact of multiple wave cut terraces of early Quaternary Ages, presently not related to sites occupied by Quaternary man, the sites probably now forever buried. A hypothetical terrace of a lower Pleistocene high sea stand is indicated in Fig. 5.

PLATE 3. *The cliffs of the Aegean Sea to the west of Troy in the vicinity of the ancient city of Sigeum. The cliffs are composed of soft sands, silts, gravels, and limestone. Rate of wave cut cliff retreat is relatively rapid leaving behind a wave cut terrace covered by a thin veneer or sediment. Any city located on a cliff site such as this would be preserved in the stratigraphic record as the destroyed remnants or artifacts of the city mixed with the thin veneer of sediments.*

Het ghefsicht vanden Hellespont en vande propontii

A. den Bergh Olimpus. B. Propontide oft de marmorifche zee. C. marmonifche eylanden. D. Gallipoli. E. de Dardanellen. F. Hellefpon. G. het
nieuw Cafteel Van Afia. H. het nieuw Cafteel Van Europa. I. de have van Suget. K. de ruwinen van troyen, den Bergh Ida. M. Conftantinopel.
Peeters. ex. op De Groen. Mart. Ant.

PLATE 4. An engraving by Jacques Peeters (1637-1695) of Antwerp, published about 1692 A.D. The
ruins of ancient Sigeum are located in the lower center of the plate in the eroding cliff of the
Aegean Sea, underneath the more modern town (abandoned) of Yenişehir.

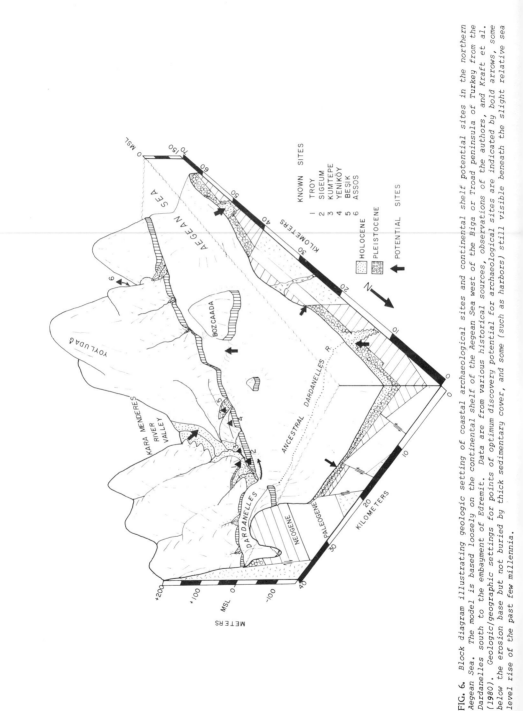

FIG. 6. Block diagram illustrating geologic setting of coastal archaeological sites and continental shelf potential sites in the northern Aegean Sea. The model is based loosely on the continental shelf of the Aegean Sea west of the Biga or Troad peninsula of Turkey from the Dardanelles south to the embayment of Edremit. Data are from various historical sources, observations of the authors, and Kraft et al. (1980). Geologic/geographic settings for points of optimum discovery potential for archaeological sites are indicated by bold arrows, some below the erosion base but not buried by thick sedimentary cover, and some (such as harbors) still visible beneath the slight relative sea level rise of the past few millennia.

Fig. 6 is a block diagram illustrating concepts described for the northern Aegean shelf. The coast is of high relief, tectonically active, and fragmented by normal faults. The Kara Menderes river valley is possibly a graben. Rising sea level has caused cliff retreat and terrace cutting, destroying many former sites. Potential sites, however, are indicated by the arrows. Known sites are shown as triangles. Other coastal features shown in Fig. 6 are: (1) a double tombolo off Bozcaada, enclosing a former lagoon, which may have high potential for discovery of sites, (2) a shoal formed by littoral drift to the southwest from the mouth of the Dardanelles, and (3) alluviation in several embayments. Note also the incision hypothesized for the former Dardanelles river valley.

We have an outstanding model for the processes that occurred along this coast from ancient Alexandria Troas and Besika embayment in the south, to the entrance to the Dardanelles in the north. Approximately 8 km to the east of the present wave cut

PLATE 5.   *The tel at ancient Troy, occupied from 5,000 to 2,000 years B.P. Twelve fortifications and one major city have overlain this tel. In the foreground is the floodplain of the Scamander River under cultivation. Under this floodplain to depths of 5 m lie potential buried artifacts and archaeological sites of ages from present to 5,000 years B.P. The site will be ultimately destroyed by cliff erosion of the Aegean Sea in the Holocene Epoch or in the next interglacial epoch of high sea level.*

terrace and eroding cliffs lies the Bronze Age site of ancient Troy awaiting in turn the arrival of coastal erosion, if not during this interglacial high sea stand, then in the next Quaternary interglacial rise of the sea (Plate 5). Here lies a steep wave cut cliff incised into sands, gravels, and marls. The ancient city of Sigeum, originally an Athenian colony, lies along this cliff coast (Plate 4). Its present site is assumed to be under the more modern but abandoned Turkish town of Yenisehir. As this is a military zone, the site has not been studied in detail with modern technologies. Nevertheless, documentation by early European visitors in the 17th and 18th centuries do suggest Classical-Roman structures being eroded away from under the site of Yenisehir (Plate 4). A more modern example is that of Yeniköy. This village was also built along this cliff and has had to be moved inland over the past 30 years and rebuilt because of the rapidity of wave cut cliff retreat. Further out on the continental shelf lie a number of islands such as Bozcaada (ancient Tenedos), Limnos (Greece), Bozcaada (Turkey), and Samothrace (Greece) (Fig. 2). These islands or outliers are in effect giant stacks of more resistant rocks that were bypassed by the wave cut terrace in the process of landward erosion. These ancient islands might also provide optimal areas for nearshore submarine studies of potential early man sites because of their accessibility. Regardless, we know that high cliffs (up to 20 meters) are undergoing active wave cut cliff retreat, wave terrace formation and finally deposition of a thin veneer in the Holocene Epoch.

To the southeast lie the ruins of the ancient City of Assos (Fig. 2, Plate 2). Its harbor was built at the base of a cliff, the citadel high above the sea on a granitic terrain. Relative sea level has risen over the ruins, preserving extant a "harbor under the sea". The cliffs above the harbor of Assos are formed of granitic rock occupied by the acropolis, not as easily eroded as at Yeniköy and Sigeum to the northwest. This results in nearshore submergence of an ancient Greek city harbor intact similar to Elaphonisos in the southeast Peloponnese (Flemming, 1971). The process could have been by seismic cataclysmic event such as at Helice (373 B.C.) in the Gulf of Corinth, now lost under alluvium of the flank of a graben, or at Gythion, still well preserved in the nearshore zone of the Gulf of Laconia in the southeastern Peloponnese.

Knowing the most probable relative rates of sea-level rise as defined by Erol previously, knowing the processes of wave-cut terrace - cliff retreat and deposition of thin sedimentary sheets overlying this terrace, we can derive fairly accurate positions of ancient shorelines in this shelf model. Two reconstructions of shoreline positions are shown on Fig. 2 as examples of this type of empirical geological exercise. The 10,000 to 15,000 years B.P. shorelines can be defined within a zone of error ± 10 kilometers assuming that the small tectonic uplift of this region was equal throughout the region. It goes without saying that in defining such a coastal zone, the eustatic or absolute sea-level curve and any local relative deflections from the curve must be known.

THE ATLANTIC CONTINENTAL SHELF: OFF DELAWARE

The geologic-tectonic settings of the northern Aegean Sea continental shelf and the Atlantic continental shelf are extremely different. But they can be compared and contrasted. The Atlantic continental shelf and coastal plain is a continuum throughout Quaternary time of the same geologic province of the emerged and submerged shelf. Coastal deposition is now on the western flanks of the Baltimore Canyon Trough geosyncline although in early Holocene time the coastal zone was centered in the geosyncline. The difference is of major import. In contrast, there is little evidence of any recent flooding of the land surrounding the northern periphery of the Aegean Sea continental shelf. It is an area of slow wave erosion and coastal cliff retreat.

Delaware Coastal and Continental Shelf Archaeological Sites

There is major evidence that the relative sea level has risen and fallen, flooding the entire portions of the low lying coastal plain of southern Delaware, Maryland, and the Virginia eastern shore. Thus, some evidences of early man on "the continental shelf" may in fact someday be discovered in the shoreline facies of earlier Quaternary period high sea stands. The likelihood is admittedly very low, nevertheless, the sediments are available for shallow drilling and outcrop studies.

On the other hand, the submerged Atlantic continental shelf is a completely different matter. The sediments undergoing submergence and emergence are all of Quaternary age and consist of unconsolidated sands, silts, and muds of the various coastal and fluvial environments that have migrated in transgressive and regressive modes across the shelf over the past two million years. Here again a knowledge of local relative and absolute sea-level change is needed in order to make projections of the potential for discovery of early human sites on the shelf. Local relative sea-level curves for the coastal zone environments of Delaware are well known (Kraft, 1976; Belknap and Kraft, 1977; Belknap and Kraft, 1981). Superimposed upon these local relative curves must be the worldwide eustatic effect (Fairbridge, 1976). Definition based on the limited data we have from the latest transgression across the shelf in Holocene times can be used to identify location and age of coastal positions that would tend to be the areas of occupance by early man. The local relative curve established in Delaware based on over fourteen basal peats and 100+ radiocarbon supporting data points has a more regional application in view of new data (unpublished) from the Pautuxent River and the St. Mary's River on the western side of the estuary, Chesapeake Bay, approximately 100 km southwest of the sources of the Delaware data.   Nevertheless, when the Delaware curve is applied to radiocarbon data from coastal environments (oysters, coastal salt marsh sediment, etc.) as dredged up by random chance on the outer continental shelf (Whitmore *et al.*, 1967), it shows that deposits of the earliest Holocene or late Wisconsin times are significantly lower than similar coastal deposits presently located and identified in great detail in the Delaware coastal zone (Kraft *et al.*, 1979; Kraft and John, 1976; and Kraft, 1971). An analysis of the radiocarbon dates from coastal sedimentary environmental lithosomes along the major estuary Delaware Bay, the west shore of the Chesapeake Bay, and the Atlantic coastal area of Delaware showed horizontality or parallelism of sea level dates vs. depth relative to the coastal plain (Belknap and Kraft, 1977). Further, the data from Whitmore *et al.* (1967), and Belknap and Kraft (1977) show that the earliest Holocene-very latest Wisconsin depth positions of sedimentary and coastal sedimentary environments of the outer shelf are much lower than those indicated by the Delaware coastal data.   The entire area is in the large and presumably actively subsiding Baltimore Canyon Trough geosyncline (greater than 35,000 feet in depth). It may be hypothesized that the latest movement of water over the coastal plain-continental shelf geomorphic provinces has led to significant tectonic subsidence of the outer shelf area as opposed to little subsidence or change along the fringe or northwest flank of the geosyncline in Delaware and Maryland. A.L. Bloom (oral communication) has attributed this to a hydroisostatic effect of "water loading".

Regardless of the reasons for the discrepancy of levels of sea relative to land, the facts speak for themselves.   During the waning of the latest Wisconsin (Würm) glaciation and the very earliest Holocene times, the shoreline lay at the outer edge of the continental shelf with deep estuarine embayments across the shelf into the coastal estuarine systems of Delaware Bay and its tributary valleys, from evidence along the coastal zone of Delaware (Kraft *et al.*, 1979; Kraft *et al.*, 1976; Kraft and John, 1976; and Kraft, 1971). To the north, the submerged canyon of the Hudson River, an extension of the present day Hudson River back to earliest Holocene times remains exposed as a valley on the continental shelf.   Further south, the extensions of the ancestral river drainage system of the Delaware River and its tributaries in early Holocene times are muted by infill of later Holocene sediments.   However, by seismic information and projection (Belknap *et al.*, 1976; Knebel *et al.*, 1977; and Sheridan *et al.*, 1974) we now have a knowledge of the location of these ancestral rivers across the continental shelf adjacent to Delaware.

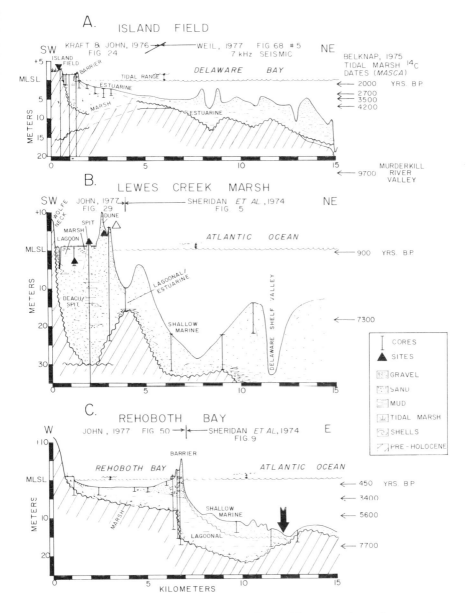

FIG. 7. *Geologic cross sections from the coast and nearshore shelf of Delaware, based on rotary auger drill holes, plastic pipe cores, vibracores and seismic reflection profiling. Radiocarbon dates on tidal marsh and basal peats from each specific section clarify sea level history. MASCA and 5730 year half-life corrected (Belknap, 1975; Kraft,*

Fig. 7. (cont.)
1976). Location of cross section given in Fig. 1. Figure 7A
based on data from Weil (1977) for Delaware Bay and Kraft
and John (1976) for South Bowers (Island Field). Figure 7B
modified and projected three miles from Sheridan et al.
(1974) for nearshore marine and modified from John (1977)
for Lewes Creek Marsh. Figure 7C modified from John (1977)
for Rehoboth Bay, and after Sheridan et al. (1974) for the
nearshore marine. Actual archaeological sites discussed in
the text are shown as black triangles. The bold black arrow
in Fig. 7C refers to the likely spot to search for a
submarine site, referring to the concept expressed by
similar arrows in Fig. 8.

Swift *et al.* (1972) developed a model geomorphic-process oriented map of the continental shelf of the region. We know from their hypotheses as to the nature of erosion, deposition and ravinement or erosion of the shoreface as the coasts transgressed landward across the Atlantic continental shelf that depositional units are very complex. Knebel *et al.* (1977), Sheridan *et al.* (1974), Field and Duane (1976) and Duane *et al.* (1972) provide us with a wealth of information regarding which elements of submarine morphology on the shelf are erosional and which are depositional. We can thus envisage an early Holocene setting of a coastal barrier system with lagoons very similar to that of the present New Jersey-Delaware-Maryland-Virginia shoreline with deep embayments across the continental shelf of the magnitude of ± 50 to 75 km inland. Surrounding these coastal environments would be the optimal areas for search for evidences of early man in the Holocene Epoch. Here again we have the problem that much of the area to be studied is below the photic zone. This is further compounded by the fact that we are dealing with American Indian traditions and life styles. Therefore, it is unlikely that any massive amounts of metal or rock would be available to aid us in the search of this area. As stated before, Whitmore *et al.* (1967) clearly demonstrated that coastal sedimentary environmental lithosomes similar to those of present time are exposed in patchy areas on the outer continental shelf. Ultimately, whether early human sites are discovered or not, may depend upon luck or new technological applications.

Data presented in Fig. 7 and studies over the past decade permit a detailed summation of the problem and solution to some of the questions about earlier human occupation of the continental shelf or the submerged areas in Delaware Bay. A recent summary of this work is given by Kraft and John (1978). This study clearly demonstrates one of the dilemmas of the researcher in locating occupation sites of earlier man. For instance, in the extreme landward estuarine positions in many areas along the Delaware

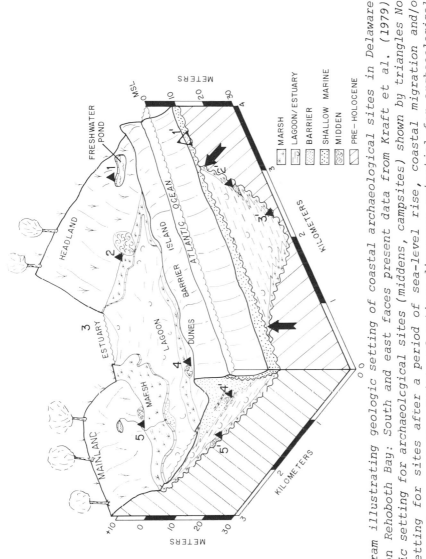

FIG. 8. Block diagram illustrating geologic setting of coastal archaeological sites in Delaware. Modeled loosely on Rehoboth Bay: South and east faces present data from Kraft et al. (1979). Geologic/geographic setting for archaeological sites (middens, campsites) shown by triangles No. 1-5. Geologic setting for sites after a period of sea-level rise, coastal migration and/or burial shown by triangles no. 1'-5'. Points of optimum discovery potential for archaeologicals on the nearby shelf are indicated by the bold arrows: the low erosion base, but not buried by thick sedimentary cover.

PLATE 6 *The Cape Henlopen lighthouse archaeological site dated to 2,000 years B.P. When occupied, it was on a tip of a recurved spit of ancestral Cape Henlopen, curved into a lagoonal type embayment of Delaware Bay. The site shown is in a deflation pit in a coastal dune field. The site has now disappeared, being buried by the advancing coastal dunes. Ultimately, it will face destruction as the dune field, berm and beachface, and shoreface undergo erosion. The only remnants will then be scattered artifacts in the nearshore marine sandy veneer overlying the transgressive surface.*

continental shelf the depositional units are buried to depths of up to 30 meters. This is a direct result of absolute sea-level rise and landward and upward transgression of the coastal sedimentary environments since 11,000 years before present. On the other hand, later Holocene sites of man in the coastal zone are being found along the tidal estuarine rivers and the Atlantic coastal spits with dates back to 6,000 years before present. One must make the assumption that these same types of sites extended along the same environments at the same time onto the submerged continental shelf and the submerged large estuary, Delaware Bay.

Fig. 8 is a block diagram illustrating concepts described above for the mid-Atlantic coast. It is conceptual, but is based on actual cross-sections from coastal Delaware (Kraft *et al.*, 1979). Archaeological sites occur in 5 basic coastal settings. Site 1, based on Island Field (Fig. 9) is a headland site near a freshwater source (Plate 7). With continued sea-level rise this site might be

completely obliterated by the shoreface erosion, as shown by 1'.
Site 2 is a midden on a lagoon and marsh edge, based on shellfish
resources. Continued sea-level rise might preserve this site, as
shown in 2'. A variation on this theme is also shown for sites 5
and 5'. Many examples of these coastal middens are found on the
mid-Atlantic coast. Site 3 would be originally far up an estuary or
tidal river. Since it would experience the longest delay between
burial and subsequent arrival of the shoreface, it would be deepest
in the column, and be most likely to survive, as shown at 3'. Site
4 is an example of a small midden on the coastal barrier island, or
on a spit, representative of the Lewes Creek Marsh spit tip sites
and the Cape Henlopen "Lighthouse" archaeological site (Plate 6).
These may be buried by dune sands or marsh, but since they are
close to a rapidly retreating shoreline, have less likelihood of long
survival, as shown by 4'. Of the three sites 1', 2' and 3' it is
obvious that preservation potential depends on the original site

PLATE 7 *An oblique air photo showing the Island Field site
on the edge of a highland surface at the fringe of the
transgressing Holocene marsh near the shoreline of Delaware
Bay. The Holocene marsh is rising landward and upward and
will tend to cover the Island Field site. Eventually,
should erosion of the shoreline continue at present rate,
the entire site will be destroyed and artifacts will be
buried in a thin veneer of nearshore estuarine sediments.*

location and the rate of sea-level rise. In looking for potential archaeological sites on the continental shelf, we would look in the areas shown by the broad arrows, in other words on the flanks of interfluves below the eroded zone, but not so deeply buried as to be inaccessible.

Figure 7 is a compilation of geologic cross-sections in the Delaware coastal zone to demonstrate the basis for the conceptual evolutionary models. They are based on drillholes, hand cores, vibracores, and seismic reflection profiling. The locations of these three cross-sections are shown on the index map for the mid-Atlantic coast, Fig. 1. Radiocarbon-dated tidal marsh peats relevant to each area demonstrate the local relative sea level at various times in the evolution of the locality. Figure 7A is a cross-section at Island Field, South Bowers, Delaware. Continuing sea-level rise and transgression have placed estuarine sands and muds over older marsh deposits. At the leading edge of the transgression, marsh deposits are overlapping a pre-Holocene highland, encroaching on the Archaic and Woodland period Indian burial site, Island Field. Future preservation of this site would depend on the rate of sea level rise, but present rates of coastal retreat would seem to doom it to destruction 1,000 years from now.

At the Island Field site along the western shoreline of Delaware Bay, a major cemetary of Woodland period occupancy (to over 3,000 years before present) was discovered on firm ground along a tidal river. Further there are indications of Archaic period (approximately 6,000 years before present) occupancy in the same area. Sites such as the Island Field site can clearly be identified as an inland sites parallel to tidal river systems in the Holocene Epoch.

The geomorphic and paleogeomorphic setting of Island Field is shown in Fig. 9. This area evolved from a tidal river 10,000 years B.P., to an arm of the ancestral Delaware Bay 6,500 years B.P., to the present wide bay 3,000 years B.P., and continued to have rapid shoreline erosion since then. Indians apparently occupied the interfluve site because it was the first site of fresh water inland from the bay. Older sites might be present in the valley, but buried below the present marsh or further bayward.

Figure 7B is a cross-section at the Lewes Creek Marsh. This area has been influenced by the growth of the Cape Henlopen spit complex over at least the past 7,000 years. The spit was prograding over estuarine deposits to the north, and sheltering lagoonal deposits to the west throughout at least the past 2,000 years. The spit was complex at several times, with recurved spit tips that protruded into a lagoon rich in shellfish resources. Middens and campsites are found on these spit tips today, surrounded by the recent Lewes Creek Marsh formed when the lagoon was nearly completely cut off by continued spit migration.

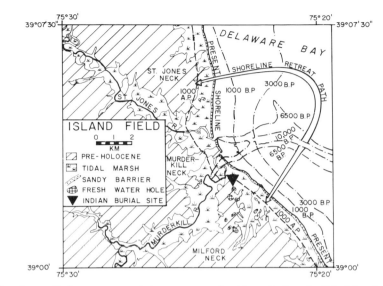

FIG. 9. *Paleogeographic map of the Island Field Indian burial site at South Bowers, Delaware, after Kraft, et al. (1976, Fig. 15). Based on more than 20 cores and auger holes and 14 radiocarbon dates.*

Atlantic coastal erosion is demonstrated by the seismic reflection profile offshore, where fragmental evidence exists for earlier lagoon and estuarine deposits, both from the ancestral Delaware estuary and coastal lagoons. Continued shoreline erosion will eventually destroy the archaeological sites, in a fashion similar to that which destroyed the Cape Henlopen lighthouse in 1926, as is shown in Plate 8.

Figure 7C is a cross-section across Rehoboth Bay and seaward. This is comparable to the southern face of the block diagram Fig. 8. This section clearly demonstrates the fact of the transgressive nature of the Delaware Atlantic coast. The leading edge of the transgression is a broad marsh-lagoon complex, sheltered from the open ocean by a sandy barrier system. The ocean front is an erosional zone scouring to 10 meters depth, erasing or preserving the stratigraphic record depending on the pre-existing topography. The preservation potential of these coastal sedimentary units has been discussed in detail by Belknap and Kraft (1981). Although no specific archaeological sites are shown on this cross-section, the broad arrow demonstrates the conditions necessary for preservation of a site on the Delaware shelf, comparable to site 2' in Fig. 8. This location is ;on the flank of an ancient interfluve, and thus has a potential for occupation. It has been buried by marsh and lagoonal sediments, it is below the zone of wave attack, and is in a window which is easily sampled by coring, or perhaps *in situ* exploration. Many more such sites should be identifiable by seismic reflection profiling.

Shoreline projection and reconstructions can and have been made based on intensive drilling programs to determine the shapes of the nearshore submarine and shoreline submarine coastal sedimentary environmental lithosomes. The logical extension of this exists throughout the submerged area of Delaware Bay, a large tidal estuary, and thence onward to the continental shelf. Weil (1976), and Kraft *et al.* (1974) formed a reconstruction of the geomorphology and location of coastal sedimentary environmental

PLATE 8. *The lighthouse and lightkeeper's house site at Cape Henlopen, constructed in the middle 18th century, one-quarter of a mile from the sea. By continuous coastal transgression of the dune upon which the lighthouse was sited, it eventually, in 1926, fell into the sea. Lighthouse sites such as this offer little potential for preservation. The debris from them will be mixed with the thin veneer of transgressive sands that overlie the surface of transgression. (Photo courtesy of J.W. Beach). Originally the lighthouse was located at the point of a cuspate foreland type of cape.*

PLATE 9. *Land surfaces that have Amerindian sites on their surfaces are infrequently exposed after "northeaster" storms when the beach-berm is removed temporarily. Plate 9 shows a pine forest with the actual forest flora pine needles and pine cones exposed. The long-term which could logically include archaeological sites is nil.*

units throughout Holocene time. What is shown is a landward and upward migration of erosion and depostion of various coastal sedimentary deposits throughout the Holocene Epoch to present time.

Thus, we can optimize areas for search of submarine earlier man sites based on models such as that of the Apoquinamink Creek, to the north (Kraft and John, 1978). Here, very clearly, a time sequence of occupancy and site increase can be shown with the rise of sea level relative to the land.

Unfortunately, the problems of locating early human sites on the continental shelf for the Holocene Epoch are much more limited. First, our model projection of paleoshorelines and, therefore, paleo-coastal environments optimal to early American Indian sites is much less definite. Also the area is much larger. Present technology does not show much promise in aiding us in attaining more precision in possible location of Holocene sites on the submerged continental shelf. Nevertheless, the works such as those of Twichell et al. (1977); Sheridan et al. (1974); Edwards and Emery (1977); and Swift et al. (1972) do allow us to optimize the areas for study in the sense of following the estuarine "drowned river valley system".

For the optimization of site search of the Atlantic Ocean

coast-parallel lagoon-barrier environments, we must at present depend on relict morphologies and the random chance discovery such as those listed in Whitmore *et al*. (1967). Fortunately, some geomorphic elements on the shelf can provide aid regarding ancient shoreline zones. A number of scarps have been identified from topographic studies of shelf bottom contour maps. A notable one is the "Franklin Shore" at the very outer part of the continental shelf. Several lesser scarps may be identified landward along the middle shelf off New Jersey. Although some would maintain that they can date these sites, factual data is in fact not available and the sites are in reality dated on a relative basis of position from the maximum low of sea stand of the present high sea stand.

In summary, regarding the Atlantic continental shelf, we then have a relatively large amount of geomorphic and environmental data but relatively poor chances of precise site location predictability.

CONCLUSIONS

The comparisons made between the wave cut terrace-cliff retreat on the northern Aegean Sea continental shelf and the Atlantic continental shelf barrier-lagoon-estuarine transgression show two dramatically different situations. Problems are revealed regarding location and/or preservation of early American man sites. For the Holocene Epoch, the possibility of eventual discovery of sites is high. However, the technology for location of these sites is poor and in the short term, random dredge data and intensive petroleum company drill site studies will provide us with the best data. Random diving and search is severely limited as a technique because of the lack of visibility over much of the middle and outer shelf bottom. In the estuaries there is a lack of visibility because of high turbidity. Clearly, Holocene sites must exist. Based on landward evidences along the deeply indented tidal estuaries in the Delaware coastal zone, we know that early man was occupying the tidal coastal zone, utilizing shellfish and finfish resources. Therefore, it is a logical assumption that this would apply to still earlier man and to possible sites on the submerged continental shelf throughout the Holocene Epoch.

Similarly, we know that the landward areas north of the continental shelf in the north Aegean Sea were occupied by Holocene man and, therefore, the potential for sites must exist on the submerged continental shelf. However, one might through empirical reasoning suggest that there is a lesser chance of locating such sites because geologic processes such as wave cut terrace incision and deposition of nearshore stratigraphic units occur as the wave cut terrace advances landward.

The search for early human sites on the continental shelves will probably lead to discoveries.   Whether this will be done by scientific and technological technique or by random chance or accident remains to be seen. Nevertheless, a full understanding of the coastal environmental units from models of present day coastal studies, and direct projection of onshore analogies seaward into the submarine record of the shelf provide us with a capability for optimizing the choice of potential occupancy zones. Without this reduction in the number of square kilometers of submerged shelf to be studied and selection of the seach areas, the study would be an almost impossible task in terms of our existing and potential "state of the art" of science and technology.

ACKNOWLEDGEMENTS

We would like to acknowledge the financial support over more than five years of the NOAA Sea Grant program of the University of Delaware, and the Office of Naval Research Geography Program. We also acknowledge the technical assistance of Maden Tetkik ve Arama Institüsü (the Turkish Geological Survey).   In particular, thanks are due to Professor Oğuz Erol, of the University of Ankara, without whom the work in Turkey would have been impossible.

REFERENCES

Belknap, D.F. (1975). *Dating of Late Pleistocene and Holocene relative sea levels in coastal Delaware*, Department   of Geology, University of Delaware, Newark, Master of Science Thesis, 95 pp.

Belknap, D.F. and Kraft J.C. (1977).   Holocene relative sea-level changes and coastal stratigraphic units on the northwest flank of the Baltimore Canyon Trough Geosyncline, *Journal   of Sedimentary Petrology*, 47, 610-629.

Belknap, D.F. and Kraft J.C. (1981).   Preservation potential of transgressive coastal lithosomes on the U.S. Atlantic shelf, *Marine Geology*, 42, 429-442.

Belknap, D.F., Sheridan R.E., Swift D.J.P., and Lapiene G. (1976). Geophysical investigations of the Delaware Shelf Valley. *Geological Society of America Abstracts with Programs* 8, 131-132.

Duane, D.B., Field M.E., Meisburger E.P., Swift D.J.P., and Williams, S.J. (1972).   Linear shoals on the Atlantic inner continental shelf, Florida to Long Island.   In (D.J.P. Swift *et al.*, eds.)*Shelf Sediment Transport: Process and Pattern* Dowden, Hutchinson, and Ross, Stroudsburg, PA pp. 447-499.

Edwards, Robert L. and Emery, K.O. (1977).   Man on the continental shelf. In (Newman, W.S. and B. Salwen, eds.) *Amerinds and their Paleoenvironments in Eastern North America*, Annals of the New York Academy of Science 288, 353-359.

Fairbridge, R.W. (1976).   Shellfish-eating preceramic   Indians in coastal Brazil. *Science* 191, 353-359.

Field, M.E. and Duane, D.B. (1976).   Post-Pleistocene history of the United States inner continental shelf: Significance and origin of barrier islands, *Geological Society of America Bulletin* 87, 691-702.

Flemming, N.C. (1971).   *Cities in the Sea.*   Doubleday and Co., New York, 222 pp.

Flemming, N.C. (1978).   Holocene eustatic changes and coastal tectonics in the northeast Mediterranean: Implications for models of coastal consumption, *Philisophical Transactions of the Royal Society of London* 298, 405-458.

John, C.J. (1977).   *Internal sedimentary structures, vertical stratigraphic sequences, and grain-size diameter variations in a transgressive coastal barrier complex: the Atlantic coast of Delaware.* Ph.D. Dissertation, Department of Geology, University of Delaware, Newark, 287 pp.

Kraft, J.C. (1971).   Sedimentary facies patterns and geologic history of a Holocene marine transgression. *Geological Society of America Bulletin* 82, 2131-2158.

Kraft, J.C. (1976a).   Radiocarbon dates in the Delaware coastal zone (Eastern Atlantic Coast of North America) University of Delaware NOAA Sea Grant Program Publication (DEL-SG-19-76), Newark, 20 pp.

Kraft, J.C. (1976b).   Geological reconstructions of ancient coastal environments in the vicinity of Island Field archaeological site, Kent County, Delaware.   *Transactions of the Delaware Academy of Science* - 1974 and 1975, Newark 7, 31-66.

Kraft, J.C. and John C.J. (1976).   The geological structure of the shorelines of Delaware, University of Delaware NOAA Sea Grant Program (DEL-SG-14-76), Newark, 107 pp.

Kraft, J.C. and John, C.J. (1978). Paleogeographic analysis of coastal archaeological settings in Delaware. *Archeology of Eastern North America* 6, 41-60.

Kraft, J.C., Sheridan, R.E., Moose, R.D., Strom, R.N., and Weil, C.B. (1974). Middle-Late Holocene evolution of the morphology of a drowned estuary system - The Delaware Bay. *Mem. Inst. Geol. Bassin Aquitaine* 7, 297-305.

Kraft, J.C., Allen, E.A., Belknap, D.F., John, C.J., and Maurmeyer, E.M. (1976). Delaware's Changing Shoreline, Technical Report No. 1, Delaware Coastal Zone Management Program, Delaware State Planning Office, Dover, 319 pp. (Prepared from an unpublished manuscript: Geologic processes and the geology of Delaware's coastal zone.)

Kraft, J.C., Allen, E.A., Belknap, D.F., John, C.J. and Maurmeyer, E.M. (1979). Processes and morphologic evolution of an estuarine and coastal barrier system. In *Barrier Islands, from the Gulf St. Lawrence to the Gulf of Mexico* (S.P. Leatherman, ed.) Academic Press, New York. pp. 149-183

Milliman, J.D. and Emery, K.O. (1968). Sea levels during the past 35,000 years, *Science* 162, 1121-1123.

Shepherd, F.P. and Curray, J.R. (1967). Carbon-14 determination of sea level changes in stable areas. *Progress in Oceanography* 4, 283-291.

Sheridan, R.E., Dill, C.E. Jr. and Kraft, J.C. (1974). Holocene sedimentary environment of the Atlantic inner shelf off Delaware *Geological Society of America Bulletin* 85, 1319-1328.

Swift, D.J.P. (1973). Delaware Shelf Valley: estuary retreat path, not drowned river valley. *Geological Society of America Bulletin* 84, 2743-2748.

Swift, D.J.P., Kofoed, J.W., Saulsburg, P.J. and Sears, P. (1972). Holocene evolution of the shelf surface, central and southern Atlantic shelf of North America. In (D.J.P. Swift *et al.*, eds.) *Shelf Sediment Transport: Process and Pattern*. Dowden, Hutchinson, and Ross, Stroudsburg, PA, pp. 499-574.

Twichell, D.C., Knebel, H.J. and Folger, D.W., (1977). Delaware River: Evidence for its former extension to Wilmington Canyon. *Science* 195, 483-484.

Weil, C.B., Jr. (1976). *A model for the distribution, dynamics and evolution of Holocene sediments and morphologic features of Delaware Bay.* Ph.D. Dissertation, Department of Geology, University of Delaware, Newark, 408 pp.

Whitmore, F.C., Jr., Emery, K.O.,Cooke, H.G.S. and Swift, D.J.P. (1967). Elephant teeth on the Atlantic Continental Shelf, *Science* <u>156</u>, 1477-1481.

LATE QUATERNARY SEA LEVELS INFERRED FROM COASTAL STRATIGRAPHY AND ARCHEOLOGY IN ISRAEL

Avraham Ronen

The University of Haifa, Mount Carmel, Haifa, Israel.

ABSTRACT

A model is suggested whereby the bulk of deposits on the coastal plain of Israel - quartz sand and fines - originated in the continental shelf. Accordingly the formation of red loams rich in fines (*ca*. 30%, "Hamra" soils) required large scale regressions which exposed the silt/clay sea bed beyond the depth of -40m. Sand beds and brown loams poor in fines were deposited during regressions of a smaller amplitude.

The Late Pleistocene and Holocene coastal stratigraphical sequence is studied, interpreted according to the model and compared with the oxygen isotope curve. The geological sequence contains archeological remains of Middle Palaeolithic, Epi-Palaeolithic, Neolithic, Chalcolithic, Bronze Age and various other historical periods. Sea level fluctuations during these periods can be postulated.

INTRODUCTION

The bulk of the coastal plain of Israel is composed of a sequence of sands and sandy loams which are thought to span the Middle and Upper Pleistocene (Ronen, n.d.). Alluvial, loessial and gravel deposits are found to smaller extent, and are confined to distinct regions. The western part of the coastal plain is characterised by a series of longitudinal and roughly parallel ridges of fossilised sand dunes. It is along these ridges that the coastal stratigraphy is seen, bearing in mind that in different segments of the coast, different stratigraphies appear. We suggest that the reason for this is that in each segment of the coast a different ridge acts as the shoreline ridge. This conclusion is supported by the long-observed fact that the number of ridges along the E - W transect steadily decreases as one goes north (submarine ridges, whose study is still very fragmentary (Almagor, 1979), excluded). Thus the coastal plain is divided into various zones which may be related to a well-known system of NW trending faults (Ginzburg et al., 1975; Neev et al., 1976), but which appear to be of an even greater magnitude than previously thought (Flexer et al., n.d.). From the point of view of coastal stratigraphy, there are three major zones:

1) The southern coastal plain between Gaza and Tel Aviv (termed Pleshet or Judea coast), which has up to seven ridges. The westernmost of these, the shoreline ridge, is unique along the Israeli littoral in that it is practically devoid of red loam, has a peculiar sand composition (Bakler, pers. comm.) and had numerous Early Neolithic settlements on its crest. This ridge disappears north of the outlet of Nahal Soreq.

2) The central, or Sharon coastal plain between Tel Aviv and Caesarea which has three to four parallel ridges. The westernmost of these is normally covered by a red loam and contains in its upper part Epi-Palaeolithic industries, 17,000 -10,000 B.P. The soil and industries are not present in the southern shoreline ridge. The typical Sharon shoreline ridge disappears near Caesarea.

3) The northern coastal plain, including that of Carmel and Galilee, which has but two to three ridges. The westernmost ridge along the entire northern segment of the coast differs from the Sharon-type ridge in that it is devoid of the covering Epi-Palaeolithic loam and its cultural remains. It is quite certain on stratigraphical and archaeological grounds that the shoreline ridge between Athlit and Rosh Haniqra is the second-westernmost in the Sharon; it follows that the shoreline ridge of the southern Carmel coast, between Maagen Michael and Athlit is the northward continuation of the Sharon shoreline ridge. There is a difficulty here in that the southern Carmel coastal ridge has a typical "northern," and not a "Sharonian" appearance, a problem which has to await further research.

The Carmel and Galilee coastal plains are separated by the Zevulun plain which, an exception along the Israeli littoral, has no sandstone ridges at all. Its ridges are submerged in the Bay of Haifa (Hall and Bakler, 1975). Thus, in at least three segments of the Mediterranean shore of Israel the eastern ridge (inland) progressively becomes the "shoreline" ridge (Fig. 1). The most complete stratigraphy is seen in the central segment, to be

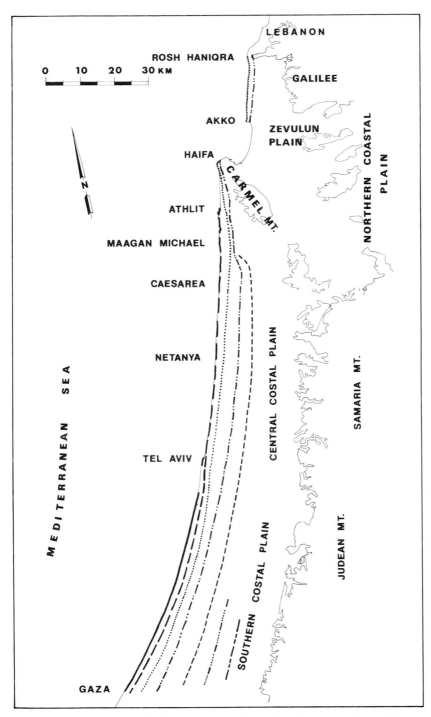

FIG. 1. *The coastal plain of Israel and schematic location of sandstone ridges.*

124   A. Ronen

described below.

A MODEL FOR COASTAL DEPOSITION

The most widely accepted explanation for the alternation of sand
beds and fines on the coastal plain is that the sand (marine and
eolian) comes from the west and the fines originate in the deserts
to the south and east (Yaalon and Dan, 1967; Dan and Yaalon,
1971, p. 256). But if the notion of different sources is accepted,
then a totally non-related pattern of distribution is to be expected
for each of the components. In reality, however, sand beds have
their corresponding loams and each pair of these (a sedimentary
cycle) has a similar distribution on an E-W transect. Furthermore,
in the inner parts of the coastal plain which were not affected by
more recent accumulations of sand, no new soil has been formed.
This is amply evidenced by the numerous Early Palaeolithic find
spots which are found on the surface of the eastern coastal plain.
Consequently, we believe that the contribution of fine material
from a southern source to soil building is negligible. In our
opinion, the bulk of continental sedimentation on the coastal plain
(alluvium and gravel excluded) originated on the continental shelf
(Fig. 2). Transgression would deposit marine sand. Regression

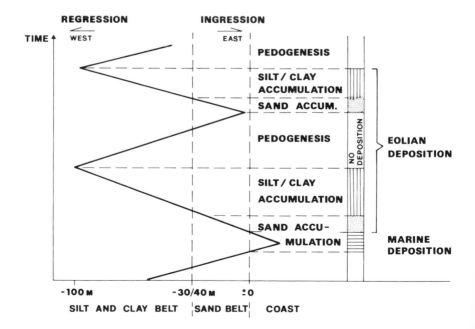

FIG. 2. *Suggested model for the formation of depositional
cycles on the coastal plain of Israel. Regression in metres
below present sea level. Time scale arbitrary.*

would enable eolian transportation by the prevailing west winds, and the nature of the eolian sediment - whether sand or fines - depends on the offshore zone which has been exposed, in other words on the amplitude of the regression. Sand will be carried on land as long as the sand belt is exposed, between 0 and -30 to -40 m. Regression beyond that depth would expose, and cause deflation of, silt and clay. The distance of transportation inland depends on wind energy and topographical features; and these conditions affect sand and fines to a similar extent. We thus consider any eolian sedimentation to be triggered by a negative sea level movement (which may or may not have been preceded by a positive movement). A sedimentary cycle of sand/loam corresponds to a cycle of regression/halt, or regression/transgression. A loam rich in fines results from a regression beyond the sand belt (Fig. 2).

In the light of the above considerations, let us examine how sea level changes are reflected in our coastal stratigraphy, best exposed in the two western Sharon ridges (Ronen, 1975a). This will be completed by observations from the northern coastal plain and its offshore zone.

THE COASTAL STRATIGRAPHY

Altogether, 10 sedimentary cycles are visible. They are, from top to bottom:

1) Recent sand, unstabilised, without vegetation or soil cover. Thickness variable up to 2 m.

2) Brown loam 0.8 m max. thick, overlying unconsolidated sand up to 2 m thick. In the loam and on top potsherds, mainly of Early Bronze I, ca. 2,700 B.C. (4,700 B.P. Gophna and Bonimovitz, 1980), are found.

3) Brown loam 0.5 m thick overlying unconsolidated sand ca. 1 m thick. Neolithic flints (7th-6th millenium B.C., Ronen et al., 1975) in the loam and the sand

4) Brown loam 0.5 m thick on top of consolidated sandstone 3 m max. thickness. Hitherto no archaeological finds turned up in this loam.

5) Red loam 1-2 m thick with, in its upper part, Epi-Palaeolithic industries (15th-9th millennium B.C.). Overlies a poorly consolidated sandstone up to 3 m thick.

6,7,8) Poorly consolidated sandstone ca. 15 m thick, intersected by three discontinuous horizons of poorly developed sandy loams, each up to 1m. thick. No archaeological remains.

9)   Brown sandy loam with abundant calcitic concretions in its
      lower third, 2.5 m max. thickness (sometimes termed
      "cafe-au-lait" soil). Overlies a poorly cemented sandstone
      up to 4 m thick.

10)   Red loam 0.5-1.5 m thick with late Middle Palaeolithic
      implements in its upper third (50,000 B.P.?). This loam
      overlies a very hard sandstone up to 3 m thick mostly of
      eolian origin but at least once (in the Carmel Coastal Plain)
      of a beachrock type, *ca*. 15 m above the present shoreline.
      Marine shells from this deposit yielded an age of 130,000
      B.P. by Amino-acid racemization (Masters, pers. comm.) and
      80,000 B.P. based on $^{230}th/^{234}U$ (Brunnacker, pers. comm.).

Submerged settlements were discovered at several points along the
northern segment of the Israeli littoral (Ronen and Olami 1978,
p.3; Wreschner 1977, 1983, this volume; Galili, pers. comm; Raban
1983, this volume). They are found under 2-3m. of water, on top
of a dark clay bed with brackish water molluscs (Galili, pers.
comm.). Prior to the settlements there existed then a lagoon or
marsh area near the shore. The settlements include walls, paved
floors and hearths and date to the Late Neolithic - Chalcolithic
periods (5th - 4th millenium B.C. or 7,000-6,000 B.P.). When
inhabited, these sites must have been situated at least 4 m above
sea level in order to be protected from storm waves. This means
that some 7,000 years ago, the sea stood 6-7 m lower than at
present (a minimum estimation). The date of these habitations
corresponds between our cycles 3 and 2. The preceding brackish
environment could have existed during cycles 4-5.

Remarks

1)   The section is not visible below cycle 10. Borings show
      another red loam immediately underneath, which we believe
      to be the Upper Acheulian-bearing soil, 100,000-200,000 B.P.
      More ancient loams exist as well (Ronen, 1975).

2)   The red loams are decalcified; the bown loams, as a rule,
      are not, and abundant snails are preserved in them,
      especially in the lowest (cycle 9), which provided the means
      for dating.

3)   Cycles 1 through 4 overlie the latest Palaeolithic
      occurrences and hence are of the Holocene. It is possible
      that additional short cycles existed within the Holocene
      which are undistinguishable. This section suggests that no
      cementation of Holocene sands has occurred after *ca*. 7,000
      B.P.

TABLE 1

Chronological framework (uncalibrated)

CYCLE BED	Material dated	C14 Dates B.P.		Archaeological evidence (B.P.)[1]
HOLOCENE 2 Loam	snails	Weiz 463E 3020±300 EB1		4700
Submerged habitation	wood	Weiz 551B 6590±100		7000-5000
Submerged site	char-coal	Hv 4256 6310±395[2]	Neo-Chalco-lithic	7000-5000
3			Neolithic	10,000-7000
Sandstone top	snails snails	Pta 2383 7130±70 Pta 2386 2370±55		
4 Sandstone base	snails snails snails snails	Pta 2385 7959±80 Pta 2373 6950±90 Pta 2384 4920±60 Weiz 463D 5530±140		
PLEISTOCENE 5 Red loam 9 Brown loam	snails	Pta 2802 30,700±500		Epipalaeolithic, 17-10,000
10 Red loam Beachrock	shell	80,000[3] 130,000[4]		Middle Palaeolithic 60-40,000

[1]Based on C14 dates obtained in numerous sites.

[2]Prausnitz and Wreschner (1971:280.)

[3]Brunnacker (pers. comm.)

[4]Master (pers. comm.)

4)   Cycles 3 and 4 were not found in a clear stratigraphical position. Both of them certainly postdate cycle 5, but by themselves might be either consecutive or contemporaneous.

5)   Cycles 1 through 9 are common to both ridges, which prove their contemporaneity. Cycle 10 is seen only in the second ridge from shore; its stratigraphical position relative to cycle 9 is not clear.

6)   Loams 9 and 10 are very different and their assumed correlation (Horowitz, 1979, p. 112) is highly improbable: the degree of pedogenesis radically differs (Bakler, pers. comm. : loam 10 is wholly decalcified while loam 9 is rich in calcareous residue); the parent material of the two loams differs (Bakler, pers. comm. : there is 30-40% of clay/silt in loam 10 as opposed to almost none in loam 9). In addition, loam 10 has relatively abundant cultural remains (Ronen, 1977) whereas loam 9 is completely sterile.

7)   The entire sequence shows a continental environment of deposition except for the high sea level attested by the beachrock at the base of cycle 10. A continuous continental environment is denoted also by the study of landsnails (below). This contradicts the Holocene sea level curve suggested by Wreschner (1977, p. 281).

ABSOLUTE DATES

Several beds of the coastal stratigraphy described above have been dated recently. These, coupled by the archaeological evidence, constitute the most complete chronological framework for the Levantine Late Quaternary available to date (Fig. 3).

Remarks

1)   The radiocarbon date of landsnail shell from loam 2 is younger than the archaeological evidence. This may suggest that a later isotopic exchange of carbon took place (Thommeret, 1976).

2)   The dates for the sandstone of cycle 4 are highly variable and seem too young. Its probable age range is 9,000-7,000 B.P. on archaeological grounds.

3)   The loam of cycle 9 may be older than its shell-derived C14 date; however we believe it to fall within the early part of the Upper Palaeolithic (*ca*. 40,000-20,000 B.P.). Not a single site from this time interval was found on the coastal plain, contrary to the relative abundance of Middle and Epi-Palaeolithic occurrences in loams 10 and 5, respectively.

INFERRED SEA LEVEL FLUCTUATIONS

The stratigraphical sequence described above reflects the following sea level fluctuations, if our model is correct (Fig. 3). After an initial relative high sea stand leaving traces at +15-20 m, probably in one of the Last Interglacial peaks, a large scale regression in the lower part of the Last Glaciation enabled the formation of the Middle Palaeolithic red loam of cycle 10. Thereafter and until the next red loam of cycle 5 (i.e., between *ca*. 50,000-25,000 B.P.), sea level fluctuated close to its present level. The fluctuations were within the range of the offshore sand belt, and the resulting deposits are all sand with poorly developed sandy loams (our cylces 9 through 6, which suggest four pulses within this time interval).

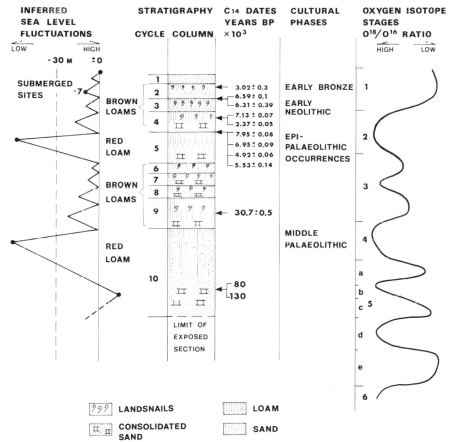

FIG. 3. *Upper Pleistocene-Holocene sea level curve as inferred from the coastal stratigraphy, compared with the oxygen isotope curve, and cultural phases.*

A new large scale drop of the sea level occurred during cycle 5, which reached far enough as to affect the silt/clay belt and to give rise to the red loam of the End-Palaeolithic industries. Thereafter, the Flandrian transgression started, which brought the sea level to its present stand. Four oscillations may be recognised within the Flandrian in our section (cycle 4 to 1), all affecting the near shore. About 7,000 years ago the sea must have been at least 6-7 m lower than today.

We have collected landsnail samples in all the loams except 10 and 5, where they were not preserved. Samples that could be studied were obtained from loams 9, 7, 4, 3, 2 and from the sandstone of cycle 4. Their study corroborated our contention that a shoreline position similar to the present one prevailed throughout (Heller and Tchernov, 1978; Schutt, in Brunnacker *et al.* 1981). The species identified* are mostly xerophile, none is aquatic or hygrophile. No change was noted between the layers, and all the species live on the coast today. Relying on the relative frequencies of *Jaminia ovularis* and *J. sulcidens,* Heller and Tchernov (1978, p. 9) suggested that during cycle 9 an important regression took place, in which the sea stood some 10 km from its present position. But, in view of the small number of *Jaminia* specimens and the different frequencies of species obtained from two localities in loam 9, we believe the evidence of the *Jaminia* to be of a local and non-significant nature.

COMPARISON WITH THE OXYGEN ISOTOPE CURVE

Our inferred sea level fluctuations fit remarkably well the oxygen isotope curve for the Upper Pleistocene (Emiliani and Shackleton, 1974). Stages 4 and 2 in the curve match the formation of the red loams of our cycles 10 and 5 (Fig. 3). Stage 3 would be the equivalent of depositional cycles 9 through 6. We would tend to place sea level during cycles 9-6 (i.e., between the two red loams) higher than suggested by Shackleton and Opdyke (1973, p. 45), 50-60 m below present sea level. However, there is no contradiction because, first, isostasy, which has not been considered by the above authors, may have played a role, and second, the maximum drop of sea level may have been less than 120 m (Blackwelder *et al.,* 1979), the figure upon which Shackleton and Opdyke's estimation was based.

*Heller and Tchernov (1978) identified *Jaminia ovularis, J. sulcidens, Trochoidea (Xerocrassa davidiana, Xeropicta vestalis* and *Monacha syriaca.* Schutt (n.d.) has identified these and also *Trocoidea (Xerocrassa) langloisiana improbata, Vertigo hebraica, Cecilioides kervillei* and *Sphincterochila aharonii.*

The model suggested here may be applied to interpret the entire sequence of sand/loam in the Israeli coastal plain, but this lies outside the scope of the present paper.

THE COASTAL STRATIGRAPHY AND ARCHAEOLOGICAL REMAINS: CONCLUSIONS

As a rule, no human occupation is found in the sandstone beds or in the sandy brown loams of the Pleistocene. The two red loams were the environment preferred for human occupation during that part of the Pleistocene which is exposed here. Sandy environments were avoided. This might have been an important reason for the lack of Upper Palaeolithic coastal settlements.

The occupation of sandy brown loam started with the neolithic inhabitants and continued, apparently with increasing density, during the Early Bronze and subsequent historical periods. This trend might reflect a growing population density, which would have caused penetration into less favorable environments.

The Middle and Epi-Palaeolithic near-shore settlements are to be sought far west of the present shoreline, perhaps between -60 to -120 m During the Upper Palaeolithic period, the shoreline was closer. But, in view of the absence of open air sites of this period, it is not believed that submerged sites exist. A close-by shoreline is also inferred for the Early Neolithic period; certainly lower than -7 m (the inferred level for the Late Neolithic), the shore of the Early Neolithic could have been around -20 or -15 m After the Late Neolithic period (i.e. from 7,000 B.P. on), the shoreline level was the same as it is at present, with only minor fluctuations.

Judging from the settlement pattern seen on the coastal plain it may be predicted that the search for submerged sites of the Upper Pleistocene and Early Holocene periods (Middle Palaeolithic through Early Neolithic phases) should be carried out on the crest of sandstone ridges near the traverse of water courses, along a strip not exceeding 1,000 m on either side of the wadi. When further underwater surveys are carried out, additional archaeologically inferred sea levels like that of 7,000 years B.P. will be recognised.

ACKNOWLEDGEMENT

The research on the Quaternary and Prehistory of the Coastal Plain of Israel was supported by grants from Stiftung Volkswagenwerk to Professor Dr K. Brunnacker and the author (AR).

REFERENCES

Almagor, G. (1979). Relict Sandstones of Pleistocene Age on the Continental shelf of Northern Sinai and Israel. *Israel Journal Earth Sciences* 28, 70-76.

Blackwelder, B.W., Pilkey, O.H. and Howard, J.D., (1979). Late Wisconsinan Sea Levels on the Southeast U.S. Atlantic Shelf Based on In-Place Shoreline Indicators. *Science* 204, 618-620.

Brunnacker, K., Schutt, H. and Brunnacker, M. (1981). Uber das Hoch und Spatglazial in der Kustenebene von Israel. In *Contributions to the Environmental History of Southwest Asia*. (Frey, W. and Uerpmann, H.P., eds). Ludwig Reichert, Wiesbaden, pp. 61-79.

Dan, J., and Yaalon, D.H., (1971). On the origin and nature of the Paleopedological formations in the coastal desert fringe areas of Israel. In (Yaalon, D.H., ed.). *Paleopedology - Origin, Nature and Dating of Paleosols*. Israel Universities Press, Jerusalem, pp. 245-260.

Emiliani, C. and Shackleton, N.J. (1974). The Brunhes Epoch: Palaeotemperature and Geochronology. *Science* 183, 511-514.

Flexer, A., Dimant, E., Polishook, B. and Livnat, A. (n.d.) Jointing of the Eocene Rocks in Israel and its Relation to the Tectonic Pattern of the Levant Subplate (in preparation).

Ginzburg, A., Cohen, S.S., Hay-Roe, H. and Rosenzweig, A. (1975). Geology of the Mediterranean shelf of Israel. *American Association of Petroleum Geologists Bulletin* 59, 2142-2160.

Gophna, R. and Bonimovitz, S. (1980). Seasonal Camps of the Early Bronze I in the South-Western Sharon. *Qadmoniot* 13, 87-88 (Hebrew).

Hall, J.K. and Bakler, N., (1975). Detailed bathymetric and shallow seismic surveys of five locations along the Mediterranean coast of Israel. Geological Survey of Israel Offshore Dredging Project, ISR/71/522, Field report 1/75.

Heller, J. and Tchernov, E. (1978). Pleistocene landsnails from the coastal plain of Israel. *Israel Journal of Zoology* 27, 1-10.

Horowitz, A. (1979). *The Quaternary of Israel*. Academic Press, London and New York.

Kukla, G. (1978). The classical European glacial stages: correlation with deep sea sediments. *Transactions of the Nebraska Academy of Sciences* 6, 57-93.

Opdyke, N.D. (1973). Oxygen isotope and palaeomagnetic stratigraphy of equatorial Pacific core V28-238: Oxygen isotope temperatures and ice volumes on a 10^5 year and 10^6 year scale. *Quaternary Research* 3, 39-55.

Neev, D., Almagor, G., Arad, A., Ginzburg, A. and Hall, J. (1976). The geology of the southern Mediterranean Sea. *Bulletin of the Geological Survey of Israel* 68, 1-51.

Prausnitz, M.W. and Wreschner, E. (1971). Newe-Yam: A submerged Neolithic settlement. *Qadomoniot* 4, 120-121 (Hebrew).

Ronen, A. (1975). The Palaeolithic archaeology and chronology of Israel. In (Wendorf, F., and Marks, A.E., eds.) *Problems in Prehistory: North Africa and the Levant*. SMU, Dallas, Texas, pp. 229-248.

Ronen, A. (1975a). Reflexions sur l'Origine, la genèse et la chronologie des grès dunaires calcifiés dits "première" et "deuxième" chaines côtières sur le littoral Israelien. *Bulletin de la Societé Préhistorique Française* 72, 72-77.

Ronen, A. (1977). Mousterian sites in red loam in the coastal plain of Mount Carmel. *Eretz-Israel* 13, 183-190.

Ronen, A. n.d. Remarks on the Quaternary stratigraphy of the coastal plain of Israel. *Géologie Méditerranéenne* (in press).

Ronen, A. Kaufman, D., Gophna, R., Smith, P. and Bakler, N. (1975). Hefziba - Hadera. An Epi-Palaeolithic site in the central plain of Israel. *Quartar* 26, 53-72.

Ronen, A. and Olami, Y. (1978). *Athlit Map*. The Archaeological Survey of Israel, Jerusalem, VI + 84 pp.

Thommeret, T. (1976). Difficultés d'interpretation des dates C14 mesurées a partire des coquilles marines. *Union International des Sciences Préhistoriques et Protohistorique*, Nice, Colloque I, pp. 160-169.

Wreschner, E.E. (1977). Newe Yam. A submerged late Neolithic settlement near Mount Carmel. *Eretz-Israel* 13, 260-271.

A. Ronen

Wreschner, E.E. (1977). Sea level changes and settlement location in the coastal plain of Israel during the Holocene. *Eretz-Israel* 13, 277-282.

Yaalon, D.H. and Dan, J. (1967). Factors controlling soil formation and distribution in the Mediterranean coastal plain of Israel during the Quaternary. *Quaternary Soils, 7th INQUA Congr. Proc.* 9, 321-338.

SURVIVAL OF SUBMERGED LITHIC AND BRONZE AGE ARTIFACT SITES: A REVIEW OF CASE HISTORIES

N.C. Flemming

Institute of Oceanographic Sciences, Wormley, Godalming, Surrey, England.

ABSTRACT

Quaternary human occupation of the continental shelf coastal zones and submerged straits has been known in principle for several decades, but it has usually been assumed that no human artifacts or settlement sites would survive the rising transgression of sea level. Conceptual models and predictive model studies have been developed to assess the survivability of submerged material, but it is equally important to consider the field examples of material found underwater in the last 10-20 years. Unconsolidated deposits of stone walls, clay floors, hearths, bones, stone tools, and other artifacts have been recovered from a wide range of marine and sedimentary conditions. This paper describes the environmental conditions and exposure of sites where materials have been recovered, dated, and preserved, and others where surveys indicate probable human occupation.

As the evidence for the survival of material *in situ* and relatively undisturbed has accumulated, more deliberate searches for lithic sites have been conducted. The key areas for the discovery of submerged sites in the context of the present study are Beringia, Sunda-Sahul, Sea of Japan, Red Sea, Gibraltar, and the Sicily Strait. No materials have been found *in situ* at any significant depth in these areas, although coastal and beach sites have been located. However, lithic and Bronze Age (3rd-2nd millenium) sites have been found from the surf zone down to 25 m in similar environmental conditions off the coasts of neighbouring

QUATERNARY COASTLINES
ISBN 0 12 479250 2

land masses, e.g. Israel, Cyprus, South of France, Brittany, Sweden, Denmark, Florida, California, South Australia.   Older material 10,000-100,000 years old has been found submerged off southern Sweden, France, and in coastal plain sink-holes in Florida.
   The known sites are grouped in terms of environmental conditions, and the circumstances of survival are considered, with reference to the artifacts recovered, and the degree of stratigraphic context.
   Optimum preservation of artifacts occurs in submerged karstic caves, sink-holes, and estuarine lagoonal or peat deposits. However, where an equilibrium sand beach exists unconsolidated remains can be preserved *in situ* under a metre or so of sand even in highly exposed positions.   We conclude that human occupation sites can survive at least one marine transgression, and that a consistent search using instrumental techniques and diving will soon provide submarine evidence for occupation sites in the critical straits and land bridges.

INTRODUCTION

The chronology of related ice sheet expansions and drops of sea level was outlined by Fairbridge (1961), and this has been greatly elaborated by Emiliani (1978), Shackleton and Opdyke (1973), and others.   It is generally accepted that there have been more than 20 cycles of glaciation and deglaciation during the last 2 million years, each cycle causing a eustatic change of sea level of the order of 100-150 m world-wide. The interaction of water and ice loading with the stability of the earth's crust has been analysed by Walcott (1972). and by Clark *et al*. (1978) and Newman *et al*. (1980).
   Archaeologists, e.g. Blanc (1937) realised that vegetation, animals, and human beings, were able to live on large areas of the continental shelf during low sea levels. Drowned forests exposed at low tide (Steers, 1948, p. 258), mammoth teeth dredged up in trawler nets (Emery and Edwards, 1966), or flint artifacts dredged up from the North Sea, all testified to this.   Clark (1969, p. 19) accepts as a matter of course that major migrations took place at periods of low sea level.
   Until the advent of cheap diving equipment, archaeologists did not have the opportunity to look underwater for archaeological remains, and only when diving became extremely common was it possible for chance finds to make a significant pattern. During the last two decades a representative sample of archaeological sites from the 3rd millenium B.C. and earlier has been discovered by divers, and this can be analysed in order to classify the locations and conditions of survival.   These discoveries have often been made by amateur divers or provincial archaeological groups, and the results have usually been published in provincial journals. Individually the sites may not seem of exceptional academic

importance when compared with the information which might be gained by the same effort on land. Collectively, however, the sites illustrate the growing body of knowledge concerning the human occupation of the continental shelf during the late Quaternary. This knowledge is based on practical experience down to a depth of about 25 m, and reasonable projections can be made into deeper water.

The fact that some of the reports and documents cited in this paper have not been published in professionally refereed journals must be borne in mind. I am sure that some underwater work by non-professional groups is extremely reliable, and the work is in many cases supervised by local museum or university staff. Local publications are often extremely detailed with clear maps, photographs, and descriptions of finds. In other cases the style of presentation is not professional, and questions or doubts are left unanswered. I have been selective. Readers of this paper should check the cited references if they are interested in specific sites, and if the publications are not fully refereed journals, they should be appropriately cautious about drawing hard and fast conclusions.

DEFINITION OF THE PROBLEM

It has commonly been supposed that human beings existed in China, Asia, and Malaysia for tens, perhaps hundreds, of thousands of years, without crossing to Australia or America. The crossings could have occurred, in theory, at any time between the first known appearance of humans on the Asiatic side, and the first known appearance on the other side of the relevant channels.With a time difference of tens of thousands of years for opposite sides of the channels there is a great deal of uncertainty as to when the first crossings took place, (Bryan, 1978; Allen et al., 1977).

This uncertainty arises, at least in part, because the people did not cross between present shorelines, but between, say, the 100 m isobaths. The culture which occupied one shore may have developed the skills necessary for a sea journey, or to migrate along a difficult coast during a glacial period, and the skills may not have been typical of those developed by people further inland. If and when they made the channel crossing, they may have been confined preferentially to the coastal plains of the continent in which they arrived, as proposed by Bowdler (1977) for Australia, and Fladmark (1978) for Canada. The early phase of colonisation of the new continent may have primarily coastal, until the rising sea level forced people to migrate inland. Archaeological studies on land today can only study those traces of occupation which were 100 m above sea level and possibly many km inland at the time of the key crossings. Thus we are bound to find inherent gaps in the evidence from studies confined to the present land masses.

There are further gaps in knowledge which are worth filling. Coastal cultures of the last 100,000 years, and older than 5,000 years, necessarily existed on coastlines which are below present sea level in most cases today. Surveys on land can reveal little specific about those coastal or maritime lithic cultures. The presence of similar tools on either side of a channel, e.g. Gilbraltar (Alimen, 1975), is evidence of trade and sea crossings; and the presence of seafood and shell middens can be evidence of shell gathering on a lower shoreline, (Jones, 1971). Nevertheless, these traces of early marine-oriented activities do not go far to elucidate the extent of human habitation over the entire continental shelf, 5.5% of the earth's surface.

If submarine archaeological sites are to be found in the region of critical straits and land bridges we must be able to predict the approximate location of sites so as to minimise the search areas, and the conditions must be known which will maximise the chance of survival of material, (see Kraft *et al.*, 1983, this volume). Wave action, ice, and currents may scatter or break up an assemblage of artifacts, bones and debris, so that nothing significant remains. Since the sea level must have transgressed across the site at least once, all underwater sites will have been exposed to more or less surf action. Sites which are stratigraphically undisturbed can only survive where the topographic and geomorphological conditions totally protect the remains from surf action, or where the wind and wave conditions are such that surf is negligible (Inman, 1983, this volume).

Conditions which would destroy sites or conceal them so that they would be difficult to detect underwater are: (a) wave erosion; (b) current erosion; (c) ice erosion; and (d) rapid sedimentation burying the site by tens of metres. I will not discuss the physics of these processes in this paper, but confine the study to the search for geomorphological situations where wave and current energy is minimal in its effect upon archaeological remains, and where sedimentation rate is not high enough to conceal remains. Wave energy will tend to be a minimum where the wind fetch is a minimum, and where the site is protected by a headland or islands or barrier bar in the immediate vicinity. Currents will be a minimum in non-tidal seas, or in large lagoons with a restricted entrance. Sedimentation is a minimum in areas without large rivers, without coastal erosion, and in the absence of longshore drift.

The geomorphological conditions which are most likely to provide protection during a marine transgression are: (a) Ria, lagoon, or estuary; (b) sheltered alluvial coast; (c) an exposed beach which is accumulating or in equilibrium; (d) sea caves; (e) karstic cave or sink-hole; (f) lee of coastal island or within an archipelago; (g) coral reefs. The following sections will analyse submerged archaeological sites which have been found in each of these environments. The global distribution of sites discussed is shown in Fig. 1. In the following sections I will estimate the wave conditions at each site in terms of the fetch exposure, and, where possible, in terms of measured wave heights.

ENVIRONMENTAL CLASSIFICATION

Ria, Lagoon, Estuary

Fonquerle (1982) describes Bronze Age and Neolithic remains including stone tools and wall foundations on the floor of the lagoon of Thau in the south of France. The remains were found when divers were searching for Roman and Greek wrecks. The location was so sheltered that the material could be surveyed and mapped by divers with a minimum of excavation. The artifacts were in a depth of 2 m and completely protected from the open Mediterranean by sand bars. Pottery, tools, and 17 wooden piles were found and surveyed by divers, (Courtin, 1978, p. 741); Fonquerle, (1982). A second Bronze Age settlement was found 300 m from the south bank of the lagoon of Thau by Freises and Pellecuer, (Courtin, 1978, p. 746). A 5th millenium Neolithic site was revealed by dredging in the lagoon Etang de Salses near Leucate, (Courtin, 1978, p. 741; see also Geddes *et al.*, 1983, this volume).

Rhys Jones (personal communication) has reported aboriginal middens on the margins of Sydney Harbour, Australia, which is a large sheltered ria valley. Similar middens occur on the shores of the ria at Little Swan Port, Tasmania, where one midden continues to a depth of 2 m below the water (Rhys Jones, personal communication).

The estuary of the Weipa river in northern Queensland, Australia, (Bailey, 1977, 1983, this volume), is bordered by very large shell middens. In view of the sheltered location similar middens could survive below present sea level. Carlson (1980, p. 110) describes midden remains and lithic scatters in the intertidal zone at river mouths in British Columbia. Schwartz and Grabert (1980, pp. 119-120) describe shell middens containing stone tools, worked bone scraps, and hearths, in beach spits at Birch Bay, Puget Sound. One hearth yielded a broken leaf-shaped projectile point, and is now exposed during marine construction, and is submerged at high tide. Sites have been found at several altitudes above sea level associated with spits formed at different sea levels. Similar spits have been detected by echo-sounding offshore, and archaeological sites would probably be found in the submerged spits. (Schwartz and Grabert, 1980, p. 119). Larsson (1983, this volume) used echo-sounding to trace the submerged channel of the river Saxån seaward from Landskrona, in

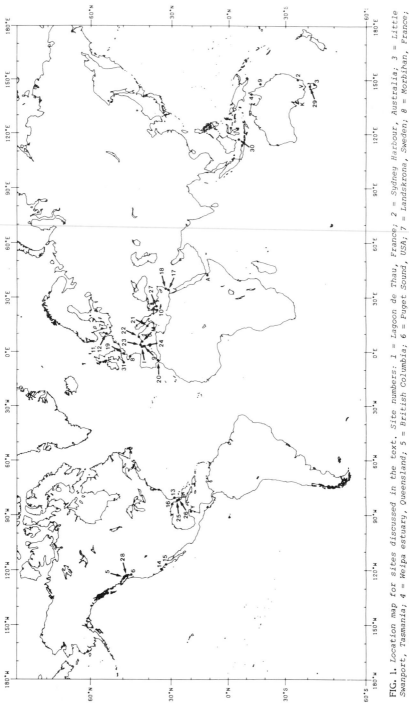

FIG. 1. Location map for sites discussed in the text. Site numbers: 1 = Lagoon de Thau, France; 2 = Sydney Harbour, Australia; 3 = Little Swanport, Tasmania; 4 = Weipa estuary, Queensland; 5 = British Columbia; 6 = Puget Sound, USA; 7 = Landskrona, Sweden; 8 = Morbihan, France; 9 = Etang de Salses, France; 10 = Pavlo Petri, Greece; 11 = Tybrind Vig, Denmark; 12 = Aerjo and Drejo jo, Denmark; 13 = Cape Canaveral, USA; 13 = Santa Monica Bay, USA; 15 = La Jolla, USA; 16 = West Florida, USA; 17 = Ashkelon, Israel; 18 = Neve Yam, Israel; 19 = Cap Levi, France; 20 = Governor's Beach, Gibraltar; 21 = Palinuro, Italy; 22 = Villefranche, France; 23 = Carry-le-Rouet, France; 24 = Sormiou, France; 25 = Warm Mineral Springs, USA; 26 = Little Salt Spring, USA; 27 = Saliagos, Greece; 28 = Montague Harbour, Canada; 29 = Tasmanian Islands; 30 = Indonesia; 31 = Isles of Scilly. Additional areas of interest are designated as follows: A = Afar coast, near Bab-el-Mandab, southern Red Sea; B = Andros Island, Bahamas; K = Kangaroo Island, Australia; V = Victoria Coast, Australia; and Y = coast of Yucatan.

southern Sweden, out into the strait of Oresund between Sweden and Denmark. Divers working at a depth of 6-8 m found worked flints dating from about 8,400 B.P., and other flints were found to a depth of 18 m.

Crawford (1927), Giot (1970), and Prigent (1978) describe the standing stone circle at Er Lannic in the lagoon of Morbihan, southern Brittany, France. The standing stones are on a sloping foreshore, and the outer half of the circle is below mean sea level. Giot (1970) and Prigent (1978) both describe other Neolithic and Bronze Age structures, tombs, and standing stones of the 4th-3rd millennium B.C. on the shores of Brittany, several located intertidally in marshes or lagoons. (See also Prigent et al., 1983, this volume.)

The sites described illustrate that lithic tools, bone tools, hearths, and uncemented stone structures can survive 5,000-10,000 years embedded in beach, deltaic, or coastal alluvial material in sheltered locations. In the rias, estuaries, and lagoons described the fetch is of the order of 1-30 km. The rate of accumulation and progradation of the shore is moderate or zero in the immediate region of the archaeological finds. If this were not so, the materials would necessarily be buried, and might be found several kilometers landward from the present shoreline, but below sea level. The coastline as a whole may be progradational, but the accumulation is uneven, with growth of spits, forelands, or deltas, interspersed with zones of zero accumulation or slight erosion. Slight erosion tends to reveal artifact sites, leaving the materials scattered on the beach or sea floor, though stratigraphy is destroyed, and the whole site will eventually be removed. Although the lagoon and deep ria sites have low current velocities, several of the sites are in areas of high tidal range.

Sheltered Alluvial Coast

Low fetch, low wave energy, sheltered sites can be created by indentations, bays, nearshore islands, or submerged reefs or rock. The Helladic submerged town at Pavlo Petri, in the Bay of Vatika, southern Greece (Flemming, 1968a, 1969, 1972; Harding et al., 1969), (Fig. 2), consists of house and street walls of uncemented stone. The ruins date from 3,500 B.P., and range from 1.0 m to 3.5 m below present sea level. The original settlement was in a protected bay, and the curved promontory protecting the bay to the east and south is now defined by the 2.0 m isobath. The fetch, 3,500 years ago and now, was limited to a few km in the northern sector, and to less than 30 km in most of the southern sector, due to shelter provided by Elaphonisos island, Kythera, and Cape Matapan. A narrow arc to the south-south-east has a fetch of about 100 km towards western Crete. It is in exactly this direction that the submerged reef or promonotory provides protection.

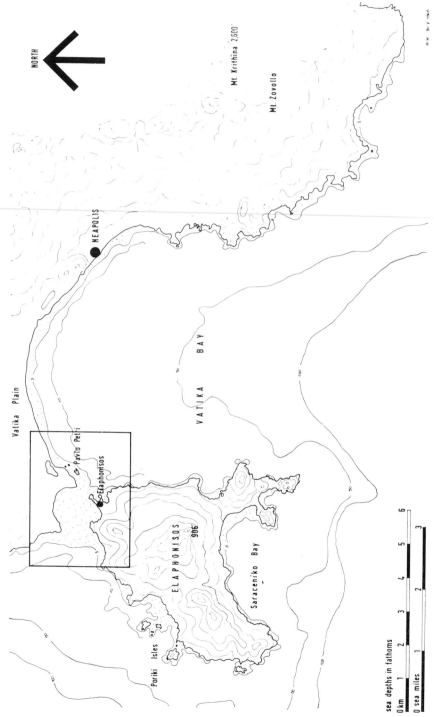

FIG. 2. *Vatika Bay, southern Greece, showing the location of the Pavlo Petri islands.*

The shore of Vatika Bay is sand, and although the beach appears to be in equilibrium both in profile and in plan, there has been erosion between Elaphonisos and the mainland, possibly resulting from land subsidence. The channel between Elaphonisos and the mainland was blocked by an isthmus in classical times (Waterhouse & Hope-Simpson, 1961). Currents observed by divers surveying the site in 1967 and 1968 were winnowing sand away from the archaeological remains on the sea floor, and gradually exposing pottery and artifacts.

Thirty five stone-lined cist graves were located by divers at Pavlo Petri, several of them with the cover stones still in place. Fragile pottery and a bronze statuette were found exposed on the sea floor. The site was sufficiently sheltered for these materials to have survived 3,500 years, but the present current regime is removing sand from the area, and making the site more vulnerable to wave damage, (Harding et al., 1969).

In Denmark diving excavation underwater in a depth of 2.5-3 m has revealed a submerged settlement of 6,000-3,600 B.P. off the beach of western Funen, (Fyn), on the Little Belt, at a location known as Tybrind Vig, (Andersen, 1980), (Fig. 3). Much of the residential part of the site has been eroded, but finds occur in a zone about 50 m long, extending along the ancient shoreline. The fetch west towards Jutland is about 10 km. The isobaths of the original shore show that the settlement was on an embayment with a narrow entrance channel, bordered by reeds. The finds were excavated from the "gyttja", a dark anaerobic freshwater mud. Objects recovered included large quantities of flint, animal bones, antler, wood and wooden artifacts, a few sherds of pottery, together with leaves, fruits, seeds and branches of trees. The preservation was excellent. The grave of a woman and child was excavated, and the scattered bones of at least 4 individuals were found.

Excavation underwater during 1980 uncovered a dugout canoe, cut from a straight lime trunk. The boat is 9 m long and about 65 cm wide, with a height of about 30 cm. The stratigraphic location of the boat indicated that it belonged to the period 3,800-3,700 B.C. The boat was buried in the gyttja, and is the first complete dugout found in settlement context in the Danish Mesolithic, (Andersen, 1980, p. 21). Other wooden objects included oars, bows, and spears.

Further south, between the islands of Aerø and Drejø a settlement of a similar date was found by Skaarup (1980). This site was also at a depth of 2.5 m, and produced pottery, flints, and antlers. The fetch ranges from 5-10 km.

This type of topographic location is usually related to headlands or islands, and is somewhat similar to the specific "archipelago" situation to be discussed later. The topography changes as the sea

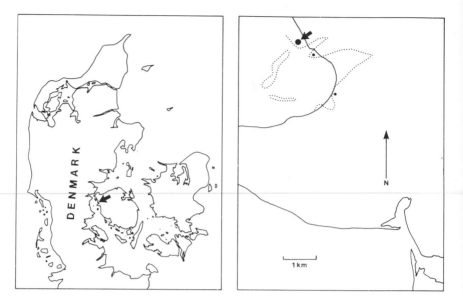

FIG. 3. *The location of Tybrind Vig, after Andersen (1980). The arrow in the left hand diagram shows the general location. In the right hand diagram the continuous line is the present shore; the dotted line is the ancient shore at the time of occupation. Note the submerged islands which originally helped to protect the site.*

rises. Pavlo Petri was a bay-headland at the time of occupation, and is now sheltered by a reef and small islands. Tybrind Vig was a lagoon site during occupation, and is now a bay, facing a channel with limited fetch. In all cases the archaeological remains are highly protected by the local topography on the scale of hundreds of metres, and broadly protected by coastal configuration which limits the maximum fetch to a few tens of kilometres. The survival of organic materials has been enhanced by the low salinity of the Baltic at the Danish sites, but wood, seeds, nuts, and other organics have been found from many wrecks buried in mud or sand below sea water of normal oceanic salinity (Bass, 1972), and with ages of 2,000-3,500 years.

Exposed Equilibrium or Accumulating Beach

An exposed high energy beach would seem to be the least likely place for the preservation of archaeological deposits over many thousands of years. However, a number of sites now provide field evidence that structures and artifacts can sometimes survive beneath a sand cover of the order of 1-2 metres at equilibrium gradient, and exposed to fetches of thousands of kilometres. I do not propose to discuss the seasonal and storm variations in beach profile which would naturally tend to exhume and re-bury archaeological strata. The dynamics of beaches are referred to elsewhere in this volume (Inman; Kraft et al.) If the extreme occurrences of erosion in cyclical beach profiles intersect the archaeological deposits, then the strata will be seriously disturbed, or even totally destroyed, in one storm. Rather than discuss the probability or improbability of such events on the basis of beach dynamics in this chapter, I will describe several discoveries on exposed shores which illustrate the circumstances in which lithic materials can survive, and those in which they may survive. These observations become data for assessing the long term stability of beaches.

During the 1960s treasure divers working near Cape Canaveral raised human bones and what were presumed to be elephant tusks. Subsequent analysis in the 1970s (Cockrell and Murphy, 1978) showed the material to be dated from about 6,000 B.P. The bones had been found in peat and clay. 11km to the south, off Fort Pierce, divers found stratified peat containing trees, a horse tooth, and a mastodon tooth, in the surf zone.

The fetch at these sites is limited to the south and south-west to 200-250 km by the Bahamas. Throughout the sector from SW to NW the fetch is of the order of 6,000 km. The divers who worked on the treasure wrecks of 1715 A.D. found metal artifacts scattered within the sand of the nearshore zone, indicating disturbance by the swell and surf. Nevertheless, the sand on the beach, allowing for onshore-offshore transport, and longitudinal transport, and seasonal and climatic cycles, has acted as a protective screen over peat and clay which has preserved human bones and animal remains.

Muche (1978) reports that a large sandstone bowl was found by a sports diver in May 1977 in Santa Monica Bay, west of Los Angeles. Diving archaeologists found three submerged creek beds bordered by rocky overhangs, with fragments of wood and occasional artifacts in the depressions. In a small pit in the rock divers uncovered a hearth of fire-blackened stones, charcoal, burnt bones, and nut shells. Two pestles were found, obsidian projectile points, and scrapers, at water depths of 4-5 m. The finds have not been dated accurately yet, but appear to be from about 5,500 B.P.

From Los Angeles southwards the continental shelf and fringes of the offshore islands are, from the reports of sports divers, scattered irregularly with stone bowls and grinding stones. Professor Glen Egstrom, UCLA, lifted several bowls from offshore during the 1960s (personal communication). Many sports divers lift one or two, but then turn to more exciting activities. Moriarty (1963) claims that divers in the La Jolla area had raised more than 2,000 Indian grinding mortars between 1950 and 1960. Whilst

Moriarty (1963) considers that the artifacts found off La Jolla and further afield are probably *in situ* though possibly disturbed by wave action and not stratigraphically preserved, there are several mechanisms that may also contribute to the presently observed distribution. (See Masters, 1983, this volume.)

In spite of the exposed nature of the South California shore the grinding stones are found at several locations in large assemblies, and some of these may indicate settlement areas or working areas. The wave climate for locations on the coast of California has been described by Powers *et al.* (1969), Pawka *et al.* (1976), Aubrey *et al.* (1980), and a series of reports by Seymour. The wave data reports for 1977 (Seymour, 1978, pp. 9-13) give the significant wave heights from the Mexican border to Port Hueneme. The maximum significant wave height is of the order of 3 m, indicating a probable Hmax-3 hours of about 6 m. Aubrey *et al.* (1980) discuss the prediction of beach profiles on the coast of California in relation to wave climate. (See also Inman, 1983, this volume.) It is important to note that submarine archaeological material is preserved even in this relatively high energy environment.

The sand movements of the beaches of Israel have been described by several researchers (Emery and Bentor, 1960; Emery and Neev, 1960; Goldsmith and Golik, 1980). At Haifa the fetch to north-west and south-west is of the order of 750 km, with a narrow arc from $275°-290°$ providing a fetch of 2,000 - 2,400 km. The wave climate has been measured during recent port construction, and is described by Goldsmith and Golik (1978), and Israel Ports Authority (1966). At Ashdod the maximum wave height is 7-8 m, and the cumulative height frequency diagram is shown in Fig. 4. The wave height exceeds 2.0 m for 20% of the time. Correlation of wave height and direction shows that waves higher than 4.0 m can only arise within the arc $260°-315°$.

Goldsmith and Golik (1980, pp. 167-169) conclude that due to the effects of refraction there is very little net transport either northwards or southwards on the whole Israel coast from Gaza to Rosh Haniqra, with the exception of a sediment sink in Haifa Bay (Fig. 5). There is some sand migration on a local scale due to migrating nodes in the pattern of wave convergence or divergence with wave direction, but this averages out on an annual time scale. The long term stability of the sand beaches on this section of the Israel coast is consistent with the discovery of Bronze Age, Neolithic, and Palaeolithic sites at over 20 places throughout the length of the shore, (Flemming *et al.*, 1978; Raban, 1983, this volume) (Fig. 6).

In particular, Perrot (1955) and Avi-Yonah and Eph'al (1975, vol. 1, p. 114) report that bone tools in association with the foundation of round stone huts were found in the beach sand at Ashkelon, and indicated Neolithic age. In January 1968 a severe storm removed much of the beach sand temporarily from the Mediterranean

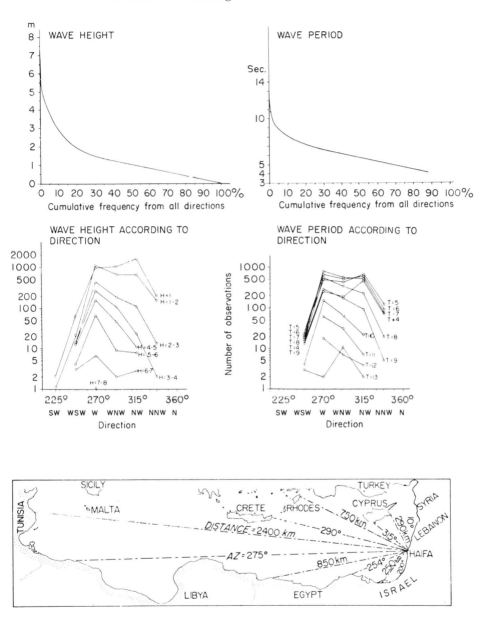

FIG. 4. *Wind fetch and wave conditions at Haifa on the coast of Israel, (reproduced from Goldsmith and Golik, with permission). From the bottom map it can be seen that the maximum fetch is restricted to the angle between 275-285°. The plot of occurrence of wave height against direction shows that for all wave heights greater than 1.0 m the most*

FIG. 4. *(continued)*
common direction is 270-280°. Long period waves also peak in
the same sector. The cumulative frequency diagrams (top)
show that for 50% of the time the wave height is greater
than 1.0 m; and for 50% of the time the wave period is
greater than 6 seconds.

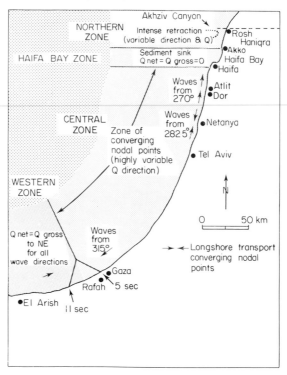

FIG. 5. *Sediment transport on the coast of Israel (reproduced*
from Goldsmith and Golik, with permission). Varying wave
directions between 270-315° produce varying convergence of
sand transport at different places on the coast between
Rafah and Haifa. The result is that, in the absence of
excavation of sand by man, the beaches are not depleted, and
coastal archaeological remains are protected from wave
action.

beaches of Israel, and stone walls, pottery, and flints, were
revealed in the surf at Neve Yam, (Wreschner, 1977; Prausnitz,
1977; Wreschner, 1983, this volume). The storm lasted from 14-16
January, 1968. On the 20 January the beach was restored more or
less to its original profile, but the walls emerged intermittently
until February 11.

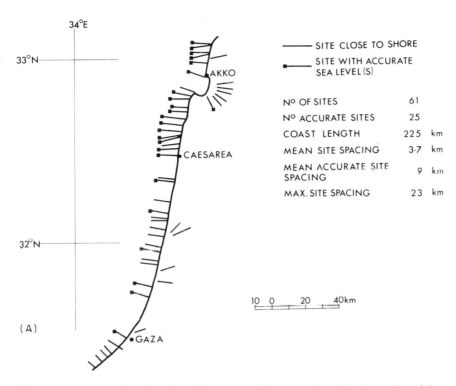

FIG. 6. *Archaeological sites on the coast of Israel, (from
Flemming et al., 1978). (A) All archaeological sites
identified on the coast, indicating those at which the
archaeological material could be correlated with an ancient
relative sea level. (B) Sites for which relative sea levels
could be derived, classified by archaeological period. Note
the concentration of Prehistoric sites between Caesarea and
Haifa.*

The walls at Neve Yam enclosed houses which were 7-9 m long
and 2.5-3.0 m wide, being of uncemented stones.   The total
occupied area appeared to be about 200,000 square metres, of
which 95% was seaward of the present shoreline. The assemblage
of finds included scrapers, burins, drills, chisels, adzes, and
obsidian tools. Carbon-14 dating provides an estimated period of
occupation of several hundred years around 6,300 B.P.   The
submerged settlement has not been seen since, and it would be
expensive to dig out the sand and conduct work underwater, or
behind a coffer dam.
    The sequence of events at Neve Yam stresses the excellent
protection which can be provided for a fragile archaeological site
by a few metres of sand, even in an exposed location. The cycle of

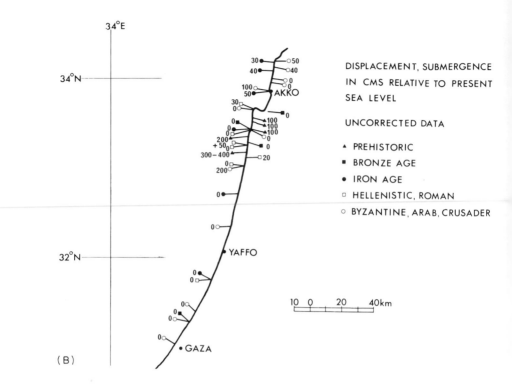

FIG. 6. *(continued)*

storm erosion followed by redeposition provided access to the site without creating severe damage. Bronze Age, Chalcolithic, and Neolithic sites in the area of Atlit and Neve Yam, (Flemming *et al.,* 1978) probably exist underwater in view of the sporadic finds by divers, (see also Raban, 1983, this volume). The preservation of the Neve Yam settlement suggests that deeper sites would be equally well protected by the sand beach during transgression, and would now be better protected since they are in deeper water and subject to less wave energy.

Ruppé (1978, 1980) has shown that shell middens survive marine transgression on the exposed coast 'of western Florida, although site protection on a local scale may be provided by barrier islands, lagoons and marshes. Fetch in the south westerly arc is of the order of 800-1,000 km across the Gulf of Mexico, and the gradient of the submerged continental shelf is low, with the 200 m isobath approximately 200 km from the shore. The low shelf gradient results in much wave energy being dissipated before it reaches the present shoreline, but, conversely, this energy is effective over a submerged area which may contain archaeological remains a considerable distance offshore. In view of the finds reported by

Ruppé it appears that the wave energy is dissipated over a wide area without destroying at least some midden sites.

Submerged forests are remnants of forest growth prior to the last rise of sea level, and they give a measure of the chances of survival of organic and other terrestrial material in the coastal zone during and after transgression. Such forest stumps and tree roots have been observed at low tide in many regions. By way of example, a few British locations cited by Steers (1948) will be given here. Submerged forests offshore with significant fetches include Drigg and Monk Moors (Steers, 1948, p. 83) with a fetch of 50 km; Criccieth (*op cit*. p. 125) fetch about 50 km; Llanaber (*op cit*. p. 140) fetch 100 km; Barnstaple Bay (*op cit*. p. 258-259). During a discussion of submerged forests Steers (*op cit*. p. 492) refers to a Mesolithic fish spear recovered from peat dredged off the Leman and Ower banks, 50 km offshore in the North Sea.

In 1970 a submerged middle Palaeolithic site was discovered near Cap Levi, 10 km north-east of Cherbourg, France. The coast is exposed to a 60 km fetch due north across the English Channel, and to longer fetches obliquely to east and west. Atlantic swell reaches the area after refraction and diffraction round Cap de la Hague. The site was discovered at a depth of 17-20 m near Cap Levi by Graindor and Scuvée, (Courtin, 1978, p. 735). A submerged river valley is bordered by lagoonal deposits, which are now being eroded by strong intermittent currents. The current creates a trough at the foot of the cliff on the east side of Cap Levi, and in so doing erodes and releases a large quantity of worked flints, which are gently deposited on the floor of the trough. The distribution of the flints has been triangulated by divers using tapes, and 2554 pieces have been lifted. Work is in progress to relate the flints to the stratigraphy of the lagoonal sediments.

This site would be classified as a lagoonal or estuarine site on the basis of the topography at the time of occupation, but the rising sea level has resulted in this section of coast being exposed to considerable wave energy. The erosion which is taking place has revealed the archaeological strata, and in the absence of erosion the artifacts would probably never have been found by divers.

Submerged Sea Caves

Blanc (1940) noted that caves south of Palinuro, southern Italy, had bone breccia cemented to the walls, even though they could only be entered now by boat, and the floors of the caves were flooded. Waechter (1964) reports studies of caves on the East side of Gibraltar. Three large caves opening onto Governor's Beach are only accessible by sea, since the beach is closed off at both ends by cliffs descending straight into the sea. The floors of the caves are concealed by sand and fallen rocks, but are probably below present sea level. The caves contain rich strata with signs of habitation, and were inhabited in a period when the sea level was lower, and access was from the coastal plain.

Many large submerged caves are known to sports divers, especially in the Mediterranean, mostly in the depth range 15-50 m. Martineau (1966) surveyed a number of caves on the coast of Malta, and other caves have been surveyed and described by diving biologists studying the fauna which cannot be sampled by normal methods from surface ships.

Flemming (1963, 1968b, 1972) has surveyed several underwater caves in order to determine Pleistocene low sea levels in the western Mediterranean. Caves with floors to depths of 50 m have been measured off Gibraltar, Marseille, Villefranche and Palinuro (Fig. 7). The author has observed caves for which plans have not been published off Corfu and Majorca. The caves are typical sea-caves, with abraded surfaces near the mouth, floors sloping upwards and backwards into the cliff, and occasionally with blow-holes high in the cliff face. Some of the caves go far back into the cliff, further than it was safe to dive, and probably connect with karstic solution channels. Stalactitic formations were found under the sea in the cave known as La Grotte de la Triperie, near Marseille. All these caves could have been used as habitations or rock shelters during the last period of low sea level. There are usually thick deposits of sand and breccia on the floors of the caves and human artifacts could survive, especially where the cave is in the lee of an island, as at La Calseraigne, Marseille.

Since, by definition, a sea cave was eroded by wave action, it follows that, when the sea returns to the same level as that which formed the cave, there will be significant wave action. Thus, if the cave has been inhabited in the intervening period of low sea level, the accumulated material in the cave will be subject to breaking waves for a hundred years or so. The same is not necessarily true of solution or karstic caves which happen to be on the coast, since they could occur in sheltered locations. Nevertheless, the material in a cave can be cemented as breccia, or buried under thick layers of sand or rocks, and could survive a marine transgression. Unfortunately, excavation under these conditions would require lifting bags to remove rocks, and water jets or power tools to dig through consolidated or cemented layers. This probably explains why submerged sea caves, although at first sight an obvious area to search, have not so far produced many signs of habitation. It is still possible that if the first trial surveys indicated important occupation levels, the resources and effort might be found to excavate through the layers of deposition in a sea cave.

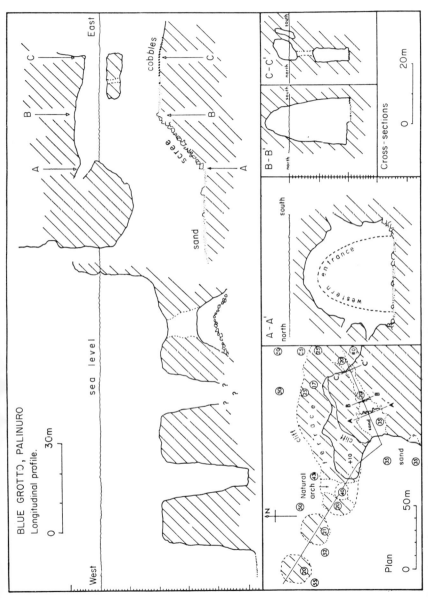

FIG. 7. *The submerged cave at Palinuro, Italy. The form of the cave and the adjacent cliff shows classic marine erosion features: the isolated pillars of rock are stacks, eroded at the base by a sea level at about −50 m; the same stacks have been planed off by a sea level at −20 m, which aligns with the floor of the cave at the east end. The natural arch just outside the mouth of the cave is partially blocked by fallen rocks, and a hole has been left in the roof of the arch. The central part of the main cave, and the arch, might both have provided shelter for human inhabitants. No vertical exaggeration.*

Karstic Caves and Sink-holes

Solution features have the advantage over erosional features in that they can be formed in areas of low wave energy. Thus archaeological deposits accumulated during low sea level may be protected during the subsequent transgression. This sequence of events can occur either at the mouth of a karstic cave opening onto the shore, or in a sink-hole in which the water level is determined by the overall water table in a karstic area, and is closely linked to sea level. Several underground rivers flow into the sea through submerged caves on the south coast of France, and these are good locations for the preservation of materials. A karstic cave or underground river also extends tens or hundreds of metres back from the cliff face, and therefore human occupation and the resulting deposits may occur in sheltered and protected areas far from the surf. Such caves have been explored by diving speleologists, although the work is naturally dangerous.

Courtin (1978, pp. 738-741) describes several submerged caves on the south coast of France which have been explored in search of archaeological deposits. Some of these have revealed interesting sequences of terrestrial and marine sediments, but finds of artifacts have not yet been reported. Stalagmitic formations and indurated layers are common. Cave 1 at Sormiou has been excavated by Bonifay and Courtin, (Courtin, 1978, p. 739) to a depth of 5 m through the sedimentary deposits at a distance of 10-15 m back from the mouth. The mouth opens at a depth of 5 m, and slopes backwards and downwards into the cliff, narrowing into a subterranean channel which at present contains fresh water. The floor of the cave would thus have been underwater as a result of the rising ground-water table before the sea broke into the mouth of the cave, and materials were thus not exposed to direct surf action.

At Carry-le-Rouet divers exploring the cave known as Grotte du Cap Méjean discovered in 1975 indurated breccias, (Courtin, 1978, p. 738). There are complex networks of galleries opening into the sea at a depth of 15-20 m. There are alternating layers of marine and terrestrial deposits, with the latter containing a fauna of birds and small mammals.

A submerged cave in the Bay of Villefranche is described by Flemming (1964, p. 144). It is known to local divers as the Grotte de Coraille, and is on the west side of the Bay. A submerged promontory of rock projects into the Bay, with the upper surface sloping from a depth of 5 m out to 15 m. The southern surface of the promontory slopes to seaward, but the northern face is vertical. The rock continues eastwards above the general level of the sea floor out to a depth of 40 m (Fig. 8). The cave is in the northern face of the promontory, completely protected from the open sea. Since the roof of the cave slopes in parallel with the upper surface of the promontory its form seems to be structurally controlled. The cave is 35 m long, 5-10 m high, and stretches about 10 m back into the cliff. There are fine sediments within the cave, and some fallen scree by the mouth. Since the cave can never have been exposed to direct wave action from the south, and the fetch within the Bay is less than 2 km, it is probable that terrestrial deposits within the cave would be undisturbed. This cave did not show erosional forms which could be equated with a low sea level, and therefore was not described in Flemming (1972).

Karstic solution caves also open onto the Bahamian shelf along the coast of Andros. (Palmer, 1981, unpublished expedition report). A series of diving expeditions have lead to at least a partial understanding of the topography and water flow through this system. No search has yet been made for strata which could contain terrestrial animal or human remains or artifacts, but further exploration is in progress.

Saline sink-holes in Florida have been excavated by Clausen et al. (1979) and Murphy (1978) and have revealed complex human remains at depths of more than 20 m below present sea level. Warm Mineral Springs is a karstic sink-hole on the west coast of Florida, 100 m in diameter at the surface, 70 m deep, and with a surface temperature of $30^{o}C$. A technically advanced diving excavation (Murphy, 1978) involving decompression diving, excavation to 1 cm accuracy, and continuous video-taping of finds underwater, resulted in accurate trenching and stratigraphy. Finds included bones, shells, plants, seeds, pollen, and human skeletal remains including skulls. Carbon-14 and pollen dating gave dates between 10,000-11,000 B.P. Warm Mineral Springs is connected to the local water table by karstic channels, and hence the water level is related to sea level. At 10,000 B.P., the eustatic sea level would be 30-40 m below present sea level, and much of the cave would have been dry and habitable.

A second Florida sink-hole has been excavated with similar results (Clausen et al., 1979). Little Salt Spring, near Charlotte Harbour, is 78 m in diameter and 60 m deep. The water level is 5 m above present sea level. The oldest remains found were of a tortoise which had been killed with a wooden stake, presumably for food. The remains were found on a ledge at a depth of 26 m below the water surface, and the wood gave a Carbon-14 date of 12,030 +/- 200 B.P. A vast range of materials associated with habitation were found with later dates and in shallower water, pointed stakes, carved oak, human bones, hickory nuts, a socketed antler projectile point, and a well-preserved portion of a non-returning oak boomerang. The rate of rise of water level in the sink-hole was estimated at 0.7 cm per year from 11,000 B.P. to 8,500 B.P., making a total rise of 25 m, by which time the level was within 1.0 m of the present surface. The level then dropped about 8.0 m by approximately 5,500 years B.P., and subsequently

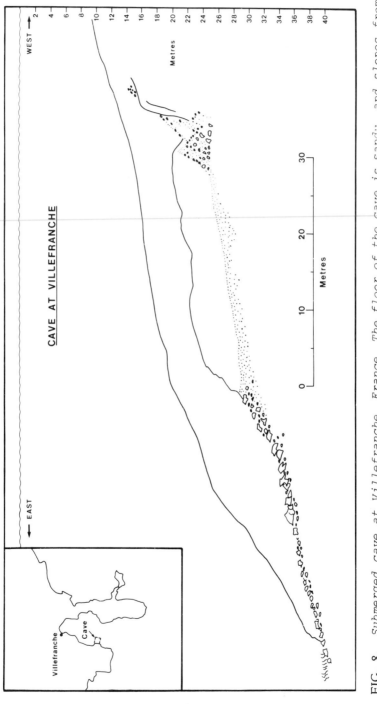

FIG. 8. *Submerged cave at Villefranche, France. The floor of the cave is sandy, and slopes from 24 m to 28 m in depth. The cave is in the north face of the submerged promontory of rock, marked with an arrow in the inset map. Thus it is only exposed to a northerly fetch across the bay of Villefranche, which is less than 2 km. The cave would have provided complete shelter from the open sea.*

rose to the present level. The finds at Little Salt Springs provide the earliest evidence so far of human activity in Florida (Clausen *et al.*, 1979, p. 613).

Sink-holes on the Yucatan peninsula, Mexico, have been explored by divers primarily searching for golden religious artifacts thrown into the water during the last 2,000 years. These sink-holes, or cenotes, are very numerous, and the water level in them is determined by the water table, and closely linked to sea level in the generally karstic terrain. Ernesto Licon (personal communication) has reported the finding of archaeological deposits in gravel beds in the wall of a cenote between ten and twenty metres below water level.

On the basis of the above evidence, karstic or solution caves therefore have a higher chance of containing significant archaeological strata intact than marine erosional caves.

Islands and Archipelagoes

Conditions of low wave energy frequently exist between islands and the mainland coast, on the lee side of islands, and between the islands of a large, relatively closely spaced, archipelago. We have already seen that submerged settlements have been found in the channels between the Danish islands, and in the shelter of the island of Pavlo Petri, southern Greece. Evans and Renfrew (1968) studied the Neolithic village on the island of Saliagos, between Paros and Antiparos, in the Aegean sea. The modern strait between Paros and Antiparos is 1 km wide, and the island of Saliagos is 100 m by 75 m, rising 5 m above the waters of the strait. Neolithic village walls are being eroded from the low cliff round the island, and clearly previously extended below sea level. An underwater survey indicated that the original shoreline was 5 m lower, and the village would then have been located on a small promontory projecting from the isthmus joining Paros and Antiparos. The spacing of the Cyclades archipelago is such that there is no fetch more than 80 km in any direction from Saliagos, except over very narrow arcs of a few degrees, and the fetch in most directions is of the order of 40 km.

Archipelago sites of particular relevance to the present study are the Indonesian islands on the route from Asia to Australia, and the coastal island chain off British Columbia, along which migration may have occurred into the Americas. No underwater archaeological finds have been made, or reported, from Indonesia, but sites on the sides of islands facing inwards into the archipelago would be exposed to an average fetch of 300 km, and often less than 50 km.

Palaeoindian material has been found on land in Alaska (Powers and Hamilton, 1978), Yukon (Morlan, 1978) and British Columbia (Mitchell, 1971; Fladmark, 1975). The evidence for coast-wise

migration has been summarised by Borden (1979) who also presents
the evidence for the survival of peoples south of the ice-cap on
the Cordilleran ranges during the last glacial maximum.
Investigations in the region of the Fraser River Delta indicate
that between 15,000 B.P. and 9,000 B.P. people migrated northwards from Washington, Oregon, and Nevada, and met other tribes
migrating south from Alaska in the area of Vancouver Island.
Borden (1979, p. 966) states that much of the migration may have
been by coastal islands, but that unfortunately, the evidence will
now be submerged or eroded away. Given the sheltered inlets and
fjord nature of much of the coast, some submerged sites in this
area may in fact be preserved, especially on the east-facing shores
of islands, protected from the Pacific. From the remains of food
materials it is evident that the Protowestern peoples south of the
ice-cap were, on the coast, exploiting shellfish.

Around 9,500-9,000 B.P., groups from Alaska and Beringia
travelled southwards down the coastal island chain of British
Columbia as far as Vancouver Island. From the wide distribution
of sites, and the remains of sea mammals, they must have had sea-
worthy craft, and considerable skill, (Borden, 1979, p. 969).

As yet, no submerged site has been discovered off the coast of
British Columbia, but Mitchell (1971, p. 78) describes a site in a
very sheltered location, Montague Harbour, which dates from 3,200
B.P., and which is being eroded by the sea at present. The site is
lower in the sea water than when it was occupied. In similar
sheltered locations, and deeper water, some older submerged sites
would almost certainly be preserved.

The coasts of Australia and its offshore islands are in places
densely scattered with large shell middens; see Coutts et al.
(1976) for an inventory of over 100 shell middens on the south
coast of Victoria, and Jones (1977) for a description of shell
middens on the north shore of Tasmania. Middens have been
reported from several offshore islands around Australia, including
Lizzard Island (Deas, personal communication), and Kangaroo Island
(Lampert, 1975). Between Tasmania and the coast of Victoria there
are many islands with fetches of 10-40 km between them, although
they would be exposed to longer fetches to the open ocean and
across the Bass Strait. Submerged middens or occupied cave sites
could survive in the relatively sheltered parts of the islands, in
spite of the stormy nature of the Bass Strait area (Fig. 9).

The Isles of Scilly constitute an archipelago 15 km by 10 km at a
distance of 40 km off the south west tip of England. Crawford
(1927) described prehistoric walls which exist on the islands, and
which continue in several locations into the water between the
islands. The area has a tidal range of 5 m and the walls can be
seen at spring low tides.

The submerged Neolithic site of Aghios Petros, Greece, was
discovered during the summer of 1981, after this paper was

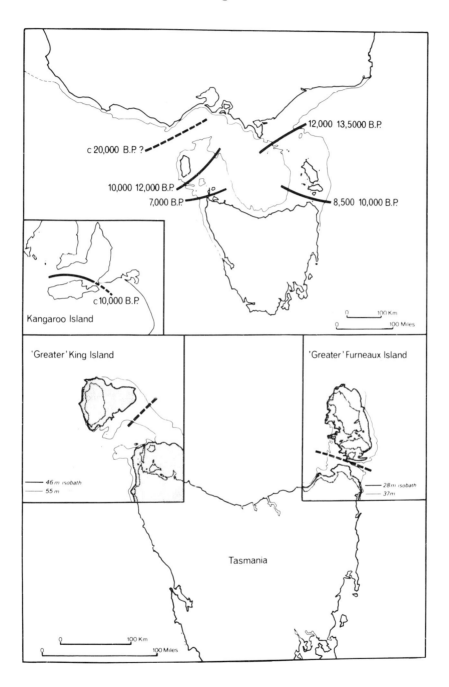

FIG. 9. (legend overleaf)

FIG. 9. *Islands of the Tasmanian archipelago (reproduced from Jones, 1977, with permission). In the top map the lines marked with dates indicate the time at which each channel was flooded by the rising sea level. The lower map shows the coastlines at different depths, when groups of islands would have been linked.*

written. The site is in an island - archipelago location (Flemming, 1983, this volume), and the fetch is of the order of 0.5-10 km.

Coral Reefs

The active growth of a coral reef tends to conceal and bury archaeological remains which may have survived on the continental shelf in that area. Faure and Roubet (1968) found an Acheulian bi-faced flint tool on the Afar coast in association with a fossil non-active coral reef. Beaton (1978) discussed the possible occupation of the Great Barrier Reef during low sea level periods, and concluded that coral growth and erosion would have concealed any possible remains.

Active coral has, by definition, extended the area of reef growth and calcification in the recent past, and it would be pointless for divers to search in an active reef. However, modern reefs are often associated with long-term accumulations of calcareous rocks in which caves or overhangs may have produced suitable habitation or shelter sites. The repeated rise and fall of sea level during the Pleistocene produced areas of fossil and dead reef above sea level, and the growth of the modern reef does not necessarily coincide with that of previous periods. The Great Barrier Reef was a coastal mountain range for much of the Pleistocene, and was certainly occupied by man during the last 30,000 years before the sea level rose. The reefs on the edge of the continental shelf between Australia and Timor (Birdsell, 1977; Van Andel and Veevers, 1967) may also have been occupied during the first migration into Australia.

Coral reefs are therefore improbable sites for the preservation of human remains, but in the long term some chance finds could occur.

SUMMARY OF SITE ANALYSIS

Ria, Lagoon Esturary

TABLE 1

Site Name	Period	Depth	Tide Range	Current	Fetch	Max Waves
1. Lagoon of Thau France	Bronze Age	2mm	0.2-03m	?	5-15km	minimal
2. Sydney Harbour Australia	?	?	1.3m	?	10km	minimal
3. Little Swanport Tasmania	?	?	0.8-1.0m	?	few km	minimal
4. Weipa Estuary Queensland	1000 BP	coastal	1.6m	?	few km	?
5. British Columbia	?	?	5m?	?	50-200km	?
6. Puget Sound Birch Bay	?	SL	2.3-2.5m	?	10-30km	?
7. Landskrona Sweden	Neolithic	6.18m	cm	strong	15-50km	?
8. Morbihan Brittany	Neolithic	0-3m	high	moderate	few km	minimal
9. Etang de Salses,	Neolithic	?	0.2-0.3m	?	15-50km	minimal

Common factors are minimal wave energy; currents and tidal range are very variable. Diving conditions for search, survey, and excavation are favourable.

Sheltered Alluvial Coasts

TABLE 2

10. Pavlo Petri Greece	Bronze Age	3.5m	0.2-0.3m	0.5 knot	30-100km	moderate
11. Tybrind Vig, Denmark	Mesolithic	2,5m	cm	?	0-10km	small

12. Aerø-Drejø Denmark	Mesolithic	2.5m	cm	?	5-10km	small

Common factors, a restricted fetch of a few tens of km, small waves, and moderate currents. Low coastal gradients. Low sedimentation rate. Good diving conditions.

Exposed Equilibrium or Accumulating Beach

TABLE 3

13. Cape Canaveral USA.	6000 B.P.	0-5m	1.2-1.3m	?	200-6000km	?
14. Santa Monica Bay, USA.	5500 B.P.	4.5m	1.5m	?	'000s	6m
15. La Jolla USA	5-8000 B.P.	0-20m	1.5m	?	'000s	6m
16. West Florida, USA	?	?	0.2-1.1m	?	1500km	
17. Ashkelon. Israel	Neolithic	0-1m	0.2-0,3m	?	2000km	7-8m
18. Neve Yam, Israel	6300 B.P.	0-1m	0.2-0.3m	?	2000km	7-8m
19. Cap Levi, France	Mid-Palaeo	17-20m	5m+	strong	60km+	?

Common factors, fetch 100-1,000's km, extreme wave exposure, generally a low beach gradient but sometimes a cliff coast, archaeological material protected by sediment cover or in rocky depressions.

Submerged Sea Caves

TABLE 4

20. Governor's Beach Gibraltar	Neolithic	0m	1.0m	?	1600km	?
21. Palinuro, Italy	?	50m	0.2-0.3m	small	500-1500km	?

Common factors, high wave exposure, calcareous rocks, steep topography.

Karstic Caves and Sink-holes

TABLE 5

22. Villefranche France	?	15m	0.2-0.3m	nil	2km	minimal
23. Carry-le-Rouet France	?	15-20m	0.2-0.3m	?	750km	?
24. Sormiou Marseille France	Wurm	10m	0.2-0.3m	small	?	minimal
25. Warm Mineral Springs, USA	11,000 B.P.	20m	zero	zero	zero	zero
26. Little Salt Springs, USA	12,000 B.P.	26m	zero	zero	zero	zero

Common factors, minimal or zero waves, currents, and tidal effects.

Islands and Archipelagoes

TABLE 6

27. Saliagos, Greece	Neolithic	0-1.0m	0.2-0.3m	?	1-80km	moderate
28. Montague Harbour Canada.	3200 B.P.	0-1.0m	1-1.1m	?	?	?
29. Tasmania, Australia.	?	?	2.3-2.5m	?	250km	?
30. Indonesia	?	?	1.3-1.7m	?	50-300km	?
31. Isles of Scilly, Britain.	Bronze Age	1-2m	5+		10-40km	?

Common factors, fetch in the 10-300 km range.

Thirty-two sites or groups of sites have been identified. Of these 24 refer to underwater sites which have been surveyed or excavated by divers or swimmers; and definitely include archaeological deposits. Five refer to specific sites or locations where the conditions are highly suitable for the occurrence and preservation of archaeological deposits (2, 4, 20, 21, 22). One refers to a cave site which contains excavated strata of climatic and environmental (24). Two refer to archipelago areas of general interest, but without the identification of individual sites (29, 30). Several other sites have been alluded to, such as the numerous caves off the south coast of France.*

DISCUSSION

No single factor in the geomorphology of the coastal zone is necessary or sufficient to ensure preservation of archaeological remains underwater, and the same is true of tidal, current, and wave exposure. Continuous erosion or continuous sedimentary deposition exclude the preservation and discovery of sites underwater respectively. However, deposition followed by erosion, as in the case of the Cap Levi site may first preserve a site, and then reveal it to divers.

Coastal human settlements, work sites, or boat landing places are likely always to be situated in sheltered spots, even when the coast as a whole is exposed. In fact, when the coast is exposed, human settlement is most probable behind islands, or in caves. This emphasises the importance of topography around a site on the scale of 1km or less. The evidence of the archaeological materials found so far confirms this conclusion. Whilst the gross topography on the scale of 10-100 km may create generally favourable conditions (Puget Sound, Sydney Harbour, Cyclades, Danish Archipelago), it is the immediate curvature or indentation of the coast which determines the existence and survival of archaeological remains.

The analysis and discussion so far has generalised coastal types on the assumption that the topography and coastal dynamics at the time of occupation were similar to those at present sea level, in general, if not in detail. (See Inman, 1983, this volume, for a discussion of this problem.) This has been a reasonable starting point, since most submarine archaeological discoveries have been shallower than 10 m, and all shallower than 20 m. Even over this depth range important changes in plan can occur when the sea level changes by a few metres. Thus the lagoon at Tybrind Vig became an open bay as the sea rose; the curving promontory at Pavlo Petri became a chain of small islands. A complete study of the survival of archaeological materials would have to include the mechanism of immediate preservation at the site of occupation in the short term; the mechanism of surviving marine transgression; and the mechanism of surviving when submerged underwater for many thousands of years. It is at this point that probabilistic and predictive models come into their own.

* No sites have been added to this list solely on the basis of other chapters in this book. The analysis is based on material published previously. Thus the present list does not include the recent work of Geddes; Raban; and Gifford reported in this volume.

The manner of discovery of submerged settlements is of three forms; (a) logical extension of a land site; (b) logical search in a new area, and (c) total chance. For many sites I do not have data, but some can be classified. Direct extension of land sites includes 3, 5, 6, 8, 27 and Aghios Petros; deliberate and logical search includes 1, 7, 10, 11, 16, 18, 24, 25, 26; chance seems to have been the dominant factor in the cases of 9, 13, 15, and possibly others. This classification may be misleading, since it is probably common for sports divers to report or describe a find, or raise a single flint or piece of pottery, after which professional archaeologists launch a detailed survey, or encourage the amateurs to continue the search and report back. The high proportion of archaeological sites resulting from deliberate searches is somewhat surprising, although the number of searches which lead to nothing is not known. My own prejudice was to expect that the discovery of most sites so far would involve a large element of chance.

The sites discussed in this paper indicate that although the factors determining the occurrence and survival of a submerged settlement are complex, there is a deterministic and logical pattern. Whilst there are too few data to derive clear predictive rules, we are not faced with a meaningless random assortment of uncorrelated or contradictory facts. Flint and stone tools, pottery, bone and even wood and other organic materials, do survive stratigraphically in the best circumstances, and scattered over tens of metres in less ideal conditions. The sites discussed above were found by chance or by using the simplest criteria to predict favourable areas, followed by labour-intensive searching by divers. Larsson (1983, this volume) and Ruppé (1980) specifically state that search was made along the axes of drowned valleys; Glen Egstrom (personal communication) discovered that indian grinding bowls could be found off Los Angeles by following drowned creek beds. It follows that where sophisticated predictive methods are used the final stages of the search should be related to topography on the small-scale. Accurate echo-sounding or side-scan mapping should reveal submerged creeks, lagoons, beach ridges, etc. Where the topography underwater is similar to that on the present shore, archaeological remains should be sought in similar locations. Thus the middens found on spits by Schwartz and Grabert (1980, p.119) suggest that similar midden materials might by found on the submerged spits which show on echo-soundings.

I have not referred to the destructive effects of ice, whether land-ice or sea-ice. The analysis of possible migration routes along the coast of British Columbia is complicated first by the depression of the land during the period of low sea level, then by the presence of land ice near the coast, then by the possible movements of coastal floating ice, and finally by marine transgression. Fladmark (1975, 1978) shows that the coastal islands were outside the main ice-sheet, but the area must have been subjected to severe peri-glacial conditions. Where fjord valleys have been subjected to the full weight of glacier ice there is no doubt that all traces of human occupancy below sea level prior to glaciation will be destroyed. In less severe conditions adjacent to glaciers the degree of survival is very difficult to estimate. There are no data on sites as yet to include in this study, and it is the premise of this study that I do not wish to speculate from a knowledge of geomorphic conditions only to an estimate of the chances of site survival.

CONCLUSIONS

The present study, based on categorisation of known underwater archaeological sites, has shown that:

(a) Lithic site structures and artifacts, uncemented walls, burials, hearths, middens, food remains, and tools and other artifacts can survive in stratigraphic context in the sea or below the coastal groundwater table after a marine transgression.

(b) Such remains are protected either because the environment is low energy (ria, lagoon, estuary, karstic cave, archipelago), or because the beach gradient provides a protective cover of sediment.

Although field evidence has not been produced on submerged sites in Arctic conditions, the variety of sites and geomorphological conditions discussed is sufficient to show that human habitation sites could be discovered below sea level in locally protected environments at all other latitudes. A search scheme based on using precision echo-sounding, bathymetric charting, and side-scan sonar would reveal the necessary topographic detail, whilst shallow penetration sonar would indicate sediment thicknesses. Such surveys in the critical strait areas between Australia and Indonesia, and Gibraltar, Sicily Straits, in the Caribbean, Red Sea, and Sea of Japan, are needed in the near future. The effectiveness of such a survey on the submerged area of Beringia is more problematic, both because of expense, and because of the possibility of ice erosion. However, the effect of ice on the southern shores of Beringia was probably not severe, and a survey could be justified. Keith (1976) has produced a preliminary topographic analysis of the areas in which a search would be most useful. (See also McManus   et al., 1983, this volume, for a review of the northern shore).

This study shows beyond any doubt that there is every reason to continue the search for submerged archaeological sites of Palaeolithic age, and every reason to suppose that submerged sites in the key bridge areas will be found. Scuba diving can be continued as the working technique to depths of 50-60 m in mid-latitude and topical waters, with a shallower depth restriction in polar latitudes. Towed camera and T.V. sledges, submersibles, or remote controlled vehicles can be used to extend the depth of survey to 100-150 m in areas of critical value.

REFERENCES

Alimen, M-H. (1975). Les Isthmes Hispano-Marocain et Siculo-Tunisien aux temps Acheuléens. *L'anthropologie* **79,** 399-436.

Allen, J., Golson, J. and Jones, R. (1977). *Sunda and Sahul.* Academic Press, London, 647 pp.

Andersen, A.S.H. (1980). Tybrind Vig, a preliminary report on a submerged Ertebolle settlement on the Little Belt. *Antikvariske Studier* **4,** 7-22

Aubrey, D.G., Inman, D.L. and Winant, C.D. (1980). The statistical prediction of beach changes in southern California. *Journal of Geophysical Research* **85.** C6, 3264-3276.

Avi-Yonah, M., and Eph'al, Y. (1975). Ashkelon. In *Encyclopaedia of Archaeological Excavations in the Holy Land* 121-130 (ed. Avi-Honah, M.) Israel Exploration Society and Massada Press, Jerusalem, **1,** pp. 339.

Bailey, G.N. (1977). Shell mounds, shell middens, and raised beaches in the Cape York Peninsula. *Mankind* **11.** 132-143.

Bass, G.F. (Ed.) (1972). *A history of Seafaring based on Underwater Archaeology.* Thames and Hudson, London. pp. 320.

Beaton, J.M. (1978). Archaeology and the Great Barrier Reef. *The Northern Great Barrier Reef. Philosophical Transactions Royal Society London, B.* **284,** 141-147.

Blanc, A.C. (1937). Low levels of the Mediterranean Sea during the Pleistocene glaciation. *Geological Society of London Quarterly Journal* **93,** 621-625.

Blanc, A.C. (1940). Industrie musteriane e paleolithiche superiore nelle dune fossile e nelle grotte litorannee del Capo Palinuro. *R.C. Reale Accademia d'Italia.* **10,** Ser.7. v.l.

Borden, C.E. (1979). Peopling and early cultures of the Pacific North-west. *Science*. 203, 963-971.

Bowdler, S. (1977). The coastal colonisation of Australia. pp. 205-246 in Allen *et al, q.v.*

Bryan, A.L. (ed.)(1978). Early Man in America. Occasional Papers, No. 1 of the Department of Anthropology, University of Alberta, Edmonton, pp. 327.

Carlson, R. (1980). Problems in archaeological site protection on the coast of British Columbia. pp. 109-112 in *Proceedings of the Commission on Coastal Environment Field Symposium, Coastal Archaeology Session.* (M.L. Schwartz Ed.) I.G.U.

Clark, G. (1969). *World Prehistory.* Cambridge University Press. pp. 331.

Clark, J.A., Farrell, W.E., and Peltier, E.R. (1978). Global changes in post-glacial sea level: a numerical calculation. *Quaternary Research* 9, 265-287.

Clausen, C.J., Cohen, A.D., Emiliani, C., Holman, J.A. and Stipp, J.J. (1979). Little Salt Spring, Florida: a unique underwater site. *Science* 203, 609-614.

Courtin, J. (1978). Direction des recherches préhistoriques sous-marines. *Gallia Prehistoire.* 21, 735-746.

Cockrell, W.A. and Murphy, L. (1978). 8 SL 17: Methodological approaches to a dual component marine site on the Florida Atlantic coast. pp. 175-182 in *Beneath the Waters of Time.* (ed. Barto-Arnold, J.) 9th Conference on Underwater Archaeology, Texas Antiquities Committee, Publication No. 6.

Coutts, P.J.F., Witter, V.C., Cochrane, R.M. and Patrick, J. (1976). Sites of special scientific interest in the Victoria coastal region, archaeological aspects. *Victoria Archaeological Survey.* pp. 96.

Crawford, O.G.S. (1927). "Lyonesse", *Antiquity* 1, 5-14.

Emery, K.O. and Bentor, Y.K. (1960). The continental shelf of Israel. *Bulletin of the Geological Survey of Israel* 26, 25-41.

Emery, K.O. and Edwards, R.L. (1966). Archaeological potential of the Atlantic continental shelf. *American Antiquity* 31, 733-737.

Emery, K.O. and Neev, D. (1960). Mediterranean beaches of Israel. *Bulletin of the Geological Survey of Israel* 26, 1-24.

Emiliani, C. (1978). The causes of the Ice Ages. *Earth and Planetary Science Letters* 37, 349-354.

Evans, J.D. and Renfrew, C. (1968). Excavations at Saliagos near Antiparos. *British School of Archaeology at Athens* Supplementary volume, No. 5, pp. 266.

Fairbridge, R.W. (1961). Eustatic changes in sea level. In *Physics and Chemistry of the Earth* 4, 99-185, Pergamon Press, Oxford, pp. 317.

Faure, H. and Roubet, C. (1968). Découverte d'un biface acheuléen dans les calcaires marin du golfe pleistocène de l'Afar (Mer Rouge, Ethiope). *Compte Rendue Académie Scientifique de Paris* 267, 18-21.

Fladmark, K.R. (1975). A palaeoecological model for Northwest Coast prehistory. *National Museum of Man Mercury Series.* Archaeological Survey of Canada No. 43, Ottawa, pp. 328.

Fladmark, K.R. (1978). The feasibility of the Northwest Coast as a migration route for early man. 119-128 In Bryan, 1978, *q.v.*

Flemming, N.C. (1963). Underwater caves of Gibraltar. *Second World Congress of the Confederation Mondiale des Activites Subaquatiques*. 96-106, Palantype, London, pp. 183.

Flemming, N.C. (1964). Submerged erosion surfaces in the Western Mediterranean. Ph.D. thesis submitted at the University of Cambridge, England.

Flemming, N.C. (1968a) Mediterranean sea level changes. *Science Journal* 4, 51-55.

Flemming, N.C. (1968b). Derivation of Pleistocene marine chronology from the morphometry of erosion profiles. *Journal of Geology* 76, 280-296.

Flemming, N.C. (19 69). Archaeological evidence for eustatic change of sea level and earth movements in the Western Mediterranean in the last 2,000 years. *Geological Society of America, Special Paper* 109 pp. 125.

Flemming, N.C. (1972). *Cities in the Sea.* Doubleday, New York, pp. 222.

Flemming, N.C. (1972). Relative chronology of submerged Pleistocene marine erosion features in the Western Mediterranean. *Journal of Geology* 80, 633-662.

Flemming, N.C., Raban, A. and Goetschel, C. (1978). Tectonic and eustatic changes on the Mediterranean coast of Israel in the last 9,000 years. 33-93 In *Progress in Underwater Science*. Proceedings of the Underwater Association 5, Pentech Press.

Fonquerle, D. (1982). Excavations in the lagoon of Thau. Proceedings of 6th Symposium of CMAS Scientific Committee, Edinburgh (ed. N. Mathers) (in Press).

Giot, P.R. (1970). La Bretagne au peril des mers Holocenes. *Travaux du Laboratoire d'anthropologie préhistorique de la Faculté des Science de Rennes* 203-208.

Goldsmith, V. and Golik, A. (1980). Sediment transport model of the south-eastern Mediterranean coast. *Marine Geology* 37, 147-175.

Harding, A., Cadogan, G. and Howell, R. (1969). Pavlopetri, an underwater Bronze Age town in Laconia. *Annual of the British School at Athens* 64, 113-142.

Inman, D.L. (1983). Application of coastal dynamics to the reconstruction of palaeocoastlines. (This volume).

Israel Ports Authority, (1966). Oceanographic observations at Ashdod, 1958-65. *Israel Ports Authority,* Coastal Studies Division, pp. 50.

Jones, R. (1971). Rocky Cape and the problem of the Tasmanians. Ph.D. dissertation submitted to the University of Sydney, Australia.

Jones, R. (1977). Man as an element of a continental fauna: the case of the sundering of the Bassian Bridge. pp. 317-386 in Allen, J., Golson, J. and Jones, R. 1977, *q.v.*

Keith, D.H. (1976). Fluctuations in sea level in late Pleistocene times and the archaeological potential of the Bering-Chukchi platform, MA thesis presented at the University of North Carolina Department of Anthropology.

Lampert, R.J. (1975). A preliminary report on some waisted blades found on Kangaroo Island, South Australia. *Australian Archaeology* 2, 45-48.

Larsson, L. (1983). Mesolithic settlement at the bottom of Oresund. (This volume.)

Martineau, M.P. (1967). The formation and significance of submarine terraces off the coast of Malta. *Underwater Association Report 1966-67* (eds Lythgoe, J.N. and Woods, J.D.) pp. 19-24.

Masters, P. (1983). Detection and assessment of prehistoric artifact sites off the coast of southern California. (This volume.)

Mitchell, D.H. (1971). Archaeology of the Gulf of Georgia area, a natural region and its cultural types. *Syesis* 4, pp. 228. British Columbia Provincial Museum.

Moriarty, J.R. (1963). The use of oceanography in the solution of problems in a submarine archaeological site. *Papers in Marine Geology*, Shepard commemorative volume, 511-522, McMillan, New York.

Morlan, R.E. (1978). Early man in northern Yukon Territory: perspectives as of 1977. pp. 78-95 in Bryan, 1978 *q.v.*

Muche, J.F. (1978). An inundated aboriginal site, Coral Beach, California. pp. 101-108 in *Beneath the Waters of Time*. (ed. Barto Arnold, J.). 9th Conference of Underwater Archaeology, Texas Antiquities Committee, No. 6.

Murphy, L. (1978). 8 SLO 19: Specialised methodological, technological and physiological approaches to deep water excavation of a prehistoric site at Warm Mineral Springs, Florida. pp. 123-128 in *Beneath the Waters of Time*. (ed. Barto Arnold, J.). 9th Conference of Underwater Archaeology, Texas Antiquities Committee, No. 6.

Newman, W.S., Marcus, L.F., Pardi, R.R., Paccione, J.A. and Tomecek, S.M. (1980). Eustasy and deformation of the Geoid: 1,000-6,000 Radiocarbon years B.P.   pp. 555-567 in *Earth Rheology, Isostasy and Eustasy* (ed. Morner, N-A.). Wiley.

Pawka, S.A., Inman, D.L., Lowe, R.L.L. and Holmes, L. (1976). Wave Climate at Torrey Pines Beach, California. *Coastal Engineering Research Centre*. Technical Paper No. 76-5, U.S. Army Corps of Engineers, pp. 372.

Perrot, J. (1955). Neolithic discoveries at Ashkelon. *Israel Exploration Journal* 5, 270-271.

Powers, W.H., Draper, L. and Briggs, P.M. (1969). Waves at Camp Pendleton, California. *Eleventh Conference on Coastal Engineering* American Society of Civil Engineers.

Powers, W.R. and Hamilton, T.D. (1978). Dry Creek: A late Pleistocene human occupation in central Alaska. pp. 72-77 in Bryan, A.L. *q.v.*

Prausnitz, M.W. (1977). The pottery at Newe Yam. *Eretz Israel. Israel Exploration Society* 13, 272-278.

Prigent, D. (1978). Contribution a l'étude de la transgression Flandrienne en Basse Loire, apport de l'archéologie. *Etude Protohistorique Pays de la Loire.* 5, pp. 177.

Raban, A. (1983). Submerged prehistoric sites off the Mediterranean coast of Israel. (This volume.)

Ruppé, R.J. (1978). Underwater site detection by use of a coring instrument. pp. 119-121 in *Beneath the Waters of Time.* (ed. Barto Arnold, J.,). 9th Conference of Underwater Archaeology, Texas Antiquities Committee, No. 6.

Ruppé, R.J. (1981) The archaeology of drowned terrestrial sites: a preliminary report. in *Burea of Historical Sites and Properties Bulletin No.6,* Division of Archives, History and Records Management, Department of State, Tallahassee, Florida, pp. 35-45.

Schwartz, M.L. and Grabert, G. (1980). Puget Sound coastal-archaeological sites revisited. *International Geographical Union, Commission on the Coastal Environment.* Proceedings of the CCE Field Symposium, August 1980. (ed. Schwartz, M.L.)

Seymour, R.J. (1978). California Coastal Engineering Data Network, Second Annual Report. State of California, Resources Agency, Department of Navigation and Ocean Development, pp. 123.

Shackleton, N.J. and Opdyke, N.D. (1973). Oxygen isotope and paleomagnetic stratigraphy of equatorial Pacific core V28-238; oxygen isotope temperature and ice volume over a 10^5 year and 10^6 year scale. *Quaternary Research* 3, 39-55.

Skaarup, J. (1980). Undersoisk stenhalder. *Tiddskriftet Skalk* 1, 3-8.

Steers, J.A. (1948). *The Coastline of England and Wales.* Cambridge, pp. 644.

Van Andel, T.J. and Veevers, J.J. (1967). Morphology and sediments of the Timor Sea. *Bulletin of the Bureau of Mineral Resources, Australia* 83, pp. 172.

Waechter, J.d'A. (1964). Excavation of Gorham's Cave, Gibraltar 1951-54. *Institute of Archaeology Bulletin, London.* 4, 189.

Walcott, R.I. (1972). Past sea levels, eustasy and deformation of the earth. *Quaternary Research* 2, 1-14.

Waterhouse, H. and Hope Simpson, R. (1961). Prehistoric Lakonia. *British School at Athens Journal,* 111-175.

Wreschner, E.E. (1977). Newe Yam - a submerged late neolithic settlement near Mount Carmel. *Eretz Israel, Israel Exploration Society.* 13, 260-271.

Wreschner, E.E. (1983). The submerged Neolithic village Newe Yam on the Israeli Mediterranean coast. (This volume.)

EARLY NEOLITHIC OCCUPATION ON THE SUBMERGED CONTINENTAL PLATEAU OF ROUSSILLON. (FRANCE)

David S. Geddes [1], Jean Guilaine [1] and Andre Monaco [2]

[1] *Centre d'Anthropologie des Societés Rurales, Centre National de la Recherche Scientifique, G.R. 44, 56, rue du Taur, 31000 Toulouse, France.*

[2] *Centre de Recherches de Sédimentologie Marine, Centre National de la Recherche Scientifique, Avenue de Villeneuve, 66025 Perpignan, France.*

ABSTRACT

An early Neolithic occupation site (6800 ± 90 B.P.) established on a deltaic levee of fluvial gravels was submerged before 5000 years B.P. by the Mediterranean, which began rising around 14,000 years B.P. according to observations in the Golfe du Lion. The Holocene transgression first invaded, downcut and channellized zones of the Roussillon continental plateau after 8000 B.P., rising particularly rapidly from 8000 to 6000 years B.P., that is during the Neolithic, and reworking the levee into a perilittoral arm or small island several meters above sea level. Excavations recovered stone and bone tools, typologically early cardial-impressed pottery of the Franco-Iberian group, and faunal remains. Taphonomic analysis of the process of burial suggests that a representative sample of animal bones was recovered. Subsistence activities included husbandry of domestic sheep and cattle; hunting for boar, deer, aurochs and birds; coastal and deep-sea fishing; and certainly the collection of mollusks and plants. The site may have played a specialized role in a subsistence system uniting the littoral and inland areas. Relationships with indigenous Mesolithic cultures, which could have had an important bearing on the diffusion of plant and animal domesticates and the shift to food production, remain uncertain. The results suggest that the coastal and

maritime   diffusion   of   Neolithic   food   production   in   the
Mediterranean would have occurred in zones currently submerged.

INTRODUCTION

As part of a multi-disciplinary research program focusing on the
changing relationships between man and the natural environment
during   the   postglacial   period   in   the   western   Mediterranean,
excavation was undertaken at the submerged, early Neolithic site
on the *Pointe de la Corrège* at Port Leucate (Aude, France).
Broadly, the project seeks to analyze human cultural reponses to
long-term   environmental   change;   the   abandonment   of
gathering-hunting in favor of food production; and the nature of a
major   diffusionary   event,   the   spread   of   agriculture,   within   a
defined geographic zone, the northern edge of the Mediterranean
basin.   The   particular   relationship   of   the   site   of   Leucate   to   the
Holocene transgression encouraged a detailed analysis of the site
in relation to the changing coastal morphology, and in relation to
known early Neolithic sites inland as a potential model for early
Holocene patterns of subsistence and settlement on the currently
submerged portion of the Roussillon continental plateau (Fig. 1).

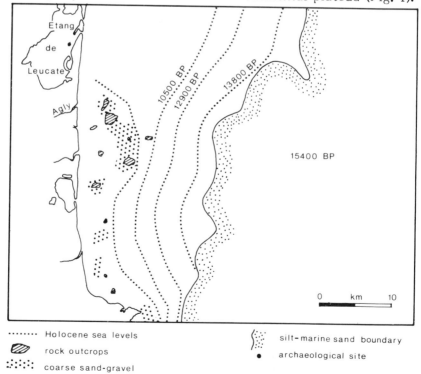

FIG. 1. *Palaeogeographic position of the site of Leucate in
relation to the formation of the Etang de Leucate.*

GEOMORPHOLOGY AND PALAEOGEOGRAPHIC EVOLUTION

The Oligocene calcareous rock formations, which form a prolongation of Cap Leucate itself, constitute the substratum to the Plio-Quaternary sedimentation of the Etang de Leucate. At depths from 20 m to 32 m, the Oligocene formation slopes to the south, and breaks up by faulting to the north of the Pointe de la Corrège. As is the case elsewhere around the basin of Roussillon, the Pliocene directly overlies this base. Grey-blue Plaisancian marls and yellow Astrian sands form a relatively regular surface between 19 m and 30 m underneath the Quaternary deposits.

The Quaternary can be grossly divided into two facies in the northern portion of the Etang de Leucate. The middle Quaternary is represented by silts, sometimes peaty silts, gravels, stones and green micaceous sands. The upper surface of this accumulation is extremely irregular, and rises to two crests of -10 m, once at the beginning of the Pointe de la Corrège, and again on its prolongation to the south (Fig. 2a). The late Quaternary accumulation is also composed of silts, muddy silts, lenticular

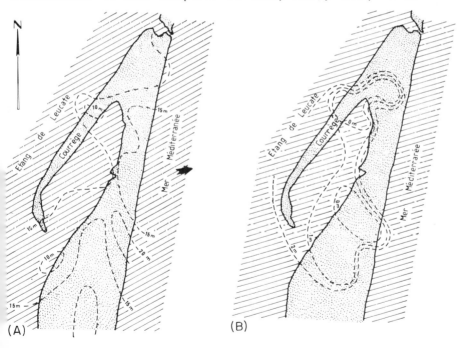

FIG. 2. (A)   Contours of the upper surface of the Middle Quaternary sediments. Note the valley deeper than -20 m trenching south west. (B) Isopach lines showing thickness of Late Quaternary sediments resting on the surface shown in Fig. 2A. Stipple = modern land surface; shading = water.

strata of gravels and superficial uncompacted sands at depths from
10 m to 20 m. The isopach lines of this subrecent formation,
which fills in the morphological irregularities remaining from the
middle Quaternary, illustrate the pattern of these minimum values
around a perimeter marked by the Pointe de la Corrège and the
facing littoral bar (Fig. 2b).

It is known from seismic profiles taken in the Mediterranean that
a very important palaeochannel traversed the sector of Leucate
and ran across a part of the adjacent continental plateau of
Roussillon (Fig 2a). From the Villefranchian through the Riss and
into the Würm, this valley migrated progressively to the south. The
Agly river spilled out over the southern part of the Etang de
Leucate until recent times when it was finally diverted and
canalized.

The various facies, as they are know from analysis of the marine
corings, are indicative of the palaeogeographic evolution of the
region.   Fluvial gravels accumulated primarily in the northern
sector of the Etang de Leucate during the middle Quaternary, and
in the southern sector during the late Quaternary, specifically at
the southern extremity of the Pointe de la Corrège (Fig. 2).
Between the latter point and the lido or barrier beach the
Quaternary gravel stratum underlies several meters of
uncompacted, subrecent formations.   These gravels represent
deltaic levees formed by the disgorging of the Agly and its
affluents into the Mediterranean, which were later reworked to a
greater or lesser degree by coastal forces.   Their deposition
precedes the invasion of this zone by the sea during the Holocene,
and the subsequent deposition of sands and euxinic oozes.   The
gravels served as the base for the Neolithic settlement.

The curve of Holocene sea levels shows a generalized rapid rise
of the transgression after 14,000 years B.P., with an acceleration
from 8,000 to 6,000 years B.P. (Aloisi *et al.*, 1975,1978). Several
intervals of relative stability are evident between 12,000 and
8,000 years B.P. Around 8,000 years B.P., the Holocene sea first
penetrated into the zones of the continental plateau of Roussillon
which had been eroded and down-cut by rivers during the Würm
and the early Postglacial, including the Etang de Leucate. Just as
the Würm can be considered a period when continental
characteristics were predominant on the Roussillon continental
plateau, the Holocene can be seen as a period when maritime
influences progressively developed. Pre-littoral bars are known
during the Holocene around -30 m, as well as laguno-marine facies
behind these bars at depths up to approximately -25 m. Remarkably
little evidence has been recovered for well-defined sea levels
around 7,000 years B.P. Possibly this results from an increased
speed of eustatic recovery between 8,000 and 6,000 years B.P.
The coarse littoral facies identified in marine corings at
Port-la-Nouvelle around -15 m are only suggestive.

Around 5,000 years B.P., the sea lay slightly below its modern level. This is the period of deposititon of euxinic oozes which started some 2,000 years earlier. The sea attained its maximum height at +2 m around 4,500 years B.P. The progressive construction of lidos during this period isolated the *étangs*, and the brackish environments resulted in the infilling of the remaining surface irregularities.

The Neolithic settlement occupied a distinctive morphological position owing its principle characteristics to the Quaternary littoral context. The site lay on a levee of fluvial gravels deposited during the Quaternary, which evolved into a perilittoral arm during the Holocene. Hence the settlement was situated at the edge of a zone of intense Holocene silting, where the lagoon and marine accumulation can surpass 10 m in thickness.

ARCHAEOLOGY

The archaeological site was discovered in 1972 during dredging of a new channel to Port Leucate. The exact location and extent of the site was never determined, nor was any stratigraphy pertinent to the archaeological deposit ever established. Hence, there is no detailed information on the emplacement of the habitation or the conditions of the archaeological deposit at the time of its submergence. The mechanically excavated sediments were being redeposited alongside the Ile Corrège, where archaeologists were able to wet-sieve the matrix and recover a large collection of stone and bone tools, animal bones and pottery. Unfortunately, mollusks from the archaeological deposit itself could not be distinguished from those subsequently deposited. Information concerning a potentially significant component of the subsistence economy is thus missing.

The ceramic and lithic materials are typologically homogeneous, and it is reasonable to treat the site as a single phase, early cardial-impressed ware occupation. In the absence of a stratigraphic section, however, it remains in question whether littoral sediments sufficiently covered the archaeological deposit at the time of its submersion to protect it from hydraulic forces which might have differentially eliminated artifactual and faunal materials.

The composition of the faunal sample suggests that the archaeological material suffered relatively little damage during the marine transgression. Research of Boas and Behrensmeyer (1976), Dodson (1973), Hanson (1980) and Voorhies (1969) demonstrates that fluvial forces transport bone as a function of several variables, currently under experimental study by these authors, such as cross-sectional surface area, resistance to torsional forces, bone weight, bone density, and gross bone morphology. Hanson's experiments with *Lepus* bones suggest that the cranium, the sacrum, the pelvis and the vertebrae are transported most readily and over the greatest distance by flowing water, while other skeletal elements are less mobile (Hanson, 1980). The lagomorph bones present at Leucate are distributed among the entire skeleton, including bones of ostensibly high mobility.

Experiments with *Ovis aries* bones reveal the same general phenomenon. The cranium, the vertebrae, and among the long bones the metatarsal would appear more vulnerable to water transport than the humerus, the femur, the tibia and the metacarpal. The large herbivore remains recovered at Leucate come from all parts of the skeleton, without any evident concentration among the bones of greatest density or least mobility. Furthermore, bird bones total approximately 20% of the faunal sample. The small, thin-walled bones of low density would probably have been preferentially removed from the deposit under the slightest hydraulic disturbance.

Certain characteristics of the bones themselves suggest that the objects underwent little physical damage during the mechanical excavation. Many thin-walled bird bones were recovered intact, without fresh breaks. The larger mammalian bone fragments have roughly worn surfaces caused by abrasion against the wet, sandy matrix. In the latter process, the broken surfaces were worn down into finely feathered edges which are preserved intact, without any evidence of damage due to the excavation and sieving. Whether the bone fractures are due to predepositional forces or damage in the ground is unclear, but it is certain that they were not the result of excavation techniques.

The pottery from Leucate belongs to typologically early cardial-impressed wares based on characteristics of form, paste and decoration. The hemi- or subspherical bowl is the most common form, but is accompanied by spherical necked vases, cylindrical jugs, and possibly shouldered vases as well. A wide variety of small and large handles, simple nipples and circular buttons is present for suspension. Decoration consists of cardium shell impression, grooves and comb impressions grouped into single and multiple bands. The form and decoration of the Leucate pottery differs from that of the eastern and central Mediterranean, where ornamentation typically covers the near totality of the vessel surface; flat-bottomed pots are common but necked vases absent. The pottery recalls the Franco-Iberian group of impressed wares which dates between approximately 7,200 and 6,700 years B.P., with impressions grouped in bands and necked vessels which are common from southern France through the Spanish Levant and into Portugal, with some similarities to North African impressed wares (Guilaine, 1976: 37-39).

Among four radiocarbon determinations obtained from wood

charcoal samples, only one can be reconciled with the material contents of the site:

6800 ± 90 B.P.   4850 B.C.   MC-788

Two dates from charcoal samples recovered floating in the dredge cannot be accepted:

5410 ± 140 B.P.   3460 B.C.   Gif-2747
3210 ± 140 B.P.   1260 B.C.   Gif-2748

A third date would be accepted if the site were still occupied at the extreme end of the Epicardial phase of the early Neolithic (Guilaine, 1976):

5900 ± 140 B.P.   3950 B.C.   Gif-2749

Guilaine notes that several potsherds with grooves surrounded by stab marks stand out from the bulk of the pottery, and may indeed by attributable to an Epicardial occupation of the site. At this time, however, the site would have lain only slightly above sea level, and an extensive occupation cannot be envisaged.

Domestic sheep and goat dominate the mammalian assemblage, with 52% of the bones. Metrically and morphologically, these domestic ovicaprids are closely comparable to early Neolithic ovicaprids from sites distributed across Mediterranean Europe: Grotte Gazel, Chateauneuf-les-Martigues, and Argissa (Geddes, 1982). The suids are represented by only 8% of the mammalian bones, none of which could be specifically assigned to wild boar or domestic pig, a remarkably low percentage for an early Neolithic site in Mediterranean Europe. Remains of *Bos* comprise 24% of the association, equally divided between domestic cattle and aurochs. In addition, red deer (5%), fox (6%) and wild rabbit (4%) are also present.

A relatively large collection of bird bones - 40 specimens from 8 individuals of 6 species -- equals a full 25% of the identified mammalian bone count. The French Mediterranean coast offered then, as it still does, a rich habitat of tidal marshes, sea coast, and adjacent open or lightly forested areas for annual or seasonal flocks. The overall bird density may have been relatively high, clustered around salt marshes and the coast, and sufficiently continuous throughout the year that birds could have formed a significant part of the diet at Leucate. The distribution of the red-throated diver *(Gavia stellata)* today, and probably during the Atlantic, when Leucate was inhabited, includes the Mediterranean coast of France only during the winter. In early spring, the diver would disappear north to its late spring/summer/early autumn habitat and breeding zone in northern Scandinavia, not to reappear permanently or in transit until late the following autumn. Although the herring gull *(Larus argentatus)*, the grebe *(Podiceps auritis)* and the rook *(Corvus corone)* occupy the Mediterranean littoral throughout the year, they exhibit seasonal concentrations along the coast during the cooler months. Adults of the royal eagle *(Aquila chrysaetos)* are relatively sedentary residents along rocky seacoasts, but younger individuals explore more widely over the littoral region in autumn and winter. Likewise, it can be supposed that the osprey *(Haliaetus albicilla)*, today nearly extinct in Mediterranean Europe, wintered on the Mediterranean coasts of southern France during the Atlantic period.

The majority of the bird species considered here occupy the Mediterranean littoral throughout the year, but preferentially cluster around estuarine, coastal and marsh habitats during the winter. The general distributional pattern of these avian species suggests a human occupation at Leucate which could encompass late autumn, winter and early spring, but not necessarily later spring, summer or early autumn. Alternatively, the subsistence economy may have preferentially exploited birds during the winter months.

Among the fish remains, two species call for attention. The swordfish *(Xiphias gladius* Linnaeus, 1758), a fish of the open sea which can attain considerable size, indicates the existence of true fishing activities, as opposed to opportunistic fish catching, from solid seacraft (Poplin, 1975). The most common fish remains belong to the gilthead seabream *(Sparus aurata)*, however, and suggest fishing activity during the summer months in waters from 4 to 20 m over sandy and rocky bottoms (Desse & Desse, in press). The absence of any fish of small size would imply fishing by the line, rather than netting. Morphological and radiographic examination of the remains of *Squatima squatima* indicate its capture in winter, and of *Lepidorhombus bosci,* capture in spring or summer. The abundance of cranial remains, especially the anterior part of the mandible, relative to vertebrae, strongly suggests processing of the fish on the site for consummation later (and elsewhere?). The numerous long, thin bone knives present at the site can probably be associated with this activity, and the traces of burning would imply smoking of the fish.

DISCUSSION

The site of Leucate is of methodological and theoretical importance because it demonstrates the existence of a network of submerged Mediterranean Mesolithic and Neolithic sites, of which reconnaissance will always be difficult if not impossible, about which we will always know little. Nevertheless the results obtained oblige us to integrate a coastal if not directly maritime facies into analyses of the Mesolithic and early Neolithic. The initial impact of coastal and maritime diffusion in the Mediterranean will have affected a region now largely submerged. Furthermore, the Holocene transgression would have closely juxtaposed the lagoonal and marine, sublittoral and Mediterranean forest environments. Such a concentration of rich Mediterranean ecosystems is precisely the type of regional environment which could have supported relatively sedentary Mesolithic gathering-hunting groups during the early Holocene. The interrelationships between such groups and those bearing newly available cultivated plants and domestic animals as well as the novel techniques of husbandry and cultivation merit the attention of future research efforts.

Leucate demonstrates once again the appearance of domestic animals along with the first cardial-impressed pottery in the central and western Mediterranean. Domestic sheep, cattle and probably goat arrive at the beginning of the fifth millennium B.C., but the case is not evident for the domestic pig. The early Neolithic sites of the Aude valley suggest to the contrary that the domestic pig appears for the first time around 4700-4600 B.C., several centuries after the first pottery (Geddes, 1982a,b). The predominance of the ovicaprids places Leucate in the same position as a number of Mediterranean early Neolithic sites. Sheep and goat, associated with domestic cattle, domestic pig and a range of cultivated plants, already constitute more than two thirds of the fauna in the first Neolithic levels in Greek and Aegean sites: 75% at Knossos, 65% to 85% at Argissa, about 70% at Nea Nikomedeia, and 70% to 80% at Franchthi Cave (see Bokonyi, 1973).

However, Leucate does not represent the earliest phases of animal husbandry in the western Mediterranean, which are earlier by as much as 1,000 years. Domestic sheep are known in late Mesolithic levels at Gazel and Dourgne in the Aude valley (Geddes, 1982a,b), at Chateauneuf-les-Martigues (Ducos, 1958), and Gramari (Dumas et al. 1971), where they are dated before 5,500 B.C. Even in the first Neolithic levels in the western Mediterranean, the domestic ovicaprids form only around 50% of the fauna, in stark contrast to the situation in Greece and the Aegean: 52% at Leucate, 17% to 50% at Gazel, around 50% of the large vertebrate fauna at Chateauneuf, and 52% at the Cova de l'Or (Geddes, 1982a,b; Ducos, 1958; Perez, 1980). Unfortunately the absence of Mesolithic sites on the Mediterranean littoral of France hinders any comparison between the late Mesolithic and the early Neolithic subsistence economies and settlement patterns.

From the perspective of the fauna, Leucate could have been a seasonal habitation utilized sporadically for the pasturage of herds of sheep, possibly goat, and cattle by an early Neolithic group which continued nevertheless, hunting for large herbivores, notably red deer and aurochs, and the exploitation of indigenous resources of coastal environments: birds, fish, certainly mollusks and plants. To judge from the bird species present, occupation could have occurred towards the end of autumn or the beginning of spring, although the fauna does not actually exclude the possibility of an occupation during the winter, the summer, or even throughout the year. The fish remains indicate summer activities, and it is necessary to consider the possibility that the utilisation of fish, mollusks, birds, plants, and domestic plants and animals varied with the seasons. Nevertheless, the exposure of the site in winter and strong heat and aridity which reign in summer (Gaussen, 1972) render occupation during the seasons of climatic extremes less likely.

The site would have thus played a specialized role in an early farming economy which also exploited resources more widely distributed in time and space. The sublittoral grasslands, which would have been impoverished during the hot and dry months, probably furnished a belt of pastureland to domestic animal herds during the cooler months. It is possible that the red deer and the aurochs, as is the case with the bouquetin of the Pyrenees (Couturier, 1962), moved down from the Pyrenees and the plateaux of the Corbières to the maritime Corbières and the Mediterranean

FIG. 3.   *Leucate and related early Neolithic sites in the Aude Valley*.

littoral during the winter. Numerous migratory birds stopped on the Mediterranean coast at the end of the autumn and the beginning of spring, while resident species preferentially clustered in the coastal *étangs* and estuaries during winter months.   By comparison it is useful to note that the fauna and macrobotanic remains from the Abri Jean Cros, situated in the Corbières at an elevation of 600 m, point to an autumn and/or spring occupation (Guilaine *et al*. 1979). The higher Pyrenean sites of Dourgne and Balma Margineda contain evidence of summer occupation, whereas the Grotte Gazel, situated on the southern slopes of the Montagne Noire, may have been occupied at all seasons of the year (Fig. 3; Geddes, 1982a).

The Mesolithic patterns of regional resource exploitation on the Mediterranean littoral are largely unknown, apart from some evidence furnished by the Grotte de la Crouzade level 4 (Sacchi, 1976) and unpublished results from La Baume Longue du Ponteau (excavations of M. Escalon de Fonton). The Mediterranean mollusks recovered at the Cauna d'Arques level 2b (6970 ± 200 B.C., Gif-2415), a site located in the Corbières near the Abri Jean Cros (Sacchi, 1976), raise the possibility of contact during the Mesolithic with coastal gatherer-hunter groups, if not seasonal movements uniting the littoral, the middle valley of the Aude, the Corbières and the Pyrenees (cf. Bahn, 1978). Confirmation of this suggestion relating submerged zones of the Mediterranean coastal plain with inland areas requires further research oriented towards problems of continuity and change between the Mesolithic and the early Neolithic in southern France.

ACKNOWLEDGEMENTS

This research was funded in its various phases by the Centre National de la Recherche Scientifique, the National Science Foundation, and the Commission Franco-Americaine d'Echanges Universitaires et Culturels, to whom the authors and associated researchers are grateful.

REFERENCES

Aloisi, J.-Cl., Monaco, A., Thommeret, J. and Thommeret, Y. (1975). Evolution paleogeographique du plateau continental languedocien dans le cadre du Golfe du Lion. Analyses comparees des donnees seismiques, sedimentologiques et radiometriques concernant le Quaternaire recent. *Rev. Geogr.phys.Geol.dyn.* 17, 13-22.

Aloisi, J.-Cl., Monaco, A., Planchais, N., Thommeret, J. and Thommeret, (1978). The holocene transgression in the Golfe du Lion, southwestern France: Paleogeographic and paleobotanical evolution. *Geogr.phys.Quat.* 32, 145-162.

Bahn, P. (1977). Seasonal migration in southwest France during the late glacial period. *J. Arch. Sci.* 4, 245-257.

Boas, N. and Behrensmeyer, A. (1976). Hominid taphonomy: Transport of human skeletal parts in an artificial fluviatile environment. *Am. J. Phys. Anth.* 45, 53-60.

Bokonyi, S. (1973). Stock breeding. In *Neolithic Greece* (D. Theochares, ed.) Athens. pp. 165-178.

Couturier, M. (1962). *Le Bouquetin des Alpes.* Grenoble.

Desse G. and Desse, J. (in press). L'icthyfaune et les activites de pêche, in *Leucate-Corrège: Site du Néolithique Cardial en Languedoc,* J. Guilaine, ed. Toulouse: Centre d'Anthropologie des Societés Rurales.

Dodson, P. (1973). The significance of small bones in paleoecological interpretation. *Univ. Wyoming Contrib. Geol.* 12: 15-19.

Ducos, P. (1958). Le gisement de Chateauneuf-les-Martigues: Les mammifères et les problèmes de domestication. *Bull. Mus. Anth. Préhist. Monaco* 5, 119-133.

Dumas, C., Livache, M., Miskovsky, J.-Cl., Paccard, M. and Poulain, T. (1971). Le camp mésolithique de Gramari à Methamis (Vaucluse). *Gallia Préhistoire* 144,- 47-137.

Gaussen, H. (1972). *Carte de la Végétation de la France 1:200,000, No 78, Perpignan.* Paris: CNRS.

Geddes, D. (1982a). De la Chasse au Troupeau en Méditerranée Occidentale: Les Debuts de l'Elevage dans la vallée de l'Aude. *Archives d'Ecologie Préhistorique* 5.

Geddes, D. (1982b). Les debuts de l'élevage dans la vallée de l'Aude. *Bull. Soc. Préhist. Franc.* 79.

Guilaine, J. (1976). *Premiers Bergers et Paysans de l'Occident Méditerranéen.* Paris: Moulton.

Guilaine, J. *et al.* (1979). *L'Abri Jean Cros.* Toulouse: Centre d'Anthropologie des Societés Rurales.

Guilaine, J. (ed) (in press). *Leucate-Corrège: Site du Néolithique Cardial en Languedoc.* Toulouse: Centre d'Anthropologie des Societés Rurales.

Hanson, C. (1980). Fluvial taphonomic processes: Models and experiments In *Fossils in the Making: Vertebrate Taphonomy and Paleoecology* (A. Behrensmeyer and A. Hill, eds). Chicago. pp. 156-181.

Perez Ripoll, M. (1980). La fauna de vertebrados. In *La Cova de l'Or. Vol. II. Servicio de Investigacion Prehistorica, Trabajos Varios 65.* Valencia. pp. 193-255.

Poplin, F. (1975). Restes de roste d'Espadon trouvés dans un gisement néolithique de l'étang de Leucate. *Bull. Soc.Préhist. Franc. 75*, 69-70.

Sacchi, D. (1976). Les civilisations de l'Epipaléolithique et du Mésolithique en Languedoc occidental (bassin de l'Aude) et Roussillon. In *La Préhistoire Française* vol. I, pt. II (H. de Lumley, ed). Paris. pp. 1390-1397.

Villette, P. (in press). Les oiseaux de Leucate. In *Leucate-Corrège: Site du Néolithique Cardial en Languedoc.* Toulouse: Centre d'Anthropologie des Societés Rurales.

Voorhies, M. (1969). Taphonomy and population dynamics of an early Pliocene vertebrate fauna, Knox county, Nebraska. *Univ. Wyoming. Contrib. Geol. Special Paper 1.*

DETECTION AND ASSESSMENT OF PREHISHORIC ARTIFACT SITES
OFF THE COAST OF SOUTHERN CALIFORNIA

Patricia M. Masters

Scripps Institution of Oceanography
University of California, San Diego,
La Jolla, California 92093, USA

ABSTRACT

Successions of prehistoric peoples occupied Southern California during the Flandrian transgression. Over the last century, their artifacts have been found in intertidal and submarine localities throughout nearshore areas of the Southern California Bight. Three possible explanations may account for the presence of artifacts underwater: secondary deposition from onshore erosional agencies, loss either intentional or accidental from seagoing craft, and survival of shelf sites following the marine transgression. In this paper the results of a mapping and diving survey of the underwater artifact localities off the coast of San Diego County are reported. The study has compiled 22 new sites in addition to the twelve previously reported. Of the 34 sites recorded, four are interpreted to be remnants of shellfishing stations, and two may have been tool factory sites when sealevel was lower at 6,000 - 4,000 years B.P. Six intertidal or beach localities probably represent secondary depositions. Fourteen localities in kelp beds at 12 - 19 meters depth may be the result of loss from prehistoric sea-faring craft, as may the seven artifact finds at depths of 14 - 31 meters on the walls of the submarine canyons. Kelp rafting also may have transported artifacts along the shelf or into the canyons. Conditions influencing preservation of the factory sites are sediment cover and physiographic location.

INTRODUCTION

A central question to the topic of land-sea migration routes is the preservation of prehistoric sites on the now submerged continental shelf. During the time of the Flandrian transgression, a number of peoples occupied the coastal areas of Southern California. Their cultural remnants above present sealevel span the time range of 10,000 years B.P. to the historic period. Prior to intensive urbanization of the Southern California coast over the last 50 years, the remains of a nearly continuous prehistoric habitation zone stretched along the coast from Point Conception south well into Baja California. Most of the sites were shell middens and represented economies reliant on marine food procurement from lagoons, estuaries, and the open coast.

Over the last 10,000 years of human occupation in Southern California, a coastal plain extended varying distances west from today's coastline. At 10,000 years B.P., the shore lay near the present 30 meter isobath (Curray, 1965). Depending on the particular area along the San Diego County coastline one considers, that contour indicates a shoreline 2 - 6 kilometers farther seaward than today's coast. At 8,000 years B.P., it was near the 20 meter isobath or 1 - 4 kilometers seaward.

Given the density of prehistoric sites known to have existed along today's coastline, one would expect that diverse hunting, fishing, collecting, and manufacturing activities took place out on the coastal plain, possibly adjacent to tidal flats, inlets, and estuaries. The archaeological evidence of these activities may be preserved on the shelf despite the rise in sealevel which has drowned the sites.

Over the past 100 years and with increasing frequency since the development of SCUBA equipment, numerous prehistoric artifacts have been reported from marine localities in nearshore areas of the Southern California Bight mainland and islands. Logically, there are three mechanisms which can account for artifacts on the continental shelf. First, they may represent secondary deposition due to erosion or disturbance of onshore sites. Second, the objects could have fallen from sea-going craft either by accident or by being intentionally jettisoned. Third, the artifacts may constitute the remnants of a prehistoric site on the coastal plain during some period of lower sealevel. In this paper, the marine sites identified off the coast of San Diego County are evaluated in terms of the three possible mechanisms. Special physiographic and sedimentary conditions contributing to the survival of the drowned sites also are discussed.

PREHISTORIC PEOPLES

The first human occupations in California may date from much earlier periods (see Bada and Finkel, 1983, or Reeves, 1983, this

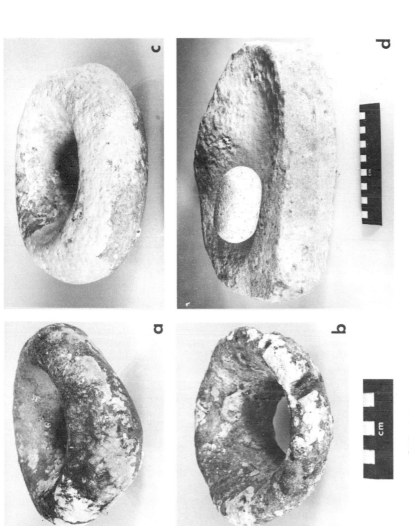

Scale a – c

PLATE 1. *Artifact types found in San Diego area. (a)Fine-grained sandstone mortar from 4 m depth at Torrey Pines Reef, site 14. (b) sandstone mortar worked all the way through the base from 14 m off Point Loma, site 2; (c) granite mortar from 14 m depth off La Jolla, site 3; and (d) sandstone metate and granite mano from the Scripps Estates onshore site.*

volume), but there is little information on their archaeological contexts. The earliest archaeological documentation comes in the range of 8 - 11,000 years B.P., with the San Diego County variant of the widespread North American hunting peoples. Known as the San Dieguito culture, the type site, the C.W. Harris site (Warren and True, 1961), is located 20 kilometers inland up the San Dieguito River Valley. The San Dieguito lithic assemblage contains points, knives, crescents, choppers, and scrapers - the tool kit of hunters. Marine shells are reported from the San Dieguito level (Warren, 1966) although they may be intrusive from later occupation.

Following the San Dieguito, the predominant culture in the coastal San Diego County archaeological record is the La Jollan, dating from approximately 9,000 years B.P., and persisting until *ca*. 3,000 years ago. Part of the larger culture complex known as the Milling Stone Horizon (Wallace, 1955) which extends along the Bight mainland and south along the Baja California coast, the La Jollan sites are represented by shell middens on seabluffs and above the lagoons of San Diego County. The diagnostic tools of the Milling Stone peoples are the flat grinding stones (metates) and hand-held mullers (manos), presumably reflecting an economy based on plant foods in addition to marine molluscs. By 5,000 years B.P., mortars and pestles appear in equal numbers with metates and manos among the Santa Barbara County coastal sites (Wallace, 1978). They occur but are rare in La Jollan middens (Plate 1).

The Milling Stone Horizon peoples were capable of ocean travel judging by cultural remains found on several of the Channel Islands. A shell midden on San Clemente has yielded two radiocarbon dates of *ca*. 8,000 years B.P. (LJ-4130 and LJ-3961). Thus, even in their earliest occupational period, the Milling Stone peoples had the ability to traverse 75 kilometers of open ocean. It is reasonable to assume that they also were able to explore and exploit nearshore marine environments along the mainland coast.

The most recent culture in the San Diego County sequence is the Diegueno, present at the time of Spanish contact. Ethnographic information on these late prehistoric peoples indicates a continuing although seasonal maritime orientation. Known shoreline usage zones (see Fig. 1) were La Jolla Shores, Mission Beach, Ocean Beach, Point Loma, San Diego Bay, and Imperial Beach (Records of the San Diego Museum of Man). Marine foods were gathered by means of fishing spears, traps, and nets; shellfish were collected using a sharp stone as a prying tool; edible seaweed was gathered; shorebirds taken; and rafts and boats were manufactured from reeds (Shipek, 1970). Temporal relationships and tool assemblages of the three San Diego area cultures are summarized in Table 1.

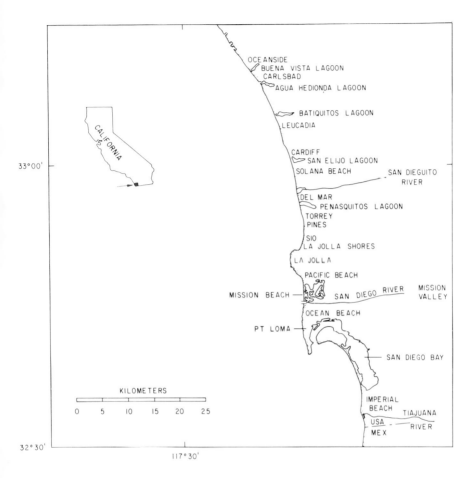

FIG. 1. *Map of San Diego coastal area.*

MARINE ARTIFACT SITES

As early as 1915, divers were finding artifacts offshore the La Jolla Beach and Tennis Club (Carter, 1955). Technical staff affiliated with Scripps Institution of Oceanography were among the first to publish on the marine artifact finds (Tuthill and Allanson, 1954; Marshall and Moriarty, 1964). Tuthill and Allanson mapped six sites along the San Diego County coast including the Beach and Tennis Club site off La Jolla where they reported collecting *ca.* 300 Indian mortars. Marshall and Moriarty cited *ca.* 2,000 mortars taken from the Beach and Tennis Club site.

TABLE 1.

Cultural sequence of coastal San Diego county

Culture	Years, B.P.	Characteristics
Diegueno		Pottery
	3,000	
La Jollan		Milling stones mullers
	7,500	
Transition		
	9,000	
San Dieguito		Hunters' lithics: bifacial points choppers, scrapers
	12,000	

Travis Hudson's 1976 study of 33 underwater sites in the northern part of the Bight marked the first involvement of a professional archaeologist in the problem. Hudson evaluated his sites in terms of ten possible explanations for the existence of the underwater artifacts:

1) Coastal outwash
2) Construction and earth-moving activities
3) Erosion of seacliffs
4) Ceremonial deposition
5) Accidental loss
6) Cairns
7) Jettisoned ballast
8) Anchors for fishing nets
9) Coastal subsidence
10) Sealevel rise.

He concluded that four (1, 4, 8, 10) of the explanations offer the most likely interpretations for the 33 sites. Ceremonial discard of a vessel accounts for six sites and possibly two others as well. The use of grooved stones to anchor fishing nets probably resulted in the net anchor finds at two sites in kelp beds. Possible offshore villages may explain nine localities along the mainland coast between Santa Barbara and Tijiguas. Based on the Milliman and Emery (1968) and Shepard (1964) sea level curves, Hudson suggests age ranges for occupation of these sites between 9,000 and 3,800 years B.P. (Re-evaluation of the sites in light of recent, local studies of sealevel change on the Santa Monica shelf (Nardin et al., 1981) may narrow the estimated times of occupation for the nine sites.)   Finally, cliff erosion due to the present high seastand may have contributed to the marine finds at four sites and possibly others.   Nine additional sites, mostly offshore of the Channel Islands, were not assigned an explanation of origin.

In the southern part of the Bight, artifacts in small numbers have been retrieved from numerous localities at depths up to 30 meters offshore of San Diego by recreational and commercial divers.   The most common type of artifact recovered is a mortar manufactured from a water-worn cobble, usually of sandstone, occasionally of granitic material (see Plate 1).   Some of these finds have been mentioned by Tuthill and Allanson (1954) and Hudson (1976).

A second category of underwater artifact localities is best represented by the La Jolla Shores Beach and Tennis Club site where hundreds of mortars have been found.   Additionally, this site has yielded a diversity of artifact types. Mortars predominate but there are occasional pestles, metate fragments, manos, and grooved stones possibly used as net weights (Tuthill and Allanson, 1954).   Some flaked lithics such as scrapers and projectile points were reported by Marshall and Moriarty (1964).

MAPPING AND DIVING SURVEY

The first step in this study was to gather as much information as possible on offshore artifact locations.   Searches were carried out in the published literature, newspaper accounts, the records of the San Diego Museum of Man, the records of the Cultural Resource Management Center at San Diego State University, and the personal files of C.L. Hubbs archived at the SIO Library.   An effort was made to talk to the people spending the most time underwater.   Five of the Scripps divers who had been involved in some of the earliest finds were interviewed (A. Allanson, D.L. Inman, J.R. Stewart, N. Marshal, and A.B. Rechnitzer).   Contacts were made with commercial divers affiliated with the San Diego Divers Association and Kelco Company.

Questionnaires were also circulated to the professional diver groups and to dive shops and sport divers' clubs.   The purpose of the questionnaire was twofold: to elicit information on artifact types and find sites and to instruct divers on responsible steps to take should an artifact be found underwater. Follow-up interviews were conducted with divers returning the questionnaires in order to verify the artifacts and the localities.

The second step in the survey was mapping and developing a data recording and retrieval system. All sites are mapped onto the U.S. Geological Survey Quadrangles, photorevised, 1975, 7.5. minute series with bathymetric contours in feet. The Imperial Beach and Point Loma quads do not include sufficient off-shore contours so they were supplemented by the National Ocean Survey Nautical

Chart 18765. Whenever possible, charting of localities was done in the presence of the informant. A file card system was established for the sites coding by geographical area, site number, depth, artifact type, and individual artifact identification number.

The third and critical step was personal on-site diving inspection of the localities. In some cases, techniques for systematic diving surveys were developed and employed (Fig. 2). Visual surveys of the bottom conditions at these localities yielded important information on general topography and sediment types which was used to evaluate the sites.

RESULTS

The survey has delineated two geographical concentrations of underwater artifacts (Fig. 3). The primary concentration of sites

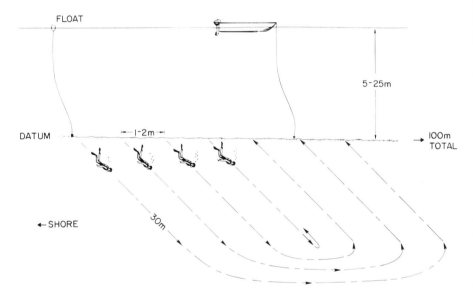

FIG. 2. *Dive Plan for underwater surveys. The plan was developed for systematic surveying in kelp beds. Divers are spaced at 1 to 2 m intervals (depending on visibility) along a baseline anchored between two end-points marked by floats. The floats are surveyed onto a chart. The lead diver, in the center of the pattern, swims a compass course perpendicular to the baseline, unrolling a 30 m line. Divers maintain visual contact while searching the bottom. At the end of the 30 m line, the lead diver signals, the others regroup, the lead diver rerolls the line and searches as well on the return path. Up to 360 square meters can be surveyed in each swing.*

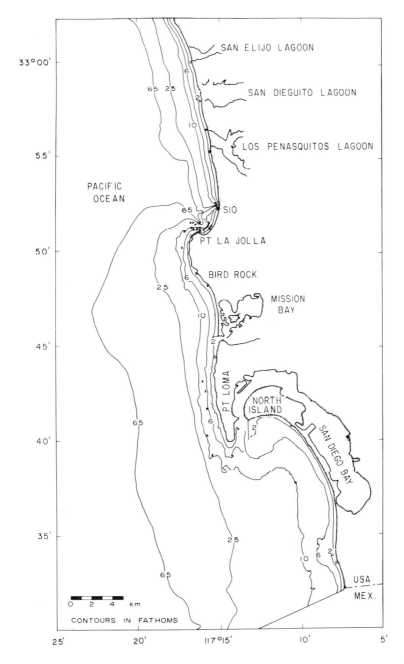

FIG. 3. *Map of underwater sites.   Solid arrows are sites located through this survey.   Open arrows indicate sites reported in earlier publications.*

occurs off La Jolla, from Bird Rock north to Scripps Submarine Canyon (north of Scripps Institution of Oceanography). In this region, 21 different localities have been charted along 11 kilometers of coastline. The second, smaller concentration of sites occurs off Point Loma where 6 localities are reported over a 9 kilometer length of coastline. From Scripps Submarine Canyon to San Elijo Lagoon at Solana Beach, there is a scattering of 4 localities. To the south of Point Loma, one was cited by Tuthill and Allanson (1954) at the mouth of the Tijuana River just north of the international border and another by Carter (1955) on San Diego Bay south of Chollas Creek. In all, prehistoric artifacts have been charted at 28 underwater and 6 beach or intertidal localities. The site information is summarized in Table 2.

TABLE 2

Summary of marine artifact sites, San Diego County.

Locality	Site Number	Reference	Depth (meters)	Bottom Conditions*	Number of Artifacts[++]	Number of Independent Reports
Solana Beach	22	1	1-8	RC	100+	6+
Del Mar	23	2	3	RS	1	1
	33	3	Intertidal	S	1	1
Torrey Pines	14	4	4-5	RBS	3	2
La Jolla	3	4	14	RBSK	2	2
	4	4	15	RK	1	1
	5	4	12	RK	2(a)	1
	6	4	15	RK	1	1
	7	4	12	RB	1(b)	1
	8	4	17	RK	1	1
	9	4	17-20 (28)	RK	6	6
	10	1	25	RW	1(c)	1
	11	1	0-6	CS	∿300(c,d,e)	
		5	0-25	CS	∿2000(a,c,d,e,f)	
	12	4	14	S	2	1
	13	4	3	RBSC	2	2
	15	1	3-5	RCS	5	4
	16	1	1-4	R	4(f)	3
	17	4	17	RW	1	1
	18	4	30	RW	1	1

*   B=boulders, C=cobbles, K=kelp, M=clay, R=rock, S=sand, W=wall of submarine canyon.

[++] Artifacts mortars unless designated as: (a) mano, (b) shaped bowl, (c) metate, (d) grooved stone, (e) pestle, (f) flaked lithics (e.g. scraper, projectile point).

TABLE 2 (continued)

Locality	Site Number	Reference	Depth (meters)	Bottom Conditions	Number of Artifacts	Number of Independent Reports
La Jolla	19	4	Intertidal	S	1	1
cntd.	24	6	Intertidal	S	1(d)	1
	25	4	15	SMW	1	1
	27	4	18	MW	1(a)	1
	30	1	31	R	1	1
	31	4	12-15	B	2	2
Pacific Beach	26	4	Intertidal	C	9	1
Point Loma	1	4	15	RSK	3	2
	2	4	14	RSK	1	1
	20	4	12	RSK	2	2
	28	4	14	RK	1	1
	29	4	12	RK	1	1
	34	7	18	RK	1	1
San Diego Bay	32	8	Intertidal	SMB	midden	1
Imperial Beach	21	1	Intertidal	C	1	1

References: (1) Tuthill and Allanson (1954). (2) Carl L. Hubbs archives SIO Library. (3) San Diego State University, Cultural Rescource Management Center, site survey records. (4) This survey. (5) Marshall and Moriarty (1964). (6) San Diego Museum of Man, site survey records. (7) Thornburgh (1956). (8) Carter (1955).

At this point it should be emphasized that the distribution of the reported sites may be dependent upon the frequency with which these areas are dived. For similar reasons, shallower sites are more likely to be discovered since free (snorkel) divers as well as SCUBA divers will be exploring nearshore areas. Artifacts at depths below 20 meters are rarely reported either because they truly are rare, or because dive times and frequencies are limited by decompression requirements.

Another factor in the apparent geographical distribution of the underwater sites is the amount of sediment cover. Neither Point Loma nor Point La Jolla have extensive offshore sand deposits. What sand exists on the two Point La Jolla pocket beaches of any size is occasionally moved offshore by winter storms, but usually not beyond *ca.* 6 meters in water depth. The presence of kelp beds off the points demonstrates a bare country rock substrate as well. Hence, sediments are not obscuring the artifacts present on the two shelves. In contrast, the nearshore shelf off Carlsbad to the north has over 12 meters of sediment (Moore, 1960). Thus, it may be premature to conclude that the apparent distribution of find localities comprises a representative sampling of the prehistoric underwater sites along the San Diego County coastline.

Some indication of the reliability of the site reports comes from the number of independent observations. Of the 34 total sites, 24 were reported by a single informant, 6 by two independent informants, and 4 by three or more independent informants. Twenty-two were located by means of the questionnaire and personal interviews. Twelve had been reported previously in the

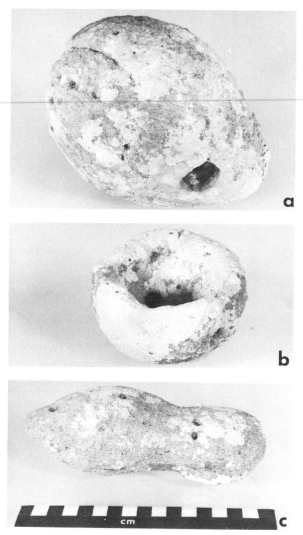

PLATE 2.   *Sandstone concretions recovered by divers off Point La Jolla and Point Loma.   These naturally occurring features can be mistaken for net weights (a), mortars or bowls (b), or pestles (c).*

literature or in the records at San Diego Museum of Man, the Cultural Resource Management Center at San Diego State University, or the Hubbs collection at the SIO Library.

All but one of the single artifact finds have been verified by personal inspection as actual artifacts. Eight additional finds were eliminated on the basis that the informants had mistaken naturally occurring geological specimens for artifacts. The sandstone Point Loma Formation which outcrops as the nearshore shelf off Point Loma and Point La Jolla contains well cemented concretions that are continuously eroded out of the poorly cemented sandstone matrix in the form of teardrop-shaped, hourglass-shaped, or flat topped basin-shaped "geofacts" (Plate 2). The concretions are frequently mistaken for artifacts by divers and reported as net weights, pestles, or grinding stones. Sea urchin scour features in globular concretions can also be mistaken for mortar holes.

Four of the 6 intertidal sites and 24 of the known depth underwater localities have been identified on the basis of mortar finds (Table 2). One intertidal and 9 underwater sites are now known from multiple mortar finds, with two of these localities reputed to have contained hundreds (Tuthill and Allanson, 1954) or thousands (Marshall and Moriarty, 1964) of mortars.

The distribution of the sites by depth is graphed in Fig. 4.

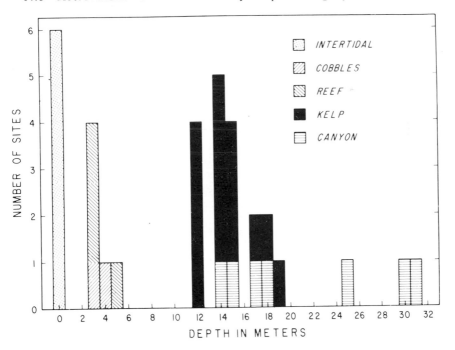

FIG. 4. *Distribution of sites by depth along the San Diego coast.*

Depths are approximate due to lack of exact time or tide
information in divers' reports, so no attempt was made to calculate
depths relative to mean sea level. For multiple artifact sites, the
average depth between the shallowest and deepest finds was used.
Excluding the intertidal localities, the sites show a basically
trimodal distribution:

1)   Nearshore rocky reefs or cobble reefs at 3 to 5 meters
       depth
2)   Kelp beds at 12 to 19 meters
3)   Walls of the submarine canyons at depths up to 31 meters.

Four sites at the heads of the submarine canyons coincide with
kelp bed depths.
   The reef sites are all within 200 meters of the shore as defined
by the mean lower low water line. The kelp bed localities off
Point Loma range between 1.0 and 1.7 km from shore, and those
along Point La Jolla lie 0.5 - 1.0 km offshore. Artifact sites along
the submarine canyon heads are 300 to 400 meters from the
shoreline datum.

DISCUSSION

The prevalence of the mortar in the marine sites off the San
Diego coast raises some interesting considerations. Mortars are
present, but in low numbers, within the onshore middens. For
example, at the Scripps Estates site, a La Jollan occupation of
5,000 to 7,000 years ago on the seabluff 2 km north of the Beach
and Tennis Club site, collections from lot 24 yielded remnants of
60 metates, nearly 300 manos, and only 3 mortars (Shumway *et al.,*
1961). Possibly a sampling problem exists offshore in that mortars
can be more easily recognized by the non-archaeologist. But the
paucity of mortars in San Diego area terrestrial sites (Warren,
1968) cannot be explained by non-random sampling. Cobble
mortars in the southern Bight clearly are associated with the
present nearshore shelf. In contrast, similar cobble material of
Eocene age outcrops 10 km inland up Mission Valley yet there is
no evidence of mortar manufacture in that vicinity.
   In the northern part of the Bight, along the Santa Barbara coast,
mortars are commonly found in late Milling Stone Horizon sites on
land (Wallace, 1978). They were utilized in the processing of
acorns, and some still exhibit asphalt traces on the rims where a
basketry funnel was glued to the stone mortar forming the
basket-hopper mortar. Usage for acorn processing does not explain
the distribution of the mortars in the southern part of the Bight.
   A more economical interpretation is that the mortars here
reflect prehistoric activities on the shelf or in nearshore areas.
One obvious possibility is that the mortars were used while

procuring marine foods or other resources. Hudson (1976) refers to an ethnographic observation of the lone Indian woman of San Nicolas Island processing dried abalone with a mortar (Anonymous, 1857). The middden sites of the La Jollans indicate a shellfish-based economy, and the Diegueno were at least seasonal collectors and gatherers in the coastal zone, but their respective technologies are unknown.

Ceremonial deposition also can result in artifacts being found on the continental shelf. Hudson (1976, 1979) discusses Chumash (late prehistoric peoples of the northern Bight) offerings being made into the sea. In the Santa Barbara Channel off Point Conception, Hudson (1979) lists 11 sites as probable ceremonial deposition localities. Ten of these are characterized by the presence of small sandstone bowls and one by a charmstone. All eleven sites occur within the kelp line (Hudson, personal communication). The bowls, however, do not closely resemble the cobble mortars from offshore San Diego.

Reef Sites

Some of the offshore find localities of the San Diego coast support a shellfish collecting or processing use for the mortars; others do not obviously do so. The first of the site groupings, the nearshore reefs, suggest shellfish or seaweed collecting stations. Here were the ideal environments for gathering mussels, rock oysters, scallops, limpets, abalone, barnacles, starfish, snapping shrimp, and edible seaweed when sealevel was 3 - 5 meters lower. In La Jolla there are four of these sites: The Casa de Manana Breakwater (15), the Cove (13), the reef connecting the terrestrial midden W-1 with the underwater Beach and Tennis Club site (11), and Dike Rock (16). To the north are the Torrey Pines (14), Del Mar (23), and Solana Beach reef (2) sites. A portion of the Torrey Pines reef with an in situ mortar is illustrated in Plate 3a.

A major concern is whether onshore sites above present sealevel contributed artifacts to the submerged localities through erosion or slumping. Four reef sites (11, 14, 16, 22) had onshore occupational components or nearby midden areas. At the other three (13, 15, 23), urbanization occurred before site records were made. None of the reef sites can be attributed easily to erosion from terrestrial middens. In each case, the artifact assemblage is nonrepresentative, the numbers of artifacts are too large, the direction of prevailing currents is wrong, or the distance from the nearest onshore site is too far. The two underwater reef sites having large numbers of artifacts can be evaluated individually.

The extensive Beach and Tennis Club site (11) consists of an ancient cobble beach thought to have formed in the range of 6,000 to 7,000 years ago (Inman, this volume). Plate 3b shows a patch of the cobbles exposed during October, 1981, after wave action had

PLATE 3. *(a) View of the Bathtub Rock reef off Torrey Pines State Reserve north of La Jolla. Diver's finger points to an in situ mortar (see Plate 1a) at 4 m below MSL. (b) Exposed section of the cobble reef at the Beach and Tennis Club site off La Jolla Shores. Sand encroachment can be seen beneath diver. Arrow points to mortar in situ at 3 m depth.*

removed the sand which seasonally covers the site. The cobbles have been reported to extend from the intertidal reefs below the bluff where the W-1 site formerly existed north approximately 320 meters (Allanson records on file at the San Diego Museum of Man).

G.F. Carter (personal communication) described the erosion of artifacts from W-1 and noted that it was general knowledge in the 1930s that artifacts could be collected from the reef below after a storm. He further stated that he saw no mortars in the W-1 midden strata. However, Tuthill and Allanson (1954) quote a local collector to the effect that mortars could be found on the beach and in shallow water after winter storms had eroded the cliff front. While it is unlikely that the multitude of mortars from the offshore cobble beds were derived from the W-1 site, the artifacts found in the intertidal reef probably were eroded out of the bluff site. Most of the mortars in Allanson's collection (San Diego Museum of Man) were fashioned on angular and subangular sandstone cobbles which are indistinguishable from the unmodified sandstone rubble comprising the bulk of the cobble reef. Scattered among these fragments of the Cretaceous Pointloma Formation are water-rounded granitic cobbles which have been washed down stream drainages to the coast and then transported south by longshore currents. Allanson's records (San Diego Museum of Man) indicate that 5% of the mortars collected were made from granitic cobbles. A fractured granite mortar from the Beach and Tennis Club site is shown *in situ* in Plate 3b.

The Solana Beach reef site (22) has been interpreted as the result of erosion from the seabluff site W-312 inshore of the mortar finds (Records, San Diego Museum of Man). But again, the ~100 mortars claimed to have been taken there at depths of 1-8 meters are not representative of the small W-312 artifact assemblage. The whereabouts of most of the Solana Beach mortars are unknown, so it is not possible to substantiate the count. However, 46 are discernible in a photograph printed in the *San Diego Union* (1952). Even this quantity exceeds by a factor of 5 the number of mortars that are catalogued at the San Diego Museum of Man from all of the county's onshore sites. Allanson (personal communication) dived at the Solana Beach site and mentioned the mortars occurring amidst cobble accumulations as at the Beach and Tennis Club site. Fifteen mortars retrieved from the underwater site in the early 1950s and now in the possession of D. McKenna, Solana Beach, are made on sandstone cobbles derived from the Eocene Delmar Formation comprising the reef complex.

A logical interpretation of the Solana Beach reef and the Beach and Tennis Club sites is that they represent prehistoric activities in the cobble areas deposited near the reefs. The 211 mortars catalogued by Allanson at the La Jolla site (Records, San Diego Museum of Man) and the 46 verifiable mortars from the Solana

Beach site suggest that the cobble beds served as natural reserves providing the prehistoric inhabitants of the adjacent middens with factory sites for mortar manufacture before sealevel rose and covered the cobbles. If the mortars were utilized in shellfish processing, they would have been fashioned conveniently near the teeming reefs.

The underwater reef sites may provide the clue for resolving a significant problem in California coastal prehistory. Bickel (1978) has attempted to relate sea level rise with changing coastal habitats and settlement patterns. She summarized evidence from San Francisco Bay area middens for a shift over time in predominant molluscan species from those requiring rocky attachment (mussels, rock oysters) to those growing in mud and sand (clams). Nelson (1909; 1910) and Greengo (1951) linked the shift to changing sedimentation conditions resulting from subsidence or sealevel rise. A similar observation concerning predominant species has been made for middens along the San Diego County coast. Analysis of the mollusc shells excavated at the Scripps Estates site (Shumway *et al.*, 1961) showed that 80% by weight of the shell derived from rocky shore species (mainly mussel), 16% from bay molluscs, and a negligible amount from sandy beach species. Shumway *et al.* remarked that this distribution and the quantity of shell on the site as a whole were not consistent with the present-day coastal environment characterized by extensive sandy beaches. An understanding of the physics and geology of the coastline as it evolved during the Flandrian transgression (Inman, this volume) has resulted in the picture of a rocky, open shore with steep cobble beaches and no sand deposits. These conditions prevailed until near-present sea level was attained *ca*. 3,000 years ago. Hence, in the 7,000 – 4,000 year range, the rocky, unsedimented coastline would have provided prehistoric peoples with ample littoral collecting and gathering locales for the shellfish species dominating their midden sites.

Kelp Bed Sites

The second of the underwater site groupings, the kelp bed localities, include all the Point Loma sites at 12-18 meters depth and the La Jolla shelf sites (3, 4, 5, 6, 8, 9) at 10-20 meters. Very similar bottom conditions characterize all of these finds: hard bottom consisting of the sandstone Point Loma Formation with an irregular, eroded surface pocked with scoured depressions where thin deposits of sand collect. Scattered over this seascape are concretions and rocks varying in size from pebbles to small boulders (Plate 4). These are the ideal bottom conditions for kelp growth in 10-30 meters of water. The finds are scattered in nature and are all mortars (except for a mano in one instance).

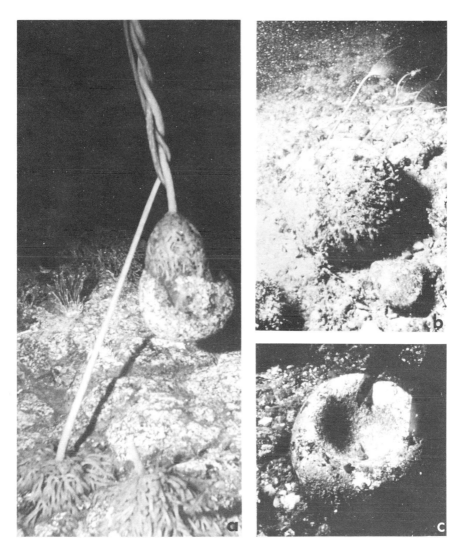

PLATE 4. *Kelp rafting of cobbles and mortars. (a) A cobble is lifted by Nereocystis kelp near Monterey, California. (b) Base of mortar found at 12 m depth off Point Loma, site 29, with three young kelp attached. (c) Same mortar inverted. Photographs courtesy of Ron McPeak.*

Because they are found on what would have been an open, high energy coastline during the last marine transgression, and because no Holocene sediment cover occurs on these areas of the shelf, it is unlikely that any cultural deposits have remained *in situ* from an occupation or activity site prior to submergence.

The ontogeny of a wave-cut terrace also has some bearing on the interpretation of these sites. The artifacts are being found on the shelf shoreward of 20 meters, an area which coicides with the 10-fathom terrace (see Inman, this volume). If Emery's (1958) explanation of the Southern California marine terraces if followed, then the wave-cut platform on which the artifacts are now found was formed during the last rise in sea level 8,000 - 10,000 years B.P. Thus cultural debris from occupation sites could not accumulate on the terrace at the same time the terrace was being cut. If the terrace was formed prior to the last sea level rise, the lack of Holocene sediments still weighs as evidence against the preservation of an *in situ* prehistoric site on the exposed, high-energy coast of California. Erosion from onshore sites above present sea level is an unlikely explanation beacuse the mortars are not the characteristic artifact in the coastal sites today, nor are they found in shallower water shoreward of the kelp beds.

Dispersal of cultural remains on the shelf would make recognition of any type of site difficult. Mechanisms of disturbance which are frequently discussed include the passage of a surf zone over the site during marine transgression. Then storm events plus normal surge and currents would tend to scatter a site.

Growth of kelp forests on the shelf introduces another dispersal mechanism: kelp rafting. The young plant attaches to the bottom or to any available rock on the seafloor. Its holdfast develops, and the stipe (stem) grows. Once the alga becomes large enough so that its buoyancy compensates for the weight of the rock or artifact to which it has attached, rafting and dispersal takes place (Plate 4). Emery and Tschudy (1941) describe rocks up to 38 cm long and weighing up to 6 kg attached to macroalgal holdfasts which were washed ashore. Cobble mortars weigh 1 - 4 kg.

Thus, the scattered finds, predominantly of mortars, the absence of Holocene sediments, and the exposed nature of the Point Loma and Point La Jolla coasts suggest that the artifacts represent accidental or intentional losses from sea-going craft following submergence of the shelf. Kelp rafting as well as currents would act to disperse the remnants of a canoe spill or ceremonial offering just as they would any midden remains. Today the kelp beds provide the highest biomass and best fishing areas of the nearshore shelf. Had Hypsithermal water temperature (see Pisias, 1979) exceeded the 16 - 18°C tolerance limit of the giant kelp during La Jollan times, the rocky bottom conditions still would have attracted a high biomass and offered good fishing areas. A high frequency of prehistoric fishing activities implies accidental losses from seagoing vessels. However, it is unclear exactly what use the mortars would have had in canoes or rafts bobbing around over the kelp beds. Intentional jettison as an offering to the sea (Hudson, 1979) could supply an alternative explanation for the kelp bed artifacts.

Scattered finds occur on both ledges and at the heads of Scripps Submarine Canyon (north arm in Fig. 3) and La Jolla Submarine Canyon (south arm) at depths of 14 - 30 meters. The branches of Scripps Submarine Canyon are rocky and precipitous and open in rather deep water, *ca*. 30 meters. The walls would have formed a rocky inlet suitable for shellfishing approximately 10,000 years ago. This predates the Milling Stone Horizon peoples. Another interpretation of the scattered mortars is unintentional loss from fishing craft putting out from the beach over the canyon heads where wave crests are low and shoaling waves do not break until close to shore. The heads of both Scripps and La Jolla Submarine Canyons lie offshore of extensive La Jollan occupation areas. Kelp rafting also could account for finds at the canyon heads as kelp collects there following storms and high waves.

Some of the artifacts discovered along the rim of the La Jolla Submarine Canyon head may have been eroding down into the canyon from areas upslope. Two informants (A. Stover and J. Stewart, personal communications) expressed caution as to the *in situ* proveniences of the mortars they retrieved beyond the canyon break. The La Jolla Submarine Canyon head opens in approximately 12 meters of water with a gradual slope increasing to a 30° slope by *ca*. 17 meters. Beyond this depth, the walls begin dropping off in series of sand-covered ledges. Given that the direction of strong, sediment-laden currents is downcanyon and that the angle of repose for granular material is generally 30°, it appears unlikely that mortars found beyond the canyon break would be *in situ*. Were they embedded in the alluvial clays underlying the sand cover the probability of *in situ* finds would be higher. While several informants found artifacts in association with the clay layers, the tools always were sighted on the eroding face of the strata rather than within the clays.

In an earlier description of the Beach and Tennis Club site, Marshall and Moriarty (1964) published a graph showing distribution of mortars by depth with the modal depth at 20 - 40 feet (6-12 meters). Although the artifacts graphed are not specifically identified as coming from the Beach and Tennis Club site, the authors state (p. 23) that "the greatest deposit of artifact material at La Jolla has been in depths to 40 feet . . . . well inside the southern head of the submarine canyon." In lmy diving surveys of the site, the cobble area and its associated artifacts were not seen beyond 5 meters depth. Although sand deposits might be obscuring cobbles further seaward, two other scientists from Scripps Institution of Oceanography who were diving the area in the 1950's and 1960's (A. Rechnitzer and D.L. Inman, personal communications) confirm my observations. In addition, Allanson's records (San Diego Museum of Man) place the modal depth at 10 - 12 feet (3-4 meters) with the deepest artifact reported at 18 - 20 feet (6 meters). Consequently, the Beach and Tennis Club site is recorded in the present study as a cobble reef at 0-6 meters depth (Table 2).

CONCLUSIONS

Both the La Jolla Beach and Tennis Club site and the Solana Beach site are located off the mouths of ancient or present-day lagoons.   But   the   proximity   of   the   lagoons   themselves   is insufficient to account for the extensive finds of mortars.   There are four lagoons or ancient lagoons along the San Diego County coastline that are not known to have underwater sites (Agua Hedionda, Batiquitos, Penasquitos, and Tijuana) versus the two that do have sites (La Jolla Shores, San Elijo). Only when lagoon mouths coincide with barrier structures such as reefs (San Elijo) or the special physiographic situation at the Shores where a westward bend of the coastline intercepts the southerly transport of sediment, do cobble patches accumulate and form natural reserves of cobbles which would be available to prehistoric peoples as factory sites for mortars during periods of lower sea level. Other types of underwater sites may exist on the continental shelf off the lagoons, but the sites discussed here are the only evidence we have of prehistoric sites surviving the marine transgression.

Concerning a chronology for underwater localities, we lack datable organic materials at present so there remain only two lines of inference: typology and depth. As discussed above, mortars appear in the range of 5,000 - 3,000 years B.P. in the northern part of the Bight and persist into historic times. Although they are rare in terrestrial sites here in San Diego County, this age range would not be inconsistent with dates inferred from the depths of the submarine cobble patches where mortars are found.

Today the patches are visible in 3-5 meters of water when uncovered by sand movement. Deposition of the cobble beds coincided with the end of the rapid phase of sea level rise between 6,000 and 7,000 years B.P. (Inman, this volume). This was a time when there were numerous cobbles in nearshore waters remaining from a period of lower sea level when the rivers carried lithic material directly onto what was to become the continental shelf.   Yet the rise in sea level was sufficiently slow to allow nearshore waves and longshore currents to roll and concentrate the fluvial material into formidable cobble beaches. Sea level then continued to rise, but more gradually, until present level was attained. Thus, a window in time existed from *ca.* 6,000 - 4,000 years B.P. during which the cobble beaches were laid down but before the more slowly transgressing sea submerged them. If this interpretation is valid, then the mortar factory sites and consequently the reef shellfishing stations date from mid to late La Jollan times. The isolated kelp bed and submarine canyon sites containing analogous artifacts probably are contemporaneous with the factory sites.

The question of site preservation during transgressive sea level changes can be approached by considering three factors. First is the nature of the site. An occupational midden composed of relatively unconsolidated sediments would be less likely to survive intact through a transgressing shoreline than would a cobble beach factory site. A second factor, location, is also critical. Certain configurations of the shelf or littoral zone would contribute to preservation: submarine canyons, headlands, reefs, or islands. But the third factor, duration of surf zone passage, may be the most important. A stillstand with archaeological materials caught in the surf zone would be the most destructive situation unless an aeolian sediment cover is deposited prior to submergence and is replenished by longshore transport (see Raban, 1982; Wreschner, 1983, this volume). The Beach and Tennis Club site exists today because the low wave energy environment at the head of the La Jolla Submarine Canyon permitted the cobble accumulation as well as its preservation. The present stillstand has not caused much disturbance due to the nearshore deep water of the canyon, seasonal sand cover, and protection afforded by the La Jolla headland. The Solana Beach reef site has been protected both by its location in a small "cove" within the reef structure and by the seasonal sediment cover. Thus, the evidence presented in this paper suggests that some prehistoric sites along the southern California coast may be expected to survive a marine transgression relatively intact.

ACKNOWLEDGEMENTS

I thank Douglas L. Inman and Travis Hudson for critical reading of the manuscript, which was greatly improved by their suggestions. George Carter also has offered helpful information. The photographs in Plate 4 were contributed by Ron McPeak. The diving surveys were accomplished with the expert assistance of Walt Waldorf and many other S.I.O. divers.

REFERENCES

Anonymous, (1857). The Indian woman of San Nicolas. Hutching's California Magazine (San Francisco) 1, 347-348. Also Document 2D, Original Accounts of the Lone Woman of San Nicolas Island. Heizer, R.F. and Elasser, A.B. (eds), Reports of the University of California Archaeological Survey, Np. 55, Berkeley, California.

212 P.M. Masters

Bickel, P.McW (1978). Changing sea levels along the California coast anthropological implications. *Journal of California Anthropology*, 5, 6-21.

Carter, G.F. (1955). On submarine archaeology about San Diego. *The Masterkey* (Southwest Museum, Los Angeles) 29, 21-27.

Curray, J.R. (1965). Late Quaternary history, continental shelves of the United States. In *The Quaternary of the United States* Wright, H.E. and Freys, D.G. (eds,) Princeton University Press, Princeton, N.J., pp. 723-735.

Emery, K.O. (1958). Shallow submerged marine terraces of Southern California. *Bulletin of the Geological Society of America* 69, 39-59.

Emery, K.O. and Tschudy, R.H. (1941). Transportation of rock by kelp. *Bulletin of the Geological Society of America* 52, 855-862.

Geengro, R.E. (1951). Molluscan species in California shell middens. Reports of the *University of California Archaeological Survey* Report No. 13, Berkeley.

Hudson, D.T. (1976). Marine archaeology along the southern California coast. *San Diego Museum Papers*, No. 9, San Diego, California.

Hudson, Travis (1979). Charmstone from the sea off Point Conception, California. *Journal of California and Great Basin Anthropology*, 1, 363-366.

Marshall, N.F. and Moriarity (sic), J.R. (1964). Principles of underwater archaeology. *Pacific Discovery* 17, 18-25.

Milliman, J.D. and Emery, K.O. (1968). Sealevels during the past 35,000 years. *Science* 162, 1121-1123.

Nardin, T.R. Osborne, R.H. Bottjer, D.J. and Scheidemann, R.C. Jr. (1981). Holocene sea-level curves for Santa Monica Shelf, California continental borderland. *Science* 313, 331-333.

Nelson, N.C. (1909). Shellmounds of the San Francisco Bay region. *University of California Publications in American Archaeology and Ethnology* 7, 309-356.

Nelson, N.C. (1910). The Ellis Landing shellmound. *University of California Publications in American Archaeology and Ethnology* 7, 357-426.

Pisias, N.G. (1979). Model for paleoceanographic reconstructions of the California current during the last 8,000 years. *Quaternary Research* 11, 373-386.

San Diego Union (1952). June 29, p. a-20.

Shepard, F.P. (1964). Sea level changes in the past 6,000 years: possible archaeological significance. *Science* 143, 574-576.

Shipek, F. (1970). *The Autobiography of Delfina Cuero, A Diegueno Indian*. Malki Museum Press, Maronga Indian Reservation, California.

Shumway, G., Hubbs, C.L. and Moriarty, J.R. (1961). Scripps Estates site, San Diego, California: a La Jolla site dated 5460 to 7370 years before the present. *Annals of the New York Academy of Sciences* 93, 37-132.

Thornburgh, M. (1956). Mystery mortars under the sea. *Natural History* 65, 464-467.

Tuthill, C. and Allanson, A.A. (1954). Ocean-bottom artifacts. *The Masterkey* (Southwest Museum, Los Angeles) 28, 222-232.

Wallace, W.J. (1955). A suggested chronology for southern California coastal archaeology. *Southwestern Journal of Archaeology* 11, 214-230.

Wallace, W.J. (1978). Post-Pleistocene archaeology, 9,000 to 2,000 B.C. In *Handbook of North American Indians*, Sturtevant, W.C. (ed.) Vol. 8: *California*, Heizer, R.F. (ed.) Smithsonian Institution, Washington, D.C., pp. 25-36.

Warren, C.N. (Ed.) (1966). *The San Dieguito type site: M.J. Rogers' 1938 excavations on the San Dieguito River*. San Diego Museum Papers, No. 5, San Diego, California.

Warren, C.N. (1968). Culture tradition and ecological adaptation on the Southern California coast. *Eastern New Mexico Contributions to Anthropology (Portales)* 1, 1-14.

Warren, C.N. and True, D.L. (1961). The San Dieguito complex and its place in California prehistory. *Archaeological Survey Annual Report 1960-1961*, pp. 246-338. University of California, Los Angeles.

SUBMERGED PREHISTORIC SITES OFF THE MEDITERRANEAN COAST OF ISRAEL

Avner Raban

Center for Maritime Studies,
Haifa University, Israel.

SUMMARY

The coastline of Israel is basically a straight one, with the coastal plain divided by long-shore low ridges of sandstone. These ridges are solidified dunes calcified during the interglacial transgressions of the Pleistocene (see Ronen, 1983, this volume). Similar ridges, formed while the sea level subsided below the present one, are now submerged off the coastline. The sunken basin between the underwater ridge and the coastal ridge is partially infilled by a thick layer of transported sand. Recent quarrying of large quantities of sand from the beaches caused a deficit and results in exposure of the substrata of the sea bottom near the shore. On these newly exposed patches of sea bottom well preserved evidences of late prehistoric coastal sites were observed. Among them are Chalcolithic settlements; remnants of oak forest (with signs of human activity); at least one Neolithic site; and some enigmatic large-scale quarries related to a sea level lower by 5-6 meters than the present one. The locations and elevations of these sites enable us to reconstruct the ancient sea levels and the Palaeotopography of the coast-line. The data can provide dating for the progress of the Flandrian transgression and some local tectonic submergence of late prehistoric shores.

INTRODUCTION

The Mediterranean coastline of Israel is basically straight but slightly curved to the south. It's character derives primarily from the fluctuating sea levels during the Pleistocene and the transgressions and regressions caused by changes of climate within the Quaternary (Emery & Neev, 1960). It can be divided into a southern and a northern segment. The southern segment, from Rafah to the southern plunge of the Mount Carmel block, is marked by a continuous, low, linear escarpment (10-50 m. high), which is interrupted by several gaps formed by Late Pleistocene rivers. These old estuaries have been filled by beach, swamp, and alluvial deposits. The coastal cliff is composed of carbonate-cemented Quaternary sandstone (kurkar), originally deposited as NE-facing Barchan dunes, interbedded with reddish-brown loams (Hamra). The cliff reaches its greatest height in the central part of this segment, between Tel-Aviv and Beth Yanai (some 35 km to the north), where the beaches are narrowest (as little as 10 m). A rocky kurkar strip extends along this segment as far as 200 m. off shore, forming rimmed terraces at sea level as well as submerged knolls, partly covered by unstable moving sand. The coastal plain of this segment narrows from about 50 km in the south to about 20 km where it approaches Mount Carmel. Three longitudinal kurkar ridges, trending subparallel to the coast-line, occur in this segment.

The northern segment extends northward along Mount Carmel and the Lebanese coast. Along this segment, the inland hills, composed mostly of Cretaceous chalk, limestone, and dolomite, occasionally reach the coast-line, leaving a narrow coastal plain or none at all. Mount Carmel appears to be a large, tilted block plunging to the SSW and terminating northward at a steep NW-trending fault escarpment.

The continental shelf off Israel, which reaches about 100 m. depth, is about 25 km wide off Rafah and narrows toward the north to 10 km off Mount Carmel. North of Haifa bay, the shape of the shelf becomes irregular. Two pronounced canyons, the Carmel Canyon, which is an extension of the Qishon Graben (Nir, 1973) and the Akhziv Canyon (Nir, 1965), cross the shelf as the extensions of onshore river valleys. Between them, the shelf broadens to about 15 km, forming the Akko and the Carmel Noses. North of Akhziv, the shelf narrows to only 3-0.5 km (Neev & Ben-Avraham, 1977).

The shelf off Israel can be divided into two main topographic belts (Emery & Bentor, 1960). The first, from the shoreline to the 30 m. isobath, is about 3 km wide with a slope of $0.5^{\circ}-1.0^{\circ}$. At least three longitudinal sunken kurkar ridges are protruding in random outcrops above the layers of recently deposited gravels, silt, and sand. The basins between these ridges contain terrestrial sediments of reddish-brown loam and black clay deposited during the low sea level of the Glacial periods. The second belt forms a wide and flat area (slope 10' - 20') extending approximately to the 80 m. isobath.

The first belt, having a steeper gradient than both the second one to the west and the present coastal plain to the east, was deeply trenched by rivers during the late Würm, some 12,000 years ago (Wreschner, 1977). These deep river courses became estuaries, flooded by the sea during the Flandrian transgression which reached its highest level some 5,000 years B.P. (Nir & Bar-Yosef, 1976, p. 115f). This rapid rise of the sea level affected the drainage system of the coastal plain and turned the basins between the kurkar ridges into lagoonal or marshy areas.

After the generally stable sea level of the Holocene was established, a continuous accumulation of wave-carried and wind blown sand was deposited on the shore and was carried a few miles inland where the coastal cliff is low or absent (as at gaps caused by river outlets. This sand accumulation reached an equilibrium stage around the end of the second millenium B.C., and now is affected only by human quarrying activities and small-scale eustatic fluctuations of sea level (Goldsmith & Golik, 1980). Wreschner (1977), following Michalson's assumptions (1968), dates the maximum Flandrian transgression to the time period between 8,000-6,000 B.C., but suggests that during the 5th Millenium B.C., the sea level was lower - at least 5 m below the present one. Neev et al. (1973) describe much later vertical tectonic displacements of the shoreline with a magnitude of over 20 m. Both these theoretical assumptions are intriguing when looking for the prehistoric coastal settlements. The data selected for this paper will have therefore, not only to illuminate the way prehistoric peoples made use of the topographical features and the ancient coastal landscape, but also to compare and analyse the various theories of fluctuating sea levels, their causes, and dates.

Sources of Information

The physiographic character of the Israeli Mediterranean coast resulted in almost uninterrupted heavy coverage of sandy sediments over all the now submerged parts of the prehistoric shoreline. Only the upper parts of the kurkar ridges are relatively silt-free today. Of those, the submerged ones were subjected to a long process of abrasion and erosion by waves and currents, and encrustation by marine biotic species. Therefore there is almost no chance that any buildings, artifacts or flint implements would have survived in situ. Even quarries, cup marks and other known types of prehistoric rock cuts would be badly eroded and heavily disguised by marine faunal growth.

The only places where prehistoric remnants would survive are at the foot of rocky ridges and in solidified loam and black mud of the submerged basins between the ridges. Exposure of these cultural materials by removal of the sediment cover is caused by modern human activities, such as sand quarrying, off-shore jetties, breakwaters, and anything that might disturb the pre-existing equilibrium of the coastal process (Nir, 1976; Goldsmith & Golik, 1980). In some cases, unusual storms would result in temporary exposure in the same way, mainly near the shoreline (Wreschner, 1977).

Tracing those sites, which would be scattered by wave action or covered again by a sandy layer sometimes in a matter of a few days, takes systematic and repetitive survey - both on the shore and on the shallow offshore sea bottom. Such repetitive surveys are necessary to avoid random and casual selection of data, without any statistic value.

The data gathered so far come from the following surveys: 1) The activities of the "Archaeological Survey of Israel", started in 1964, with the field group headed by A. Ronen and Y. Olami. The first area chosen by this group for their systematic survey covers the shoreline south of Haifa. Up to 1971, they surveyed as far south as the Nahal Dalia outlet, some 30 km to the south. The facts that both directors of this group are well trained prehistorians and that the northern half of this shoreline segment (between Atlit and Haifa) was under heavy sand quarrying activities, through 1965, helps to enrich the data gathered from prehistoric sites near the shoreline (Ronen & Olami, 1978; 1980). 2) The continuous activities of volunteer divers of the Undersea Exploration Society of Israel, since 1960, concentrated around its center in Haifa.

Having noticed the repetitive random exposure of dark consolidated loam patches, mainly along the inshore water between Hof Harcarmel and Dor, and campaigning against diving ex-fishermen who had become well organized treasure hunters, they try to be the first in surveying any newly exposed submerged material. The collaboration between these diving volunteers and the Archaeological Survey of Israel helped to ensure the continuation of the surveyed area from the coastal plain and the shoreline to the inshore sea floor (Raban, 1973; 1980a). 3) Emergency surveys were carried out in recent years along the shoreline, arising from the necessity to trace archaeological remains threatened by new road construction and other coastal development. Such surveys along the shoreline of the Gaza strip (Biran, 1974), near Ashkelon (Noy & Berman, 1974), along the course of the new highway from Haifa to Tel-Aviv, and at the site of the new electric power station south of Caesarea added valuable data, though not of continuously systematic surveyed areas.

Selected List of Sites (see Fig. 1)

As mentioned above the best surveyed area is the coastal segment just south of Haifa. All the sites in this segment are located

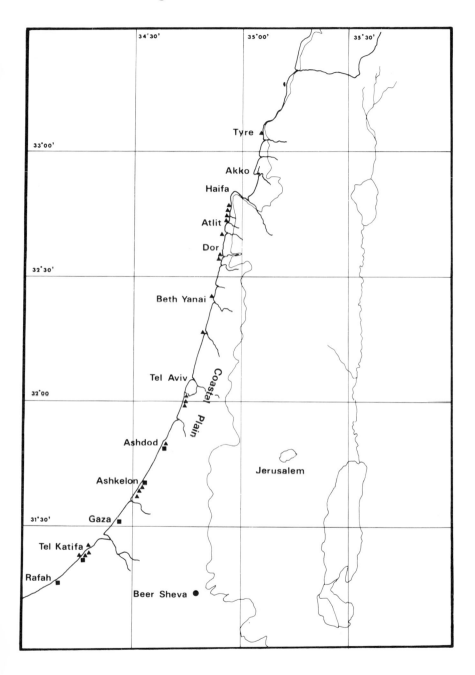

FIG. 1. *The Mediterranean coast of Israel and adjacent coasts indicating principle sites mentioned in the text.*

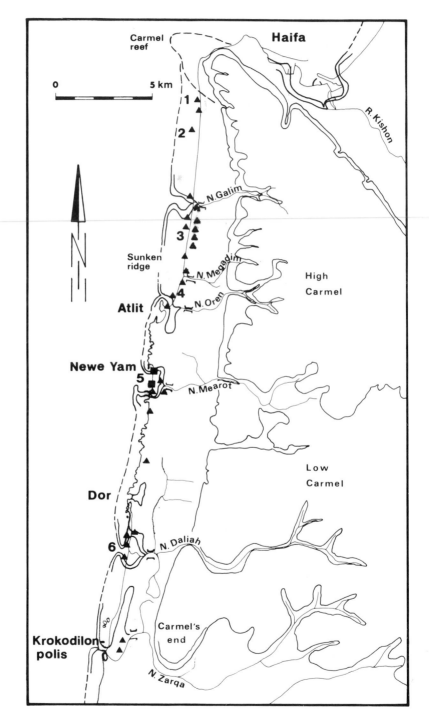

FIG. 2. *Coastline in the region of Haifa and Mount Carmel illustrating the submerged ridges west of the present shore. Numbers indicate sites discussed in the text.*

along a narrow belt (100-200 m) which includes the western side of the main kurkar ridge (the eastern-most between the Carmel and the sea), the beach at its foot, and the shallow sea bottom next to it to the west (Fig. 2). As shown by Ronen (1977), the Palaeolithic surface is now buried under the Upper Sandstone and therefore visible only in quarried sections of the kurkar ridge. In places where the waves eroded off this Upper Sandstone layer, the Palaeolithic man-made artifacts which were carried and scattered can now be found out of context on the sea bottom. All the submerged prehistoric sites to be found *in situ* are located on, or in, the uppermost layer of Epipalaeolithic Loam that gains increasing thickness in the submerged basin, west of the kurkar ridge (as much as 4-6 m).

1. *Hof Dado (Fig. 2:1)* *On the sea bottom, some 10-20 m, from the shoreline and at depth of 1.2 m found by E. Galilee, of the Undersea Exploration Society of Israel after the winter storms of December, 1980 had exposed a patch of brown loam. The site

PLATE 1. *Floor of sandstone slabs, submerged at Hof Dado.*

*This site is currently being studied by E. Galilee and M. Weinstein-Evron and the scientific paper of their findings is in preparation.

is 30 x 15 m, and includes remnants of habitations with floors
made of flat sandstone slabs which had been laid directly on the
loam (Plate 1).   The floors are encircled by what seems to be a
foundation course of walls, made of rubble (Plate 2).   There are at

PLATE 2. *Submerged wall at Hof Dado.*

least 6-7 separate units, with stone-made hearths (Plate 3).   The
small finds are numbered and consist mostly of flakes and chisels
of late Neolithic or Chalcolithic type.

2.   *Kefar Samir   (Fig. 2:2)*   Some 300 m off the shoreline,
under 5.4 m of water, a wide patch of brownish-black loam
exposure was surveyed by the writer in 1978. This loam, wherever
exposed, is rich with partly carbonized tree roots and trunks.   In
one place we found a stone circle about 2.3 m across, made of
carefully laid pebbles (Plate 4). In the middle of this stone circle
there was a tree-trunk, which protruded as high as 60 cm. above
the bottom.   A sample extracted from it was sent for C-14 dating
and for identification of its species.   The corrected C-14 date is
5,700 B.P. ± 140 and the tree's species is *Quercetum   ithaburense*
(Tabor oak), which matches other samples of roots extracted

PLATE 3. *Circular submerged hearth at Hof Dado.*

PLATE 4. *Submerged circle of stones at Kefar Samir.*

elsewhere from this type of fossil loam exposure on the sea bottom
between Haifa and Atlit.

3. *Tel Harez (Chreiz)* *(Fig. 2:3)* During the winter of 1964
a group of volunteer divers from the Undersea Exploration Society
of Israel carried out a series of underwater surveys, in order to
complete the land and coastal archaeological survey directed by A.
Ronen and Y. Olami on behalf of Israel Archaeological Survey. The
most interesting site surveyed during that winter was opposite the
Chalcolithic site of tel Harez (Ronen & Olami, 1978, No. 2). A
random exposure of brown loam patches was traced, some 60-70 m
off-shore and at a depth of 2-2.6 m. The total length of the
exposed area was over 200 m, and at its south part there were
rubble pavings and some irregular platforms of sandstone slabs,
laid on thin layer of pebbles. Here we found flint utensils (Fig. 3)

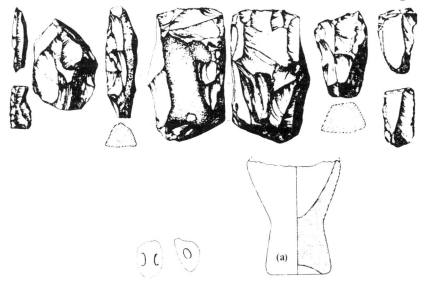

FIG. 3. *Flint tools from Tel Harez. (a) Basalt mortar and*
"Pierced Handle" of Chalcolithic clay vessel.

and a basalt mortar, of the Chalcolithic era (Plate 5), with pottery
sherds of the same period. Some 40 m farther to the south, the
spring storms of March, 1965, exposed another part of the site.
Here we found a hearth, defined by large pebbles. In it, directly
on the loam, there were partly burned twigs and branches and
some bones, including the lower jaw of *Dama mesopotamica,*
Fallow-deer (Raban, 1965; and see Plate 6).

4. *Atlit, North* *(Fig. 2:4)* At the south-east corner of the

PLATE 5. *(Left) Chalcolithic basalt mortar with pottery sherds lying on the sea floor off Tel Harez.*
PLATE 6. *(Right) Twigs and bones of fallow deer, Dama Mesopotamica, embedded in loam off Tel Harez.*

marine intrusion which flooded the area north of Atlit's peninsula, halfway between the River Oren outlet and the submerged Phoenician harbour (Linder, 1967), both in exposures of brown loam on the sea bottom and on the beach (Plate 7), there are many flint flakes and partly abraded utensils, broken sherds of pottery, and scattered sandstone slabs, mixed with remnants of roots and trunks of a forest of Tabor oaks. The finds were traced as far as 300 m off shore and down to a depth of 5 m below sea level.

On the shore, east and south of this bay, the winter storms sometimes remove the sand cover exposing a stratigraphy of:

a) Dark brown loam, with Chalcolithic and Late Neolithic remains.
b) Brownish-red loam (30-50 cm thick), into which burials of Middle Bronze Age IIa (MB IIa) were dug.
c) Sandy layer, mostly consolidated and partially lithified, with floors, walls and pottery of 7-6th century B.C. The top of this stratum is leveled by wave erosion and its elevation is 1.4-1.6 m above the MSL.

5. *Newe - Yam (Fig. 2:5)* Like Atlit, the submerged site of Newe Yam is located on the lee side of the western kurkar ridge, at a place where the sea invaded and flooded the basin behind it. Here, there was in antiquity the estuary of the River Me'arot (Wreschner, 1977, p. 260). (See also Wreschner, 1983, this volume.) In January, 1968, an unusual storm generated waves of extraordinary height (6-7m) that swept away much of the sand

PLATE 7. *(Left) Exposure of flints and utensils on the shore north of Atlit.*
PLATE 8. *(Right) Neolithic wall exposed in the surf zone at Newe Yam.*

cover from the beach, and exposed remnants of buildings, flint tools, pottery sherds, and patches of brownish black loam. The strong eastern wind a few days later caused a drop in sea level and made a salvage dig possible. This was carried out by E.E. Wreschner and M.W. Prausnitz, on behalf of Israel Department of Antiquities.

The better preserved houses were exposed in shallow water; they are rectangular structures 7-9 m long and 2.5-3.0 m wide. The stone walls are relatively thick (80cm) and composed of two rows of undressed blocks (Plate 8). The excavators defined two distinct occupation levels of the late Neolithic (Neolithic Pottery B=5th millennia B.C.) and Early Chalcolithic (Pre-Ghassulian = around 4,000 B.C.). The silos, fireplaces and courtyards, and the used sickleblades, point to an agricultural settlement, with additional herding and fishing (Wreschner, 1977, p. 271).

Though the storm exposed an inhabited area of as much as 20,000 sq.m, later underwater surveys showed that it was much larger and stretched as far south as Tell Nami, almost 2 km further south (cf. Ronen & Olami, 1978, No. 121). An interesting find is the group of four obsidian blades, which must have come from abroad, probably originating in central Anatolia (Perlman & Yellin, 1980).

6.   *Tantura - Nahal Dalia (Fig. 2:6)* South of Tantura's lagoonal bays the shoreline recedes and the low eastern kurkar ridge disappears under the present day marshes of what was in antiquity the estuary of the River Dalia. The marshes were drained into a series of fish ponds. When the ponds were dug to a level below MSL, a very large settlement from the Late Neolithic and Chalcolithic periods was unearthed and demolished. But even

now one can easily trace their remnants along the shore and in shallow water when the storms sweep off part of the sand sediment as far north as the last rocky hill of Tantura (where foundations of stone-built rectangular houses are visible) and for several hundreds of metres south of the river outlet.

The site resembles the ones at Newe Yam and Tel Harez, yet is bigger and richer in small artifacts, flint tools, obsidian blades and variety of pottery vessels. Its location fits the theory that during the 5th millennium B.C. an intensive settlement process started along the shore, with preference for the newly created estuaries (Olami, Burian & Friedman, 1977), and later spread on to the top of the coastal sandstone range and into the low ground on its west side (Ronen & Olami, 1980).

7. *Further South* The continuous cliff and the narrow beach, from Hadera to the Gaza Strip, the larger quantities of sand deposits, the developed beach-rock and the rarity of underwater survey activities, are the reasons for absence of data on submerged prehistoric sites in this segment. This picture contrasts with the information about numerous Neolithic and Chalcolithic sites surveyed and partly excavated on the hills just inshore (Noy, 1977), sometimes a few dozen metres from the waterline (Noy & Berman, 1974; Biran, 1974). In those places where the volunteer divers of the Israel Undersea Exploration Society occasionally surveyed the sea bottom near the shore, after exceptionally strong winter storms, enough data were gathered to show that some of

PLATE 9. *Neolithic-Chalcolithic tools exposed on the beach at Yavneh-Yam after a storm.*

PLATE 10. *Shore at Tel Qatifa, north of Gaza.*

the sites continue into the sea. This is the case for the Early
Neolithic site near the outlet of River Poleg (The Green Beach,
south of Natania); at Yavneh-Yam (PPB Neolithic-Chalcolithic
tools, see Plate 9), and the coastal stretch of water over two km
long, from Tel Qatifa north, in the Gaza Strip. There, the red
loam range of long-shore hills (Plate 10) exhibits scattered
remnants of buildings, stone foundations for seasonal huts, flat
paving slabs of beachrock and flint and pottery of PP Neolithic,
Late Neolithic and Chalcolithic settlements. Remains of all three
periods (including obsidian blades) are also to be found in shallow
water just off shore.

SEA LEVEL CHANGES DURING THE EARLY HOLOCENE

Two recent papers (Wreschner, 1977; Flemming *et al.*, 1978) deal
with tentative reconstructions of the Late Prehistoric sea level
(8,000-4,000 B.C.), based on archaeological data. Flemming's
reconstruction is mainly concerned with the Bronze Age and later
periods, with only one submerged Neolithic site (Newe-Yam) and
three Chalcolithic (around Atlit). The rough reconstructed trend
of Eustatic rise, from 5-4 m below the present sea level, at the
Early Neolithic period to 3-2 m below the MSL in the 4th
millenium B.C. is based on inadequate data and only provides a
highest possible sea level for each date. Wreschner based his
reconstruction on two main assumptions: a) The Flandrian

maximum transgression occurred during the earlier Holocene (Wreschner, 1977, p. 280). b) absence of data for the Natufian and Pre-Pottery Neolithic periods in the coastal plain and near the shoreline. His reconstructed oscillation of the early Holocene sea levels (*ibid*, Fig. 3) shows a tentative eustatic rise to as high as 3 m above MSL in the 8th millenium B.C.; lowering of the sea to about the present height in the 7th (the beginning of Pre-Pottery B period); another rise to about 1 m above modern MSL during the next millenium (= Pottery Neolithic A) and a distinct drop to as low as 5 m below the present sea level just before 4,000 B.C. The data for this reconstruction of sea levels based on site distribution is far from being complete at the time of writing (and see Noy, 1977; in the same volume), and the scale of oscillations seems to be over-estimated. The early date for the Flandrian maximum transgression can be discarded for several reasons:

a) The elevation and proximity to the shore of the Pre-Pottery Neolithic sites near Tel Qatifa and the River Poleg outlet (see above, section 7).
b) There are some indications of significant vertical tectonic movements along the shoreline during the Holocene (Neev *et al.*, 1973) which have been rejected or minimised by Wreschner (1977) and Flemming *et al.* (1978). A westward downwarping of the coastal plain during the early Holocene (Neev & Ben-Avraham, 1977, p. 370 ff.) might have caused its submergence before the eustatic maximum transgression occurred.
c) Both Wreschner (1977) and Noy (1977) provide an alternative explanation for the absence of Early Neolithic sites near the coastline by assuming that either they are now covered by thick layers of silt or sand, or that the societies of the pre-agricultural stage were settled on the ancient beaches and living mainly by fishing.

At this stage we can not reconstruct the early Holocene sea level of the Mediterranean coast of Israel more accurately than by saying that there are indications for it being generally lower than the present one. In fact, there are indications that in some segments of this coast the actual shoreline was west of the present day sunken kurkar ridge. The increasing settlement of the shore during the Bronze Age, with the numerous harbour sites of MB IIa (around 2,000 B.C.), often made use of the wave abraded shelves on the coastal ridge 2.5-3.0 m above the present sea level (Raban, 1981). These abraded shelves are never found with prehistoric remains on them. Thus they seem to indicate transgression of Post-Chalcolithic date. The siting of the Bronze Age harbours implies an extensive use of estuaries and deeply entrenched river outlets (Raban, 1980b, p. 753 ff.). This type of

230   A. Raban

topography fits the final stage of rapidly rising sea level and somewhat contradicts reconstructions of high sea levels for most of the previous millennia (8,000-5,000 B.C.). The coastal dunes which now cover sites as early as Epipaleolithic (Ronen, 1977) seem to be a late historic intrusion (pre- and post-Roman) resulting from a sea level near the present height (Neev & Ben-Avraham, 1977).

CONCLUSIONS

The late Prehistoric archaeological data from the Israeli shoreline, though little of it is satisfactorily surveyed so far, proves its important place in the Neolithic settling process observed elsewhere in the Levant. These data emphasise the importance of the well watered coastal plain and its loam filled basins for the first agricultural societies.

The locations and distribution of these sites indicate a much better drained plain, with an appropriate drainage gradient to a lower base level. The first transgression of the sea above present sea level during the Holocene did not occur before the abandonment of the site at Nahal Dalia, at the beginning of the third millennia B.C. (see Fig. 3). Though some scholars call that transgression "The Shephelien" (Rossignol, 1969; Nir & Bar-Yosef, 1976) and distinguish it from the earlier Flandrian, some new archaeological data and palaeotopographic reconstructions contradict that definition. Both the Chalcolithic and the Late Neolithic coastal sites contain imported obsidian. The obsidian could have been transported by land or by sea from Turkey, but no scholar has yet referred to the maritime function of these coastal sites.

There are strong indications, therefore, that the earlier Neolithic coastal sites where maritime activities were probably initiated are to be looked for in deeper water and further off shore.

REFERENCES

Bar-Josef, O. (1971). Prehistoric sites near Ashdod, *Palestine Exploration Quaterly*, pp. 52-64

Emery, K.O. and Neev, D. (1960). Mediterranean Beaches of Israel. *Bull. Geol. surv. Israel* 26, 1-24.

Emery, K.O. and Bentor, Y.K. (1960). The Continental Shelf of Israel *Bull. Geol. surv. Israel* 26, 25-41.

Flemming, N.C., Raban, A. and Goetschel, C. (1978). Tectonic and Eustatic Changes on the Mediterranean Coast of Israel in the last 9000 Years. In (J.C. Gamble and R.A. Yorke, eds) *Progress in Underwater Science* Vol. 3, pp. 33-93.

Goldsmith, V. and Golik, A. (1980). Sediment Transport Model of the Southeastern Mediterranean Coast *Marine Geology* 37, 147-175.

Linder, E. (1967) La Ville Phénicienne d'Atlit. *Archéologia.* 17, 25-29.

Michalson, C. (1968). *Sea Level Fluctuations of the Mediterranean* MSc Thesis, Hebrew University, Jerusalem (Hebrew).

Neev, D., Almagor, G., Arad,A., Ginzburg, A. and Hall, J.K. (1973). The Geology of the Southeastern Mediterranean Sea. *Report Geol. surv. Israel,* No. MG/73/5, 43 pp.

Neev, D. and Ben-Avraham, Z. (1977). The Levantine Countries: The Israeli Coastal Region. In (A.E.M. Nairn, W.H. Kanes and F.G. Stehli, eds). *The Ocean Basins and Margins,* Vol. 4a, pp. 355-377.

Nir, Y. and Bar-Yosef, O. (1976) *Quatenary Environment and Man in Israel* Tel Aviv, (Hebrew).

Nir, Y. (1965). Bottom topography. In (D. Neev ed.) *Submarine Geological Studies in the Continental Shelf and Slope off the Mediterranean Coast of Israel, Report Geol. surv. Israel* No. QRG/1/65, pp. 4-6.

Nir, Y. (1973) Geological History of the Recent and Subrecent Sediments of the Israeli Mediterranean Shelf and Slope, *Report Geol. surv. Israel,* No. MG/73/2, 179 pp.

Nir, Y. (1976). Detatched Breakwaters, and other Artificial Constructions on the Mediterranean Coast of Israel and their Effect on the Israeli coast. *Report Geol. Surv. Israel,* No. G1/72/2, 34 pp. (Hebrew).

Noy, T. (1977). Neolithic Sites in the Western Coastal Plain, *Eretz-Israel,* Vol. 13 (Stekelis volume), pp. 18-33 (Hebrew, English sum.).

Noy, T. and Berman, A. (1974). Neolithic-chalcolithic site south of Ashkelon, *Israel Exploration Journal* 24, 132 ff.

232   A. Raban

Olami, Y., Burian, F. and Friedman, E. (1977). Givat HaParsa - A Neolithic site in the Coastal Region, *Eretz-Israel*, Vol. 13 (Stekelis volume) pp. 34-47 (Hebrew, English sum.).

Perlman, I. and Yellin, J. (1980). The Provinience of Obsidian from Neolithic sites in Israel, *Israel Exploration Journal* 30, 83-88.

Raban, A. (1965). Tel Harez: Chalcolithic and Persian remains in the Sea. *Bematzuloth Yam* 3-4, 6-9 (Hebrew).

Raban, A. (1973). Survival of Ancient Wrecks in varying conditions off the Israeli coast. In (N.C. Flemming, ed.) *Science Diving International*. London, pp. 29-40.

Raban, A. (1980a). Archaeological remains, Carmel Coast. In (A. Soffer and B. Kipnis, eds) *Atlas of Haifa and Mount Carmel*. Haifa University, pp. 56-58.

Raban, A. (1980b). The Siting and Development of Mediterranean Harbors in Antiquity. In (M. Sears and D. Merriman, eds) *Oceanography, The Past*. New York, pp. 750-764.

Raban, A. (1981). Some Archaeological Evidence for Ancient Maritime Activities at Dor. *Sefunim* VI, 15-26.

Ronen, A. (1977). Mousterian Sites in the Red Loam in the Coastal Plain of Mount Carmel, *Eretz-Israel*, Vol. 13 (Stekelis volume), pp. 183-190.

Ronen, A. and Olami, Y. (1978). *Archaeological Survey of Atlit Map* Israel Archaeological survey, Jerusalem.

Ronen, A. and Olami, Y. (1980). Prehistory - Mount Carmel. In (A. Soffer and B. Kipnis, eds) *Atlas of Heifa and Mount Carmel*. Haifa University, pp. 32-33.

Rossignol, M. (1969). Sédimentation palynologique récente dans la Mer Morte. *Pollen et Spores* XI, 17-38.

Wreschner, E.E. (1977) Sea-level changes and settlement locations in the coastal plain of Israel during the Holocene *Eretz-Israel* Vol. 13 (Stekelis volume), pp. 276-281.

PRELIMINARY GEOMORPHOLOGICAL SURVEY OF AN EARLY NEOLITHIC SUBMERGED SITE IN THE SPORADHES, N. AEGEAN.

N. C. Flemming

*Institute of Oceanographic Sciences,
Wormley, Godalming, Surrey, England.*

ABSTRACT

The northern Sporadhes islands are separated by straits which were flooded throughout the last 10,000 years. Palaeolothic and Neolithic occupation of the island of Kyra Panagia indicates seafaring inhabitants during the period 10,000 to 5,000 B.P. Sea level indicators on Kyra Panagia and the small islands of Pelerissa and Aghios Petros show two events. A subsidence of the order of 30-50 cm has occurred during the last thousand years, and this subsidence is limited to the western part of Kyra Panagia and its associated islands. Submerged terraces and small cliffs around Aghios Petros relate to sea level still stands deeper than 9 m, and earlier than 7,000 B.P. There is some evidence for tectonic subsidence of 1.5 m between 5,000 B.P. and 1,000 B.P. A submerged area of Neolithic and Bronze Age ceramics, bones, obsidian, and flint was found extending from the shoreline to a depth of 10 m, and over 50 m by 35 m in extent. Measurements were made of rock profiles, sediment thickness, and sediment movements so as to analyse the effects of marine transgression over the archaeological site. It is concluded that at least the shallower half of the site has been disturbed by wave action, which has moved the artifacts several metres downslope, but without completely destroying them. The lower part of the site is in thicker sediments and may be better preserved. Further rise in sea level would not alter the disposition of the existing underwater remains, and thus Aghios Petros indicates the kind of

QUATERNARY COASTLINES
ISBN 0 12 479250 2

site survival which could be expected in deeper water. The sea floor gradient is 1 in 4 at the site, and preservation would have been better if the gradient were flatter.

INTRODUCTION

During the last decade the study of underwater remains of harbours and coastal settlements has progressed further into the past. The analysis of Greek and Roman classical harbours, and their relation to sea level was described by Blackman (1973); Bronze Age harbours by Harding et al. (1969) and Flemming et al (1978). Neolithic, Mesolithic, or Chalcolithic materials underwater have been reported by Wreschner (1977), Andersen (1980) and Raban (1983, this volume). The site of Epiktitos Vrysi in northern Cyprus extends into the water, but has been heavily eroded (Peltenberg, 1975). No Mediterranean Neolithic site has previously been found below present sea level which consists of the concentrated remains of a settlement, preserved in such a way that they could be surveyed and excavated as a site, rather than as scattered individual artifacts found over hundreds of metres or, kilometers of sea floor.

The Northern Sporadhes are a chain of six principle mountainous islands extending eastwards into the North Aegean, (Fig. 1). The principle islands consist of Cretaceous and Jurassic limestones with some metamorphism, and zones of schist and marble. There is a close-spaced-faulting, and beds of boulders and breccia. There are scattered eruptive greenstones (Philippson, 1901, p. 139) which were also observed during the present study in the ravines on the south east coast of Kyra Panagia. Psathura is basaltic (Philippson, p. 1901, p. 169). The chain of islands border to the north a deep trough which extends north-eastwards towards the Dardanelles, and is known as the Anatolian Trough. It is an active graben (McKenzie, 1978) with a central depth of over 1,000 m within 30 km of Kyra Panagia. An exceptionally deep elongated depression of 1,800 m extends parallel to the north-west shore of Alonnisos only 7 km offshore. McKenzie (1978, Fig. 11) shows 15 instrumentally measured epicentres shallower than 50 km in the Sporadhes, with a concentration on Alonnisos, and one epicentre beneath Kyra Panagia. Major recent earthquakes in the north Aegean (Magnitudes $M = 7.1$, Feb 19, 1968; $M = 5.5$, May 24, 1978; $M = 6.5$, June 20, 1978) are described by Drakopoulos and Ekonomides (1972) and Mercier et al (1979).

The islands are thus located in a vertically unstable area, and are subject to the seismic activity associated with normal faulting in the walls of the Graben of the Anatolian Trough. The channels between the main islands range in depth from 100 m to 148 m so that the deeper channels are not likely to have dried out during the late Quaternary unless considerable earth movements have

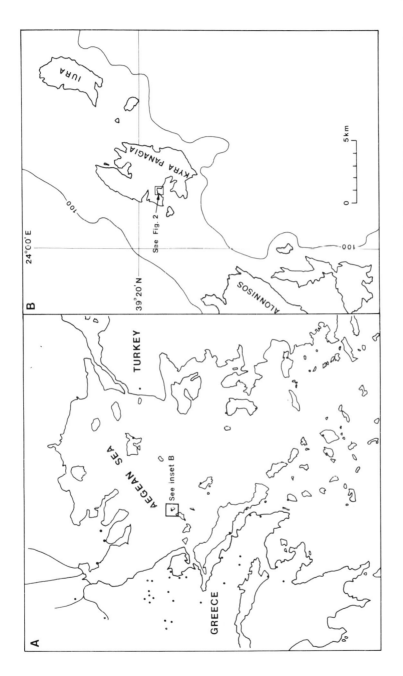

FIG. 1. (A) *North and central Aegean showing locations of coastal Neolithic sites, and those in the region of the Sporadhes, after Theocharis.* (B) *Kyra Paragia and neighbouring islands.*

increased the depth of the channels subsequently. The small islet
of Aghios Petros is situated in the bay on the south west side of
Kyra Panagia. An early Neolithic site (7,000 - 6,000 B.P.) was
excavated on the south west end of Aghios Petros by Theocharis
(1970), and a superficial survey of the island revealed Bronze Age
and Palaeolithic artifacts as well (Michos, personal communication).
Palaeolithic tools were also found on the shore of the inlet just
north east of Aghios Petros (Michos, personal communication).
These finds suggest that Kyra Panagia was occupied by peoples
capable of crossing the channel from Alonnisos in the Palaeolithic
period, and that early Neolithic people occupied the present island
of Aghios Petros.

PLATE 1. *Aerial view of Aghios Petros, looking south. The*
submerged archaeological site is at the bottom of the
picture, between the cleft in the rocky shore and the south
west end of the island.

In 1980 and 1981 a further excavation was conducted on Aghios Petros under the leadership of Nikolaos Efstratiou, and supervised by representatives of the Efor at Volos. The area of material found on the island was extremely small, extending about 20 m along the shore, and only a few metres inland. In spite of this, the quality and quantity of ceramics, bones, obsidian, and other artifacts indicate a prosperous settlement (Efstratiou, personal communication). From this anomaly Efstratiou deduced that a relative change of sea level had occurred since the early Neolithic, and that the site probably extended below the sea at some point around the island of Aghios Petros. This had previously been suggested, but with less evidence, by Theocharis (1970).

Accordingly, a team of six snorkel divers visited the site to work in parallel with the land excavation of 1981, and to examine the evidence for a relative change of sea level. The purpose of the coastal and submarine survey was to establish the ancient shoreline at the time of occupation, to find a water supply for the settlement, to examine the submarine topography so as to estimate whether a harbour had existed at the time for occupation, and to assess the qualities of the harbour and its relation to the settlement so as to deduce whether the occupants had most probably been seafarers, or whether the location of the site on the shore was coincidental.

The present paper will describe briefly the geology and geomorphological background of the site, the submarine topography, the methods of work used, the findings, and provide a preliminary analysis of the results. It should be stressed that no underwater archaeological excavation or stratigraphic work was conducted, and that such work needs to be done before firm conclusions can be reached.

GEOLOGY AND GEOMORPHOLOGY

The islet of Aghios Petros consists of massive bedded limestone with a dip varying from 25° to 34° and strike varying from 350° to 50°. At the south west end of the islet the topography is controlled by the lithology. A strike ridge extends at approximately 220° (SW), sloping gently to the NW, and with successive beds of rock producing parallel ridges 0.5 - 1.0 m high. The main ridge has a steep south-easterly face, dropping to 9 - 10 m depth, with a small cliff at that depth.

The surface of the islet above the swash zone is covered with a layer of red earth, terra rossa, about 1.0 m thick. A coarse scrub of thorns grows over the upper part of the island. The swash zone is about 2.0 m high on the south west tip of the islet, and there is a strip of heavily eroded rock about 7 - 8 m wide. The swash zone narrows both verticaly and horizontally as one proceeds progressively to the lee of the islet, and is about 1.0 m high at the

PLATE 2. *View of Aghios Petros islet from the north east showing the way in which the scrub growth is related to wave exposure. The submerged archaeological site is just off the right hand edge of the island in this view.*

most sheltered point.

The bay in which Aghios Petros is located is shown in outline in Fig. 2. A swash zone within which no vegetation grows is visible all round the bay, and the height is determined by the exposure of each point. On the south and south eastern shores of the bay the swash zone extends to a height of 3 - 4 m, but on the northern shore it drops to 2 m, and the most sheltered part of the bay to the north west of the Aghios Petros islet the scrub grows down to within 1.0 m of the sea.

This variation is indicative of the storm waves which reach each part of the shore, and these are determined by a combination of total straight-line fetch, frequency and strength of winds, and refraction and diffraction of waves entering the bay. Beaches of rounded and sub-angular cobbles exist in several of the inlets around the bay, and the stones are consistent in shape and size with the angular cobbles in the terra rossa.

Figure 3 shows the straight line fetch from Aghios Petros itself. In the northern arc from west through north to east the fetch is never more than 300 m. This increases in the south to 900 m. In an arc of about 30° centred on SW the fetch ranges from 2 km to

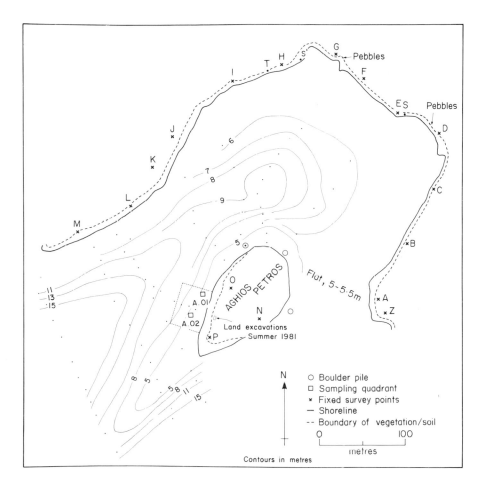

FIG. 2. *Aghios Petros and the adjacent coast. Points marked with letters A-P and Z are survey points fixed by theodolite. S and S' are submarine springs. T marks the location of the tide staff. A.01 and A.02 are the two quadrats within the grid which were most completely excavated. Contours of depth are based on soundings measured by weighted tape. The unmarked points indicate sounding locations.*

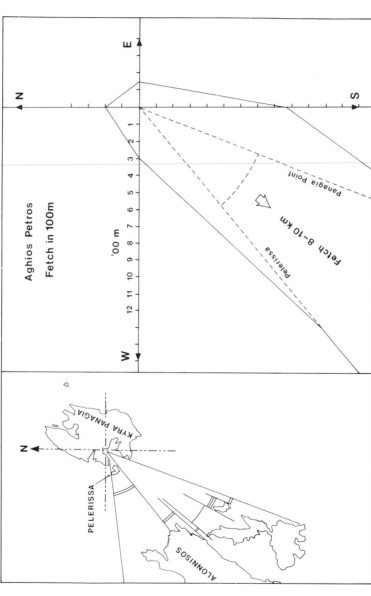

Aghios Petros

Fetch in 100m

'00 m

Fetch 8-10 km

panagia point

pelerissa

N

E

S

W

12 11 10 9 8 7 6 5 4 3 2 1

KYRA PANAGIA

PELERISSA

ALONNISOS

N

FIG. 3. (A) Directions of maximum fetch as measured from Aghios Petros. The circumferential arcs label the distinct arcs within which different fetches apply. (B) Large scale plot of the fetch centred on Aghios Petros. Note that wave action is only significant from the south west.

10 km, and back to 1.7 km. In every direction the open sea fetch is blocked, as viewed from Aghios Petros, by the headlands enclosing the bay, by the island of Pelerissa, and beyond that, by Alonnisos. Thus Aghios Petros itself is very sheltered, and the lee of the islet is even more sheltered.

The extreme shelter around Aghios Petros is in marked contrast to the south and south east parts of the bay. From here there is a fetch of 200 km on a straight line through the channel to the north of Pelerissa, and extending the length of the Gulf of Salonika. This accounts for the broad swash zone on the south side of the bay. On the 20-21 July 1981 a strong NW wind produced waves of several metres in the open sea, and heavy surf on the shore with spray breaking tens of metres into the air. Aghios Petros was in an area of calm water. The implications of the observations made during this storm will be discussed later.

The submarine topography, based on soundings from an unpublished report by Theocharis and soundings made during 1981, indicates the form of shoreline which would have existed at different lower sea levels (Fig. 2). At -50 m the gap between Pelerissa and the northern side of the bay would be closed, and there would only be a small inlet between Pelerissa and the southern side, opening into a small lagoon in the centre of the present bay. During a pluvial period several small streams would have crossed the floor of the bay to flow into the inlet. At a depth of -20 m the contour passes to the SW of Aghios Petros, so that the islet would then have been simply a spur of high ground projecting towards the sea, with a valley to the north of it. At -10 m the sea invades the valley to the north of Aghios Petros and forms a long narrow inlet, protected from the south by the extended ridge of the islet which is now submerged. These various topographic shorelines will later be considered in relation to different sea levels during the Flandrian transgression.

METHODS

Owing to the nature of the provisional permit for the underwater survey, work could be conducted only by snorkel diving; aqualungs (scuba) were not permitted. This made much of the work slow and laborious, but did not prevent the achievement of reasonable accuracy.

Survey

Thirteen base points on the shore of the bay were surveyed in by theodolite, and marked with paint. Three points were fixed on Aghios Petros islet. The shore of the bay was plotted by measurements with a 50 m tape from the base points, and by reference to low-level colour aerial photographs. The shore of the islet was similarly plotted. Preliminary submarine survey by snorkel swimmers revealed the key features, and transects were selected which would provide the most relevant information. These transects were then measured by sounding with a 50 m plastic tape marked in centimetres. The tape was held at each survey point by a snorkel swimmer who could see when the weighted tape touched the bottom. The tape could be read to an accuracy of 5-10 cm in a water depth of -10 to -20 m. The snorkel swimmer could also note the type of bottom, rock, sand, gravel, patchy, and the roughness or local gradient. The position of each sounding was fixed by theodolite fixes from the base points. Soundings and theodolite fixing were co-ordinated by radio communication. No echo-sounder was available to provide continuous transects.

Tide Staff

A tide staff was fixed in the NE corner of the bay at the point marked "T" on Fig 2. The staff was marked in centimetres, and was in a very sheltered position. When the water was still it could be read to an accuracy of 1.0 cm; when there was a swell of 10-15 cm reaching the staff, the mean level was derived by taking the mean of the crest and trough measurements, giving an accuracy of about ± 2.0 cm. The tide staff was read at approximately hourly intervals when work was being conducted in the area during the days from 11-18 July 1981. The staff was read at every hour for 24 hours throughout 16 July, on a monthly spring tide. The 24 hour record produced a marked diurnal assymetry, with one cycle of amplitude 17 cm, and the second of amplitude 26 cm. Mean sea level on the tide staff was determined, and this was surveyed into the theodolite levelling chain.

No changes of sea level due to meteorological events were noted, though this may have been due to the incompleteness of the record. Observations were not recorded during the storm of 20-21 July, but a single observation of the staff showed that even when the storm was at its height the swell reaching the staff had an amplitude of only 30 cm and a period of over 10 seconds.

Observations of depths were corrected to mean sea level using tidal data when not to have done so would have introduced an error of more than 10 cm.

Sediments, and Solution Notches

As noted above, the bottom type was recorded visually at each sounding position, (Fig. 4). In addition, divers obtained samples of 1-2 kg of sediment at several locations so as to determine if there were significant gradations of sediment size or sorting across the site area. Rock features were measured and photographed, and particular attention was given to vertical cliff features, overhangs

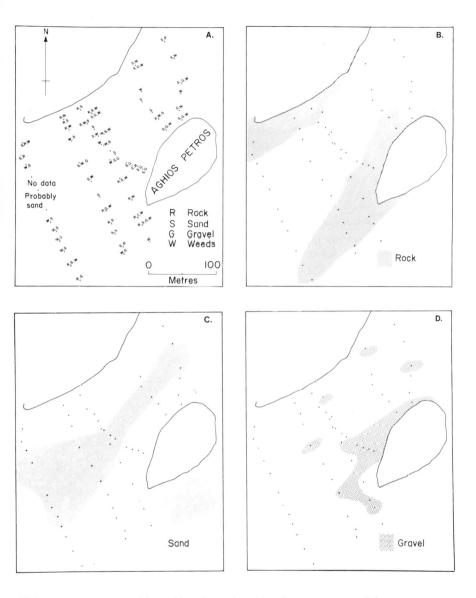

FIG. 4. *Sediment distribution in the bay near Aghios Petros.*
(A) Each observation point is indicated by a dot, and the
letters indicate the bottom type observed; S = sand; R =
rock; G = gravel; W = weed. Most points are composite. (B)
indicates the area where rock was observed. (C) indicates
the area where sand is dominant. (D) indicates the areas
where gravel is dominant.

or apparent solution notches, terraces, and other possible indicators of erosion or solution at previous sea levels. Higgins (1980) discusses the numerous theories of notch formation, and concludes that, at least in Greece, solution notches only occur in proximity to freshwater springs, or groundwater.

Within the bay there was no visible solution notch at present sea level. In contrast, a large solution notch and overhang was found all round Aghios Petros, and on all shores of the bay, and on the east side of Pelerissa at a depth of 30-35 cm. (See Fig 5.) This notch was measured and photographed at several locations. During a boat trip from Kyra Panagia to the next island to the east, Iura, the cliff was observed continuously so as to identify a notch at present sea level, if it existed. The notch on Iura itself was at present sea level, and along the whole southern and eastern shore

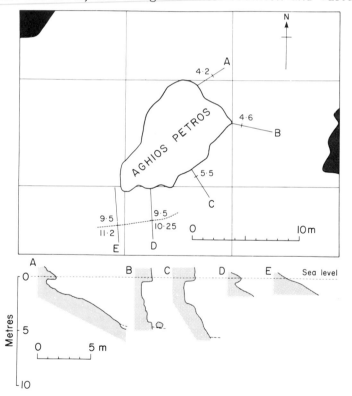

FIG. 5. *Rock profiles and notches in shallow water close to Aghios Petros. The profiles are shown without vertical exaggeration. Numbers indicate depth in metres. Two adjacent depths indicate top and bottom soundings at a vertical cliff. Note that the notch becomes less pronounced as the exposure increases towards the south west.*

of Kyra Panagia. Unfortunately the southern entrance to the bay, known as Panagia Point, has a low gradient of extremely weathered and pitted rock. The waves break continuously on the low gradient, and no solution notch was formed. Thus the junction between the area with the submerged notch within the bay, and the cliff with the notch at present sea level, was not determined to within a kilometer. Nevertheless, the junction must be within 2 kilometers of the entrance of the bay on the south. No investigation of the notch was made outside the bay to the north.

Freshwater Springs

The swimmers quickly detected very cold water near the north east shores of the bay adjacent to Aghios Petros. A layer 10-20 cm thick lay on the surface of the sea on calm days, and a search was made for submarine springs. The spring emerged from the rocks at point "S" on Fig. 2, close to the shore, and did not well up from the sandy sea floor as at first suspected. The lense of cold fresh water extended about 40 m from the beach and could be detected within 9 m of the beach. Closer to the beach it was broken up by water movement even in calm weather. The lens extended about 50 m along shore from the point of exit and was 22 cm thick, with a visible density interface with the salt water, at its thickest point. Over much of the area the fresh water was 3-5 cm thick.

   The rate of flow was not measured, and it was in fact difficult to find a single exit point for the freshwater amongst the rocks. A rough calculation suggests that the volume of freshwater in equilibrium within the cold lens was about 30 x 50 x 0.1 = 150 cu m. However, there was no way of knowing how quickly the volume of freshwater accumulated, or how rapidly the fresh water mixed with the salt water. Accurate measurements of salinity and temperature would have been needed to calculate this, and it would have been useful to observe the formation of the fresh water lens after the waters had been mixed by a wind.

   A second and similar spring was found further north at point "S¹" on Fig. 2, but no measurements were made of the volume of freshwater.

Underwater Survey Grid

The area of sea floor which contained archaeological remains was found to be about 50 m along the shoreline and 35 m wide in the offshore direction (see below). In order to survey this area accurately a rectangular grid of white nylon cord was laid over the site, with a line spacing of 10 m, with the exception of the row nearest the shore which was only 5 m wide. (See Fig. 6.) Since aqualungs were not available on site, and the outer edge of the

site was over 10 m deep, the grid had to be pre-assembled and
towed into position. It could not be laid down as separate lines,
and knotted on the sea floor. In order to achieve this a series of
50 m lines and 35 m lines were laid out on land and marked every
5 m with coloured plastic tape.

The lines were transported by rowing boat to the archaeological
site off Aghios Petros, uncoiled on the rocky shore, and knotted
together at the junction points. The seaward segment of the grid
was passed into the water and pulled out by snorkel swimmers.
One person on land walked backwards and forwards lifting
successive lines off the jagged rocks and passing them to snorkel
swimmers, whilst the grid as a whole was slowly pulled seawards.
The shoreward corners were secured to heavy stones and dropped
into the water. The whole grid was then pulled tight, and the
outer corners were sunk with heavy stones. In spite of the very

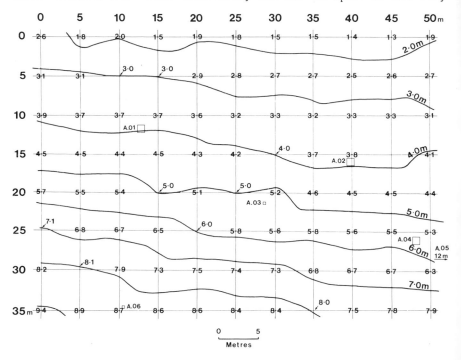

FIG. 6. *The archaeological survey grid, with the shoreline at
the top. The contours were obtained from plots of soundings
at all grid intersections, and at 5 m mid-points. Excavated
quadrats are shown A.01 to A.06. For reference purposes and
photographic identification the 10 m x 10 m squares were
numbered I–XV; that is I–V in the shallowest row; VI–X in
the middle row; and XI–XV in the deepest row. (See also
Plate 3.)*

primitive conditions of launch the grid was remarkably rectangular, and only a few slack sections or kinked lines were present.

The distribution of sand, gravel, rock, weed, etc., was then sketched for every 10 m square by drawing on plastic board. This was a preliminary survey precaution in the event of failure of the photographic coverage. The entire grid area was then photographed in 5 m squares, using both black and white and colour film. Because of the lack of aqualung diving gear all the work had to be done by snorkel swimmers. In each photograph a 1.0 m quadrat marked with 5 cm scale was placed in the centre of the square, together with a key number, and a small buoy to indicate the required height of the camera. The photographer then swam down to the buoy with a Nikonos camera fitted with a 15 mm wide-angle lens, and took the picture. Snorkel swimmers then picked up the quadrat and numbers, and moved them into the next square. One hundred and forty photographs were taken in this way, each involving several snorkel dives to -5 -10 m, often with a swim of 5-10 m along the bottom. It is not very hard to photograph one or two squares like this, but 140 photographs requires a great deal of stamina in breath-hold diving.

The sediment thickness was tested by prodding with a diving knife at every 10 m intersection of the grid. The knife was marked in cms. In addition, test profiles were made across gulleys and sediment patches to estimate the thickness of obvious concentrations.

Two 1.0 m square quadrats were dropped more or less at random in about -3.7 m of water, and material was excavated as a test to see if there was any archaeological material. These quadrats did show archaeological remains, and subsequently one more 1.0 m quadrat was excavated, and three 0.5 m quadrats were sampled but not fully excavated, (see Table 1). In order to raise useful quantities for study, a canvas kit-bag was lined with polythene, and the mouth propped open with a ring of stiff wire. The bag was weighted with stones and laid next to the quadrat. Snorkel divers then descended in rota, each digging with his hands or a knife, and sweeping the material complete with sand and stones into the bag. The bag was lifted to the rowing boat when it was about half full, since it was then almost too heavy to lift out of the water. The material from each quadrat was washed free of sand, and sieved. All materials were checked and photographed, including sand, gravel, stones, artifacts, shells and bones. The archaeological materials were labelled and transferred to the Museum at Volos. The sediments were stored for grain-size analysis.

The depth of every 5 m intersection of the grid was measured to an accuracy of the nearest 10 cm, that is, ± 5.0 cm, by sounding with a plastic tape. The area of maximum archaeological importance was then contoured at 1.0 m intervals (Fig. 6). This

TABLE 1

Location and sampling of quadrats.
For locations of quadrats see figures.

Quadrat Number	Size	Depth	Sample procedure
A. 01	1 m^2	3.8 m	Excavated to bedrock
A. 02	1 m^2	4.0 m	Several layers excavated but not to bedrock
A. 03	0.25 m^2	5.3 m	Excavated down to silt layer. Stones and shreds removed
A. 04	1 m^2	5.5 m	Cleared completely to bedrock
A. 05	0.25 m^2	8.6 m	Hand samples only
A. 06	0.25 m^2	8.8 m	Hand samples only

(Sherds found on sandy bottoms 10 m seaward from quadrat A.06)

survey took place near mid-tide level, with a maximum tidal displacement of 8.0 cm during the two hours of the survey, and no tidal correction was applied.

RESULTS

Before the survey was started it seemed possible that the submerged area of the settlement might be either on the submerged isthmus between Aghios Petros and Kyra Panagia, or in the shelter of Aghios Petros to the north. Preliminary surveys indicated nothing at all suggestive of a Neolithic settlement. There were large quantities of Byzantine pottery, presumably scattered from a wreck known to lie to the south-west of Aghios Petros. Comparison with the excavation on the islet did not give any clue as to what might be found underwater, especially since no definite walls or foundations of stone were found, and houses were probably of mud-brick. In the absence of aqualungs it was not possible to search continuously close to the bottom, or to turn over likely looking artifacts or sediments on a continuous basis.

All areas of pure sand and exposed rock were eliminated, although one could not exclude the possibility that remains might

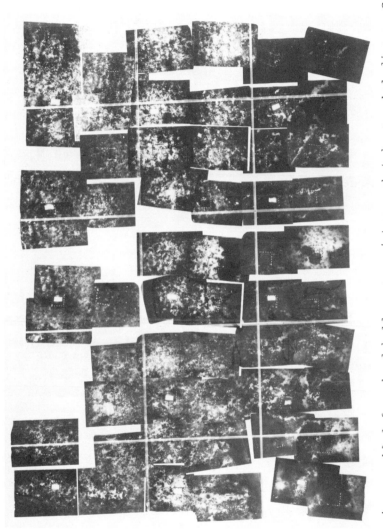

PLATE 3. *Mosaic assembled from hand-held camera pictures shot by snorkel divers. Coverage was not complete on the short axis of the frames. Note the gulley of sand on the left hand edge of the grid; the bright area in square II where quadrat A.01 has been excavated down to bedrock, and the quadrat A.02 is already in position.*

The white cords of the grid squares are not rectangular in arrangement because of erratic camera angles. An approximate fit grid has been drawn over the mosaic.

PLATE 4. *Bone fragments from one half-sack sample from quadrat A.02. There are 123 pieces of bone, provisionally identified as sheep and goat.*

PLATE 5. *Ceramic fragments from one half-sack sample from quadrat A.02. The 347 sherds are graded in approximate size order. The scale is in cm.*

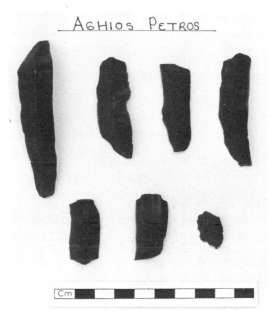

PLATE 6. *Obsidian blades from quadrat A.02.*

PLATE 7. *Simple ceramic figurine from A.02. A similar artifact was found in quadrat A.01.*

be concealed under sand. The bed rock was normally covered with a sparse growth of algae giving it a dark green-black appearance. In one area adjacent to the islet there was an anomalous zone of paler rocks, less weed, and scattered patches of gravel and sand with occasional cobbles. In sedimentological terms the material was extremely poorly sorted. The boundaries of the anomalous area were quite abrupt, with no patches of similar material outside well defined lines. The zone was located and defined entirely by swimming and by underwater observations, without reference to the shore. The alongshore limits of the underwater zone turned out to coincide roughly with the limits of the onshore test pits which had produced Neolithic artifacts. The outer limit appeared to be in a depth of about 10 m.

After discussion with the representative of the Museum of Volos, it was agreed that several 1.0 m square quadrats could be placed on the bottom, and the contents of the quadrats excavated to test for the existence of artifacts. The first quadrat, designated A.01 (see Fig. 6) was laid in 3.7 m of water, and excavated as described above. Two kit-bag loads of material were removed, and the bedrock was cleaned with a brush. The bare area of rock shows in the section of mosaic shown in plate 3. The first sample, on inspection after washing and sieving, proved to contain several hundred sherds of Bronze Age and Neolithic Age, as well as many tens of bones, shells, and a few fragments of obsidian, flint and quartz. The bones were mostly of sheep and goats (Schwartz, personal communication). The second sample from A.01 contained a similar assemblage, and included a small ceramic figurine. The thickness of the sediment layer to bedrock was less than 10 cm.

Quadrat A.02 was thicker than 25 cm, and although several loads of material were removed, sieved, inspected, and photographed, bedrock was not reached (Plates 4,5, and 6). The lowest layers were black, and may have contained organic sediments. Probing with a knife did not reach bedrock. A second ceramic figurine was found in A.02 (Plate 7).

All subsequent quadrats (see Fig. 6) produced high concentrations of artifacts and bones. In the deeper 0.5 m square quadrats only a few handfuls of material were obtained, but this was sufficient to show the presence of archaeological evidence.

Within the grid area the artifacts and bones appear to be concentrated in patches and gulleys, interspersed with areas of rock which are almost bare. (See plate 3). Assuming a limited supply of coarse clastic sediments, it is natural that the material would collect in depressions in the bedrock. Regular testing of sediment thickness by probing at 10 m grid intersections produced the results shown in Fig. 7. A band of thicker sediment, 8-25 cm, appears to extend from the northern seaward corner of the site, along the bottom edge, and then swings into shallower water towards the landward southern corner. This continuity of grading

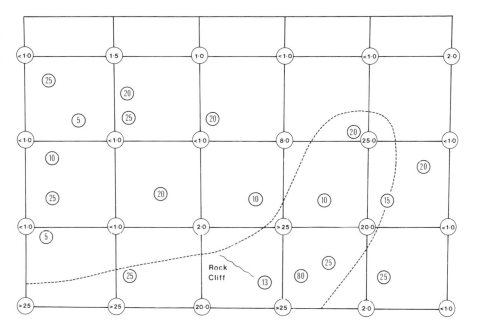

FIG. 7. *Thickness of clastic sediments over the archaeological site. Numbers indicate thickness in cm. Probes were made at 10 m grid intersections, and at selected places where the sediments looked thick. Compare Fig. 8 and Plate 3. The dashed lines enclose the area where the majority of probes are over 15 cms.*

is not so evident from visual inspection, except for the general observation that there is much more sand in the deeper than the shallower parts. Outside this zone the probe survey seldom reveals more than 1.0 cm of sediment thickness.

The regular probe survey fails to record the gulleys and ridges trapping sediment which are immediately apparent to the eye, and on photographs. Eighteen sample areas (see Fig. 7) were selected for the obvious concentration of sediments, and were tested for thickness by probing with a diving knife. Five locations produced a thickness of 25 cm or greater, six were over 20 cm, five 10-20 cm, and two in the range 5-10 cm. Many of these gulleys and patches were outside the area of generally thicker sediment registered by the regular grid sampling. On this limited evidence it appears that seven 10 m x 10 m squares can be classed as having sediments of 20 cm or thicker, that is 700 sq m out of 1750 sq m, or 40%. To this should be added several tens of square metres, perhaps 100, from the gulleys and patches, also with sediment thickness in the 10-25 cm range. Thus about 50% in all of the grid area contains sediments which could produce material on the scale of quadrat A.02. Additionally, two of the gulley-patch probes produced black muddy silt layers.

At the deeper edge of the site the gravel-sand layers extend in patches outside the grid, by 10-20 m in each direction, and artifacts were also found in hand samples taken from seaward of the grid. Thus the extent of the site and the estimate of the volume of archaeologically significant material are both minima.

The material raised from the few test quadrats produced so many artifacts that it was difficult to sort and classify them. Systematic excavation of large areas of the site would produce enormous quantities. The high proportion of artifacts and bones is probably due to the matrix of earth in which they were originally embedded having been washed away. Thus the coarser gravel, pebbles, and archaeological remains have sunk to the bottom, and have become mixed with marine sands. This process will be discussed more fully later.

A sketch map based on overlay tracing of the photo-mosaic and the direct visual sketching of the site is shown in Fig. 8.

After the storm of 20-21 July the clean swept rock of quadrat A.01 was inspected and it was found that no silt or sand had been moved onto the rock by wave action. It was concluded from this that ordinary storms could not move fine sand at a depth of 3.7 m on the archaeological site. In contrast to this, there was silt in the superficial sediments at a depth of 4-5 m, but not at 3.5 m. Thus it would appear that the silt fraction has been washed out of the sediments shallower than 4.0 m, and redeposited in deeper water. Many of the ceramic fragments were in the size range 1.0-5.0 cm and their edges were only slightly abraded. Thus the coarser ceramics were probably only abraded during marine transgression, and are not being moved now. In contrast, the large number of small ceramic fragments from A.01 and A.02 of about 0.5-1.0 cm were sub-angular and had rounded edges, indicating longer periods of abrasion. These observations indicate that the coarser artifacts are probably not moved at all in the sheltered conditions in water deeper than 2.0 m. Since the rock drops almost vertically to 1.9-2.0 m, there is no opportunity to observe the transport phenomena in shallower water. The rock adjacent to the shore is very steep and irregular, and there are no sediments except in gulleys.

As against these factors suggesting minimal sediment particle movement, it should be noted that an indicative characteristic of the submerged archaeological site is the relative lack of weed in comparison with the surrounding rock. This may be due to the inability of algae to grow on the sand and gravel present, whether it moves or not; or it may be due to occasional movement and abrasion.

Vita Finzi (personal communication, 1982) made a preliminary

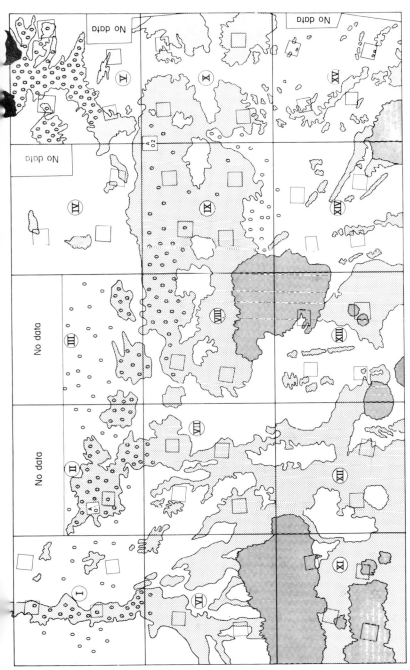

FIG. 8. *Distribution of natural surface materials within the grid area. Fine stipple = sand; wavy lines = thick weed; scattered circles = gravel; stipple and circles = sand and gravel; solid black = large boulders. The unshaded white area is almost bare rock in the shallower part of the site; in the deeper part of the site it is rock or sediment covered with a thin layer of weed giving the superficial appearance of rock. The small quadrilaterals represent the scale frames placed in each photograph, and are 1 m square. The frames do not appear square in every case, since the bottom was not flat, and the frames are tilted. The map was compiled by direct tracing from photographs (see Plate 3). There is a tendency for the centre of each photograph, where the angle of view is vertical, to show sand; whilst near the edge of the photographs the irregularities or scattered weed conceal the sand. The grid spacing is 10 m.*

analysis of the sedimentary material and commented that samples contained stained gravel and a sufficiently large silt/clay proportion to indicate rapid submergence and minimal wave action, at least for the deeper samples. He considered that submergence was at times rapid enough for alluvial deposits to be drowned without prolonged exposure to the sorting effects of wave action. During the search for the Neolithic site remains several other artificial structures were discovered offshore from the Aghios Petros islet. Three rectangular piles of boulders were found in depth ranging from 1.5 to 5 m, for locations, see Fig. 2. Each pile of stones was about 3 m by 2 m in plan area, and composed of large pale coloured rounded stones 10-20 cm in diameter.

No explanation of the origin or function of these stones can be suggested. They are not connected to the island, and so do not appear to be moles or jetties or mooring places; it is unlikely that they are dumped ballast because of the compact shape of the mounds; it is also unlikely that they are ballast from wrecked boats. On the other hand, if they are submerged structures originally built on land, there is no obvious function for them. They would have been close to the shore during the last phase of marine transgression during the Late Neolithic-Early Bronze Age, but no similar structures have been reported by archaeologists working on the island.

DISCUSSION

Introduction

It is not the purpose of the present paper to interpret the archaeological artifacts in any way in terms of cultural associations, or even function. Suffice it to say that the submarine quadrats produced Early Neolithic and Bronze Age ceramics. The questions which have to be addressed are: does the evidence suggest that the archaeological materials are *in situ*, or have they been transported or scattered by wave action? What was the sea level at the time of occupation, what was the topography of the site, and was there a specific harbour area? How did the occupation area react to marine transgression? How was the occupation of the site influenced by the continuously changing sea level during the period of occupation? These questions will be considered in the following sections.

Topography and Sea Levels

The pronounced submerged solution notch and undercut which occurs all round Aghios Petros islet and the neighbouring coast indicates tectonic submergence of 30-50 cm recently. For a review of the various theories of the process of solution of limestones by sea water see Higgins (1980). The submerged notch is undercut by 1.0-2.0 m in some places, indicating a prolonged stillstand. The submerged notch is similar in the depth that it is cut back into the cliff to those sea level notches outside the bay at present sea level. Within the bay there is no notch at present sea level. The simplest interpretation of these facts is that the sea level reached present sea level and maintained constancy, or near constancy for several thousand years. Within the last few hundred years a part of the coast, including Aghios Petros, subsided by 30-50 cm, and there has not been a new notch cut in the subsequent short period.

There is a complicating factor. The undercut notches around Aghios Petros are not sharp solution notches, but in many places continue downwards in deep scalloped undercuts, forming small curved cliffs which only flatten out into terraces at depths of 1.5 - 2.25 m. (See profiles in Fig. 5 and Fig. 9.) An alternative interpretation is that the eustatic sea level rise terminated with the sea at a relative level at -2 m abutting against Aghios Petros, and that subsequent gradual or periodic tectonic submergence totalling 1.5 m created the deep undercut up to the 0.3 - 0.5 m level. A final and more abrupt submergence of 0.5 - 0.3 m caused the notch system to drop below the sea level altogether.

Complete profiles (Fig. 9) across the archaeological site show that there is a terrace feature immediately seaward of the low cliffs. Fifteen metres seaward, on the NE profile, the gradient increases, and becomes realigned with the overall gradient from sea level to -10 m. The change of gradient on each profile takes place at a depth of about -4.5 m. The presence of sand and gravel at this depth, the absence of rounding of pottery, and the observation of zero sediment movement during the storm of 20-21 July indicate that no erosion is taking place at depths of -4.0 - 4.5 m in present conditions. This suggests that the terrace undercut feature was initiated at a relative sea level of about -1.0 - 2.0 m, since the water depth at the outer edge of the terrace would then only have been 2.5 - 3.5 m, which would be within the equivalent depth of maximum wave action today.

On this hypothesis the archaeological site would have been exposed to wave action and solution over a 15-20 m wide zone which would have removed large quantities of solid rock. The site deeper than 4.5 m would have been exposed to steady marine transgression, whilst the site above that depth would first have been exposed to a relatively long stillstand, and then progressively decreasing wave action as the subsidence continued. When the relative sea level attained the present level, the terra rossa on land was washed down by spray action, and the archaeological materials scattered over the previously eroded and dissolved area. The original archaeological objects from the eroded/dissolved zone would have been scattered down-slope before erosion commenced.

This hypothesis is complex and based on circumstantial evidence. Granted that there was a prolonged stillstand at -0.3 to -0.5 m, the wave action at that time was effective to about -3.5 m, which is close to the observed break of slope at -4.5 m. Exceptional storms from the west or south west might create sufficient water movement to deepen the outer edge of the terrace. The cliff-terrace feature is not present at all points around Aghios Petros, and the lower parts of the scalloped undercut may be exceptionally deep solution features. Tectonic subsidence is not the direction of motion to be expected on the up-throw side of the graben wall of the Anatolian Trough, but such movements are often associated with frequent local reversals and stick-slip phenomena (Flemming, 1978; Le Pichon and Angelier, 1980). On the available evidence it seems most probable that there was a gradual or periodic phase of tectonic subsidence followed by recent abrupt submergence by 0.3 - 0.5 m.

The submarine topography is shown by Fig. 2. As stated by Theocharis (1970) the northern corner of the bay, near Aghios Petros, is the best natural harbour for many kilometers in all directions, and a lowered sea level would improve the shelter. The prolongation of the islet to the SW below present sea level means that the shelter provided at a period when the sea level was 10 m lower than present would be extraordinarily secure. Various potential sea level indicators were checked inconclusively. The small cliffs to the south of the islet from 9 - 11 m suggest erosion as does the small cliff in square XIII of the grid, but there is no way at present of dating them. The contact between the rocky substrate of the archaeological site and the sandy bottom to the north suggests a shoreline or beach, but the sand may have accumulated considerably after marine transgression. On the other hand, the presence of sherds in the sand indicates allow rate of accretion, and also suggests that the occupied area may have extended north-west from the rock-sand junction.

The contours of the inlet to the north-west of the islet show that, assuming no sediment infill, a sea level at -9 m would have produced a long narrow inlet extending well to the north-east of the archaeological site. This long narrow inlet would have had two small streams draining into it, and would have made a perfect natural harbour about 1.0 m deep. A sea level at -10 m to -11 m would produce a much less indented bay, but still a sheltered water area adjacent to the settlement. A sea level at -13 to -15 m would result in a 40 m wide zone between the present sand-rock boundary at the edge of the site and the contemporary waterline. The topography of the rock ridge extension of the islet was not sounded beyond a depth of 11.0 m, and so the degree of shelter provided is not certain at the -15 m level.

Typical eustatic sea level curves for the Mediterranean (Labeyrie *et al.*, 1976; Kraft *et al.*, 1977) predict sea level of -20 m at 8,000 B.P., -15 M at 6-7,000 B.P., and -10 m at 5-6,000 B.P. These figures are all consistent with the occupation of the site to a depth of 10 m at 7,000 B.P. Thus, apart from indicating that the sea level must have been lower than -10 m at 7,000 B.P., the evidence obtained so far from Aghios Petros does not provide accurate data on sea levels. Since the sea level was rising progressively during the period 8,000 - 5,000 B.P., it is not surprising that no signs of stillstand, erosion, or solution, are detected. On the other hand, older ceramics might be found deeper than -10 m and younger ceramics shallower, indicating response to the rising sea level. This possibility will be discussed further below.

Sequence and Effects of Inundation

An isometric projection of the grid area is shown in Fig. 9, for reference in the following discussion.

The land site consists of artifacts and bones embedded in terra rossa up to 1.4 m thick (Theocharis, 1970). The red earth itself is fine grained, and, if we assume that the archaeological deposits of the submerged area were similar to those now on land, it is natural that all the fine-grained materials have been washed away, even in the absence of strong wave action. The angular stones and pebbles of the terra rossa, together with the archaeological objects, then settled to the sea floor, and became mixed with marine sands and silts. This sequence could be checked by analysis which there was not time to carry out. Firstly, the total quantity of both natural stones and artifacts and bones in a column of terra rossa on the island could be measured, and the quantity compared with that found at present on the sea floor. Comparison of the size and shape composition of the cobbles on the sea floor with those in the terra rossa would add further confirmation.

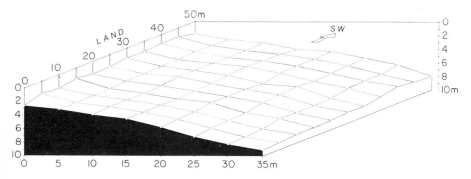

FIG. 9. *Isometric view of the grid from the north, based on the soundings shown in Fig. 6. No vertical exaggeration.*

The principle ambiguity in interpretation of the site is estimation of the degree of erosion and scattering of materials during transgression. The simplest model implies that the artifacts and bones in a column of terra rossa settle vertically to the sea floor. This is an oversimplification. At the present shoreline the run-up of waves and spray washes terra rossa into the sea from a height of 1-2 m above still water level. The width of the swash zone between the land trenches and the submerged site is 7-8 m of bare rock. Is it possible that all the archaeological objects found in the submerged site area could have been washed off this zone of bare rock?

On the basis of gross quantities, it is unlikely that 1.4 m thickness of terra rossa spread over an area about 8 m by 50 m could contain sufficient archaeological material to cover a trapezoidal area 50 m on one edge, 75 m on the long edge, and 35 m wide. The area of the swash zone is about 400 sq m, and that of the whole submerged site (including deposits outside the grid) about 2,000 sq m. The ratio is 1 to 5. The land archaeologists (Efstratiou, Michos, personal communications) stated that the volume of artifacts and bones recovered from 1 sq m underwater would only be produced by excavating a considerable depth of soil on land. Thus the concentration of archaeological objects in the 400 sq m swash zone would have to be quite extraordinary to produce a distribution of objects over 2,000 sq m underwater. This explanation is therefore very unlikely, even granted that only half the submarine area is thick with archaeologically rich deposits.

Terra rossa and archaeological objects clearly have been washed off the swash zone, and from the first 3-5 m of the underwater zone. Thus a zone 10-12 m wide has been cleared of artifacts and bones by wave action at present sea level. In this case all items are moved 10-12 m offshore and redeposited, with additional lateral movement randomly alongshore which would probably be of the order of several metres.

As discussed above, the erosion or solution of the cliff-terrace feature is problematical. Let us consider first the simpler case of the marine transgression over a smooth gradient of 1/4, between the depths of -10 up to -5 m. At each level the spray or wave run-up would wash away the terra tossa up to about 2.0 m above still water level, whilst submarine wave action would tend to move material downslope to a depth of -2 to -3 m. Thus material could be moved about 4.0 m vertically, or 16 m horizontally. Archaeological material from a depth of -10 m could be moved, for example, offshore into an area which was previously open sea, and this may account for the sherds found on the open sand. Similarly, sherds from 15 m offshore could have been moved downslope to a distance 30 m offshore, and sherds from the present shoreline could be moved 15 m offshore.

It is however notable that sherds, flints, etc., are not heavily abraded or rounded, with the exception of the smallest fragments of pottery.   There are two possible explanations: the downslope transport is arrested, either by irregularities of the bottom, or by accumulations of stable sediments.   The drawings and photographs of the grid area show that irregularities in the sea floor, gulleys downslope, and bedding planes across slope, create concentrations of that sediment which is in the zone shallower than -5.0 m. These thick concentrations (10-25 cm thick) are separated on a scale of 5-10 m.   Thus few archaeological fragments would move more than 5-10 m before getting trapped.

The bands and patches of clastic material within irregular depressions are stable under present conditions, but possibly only because of the supporting projections of bedrock nearby.   At depths greater than -5.0 m there are thicker layers of sand, together with weed, which indicate that the sediments are stable. Archaeological materials reaching the sand would become embedded, and protected from further abrasion.

Assuming maximum disturbance of the site, every archaeological object could have been removed from its original point of deposition on land, and transported 10-15 m downslope by swash and wave action, and moved randomly several metres alongshore. Still assuming worst case disturbance, the sea level reached to within one or two metres of present sea level, washed the archaeological materials off a 10-15 m wide zone, and dissolved and eroded out the cliff-terrace feature.   Tectonic subsidence brought the wave action into contact with more terra rossa and archaeological fragments, and the latter were then deposited on the rock terrace.

A model assuming less disturbance would suggest that only the smaller fragments were moved as much as 10-15 m during the transgression, and that many of the larger ones were only moved 5-10 m, or less, before becoming embedded in stable fine-grained sands.   When the eustatic stillstand occurred the dominant effect was solution of the limestone, and mechanical erosion and abrasion were minimal.   Artifacts within the solution/erosion zone were transported downslope relatively unabraded, whilst objects washed off the land were transported through the zone.   After the final tectonic subsidence materials were washed off the land and redeposited on the shallower edge of the terrace.

It is impossible to distinguish between these two models on the present evidence.   In both cases stratigraphic vertical context has been destroyed, though in the second model assemblages might still preserve considerable relational context.   There is a close analogy with the assemblages which have been analysed in archaeological excavations of shipwrecks which have been disturbed by waves and currents (Muckelroy, 1979).   One very important point must be stressed.   The site does exist underwater as an assemblage of Neolithic and Bronze Age objects covering an area similar to that which is common for neolithic settlements. Even if every object has been displaced 10 m downslope, the total assemblage does still exist as a concentration of archaeologically significant materials. If the sea level were to rise a further 50 m the present submarine site would be enriched by some more artifacts and bones from the present land area, and it would then be totally protected from any further wave or current action. If divers were to find such a site under 55-60 m of water they would be rewarded by discovering a very substantial and complex site, albeit slightly displaced from its original location.

The Aghios Petros submarine site has already survived the most extreme levels of marine attack which it is ever likely to undergo, and it is still recognizable. It has even survived a 3,000-5,000 year stillstand and continuous wave attack and rock solution cutting through the site area. From the point of view of maximum survival potential it is a disadvantage that the gradient of the site is 1/4 rather than 1/10 to 1/20. Because of the relatively steep gradient it was not possible for stable beach sands to accumulate in the wave zone. If such beaches had formed, it is possible that artifacts and bones might have been moved less than a metre, or even preserved *in situ* (see, for example, Wreschner, 1977; 1982, this volume).

Archaeological Site Interpretation, and the Harbour

It has been known for many years that seafaring voyages were made during Neolithic times, (Renfrew, 1972; Mellart, 1975, p. 244; Peltenberg, 1975; Theocharis, 1970; Cherry, 1981), and the presence of Neolithic sites on Cyprus, Crete, and Saliagos leaves no doubt. However, nothing is known about the seafaring competence of Neolithic peoples, the efficiency of vessels, the frequency of voyages, the existence of harbours, or the existence of specialisd maritime communities or cultures. Since all Mediterranean Neolithic sites on the sea shore must now be submerged to more or less the same extent as Aghios Petros, only study of these sites can answer the questions.

The first question about the Aghios Petros settlement is, was it a true maritime community, or merely a farming village which happened to be close to the sea? No tools have yet been identified that would confirm a predominance of maritime activity, but circumstantial evidence can be drawn from the topography of the settlement area and the harbour. As Theocharis (1970) pointed out, and as has been explained in the present paper, the north east corner of the bay around Aghios Petros is an extremely secure natural harbour, and would have been much better when the sea level was 5-10 m lower than at present. The bay is used today by fishermen seeking shelter, as well as by luxury yachts and small sailing cruise boats. It is noteworthy that fishing boats always make for the north east corner of the bay and tie up or anchor close to the point selected for the tide staff. Tourist boats anchor in the south east corner which looks prettier because of its proximity to low lying land and an olive grove. The latter anchorage proved to be extremely dangerous during the storm of 20-21 July, and a large motor cruiser of over 100 tons trying to leave the bay was in considerable danger. Local knowledge is correct in selecting the best anchorage.

The fact that the Neolithic settlement is located in the best anchorage for several tens of kilometers does not prove that it was a seafaring community. But consideration of the extreme shelter provided when the sea level was 10 m lower, and the fact that the settlement area seems to broaden towards the ancient waterline, lend further weight. The proximity of the two freshwater springs which flow even in mid-summer increase the suitability of the site for a major settlement.

A settlement in open land tends to be more or less equiaxial, and the town maps of the Neolithic and Early Bronze Age published by Renfrew (1972) and Mellart (1975) illustrate this. A settlement which is on the shore, and oriented towards the sea tends to be more or less semi-circular with the diameter on the waterline. The distribution of artifacts at Aghios Petros tapers to less than 50 m in the longshore direction above present sea level, and broadens out progressively towards the 10 m depth, where the extent is 50-75 m. Even allowing for some spreading during downslope transport, it seems probable that the site was originally wider at the ancient waterline.

The circumstantial evidence is, then, that the community was probably maritime in the nature of its activities. Publication of the full archaeological reports, considering finds from land and under the sea, will provide evidence as to trade connections. More detailed studies underwater may reveal tools such as fish-hooks, net-sinkers, or other equipment related to fishing.

Theocharis (1970) describes a Middle Palaeolithic site on Alonissos, and points out that the Sporadhes islands from the mainland up to Alonnissos are separated by relatively shallow straits which would have been dry 15-20,000 years ago. He also states that the channel between Alonnissos and Kyra Panagia would have been dry. The depth at the shallowest point is 80 fathoms, or 148 m. It is therefore not certain that the channel would have been dry, since the absolute level of the eustatic minimum sea level is not certain. Nevertheless, Theocharis reports Palaeolithic finds on Kyra Panagia, as do Efstratiou and Michos (personal communications). Whether the strait was flooded or not at the time that Kyra Panagia was first occupied, it was certainly flooded soon afterwards.

The environment was thus one in which primitive seafaring may have been forced into existence 15-18,000 years ago. One may speculate as to why people with only primitive and dangerous means of sea transport should sail or paddle from Turkey to Cyprus, or from Kythera to Crete. There is no mystery as to why Palaeolithic communities should have taken to boats when they found that neighbouring settlements were being separated by the rising sea level. Assuming a relative rate of rise of about 10 m per millenium, or 1.0 m per century, the inundation of the channel would have provided a natural nursery for the progressive development of seafaring skills. The same process would have taken place at later dates in other parts of the Sporadhes. At first people moving between settlements, temporary shelters, and hunting grounds would have waded through shallow water. Over the course of a century the water would have become inconveniently deep, especially in windy weather. At some time a simple craft had to be used.

There is no point in speculating in this paper as to the nature of the first craft used in the Sporadhes, or whether the technique was invented locally, or imported, or re-invented again and again over millenia. It is important only to note that it is almost inconceivable that sea travel between the Sporadhes islands should not have been developed during the Palaeolithic.

By the 6th millenium B.C. seafaring and fishing in the Sporadhes islands would have been established and developed arts. The rising sea level would have forced the Neolithic peoples back from the floor of the bay on Kyra Panagia to seek good settlement sites and harbours within 10-20 m vertically of present sea level. The northern slope of the promontory of Aghios Petros was the perfect location.

The sea level did not stop rising. How did the community react? Was the Aghios Petros site only occupied briefly, or did the inhabitants adapt and adjust continuously to the rising sea? The existence of Bronze Age materials suggests the possibility of continuous occupation, although abandonment and re-occupation are equally possible. If the site was continuously occupied, were the waterside sectors rapidly abandoned, or did the cautious occupants always build several metres back from the water, knowing that the sea would overwhelm them within a few generations? The behaviour in this respect depends on whether houses, or other waterside structures, were built to last a few years, a few decades, or generations.

Whether the inhabitants tried to anticipate the sea level rise, or whether they built houses which soon had to be abandoned, it is certain that they all had to be abandoned to the sea sooner or later. It is possible that the lower part of the site may be considerably older than the upper part, and that the settlement was in effect forced uphill by the sea over a millennium or more. This could be demonstrated if, on average, older artifacts were found in the lower part of the site.

No structures or buildings other than the most rudimentary house foundations were found on the land site (Theocharis, 1970; Efstratiou, personal communication), and so it is not surprising that no special structures were found underwater related to maritime activities, fishing, boat-building, quays, etc. Evidence from Bronze Age coastal sites (Harding et al., 1969; Flemming et al., 1978) shows that in spite of advanced shipping, sea trade, and sea warfare, artificial breakwaters and landing places were not built. Thus a Neolithic harbour is unlikely to have had any specialised waterside structures other than the simplest wooden jetties. During a period of rising sea level there were numerous deep inlets, bays and estuaries completely free of alluvial barriers, and therefore there would have been meagre incentive to build artificial harbours.

CONCLUSIONS

The Aghios Petros site illustrates that, on a gradient of 1 in 4, in a sheltered location, the archaeological materials, artifacts, ceramics, bones, and tools, are not destroyed by marine transgression, but are scattered several metres downslope. The slow subsidence between 5,000 B.P. and the present has exposed the shallow half of the site to exceptionally prolonged wave action over a wider zone than would have occurred during a true relative stillstand. If the sea level rose further by several tens of metres the site would be preserved albeit in a disturbed configuration. Preliminary survey and trial sampling provides evidence concerning the original extent of the Neolithic site, shows that it was probably a centre for marine activities, and that it was situated on a perfect natural harbour. Boats were probably built on the beach, and launched or pulled out of the water as required. Although the present coast is devoid of freshwater supply, there are two submarine springs which would have supported the community at Aghios Petros.

Further survey and thorough excavation are required to solve the many questions raised: Date of first occupation? Existence of tools related to marine skills and activities? Archaeological materials in stratigraphic context under the sand in the deeper part of the site? The distribution of artifacts and bones should be analysed to try and establish a pattern of cultural activity within the site area, and to unravel the redistribution which has occurred as a result of marine transgression. An understanding of the processes which have disturbed the Aghios Petros site would be of great value in discovering and understanding older sites in deeper water.

ACKNOWLEDGEMENT

The author is deeply indebted to Mr. Nikos Efstratiou for arranging the archaeological permit to conduct this survey, and for providing facilities in association with the land excavation. I am indebted also to Mr. Peter Nomikos for financial support to the diving team; and to the Royal Geographical Society for loan of equipment. My greatest thanks are due to the divers, T. Alexander, C. Giangrande, S.J. Kleinberg, N. Lowe, and J. Wood, who conducted the survey under extremely arduous conditions. The divers were members of the University of London Underwater Research Group and Cambridge University Underwater Exploration Group. G. Michos of the Museum of Volos represented the Greek Inspectorate of Antiquities, and provided extremely helpful advice and discussion during the work.

REFERENCES

Andersen, S.H. (1980). Tybrind Vig, a preliminary report on a submerged Ertebolle settlement in the Little Belt. *Antikvariske Studier* 4, 7-22

Blackman, D.J. (1973). Evidence of sea level change in ancient harbours and coastal installations. In: *Marine Archaeology*, (ed. D.J. Blackman) pp. 115-139. Butterworths, Colston Papers, London.

Cherry, J.F. (1981)   Pattern and process in the earliest colonization of the Mediterranean islands. *Proceedings of the Prehistoric Society* 47, 41-68.

Drakopoulos, J.C. and Ekonomides, A.C. (1972). Aftershocks of February 19th 1968 earthquake in Northern Aegean Sea and related problems. *Pure and Applied Geophysics* 95, 100-115.

Flemming, N.C. (1978). Holocene eustatic changes and coastal tectonics in the northeast Mediterranean: implications for models of crustal consumption. *Philosophical Transactions of the Royal Society, London, A* 289, (1362) 405-458.

Flemming, N.C., Raban, A. and Goetschel, C. (1978). Tectonic and eustatic changes on the Mediterranean coast of Israel in the last 9000 years. In: *Progress in Underwater Science, Proceedings of the Underwater Association* 5 .Pentech Press, London. pp. 33-93.

Harding, A., Cadogan, G. and Howell, R. (1969). Pavlopetri, an underwater Bronze Age town in Laconia. *Annual of the British School at Athens* 64, 113-142.

Higgins, C.G. (1980). Nips, notches and the solution of coastal limestone: an overview of the problem, with examples from Greece. *Estuarine and Coastal Marine Science* 10, 15-30.

Kraft, J.C., Aschenbrenner, S.E. and Rapp, G. (1977). Palaeogeographic reconstructions of coastal Aegean archaeological sites. *Science* 195, 941-947.

Labeyrie, J., Lalou, C., Monaco, A. and Thommeret, J. (1976). Oceanographie: Chronologie des niveaux eustatiques sur la cote du Roussillon de 33,000 ans BP a nos jours. *Académie des Sciences de Paris, Comptes Rendu* 282, 349-352.

McKenzie, D. (1978). Active tectonics of the Alpine-Himalayan belt: the Aegean Sea and surrounding regions *Geophysical Journal of the Royal Astronomical Society* 55, 217-254.

Mellart, J. (1975). *The Neolithic of the Near East*. Thames and Hudson, London, pp. 300.

Mercier, J.L., Mouyaris, N., Simeakis, C., Roundoyannis, T. and Angelidhis, C. (1979). Intraplate deformation: a quantitative study of the faults activated by the 1978 Thessalonika earthquake. *Nature* 278, 45-48.

Muckelroy, K. (1979). *Maritime Archaeology* Macmillan, New York, and Cambridge University Press.

Peltenberg, E.J. (1975). Ayios Epiktitos Vrysi, Cyprus: preliminary results of the 1969-1973 excavations of a neolithic settlement. *Proceedings of the Prehistoric Society* 41, 17-45.

Philippson, A. (1901). Beitrage zur Kenntnis der griechischen Inselwelt. *Petermann's Geographische Mitteilungen*, Erganzungsband XXIX, Heft 132-137, Nr. 134, 172 pp.

Pichon, X. le. and Angelier, J. (1980) The Aegean Sea. *Philosophical Transactions Royal Society London. A.* 300, 357-372.

Raban, A., 1983 (this volume) Submerged prehistoric sites off the Mediterranean coast of Israel.

Renfrew, C. (1972). *The Emergence of Civilisation: the Cyclades and the Aegean in the third millennium B.C.* Methuen, London, pp. 595.

Theocharis, D.R. (1970). Excavation on the island of Aghios Petros at (Kyra Panagia). *Archeologikon Deltion:* <u>25</u>, Chronica, Thessaly, Museum of Volos.

Wreschner, E.E. (1977). Newe Yam - a submerged late Neolithic settlement near Mount Carmel. *Eretz Israel* <u>13</u>, Israel Exploration Society, pp. 260-271,

CORE SAMPLING OF A HOLOCENE MARINE
SEDIMENTARY SEQUENCE AND UNDERLYING NEOLITHIC
CULTURAL MATERIAL OFF FRANCHTHI CAVE,
GREECE

John Gifford

Archaeometry Laboratory,
University of Minnesota,
Duluth, MN 55812, USA

ABSTRACT

Van Andel and co-workers (1980) have reconstructed the paleogeography of the landscape around the important archaeological site of Franchthi Cave (on the coast of the Argive Peninsula of Greece) as it evolved from a terrestrial to a present marine setting during the post-glacial eustatic sea level rise. In August of 1981 this sediment sequence was cored at two localities in the outer part of Koiladha Bay, between the Franchthi headland and nearby Koronis Island. The sediment sequence in both cores is a dark grey (N4), slightly sandy, organic-rich mud with bioclastic material (mollusc shell fragments, foraminifera tests, bryozoan skeletal fragments, and ostracod valves) distributed unevenly downcore. At the base of core FC1, 5.5 meters below the present bay bottom (in a water depth of 4.5 meters), a stratum rich in mollusc shell fragments and subangular limestone pebbles was found to rest on a hard layer that stopped the corer. From this coarse stratum over 30 pottery sherds were recovered from inside the core casing. Almost all are non-diagnostic coarseware, but the exceptions have fabrics characteristic of Neolithic wares. This was not unexpected, as traces of Neolithic structures, downslope from Franchthi Cave along the present shoreline, were excavated in 1973-74 and 1976(Jacobsen, 1978, p. 83). The nature of these sherds, plus the ecofactual material also recovered from the bases of the two cores, suggest that remains of Neolithic habitation or

QUATERNARY COASTLINES
ISBN 0 12 479250 2

other activity lie *in situ* several hundred meters offshore from Franchthi Cave, buried under 2-6 meters of more recent marine sediments.

INTRODUCTION

Franchthi Cave, on the western coast of the Argive Peninsula of the Peloponnesus, was almost continuously utilized by humans between approximately 26,000 and 5,000 years ago. The extraordinarily deep cultural sequence within the cave was

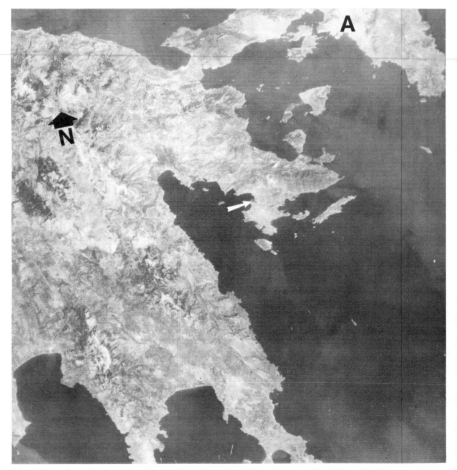

PLATE 1. *A Landsat MSS (Band 4) view of the Peloponnesus (Scene I.D. 8101008375500). North is indicated by the black arrow, while the white arrow points to Koiladha Bay on the west coast of the Argive Peninsula. Athens is indicated by the letter "A".*

excavated and is being studied by a multi-institutional, inter-disciplinary group under the direction of T.W. Jacobsen of Indiana University (see Jacobsen, 1976, for a general account of the site's excavation).

Toward the end of this long cultural sequence, at the beginning of Early Neolithic times *ca.* 8,000 years B.P. utilization began of the slope outside and northwest of the cave entrance. This area, called *Paralia* by the excavators, now lies along the shore of a small, structurally-controlled cove eroded in massive limestone of the Franchthi headland (Fig. 1), at elevations of only 1-2 meters

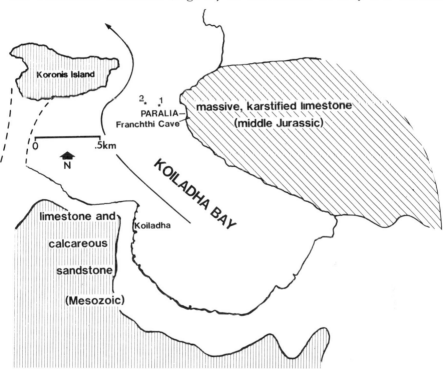

FIG. 1. *Index map of Koiladha Bay and vicinity. The fishing village of Koiladha lies across a shallow bay of the same name from the karstified limestone headland in which Franchthi Cave developed. On the present shore immediately downslope from the cave's original entrance is the Paralia site. Koiladha Bay shallows to a few decimeters along its eastern and southern shores, which are composed of Late Pleistocene and Holocene alluvium and colluvium. The approximate locations of cores FC1 and FC2 are indicated by asterisks. The course of the paleo-Koiladha river channel is shown by the solid arrowed line, and the bedrock (?) saddle southwest of Koronis Island by two dashed lines.*

above present sea level. The site is some 75 meters in horizontal distance and 15 meters vertically from the Franchthi Cave entrance (Plate 2). Interpretation of the stone wall-like structures at Paralia was complicated both by their closeness to modern sea level and by the quantity of post-cultural colluvium (including many limestone boulders) that had accumulated over them. The excavators decided that "There may be vestiges of dwellings here, but much of the seaside Neolithic settlement could now be submerged in Franchthi Bay" (Jacobsen, 1976, p. 84).

Exploration of this intriguing possibility was partially responsible for the marine seismic reflection survey of the area directed by Tj. H. van Andel in the summer of 1979 (van Andel *et al.*, 1980). Sub bottom profiles were obtained in both the inner portion (south of the Franchthi headland) and the outer part of Koiladha Bay; their interpretation produced an evolutionary scheme of post-glacial sea level rise and sedimentation in the area during its transformation from a terrestrial to a marine setting.

Several major conclusions of van Andel *et al.* (1980) that bear on the project described here are paraphrased as follows:

1) Outer Koiladha Bay is now filled with some 2-9 meters of marine sediments representing five successive stages in the post-glacial flooding of the valley now occupied by the bay. The sediments rest on a basal acoustical reflector identified as the Late Pleistocene-Early Holocene land surface.

2) The areal distribution of these sedimentary units is controlled by the pre-transgressive topography of the valley's land surface, which is dominated by a paleo-river channel trending northwestward to the southeast corner of Koronis Island, thence northeastward out to the shelf of the Gulf of Argos (Fig. 1).

3) *Ca.* 7,000-6,000 B.P. sea level was approximately 15 meters lower than at present. A river larger and possibly more permanent than any extant in the local area flowed through the valley south of the Franchthi headland and into a (seasonally-brackish?) slough occupying the lower end of the channel between the headland and Koronis Island. During the period 6,000-4,000 B.P. the slough deepened and migrated upchannel as sea level rose.

4) From approximately 7,000-5,000 B.P. the river channel formed the western scarp of a 300-500 meter wide alluvial slope extending continuously up to the base of the Franchthi headland. On this level area of several hectares may have been the main part of the Neolithic activity area known from the Paralia excavations situated.

In the following preliminary report I will describe the core sampling and analysis of probable Neolithic-age surface sediments underlying the transgressive marine sediments between Franchthi Cave and Koronis Island.

FIELD WORK

From van Andel's reconstruction of the landscape evolution around Franchthi Cave (described previously), it was apparent that, depending on the locality, some 3-6 meters of fine-grained, water-saturated sediments would have to be penetrated to reach any cultural material at or near the Early Holocene land surface. Present water depths between the headland and Koronis Island range from 2-8 meters. The total water/sediment column depth range of 5-14 meters is somewhat too deep for hand coring from a surface-moored platform, and too shallow for effective piston or gravity coring using standard oceanographic equipment. A compromise was found in a hand-operated coring system using a cased hole. Although the equipment was designed for subaerial use in water-saturated sediments, in this project it was operated successfully from the bottom by two SCUBA-equipped divers.

PLATE 2. *Looking northwestward from near the entrance to Franchthi Cave, across the outer portion of Koiladha Bay to Koronis Island. Trenches of the 1973-74 Paralia excavation are visible along the shore of the small cove in the right foreground. An inflatable boat is anchored between Paralia and Koronis Island, over core site FC2. (Photo by R.K. Vincent, Jr.)*

The corer itself is a small (75 cm long x 4 cm o.d.) piston type device fitted with quick-disconnect couplings and meter-long extension rods for incremental coring to a sediment depth of 7 meters. To prevent hole collapse between removal of the core sections, a casing of thick-walled, 7 cm i.d. plastic tubes is manually pushed into the bottom around and ahead of the corer. Additional meter-long casing sections are joined as needed to the top of the string by means of internal threads on each tube section. The corer only partially removes all the sediment within the casing due to the disparity in their diameters; therefore an open-ended steel tube, 6 cm in o.d. and fitted with a one-way flapper valve at its lower end, is inserted into the cased hole alternately with the corer to churn up the excess sediment and remove it from the casing before the next deeper core section is recovered. In this way almost no core contamination from slumping can occur.

In the photograph of Plate 2, taken from near the entrance to Franchthi Cave, a general view of the area of concern is shown, as well as the surface position of core site FC2.

Plate 3 is a closer view of our work boat anchored over core

PLATE 3. *Core site FC1, with the entrance to Franchthi Cave visible above the standing figure, and the Paralia excavation site on the shore above the bow of the inflatable boat. Water depth here is 4.5 meters. Two divers have just brought up the lowermost 2 meters of the plastic core casing (with handle still attached) after manually pulling the casing free of the bottom. (Photo by R.K. Vincent, Jr.)*

TABLE 1.

Field description of cores taken between the Franchthi headland and Koronis Island.

FC1   Water Depth: 4.5 meters

                      Total Core Length: 5.5 meters

0-200 cm   Dark grey (N4), clayey mud, homogenous, with many finely comminuted shell fragments. One articulated *Donax* sp. at 100 cm. Increasing fine sand content toward 200 cm

200-220 cm   Shelly, slightly pebbly dark grey (N4) sandy mud

220-350 cm   Dark grey (N4) mud with scattered broken mollusc shell fragments; increasing percentage of shell fragments downcore.

350-425 cm   Dark grey, shelly slightly pebbly mud

425-550 cm   Shelly, pebbly, muddy sand, increasing pebble percentage downcore.

(Hard surface at 550 cm)

FC2   Water Depth: 5.5 meters

                      Total Core Length: 5.65 meters

0-450 cm   Dark grey (N4), homogenous, clayey mud with slight H$_2$S odour; several large (3-4 cm long) *Cerithium* sp. shells scattered throughout; concentration of small (1 cm) *Donax* sp. shells (many articulated) at 440 cm

450-565 cm   Slightly pebbly, shelly, sandy mud

(Hard surface at 565 cm)

---

site FC1. The coring proceeded more slowly than expected due to the zero visibility conditions that developed soon after the excess muddy sediment was removed from the core hole. Each pair of divers generally spent 60-80 minutes working on the bottom before being relieved by another team.

In a useful modification of the standard operating procedure for this corer, we extruded each core section underwater immediately after it was taken, using as a receptical a pre-labled plastic tube section of suitable length and i.d. After capping, these tubes prevented damage to or contamination of the core sections.

Upon our twice-daily return to the small fishing village of Koiladha, the core sections were sliced lengthwise, described, and sampled every 20 cm. Two cores were taken down to an impenetrable hard substrate; both were located in the area between Franchthi headland and Koronis Island (Fig. 1). A field description of the cores is given in Table 1.

After discovering a 1 cm long pottery sherd in the 480-500 cm. interval of core FC1, we retained all the sediment (about 2 kg) found inside the casing from 500-550 cm (bottom of core). This material was screened through a 1 mm plastic mesh and an additional 32 sherds were picked from the gravelly, shelly sediment residue. All the sherds are in the 0.5-3 cm size range, and all were deposited with the Ephoria Enalion Archaiotition (Underwater Archaeology Branch) of the Greek Antiquities Service in Athens. The sherds are from different coarseware vessels (no joins), and are mostly undiagnostic. One, however, exhibits a black burnish surface treatment that is characteristic of Late Neolithic pottery in the Argolid, and another is of Neolithic Urfinis ware that was in use *ca*. 7,000-6,000 B.P. Four sherds less than 1 cm in maximum dimension were also recovered from the 540-565 cm interval of core FC2 during sediment analysis.

In addition to the sherds, a number of ecofacts - ecological indicators of cultural activity - were found in the basal sediments of both cores: many charcoal fragments (one of *Ficus* sp.) several carbonized *Triticum* sp. caryopses, several small fish vertebrae, possible mud daub fragments, and microscopic flakes of oxidized copper were recovered.

Some edge rounding is evident on most of the sherds recovered from FC1 and FC2, but they are significantly less worn than Neolithic sherds presently found in the swash zone at Paralia. Here (Plate 2), on a narrow, pebble/cobble beach, small sherds occasionally weathering out of the 1973-74 excavation scarps have been abraded by a maximum of seven years of wave activity. Almost all these sherds exhibit advanced edge rounding and complete loss of surface treatments (burnish, paint, incisions). If the sherds from the bottom of cores FC1 and FC2 are comparable in a mechanical strength to those presently on the Paralia beach, then the former were never subject to the degree of wave activity that characterizes this beach.

LABORATORY ANALYSES

Information on local vegetation, paleoecology of local marine habitats, and sedimentary depositional environments can be extracted from the core sediment samples.

For reconstructing the vegetation around the core sites, pollen and phytolith samples are being prepared from each 20 cm section. To compensate for the relatively low pollen concentrations usually found in marine sediments, 30 cm^3 samples are treated in a modified heavy liquid flotation procedure. Counts of 50-100 grains per slide have been obtained for most of the FC1 core samples, and a pollen diagram will be prepared when absolute dates are available for the base of the core (see below).

Splits of the sediment samples are also being processed for their phytolith assemblages. Phytoliths are microscopic opaline silica bodies that form in the tissues of plants, particularly grasses; some have shapes that are diagnostic of certain families or genera of grasses. While the usefulness of phytoliths in vegetation reconstruction is presently more limited than that of pollen grains, their opaline silica composition may resist corrosion better than sporopollenin in an oxidizing microenvironment. Ideally, the two approaches should complement each other.

The marine mollusc assemblages from core FC1 are being examined by J.C. Shackleton (Cambridge University). Variation in shell assemblages downcore may add more detail to reconstructions of coastal zone paleoecology near Franchthi Cave during the Holocene (cf. Shackleton and van Andel, 1980).

Some chronological control on the age of the sediment sections in both cores will be provided by radiocarbon dating. Sufficient charcoal fragments (20-30 mg) have been recovered from the base of both FC1 and FC2 to allow their dating by the accelerator technique.

Granulometric analysis of the core sediments, in combination with mineralogical analyses of individual size fractions, gives some idea of the contemporary depositional environment. Figure 2 illustrates the percentage variation in three size classes down the length of core FC1. Strata at 210 cm and 350 cm below the water-sediment interface are coarser due to a higher percentage of included mollusc shell fragments. Above 400 cm the sediment type is an extremely poorly sorted, slightly gravelly, sandy mud (using Folk's terminology).The medium sand fraction (0.35-0.50 mm diameter) of samples above this level generally comprises 35-40% micro- and macromollusc shells and fragments (most angular and fresh), 15-20% foraminifera tests (without dissolution features), 15-20% bryozoan skeletal fragments, 10-15% non-carbonized plant fragments (probably of the marine grass *Poseidonia*), 5-10% rock fragments (mostly angular, translucent quartz and sub-angular, grey microcrystalline limestone), and 0-5% ostracod valves.

Core FC1: Grain Size Distribution

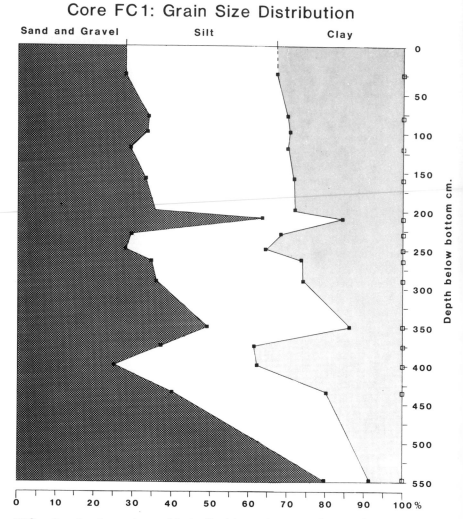

FIG. 2. *Grain size distribution in samples of core FC1;*
sample positions indicated by the open squares along the
right vertical axis. See text for discussion.

In contrast, the sediment in core FC1 from 400-550 cm (bottom)
coarsens downcore to a very poorly sorted, gravelly, muddy sand.
Composition of the medium sand fraction of the 500-550 cm
interval is: 70-75% rock fragments (both igneous and sedimentary,
with subround to round/polished igneous grains common), 10-15%
micro-and macromullusc shell fragments (many showing dissolution

features), 5-10% bryozoan skeletal fragments, and 0-5% foraminifera tests, plant fragments, echinoid spines, and crab claw fragments. Thus the cultural material (microartifacts and ecofacts) discovered in the 500-550 cm interval of core FC1 lay in a sedimentary matrix considerably different than the overlying marine muds of the Holocene transgression.

Yet a third sediment type of relevance to interpreting the depositional environment at the base of core FC1 was documented in the excavations at Paralia. The Neolithic stonework at Paralia was built on an undisturbed "basal red soil" that probably represents a Pleistocene terra rossa deposit. Such a soil is believed also to form part of the basal acoustical reflector identified in the profiler sections from Koiladha Bay (van Andel *et al.*, 1980, p. 394). A subsample of the basal red soil underlying the Paralia excavation was kindly supplied by S. Duhon (Geology Department, Indiana University). Its medium sand fraction differs considerably in composition from the two described above. In this sample (Q10), approximately 40% of the 0.35-0.5 mm size fraction comprises angular mineral grains (translucent quartz and hematite), 30% is of botryoidal carbonate aggregates (secondary), and 30% is of pulverized pulmonate gastropod shells. All these grains are slightly to moderately red stained by iron oxide films.

DISCUSSION AND PRELIMINARY CONCLUSIONS

The coring both at sites FC1 and FC2 was stopped at 550-560 cm below the water-sediment interface by a hard substrate, either in the form of large cobbles or of bedrock. In light of the grain composition and characteristics of the sand fraction overlying this surface, the substrate more likely represents alluvial cobbles and finer alluvium of the drowned Koiladha River bank. Its grain mineralogy is so different from the local terra rossa soil at Paralia that the latter sediment can also be eliminated as being present at the base of the two cores.

Some Neolithic habitation or other activities presumably were located on this small alluvial slope, as was suggested by van Andel *et al.* (1980, p. 400). Although our evidence from two cores is not conclusive, it is unlikely that the cultural material recovered from the bottom of both was redeposited from any great distance upslope, nearer the excavated structures at Paralia. The basis for this supposition rests on: 1) the relatively unabraded appearance of the sherds recovered, and their high density in the sediment volume sampled, and 2) the large quantity of ecofactual material also recovered from both cores. The homogeneous distribution of all these materials of differing densities, weights, and shapes within the sediment volumes sampled by the corer also indicates minimal downslope movement, which would tend to segregate such disparate materials (Rick, 1976).

If it is assumed that Neolithic cultural material does rest *in situ* on the alluvial slope 200-300 meters northwest of the Paralia excavation site, then consideration of how this material was affected by the subsequent shoreline transgression that occurred *ca*. 4,000-3,000 B.P. is in order.

Here two factors of local geomorphology are of importance. First, the alluvial slope representing the presumed Neolithic surface is low angled: from the profiler sections of van Andel *et al*. (1980, p. 395) it must be less than 5%. Secondly, this slope lies in the lee of Koronis Island. Between the southwest corner of this island and the adjacent mainland (Fig. 1) there is a (bedrock?) sill with a controlling depth of 5-6 meters below present sea level. Thus the Bronze Age shoreline transgression could have proceeded up the valley only via the eastern pass between the Franchthi headland and Koronis Island; the alluvial slope and its cultural material remained completely sheltered from any long wave fetch from the Gulf of Argos. That the sedimentary depositional environments accompanying this transgression were always of low energy is demonstrated by the sediments' fine grain size above 400-450 cm depth in both cores.

As a first approximation it is therefore assumed that Neolithic cultural material lay on and partly buried in alluvium on the east bank of the paleo-Koiladha River. A relatively rapid shoreline transgression of minimal energy vertically mixed the upper layer of alluvium (and its included cultural material) with marine muds, but evidently did not sort or horizontally transport this material any distance over the slope. To investigate this point in detail, more cores would be needed to describe adequately the areal distribution of cultural material.

ACKNOWLEDGEMENTS

I thank T.W. Jacobsen (Indiana University) and Tj. H. van Andel (Geology Department, Stanford University) for their encouragement and assistance in planning this project and in discussion of its results; the Ephoria Enalion Archaiotiton (Underwater branch of the Greek Archaeological Service) for granting the necessary permissions for the field work; T. Cullen (Indiana University), K. Pope (Stanford University), V. Arvanitopoulos (Hellenic Institute of Underwater Archaeology), and N. Lianos (Ephoria Enalion Archaiotiton) for their crucial assistance in the underwater coring; J. Hansen (University of Minnesota) for identification of charcoal and carbonized seeds; J.C. Shackleton (Cambridge University) for comments on the molluscan fauna at Franchthi; and C.L. Hill (Archaeometry Laboratory, University of Minnesota) for undertaking the granulometric analyses and drafting the accompanying figures. This project was funded by a grant from the Committee for Research and Exploration of the National Geographic Society.

REFERENCES

van Andel, Tj. H., Jacobsen, T.W., Jolly, J.B. and Lianos, N. (1980). Late Quaternary history of the coastal zone near Franchthi Cave, southern Argolid, Greece. *Journal of Field Archaeology* 7, 389-402.

Jacobsen, T.W. (1976).   17,000 years of Greek prehistory. *Scientific American* 234, 76-87.

Jacobsen, T.W. (1979). Excavation at Franchthi Cave, 1973-74. *Archaiologikon Deltion* 29B, 269-282.

Rick, J.W. (1976).   Downslope movement and archaeological intrasite spatial analysis. *American Antiquity*, 41(2), 133-144.

Shackleton, J.C. and van Andel, Tj.H. (1980). Prehistoric shell assemblages from Franchthi Cave and evolution of the adjacent coastal zone. *Nature* 288, 357-359.

MESOLITHIC SETTLEMENT ON THE
SEA FLOOR IN THE STRAIT OF ÖRESUND

Lars Larsson

*Institute of Archaeology, University of Lund,
S-223 50 Lund, Sweden*

ABSTRACT

Submarine bogs have been found in the strait of Öresund, the
stretch of water separating the Island of Zealand in Denmark from
Scania, Sweden. Stratigraphic studies of these have provided
information regarding sea-level during the Boreal period
(7000-6000 B.C.) and indicated that large areas, now submerged,
were then habitable and suitable for settlement by man. A
reconnaissance was made in 1979 and 1980, in an effort to localise
settlement sites in the area of the now submerged western-most
channel of the river Saxån outside Landskrona. Artifacts
uncovered during dredging etc. had earlier indicated that such
sites existed, both here and elsewhere in the Öresund. By means
of sea-bottom samples obtained from ship-board and skin-diving
searches, two sites were located. One of these yielded artifacts
datable to between 6400 and 6000 B.C. Together with earlier
finds within the reconnaissance area three, and probably four sites
have now been indicated. Results show that coastal settlement
during the Boreal period tends to follow a pattern of localisation
similar to that which applied to settlement-area preferentials
during the later Atlantic period.

INTRODUCTION

Recent years have seen a marked increase in the investigation of
sub-aqua antiquities in Sweden. This is largely due to a mutually
rewarding rapport between the antiquarian authorities and the

many sub-aqua diving clubs, whose number and membership are
steadily increasing. This good relationship has made it possible to
embark on more extensive projects, such as the surveying of
shipwrecks along parts of the Swedish coast (Cederlund, 1976). The
inventory has hitherto been concentrated upon constructions and
remains connected with maritime activities such as ships, harbours
and blockades (Ingelman-Sundberg, 1972; Lundstrøm, 1978).
Documentation of constructions not directly connected to
navigation has been exceptional - one such exception being the
excavation of Bulverket in Tingstäde Marsh on the island of
Gotland (Zetterling, 1927, 1928). This can be nominally compared
to the extensive excavation of submerged sites from the Neolithic
and Bronze Age carried out in Switzerland (Ruoff, 1976,1981;
Stickel, 1976). These excavations have, however, been made in
lakes, where conditions are quite unlike those in a marine
environment.

The Basis for a Reconnaissance

Traces of sea-bottom Boreal human settlements have not been
observed earlier because the major part of Scandinavia has been,
over a long period of time, in a state of isostatic movement, and
still is. It is only in the southernmost part, i.e. Denmark and
Scania, that the isostatic uplift has culminated and been replaced
by a lowering, and where the original shore-line has been
submerged since the Mesolithic. In Scania, as well as further to
the north, there are several examples of sites that have been
submerged for longer or shorter periods of prehistory, where the
whole scale of damage by sea-erosion can be observed, from sites
only marginally effected to those almost obliterated. In some
cases it is even possible to ascertain both extremes on the same
site.

Information regarding the position of the original shore line and
the eustatic movements which caused large areas to become
submerged during the middle part of the Mesolithic is very
fragmentary. In a reconnaissance sense, this poor basis becomes
even more apparent when compared to knowledge about later
sea-level changes (Berglund, 1964, 1971; Digerfeldt, 1975).

The existence of submerged bogs along the coast of Denmark and
Scania has been known for a long time. By studying the
stratigraphy of these bogs, scattered but still usable, information
about sea-level changes during the Early Post-Glacial period can
be obtained. Special attention has been paid to the bogs found at
the southern part of the Öresund strait, where several
core-samples have been taken in bogs as deep as about 20 m below
the present sea-level (Jessen, 1920, 1935; Ødum, 1951; Krog, 1965).
Some of the bogs have a stratigraphy showing thicker or thinner
layers of organic litter deposited in a limnic environment. Above

this layer one or several layers which have been formed in an environment with brackish water, probably some kind of lagoon, are found. The problem of studying the eustacy has been to fix exactly the level of the change from a limnic to a more marine-influenced environment, and to determine when this change occurred. Most of the core samples have been subjected to pollen analysis. However, since few samples were taken, information about the exact age of the deposition is very scanty. The analyses show, however, that Öresund at the latitude of Copenhagen held fresh-water basins down to a level of more than 19 m below the present sea level during the early part of the Boreal period (Fig. 1). It is not possible to achieve a fixed standpoint from which to identify which changes occurred, apart from ascertaining that the sea level rose during the Boreal period. On the basis of stratigraphic studies made along the coast of Halland, the province adjoining Scania in the north, Mörner thinks that certain levels of the core samples from the Öresund strait can be correlated to three stages during the Boreal period, named ALV-1, ALV-2 and ALV-3 (Mörner, 1969, p. 276 ff.). During the Late Boreal period the shore should be situated at a level of between 15.3 m and 12.8 m below sea level. Iversen places the same shoreline at 13 m below sea level (Iversen, 1973, p. 73).

At the transition from the Boreal to the Atlantic period there are some radio-carbon datings giving some information about the location of the original shore. A tree found at -5 m in the Landskrona harbour has been dated to 6150 ± 100 B.C. (Mörner, 1969, p. 358). The heart-wood from a tree deposited in a peat bog at a depth of -3.7 m at Sjölunda at the mouth of the River Sege å was dated to 6125 ± 100 B.C. (Sigling, 1963, p. 54; Mörner, 1969, p. 360). Finally there are two dates, with a variation of 6040 ± 160 B.C. and 5945 ± 115 B.C. from wood found in a peat bog at a level of -8 m in the Limhamn harbour (Persson, 1962, p. 15). This means that the shore of the bay open to the Kattegat and running down to the latitude of Malmö had not reached the level of about -5 m in Landskrona nor the level of about -8 m in Limhamn. On the other hand, there is no acceptable information about how much lower the shoreline was situated. It is not until almost a millennium later that a situation more rich in information occurs, in which a transgression raised the sea to a level almost the same as the present one.

We have finds indicative of human activity in areas now submerged. A tool determined as some kind of knife made of reindeer antler has been found on the Danish side of the Öresund. It is dated to the Older Dryas period and as such constitutes one of the earliest indications of human activity yet known in Scandinavia (Iversen, 1973, p. 36 ff.). During the dredging of the harbour at Limhamn in 1891, artifacts were found at a level of about 2 m below sea level. The finds included core axes, blade

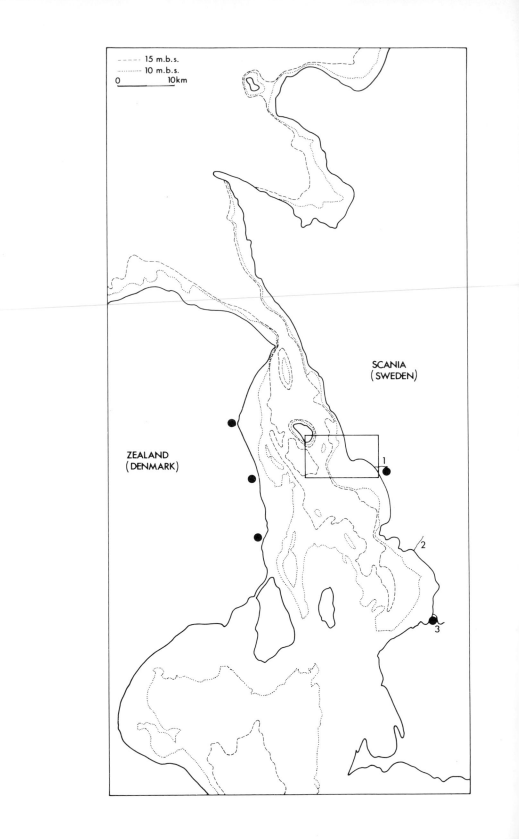

FIG. 1. *The strait of Öresund with the surrounding land. The framed part shows the position of the area of reconnaissance. The dots mark concentrations of sites from the Atlantic period. 1: river Saxån; 2: river Lödde å and 3: river Sege å.*

scrapers and a large amount of waste. Some bones and a slotted bone point were also found (Salomonsson, 1971, p. 41). Based on the knowledge of sea level changes, this assumed site should be dated to the middle or to a relatively late part of the Early Atlantic period, as the refuse layer of a coastal site like Segebro, dated to the centuries prior to 5000 B.C. is found at a level of between 0 and 1 m below sea level (Larsson, 1982).

A rich amount of material exists from the Boreal period of inland settlement of South Scandinavia. That some contact was maintained with the coast is testified by finds of seal bones or seal teeth at inland sites both on Zealand in Denmark and in Scania (Degerbøl, 1933, p. 376; Larsson, 1978, p. 51 ff.). Some sites like Melsted on the Island of Bornholm and Tobisborg in southeastern Scania were situated in a coastal environment but cannot be considered as true coastal sites (Becker, 1952, p. 97 ff. Strömberg, 1976, p. 11 ff.). Furthermore, important indications of contact between Zealand and Scania during the Boreal period are the several striking parallels in the tool kits from the two areas. The stretch of water, then relatively narrow, was easily navigable while a land bridge, which joined Zealand with Scania in their southern parts during the whole period, facilitated such contacts.

METHODS AND FIELDWORK

Choice of Reconnaissance Area: The Atlantic Model

In order to find true coastal sites, it was necessary to reconnoitre the Öresund at the sea bottom. On the face of it, this seemed to reflect the old adage of seeking the needle in the haystack. However, applying the knowledge of the geography of Atlantic period settlement and using this as a basis, it was possible to reduce the search-area and limit it to locations within which settlement remains might reasonably be expected to be found.

Excavation of coastal sites on both the Danish and Scanian sides of the Öresund, dated to the Early and Late Atlantic periods (6000-3000 B.C.), indicates a certain systematization in terms of settlement-area preferentials. The sites do not seem to be spread randomly, but rather have formed clusters at narrow bays, as on the Danish side, or close to the mouths of rivers, as on the Scanian side (Vang Petersen, 1976, p. 85 ff.; Larsson, 1980a, 1980b, 1982). The reason for this is probably the desire to place the site

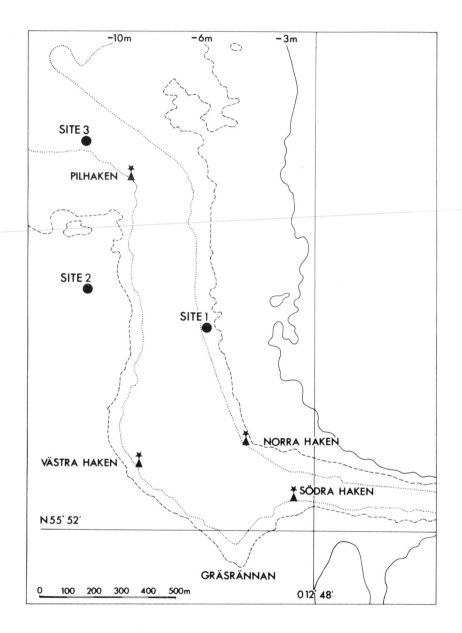

FIG. 2. *The area of reconnaissance. The above map shows the position of the area. The map opposite shows the position of the three underwater sites. Legend; 1: contour of 30 m below sea level, 2: contour of 20 m below sea level and 3: the submerged river channel.*

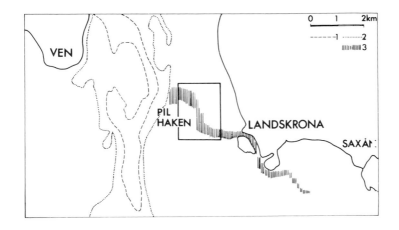

FIG. 2. *(cont)*.

close to the sea while at the same time protecting it from direct exposure to heavy wave or current action. A river-mouth environment provided excellent opportunities for hunting and fishing in different ecological zones - the densely forested hinterland, the river valley with fresh water, the delta with brackish water and the sea close by with its salt water - each abundant in a wide variety of species peculiar to their milieu. This combination of several zones within a limited area ensured optimal production of biomass and facilitated a more than tolerable level of subsistence. These will have been the determining factors in settlement-area location and ones which ensured that the site could support a permanent, or at least a semi-permanent settlement lasting most of the year, without causing any great changes in the ecological balance.

The basis for the reconnaissance has, therefore, been the assumption that the submarine Boreal sites would have been located in a similar environmental situation, despite a somewhat different combination of flora and fauna. It was decided that we should attempt to follow the streams of present rivers into the sea bottom and out to presumed submerged deltas down to a depth of 20 m below sea level at the most. A study of the nautical charts covering the Öresund showed that the marks of only a few rivers could be ascertained on the sea floor. Of these, only the submarine valleys of the rivers Löddeå and Saxån could be documented in detail in the bottom topography. Most distinct was the submarine valley of the latter river which, from a point some hundred metres outside the present mouth, is marked by a channel several metres deep running in a sharp S-shape, starting at almost right-angles to the present mouth and ending in a delta between Landskrona and the Island of Ven (Fig. 2). That Landskrona has such a good harbour is precisely due to the presence of this submarine river channel.

Just outside Landskrona the channel is a few hundred metres wide and about 10 m deep, while at the former delta the channel is twice as wide and has a depth of about -20 m. To the west of the upper part of the submarine river there is a bank called Pilhaken with a width of 1 km and a top reaching up to between 5 and 3 m below the present sea level. Comparison with site localization during the Atlantic period, as exemplified by Häljarp situated near the River Saxån, or by Segebro, situated near the River Sege å, indicates that the area around the distal part of the submarine river channel would have been highly attractive to hunter/gatherers (Larsson, 1980a, 1982). That submarine sites might be found there was indicated by earlier finds of worked flint from Pilhaken. When taking core samples in the 1930's for the purpose of making an examination of sea-bottom fauna, marine biologists found these artifacts in borings at the distal part of the bank. This was also confirmed by scraping the bottom at right angles to the bank in the autumn of 1975, when several flints were torn up from a depth of between -12 m and -20 m (Rausing and Larsson, 1977, p. 3 ff.).

The reconnaissance

A closer assessment of both submarine river banks was carried out during two weeks in August 1979, using the survey ship Carolina from the University of Lund. The survey included scraping the bottom at fixed places at intervals of 50 m, as well as inspection and sample-collection by skin divers. A scraper with a round front proved to be the most suitable for this method of sampling. A rather small number of samples revealed that the area which could be surveyed was limited, due to a variety of factors. The bottom of the northwestern part of Pilhaken proved to consist of large stones, where the scraper would not work. On the other hand, such a surface was not suitable for settlement, either. More problematic was the limitation caused by modern pollution; namely layers of hydrocarbon compounds with a thickness of more than 10 cm covering the bottom of the submarine river banks and channel at a depth of more than -8 m.

The abundant presence of common sea mussels complicated the scraping (Plate 1). The position of the survey area close to a heavily trafficked sailing lane, as well as fishing nets, was a factor which caused inconvenience during the sampling.

About 150 bottom samples were taken along lines marked by buoys. Every sample, with weights varying from five to twenty-five kilos, was water-sieved and sorted at sea. The sampling showed that the bottom close to the submarine river mouth consists of sand. Core samples taken by skin divers using a

PLATE 1. *A typical view of the bottom inside the area of reconnaissance with the sand covered by sea mussel. The open area marks the track of a bottom scraping. Photo by Johnny Bengtsson.*

drill sampler demonstrated that the sand had a thickness that in places was thinner than 10 cm and that the sand covered a much thicker layer of boulder clay. A few large stones were registered inside the research area. In addition there was an abundance of flints showing a dull greyish surface and with clear marks from frost splitting. Marks of preparation were not observed on these flints.

The Sites

Worked flints were found in two places. The first documented site is situated on the eastern side of the submarine river channel at a depth between -8 and -6 m (Fig. 2). At this site, named Site 1, no more than 12 flints were found within an area with a diameter of less than 20 m. In spite of the fact that several scraping samples were taken directly at sea bottom by divers, no more artifacts were found. In this connection, however, it should be noted that an area, the topography of which has been altered by dredging, adjoins with this presumed site. A furrow was cut into the bottom and the stratigraphy registered. This shows a sand layer with a thickness of 15 cm underlain by clay. Probably Site 1 is either the remains of a short stay, or the distal part of a larger site now destroyed by dredging.

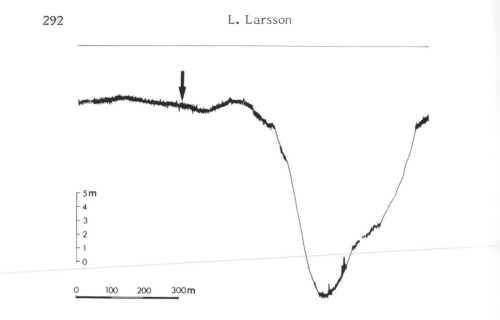

FIG. 3. *Profile of the bottom close to Site 2, based upon sonar soundings.*

More information could be gained from a second find spot that was first found on the next to last day of the 1979 summer season. Worked flints were found inside an area which diving in the autumn of 1979 and early summer of 1980 showed to have an extent of about 40 m in a north-south direction and about 35 m in an east-west direction. This site, named Site 2, is situated at a depth of between -5 and -6 m on a slight slope grading to the east, towards the river channel. The distance to the channel is about 100 m. The profile in Fig. 3 is based on sonar soundings and shows the location of Site 2. The slope mentioned above can also be seen. Close to the river channel there is a gentle rise. About 200 m towards the west the area reaches its highest point at about -4 m and thereafter slopes gradually off to the western side of the bank. The stratigraphy showed a sand layer with a thickness of 25 cm and lacking the characteristic dark coloring associated with human activity. Remains of organic sediments such as peat or mud were not found within or close to Site 2. This condition is, of course, not unusual in these climates. Several instances are known of Atlantic sites which, due to transgressions above present sea level during the Early Neolithic phase, have lain submerged for longer or shorter periods. The highest transgression was approximately 5 m above present sea level, but these sites are today found on dry land. Among these some display remnants of organic sediment while others display none at all, without, in the latter cases, detracting from the fact that the sites are *de facto* settlement areas.

PLATE 2. *The appearance of the seabed at Site 2. Besides the dark, living sea mussel, many of those shells having the same distribution as the worked flints can be seen. Photo by Johnny Bengtsson.*

Inside the find area the bottom consisted of sand with a mixture of shells from *Mytilus edule, Cardium edule, Tapes aureus* and *Litorina litoria*. This mixture of sand and shells could only be found inside the same area as the distribution of worked flints, indicating that this accumulation of shells has some connection with the remains of human activity on the site (Plate 2).

Due to the limited resources at our disposal, no systematic collection of flint artifacts could be carried out. It was, however, ascertained that the flints collected represent only a small part of the remains from knapping on Site 2.

In contrast to the greyish-coloured flints from Site 1, those found in Site 2 show a blue or blue-white patination. There was a marked variation as to degree of rolling - from a few examples with well-smoothed edges to those with little or no signs of weathering. Twenty nine per cent of all flints found at Site 2 fall into the latter category. While the possibility that the area containing artifacts is a result of secondary deposition by currents cannot be totally excluded, the protected locality, the limited distribution of artifacts and the large number of non-eroded or only slightly eroded flints are factors which strongly suggest that

TABLE I

The artifacts found at the sites of Pilhaken

Site 1

Flake burin	1
Bulbar flakes	6
Bulbar flakes with retouch	1
Flakes	4

Total	12

Site 2

Blade scraper	1
Flake scrapers	2
Flake burin	1
Micro-blade core	1
Flake cores, irregular	3
Flake core with platform	1
Blades	3
Blade fragments	2
Micro-blades	3
Bulbar flakes	95
Bulbar flakes with retouch	2
Bulbar splinters	2
Flakes	83
Flake damaged by fire	1
Flake with retouch	1
Splinter	1

Total	202

Site 3

Blades	2
Bulbar flakes	9
Flakes	5
Flake with retouch	1

Total	17

the site has remained relatively undisturbed since it was abandoned.

The artifact collection has, for reasons given above, the character of a sporadic selection of surface finds, meaning that the composition of flints is not representative of the waste left by the inhabitants. Stronger criteria than usual were applied for separating flints worked by man from natural flints. Only waste showing the clear characteristics of manual working was accepted. As can be seen in the list of finds (Table 1), the majority of worked flints consists of bulbar waste, the bulb of percussion being an easy feature to distinguish. As the total number of artifacts is low, one cannot expect to find a large variety in the tool kit. Classified tools number only four; one small blade scraper with convex end retouch, two flake scrapers - both with retouch of the distal part - and one small flake burin showing one burin edge. The number of blades is low, with only three intact examples and two fragments.

The only artifacts that can be used as chronological indicators are the fragments of a micro-blade core and three micro-blades, (Plate 3). By pollen analysis combined with radio carbon dating,

PLATE 3. *Flint artifacts from Site 2 (Nos. 2-5) and Site 3 (No. 1). 1: blade, 2: flake scraper, 3: fragment of a conical shaped micro-blade core and 4-5: microblades. Photo by Bertil Centerwall.*

the introduction of micro-blade production can be dated to a late part of the Late Boreal period, more precisely to subzone BO 2c, dated to about 6400 B.C. (Welinder, 1971, p. 137; Nilsson, 1964, p.4). This means that Site 2 was not submerged before this time. The type of micro-blade core represented at Site 2 belongs to the earliest type, the conical shaped type, with a rather short period of use. At sites dated to about 6000 B.C. they represent only a small percentage of the total number of micro-blade cores, with the handle core as the dominating type (Larsson, 1978, p. 54 ff.). This is an indication that Site 2 cannot have been used much later than about 6000 B.C., i.e. the transition from the Boreal to the Atlantic period. The previously mentioned peat from the harbour of Landskrona at a depth of -5 m belongs to a very late part of the Late Boreal period. The peat has been formed at the bottom of the river channel or in a basin directly connected with this channel. The depth of formation cannot be used as a basis for a specified sea level determination, as the bottom of a river channel in connection with the river mouth might have a level of one or two metres below the sea level. However, the sea level during the latest part of the Late Boreal can hardly have reached higher than about -4 metres; although it might also have been several metres lower. The location of Site 2, with very small level variations, suggests that it was used before or up to the time when the sea level was situated at the edge of the former bank, i.e. at a level of -6 m or less. Even before this time the area east of Pilhaken constituted a narrow bay with an inflow of salt water from the north and fresh water from the south.

The worked flints found during the 1976 scraping do not have the same patination as the flints from Site 2, meaning that they do not originate from the same site. On the other hand, they were found at a greater depth than the flints from Site 2, namely on a level of between 18 and 12 m below sea level, which indicates that they belong to one or several sites used during an earlier part of the Boreal period.

As mentioned earlier worked flints were found by marine biologists in the 1930s when core samples were taken. The flints, of which the worked ones numbered 17, were found when scraping the bottom at a depth of -23 m in an area close to the northern end of Pilhaken. According to the material brought up by the scraper, the bottom in this particular area contains a lot of small stones that might be the remains of a beach ridge. The worked flints do not give any clue to the dating. The position of the flints, however, indicates that the human activity on this site, named Site 3, must be older than that of Site 1 and Site 2. By sonar soundings of the submerged mouth of the river Saxån, Mörner is able to document the mouth at a level between -24 m and -21 m (1969, p. 274). Mörner connects the stage ALV-1 to a level in this area of -31 m. He puts the transgression from ALV-1 up to ALV-2 at a level of about -13 m starting at 7330 B.C. and ending at about 6900 B.C. This means that Site 3 must be older than the latter date (Mörner, 1969, p. 301). If the flints are directly connected to a beach level then that date can be framed in the interval between 7300 B.C. and 6900 B.C.

In 1976 indications of Mesolithic settlement were also found close to the submarine channel of the river Lödde å, mentioned earlier as a suitable place, like Pilhaken, for finding early coastal settlement (Fig. 1). In 1976 a submarine excavation was made of a quay construction from the Viking period, named Lödde kar and situated about a kilometre out from the present river mouth (Lindqvist, 1976, p. 19 ff.). Close to the construction a large number of flints were found, and some of them showed clear marks of having being worked. Unfortunately, the time for flint collecting was very limited and no finds were made of artifacts giving any clue to the chronological setting of the assumed settlement. The depth of the site is 4 m below sea level. According to our knowledge the site was submerged shortly after Site 2 at Pilhaken, i.e. at an early part of the Atlantic period. A submerged bog was found just some 10 metres from the distribution area of the flint artifacts, although so far no detailed analysis of the stratigraphy has been carried out.

DISCUSSION

These researches indicate that there might still be a large number of settlement remains around the coast of the southern-most part of Sweden which should be taken into account during antiquarian control of marine exploitation such as sand removal, harbour enlargement and bridge construction. All three activities are planned for the Scanian Öresund coast in the near future.

It is evident that the conditions conducive to preservation in cases which are not too extreme might be far better than at Pilhaken. This is confirmed by the sites that today are situated above sea level which have been submerged previously for several millennia. One such example is the Atlantic occupation layers at Segebro (ur 3 in Fig. 1), formed somewhat before 5000 B.C. and covered by the sea shortly after and up to the Bronze Age, i.e. for a time span of at least three millennia (Larsson, 1982). The study of the find conditions showed that those areas not directly oriented towards the sea had not been marked by the transgressions, whereas other areas oriented towards the open water had been exposed to heavy erosion. Later transgressions and ocean currents do not seem to have caused any disturbance in the stratigraphy. A large part of the site was covered by mud and sand so that only the highest part of the settlement area was exposed on the bottom of the sea.

That some submarine sites do contain remains of artifacts made of wood, very seldom preserved on supramarine sites, even in waterlogged areas, is proved by two sites from the Ertebølle Culture excavated in Denmark at Tybrind Vig on the west coast of the island of Fynen and at Dejrø at the north coast of Aerø (Andersen, 1980, p. 7 ff; Skaarup, 1980, p. 3 ff).

The research on Pilhaken is too limited to form a good basis for a detailed description of coastal settlement during the Boreal period. But some conclusions can be drawn. The assumption that the Boreal settlement had a pattern of localisation similar to the Atlantic one, with a clustering at the river mouths, has been confirmed. The possibility that settlement existed along other parts of the coast is not excluded, but it does not change the conclusion that there is a resemblance between Boreal and Atlantic coastal settlement. The study of inland settlement during the Boreal period has given a basis for a model where groups of people 25 to 50 in number formed self-sufficient units that could find their subsistence inland during the whole of the year by seasonal movements. In the Atlantic environment with a dense mixed oak forest and with a large number of lakes overgrown with organic litter, the conditions for a self-sufficient settlement through the whole of the year were worse in the inland of Scania. For this period a model has been suggested whereby the main activities are concentrated on the coastal area, while the inland, here referring to an area situated farther than 10 km from the coast, was used extensively during seasonal settlement by smaller units such as one or two families and during shorter periods, such as the autumn (Larsson 1980a). During the Boreal period the access to food was so favourable that year-round activities could have existed on the coast as well as inland. The finds of seal bone and amber show that the same kind of contact existed between these two settlement zones. The extent of Site 2 at Pilhaken is about 1500 m², which is the same size as the largest inland sites during the Boreal period and coastal sites during the Atlantic period. This area might be interpreted in the same way as those of contemporary or later periods where large settlement areas have been looked upon as the remains of larger and self-sufficient units of several families. Thus the find from Pilhaken gives important information about how future research on the sea bottom should be conducted.

ACKNOWLEDGEMENTS

The flint artifacts found by the marine biologists in the 1930s as well as information about them were kindly provided by Professor Hans Brattström, Biological Station, Blomsterdalen, Norway. Great help was given by the crew on m/s Carolina, Å. Möller and W. Wiberg as well as the diving assistants J. Bengtsson and P. Söderhielm. Deborah Olausson and William Troy have been of great help in the English revision of the article.

REFERENCES

Andersen, S.H. (1980). Foreløbig meddelelse om en undersøisk stenalderboplads ved Lillebaelt. *Antikvariske Studier* 4, 7-22.

Becker, C.J. (1952). Maglemosekultur på Bornholm. *Aarbøger* 1951, 151-263.

Berglund, B. (1964). The Post-Glacial Shore Displacement in Eastern Blekinge, South-eastern Sweden. *Sveriges Geologiska Undersökning*, Ser C. No. 599, 47 pp.

Berglund, B. (1971). Littorina transgressions in Blekinge, South Sweden. A preliminary survey. *Geologiska Foreningens i Stockholm Förhandlingar* 93, 625-652.

Cederlund, C.O. (1976). Fornminnesinventering under vatten. *Fornvännen* 70, 124-136.

Degerbøl, M. (1933). Danmarks Pattedyr i Fortiden i Sammenligning med recente Former. *Videnskabelige Meddelelser fra Dansk naturhistorisk Forening i København* 96, 357-641.

Digerfeldt, G. (1975). A standard profile for Littorina transgressions in western Skåne, South Sweden. *Boreas* 4, 125-142.

Ingelman-Sundberg, C. (1972). Undervattensarkeologisk undersökning utanför Birka. *Fornvännen* 66, 127-135.

Iversen, J. (1973). The Development of Denmark's Nature since the Last Glacial. *Danmarks Geologiske Undersøgelse* V. Raekke, No. 7-C., 125 pp.

Jessen, K. (1920). Moseundersøgelser i det nordøstlige Sjaelland. *Danmarks Geologiske Undersøgelse*, II Raekke, No. 34, 1-268.

Jessen, K. (1935). The Composition of the Forest in Northern Europe in Epipalaeolithic time. *Kongelige Danske Videnskabernes Selskab. Biologiske Meddelelser* XII. I, 3-64.

Krog, H. (1965). On the Post-glacial development of the Great Belt. *Baltica* 2, 47-58.

Larsson, L. (1978). Ageröd I:B - Ageröd I:D. A Study of Early Atlantic Settlement in Scania. *Acta Archaeologica Lundensia*, No. 12, 258 pp.

300 L. Larsson

Larsson, L. (1980a). Some Aspects of the Kongemose Cultur in Southern Sweden. *Meddelanden från Lunds universitets historiska museum* 1979-1980, 5-22.

Larsson, L. (1980b). Stenåldersjägarnas boplats och gravar vid Skateholm. *Limhamniana* 1980, 13-39.

Larsson, L. (1982). Segebro. En tidigatlantisk boplats vid Sege ås mynning. *Malmöfynd* 4 (in press).

Lindqvist, P.-I. (1976). Marinarkeologi i Öresund. *Ale. Historisk tidskrift för Skåneland*. No. 1. 1976, 17-29.

Lundström, P. (1978). Östersjöhamnar. *Förtryck av mötesföredrag*. XV Nordiska arkeologimötet 1978, 22 pp.

Mörner, N.-A. (1969). The Late Quaternary history of the Kattegatt Sea and The Swedish West Coast. *Sveriges Geologiska Undersøkning*, Ser. C. No. 640, 487 pp.

Nilsson, T. (1964). Standardpollendiagramme und C-14 Datierungen aus dem Ageröds Mosse im mittleren Schonen. *Lunds Universitets Årsskrift*. N.F. Avd. 2. Bd 59. No. 7, 52 pp.

Persson, G. (1962). En transgressionslagerföljd från Limhamn. *Geologiska Föreningens i Stockholm Förhandlingar* 84, 47-55.

Rausing, G. and Larsson, L. (1977). Pilhaken, en stenåldersboplats under Öresund. *Ale. Historisk tidskrift för Skåneland*, No. 2, 1-5.

Ruoff, U. (1976). Eight years of diver excavation in Switzerland. *Underwater* 75. Proceedings of the fourth world congress of underwater activities, 149-154.

Ruoff, U. (1981). Der "Kleine Hafner" in Zürich. *Archäologie der Schweiz* 4 (1), 2-14.

Salomonsson, B. (1971). Malmötraktens förhistoria. *Malmö Stads Historia* 1, 170 pp.

Sigling, A. (1963). *Sege å's pre-atlantiska dalmynning - transgressionslagerföljder NO om Malmö*. Duplicate, Dept of Quaternary Geology, Lund.

Skaarup, J. (1980). Undersøisk stenalder. *Skalk* 1980:1, 3-8. (1976)

Stickel, E. (1976). *A Temporal and Spatial Analysis of Underwater Neolithic Settlements in the Alpine Foreland of Switzerland.* Ann Arbor. 247 pp.

Strömberg, M. (1976). Forntid i Sydöstskåne. *Föreningen för Fornminnes - och Hembygdsvård i Sydöstra Skåne Småskrifter* 14, 84 pp.

Vang Petersen, P. (1976). Bosaettelsemønstre i atlantisk tid i Nordøstsjaelland. *Kontaktstencil* 12, 77-94.

Welinder, S. (1971). Tidigpostglacialt mesolitikum i Skåne. *Acta Archaeologica Lundensia.* No. 1, 227 pp.

Zetterling, A. (1927). Bulverket. En svensk pålbyggnad i Tingstäde träsk på Gotland. *Fornvännen* 22, 161-178.

Zetterling, A. (1928). Bulverket i Tingstäde träsk. 1927 års undersökning. *Fornvännen* 23, 27-37.

Ødum, H. (1951). En faelles dansk-svensk undersøgelse af Østersøområdets sen- och postglaciale sedimenter. *Meddelelser fra Dansk Geologisk Førening* 12, 175-177.

HUMAN OCCUPATION OF THE SUBMERGED COAST OF THE MASSIF ARMORICAIN AND POSTGLACIAL SEA LEVEL CHANGES

D. Prigent[1], L. Visset[2], M.T. Morzadec-Kerfourn[3], and J.P. Lautrido[4]

[1]*Service archéologie, Départment de Maine-et-Loire, 106 rue de Frémur, 49000 Angers, France.*

[2]*Laboratoire d'Ecologie et de Phytogéographic, Université de Nantes, 44072 Nantes Cedex, France.*

[3]*Insitut de Géologie et Equipe du CNRS Anthropologie Préhistoire, Protohistoire et Quaternaire armoricain, 35042 Rennes Cedex, France.*

[4]*Centre de Géomorphologie de CNRS, rue des Tilleuls, 14000 Caen, France*

ABSTRACT

The postglacial sea level variations along the coast of the Massif Armoricain (France) have been the subject of various studies for ten years. The results indicate a rapid sea level rise during the first part of the Postglacial, then a lower rate since the beginning of the Neolithic, with some differences according to the studied areas.

Numerous traces of human occupation (megaliths, settlements, salt sites) are now partly under water or embedded in peat or mud. They attest to an important occupation of the Armorican coast during the Postglacial, an occupation which is partly linked to the shoreline evolution.

INTRODUCTION

The Massif Armoricain situated in the West of France is essentially made of ancient rock formations. Its shoreline stretches over several thousands kilometers and presents very diverse aspects: The indented rocky coast of the Léon, the rias of the Vilaine and the Rance, the tidal marshes of Brière and of the bay of Mont-Saint-Michel, and numerous islands of different sizes.

One of the characteristics of this coast is the great amplitude of the tidal range. This tidal range is close to 6 m in the Atlantic but increases quickly in the Channel to reach 15 m in the bay of Mont-Saint-Michel.

Since the end of the Palaeolithic the coastal area has been intensively occupied. Numerous sites are now to be found beneath the level of the highest tides.

HUMAN OCCUPATION OF THE COAST

The traces of human occupation consist of occupation floors, remains of buildings and burial monuments (Neolithic megaliths and Bronze Age cists), and of installations connected with the salt industry or with fishing (Giot, 1978; Delibrias *et al.*, 1971; Prigent, 1978, 1979a,b).

Originally some of the sites were on dry land and hence only give a maximum indication of the level of the highest seas. On the other hand, others, in close relation with tidal movements (briquetages and salt marshes) are most useful for fixing the former coast line.

The preservation of the different sites is variable:

1) the sites located on cliffs, which are the most numerous category are subject to erosion and mlay have been extensively damaged;
2) the sites of the intertidal zone are incompletely revealed to an extent which is dependent on the degree of the retreat of the beach. The archaeological material has been often spread out but has sometimes been protected either by the monument or by a later formation (peat, dune);
3) the sites of the tidal marshes and estuaries, embedded in peat, mud or sand are generally in a satisfactory state.

Early Postglacial

Dating from the first part of the Postglacial period are several settlements (Epipalaeolithic, Mesolithic) which have been found on the marine cliffs [Beg an Dorchenn at Plomeur (1), Le Croisic (4) or La Pointe Saint-Gildas near the Loire mouth] and on islands which are now away from the shore [Téviec (2), Hoédic (3)] (see Fig. 1). The absence of sites situated on the present shore can be explained either by the destruction of the Pleistocene deposits (head, loam, loess) on which they may have rested, or by the

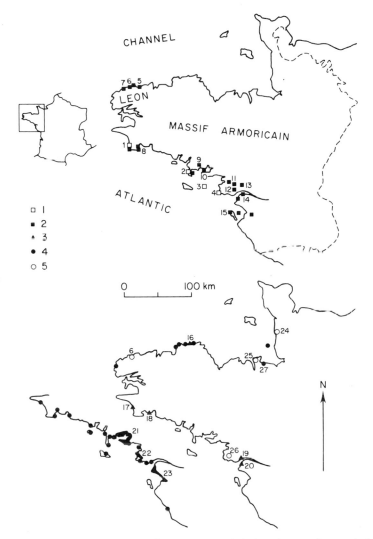

FIG. 1. *Map of localities of prehistoric and protohistoric sites on the coast of the Massif Armoricain. Explanation of symbols:- 1 = Epipalaeolithic and Mesolithic sites; 2 = Neolithic sites; 3 = Bronze Age sites; 4 = briquetages; 5 = gallo-roman sites.*

position of these sites in the present-day subtidal zone. The coastal morphology was very different because of the lower sea level and the slight slope of the platform. At this time some islands were linked to the mainland or at least presented a much larger dry land area than nowadays.

Neolithic

During the Neolithic the first megaliths were built in Armorica (at about 6,000 B.P.); they continued to be built up to 4,000 B.P. Some of them are now at various levels in the intertidal zone (Giot, 1968; Prigent, 1979a). We can make a broad distinction between standing stones (menhirs) and megalithic tombs. The menhirs were erected during a long period from the beginning of Neolithic to Early Bronze Age. That is to say that in the absence of firm stratigraphical or archaeological indications the available data remain rather vague. For example, it is suggested that the Men Ozac'h standing stone at Plouguerneau (7) (Plate 1b), the base of which is situated at about -7 m MHWS* may have been erected between 5,000 and 4,000 B.P. (Delibrias *et al.*, 1971). In the same way, the organic mud sealing the base of the menhir "la Pierre blanche" in Brière (12) at -3 m MHWS only allows one to say that this had been erected before 4,300 B.P. On the other hand the menhir of Hêlé at Donges (13), also situated in the marshland of Brière at about -3 m MHWS is better dated; it was erected after the end of the deposition of fluvio-marine mud and before the formation of the peat (Plate 2b), towards 4,500 - 4,200 B.P.

PLATE 1a. *Gallery grave of Kernic at Plouescat, Léon.*

*All the heights are given in relation to the present Mean High Water Spring Tides (MHWS).

The megalithic enclosure of Er Lannig (10) in the Bay of Morbihan the lowest menhir of which would be situated at about -6 m MHWS, could date to about 5,000 - 4,500 B.P.

b

PLATE 1b. *Menhir of Men Ozac'h at Plouguerneau, Léon.*

The megalithic tombs are relatively well known and the broad lines of their chronological distribution are established (Giot *et al.*, 1979a). The passage graves of the Middle Neolithic (6,000 - 4,500 B.P.) such as Ezer at Loctudy (8), L'Herbaudiere on Noirmoutier (15), Kerroyal at Plougoumelen (9) are situated in the upper part of the strand zone. The late gallery grave "Le Moulin Neuf" at Corsept (14) is situated at the limit of the highest tides. The gallery grave of Kernic at Plouescat (5)(Plate 1a), which was in use around 4,500 - 4,000 B.P., is lower, at about -3 m MHWS.

As for the settlements, the most important is that of Curnic at Guisseny (6) situated at mean sea level. The site seems to have been occupied from 6,000 to 4,000 B.P. Another important settlement protected by the bar separating the marshland of Brière from the Loire is that of la Butte aux Pierres in the centre of the marshland (11). This mound, the lowest parts of which are at about 2 m below MHWS was also occupied for a long period during the Neolithic (Plate 2a).

PLATE 2a. *Neolithic settlement of "La Butte aux Pierres" Grand Brière.*

PLATE 2b. *Menhir of Hêlé at Donges, Grande Brière.*

Bronze Age

For the Bronze Age (3,800 - 2,800 B.P.) the data are more scarce. The cist graves which may have been used from the end of the Neolithic to the beginning of the Iron Age (Giot et al., 1979b) are to be found on the strand zone at Penvenant (16), Ty Anquer at Ploeven or Mousterlin at Fouesant (18). At la Roussellerie at Saint-Michel-Chef (20) hearths at -3 m MHWS belong to a settlement of the Late Bronze Age, circa 3,000 B.P. (Tessier 1965).

Numerous artifacts have been discovered in the wetlands (marshlands, estuaries) but they give little indication of the position of the shoreline; so the site of Penhouet at Saint-Nazaire (19) during the last century yielded many objects dating from the Bronze Age and particularly from the Late Bronze Age, but the interpretation of these discoveries is still under discussion (Prigent, 1978).

Iron Age

During the Iron Age (2,800 - 2,000 B.P.), and particularly during the second part of this period, numerous briquetages (installations for the processing of salt) were established along the Breton coast, with important concentrations in the bay of Morbihan (21) and the Pays de Retz (23) (Gouletquer 1968). These sites demonstrate in many cases a distinct slowing down of the transgression and perhaps even a regression around the beginning of our era. The relative sea level would have been at this time lower by 3 or 5 m than at present (Delibrias et al., 1971; Prigent, 1979b). One may quote the briquetage of Curnic (6) for the Late Bronze Age (-5 m MHWS), and those of the marshes of Dol (27) ($\sim$-2 m MHWS, Langouët et al., 1974), and of Guérande (22) ($\sim$-2 m MHWS), for the Late Iron Age and the Gallo-Roman period. The fortified sites on the marine cliffs also attest to a period of sea level close to that of the present.

Historical Period

In the historical period, during the four first centuries of our era some sites show that the sea level was lower than nowadays. For example, the water pumping mechanism at the foot of the promontory occupied by the city of Alet (Saint-Malo, 25) is placed at 5 m below the MHWS. It is true that the site was probably protected by an offshore bar (Langouët and Meury, 1973). On the other hand at Lingreville (24) a peat yielded material dating from the second century A.D. at about -0.5 m MHWS. The fish reservoir of Curnic is now about -1 m MHWS (Sanquer, 1968). In the marsh of Guérande a gallo-roman site (26) was built on Holocene marine clay. Then the indications of the sea level changes situated on tidal flats date from the end of the first and from the second

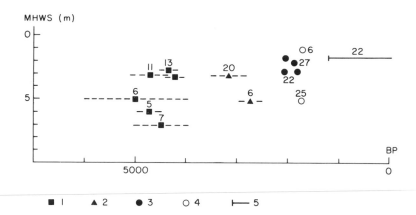

FIG. 2. *Situation of the most important sites in relation to present mean high water springs. Explanation of symbols:- 1 = Neolithic sites; 2 = Bronze Age sites; 3 = briquetages; 4 = gallo-roman sites; 5 = salt marshes. Horizontal dotted lines indicate the probable age range of the sites.*

millenium A.D. These sources of evidence (oysters mounds, salt marshes, fish weirs) show that the shoreline has not changed very much since that time and that the present sea level had already been reached.

The indications for the sea level during the different periods and its relationship to human occupation show that the level has varied considerably, but that there has been no divergence between the North and the South of the Massif armoricain (Fig. 2). In general terms they show a sea level lower than the present one, sometimes by several metres, during the whole Neolithic and up to the Gallo-Roman period, and perceptibly close to the present one for the last mlillenium at least. However the data supplied by archaeology are sometimes insufficient by themselves to determine the shoreline variations. It is necessary to refer to the results given by the corings carried out in the estuaries and the tidal marshes.

SHORELINE   VARIATION   IN   THE   ESTUARIES   AND   TIDAL MARSHES

The corings carried out in the estuaries and the tidal marshes yield more precise data concerning the coastal variations, through their   sedimentology,   micropalaeontology,   palynology   and radiocarbon dates.

The   results   obtained   are   somewhat   different   according   to whether one is dealing with estuaries, tidal marshes or small pools on the rocky coast (Morzadec-Kerfourn, 1979). The estuaries of the Loire and of the Vilaine, and the northern coast of Brittany (the Léon) and the bay of Mont-Saint-Michel are at present the better studied areas.

Basse-Loire

In Basse-Loire (Figs 3A and B) the most important data are at present supplied by the fill of the Loire estuary (Core AI and CII), the marshes of l'Acheneau, (Core CPII), and above all by the marshland of Brière, (Core Canal des Fougères), which spread over 20,000 ha (50,000 acres). In the Loire estuary, the Holocene sedimentation sequence begins at about 6,300 BP (6270 ± 160 Gif 1811) in fairly deep water conditions (about 30 m) at -45 m NGF*, whereas in the Acheneau valley at the same period (6345 ± 145 Ny 747), the first marine deposits are situated at -14 m NGF. The oldest sediments cored at present, dating from about 8,000 B.P., have been sampled at a depth of -20 m NGF (Visset, 1979).

At about 8,000 B.P., there is a silty clay sediment containing pollen of brackish Chenopodiacea (25 to 75%); these pollen rates indicate the penetration of the sea into the Brière marshland area along the thalwegs, which is related to the rapid rise in sea level at that time.

Between 7,800 and 7,000 B.P. the Chenopodiacea noticeably decrease; this decrease seems to correspond to a slowing down of the sea level rise with less sea water in Brière.

Between 7,800 and 6,100 B.P. the sea level rise is rapid; a deposit of silty clay is observed. The percentage of Chenopodiacea is about 50%** and schorres become established along the valleys; the Foraminifera which vary in abundance from level to level are essentially represented by *Protelphidium paralium* together with *Elphidium gunteri* and *Ammonia beccarii*. Only four genera of molluscs are observed in this sequence: *Cardium, Scrobicularia, Ostrea, Hydrobia;* they correspond to the fauna of an intertidal slikke, mudflat, or lagoonal environment. The Dinoflagellate cysts have a variable representation and never exceed 4%.

Between 6,100 and 4,500 B.P. there is a noticeable slowing down in the sea level rise (in the same way the marine influences

*Nivellement general de la France, corresponding approximately to mean sea level.

**A schore is a salt marsh or zone of halophytic vegetation covered by the sea only at spring tides.

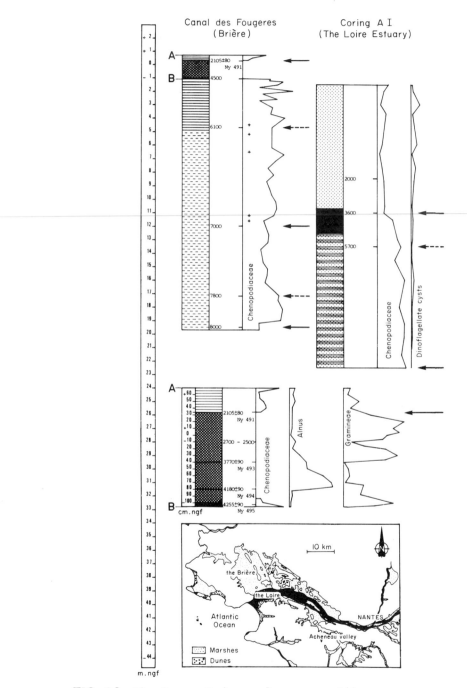

FIG. 3A. *The Basse-Loire and core profiles.*

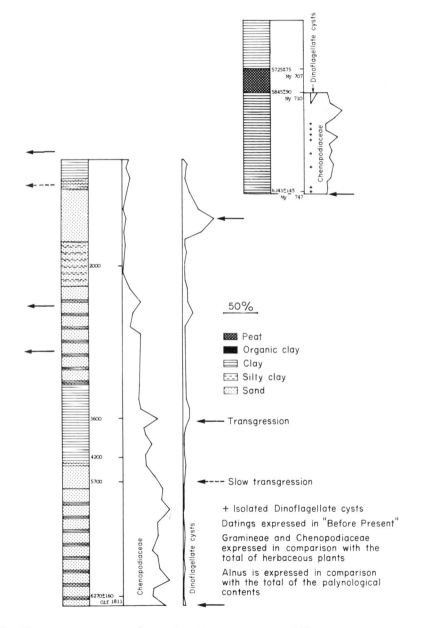

FIG. 3B.   *The Basse-Loire, further core profiles.*

disappear from the Acheneau at about 5,800 B.P.) and the first peats are formed; the schorres reach their greatest development at this point. The Chenopodiacea show percentages which can reach 60%. The clay deposits contain at their base a few rare Foraminifera among which appear *Trochammina inflata* and *Jadamina polystoma*.

At about 4,500 - 4,200 B.P., after the sea level had reached its maximum height in Brière, approximately -3 m MHWS, there are late marine influences, more and more toned down. This episode is marked in the estuary of the Loire by a reduction in the deposits at this period, and in the Brière by the disappearance of the schorres (the Chenopodiacea diminish then vanish), the raising of megaliths by the Neolithic inhabitants on the clay now no longer covered by water, and the establishment in some areas of clusters of high trees *(Quercus)* on ground prone to flooding. At the end of this period in this closed basin the fresh water level became high enough to drown the clusters of trees, and marshes with Gramineae and Cyperaceae are established.

Between 4,200 and 3,700 B.P. the extinction of the haelophytes and the general establishment of alder groves attest a relative drying of the basin.

From 3,700 B.P. there is a phase after the drowning of the alder groves, when Gramineae, Cyperaceae become established once more, corresponding, in the basin of Brière to a rise in the fresh water level.

At about 2,500 B.P. there is another fall in the extinction of the halophytes and re-establishment of alder groves sometimes mixed with oaks.

Later, a transgressive movement after 2,100 B.P. allowed the sea to invade Brière again (at least in its Southern part) and to deposit a fluviomarine mud which sealed the underlying peat. At about the beginning of our era, in the estuary of the Loire, significant percentages of Dinoflagellate cysts (up to 45%) above all of the genus *Spiniferites* attest the increasing saltiness of the water.

The Vilaine Valley

The Flandrian transgression penetrates the Vilaine valley in the vicinity of Arzal from 8,000 B.P. at ∿-29 m MHWS and reaches as far upstream as Redon, 50 km from the mouth (Morzadec-Kerfourn, 1974) (Fig. 4). This transgression shows itself by the deposition of clay and silt containing estuarine plankton. The sea level rise is at first irregular and at two points around 7,800 B.P. a soil comparable to the one of a schorre becomes established over a large area of the valley. These soils are present at Arzal and at Redon where they are contemporaneous with the extension of *Corylus* and the appearance of *Alnus*. Each marine phase is

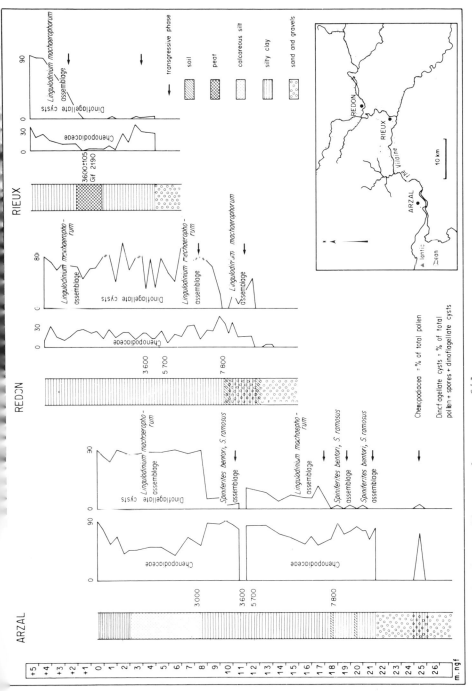

FIG. 4. *The Vilaine Valley, and core profiles.*

underlined by the appearance of Dinoflagellates belonging to the coastal assemblage of *Spiniferites bentori, Spiniferites ramosus* (Morzadec-Kerfourn, 1976). Up to 5,700 B.P. there is a regular sedimentation in the whole valley; it is marked by the abundance of Chenopodiaceae (70% at Arzal, 25% at Redon) and the homogeneity of the assemblage of Dinoflagellate containing *Lingulodinium machaerophorum,* characteristic of brackish conditions.

Between 5,700 to 3,600 B.P. the sedimentation is strongly disturbed everywhere: no deposition at Arzal, intermittent sedimentation at Redon and establishment of marshes with Cyperaceae at Rieux. This peaty level widespread in the marshes of Redon has been dated to 3,600 ± 105 (Gif 2 190).

After 3,600 B.P. the estuarine sedimentation starts again in the whole valley with the arrival of the coastal assemblage of Dinoflagellates containing *Spiniferites bentori* and *S. ramosus.* This marine phase reaches its maximum after 3,000 B.P. particularly at Arzal with the deposition of limey silt with planktonic Foraminifera and Coccolithophoridae. The deepening of the estuary is marked by the decrease of the Chenopodiceae in the schorre deposits whereas the assemblage of *Lingulodinium machaerophorum* becomes established in the whole valley of the Vilaine.

A slight regression of the limit reached by the high seas is noticeable at Arzal. It is underlined by the extension of Chenopodiaceae. This regression linked to the sedimentary dynamic of the estuary which has led to the formation of the present water meadows is later than the introduction of *Juglans* in Brittany and therefore close to the beginning of the historic period.

The Coast of Léon

Besides the megalithic monuments many peaty deposits exist in the strand zone of Léon. They are not very thick and generally rest on periglacial loam or on the bedrock (Morzadec-Kerfourn, 1969).

At about 5,700 B.P. the highest tide level is the same as the present mean low water, at about -9 m MHWS. Between 5,700 and 4,000 B.P. the marine progession is slow. Most of the peats of this period which outcrop on the strand zone occur in the marshy meadows of the valley floor (Morzadec-Kerfourn, 1979). The sea ievel stays between -8 and -5 m MHWS.

From 4,000 to 3,000 B.P. the transgression becomes more marked. The peats located at the top of the strand zone correspond to tidal zone.

At about 3,000 B.P. the shoreline was close to that of the present, while remaining at a lower level.

Next, the tidal marshes spread at many points to the strand

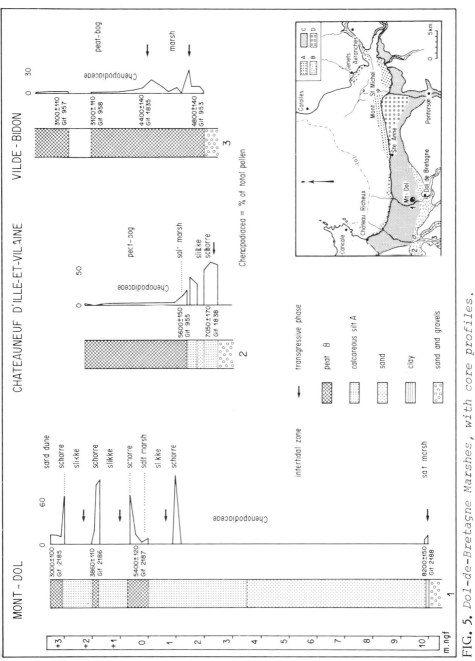

FIG. 5. *Dol-de-Bretagne Marshes, with core profiles.*

zone. At Santec two marshes succeded one another in the innermost part of the bay at ∿-3 m MHWS. They are separated by a thousand years and probably by a transgressive episode. One of them, dating from about 4,200 B.P. is a marshy meadow, the other one in direct contact with the preceding one is a tidal marsh; it dates from 2,330 ± 150 (Gif 818).

No peat deposit of more recent date has been found on the tidal shore of Léon.

The Tidal Marsh of Dol-de-Bretagne

The tidal marsh of Dol-de-Bretagne fills the south east angle of the bay of Mont-Saint-Michel (Fig. 5). The Flandrian transgression can be detected at -15 m MHWS from 8,200 B.P. and caused the formation of marshes in the thalwegs (Morzadec-Kerfourn, 1974). Up to 5,000 B.P. the floor of the bay lay within the intertidal zone. Some schorres, evidence of which remains in the form of tangue (calcareous sandy shelly mud) with *Hydrobia*, spread out to the North up to the Mont-Dol itself at about 7,000 - 6,500 BP. After this period the speed of the progression of the transgression slowed down and the deposition of tangues followed the sand.

About 5,500 B.P. a tidal marsh became established above the schorre in the whole of the Western part of the bay up to the vicinity of Mont-Dol. Between 5,400 and 3,800 B.P. the sea covered again the whole floor of the bay. Marine influence between 4,800 and 4,400 B.P. in the upper part of the Biez Jean valley is undeniable. The formation of a marsh with Cyperaceae and Gramineae at about 3,600 B.P. again involved the displacement of the shoreline to the North. The tidal marshes were protected by offshore bars but the evacuation of water was essentially via the Biez Jean.

The establishment of the present offshore bar dates from about 3,000 B.P. While the western part of the marsh of Dol has remained sheltered from the marine influences, it has been deeply cut into by the Biez Jean for a very long time.

Bay of Mont-Saint-Michel and the Western Coast of the Cotentin

In the eastern part of the bay, more subject than the marsh of Dol to marine influences and the variations in the courses of the major rivers (Sélune, Sée, Couesnon), the peaty formations are less extensive and less thick. Nevertheless the overall picture of the marsh of Dol is valid for the Eastern part of this bay. The most important period of peat formation lay between 3,700 and 3,000 B.P. These peats are covered by homogeneous littoral deposits (tangues) without any peaty intercalation. The upper part containing Juglans and Castanea dates from the historical period. There is no proof either of the existence of a forest of Scissy surrounding the Mont-Saint-Michel nor of its destruction around the 8th century A.D.   The only proof of marine invasion is in Pontaubants in the estuary of the Selune (Fig. 6) where sands with marine fauna are eroding a peat which contains Roman artifacts (Clet-Pellerin *et al.*, 1982).   The Western coast of the Cotentin has the advantages of presenting many stratigraphic sequences.Owing to the thickness of the Weichselian eolian deposits on the wave-cut platform the sea reached the present shoreline later than in the marsh of Dol.   The peats with brackish

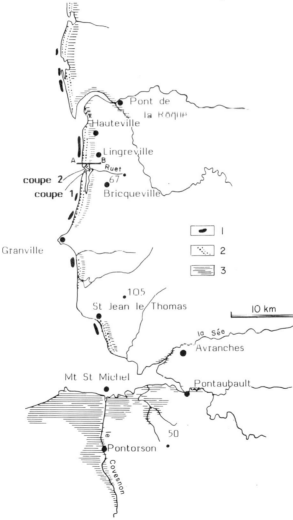

FIG. 6. *Eastern part of the Mont-Saint-Michel bay; map of localisation. 1. Peat, 2. Dune, Coastal barrier, 3. Lagoonal and estuarine formations*

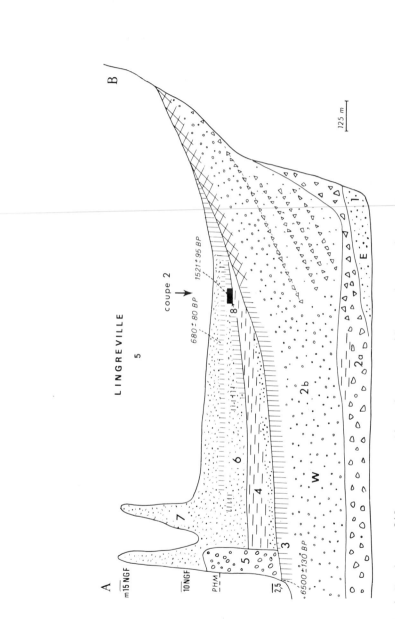

FIG. 7. *West–East profile across the "havres" (lagoon) of Lingreville – Brigueville; 1. Marine sands and gravels: end of Eemian (E); 2–2a. Weichselian head, 2b. Pleniglacial Weichselian sands (aeolian) (W); 3. Peaty sand or podzolic soil (east of section 2); 4. Lagoonal brackish formations; 5. Gravel coastal barrier; 6. Older dune sands (dune plain) with peaty layers; 7. Younger dune barrier; 8. (black rectangle) Archaeology from Lingreville, section 2 first and second century A.D.*

episodes which have been discovered in the intertidal area to the North of Granville at the mean sea level date from 6,500 to 6,000 B.P. Following this, brackish deposits piled up behind the offshore bar. At about 4,700 B.P. (Saint-Jean-le-Thomas) sea level was 3 m below that of the present. The sea level rise was important and ended up by breaking through the Lingreville offshore bar around 4,000 B.P., involving the erosion of the lagoonal deposits (Fig. 7). The rapid silting up of the breach in the offshore bar produced filling of the erosion gullies between 3,900 and 3,600 B.P. The lagoonal sedimentation began again in the upper part of these marshes, called "havres", and continued up to the Roman period. In fact, a peat covers the brackish deposits; in Lingreville it dates from 1,520 B.P. (Elhai, 1963), and recent archaeological discoveries there attest a human occupation which indicates the age of the peat (1st, 2nd century A.D.). A plain of dunes (lowland) covers and preserves the marsh in its inland part. The small peat at the top of these dunes, situated slightly above the level of the present MHWS, dates from 680 B.P. Just after 680 B.P. the sea again broke through the Lingreville offshore bar, and this bar has remained broken up to the present day.

In the Sienne estuary at Pont de la Roque the raised schorre which seemed to be an argument for a sea level perceptibly higher than the present one in a very recent period is in fact anthropogenic.

Shoreline of the Massif Armoricain

On the edge of the Massif Armoricain, local differences in the evolution of the shoreline show themselves essentially to depend on the coastal geomorphology but differential compaction of sediments and possible tectonic re-settlement may have interfered.

Everywhere a rapid rise in the sea level is observed at about 6,000 B.P. The slowing down which follows is expressed by the establishment of a schorre in Brière, by the end of marine influences in the Acheneau valley (about 5,800 B.P.), and by the formation of the first tidal marsh in the Western part of the bay of Mont-Saint-Michel. But in this part of the bay it is between 4,800 and 4,400 B.P. that the sea reaches the furthest point inland along the course of the Biez Jean. Then, at around 3,700 B.P. comes the main period of the peat formation in the whole bay. During the same period in Brière, between 4,200 and 3,700 B.P., the extension of the alder grove attests a phase of drying. In the Vilaine valley around Redon and Rieux, marshes form, covered by tangues or fluvio-marine deposits. A regression of the shoreline is however perceptible in some places, especially in Brière and in Léon, around 2,500 - 2,300 B.P. But everywhere along the Armoricain coast the beginning of the historical period is characterized by a sea level close to that of the present day.

CONCLUSION

The human occupation of the coast during the Holocene depends on the geomorphology which varies considerably according to the rise in sea level.

At the beginning of the Holocene the coast line was several kilometres seawards of the present coast. The islands on which most of the settlements lie (Epipalaeolithic, Mesolithic) were linked to the mainland or were much larger than at present. The initial rapid sea level rise up to 6,000 B.P. slowed down at the beginning of the Neolithic. The shoreline was close to the present one. The high tide level of this period was similar to the present low tide level. The cliffs masked by the deposition of Pleistocene sediments show a less scarped aspect. The present tidal flat was covered with loam or loess allowing cultivation during the Neolithic (Plouescat, le Gurnic). During this period the rise in sea level was very slow (less than 3 m during about 2,000 years) and the conditions did not vary very much. This fact explains the abundance of mlegalithic remains in the submerged area, and the long occupation of the site of Curnic in Guisseny on the strand zone.

For the Bronze Age period in Armorica we have little information about the relation of people to the coast. It seems that at the end of Bronze Age or at the beginning of Iron Age, the sea reached the foot of the present cliffs. Then, at the end of the Iron Age and the beginning of the Gallo-Roman period, when there was a noticeable slowing down of the transgression (and possibly even a regression), and after the infilling of the bays, the salt-makers settled on the deserted schorres while others established briquetages on the cliffs.

At the end of the Gallo-Roman period it seems that a transgressive episode occurred raising the sea level to an elevation very close to the present one by the end of the first millennium A.D. at the latest. Since that period only decimetric variations could have happened as is attested by the continuous functioning of the salt marshes on the south side of the Massif Armoricain. The main modifications to the coast are the dune formation, the erosion of some of the less resistant coastal deposits and the extension of some of the tidal marshes, such as the Marais Breton.

ACKNOWLEDGEMENTS

We wish to thank Professor P.R. Giot who reviewed the manuscript, and M.T. Prigent and C. Scarre for their translation.

REFERENCES

Clet-Pellerin M., Lautridou, J.P. and Délibrias, G. (1982). Les formations holocènes et pleistocènes de la partie orientale de la baie du Mont-Saint-Michel. *Bull. Soc. Linn. Normandie,* Caen (in press).

Delibrias G., Giot, P.R., Gouletquer, P.L. and Morzadec-Kerfourn, M.T. (1971). Evolution de la ligne de rivage le long du littoral armoricain depuis le Néolithique. *Quaternaria,* 14, 175-179.

Elhai H. (1963). La Normandie occidentale entre la Seine et le golfe normand-breton. Etude morphologique. Thèse Lettres, Paris, impr. Bière, Bordeaux.

Giresse P. and Lautridou, J.P. (1973). Les formations quaternaires du littoral du golfe normand-breton entre Coutainville et Avranches. *Bull. A.F.E.Q.* 2, 89-101.

Giot, P.R. (1968). La Bretagne au péril des mers holocènes. In : *La Préhistoire, problèmes et tendances,* pp. 203-208. Paris, C.N.R.S.

Giot, P.R., L'Helgouac'H, J. and Monnier, J.L. (1979a). *Préhistoire de la Bretagne.* Rennes, Ouest-France, 444 pp.

Giot, P.R., Briard, J. and Pape, L. (1979b). *Protohistoire de la Bretagne.* Rennes, OuestFrance, 444 pp.

Gouletquer, P.L., Lejards, J., Pinot, J.P. and Tessier, M. (1968). Etudes sur les briquetages. *Ann. Bretagne* 75, 117-148.

Langouet, L. and Meury, J.L. (1973). La machinerieen bois du Haut Empire retrouvée à Alet. *Ann. Bretagne* 80, 163-184.

Langouet, L., Bardel, A. and Gouletquer, Pll. (1974). Découverte de briquetages gallo-romains dans les marais de Dol. *Bull. Soc. Archéol. Ille-et-Vilaine* 78, 17-34.

Morzadec-Kerfourn, M.T. (1974). Variations de la ligne de rivage armoricaine au Quaternaire; analyse pollinique de dépôts organiques littoraux. *Mém. Soc. géol. minéral. Bretagne* 17, 208 pp. Rennes.

Morzadec-Kerfourn, M.T. (1976). La signification écologique des Dinoflagelles et leur intérêt pour l'étude des variations du niveau marin. *Rev. Micropal.* 18, (4), 229-235.

Morzadec-Kerfourn, M.T. (1979).   Indicateurs écologiques du domaine littoral végétation et plancton organique. *Oceanis* 5, (H.S.), 207-213.

Prigent, D. (1978).   Contribution à l'étude de la transgression flandrienne en BasseLoire.   Apport de l'Archéologie.   *Et. Préhist. Protohist. Pays de la Loire* 5, 177 pp.

Prigent, D. (1979a). Megalithes côtiers bretons et niveaux marins à l'Holocène. *Oceanis* 5, (H.S.), 183-189.

Prigent, D. (1979b).   Briquetages de la côte méridionale bretonne et niveaux marins. *Oceanis* 5, (H.S.), 167-173.

Sanquer, R. (1968).   Découvertes récentes aux environs de Brest. *Ann. Bretagne* 75, 231-265.

Tessier, M. (1965).   Sites côtiers de l'Age du Bronze du Pays de Retz (Loire-Atlantique) *Ann. Bretagne* 72, 75-85.

Visset, L. (1979).   Recherches palynologiques sur la végétation pleistocène et holocène de quelques sites du district phytogéographique de Basse-Loire.   *Soc. Sci. nat. Ouest de la France* (H.S.). 282 pp.

THE SUBMERGED NEOLITHIC VILLAGE "NEWE YAM" ON THE ISRAELI MEDITERRANEAN COAST

Ernst. E. Wreschner,

*Department of Anthropology,
University of Haifa, Haifa, Israel.*

ABSTRACT

The exposure of the submerged neolithic village of Newe Yam was due to a heavy south-western storm in January 1968. The circumstances of discovery and the objects found suggest that, since its population was forced to abandon its habitation around 5,000 B.C. by the rapid accumulation of sand, the site has not been previously exposed. The location of neolithic Newe Yam and the archaeological evidence support the conclusion that on this part of the Mediterranean coast the sea level was then at least five metres lower than at present. Isostatic factors for the present submerged location of the site can, according to recent investigations, be ruled out.

INTRODUCTION

The Neolithic settlement, which derives its name from the nearby modern communal village of Newe Yam, is located about 3.5 kilometres due west of the Carmel Caves of the Wadi Mughara (Nahal Me'arot). It was probably situated adjacent to the then existing estuary of the Mughara river on the marshy flat stretch of land which was protected against the northern winds by a rocky promontory. About 250 metres from the present shoreline exists a chain of small islets which are the remnants of a former shore. The sand beach is bordered by low dunes which support a vegetation of brush and scrub that prevents the sand from moving farther east. Behind these narrow dunes lies a 300 metres wide

QUATERNARY COASTLINES
ISBN 0 12 479250 2

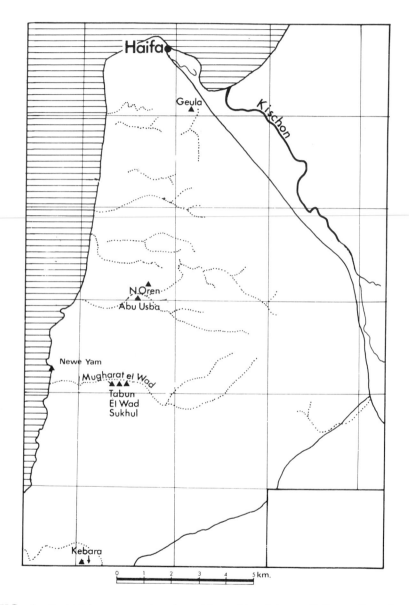

FIG. 1. *Location map showing the situation of Newe Yam to the Mount Carmel caves.*

stretch of alluvial soil bordered by a kurkar ridge which attains a height of up to 30 metres and runs parallel to the shore. East of this ridge extends the alluvial coastal plain to the foot of the Carmel range.

The site became exposed in the wake of an exceptionally heavy south-western storm which struck the beach unabated for 72 hours. Usually this part of the coast experiences north-western gales which accumulate sand on the beach and off shore. The south-western gale denuded the beach of its sand cover to a width of about 50 metres and swept it into the sea. Along the shoreline and under the shallow water a stretch of blackish loamy soil became exposed. The waves carried and deposited flints, pottery fragments, basalt and limestone fragments about 50 metres inland.

When the storm abated, the direction of the wind changed and it blew now from the east. On the shore and in the calm water foundation structures of rectangular houses, silos and storage pits were revealed and it was found that the dark soil contained flint implements, animal bones, pottery and fragments of basalt grinding stones and limestone bowls.

THE EXCAVATION

Soundings and excavation were undertaken immediately near the shore and up to 30 metres inland. Working conditions were extremely difficult because of the water seeping in from below. After removing the deposit of sand we could expose the loamy

PLATE 1. *The shore at Newe Yam showing foundations of a rectangular stone structure underwater in the surf zone. The low island in the background indicates the probable line of the ancient shoreline at time of occupation.*

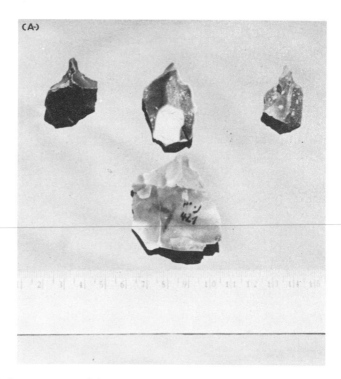

PLATE 2. *A & B Flint tools from the submerged site at Newe Yam.*

dark soil. Its top twenty centimetres contained similar material to that scattered and deposited by wave action during the storm (Wreschner, 1977a). We retrieved 936 flint implements, 18 bone tools, 5 obsidian sections, 13 fragments of basalt mortars and limestone bowls and grinders and a great number of pottery sherds, (Prausnitz, 1977). Besides the bone tools, animal remains evidenced the presence of *Capra sp.* at Neolithic Newe Yam. The foundation structures were found to be 7 to 9 metres long and 2.5 to 3 metres wide. The 80 centimetres wide walls consisted of two rows of undressed limestones, similar to the architecture of the "néolithique moyen" and the "néolithique récent" at Byblos (Cauvin, 1968).

The combination of diverse elements at Newe Yam give this site an importance in the archaeological record which exceeds its archaeological significance in the frame of discoveries from the later neolithic cultures: its location, the phenomenon of its exposure, the characteristics of its assemblage and the fortunate possibility for C-14 dating. All together hold clues for an evaluation of its history in relation to environmental events and its placement concerning the time scale and sea level height in

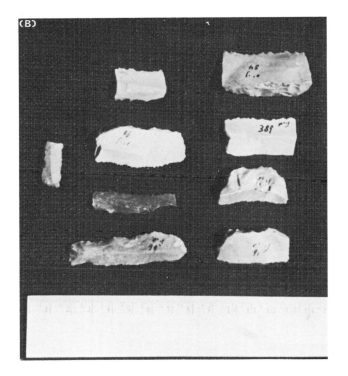

PLATE 2. (contd)

this particular part of the coast (Wreschner, 1977b).

Among the 936 flint tools and flakes 10 only were rolled or abraded whereas all others have very sharp edges. Only 12 have patina which means that only these very few had been exposed after use. About 50% of the pottery fragments show sharp unabraded breakage fractures and are not rolled. The remainder have different degrees of rounding of the edges which might be due to a short exposure to the turbulent wave action and sand grinding. That this can happen with sherds on the shore was observed a month after completion of the work at Newe Yam on abandoned material. Some big lumps of pottery which were part of a kiln were found to contain and enclose charcoal and permitted a C-14 test with sterile material. They gave a date of 4.360 ± 395 (Hannover). Allowing for an additional 500 years (Suess effect) we may conclude that the village was occupied around 5,000 B.C.

DISCUSSION

The present maximal depth of the sea between the shore and the islets of a former shore, about 250 metres west, is 5 metres. When the village was flourishing seven thousand years ago, the sea level

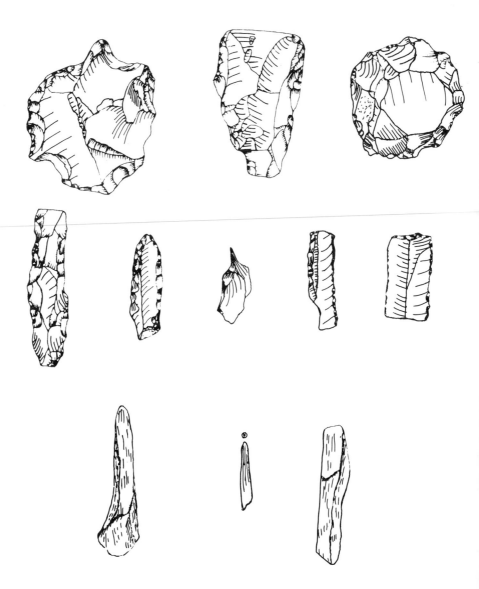

PLATE **3.** *Drawings of flint and stone tools from Newe Yam.*
Upper two rows are flint tools: the lower row shows bone
tools.

had then to be at least five metres lower than today.
Investigations by a team of scientists of the Weizman Institute led
to the conclusion that the influence of isostatic phenomena is not

significant at this particular part of the coast (Dr Bakler, personal communication).   Sporadic archaeological finds indicate the presence of another late Neolithic site about 8 kilometres north of Newe Yam, now submerged under water. Cauvin (1962) reported finds of Chalcolithic implements below two metres of water at Minet al-Dalieh, south of Beiruth.

These findings suggest, and Newe Yam provides the evidence, that during the Late Neolithic and early Chalcolithic about 5,000 B.C. to 4,000 B.C. a sea level of at least -5 m added a substantial area to the now existing coast (Wreschner, 1977b). This added a substantially increased exploitation potential for coastal populations in the northern part of the Israeli coast and the southern Lebanese littoral.

The Newe Yam lithic assemblage shows a prominent component of hide working tools and the bone tools found reinforce this indicator.   These and the remains of *Capra sp.* suggest a pastoralist subsistance of the Newe Yam settlers with some additional hunting, as evidenced by faunal remains. It is feasible that the nearby salt sources from the sea, the result of evaporation, were utilised for hide and leather working, which could have been the main items for trade. Substantial quantities of salt are found today in summer in the crevices of the rocks on the coast.

Trade connections point to the north and are manifested by the presence of obsidian and by a figurine in stone of Syrian origin. The figurine was found after the excavation by a diver. Basalt is not found on the coast or on Mount Carmel, the nearest sources

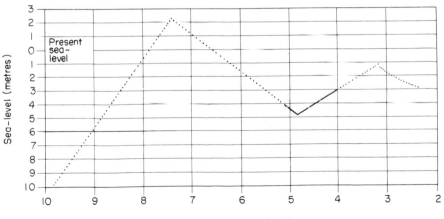

Thousand years (B.C)

FIG. 2. *The hypothetical curve of relative sea level at Newe Yam indicates that the sea level was relatively 5 m lower at 5,000 B.C., and that increased littoral land was available to the settlement at that time.*

are about 30 kilometres inland. But basalt is abundant in northern Israel, Lebanon and Syria. Whether these trade connections with the northern nucleus of the Late Neolithic culture on the coast at Byblos were by coastal shipping or by overland routes is difficult to establish. On the other hand the findings of Anati at Hazorea (1973) and Kaplan at Ein el-Jarba (1969) in the Esdraelon valley suggest cultural affinities between the material assemblages of the former and Newe Yam. This leads us to the problem of the duration and the causes for the abandonement of Newe Yam and the probable migration of the coastal village population towards the inland valleys. We suggest that the estimated life span of the Newe Yam settlement did not exceed 300 years. There was only one level which contained archaeological remains at Newe Yam, but it was found that the architecture contained two phases. We are not in a position to enlighten the problem of the migration direction of the displaced Newe Yam population, but we can conclude that Newe Yam ceased to be habitable owing to fast accumulating sand and subsequently to the encroaching sea.

The significant absence, numerically, of abraded and patinated material in the overall assemblage, as well as the preservation of fauna, indicate that the covering of the site with sand must have been fast. Thus flints, pottery and bones have not been exposed to the action of sand and wind and water for a long period. After its fast burial by sand, Newe Yam became inundated by the rising sea.

The same observations which lead us to conclude that the conditions for the uninhabitability of the neolithic village developed fast, have a bearing on the time and causes for its exposure. If the site had experienced such an exposure once or more during about seven thousand years we should have a much greater percentage of rolled and abraded material. It is noteworthy that among the great amount of sand removed during sounding and excavation we could not find a single piece of flint, pottery or stone. All these factors lead us to conclude that, since its disappearance under sand and water, the village was freed from its overburden of sand and exposed for the first time in 1968.

This conclusion requires an investigation of the frequency and velocity of sand movement as well as the resulting phenomena on this part of the Mediterranean coast. The speed with which a north-westerly moderate wind and wave action can build up a denuded beach has been experienced during our work at the site during the month of February 1968. After 72 hours of a heavy south-west storm and five days of east wind, a moderate north-western breeze led to a steady buildup of the shore and to accumulation of sand. After 33 days the beach was restored to its former shape, the rods of our grid were buried under sand and the archaeological layer with its stone foundations were submerged under water. The shore was covered by one to one and a half metres of sand.

Thirteen years have passed since then. The site is now buried under more than three metres of sand and occasionally one encounters a sherd, heavily rolled, smoothed and reduced to a thin fragment, a reminder of a fortunate coincidence: the temporary disclosure of the past and my chance visit to the shore at Newe Yam during the stormy days in late January 1968.

REFERENCES

Anati, E. (1973). *Hazorea I Archivi* 5, 84-85

Cauvin, J. (1962). Les industries lithiques du Tell de Byblos. *L'Anthropologie* 66, 488-502.

Cauvin, J. (1968). Les outilages néolithiques de Byblos et du littoral libanais. Paris.

Kaplan, J. (1969). "Ein el-Jarba", Chalcolithic Remains in the Plain of Esdraelon. *Bulletin of the American Schools of Oriental Research,* 159, 32-36.

Prausnitz, M. (1977). The Pottery at Newe Yam. In *Eretz-Israel* Vol. 13 (Arensburg, B. and Bar-Yosef, O., eds) pp. 272-276. Israel Exploration Society, Institute of Archaeology of the Hebrew University, Jerusalem.

Wreschner, E.E. (1977a). Newe Yam - A Submerged Late-Neolithic Settlement Near Mount Carmel. In *Eretz-Israel* Vol. 13 (Arensburg, B. and Bar-Yosef, O., eds) pp. 260-271. Israel Exploration Society, Institute of Archaeology of the Hebrew University, Jerusalem.

Wreschner, E.E. (1977b). Sea Level Changes and Settlement Location in the Coastal Plain of Israel During the Holocene. In *Eretz-Israel* Vol. 13 (Arensburg, B., and Bar-Yosef, O., eds) pp. 277-282. Israel Exploration Society, Institute of Archaeology of the Hebrew University, Jerusalem.

QUATERNARY SHORELINES IN THE REGION OF CORFU AND ADJACENT ISLETS, WESTERN GREECE

Augustus Sordinas

Kothoniki, Corfu, Greece

ABSTRACT

Archaeological evidence on the island of Lefkas, in large areas with *terra rossa* on the island of Corfu, and on heavily eroded surfaces of the adjacent islets of Dhiapl, Mathraki, and Othonoi, to the northwest of Corfu, indicates substantial human occupation at 'least during the Middle Palaeolithic and the terminal Upper Palaeolithic.

Typologically, the greatest amount of artifacts belong to the Circum Mediterranean Levalloiso-Mousterian cultures. The artifacts were struck on honey colored or chocolate brown flints that are characteristic of the palaeolithic flints of the Greek mainland. Most of the artifacts are found on the surface of heavily eroded masses of *terra rossa*. Others, however, are now submerged around the present coastline of Corfu from which they are often detached by wave action and rolled to the beach.

In addition, a typical Romanellian industry was determined by the author in the shelter of Grava, Ayios Mathias, in the southcentral Corfu. The fauna was rich including such large animals as horse and *Bos primigenius*.

These factors strongly indicate major lowering of sea level, and a land bridge between the Greek mainland and the island during Wurm I and III at least. The Romanellian typology must be further borne in mind in terms of a land bridge somewhere across the Adriatic.

INTRODUCTION

Their notorious tectonic instability notwithstanding, the Ionian

QUATERNARY COASTLINES
ISBN 0 12 479250 2

Islands provide eloquent evidence of a variety of sea level
ooscillations. Because of the location of these islands at the
entrance of the narrow Adriatic Sea, this evidence becomes
indispensable in a discussion of possible migration routes in
Central Europe and the northern Mediterranean during periods of
marine regression.

The observations presented in this paper are limited to the island
of Corfu and the adjacent islets of Dhiáplo, Mathráki, Erríkousa,
and Othonoí, to the northwest of Corfu (Figs 1 and 2). Similar
observations, however, were documented by me on the islands of
Lefkas (and the adjacent mainland from which Lefkas was
artificially separated), Kefallinia, and Zakinthos or Zante
(Sordinas, 1970). All these observations were frankly ancillary to
a comprehensive archaeological survey of the prehistory of the
Ionian Islands which I initiated in 1964. Some of the finds were
published in English (Sordinas, 1969). Others were the subject of
an oral communication in English (Sordinas, 1973), and a
publication in Greek (Sordinas, 1974). The present paper
summarizes all the pertinent evidence. Listing of sites is kept to
the minimum here for convenience in reading, but a comprehensive
list of sites and inventories can be found in the references cited.

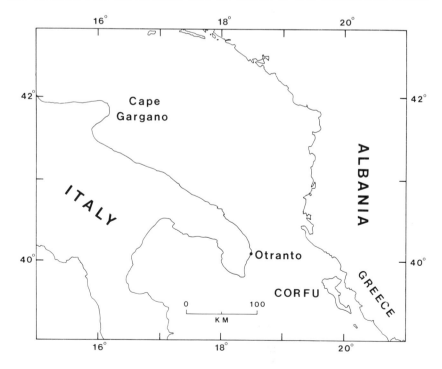

FIG. 1. *The south Adriatic showing the location of Corfu.*

WARM SEA TERRACES

30 Metre Terrace

This was discovered at Solári, central Corfu, resting on Pliocene clays. It consists of a soft calcareous sediment of unrolled molluscs including microfaunal elements. There is no evidence of shingles, and the terrace is not associated with artifacts. The fauna includes warm sea molluscs. Some of them had attained large sizes (e.g. *Strombus coronatus*, 18 cm long; *Xenophora crispa*, 12 cm in diameter; *Conus mediterraneous*, 15 cm long). The fauna was partially identified by Dr John D. Taylor, Department of Palaeontology, British Museum of Natural History, as shown in Table I.

A similar deposit was located below the ruins of the Byzantine church Neranzícha near Corfu's airport. This deposit, however, now stands 6-8 m above present sea level. But it must be pointed out that it consists of fine silty sediments in layers, some of which contain a great number of molluscs while others none at all. The evidence points to sediments formed in deep water away from the shoreline.

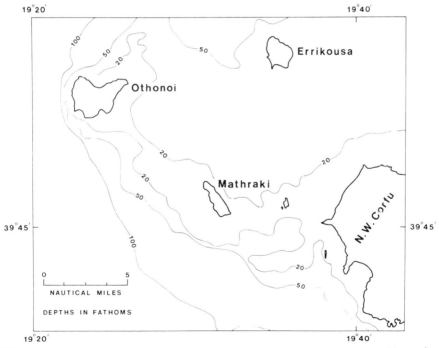

FIG. 2. *Bathymetry around northwest Corfu. Depths in fathoms. The shallower part of the sill between Corfu and Errikousa is 37 fathoms, or approximately 72 m.*

TABLE 1

Macrofauna

Strombus aff. coronatus
  Defrance
Conus mediterraneus
Triton corrugatus
Apollon Marginatus
Xenophora crispa
Calyptraea chinensis
Nassa semistriata
Peratotoma concinna
Murex sp.
Actaeon tornatilis
Glycymeris pilosa
Ostrea edulis Linne, var.
  ungulata Nyst
Amussium cristatum
Spondylus crassicosta
Cardium lians
Acanthocardium aculeatum
Callista chione
Solen marginatus
Corbula gibba
? Pitar sp.

Microfauna (including microfaunal elements, immature
shells of naturally small
forms)

Nuculana fragilis
Area tetragona
Aequipecten afercularis
Similipecten similis
Limatala sulcata
Anomia sp.
Chama gryphoides
Parvicardium papillosum
Myrtea spinifera
Venus multilmellae
Divaricella divaricata
Turritella tricarinata
T. subanculata
Nassa Lineata
Fusus sp.
Enlimella scillae
Calliostoma cingulatum
Ringicula ventricosa

Natica leicina
Margillia bertrandi
Epitonium communis
Bulinella cylindracea
Rissoina sp.
Fissurella graceca
Biltium reticulatum
B. palludosium
Risoa cimex
Cerithium mulgatum
Turbinella lactea
Chama gryphides
Acanthocaria aculeata
Cardita trapezium
Loripes lucinalis
Thyasina lacteus
Dossinia lupinus
Venus verruscosa
V. striatula
Tellina pulchella
T. donacina
Abra cf. longicallus
Gastrona fragilis
Mactra corallina
Murex blainvillei
Cerithium vulgatum
Bittium reticulatum
Rissoa cimex
Gibbula filiformis
Nassa mutabilis
Vermetus sp.
Bullinella cylindracea
Emarginula elongata
Chiton olivaceus
Turbinella pallida
Gibbula sp.
Buccinum sp.
Vermetus sp.

Scaphopoda
Cdulus gadus
Dantalium sexangulum

Echinodermata
Maretia sp.
Astropecten sp.

Also various bryozoa,
Ostracoda and Foraminifera

Low Warm Sea Terrace (?10-20 m)

The entire western coastline of Corfu is the product of the Adriatic fault. Indeed, the whole island can be described as a syncline dipping toward the East. The present western shoreline of the island consists of an almost perpendicular cliff of raised Pliocene clays and marls, upon which rests a two-meter bed of hard coquina. A similar bed can be seen on the offshore islets of Mathráki, Dhiáplo, and Othonoí northwest of Corfu, and the islets of Lagoúdhia, southwest of Corfu. This coquina can be seen submerged in the rather shallow sea between Corfu and the above mentioned islets. Characteristically, some of these submerged formations jut out of the sea to form reefs of this hard rock (e.g. the reef of Trakhiá, NW of Mathráki, shown in Fig. 2. The name means "hard" in Greek). In traditional times the islanders used these formations extensively for quarrying. Diagnostically, this coquina bed has large numbers of rolled *Strombus bubonius* (with lengths never exceeding 12 cm), and rolled shingle. No artifacts incorporated or associated with this beach have been observed to date. This coquina bed is covered by extensive accumulations of *terra rossa* containing heavily altered but unrolled Levalloiso-Mousterian assemblages (see below).

TERRA ROSSA

Extensive *terra rossa* accumulations (at Kombitsi 30 m thick, but elsewhere much less) always uncomfortably resting on Pliocene formations, have been located and mapped in the interior of the island of Corfu, and the islets of Dhiáplo, Mathráki, and the southern tip of the islet of Othonoí. What is pertinent here is that these accumulations invariably contain a rich assortment of Levalloiso-Mousterian artifacts and debitage. They are characterized by the following attributes:

a)   Considerable weathering, rounding of edges, deep alteration of the chemical properties of the flint. No rolling.

b)   Heavy glossy patina (an easily recognizable orange yellow).

c)   A fine Levallois technology as evidenced by rather thin flakes with multi-faceted butts.

d)   A clear palaeolithic typology (racloirs, thick end-scrapers, burins).

The analysis of hundreds of flints exhibiting these attributes, from a variety of sites, is strong evidence for the presence of elements of the Circum-Mediterranean Levalloiso-Mousterian cultures which must have reached these regions during a marine regression allowing the formation of a bridge with the mainland.

Interestingly, *terra rossa* accumulations, with the attendant artifacts, were not located on the islet of Erríkousa which yielded neolithic materials only. On this matter, the present sea depths round this islet may be of some significance (Fig. 2).

SUBMERGED LANDS

Additional observations further attest to the stage of marine regression reported above:

Submerged Shorelines

To the East of the solid rock mesozoic formations upon which the "Old Fortress" of the city of Corfu was built, and specifically, at locality Capo Sidero, at depth of 10 meters and possibly more (determinable only by underwater exploration), once can see on clear days beach strands of large and small rounded shingles and pebbles. The nature of this rocky promonotory precludes any possibility that these pebbles could have been recently formed or transported from elsewhere.

Rolled Levalloiso-Mousterian Artifacts

Importantly, in various parts of the island of Corfu, for instance at localities Koríssia-Glyfonéri (Southwest), Ay Iannis Peristeron-Messonghi (East), or Ai Stefanos Avlioton (Northwest), rolled Levalloiso-Mousterian tools or debitage, including fist-sized cores - all heavily rolled - are washed up from the sea by the waves and are incorporated in the sands or the shingle of the present beach at high water mark but not beyond.

LAND BRIDGE DURING THE UPPER PALAEOLITHIC: (EPIROS-ISLAND OF CORFU)

The Shelter of Gráva

A terminal palaeolithic shelter was discovered in May 1966 on the southern side of Mount Áyios Mathiás in south-central Corfu. It is a fine living shelter *ca.* 18 m deep, with a large entrance and ledge facing South, and with a commanding view of the entire southern region of the island. The occupation floor of the shelter extends to *ca.* 5 x 14 m of the present surface. Considerable erosion in the southern area of the floor and various rock dislocations have disrupted the occupation layers. Exploratory trenches scratched the top layers only. The talus under various rock-falls was not examined. The top layers form a hard ossiferous breccia containing a rich backed-blade industry.

The Faunal Elements

The fauna is rich. Particularly interesting is the great number of large birds which I was not able to identify. Most of the bones were examined and partially identified by the late Eric Higgs and J. Jarman of Cambridge University with the help of Ms. Heather Stokes, Department of Palaeontology, University of California at Berkeley. The fauna is richly represented by many *Cervus elaphus* individuals, *Equus* of various sizes, and less by *Dama* and *Capreolus*, rare *Sus*, and some *Lepus*, *Vulpes*, *Hyaena*, *Meles*, *Mustella*, various rodents and snails. Most importantly for the present paper, many bones of a large *Bos* were identified, the size of which falls within the range of the eastern European *Bos primigenius*.

The Industry

The shelter yielded no indications of cultures postdating the Upper Palaeolithic. The top layers of the breccia yielded 870 flints including debitage (but excluding hundreds of small fragments of manufacture which were bagged separately). All the materials were mint fresh, struck on translucent gray flint and some chocolate brown flint of the kind that is common in Épiros. The analysis clearly showed that the industry is the product of a fine backed blade technology manufactured *in situ*. The inventory comprises:

Blades and Bladelets (worked and unworked)	234
Cores (mostly small or spent)	58
Scrapers	78
Burins	50
Pointed retouched blades	15
Small Gravettoid points	39
Worked bone (?polisher), fragmented	1
Bone point with incisions, fragmented	1
Globular bead	1
Various hammerstones, choppers, splintered or utilized flakes, fire-reddened pebbles abound.	

The cores are atypical or small pyramidal when spent. The blades have thin nondescript butts, but are generally small and assymetrical. There is a variety of scrapers but thick planoconvex end-scrapers are very characteristic of the shelter. There is a fairly large number of nucleiform burins and atypical angle burins with beaked pointed ends, generally with many and clumsy spall removals. Various composite burin-scrapers were obtained. There are comparatively few pointed backed blades or flakes, but then, some are carefully worked bilaterally.

The most characteristic implements are several small Gravettoid points on dextrously backed and further retouched (but not truncated) bladelets, often with partial bifacial retouch at the base and/or the tip. The bone point has a fine cylindrical cross-section and symmetrically arranged clusters of short parallel incisions on both sides - very much the kind of incisions made by ethnographic parallels for the retention of poison. The length of the fragment is 6 cm slightly tapering toward one end.

The bead is of the globular peduncular variety, common in similar contexts in various Mediterranean sites. It was made on a polished trunk of a tooth. The perforation is of the round hour-glass type with thin inner walls. Identical beads were discovered by Higgs in the Upper Palaeolithic shelter of Kastritsa in Épiros.

Taken as a whole the features found at the shelter of Gráva indicate strong affinities with the Romanellian cultures. Thus, Corfu can be considered an outpost of a geological and cultural bridge connecting - during the Terminal Palaeolithic - the Southern Balkans and Southern Italy into a large province with strong environmental and cultural ties. But by this we do not imply that the entire Adriatic was a land bridge. Rather, that it was a much smaller sea barrier perhaps not penetrating any further than the Gargano peninsula.

POSTGLACIAL SEA RISE

The site of Sidari, NW Corfu, has yielded a mesolithic kitchen midden (with a single uncalibrated radiocarbon date of 5820 ± 340 years B.P.) formed on a peaty deposit of an old river bed, hence deflected to the east by successive silting. A thin layer of sand and pebbles resting on the peaty deposit is indicative of a relative sea level 80-100 cm above present sea level. Interestingly, our studies have shown that the typology as well as the lithic sources of the mesolithic midden are foreign to Corfu, and indicate marine contacts (Sordinas, 1977, p. 174 ff.). This is the first certain evidence that Corfu had become an island in postglacial times. The apparently high postglacial sea level may be influenced by tectonism.

These marine contacts were followed by a succession of others, the wide spreading of Campignian industries on the islets northwest of Corfu, the introduction of domestication at Sidari, the appearance of various types of early neolithic pottery, and the appearance of polished celts made of serpentine (foreign to Corfu and the adjacent islets).

Although outside the scope of this report, it may be of some interest to add that the area of Sidari, NW Corfu, indicates further rises of the sea level and heavy erosional features postdating the local Early Bronze Age. This can be confirmed from the heavy erosion that seems to have set in after the land was occupied by settlements with characteristic Early Bronze Age utilitarian ware. The sea invaded the land and cut off whole tracts turning them into virtually inaccessible rocks the tops of which are covered by a thin layer of soil with EBA potsherds.

SUMMARY

The following conclusions can be reported:

1) Two terraces with warm sea faunas. The higher terrace, at least 30 m, yielded various large specimens including *Strombus coronatus*. The lower terrace is a very distinctive bed of hard coquina, rich in *Strombus bubonius*. Heavy tilting does not permit the accurate pin-pointing of its elevation which can be averaged in the vicinity of 10-12 m.

2) Evidence suggests that some of the islets were occupied at times when the sea level was lower than -20 m, but probably not lower than -80 m, thus effectively connecting Corfu, and the islets of Dhiáplo, Mathráki and Othonoí (to the exclusion of Erríkousa) to the mainland of Greece-Albania during Würm I-II, permitting the widespread distribution of Levalloiso-Mousterian elements in the aforementioned region (see also Davies, 1980 pp. 166-167; Labeyrie *et al.*, 1976).

3) A land bridge between Corfu and the mainland seems to have existed during Wurm IV during which the island of Corfu was inhabited by large herbivores supporting Romanellian-type hunters permanently stationed in shelters.

4) Such a land bridge was submerged after the Romanellian occupation by seas reaching about 80-100 cms. above present sea levels possibly a little prior to the sixth millennium B.C. At any rate, late in the sixth millennium a Mesolithic settlement appeared on the island of Corfu, indicating maritime contact. Soon after, this was succeeded by Neolithic camps with imported pottery attesting to further maritime diffusion.

5) Slightly raised sea levels, with attendant heavy erosional features, occurred after the local Early Bronze Age.

REFERENCES

Davies, Oliver (1980). Last Interglacial Shorelines in the South Cape *Palaeontologia Africana* 23, 153-171.

Labeyrie, J., Lalou, C., Monaco, A. and Thommeret J. (1976). Chronologie des nivaux eustatiques sur la côte au Rousillon de -33,000 ans B.P. a nos jours. *C.R. Acad. Sci. Paris* <u>282</u>, 349-352.

Sordinas, Augustus (1969). Investigations of the Prehistory of Corfu during 1964-1965. *Balkan Studies* <u>10</u>, 393-424.

Sordinas, Augustus (1970). Líthina Ergaleía apó tén Proistorikí Zákyntho. *Kerkyraiká Chroniká* <u>15</u>, 122-130.

Sordinas, Augustus (1973, 1974). Stone Age Sites on Offshore Islets Northwest of Corfu, Greece. Paper read at the 72nd Annual Meeting of the American Anthropological Association, New Orleans, La. Published, in Greek, (1974) in *Kerkyraiká Chroniká* <u>19</u>, 88-93.

Sordinas, Augustus (1977). E Papyrella. *Deltion Ioniou Akademias* <u>I</u>, 171-184.

HARD TIMES IN BERINGIA : A SHORT NOTE

David M. Hopkins

U.S. Geological Survey
Menlo Park, California 94025, USA

Recent studies indicate that glaciers covered the coastal mountains of southern Alaska and Yukon Territory and probably also the Koryak Mountains in northeastern Siberia almost constantly for at least the last 80 thousand radiocarbon years (krcy), but in more northerly parts of Beringia, mountain glaciers were of extremely limited extent after 60 or 70 krcy ago. The older history of the Laurentide ice to the east is still obscure, but it lay near its maximum position in northwestern Canada most of the time from 30 to 14 krcy ago.

The Bering Land Bridge was probably in existence most of the time between 80 and 14 krcy ago, but it may have been shallowly flooded on one or two occasions between about 45 and 35 krcy ago. It seems unlikely that this possible flooding significantly affected the ability of humans to move through the region, but it would have had substantial effects upon climate and vegetation. Flooded shelves mean relatively mesic climate and exposed shelves result in moisture deficiency throughout most of Beringia.

After a brief interval of mild, mesic climate perhaps 60 krcy ago, the climate of Beringia was almost constantly dry until about 14 krcy ago. Conditions were most severely dry between about 25 and 14 krcy ago. Large areas of dunes were active in lowlands of Alaska and northeastern Siberia and probably also on the now-submerged continental shelves. Organic productivity was limited as much by lack of soil moisture as by temperature or length of growing season. Low pollen influx rates indicate a very sparse tundra-steppe vegetation cover. Spruce and tree birch and perhaps aspen and larch became regionally extinct, and cottonwood and alder were confined to small refugial areas somewhere near Bering Strait. Dwarf birch was widely distributed but evidently persisted as scattered prostrate shrubs that constituted only a very minor element in the vegetation. Willow thickets persisted on river flood plains, providing essential brows for the three wide-ranging large-bodied ungulates (mammoth, horse and bison) that comprised something like 90% of the vertebrate biomass. The long period of winter plant dormancy was the most important limiting factor affecting the large mammals. The now-submerged continental shelves of Bering and southern Chukchi Sea, though vegetated with tundra-steppe, were nevertheless the most mesic and probably the most productive sector of Beringia between about 25 and 14 krcy ago.

A rapid and drastic climatic change, 14 krcy ago, was related at least in part to flooding of the continental shelves by rising sea level (see McManus *et al.*, 1983, this volume) and resulted in a sudden bloom of dwarf birch accompanied by an expansion of cottonwood and alder from central Beringian refugia. Mammoth and horse disappeared, bison became rare, and reindeer/caribou proliferated throughout Beringia during the next one or two millennia. Wapiti became widely dispersed though not abundant in eastern Beringia during the "birch period", possibly representing a dispersal from south of the ice sheets. The "birch period" came to an end with the time-transgressive re-appearance of spruce and tree birch, which also re-invaded eastern Beringia from sources south of the Laurentide ice. Spruce reached the lower MacKenzie River valley in northwest Canada 11,500 years ago and the Tanana Valley of central Alaska 9,000 years ago. A further climatic change, probably also time-transgressive, resulted in a still more humid climate that encouraged bog development and peat accumulation throughout Beringia during early Holocene time.

During the drastic dry period 25 to 14 krcy, such human populations as may have been in Beringia must have been almost entirely dependent upon land mammals for food as well as for other essential requirements. Because it had the most mesic climate and probably the highest organic productivity, the submerged shelf of Bering Sea and the Bering Strait area might be expected to have been the areas most attractive to human hunters. Late winter (e.g. February through mid-April) should have been the most acute stress period for human populations. Two northeast Siberian archaeological sites Dyukhtai Cave and Berelekh seem likely to have been winter base camps. Bone remains indicate that mammoth was the overwhelming major prey item and that a broad spectrum of other ungulates were utilized with hare and fur-bearing mustelids and canids.

The change in game populations during the "birch period" led to a gradual shift in concentration away from mammoth. Sheep and caribou evidently became the major prey species, but plant resources would have become more abundant during this period, too. The earliest evidence of concentration of coastal and riverine resources seems to date from about 10 krcy ago.

THE STAGES AND ROUTES OF HUMAN OCCUPATION OF THE BERINGIAN LAND BRIDGE BASED ON ARCHAEOLOGICAL DATA

Nikolai Nikolaevich Dikov

Corresponding Member, USSR Academy of Sciences, Portovaya St 11/2, Aptm. 22. Magadan 685013, USSR

ABSTRACT

Four stages of the peopling of Beringia can be singled out with different degrees of precision. Two first ones are hypothetically of Ziryansk glaciation (70,000-50,000 years ago) and of the beginning of Sartansk glaciation (more than 27,000 years ago). The third one refers to Sartansk glaciation (15,000-13,000 years ago) and is connected with bifacial projectile stemmed points of Ushki I type (Layer VIII) and Ul'khum on Chukotka at the end of Sartansk glaciation. The fourth stage (at the end of Sartansk glaciation - 11,000-10,000 years ago) corresponds to artifact sites of the Beringian tradition, containing wedge-shaped cores and leaf-shaped bifacial points (Ushki I, Layer VI; Kurupka I on the Chukotski Peninsula; and others).

INTRODUCTION

As a geologic and palaeogeographic basis of the present report, I take D.M. Hopkin's theory of the Beringian Land Bridge between Chukotka and Alaska which was exposed during the Quarternary glaciation periods. The extent of Beringia included the present continental shelves in consequence of marine regression, which is becoming generally recognized (Hopkins, 1979). I shall remind the reader that the term of "Beringia" was first introducd by P.P. Sushkin, a Soviet palaeozoologist (1925), but the general idea of such a link between Asia and America had appeared much earlier, with S.P. Krasheninnikov (1756). Most authors think that there was a continuous land junction between Asia and America, but there is another opinion: the bridge might be in the form of an archipelago - a group of closely situated islands (Portenko, 1968). In one way or another, between the greater continents, across this continuous or interrupted "bridge", an intensive exchange of flora and fauna took place. Beginning with some not quite definite period, human migrations first began from Asia to America, which led to its primary peopling.

Here we shall consider the stages and routes of peopling Beringia, especially in connection with the problem of primary peopling of America.

THE ARCHAEOLOGICAL BACKGROUND

The essence of the problem is in the still existing contradiction between anthropological and archaeological data. Anthropological materials have ascertained the Asiatic origin of the earliest American population. In contrast, archaeological data tend to emphasise radical differences rather than specific similiarities between palaeolithic cultures of the Old and New Worlds, and witness the lack of the earliest Asian cultures which might be taken as starting-points for the most ancient American cultures with bifacial projectile points.

Very many sometimes ingenious, but finally unsuccessful, attempts have been made to overcome this contradiction. An outstanding role belongs to Müller-Beck's and Chard's hypotheses of the stages and routes of peopling of America from Asia being controlled and limited by the system of Beringian land bridges and interglacial corridors functioning simultaneously only in short periods: 28,000-23,000 and 13,000-10,000 years ago (Chard, 1959, 1960; Müller-Beck, 1966). Different aspects of the hypothesis of peopling America from Asia, and of introducing various cultural traditions from there at the most ancient stages, have been elaborated by many American and Soviet scientists (Campbell, 1963; McNeish, 1964; Haynes, 1971; Borden, 1970; Wormington, 1971; Dikov; 1968, 1979 *et al*. The latest and the most complete investigation of the Beringian archaeology from this standpoint belongs to F.H. West (West, 1979).

However, most recently some cooling towards the cultural adoption hypotheses can be observed, and more and more frequently emphasis is given to the evolution of man and his earliest cultures in America being convergent rather than dependent on the Old World (Bryan, 1978). The antiquity of the peopling of America dating back to the period of 30,000 years ago and more is becoming more accepted due to new discoveries (Morlan, 1980; Bryan, 1978). The problem enters into the third phase of dialectical negation of negation, bringing us back if not to former and complete autochthonism of man's origin in America, then at least to the assumption that America might have been peopled from Asia by palaeoanthrops (Bryan, 1978), although there is no evidence to corroborate this idea.   The earliest American population is acknowledged to have been capable of independent historical creative work manufacturing its own bifacial tool technology, and of inventing its own quite peculiar stone points for projectile weapons.   Later indigenous peoples founded the New World civilizations independently based on cattle-breeding, agriculture, trades, writing and so on.   This surprising convergence, starting from the early Palaeolithic, gives us a very obvious and inspiring example of independent development of a tremendous part of the globe in almost full isolation, as if on another planet.   This comparison gives an additional sense to the theme under discussion, as far as the world outlook is concerned, making us pay more attention to those possible migrations and ties which have affected ancient America, and to those peoples who were moving towards it through Beringia submerged 10,000 years ago.

From the standpoint of the archaeology of Northeastern Asia, I start from the thesis acknowledged by many, that America was populated from Asia through Beringia by the people of the modern type *(Homo sapiens)*, with yet un-specialized Mongoloid features. But, taking into account some new data, I am somewhat cautious and do not exclude the possibility that the first entry into America could have been made by palaeoanthrops, who for some reason did not leave any visible tracks in the anthropological record of Amerinds (probably because of having been forced out, eliminated or assimilated by the modern type of man).

As discussed previously by Dikov (1969, 1979), and West (1979), primary migrations to America were accomplished very slowly and unconsciously as a result of natural population growth and gradual mastering of the adjacent, unoccupied hunting grounds.   Naturally, such slow and unconscious dispersal of palaeolithic hunters did not have any ecological barriers for them if there was enough game. Such a state of things applied until there appeared a productive type of economy in the Neolithic.

THE STAGES OF MIGRATIONS

At present, the available data permit us to single out four stages of the peopling of Beringia with different degrees of precision.

The First Stage

This stage is as yet only hypothetical, but necessary from the point of view of logic.   It is the most indefinite as far as its chronology is concerned.   It is connected with the initial entry of man into Beringia, and it appears to correspond either to the last but one so called Ziryansk glaciation (70,000-50,000 years ago) or to the beginning of the last Sartansk glaciation which lasted between 28,000 and 10,000 years ago. The remains of the so-called "pre-projectile-point stage", including the bone industry of Old Crow with prevailing pebble and flake tool technology lacking any developed forms of bifacial points (Kreiger, 1964; Morlan, 1980; Grabert, 1979) may belong principally to this stage in the history of Beringia (28,000-10,000 years ago, or more). In the Soviet Far East Philimoshki, Kumary I, the southern examples of pebble tool technology, appear to be prototypes of these most ancient American artifact sites (Derevyanko, 1978). Moreover, the well-stratified sites of Kongo (9470 ± 530 [Kril-314]; 8655 ± 220 [Mag-196]) and Siberdik (8480 ± 200 [Kril-249]) on the Kolyma (Dikov, 1977, 1979), Lopatka IV in Kamchatka (Dikova, 1979) and the complex of Pasika in northwestern North America dating back to approximately the twelfth millennium B.P. (Borden, 1970) appear to be late relics of this archaic Early Palaeolithic East-Asian-American pebble tool technology. Naturally, only some elements of the named complexes can be regarded as relics of the "pre-projectile-point" stage: these are the flake tools and pebble tools, but without bifacial points occurring amongst them.

In connection with the discovery of worked bones of this Early Paleolithic period in northern Yukon Old Crow one can only regret that we know too little about the fractured mammoth bones discovered in the 1950s by Brykin on the Mukhomornaya River in central Chukotka and by Arsenyev also in Chukotka earlier (Dikov, 1979; p. 14).

The Second Stage

This stage of peopling Beringia (20,000-14,000 years ago) is still hypothetical in some aspects, and corresponds to the stage of the greatest spread of the last (Sartansk) glaciation glaciers and to the maximum size of Beringia itself. At that time, under the pressure of the approaching and then blocking gigantic Canadian and Laurentian ice sheets the population had to depart from the inner Alaskan periglacial areas to the Beringian bridge, especially to its southern edge which was gradually drying out.

At this stage the tundra-steppe of northeastern Asia, Alaska and the Beringian land "bridge" was a continuous ecological zone populated with megafauna. This region was bounded by glaciers to the west and east, by the ice cap of the Arctic Ocean to the north and by the relatively warmer Pacific Ocean to the south. It appears that within this blocked region we must consider a division into two cultural zones - the inner continental zone of land hunters for large tundra-steppe mammals, and the scarcely defined North-Pacific littoral zone of hunters sporadically exploiting marine bioresources. As for technology, on the whole it was still

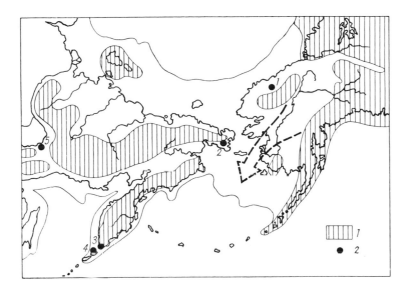

FIG. 1. *The second stage of peopling of Beringia (20,000-13,000 years ago). (1) glaciers; (2) ancient sites (1-British Mountain; 2-Chel'kun II, III; 3-Lopatka IV; 4-Kozyrevsk I, Bolshoye I (Shumshu Is.) The dotted arrow shows probable human departure from the glacier.*

a united cultural zone with a relatively uniform culture, probably in the process of transition from pebble tools to bifaces.

The artifacts of the British Mountain type in the northern Brooks Range in Alaska with their pebble tools and primitive flake points (McNeish, 1964), and also the sites of Lopatka IV in southern Kamchatka (Dikova, 1979), Kozyrevsk I and Bolshoye I on Shumshu Island (Salova, 1976), having pebble tools as well, perhaps give some idea of this culture. But, unfortunately, all of these non-stratified artifacts lack well founded dates.

In spite of the vast field investigation in Alaska, no Dyuktai-Denali artifacts have been found for this stage, (they occur only 12,000-11,000 years ago). Apparently at that time the reverse migrations of hunters from Alaska to Northeastern Asia under the pressure of advancing North American glaciers prevailed, and, prevented the dispersal of the Dyuktai population to Chukotka, Kamchatka, and Beringia. This effect is increased because the glaciers of the Chersky Range made an obstacle too (Fig. 1). Thus it is necessary to agree with Haynes (1976) and Irving (1978) who reject any influence of the Dyuktai culture of Yakutia on the formation of paleo-Indian culture.

Consequently, 20,000-14,000 years ago in Beringia some other

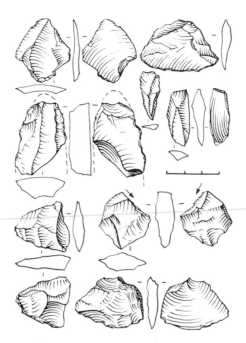

FIG. 2. *The complex of stone implements from Chel'kun site III on the Chukotski Peninsula.*

culture may be expected to have developed, and it might be a direct and immediate predecessor of the Early Ushki culture (the Ushki Site I, II, Layer VII) with developed bifacial stemmed points which has been discovered so far only in Kamchatka and which will be discussed below. It appears that this hypothetical culture contained the same bifacial points as the Trail-Creek Cave in Alaska (Larsen, 1970) or the same rudimentary primitive projectile flake points as the sites of Chel'kun II, III in Chukotka where I found them in 1977 on the surface of the fluvioglacial terrace together with scrapers, burins, and fragments of bifacial knives (Fig. 2). But, unfortunately, the complex of Chel'kun II, III dating is very problematic, as it is based only on its similarity with the problematic British Mountain complex, and on being relatively more primitive than the successive Chel'kun stemmed points which are of Early Ushki culture character.

The Third Stage

The third stage of peopling Beringia, quite definitely brought to light, corresponds to the dispersal of the Early Ushki culture on its western approaches and is dated 14,000-13,000 B.P. Beginning

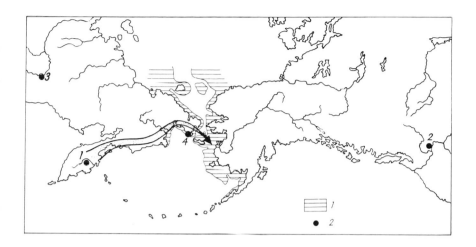

FIG. 3. *The third stage of peopling Beringia (14,000-12,000 years ago. (1) The remains of the Beringian "bridge" 13,000 years ago. (2) The ancient sites (1-Ushki I,V; 2-Marmes; 3-the Dyuktai Cave; 4-Ul'khum). The arrow shows the probable direction of littoral dispersal of the Early Ushki culture.*

with this period we can speak quite materially and definitely about cultural relations between Asia and America through Beringia. Moreover, it was the last period when these connections and population migrations could take place purely on dry land, as Beringia had not yet been divided by a sea strait. The cutting of the isthmus by the sea occurred at the beginning of the thirteenth millennium (Fig. 3).

Large sites on the Ushki Lake shores have been discovered so far only in Kamchatka and refer to the Early Ushki culture - Ushki I and Ushki V in the deposits of cultural Layer VII. They lie on the bench of the fluvioglacial plain of Sartansk age which is 3-4 m above the flood plain. The fluvioglacial facies of the loose deposits of the terrace consists of gravel and fine-grained sand. Soil pyroclastic facies of the upper deposits with a total thickness of 2.6 m are formed of sand and clay loam horizontally stratified layers containing several cultural horizons of wide chronological range - from the Neolithic to the Palaeolithic. The lowest Layer VII lies at the depth of 2.1-2.2 m.

As for stratigraphy, all the Ushki sites are beyond criticism. The cultural layers are clearly divided by sterile bands of volcanic ash and the material cultural remains mainly occur directly in the charcoal ground floors of the dwellings. The same stratigraphic precision is notable in particular for Palaeolithic Layer VII having two radiocarbon dates: 13,600 ± 250 (GIN-167); 14,300 ± 200

354 N.N. Dikov

(MAG-550).
Paleolithic sites Ushki I and V of Layer VII are the only ones of such age in the Far East which have preserved house remains and a burial in a special pit among them.

The Early Ushki houses are characterized by their very large size (over 100 sq. m.) and their double nature. There were three hearths in each part of a house. The framework of wooden poles anchored in the ground probably supported tents made from animal skins. The primitive arrangement of the hearths without any stone border gave a very archaic appearance to these houses. Judging by considerable accumulations of bone and charcoal the houses

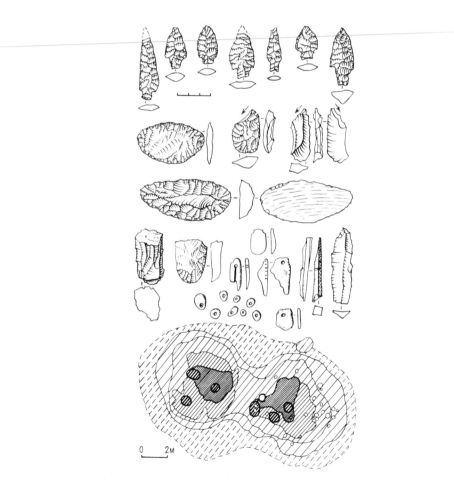

FIG. 4. *The complex of stone implements and the scheme of a doubled house of the Early Ushki culture (Kamchatka).*

were occupied for a long duration. Most probably, in Palaeolithic villages there was a tribal community consisting of paired families and keeping a communal household.

Considering the stoneworking manufactured items of the Early Ushki Palaeolithic sites there was a technology of flake detachment from amorphous cores and blade detachment from prism-like cores and probably from Levalloisian cores. The inventory of stone tools consists of arrowheads with bifacial continuous retouch on a triangular blade having convex edges, and a stem; knives of mainly leaf-like shape treated with side retouch either unifacial or bifacial; scrapers of various form, including end ones; and diagonal or side burins. Stone beads and small flat pendants are numerous (Fig. 4).

The complex economy of the Early Ushki culture people resulted from fishing, hunting by means of bow and arrows, and gathering. On the whole, the economic and technical level in Kamchatka was quite high (bows with arrows, polishing of stone adornments) - not a bit lower than in the European Palaeolithic.

There are grounds to suppose that this most ancient Kamchatkan culture, or at least its influence, actively spread towards America. A great number of beads and pendants - a typically Indian wampum - which have been preserved in one of the Ushki graves, appear to indicate deep Kamchatkan and finally Asiatic sources of the Indian custom to wear adornments like these. The very custom of magic ochre utilization in a funeral ritual can be also regarded as a considerable linking element between the Palaeolithic cultures of the New and Old World. Finally, the Ushki stemmed arrow points also display much in common with the later American ones.

The relations with America are particularly clearly expressed in similarity of bifacial stemmed points with those of the Palaeo-Indian Tradition of Lind Coulee in the northwestern USA (the sites of Marmes, Lind Coulee) dated about 11,000-10,000 years ago (Fryxell et al., 1970) and the consequent San Dieguito culture in the southwestern USA. Taking into account the chronological priority of the Kamchatkan stemmed points and the relatively small chronological gap between them and western American ones it is possible to admit that the Kamchatkan points somehow influenced the development of stem types. It goes without saying, this does not mean that I think all the American points have originated from the described stemmed points from Kamchatka - the opinion very often ascribed to me (Bryan, 1978). This is rather A. Jelinek's opinion, who thinks it possible to infer that the Llano Complex is derived from the Ushki sites culture of Layer VII (Jelinek, 1971).

Taking into account the possible influence of the Early Ushki culture on the cultures of northwestern North America, we may accept the possibility of its dispersal from the region of Kamchatka, which was no dead-end in glaciated periods as is sometimes thought. The dispersal towards Alaska could be along two routes: the inter-continental and the littoral one. The last way seems more convenient and probable for the Ushki people with such complex site economy. Besides, until the thirteenth millennium the route could pass completely by land along the southern Beringian shore and then along the northwestern coast of North America, when the glaciers had somewhat retreated and were no obstacles for human settling on the Pacific coast (Fig. 3).

The Fourth Stage

The fourth and best defined stage of peopling Beringia refers to the terminal Sartansk glaciation (12,000-10,000 years ago). It is connected with further erosion and ecological reconstruction: widening the strait between Chukotka and Alaska, gradual swamping of the tundra-steppe, and reducing the species diversity and the number of megafauna. As for archaeology, this stage is characterized by the dispersal of a peculiar culture with wedge-shaped cores and with microblades detached from them, and leaf-shaped bifacial spear and arrow points (Fig. 5). These spread from Chukotka to the Beringian territory and further into Alaska.

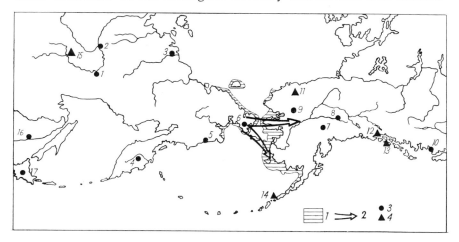

FIG. 5. *Peopling of Beringia 12,000-9,000 years ago. (1) the remains of the Beringian "bridge" about 12,000 years ago; (2) probable direction of migrations from the side of Chukotka to Alaska 12,000-10,000 years ago; (3) the monuments of the Dyuktai-Denali-Akmak type with bifacial tools (1-Dyuktai, 2-Ikhine, 3-Berelyokh, 4-Ushki I,II,IV,V,VI, 5-Inas'kwaam II, 6-Kurupka I, 7-Dry Creek, 8-Healy Lake, 9-Akmak, 10-Namu; 16-Ustinovka-Tadushi, 17-Shirataki). (4) the monuments with bifacial tools (11-Galaher Flint, 12-Ground Hog Bay, 13-Hidden Falls, 14-Anangula, 15-Sumnagin).*

Because of the previously mentioned ecological changes this
so-called Beringian cultural tradition (West, 1980) of northeast -
Asian origin underwent considerable transformation.   After its
entry into the Pacific coast, sea hunting apparently developed
more and more intensively. This gradual maritime adaptation may
have permitted those ancient Beringians to traverse the sea strait
not only by ice, but by boat too and cross over to the eastern side
of Beringia 12,000 years ago, bringing to Alaska the culture known
there as Denali-Akmak (Anderson, 1970; West, 1979).

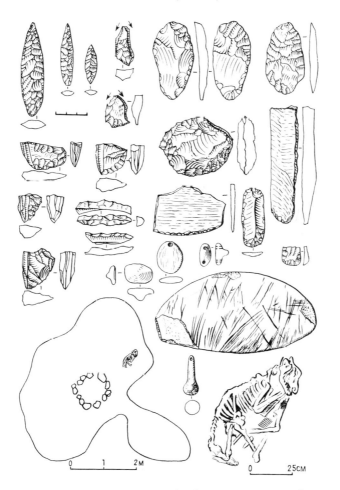

FIG. 6. *The complex of stone implements, a pendant, labrets,
a sandstone plate with the image of a dwelling and the
dwelling itself with the domestic dog's burial excavated on
site Ushki I in Layer VI (the Late Ushki culture in
Kamchatka).*

It is not excluded that the Dyuktai mammoth hunters from
northern Yakutia had by the twelfth millennium, settled down on
the site of Berelyokh on the lower Indigirka River (Mochanov,
1977) and penetrated to Alaska by the northern route. But the
main migration flow had to be achieved by the southern Pacific
route. In this southern region the so-called Late Ushki culture
formed consisting of bison hunters and fishermen, and this complex
culture was easily adaptive to the new ecological conditions. (It
has been well studied on the Ushki Lake shores on the peninsula of
Kamchatka.) It is characterized by large sites with remains being
preserved to a depth of two metres in Layer VI of Ushki points I,
II, IV, V and VI, dated by radiocarbon 10,860   ±   400 (MAG-400);
10,760 ± 110 (MAG-219); and 10,360 ± 350 (MO-345) (Dikov, 1977,
1979).

Ushki I, one of these Kamchatkan Palaeolithic sites, includes
more than 20 excavated houses of different types, the
semisubterranean ones among them having an entrance hallway and
a ring-like stone hearth always abundant in charcoal (Fig. 6). These
houses had a framework of poles, probably covered with skins, and
in their style of construction and smaller size radically differed
from the large double tents of the underlying Layer VII. There are
differences in stone implements, too: together with leaf-shaped
points and wedge-shaped cores lacking in Layer VII, unique stone
lip perforator labrets occur (Fig. 6). Bone implements have been
also found here: various spurs and dagger-like tools of large
tubular bones and, besides, very finely made shovels for
housekeeping. Throughout Layer VI fragments of bison, horse,
lemming and salmon bones occur. In one of the houses a husky-like
domestic dog burial has been found (Fig. 6). Primitive works of art
are also known here, in particular, a sandstone plate with an
image of a tent-like house in a wood (probably of larches), and on
the floor of one of the houses the image of a red ochre fish has
been discovered.

The relationship between the Late Ushki culture and America
are traced in similarities of bifacial leaf-shaped points,
wedge-shaped cores, ski-like spalls and microblades detached from
them, knife-scrapers and burins with the same implements of the
Denali culture and, in part, the Akmak Complex in Alaska. Some
general technological affinity with the blade industry of the most
ancient Aleutian site of Anangula has been also found. All these
connections and analogies lead us to suppose that the Late Ushki
culture, like its predecessor the Early Ushki culture, dispersed
from Kamchatka to Chukotka and Alaska during the final
Pleistocene and played a definite role in the formation of
proto-Eskimo-Aleuts.

The artifact sites discovered in Chukotka not long ago can be
regarded as intermediate. The first one - the site of Inas'kwaam
in southern Chukotka - contains two complexes of stone artifacts:

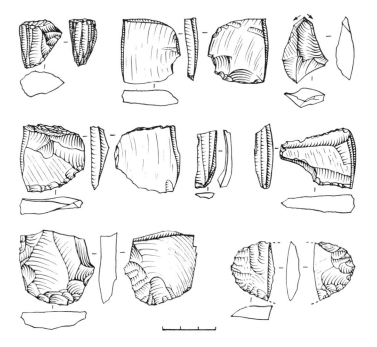

FIG. 7. *The complex of stone implements of Kurupka I site on the Chukotski Peninsula.*

1) slightly pointed flake cutters, like the Ushki Layer VII finds; 2) a miniature wedge-shaped core and a fragment of a narrow leaf-shaped bifacial projectile point typical for Ushki Layer VI. The other artifact site - the closest to America - is a complex of bifacial stone implements from a high (15-20 m) fluvioglacial terrace on the side of the Kurupka River on the Chukotski Peninsula close to the Bering Strait. Not long ago (1978-1979) wedge-shaped cores of grey flint were found there (some of them had a very peculiar archaic appearance of flat plate-like flakes from the butt of which microblades had been detached), together with leaf-like bifacial knives, crudely worked scrapers, and burins (Fig. 7).

The third one, which was discovered in 1981 close to Chaplin Cape just opposite St Laurence Island, is the Ul'khum Site on the bank of the river of the same name flowing into Lake Naivan. Here, on the fine road metal surface of a fluvio-glacial terrace 12 m high and also in the surface cultural layer as thick as 15-20 cm, there occurred numerous flakes of grey siliceous slate stone implements very typical of the Palaeolithic Beringian tradition: a bifacial butted core and an ordinary wedge-shaped core, fragments

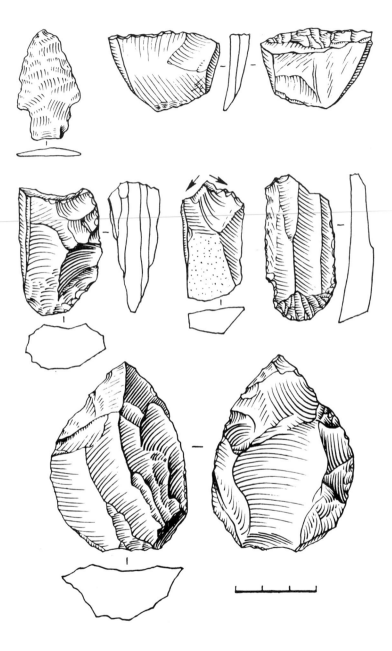

FIG. 8. *The stone artifacts of the Palaeolithic Site Ul'khum on the Chukotski Peninsula.*

of bifacial knives and projectile points, burins, scrapers, blades and microblades, and some other artifacts of the same siliceous slate. Of particualr interest are original handaxe-like tools with a slightly pointed cutting and pricking working end and a stemmed arrowhead - exactly of the same type as in Palaeolithic Layer VII of the Ushki Sites in Kamchatka and probably left on the site much earlier than the wedge-shape and butted cores (Fig. 8). Thus the mixed complex of the Ul'khum Site finds dating back to different periods in general is more close to the Kamchatkan Palaeolithic, than to the Dyuktai Palaeolithic in Yakutia, where stemmed points in Palaeolithic assemblages are totally absent.

As the Beringian Tradition at its final stage is connected with the ethnogeny of proto-Eskimo-Aleuts its remains and artifacts can be situated not only on river terraces, like most of the preceding cultures, but also on the sea coastline of ancient Beringia. To a great extent it is related to more recent Early Holocene sites of the type of ancient Aleut Anangula, the economy of which was closely tied up with sea. For all this, it is necessary to reject completely a commonly held idea (Lauglin, 1979) that the ancient Anangula people came to their site on the present Anangula Island by land migration along the continuous southern Beringian coast. This coast has not existed since the thirteenth millennium, B.P., and by the time of the start of the Anangula culture the Chukotka and Alaska coastlines had already been close to their modern positions for many years. That is why the search for ancient sites with the Beringian Tradition of the Anangula type is very likely to succeed in some stable parts of the coastline of southeastern Chukotka and on the Beringian shelf underwater, comparatively close to the present coastline.

To date there are only two uncertain finds underwater of rather questionable artifacts, in the form of thin fragments of slate, found by geologist Y.I. Goldfarb drilling in two locations on the shelf of the Okhotsk Sea: in the Gizhiga Bay and close to it.

REFERENCES

Anderson, D.D. (1970). Akmak: An early archaeological assemblage from Onion Portage, Alaska. *Acta Arctica*, fasc. 16.

Borden, C.E. (1970). New Evidence of early cultural relations between Eurasia and Western America. Proceedings VIII ICAES (Tokyo), Vol. III.

Bryan, A.L. (1978). An Overview of Paleo-American Prehistory from a Circum-Pacific Perspective. In *Early Man in America from a Circum-Pacific Perspective* (A.L. Bryan, ed.). Edmonton.

Campbell, J.M. (1963). Ancient Alaska and Paleolithic Europe. In *Early Man in the Western Arctic. A symposium. Anthropological papers of the University of Alaska*, Vol. 19, No. 2.

Chard, C.S. (1959). New World Origins: a Reapprisal. *Antiquity*, 33.

Chard, C.S. (1960). Routes of Bering Strait. *Arctic Anthropology*, 26.

Derevianko, A.P. (1978). On the Migrations of Ancient Man from Asia to America in the Pleistocene Epoch. In *Early Man in America from a Circum-Pacific Perspective* (A.L.Bryan, ed.). Edmonton.

Dikov, N.N. (1968). The discovery of the Paleolithic in Kamchatka and the problem of initial occupation of America. *Arctic Anthropology* V (1) (In Russian).

Dikov, N.N. (1969). *The Ancient Fires of Kamchatka and Chukotka*. Magadan. (In Russian).

Dikov, N.N. (1977). *The Archaeological Monuments of Kamchatka, Chukotka and the Upper Kolyma (Asia Joining America in Ancient Times)*. Moscow (In Russian).

Dikov, N.N. (1979). *The Ancient Cultures of Northeastern Asia (Asia Joining America in Ancient Times)*. Moscow (In Russian).

Dikova, T.M. (1979). The first Paleolithic finds in Southern Kamchatka (the Cape of Lopatka). In *The New Archaeological Monuments of the Far East North*. Magadan (In Russian).

Fryexel, R., Bielicki, T. and Daugherty, R. (1970). Human Skeletal Material and artifacts from Sediments of Pinedate (Wisconsin) glacial age in Southeastern Washington, United States. In *Proceedings VIII ICAES* (Tokyo and Kyoto, September, 1968), Ethnology and archaeology. Tokyo. Vol. III.

Fladmark, K.R. (1978). The Feasibility of the Northwest Coast as a Migration Route for Early Man. In *Early Man in America From a Circum-Pacific Perspective* (A.L. Bryan, ed.). Edmonton.

Grabert, G.F. (1979). Pebble Tools and Time Factoring. *Canadian Journal of Archaeology*, No. 3.

Haynes, V.C. (1971a). Time, Environment and Early Man. *Arctic Anthropology*, Vol. VIII, No. 2.

Haynes, V.C. (1971b). Mammoth Hunters in the USA and the USSR. In *Beringia in the Cenozoic*. Khabarovsk (In Russian).

Hopkins, D.M. (1979). Landscape and Climate of Beringia during Late Pleistocene and Holocene Time. In *The First Americans: Origins, Affinities and Adaptations*. New York.

Irving, W.N. (1978a). Pleistocene Archaeology in Eastern Beringia. In *Early Man in America from a Circum-Pacific Perspective* (A.L. Bryan, ed.). Edmonton.

Irving, W.N. (1978b). An Approach to the Prehistory of the Far East, From Farther East. In *Early Paleolithic in South and East Asia*. (F. Ikawa-Smith, ed.). Mouton Publishers. The Hague, Paris.

Jelinek, A.J. (1971). Early Man in the New World: a Technological Perspective. *Arctic Anthropology* VIII.

Krasheninnikov, S.P. (1756). The Description of the Land of Kamchatka. Saint Petersburg (In Russian).

Krieger, A.D. (1964). Early Man in the New World. In *Prehistoric man in the New World*. Chicago.

Larsen, H. (1970). Trail Creek. *Acta Arctica* Fasc. XV, Copenhagen.

Laughlin, W.S., and Wolf, S.I. (1979). Introduction. In *The First Americans: Origins, Affinities and Adaptations*. New York, Stuttgart.

McNeish, R.S. (1964). Investigations in Southwest Yukon. Papers of the Robert S. Peabody Foundation for Archaeology, Phillips Academy, Andover, Massachusetts, Vol. 6, No. 2.

Mochanov, Yu.A. (1977). The Ancient Stages of the Human Settlement of Northeastern Asia. Novosibirsk (In Russian).

Morlan, R.E. (1980). *Taphonomy and Archaeology in the Upper Pleistocene of the Northern Yukon Territory: a Glimpse of the Peopling of the New World*. Ottawa.

Müller-Beck, H.G. (1966). Paleohunters in America: Origins and Diffusion. *Science* 152, (3726).

Portenko, L.A. (1968). The Beringian Connections Between Eurasia and North America in the Notion of Zoogeographers. In *The Arctic Ocean and Its Coastline in the Cenozoic.* Leningrad (In Russian).

Salova, O.A. (1976). To the Problem of the Paleolithic on the Kuril Islands. In *Siberia, Central and East Asia in Ancient Times.* Novosibirsk (In Russian).

Sushkin, P.P. (1925). Zoological Regions of Middle Siberia and the Nearest Parts of Mountainous Asia and the Historic Experience of Modern Fauna of Paleoarctic Asia. *The Bulletin of the Moscow Society for Testers of Nature.* New series, the biological department, 34 (In Russian).

West, F.H. (1979). *The Archaeology of Beringia.* Columbia Press, Williamstown.

Wormington, H.M. (1971). Comments on Early Man in North America, 1960-1970. *Arctic Anthropology* VIII (2).

THE HOLOCENE TRANSGRESSION ON THE ARCTIC FLANK OF BERINGIA: CHUKCHI VALLEY TO CHUKCHI ESTUARY TO CHUKCHI SEA [1]

Dean A. McManus [2], Joe S. Creager [2], Ronald J. Echols [2*], and Mark L. Holmes [3]

[2] *School of Oceanography, University of Washington, Seattle, WA 98195, USA*
[3] *United States Geological Survey, Seattle, WA 98105, USA*

ABSTRACT

Modern assemblages of benthonic foraminifera have been used to define biofacies in 26 cores of Holocene transgressive sediments in the southern Chukchi Sea. Based on these biofacies and on radiocarbon dates that contain corrections for inactive carbon, the following sequence of events is inferred: the low sea level of the last glaciation exposed the inner and central parts of the shelf as a broad, steppe-tundra valley, down which flowed a stream system that entered the Arctic Ocean through a canyon near Wrangel Island. With rising sea level, the encroaching ocean extended quickly up the valley to form a narrow, shallow estuary (10 m deep). Although probably ice-covered almost year round, the estuary apparently received sufficient river water during brief summers to nourish an inner shelf benthonic foraminiferal assemblage. The ice cover of the estuary may not have formed a significant barrier to land migration, however. Increasing water depth brought a higher arctic assemblage comparable to that in the ice-covered East Siberian Sea today. The flooding of Bering

[1] Contribution 1236 of the School of Oceanography, University of Washington.

*Present address: Mobil Oil Corporation, Dallas, Texas 75221, USA.

Strait ($\sim$ 15,500 B.P.) and, soon after, Long Strait and the sill between Herald Shoal and Cape Lisburne ($\sim$ 14,600 B.P.) changed the estuary into an embayment of the Arctic Ocean with shorelines only 50-100 km from today's. The flooding of Anadyr Strait ($\sim$ 14,400 B.P.) terminated the land connection and joined Bering Sea water to the Chukchi Sea along a narrow passage through which came a lower arctic assemblage. Approximately 13,500 B.P. an assumed dramatic warming of the climate accelerated the melting of nearby glaciers and the accumulation of sediment in a possibly turbid sea. On the flooding of the final sill, Shpanberg Strait ($\sim$ 12,000 B.P.) warm water entered the Chukchi Sea from the Bering Strait in abundance, bearing a lower arctic assemblage and silt from the Yukon River. Since then, the water circulation has been essentially unchanged, around lower capes that may have served as habitation sites like similar ones today. Approximately 5,000 years ago a mixed assemblage appeared, suggesting more episodes of southerly transport of water through Bering Strait. Throughout this time the deltas of the Noatak and Kobuk rivers migrated 200 km southeast with rising sea level to their present positions. These deltas, like other coastal features in the southeast Chukchi Sea, can be followed seaward from their present sites and back in time over much of the Holocene transgression.

INTRODUCTION

The waters of the Chukchi Sea today cover much of the Arctic flank of Beringia (Fig. 1). The sea is wide and shallow over its almost featureless inner and central parts. The geological oceanography of these parts is discussed by Creager and McManus (1967) and McManus, Kelley, and Creager (1969). The following comments on the physical oceanography come from Coachman, Aagaard, and Tripp (1965) and Coachman and Aagaard (1981). The outer part of the sea, north of Herald Shoal, is not well known.

For approximately eight months of the year the entire Chukchi Sea is covered by winter ice and polar pack ice. Although the net flow of water during this ice-covered period is at times to the south, the principal feature of the mean annual water circulation is that water enters the sea through Bering Strait and exits around both ends of Herald Shoal, to produce a quasi-permanent northward-setting current. The part of this current near the Alaskan shore is the warmer, less saline Alaskan Coastal Water, best developed during the ice-free season and moving at speeds of 10-40 cm/sec. The water that moves direct across the Chukchi Sea from Bering Strait to Herald Canyon, between Herald Island and Herald Shoal, is the colder, more saline, slower-moving Bering Sea Water. Water also enters the Chukchi Sea in two other, but minor, ways. Some cold, low salinity waters enters through Long

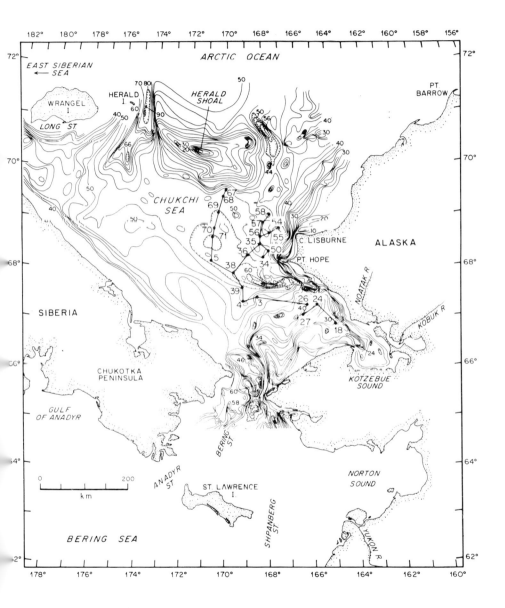

FIG. 1. *Bathymetry of the Chukchi Sea, showing location of cores used in this study. Contour interval is 2 m to 70 m, 10 m thereafter. (From Holmes, 1975, Fig. 4).*

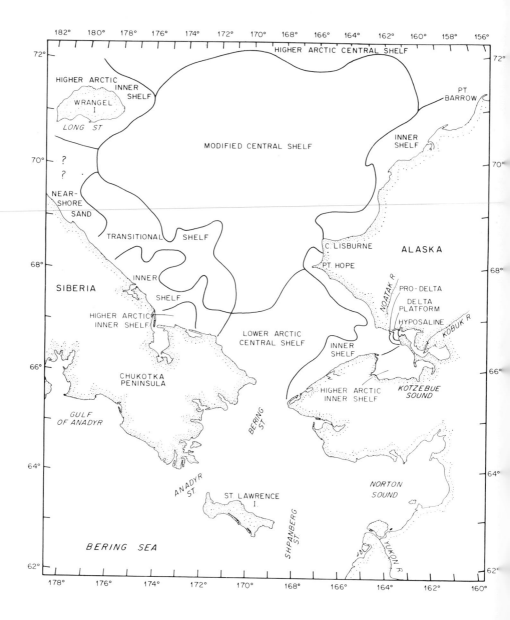

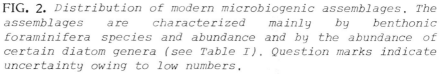

FIG. 2. *Distribution of modern microbiogenic assemblages. The assemblages are characterized mainly by benthonic foraminifera species and abundance and by the abundance of certain diatom genera (see Table I). Question marks indicate uncertainty owing to low numbers.*

Strait from the East Siberian Sea and moves southeastward along the Siberian coast, sometimes almost to Bering Strait. And at times cold, saline water enters from the Arctic Ocean along the bottom of the sea by rising up Herald Canyon and another canyon near Pt. Barrow.

For this study samples from 26 piston cores (locations shown in Fig. 1) of up to 8 m in length were analysed, using sieve and pipette analysis for grain size and microscopic analysis for the microfossil identification. The sediments in the cores consist mainly of clayey silt and very clayey silt, but significant variations are observed. The organisms present as microfossils in the cores are also present in the modern Chukchi sediments. The modern organisms have been grouped into modern assemblages, based mainly on benthonic foraminifera and on diatoms, that we believe contain significant ecological information. These assemblages are characterized in Table 1, and their distribution in the bottom sediments is shown In Fig. 2. The appearance of these same assemblages at depth in the cores is inferred to represent the same ecologies; the assemblages are defined as biofacies of the sediments containing them (Fig. 3). It is from these presumed ecologically-sensitive biofacies that the following historical development of environments is constructed for the transgressing Chukchi Sea.

SEA LEVEL CURVE

Radiocarbon dates of carbonate-free carbon in the sediments were determined. In an attempt to correct these dates for contamination by the inactive carbon observed in the sediment as microscopic particles of coal-like material, the "readily oxidizable organic material" was determined by the Walkley-Black analysis (Jackson, 1958, p. 214) and subtracted from the carbonate-free total carbon content. The remaining carbon was attributed to inactive carbon. The corrections in the dates follow the procedure of Broecker and Kulp (1956) for per cent of inactive carbon. Nevertheless, these dates (Fig. 3) must still be viewed as questionable, because of the need for such corrections and of the large thickness of cored section (10-15 cm) usually required for sufficient carbon to date. Despite the uncertainties in dating, a sea level curve for the period 16,500 to 12,000 B.P. is estimated (Fig. 4) from the following kinds of data: lagoon or coastal pond with the freshwater or hyposaline algae *Chara* (L in Fig. 4); nearshore sand, < 10 m (N in Fig. 4); the contact between pro-delta and inner shelf assemblages, 5-15 m today (P in Fig. 4); and 12,000 B.P. as the opening of Shpanberg Strait, -30 or -32 m (McManus *et al.*, 1974) (triangle in Fig. 4). Straight lines through these points give the estimated sea level curve of Fig. 4. This curve diverges from worldwide curves such as those of Curray

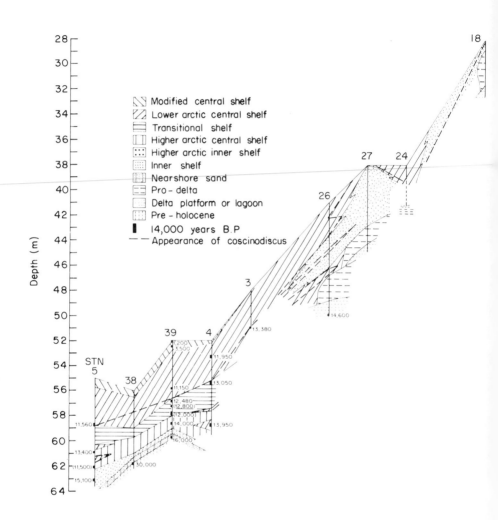

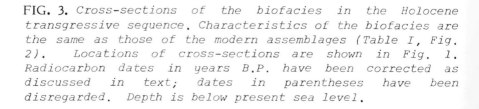

FIG. 3. *Cross-sections of the biofacies in the Holocene transgressive sequence. Characteristics of the biofacies are the same as those of the modern assemblages (Table I, Fig. 2). Locations of cross-sections are shown in Fig. 1. Radiocarbon dates in years B.P. have been corrected as discussed in text; dates in parentheses have been disregarded. Depth is below present sea level.*

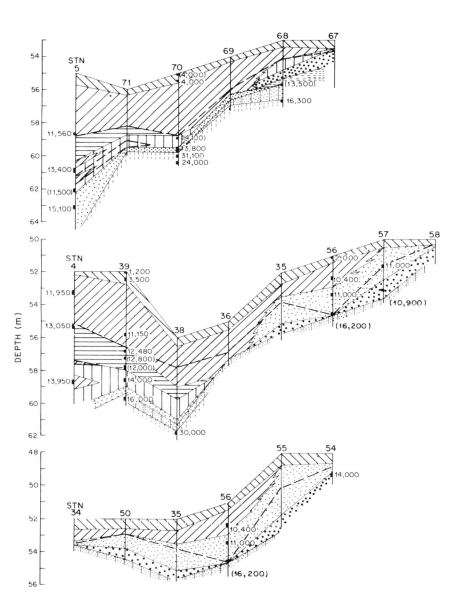

FIG. 3. (contd)

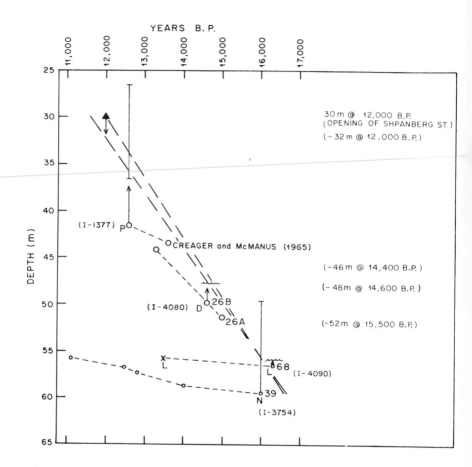

FIG. 4. *Estimated sea level curve for the Chukchi Sea (16,500 to 12,000 B.P.). Lines of short dashes connect sample data in cores 26 (A and B), 39, and 68 (for locations see Fig. 1) and the core described by Creager and McManus (1965). Circles represent dates and depths below present sea level of samples in these cores. X represents an apparently unreliable date. The types of data used in estimating sea level positions (L, N, D, P, and the triangle) are described in the text. Cores 26A and B are replicate cores at station 26. Laboratory C-14 numbers are as follows: P = I-1377; D = I-4080; L = I-4090; N = I-3754.*

(1965) or Mörner (1971), as might be expected from local differences in the hydro-isostatic response of shelves (Clark, Farrell, and Peltier, 1978; Clark and Lingle, 1979), the Chukchi shelf being an unglaciated shelf near glaciated uplands. In addition, mild Quaternary tectonism has apparently uplifted areas bordering the Chukchi Sea, as well as features within it (Holmes and Creager, 1981, p. 298), and produced some recently active faults within the Chukchi basin (Holmes, 1975, p. 103) and between Bering Strait and St. Lawrence Island (Hopkins, 1972, p. 134). Nevertheless, the curve in Fig. 4 does fall within the uncertainty of compiled sea level data for the Bering and Chukchi continental shelves over this period (Hopkins, 1979, Fig. 1.3).

THE TRANSGRESSION SEQUENCE

Chukchi Valley: Time of Lowest Sea Level (18,000 B.P.)

At the time of lowest sea level, the Chukchi Sea was exposed as a broad, low valley separated by the subdued hills of the Herald Shoal-Cape Lisburne Peninsula (40 m relief) from the outer plain dipping northward to the Arctic Ocean shoreline (Fig. 5). Crossing this unglaciated valley was a stream system composed of (1) Hope Valley (Creager and McManus, 1965), which included the ancient Kobuk, Noatak, and other rivers fed by the mountain glaciers north and east of Kotzebue Sound, (2) valleys of Siberian streams fed by glaciers in the uplands of Siberia (Hopkins, 1979, Fig. 1.4), and (3) a valley fed by a large pro-glacial lake south of Bering Strait adjoining the glaciated end of the Chukotka Peninsula (Hopkins, 1979, Fig. 1.4). Sediments of this pre-transgression environment were reached in six of the cores; they ranged from a hard, compact, laminated silty clay devoid of microfossils to fossiliferous silty clay. The former resembles the pre-transgression silty clay beneath 0.2 to 0.5 m of transgressive sediment around Wrangel Island (Lapina et al., 1970, p. 519). The fossiliferous silty clay contains abundant pollen grains of Artemisia, grass, and sedge (P.A. Colinvaux, personal communication, 1972) of the steppe tundra vegetation that covered this part of Beringia (Colinvaux, 1967).
   Although the Chukchi Valley was apparently swept by strong, persistent winds, as recorded in the dunes and loess of northwest Seward Peninsula (Hopkins, 1972, p. 134) and the loess of the Arctic coastal plain of Siberia (Pewe, 1976, p. 48), the few samples of pre-transgression sediment in our cores have none of the characteristics of loess. This windy, steppe tundra valley leading gently upward to the southeast toward ice-free central Alaska was an open route for migration of humans and mammals at this time (Hopkins, 1972, p. 137).

TABLE 1

Modern Microbiogenic Assemblages and Holocene Biofacies

	Benthic Foraminifera	
Name	Arenaceous vs. Hyaline	Species Dominance
1. Modified Central Shelf	Abd. arenaceous	Dom: *R. arctica* or *E. advena* Sub: *S. biformis* or *P. torquata*
2. Lower Arctic Central Shelf	Arenaceous 1/5 to 1/2 as abd. as in 1	Dom: *E. advena* Sub: *R. arctica* Other arenaceous spp rare.
3. Transitional Central Shelf	Abd. hyaline No dominant arenaceous	Dom: *E. clavatum* Sub: *B. frigida*
4. Higher Arctic Central Shelf	Moderately abd. arenaceous	Dom: *S. biformia* or Sub: *P. torquata* or *E. advena* *R. arctica* absent
5. Higher Arctic Inner Shelf	Arenaceous and hyaline about equal abd.	Dom: *E. advana* Sub: *S. biformis* Hyaline: *E. clavatum B. frigida, A. pulchella* and *E. frigidum*
6. Inner Shelf	Abd. to very abd. arenaceous	Dom: only *E. advena* Other arenaceous spp. not even sub.
7. Pro-delta	Hyaline abd. Arenaceous com.	Dom: *E. clavatum* Sub: *B. frigida* Most important: *C. incertum* and *E. subarcticum E. advena* < 10%
8. Delta platforms; lagoon	Hyaline abd.	Dom: *E. clavatum* and *P. orbiculare E. advena* < 10%
9. Hyposaline	Hyaline present Arenaceous absent	Char: *E. sp* cf. *E. selseyense* and *P. orbiculare*
10. Nearshore sand	Hyaline present: Few fossils.	Char: *A pulchella* and *E. subarcticum*

Arenaceous Foraminifera

Reophax arctica
Eggerella advena
Spiroplectammina biformis
Pseuodobolivina torquata

Diatom Content	Present Location	Ecological Significance
Coscinodiscus and *Melosira* abd.	Main central	Silty sediment central shelf under present-day environment of mixed higher and lower arctic environments
Coscinodiscus may or may not be present *Melosira* absent	Central shelf near Bering Strait	Silty sediment central shelf under a surface water environment supplied from the Bering Sea, but not reaching the bottom
Coscinodiscus and *Melosira* absent	In deeper, fine-grained sediment of central shelf off Siberia	Silty sediment under an environment of apparently rapid sediment accumulation, but not marginal marine
Melosira abd. *Coscinodiscus* absent	Outer shelf	Silty sediment under a central or outer shelf ice-covered environment dominated by the Arctic Ocean
Melosira may be present (plant fragments common)	Inner shelf at high latitudes and near bays with cold, winter water	Sandy sediment under a higher arctic, cold, small variability inner shelf environment
Melosira may be present (plant fragments may be present)	Inner shelf of part of Alaskan Coastal Water and part of East Siberian Water	Sandy sediment under a highly variable inner-shelf environment.
Melosira abd. (Tintinnids present)	Kotzebue Sound	Fine-grained sediment seaward of delta platform
Plant fragments abd. (Tintinnids present)	Kobuk-Noatak delta platform, Kotzebue Sound	Delta platform or lagoonal environment. Water depth: ∿2 m
Plant fragments abd. (Tintinnids present)	Kobuk Inner Delta $< 10°/oo$ salinity	Sands to sandy silts of hyposaline environment, very shallow water
None	Off western Siberia coast	Sandy to very sandy sediment under a nearshore environment near the beach.

Hyaline Foraminifera

Elphidium clavatum
Buccella frigida
Elphidium frigidum
Asterellina pulchella
Cribrononion incertum
Elphidium subarcticum
Elphidium sp. cf. *E. selseyense*
Protelphidium orbiculare

Shallow Chukchi Estuary: ($\sim$18,000 to $\sim$15,000 B.P.)

The beginning of the transgression went unnoticed over most of the Chukchi Valley, because the first rise in sea level would have been at depths within Herald Canyon, still below the level of most of the Chukchi Valley. The history of the outer shelf, north of Herald Shoal, is unknown. Until sea level had risen to approximately -70 m, the floor of the Chukchi Valley was little affected. But by the time it rose to -60 m ($\sim$17,000 B.P., Fig. 4), a long, narrow, shallow estuary had been formed (Fig. 5) and formed quickly, with each 1 m rise in sea level flooding another 30 km of the valley to the southeast. By then, the headward retreat of the stream mouths would have separated the Kobuk-Noatak, Bering Strait, and Siberian streams from their former tributary attachment.

The first sediments to be deposited in this estuary were either mixtures of sand, silt, and clay containing few microfossils, the Nearshore Sand (Cores 38, 39, Fig. 3), or the sandy sediment of the Inner Shelf (Cores 70, 71, Fig. 3). Eventually the Inner Shelf assemblage came to dominate. Today this assemblage tolerates a highly variable temperature and salinity, from the cold, saline bottom conditions produced by vertical mixing during ice-formation in the surface water to the warmer, less saline conditions produced by stream runoff and insolation along the Alaskan coast in the summer (Fig. 2). Perhaps the most similar location today, however, is a large area of the ice-covered East Siberian Sea off the mouth of the Kolyma River, where this assemblage occurs. The Shallow Chukchi Estuary, therefore, could well have been ice-covered almost year round, with a brief summer to provide warmer, less saline water to the estuarine environment. The water in the estuary was certainly shallow, as can be shown as follows: radiocarbon dates of its sediments are as young as $\sim$15,000 B.P.; the sill at Bering Strait gives a datum of -52 m, which the sea level curve shows to have been breached $\sim$15,500 B.P. Therefore, the Shallow Chukchi Estuary was mostly less than 10 m deep (Fig. 3). (The average depth of Norton Sound today, even with the presence of the delta of the Yukon River, is almost twice this, as is the average depth of Kotzebue Sound.)

Chukchi Higher Arctic Estuary and Sea: ($\sim$15,000 to $\sim$13,500 B.P.)

As the waters of the Chukchi Estuary continued to deepen with rising sea level, the Inner Shelf biofacies of sandy sediment in the middle of the estuary was superceded by the Higher Arctic Central Shelf biofacies of very fine-grained sediment (Fig. 3 - Cores 5, 71, 70, 4, 39, 38). Today this assemblage is most extensive on the Chukchi outer shelf (Fig. 2) and in the East Siberian Sea in an environment of little variation under general ice

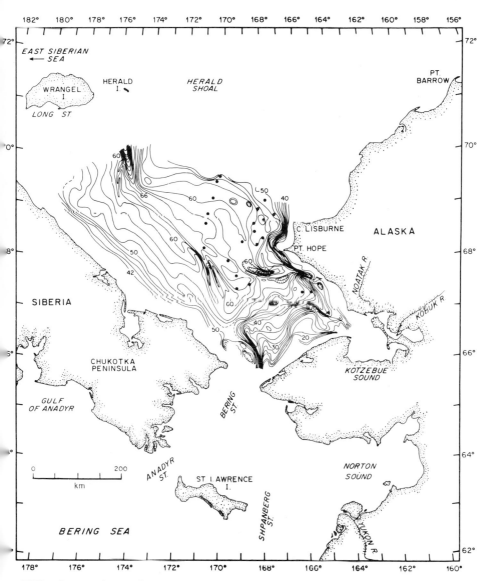

FIG. 5. *Estimated topography of the exposed Chukchi Valley during low sea level. Contour interval is 2 meters. Note the stream valley, with tributaries to Kotzebue Sound, Bering Strait, and Siberia. These contours mark the topography on the top of a seismic reflector (3.5 kHz) that corresponds with the basal sandy sediment of the transgression sequence. The thinness of the basal sediment should make the reflector a reliable expression of the underlying subaerial topography. (From Holmes, 1975, Fig. 17). Dots show core locations. Interpretations of sea level rise based on this chart have assumed no significant isostatic or tectonic change in this surface during the rise.*

cover with highly saline bottom water of very low temperatures. We assume the same environment applied at that time in the Chukchi Estuary, although we should note that today this assemblage also occurs in Kotzebue Sound and the Gulf of Anadyr where cold, saline water residual from winter ice formation persists on the bottom through the ice-free season. This summer preservation is due to the stable, two-layer water column that develops when insolation warms the lighter, less saline, surface water containing the river runoff (Coachman, Aagaard, and Tripp, 1965). We prefer the ice-covered interpretation because the great size of the Chukchi Estuary then, which was still relatively shallow ($\sim$ 15 m), would require considerable insolation and fresh water run-off to maintain the stable, two-layer water column, and we find no other evidence of warming at this time.

With the continued rise in sea level, the estuarine phase of the Chukchi Sea approached its end. The Bering Sea was still beyond the sill in Anadyr Strait (-46 m), and the Arctic Ocean lay beyond the other side of the estuary behind the Cape Lisburne-Herald Shoal Peninsula (sill depth = -48 m) and the sill in the Long Strait (-48 m). All these sills were by then only a few meters above sea level and several tens of meters wide, but shrinking. The land bridge had been reduced to the sill in Anadyr Strait, although the water passage near Bering Strait was only about 25 km wide, and that separating Wrangel Peninsula and Herald Peninsula about 75 km. Surface currents, though subject to wind effects, would be expected to follow an estuarine pattern of setting southeast along the southern shore and northwest along the northern shore. With the flooding of Long Strait (-48 m) and the sill between Herald Shoal and Cape Lisburne (-48 m), the Chukchi became an embayment of the Arctic Ocean, and a short time later, when Anadyr Strait was flooded ($\sim$ 14,400 B.P., Fig. 4), the land bridge finally disappeared.

The first record in our cores of the connected waters of the Bering and Chukchi seas is in Cores 4 and 5 (Fig. 3). Into the Higher Arctic Central Shelf biofacies of the Chukchi Sea there were intruded pulses of the Lower Arctic Central Shelf biofaces, as distinct pulses in Core 4, nearest Bering Strait, and as mixtures of the two biofaceies in Core 5. The Lower Arctic Central Shelf assemblage today occurs just north of Bering Strait (Fig. 2) and is the same assemblage as that on the central shelf of the Bering Sea south of St. Lawrence Island (Knebel, Creager, and Echols, 1974). The pulses affect only the biota; the sediment is unchanged. Because no pulses of the Higher Arctic Central Shelf biofaces are reported in cores south of St. Lawrence Island (Knebel, 1972; Knebel, Creager, and Echols, 1974), except for the surface sediments in the Gulf of Anadyr with its residual bottom water (Kummer and Creager, 1971), we assume that the flow of water was from the Bering Sea into the Chukchi Sea, then as now. The flow direction today is presumably due to sea level being higher in the Bering Sea, although this sea level differential is still unexplained (Coachman and Aagard, 1981, p. 108). The proposed role of atmospheric circulation in driving the shelf circulation (Coachman and Aagaard, 1981) can be used with Lamb and Woodroffe's (1970, p. 50) model of atmospheric circulation here over the last 20,000 years to suggest that the mean flow direction has continually been from the Bering into the Chukchi. Just after the flooding of Anadyr Strait, however, this flow would have been along a narrow, even tortuous passage to the Bering Strait, quite possibly with glaciers still nearby along the end of the Chukotka Peninsula (Hopkins, 1979, Fig. 1.4). Presumably it was only at times of some increase in the flow from the Bering Sea that the pulses of the Lower Arctic Central Shelf assemblage were carried into the southern part of the Chukchi Sea in sufficient abundance to be preserved. Otherwise, the ice-covered Higher Arctic assemblage dominated the sea entirely.

The Transition: (∿13,500 to ∿12,000 B.P.)

Sometime after the opening of Anadyr Strait, the Higher Arctic Central Shelf assemblage was superceded by a different, a transition assemblage. We are not certain about the significance of this new assemblage, even though it is present today off the coast of Siberia. In both the modern assemblage and the cored biofacies it is characterized by hyaline benthonic forminifera (Table I) but not of marginal marine species. Although we have no data on its modern accumulation rates, rates in the cores were more than twice those of the previously described environments (140 to 500 cm/1,000 years vs. 50 to 60 cm/1,000 years). This same environment is recognizable in the cores taken by Knebel, Creager, and Echols (1974) on the shelf south of St. Lawrence Island. It forms the inner shelf environment prior to 14,000 B.P. and has an accumulation rate of 180 cm/1,000 years, compared with rates of 20 to 30 cm/1,000 years for the equivalent of our Inner Shelf environment during the last 14,000 years. Therefore, we assume that this biofacies marks an environment of very rapid sedimentation. And because it does not contain deltaic assemblages, its condition of rapid sedimentation is assumed to have extended far from shore. But the sediment is not from the Yukon River; that sediment arrived later.

The silts and clays deposited in this environment, like those in the underlying sediments, but unlike those from the Yukon River, contain a prominent tail of particles finer than 0.5 μm. Such a distribution may characterize more than one mode of particle formation, as far as we know, but in a polar environment it seems to be closely associated with melting ice. It characterizes sediment from melting glaciers in southeast Alaska (Slatt and

Hoskin, 1968, p. 445; Sharma, 1979, p. 48), from much of the pack
ice-covered outer Chukchi shelf, from much of the pack
ice-covered shelf of the East Siberian Sea (Naugler, Silverberg,
and Creager, 1974, p. 198), and from the classical winter layers of
the varves from glacial lakes (Ashley, 1975, p. 316). Combining
this interpretation with the rapid sedimentation rate leads us to
infer that a marked climatic warming at this time greatly
accelerated the melting of glaciers in Chukotka and the Brooks
Range. A drastic warming about 14,000 to 13,000 B.P. is inferred
by Hopkins (this volume) from independent data on land.

The Last Sill: ($\sim$12,000 to $\sim$5,000 B.P.)

The last sill, in Shpanberg Strait (-30 or -32 m), was flooded
approximately 12,000 B.P. (Knebel and Creager, 1973; McManus
et al., 1974), which provided the Alaskan Coastal Water a direct
passage to Bering Strait. The lower Arctic Central Shelf
assemblage reappeared, this time pervading the entire Chukchi
central shelf and this time accompanied by the silt from the Yukon
River, which is almost devoid of the clay-sized particles (Dupre
and Thompson, 1979, p. 662) that characterized earlier Chukchi
sediments. The mouth of the Yokon was still south of Shpanberg
Strait at this time (Knebel and Creager, 1973).

The wide dispersal of the assemblage shows that all the sampled
part of the Chukchi Sea was dominated by the flow from Bering
Sea. Near Point Hope an Inner Shelf assemblage developed (Fig.
3), superceding the Higher Arctic Inner Shelf assemblage. But
farther northwest, along Herald Shoal, which was finally flooded,
the Higher Arctic Inner Shelf assemblage thrived, probably because
most of the warmer water turned round Point Hope to flow into
the Arctic Ocean and did not reach Herald Shoal. The currents at
that time were apparently comparable in speed to those of today,
for the sites of Cores 36 and 69 (Fig. 3) contain hiatuses that
make those sites at that time resemble the platform south of Point
Hope today, which is now kept clean of sediment by the curents.
One intrusion into this current pattern, however, was the delta of
the Kobuk/Noatak rivers.

This delta formed much earlier at the head of the estuary.
Probably as soon as the rapid, early flooding of the Chukchi Valley
had been completed, a delta formed at the head of the estuary.
Our oldest radiocarbon date from a delta platform biofacies is
14,600 B.P. Although a delta is usually interpreted as evidence of
a sea level stillstand, this one may not signify that, after all. It is
10 m deeper than the delta previously discussed by Creager and
McManus (1965) as a basis for a stillstand. And deltaic sediments
are present in several cores at shallower present-day water depths
until the modern deltas are reached at the north end of Kotzebue
Sound (Fig. 3). Although the Delta Platform biofaces was sampled

in several cores, a lithology of platform sands, as occurs in Kotzebue Sound today, was never present; the sediments are clayey silts. Possibly stillstands are represented in this sequence, but such a sequence could also be produced during a rapid rise in sea level (Van Straaten, 1960, p. 431). Regardless of the stillstand significance, this sequence marks a persistent deltaic environment for the past 14,600+ years that migrated eastward with rising sea level into Kotzebue Sound.

The Modern Shelf: (since ∿5,000 B.P.)

Modern conditions are assumed to have begun with the appearance of the Modified Central Shelf assemblage, approximately 5,000 B.P. (Fig. 3). Also at this time the percentage of silt lessened in much of the area, possibly owing to the formation of the modern Yukon Delta at that time and the retention of more of its silt in Norton Sound (Nelson and Creager, 1977). There was still enough silt reaching the Chukchi Sea, however, to transgress with the Modified Central Shelf environment over previous inner shelf environments (Fig. 3).

The Modified Central Shelf assemblage is a mixture of higher and lower arctic forms (Table 1). The reappearance of higher arctic forms might signify more common episodes of southerly water movement across the Chukchi Sea, and into the Bering Sea. Such episodes occur today when the atmospheric pressure gradient produces extensive north winds, which can reduce the mean monthly northward water movement through Bering Strait to very low values at times (Coachman and Aagaard, 1981, p. 109).

DISCUSSION

During the last glaciation the Chukchi Valley was a windswept, steppe tundra, like the rest of the exposed polar shelves that formed parts of a possible migration route into central Alaska. At that time there was no topographic or marine obstruction to migration across the Chukchi Valley; there was, however, a large stream system running down the valley to the northwest and emptying into the Arctic Ocean. As sea level rose, this stream system was drowned to form a headward-lengthening, shallow estuary. By the time sea level had risen to -60 m (∿17,000 B.P.), the estuary had extended at least 500 km up the valley. It was only a few meters deep, shallower than Kotzebue Sound or Norton Sound today, and had a narrow width, comparable to that of Bering Strait today. Its trend from its mouth near Herald Island to its broad head some 150 km north of Bering Strait might have formed a northwest-southeast, narrow, shallow, marine obstacle to land migration. Because the estuary was probably ice-covered most of the year, however, it might not have been a significant obstacle. To maintain a land migration route around the estuary, ice-covered or not, would have required the route to be deflected along the south shore and through the 150 km-wide section between the head of the estuary and Bering Strait to the south.

With the continued rise of sea level, the estuary began to widen over coastal ponds and tundra. Our cores obtained few samples of these environments - principally because these environments are preserved as stiff clays that stop penetration of the piston core barrel beneath 5 m or more of Holocene silts. It seems possible that a different coring technique, for example, vibrocoring (Bouma, 1969, p. 328), could sample these sediments throughout much of the Chukchi Sea. This technique should also allow coring through sand. A comparison of the core distribution in Fig. 1 with the surface sediment type (Creager and McManus, 1967, Fig. 6) will show the cores to be absent from sandy bottoms (and bottoms in Soviet jurisdiction).   Consequently we have little information on older sandy sediments, for example, beaches. Vibrocoring should provide such information.

The widening estuary was probably ice-covered almost year round, with only a brief summer to provide melt water from the stream. The estuary was still mostly less than 10 m deep, and its environment with an inner shelf assemblage might well have resembled that off the Kolyma River today. The further rise of sea level widened the estuary considerably. The effect of river flow was reduced, for a high arctic assemblage developed on the estuary bottom. The estuary was then approximately 15 m deep and probably ice-covered still for most all the year, perhaps a very shallow version of the East Siberian Sea or outer Chukchi shelf today. General surface water circulation would have tended to be toward the head of the estuary along the south shore and seaward along the north shore. The south shore, like the Siberian shore today, would have been the colder-water shore, bordered by a current flowing eastward in the direction of migration.

The flooding of Bering Strait (-52 m, $\sim$15,500 B.P.) seems not to have made a major mark in the stratigraphic record. By that time the estuary's southern shore lay only 100 m off the present Siberian shore, reducing the width of an exposed-shelf migration route to a narrow belt along there. The north shore was along the low (30 m relief), wide peninsula of Herald Shoal-Cape Lisburne. The end point of this low, open peninsula varied little in location throughout this rise of sea level, as did the Herald Island end-point of the opposite peninsula, because of steep slopes. Between them passed the water and ice exchange between the Arctic Ocean and the estuary and also passed the introduction and migration of any Arctic-Sea creatures into the estuary.

When the estuary had begun to widen rapidly, the pre-existing topography was such that the head of the estuary had ceased to advance as rapidly as before. As a result, a delta probably formed at the head of the estuary. Since then, the delta has retreated 150 km southeast from that somewhat protected position to the present protected position of the Noatak and Kobuk deltas at the north end of Kotzebue Sound. These two positions are presumably connected by a continuous, buried sequence of deltaic deposits filling the baylike depression shown in Fig. 5 at the sites of cores 18, 24, 26, and 27. On the north and south sides of this depression are elongated elevations that at appropriate sea levels may have served for human habitation sites as Point Hope and the capes around Kotzebue Sound did later. Although our cores of the deltaic sediments mainly sampled submarine deltaic environments (some presumably < 2 m deep), one short core bottomed in peat, and many more subaerial deposits might be preserved in the complex sequence. The sediment accumulation rates in the silty deltaic sequence are high (350 cm/1,000 years). Creager and McManus (1965) report an even higher rate. In the silty sediments of Core 39, by contrast, the accumulation rates vary from 115 cm/1,000 years at the bottom to 3 cm/1,000 years at the top. The deltaic sediments would seem to record appropriate conditions for preservation of a variety of remains.

With the flooding of Long Strait (-48 m, ∿ 14,600 B.P.) and the sill between Herald Shoal and Cape Lisburne (-48 m), the Chukchi changed from a wide estuary narrowly connected to the Arctic Ocean into an embayment of that ocean. Not long afterwards, the low sill in Anadyr Strait (-46 m, ∿ 14,400 B.P.) was flooded to connect the Bering Sea with the Chukchi Sea along a narrow passage. Through the passage came a lower arctic assemblage from the Bering Sea that at times of possibly increased flow was abundant enough to be preserved in Chukchi sediments. The land bridge, though by then severed, still retained a narrow band of exposed shelf along the Siberian coast and, on the other side of this narrow water passage, it continued as the broad lowlands stretching eastward into what later would become Norton Sound.

Approximately 13,500 B.P. a drastic increase in warming accelerated the melting of the remaining glaciers on the Chukotka Peninsula and in the Brooks Range of Alaska. The resulting meltwater carried considerable sediment to the sea that was deposited rapidly. The water may well have been turbid during this period, which can be thought of as a brief transition leading to the time of flooding of the last sill, Shpanberg Strait (-30 or -32 m, ∿ 12,000 B.P.). Even at this stage, however, two points of land extending into the sea may have proved as attractive for habitation sites as their modern day counterparts.

Once the flow of water from the Bering Sea began and could continue past Cape Lisburne, the pattern of the modern circulation was established. Just as today Cape Prince of Wales and Point Hope are thrust outwards into the modern flow and the migrations of marine organisms, so too at that earlier time were the north end of the shoal extending north from Cape Prince of Wales (Holmes, 1975, Fig. 24) and the Point Hope of that time thrust outwards. These exposed, rocky or gravelly sites might have been swept clean of remains by the advancing waves and currents of rising sea level, however.

On the flooding of Shpanberg Strait warm water entered the Chukchi Sea direct, bearing a lower arctic assemblage and silt from the Yukon River. Norton Sound itself was still dry land. The water circulation was essentially that of today with perhaps fewer episodes of southerly water transport. For the next 7,000 years this environment persisted, until beginning approximately 5,000 years B.P. the episodes of southerly flow apparently increased, producing a modified assemblage of higher and lower arctic forms. The net result was to give a colder water appearance to the central shelf assemblage. At about the same time the Yukon River shifted to its modern delta in Norton Sound, thereby slightly reducing the supply of silt to the Chukchi Sea. And the persistent delta of the Noatak/Kobuk rivers had almost retreated to the location of the two separate deltas today.

CONCLUSION

A history of the Holocene transgression can be reconstructed for the Chukchi Sea. The relative sequence of events progresses from a windswept, steppe-tundra valley to a shallow, partly ice-covered estuary. A broader, more continuously ice-covered estuary became an embayment of the Arctic Ocean and began to receive pulses of warmer water from the Bering Sea. With the advent of a climatic warming, considerable sediment was brought to the sea. Rising sea level finally opened the last strait, bringing warmer Bering Sea water and Yukon River silt throughout the Chukchi Sea. A final change has given a colder water appearance to the Chukchi Sea, possibly by increasing the episodes of flow into the Bering Sea.

Although this relative sequence of events has been given dates, the nature of the corrections required for the radiocarbon dates should be kept in mind.

During at least the last 12,000 years of this history in the southeastern part of the Chukchi Sea a continuity of coastal features can be illustrated. As shown in Fig. 5, Cape Prince of Wales had an antedated cape in the form of the shoal extending northward from it. Northwest of both capes at the entrance to Kotzebue Sound are similar, older capes. The continuation of the deltas backward in time to the northwest has been mentioned. An older Point Hope extends westward from the modern one. In general, a line drawn normal to the shoreline at the coastal feature will trace that feature's historical positions over much of the last transgression.

ACKNOWLEDGEMENTS

This paper has benefited from discussions of our results and of problems in Beringia in general with David M. Hopkins. Discussions with several participants in the symposium have also been very helpful. This research was funded by grants from the National Science Foundation.

REFERENCES

Ashley, G.M. (1975). Rhythmic sedimentation in glacial Lake Hitchcock, Massachusetts-Connecticut. In *Glaciofluvial and Glaciolacustrine Sedimentation* (A.V. Jopling and B.C. McDonald, eds). Society of Economic Paleontologists and Mineralogists Special Publication no. 23, pp. 304-320.

Bouma, A.H. (1969). *Methods for the Study of Sedimentary Structures*. Wiley-Interscience, New York, 458pp.

Broecker, W.S. and Kulp, J.L. (1956). The radiocarbon method of age determination. *American Antiquity* 22, 1-11.

Clark, J.A., Farrell, W.E. and Peltier, W.R. (1978). Global changes in post-glacial sea level: A numerical calculation. *Quaternary Research* 9, 265-287.

Clark, J.A., and Lingle, C.S. (1979). Predicted relative sea-level changes (18,000 years B.P. to present) caused by late-glacial retreat of the Antarctic ice sheet. *Quaternary Research* 11, 279-298.

Coachman, L.K. and Aagaard, K. (1981). Reevaluation of water transports in the vicinity of Bering Strait. In *The Eastern Bering Sea Shelf: Oceanography and Resources*, Vol. I. (D.W. Hood and J.A. Calder, eds). National Oceanic and Atmospheric Administration, Washington, D.C.,p p. 95-110.

Coachman, L.K., Aagaard, K. and Tripp, R.B. (1975). *Bering Strait: The Regional Physical Oceanography*. University of Washington Press, Seattle. 172 p.

Colinvaux, P.A. (1967). Quaternary vegetational history of arctic Alaska. In *The Bering Land Bridge* (D.M. Hopkins, ed.). Stanford University Press, Stanford. pp. 207-231.

Creager, J.S. and McManus, D.A. (1965). Pleistocene drainage patterns on the floor of the Chukchi Sea. *Marine Geology* 3, 279-290.

Creager, J.S. and McManus, D.A. (1967). Geology of the floor of Bering and Chukchi seas - American Studies. In *The Bering Land Bridge*. (D.M. Hopkins, ed). Stanford University Press, Stanford, pp. 7-31.

Curray, J.R. (1965). Late Quaternary history, continental shelves of the United States. In *The Quaternary of the United States*. (H.E. Wright Jr. and D.G. Frey eds). Princeton University Press, Princeton. pp. 723-735.

Dupre, W.R. and Thompson, R. (1979). The Yukon delta: A model for deltaic sedimentation in an ice-dominated environment. *Proceedings Offshore Technology Conference* 1, 657-664.

Holmes, M.L. (1975). Tectonic Framework and Geologic Evolution of the Southern Chukchi Sea Continental Shelf. Unpublished Ph.D. dissertation. University of Washington, Seattle, 143 pp.

Holmes, M.L., and Creager, J.S. (1981). The role of the Kaltag and Kobuk faults in the tectonic evolution of the Bering Strait region. In *The Eastern Bering Sea Shelf: Oceanography and Resources*, Vol. 1. (D.W. Hood and J.A. Calder, eds). National Oceanic and Atmospheric Administration, Washington, D.C., pp. 293-302.

Hopkins, D.M. (1972). The paleogeography and climatic history of Beringia during Late Cenozoic time. *Internord* 12, 121-150.

Hopkins, D.M. (1979). Landscape and climate of Beringia during Late Pleistocene and Holocene time. In *The First Americans: Origins, Affinities, and Adaptations*. (W.S. Laughlin and A.B. Harper, eds). Gustav Fischer, New York. p. 15-41.

Hopkins, D.M. (1983). Hard times in Beringia (this volume).

Jackson, M.L. (1958). *Soil Chemical Analysis*. Prentice-Hall, Englewood Cliffs, 298 pp.

Knebel, H.J. (1972). Holocene Sedimentary Framework of the East-Central Bering Sea Continental Shelf. Unpublished Ph.D. dissertation. University of Washington, Seattle, 186 pp.

Knebel, H.J. and Creager, J.S. (1973). Yukon River: Evidence of extensive migration during the Holocene transgression. *Science* 179, 1230-1232.

Knebel, H.J., Creager, J.S. and Echols, R.J. (1974). Holocene sedimentary framework, east-central Bering Sea continental shelf. In *Marine Geology and Oceanography of the Arctic Seas* (Y. Herman, ed.). Springer-Verlag, New York, pp. 157-172.

Kummer, J.T. and Creager, J.S. (1971). Marine geology and Cenozoic history of the Gulf of Anadyr. *Marine Geology* 10, 257-280.

Lamb, H.H., and Woodroffe, A. (1970). Atmospheric circulation during the last ice age. *Quaternary Research* 1, 29-58.

Lapina, N.N., Byelov, N.A., Kulekov, N.N., Syemyenov, U.P., and Spiridonov, M.A. (1970). Bottom sediments of the arctic seas. In *Geology of the U.S.S.R.*, Vol. 26 (D.B. Sidoryenko, ed.). Nyedra, Moscow, pp. 485-530, (in Russian).

McManus, D.A., Kelley, J.C. and Creager, J.S. (1969). Continental shelf sedimentation in an arctic environment. *Geological Society of American Bulletin* 80, 1961-1983.

McManus, D.A., Venkatarathnam, K., Hopkins, D.M., and Nelson, C.H. (1974). Yukon River sediment of the northernmost Bering Sea shelf. *Journal of Sedimentary Petrology* 44, 1052-1060.

Morner, N.A. (1971). Eustatic changes during the last 20,000 years and a method of separating the isostatic and eustatic factors in an uplifted area. *Paleogeography, Paleoclimatology, Paleoecology* 9, 153-181.

Naugler, F.P., Silverberg, N. and Creager, J.S. (1974). Recent sediments of the East Siberian Sea. In *Marine Geology and Oceanography of the Arctic Seas* (Y. Herman, ed.). Springer-Verlag, New York, pp. 191-210.

Nelson, C.H., and Creager, J.S. (1977). Displacement of Yukon-derived sediment from Bering Sea to Chukchi Sea during Holocene time. *Geology* 5, 141-146.

Pewe, T.L. (1976). Wind-blown dust in hot and cold deserts during the last glaciation. Abstracts, Fourth Biennial Meeting, American Quaternary Association, pp. 47-51.

Sharma, G.D. (1979). *The Alaskan Shelf*. Springer-Verlag, New York, 498 pp.

Slatt, R.M. and Hoskin, C.M. (1968). Water and sediment in the Norris Glacier outwash area, upper Taku Inlet, southeastern Alaska. *Journal of Sedimentary Petrology* 38, 434-456.

Van Straaten, L.M.J.U. (1960). Some recent advances in the study
of   deltaic   sedimentation.   *Liverpool   and   Manchester
Geological Journal* 2, 411-442.

BERGS, BARRIERS AND BERINGIA: REFLECTIONS ON THE PEOPLING OF THE NEW WORLD

Brian O.K. Reeves

*Department of Archaelogy,
University of Calgary, Calgary, Alberta,
Canada T2N 1N4.*

ABSTRACT

The debate on the time and entry of Early People into the New World generally focuses on the nature and extent of Western Canadian Ice Free Corridors - coastal, Cordilleran and interior - as the controlling mechanisms. The Late Wisonsin (*ca.* 20,000-14,000) glaciation was limited, in extent, and while the Cordillera was covered by an ice dome, both coastal and interior routes were open. A 100-200 km wide corridor existed at the height of glaciation, from the unglaciated regions of the Central Yukon south along the entire western border of the interior plains and foothills to the unglaciated regions of the continental interior of the United States.

Rocky Mountain glaciers were very limited in extent, and did not advance beyond the mountain fronts. The corridor's environment appears to have been characterized throughout by a cold, dry steppe tundra capable of supporting Rancholabrean grazers and man. Man was present by this time in both Eastern Beringia and the unglaciated regions to the south, which indicates that man could have entered during Mid-Winconsin (54,000-20,000) and/or earlier non-glacial times - the Sangamon (*ca.* 120,000 years ago). Ice distributions and environments in Western Canada were at these times analagous to today's, and more than sufficient time was available to populate the entire Western Hemisphere by people resident in Eastern Beringia throughout the time period.

QUATERNARY COASTLINES
ISBN 0 12 479250 2

While the nature and extent of Early Wisconsin glaciation is poorly known, the Western Canadian corridors were effectively sealed by barriers of water and ice at the height of Late Pleistocene glaciation during Illinonian times (*ca.* 150,000 + years ago).   It was during the close of this glaciation that the Rancholabrean fauna passed south through the open corridor with it steppe tundra environment on the freshly deglaciated and de-watered surfaces.   Man, present in Eastern Beringia at that time, could have followed the herds south eventually reaching the continental interior.

INTRODUCTION

The time(s) of entry and subsequent spread of Early People south of Beringia in Late Pleistocene time is a contentious issue in New World archaeology.   Speculations on early peopling generally fall into three categories:

(1)   The moderate - occupation during the Mid-Wisconsin or earlier (e.g. Adavasio *et al.*, 1983 (this volume))   The debate centres on dating the archaeological evidence, and geochronological control.

(2)   The radical - Sangamon or earlier peopling (e.g. Carter, 1957).   The Valsequillo (Steen-McIntyre   *et al.*, 1981, Irwin-Williams, 1981) and Calico (Schuiling, 1979; Simpson *et al.*, 1981) sites the two most widely debated cases. At Valsequillo the problem is dating, not the evidence, as the objects are artifacts and associated with butchered Pleistocene mammals.   In contrast, at Calico, the problem involves both the objects and dating.   There were no bones.   Had there been bones, I suspect, the argument would be dating, not the stones.

(3)   The absurd - as represented most recently by Goodman (1981) in *American Genesis* - who distorts data, evidence, and archaeologists to support his thesis of a New World origin for *Homo sapiens sapiens*.

The problems are many and complex, as are indeed the personalities, and far beyond the scope of my paper. Suffice it to say that the arguments in favor of early migration are not advanced by continued use by some archaeologists of terms such as the Lower Paleolithic for early New World assemblages. These terms invoke an immediate reaction and rejection by the conservative school.
    People may have been present in Beringia, at sites such as Old

Crow, from Sangamon times on. The evidence consists now not only of big bones but tiny stones (Morlan, 1981). Data presented by Irving and his associates (Jopling *et al*, 1981) suggests the possibility of Late Illinoian occupation, 150,000 or so years ago.

With man present in Beringia from possibly Late Illinoian on, he could have moved south then or later through any one or all of the Western Canadian Corridors - Coastal, Cordilleran, Eastern Slopes, and Interior Plains. Use of these does, however, require certain kinds of cultural adaptations - coastal, mountain, interior forest and plains - factors one should always bear in mind when considering the first peopling of the New World. Further, a littoral adaptation requires a less sophisticated technology than exploitation of high latitude mountains, plains and forests.

Life on the plains, or in the forests and mountains requires reasonably sophisticated extractive technologies for effectively hunting the game, and surviving the long cold northern winters. The northern boreal forests, are the least attractive of all. Land mammal resources are at present thin and widely scattered. Historically, life was difficult, the native population few, and winter settlement focused on the fish lakes. The Old Crow data, however, indicates people adapted to interior and high latitude steppe/tundra and forest conditions from Sangamon times on (Jopling *et al.*, 1981, Morlan, 1980).

The nature of the Western Canadian Corridors, the windows and their temporal duration, would place limits on human migration south particularly along the Eastern Slopes, or the so called Ice Free Corridor, which still in many peoples' minds was the principal migration route despite arguments by Fladmark (1979, 1981) for consideration of other routes.

Late Pleistocene windows are of two kinds: non-glacial intervals (Sangamon and Mid-Wisconsin), which would place no environmental limitations on peoples' movement south; and glacial intervals (Illinoian, Early and Late Wisconsin), when altered climatic conditions would limit and direct movement.

LATE WISCONSIN (*ca*. 20,000-10,000)

Both the Coastal and Eastern Slope corridors were open during the height of Late Wisconsin glaciation (*ca*. 20,000-15,000 B.P.) for use or movement through by people adapted to coastal and interior environments.

Cordillera

Accumulating evidence suggests that while the Cordillera was covered by an ice sheet the situation was complex, particularly in northern British Columbia (Fladmark, 1981). Cordilleran glaciation began *ca*. 19,000-17,000 years ago climaxing *ca*. 14,500-15,000 years ago. It was deglaciated by *ca*. 12,000 years ago. Use of the Cordillera as a corridor could occur during the initial Alpine and Valley glacial phases and, during drainage of the large proglacial lakes *ca*. 12,000 years ago. Upland areas, however, would be available to people during the late deglaciation phase.

Coastal

The Coastal corridor has been examined in some detail by Fladmark, who proposes it as a route for early movement (1979, 1981). While noting the uncertainty of the evidence for ice free areas along the North Pacific coast and problems in glacial limits and chronology, he remains of the opinion that it was a viable route; not only during the climax of the Late Wisconsin, but definitely before 17,000 or after 15,000 B.P.

As Fladmark points out (*ibid*., p. 43), evidence indicates the marine environments were then biologically productive and available for use by man particularly if he had the use of water-craft. The latter he feels would be required during the short glacial maxima.

Ice Free Corridor

The proposed ice free corridor along the western border of the Interior Plains and Eastern Foothills of the Rocky and Mackenzie Mountains (Fig. 1) was once considered a 1,600 km long, 1,500 m thick, continuous barrier of coalesced Cordilleran and Continental ice persisting until *ca*. 12,000 years ago. Our view of this event is rapidly broadening as is the corridor itself, particularly south of 60 degrees north.

Southern Alberta. Late Wisconsin glaciation in the Rocky Mountains now appears to have been a relatively minor event and represented by termini at or well behind the mountain fronts (Alley, 1973; Jackson, 1979; Jackson *et al.*, 1981; Reeves, 1973; Rutter, 1980). From the Bow Valley, near Banff, a radio-carbon date of approximately 25,000 (Wilson, pers. comm.) years has been obtained on a horse bone from gravels which may not be overlain by till, 32 km inside the mountain front, suggesting the Late Wisconsin Bow Valley glacier terminated some distance up-valley from the mountain front. Perhaps the contemporary ice front is represented by the Eisenhower Junction advance (Rutter, 1972); Kostashcuk, 1980). Eighty kilometers southeast in the Elk Valley, a date of 13,430 +/- 450 (GLX-5599)(Ferguson and Osborn n.d.) has been obtained from the base of a bog less than 40 km from the ice accumulation area of the Mount Joffre ice fields (Ferguson, 1978). In the Elk, the maximum down valley extent of the Late Wisconsin

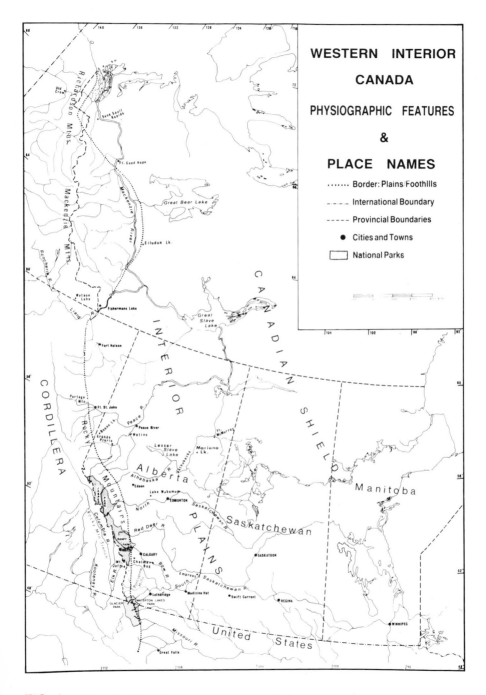

FIG. 1. *Topography and site names mentioned in the text.*

ice appears to have been on the order of only 53 km. Glaciers
appears to have retracted within a few kilometers of the present
limits on the Continental Divide by 10,000 years ago (Luckman and
Kearny, 1978).

These data suggest then that Late Wisconsin Mountain "Pinedale"
ice was limited both in extent and duration. Early people if
present could easily exploit not only unglaciated lands in the
foothills and lower mountain valleys, but the higher slopes above
the valley glaciers. Pollen profiles from the Elk Valley indicate
the presence of a birch, sage, grass, mountain shrub/herb tundra at
13,500 B.P. Pine, spruce and fir were present down valley
(Ferguson, 1978). The river had significantly downcut itself by
11,000 years B.P. (Harrison, 1976).

The Eastern Slopes, then as today, would be relatively moisture
deficient, subject to the dry chinook winds. Eastern slope pollen
profiles suggest a cold steppe tundra grassland environment. A
site, known as Chalmers Bog, in excess of 13 m thick, on the
Sheep River, 80 km southwest of Calgary, yielded a date of 18,300
+/- 380 (GSC-2668) and 18,400 +/- 1,090 (GSC-2670)(Jackson,
1979), at the 9-10 m level, and pollen indicative of a steppe
tundra. Other profiles from southern Alberta show generally
similar vegetation associations in the Porcupine Hills (Alley, 1972)
and Bow Valley (MacDonald, 1980). Post-glacial forests appear ca.
12,000-10,000 years ago in the mountain valleys and forested
eastern slopes (Jackson et al., 1981; MacDonald, 1980).

In summary, the evidence now clearly indicates that Late
Wisconsin mountain ice in Southern Alberta was restricted in
extent and did not coalesce with Laurentide ice along the
mountain front (Alley, 1973; Alley and Harris, 1974; Boydell, 1978;
Jackson, 1979, 1980; Reeves, 1973; Rutter, 1980; Stalker, 1975,
1980; Stalker and Harrison, 1977). Positive evidence for this
coalescence in Late Pleistocene times only comes from the
Athabasca Valley (Roed, 1975). Here, ice flowing out from the
mountains along the Athabasa Valley, coalesced with southwesterly
flowing Laurentide ice, deflecting both glaciers to the southeast
along the Foothills Front. This event is known as the Foothills
Erratic Train Glaciation and is Pre-Wisconsin in age. A
radiocarbon date of 49,400 +/- 1,000 (GSC-2409) has been obtained
from till of this glaciation in the Calgary area (Jackson, 1979). It
is considered a minimum date. The date provides support for
earlier determinations from 25 km north of Calgary on peat in
fluvial deposits of >35,000 (S-204), 33,500 +/- 200 (S-205) and
26,700 +/- 1,400 (S-206(Reeves, 1973; McCallum and Wittemberg,
1968: 365).

In Late Wisconsin times ca. 20,000 years ago the ice appears to
have stood at its maximum, well east of the foothills front (Fig. 2)
(Reeves, 1973; Stalker, 1975; Rutter, 1980). A physical corridor
between 100-200 km wide existed, depending upon which ice

frontal position in southern Alberta represents the Late Wisconsin maximum. It may correlate with the Lethbridge End Moraine (Reeves, 1973; Stalker, 1975) or lie some considerable distance east towards Medicine Hat (Reeves, 1973).

Recent support for a Late Wisconsin ice frontal position, passing through the Edmonton area (Bretz, 1943; Reeves, 1973), comes from a pollen profile at Wabamum Lake (Holloway, 1978), with basal dates of ca. 15,000. Steppe tundra vegetation was replaced at 11,000 B.P. by a boreal forest assemblage.

The ice frontal positions east of the Foothills Front still remain to be "fine tuned", but by 14,000 years ago most of the interior plains of Alberta and western Saskatchewan below 52 degrees north were ice and water free (Christianson, 1979, 1980; Mott and Christianson, 1980; St. Onge, 1980) (Fig. 2). A cold steppe grassland/parkland existed. A Rancholabrean grazing community dominated by bison were present. At Empress, Alberta, the faunal assemblage included mammoth, horse, camel, caribou, and bison. These were recovered from the 15 m post-glacial terrace of the Red Deer River. The assemblage is dated at 14,200 +/- 1,120 (GSC-1199) and 20,400 +/- 320 (GSC-1387)(Lowdon and Blake, 1975:16).

Northern Areas   The Late Wisconsin maximum in the Peace River country of northern Alberta and British Columbia is becoming increasingly well defined. The critical area is the Peace River Valley in northeastern B.C. (Mathews, 1978, 1980; Rutter, 1977). Until very recently, the data suggested that Late Wisconsin Cordilleran Ice (Early Portage Mountain Advance [Rutter, 1977]) and Laurentide Ice coalesced. Evidence for coalescence consists of a thin continuous till sheet, absence of end moraines and some drumoloid features showing a southward deflection (Rutter, 1980). It is not particularly "strong" in comparison to the Athabasca where a very vigorous deflection of the Athabasca Valley glacier occurred (Roed, 1975).

Dating of the Peace River Valley coalescence was based on a mammoth tusk recovered from outwash deposits assigned to the Late Portage Mountain Advance (Rutter, 1977). Recent re-dating of the specimen, originally dated at >11,600 (I-2248) and incorrectly reported as 11,600 +/- 320 (e.g. Rutter, 1977), has given a value of 25,800 +/- 320 (Mathews, 1980). The sample may well have been contaminated (it was earlier covered with preservative) or is redeposited (Clague, 1980:8; Lowdon and Blake, 1980:28) as it conflicts with one of 25,940 +/- 380 (GSC-573) from non-glacial sediments 135 km west (Clague, 1980, 1981; Mathews, 1980). The data suggests (*ibid.*) that the Early Portage Mountain Advance is Pre-Wisconsin in age and that Late Portage Mountain is Pre-Late Wisconsin in age.

The post Late Portage Mountain Cordilleran advance [Deserter's Canyon Advance (Rutter, 1977)] was a limited advance terminating 40 km upstream (Mathews, 1978:11). The sample dated (GSC-573) came from below till-like lenses which were considered by Rutter (1977) to be Early Portage Mountain. However, it would appear these lenses relate to the post Late Portage Mountain event (Mathews, 1980: 7-8, 14; Fladmark, 1981).

Other data supports this interpretation. A date of 27,400 +/- 580 (GSC-2034) was obtained by Mathews from a mammoth tooth in non-glacial gravels beneath a post-glacial river terrace at Fort St. John (Mathews, 1978: 17). Mathews originally considered the date to be from inter-glacial deposits with the Late Wisconsin till removed by erosion. However, redating of the Portage Mountain tusk suggests to Clague (1980: 13) that GSC-2034 is from a post-glacial context and ice did not cover the Fort St. John area in Late Wisconsin time.

While the Late Wisconsin coalescence and dating problem in the Peace (Reeves, 1973: 9) now appears to be satisfactorily resolved, the overall extent of Late Wisconsin ice and proglacial lakes requires delineation. Glacial Lake Peace (Mathews, 1980) consists of two separate stages. The earliest, the Bessborough stage, formed shortly after the maximum advance of Laurentide ice. This lake cut a beach into the Late Portage Mountain Moraine, now considered to be of Pre-Late Wisconsin age. At this time, Laurentide ice stood in a NW/SE trending front along the western edge of the higher foothills and plateaus (Mathews, 1980: Fig. 5B), some of which have been unglaciated since Mid-Early Pleistocene times.

Clayhurst is the next major stage of Glacial Lake Peace (Mathews, 1980: Fig. 5D). It formed when the Peace River Lobe of the Laurentide ice entered the area from the north and east in Late Wisconsin times (Mathews, 1980). Clayhurst drained to the southeast via Lesser Slave Lake (Fig. 2) and into the Saskatchewan River. By 11,000 years ago, Slave Lake and the Athabasca lowlands in north-central Alberta were deglaciated and the Mackenzie system open. Clayhurst persisted for some period of time, beach lines are well defined and varves indicate a minimum of 300 years. The lake drained some time prior to 12,000 years ago as Clovis complex sites occur within the basin.

An early drainage of Clayhurst is suggested by a radiocarbon date of 10,200 +/- 100 (GSC-2902) on a bison tibia from the 40 m terrace of the Smoky River at Watino, 130 m below prairie level, indicating either extremely rapid down-cutting or a very limited effect of Late Wisconsin ice in the area (Lowdon and Blake, 1979: 19).

Early drainage of Glacial Lake Peace is further substantiated by dates from the Athabasca area. Dates of 10,200 +/- 160

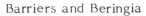

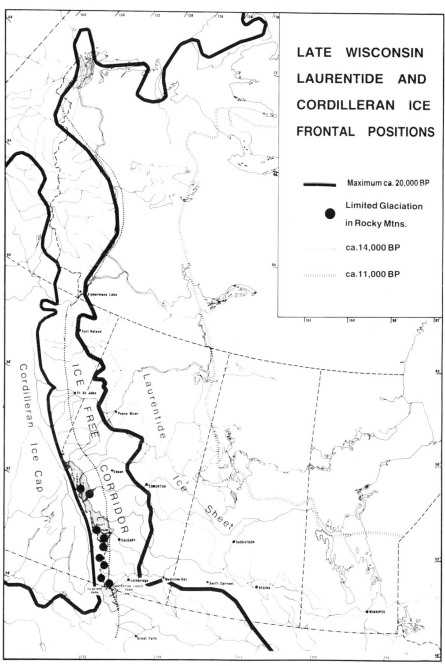

FIG. 2. *Ice front positions of the Cordilleran Ice Cap and Laurentide Ice Sheet at the time of maximum Late Wisconsin glaciation.*

(GSC-1205) on a bison bone from a high terrace 0.6 km north of the town of Athabasca (Lowden and Blake, 1979: 17) and of 11,300 +/- 110 (GSC-2038) on basal gyttja at Mariana Lake, 100 km southwest of Fort McMurray indicate the lower Athabasca River existed in its present location by that time. These dates suggest a much earlier drainage of Clayhurst than had generally been considered, based on dates from adjacent north-central Alberta (St. Onge, 1972).

Support for a limited Late Wisconsin advance in the Peace Valley well back from the Foothills front also comes from a radiocarbon dated section which lacks any evidence of Late Wisconsin Glaciation. A pollen core from Boone Lake in the Saddle Hills, 60 km northwest of Grande Prairie, Alberta, has a series of dates in stratigraphic succession of greater than 30,000 (WAT-361); 17,570 +/- 650 (WAT-406); 12,650 +/- 320 (WAT-408); and 10,740 +/- 395 (WAT-362)(White *et al.*, 1979). While the dates may be contaminated (Fladmark, 1981), the pollen core does suggest the presence of vegetation in the vicinity of Glacial Lake Peace in Late Wisconsin times.

A second "non-glacial" section, also in Alberta, is from fluvial deposits at Watino along the Smoky River, 110 km southeast of the Saddle Hills. Here a stratigraphic series of dates range from 43,500-27,400 B.P. (Westgate *et al.*, 1972). Glaciolacustrine sediments overlie the section. Till is absent.

The next major valley north of the Peace where Cordilleran Ice broke through is the Liard. Between it and the Peace lies an extensive tract of unglaciated foothills and mountain ranges. Recent studies by Klassen (1978) on the Liard have indentified a long and complex Pleistocene glacial record. Two dates have been obtained from below the latest till of the Liard Lobe on the Rancheria River near Watson Lake. The lower is a greater than 40,000 year old date from the base of the section. Higher in the interglacial sediments a date of 23,000 has been obtained. Palynological analysis indicates the presence of a grassland steppe at this time (Klassen: personal communication, 1981).

The relationships between the Liard lobe and the Fort Nelson lobe of Laurentide ice remain to be examined. However, in Late Wisconsin times, if the Glacial Lake Clayhurst stage correlation is correct, the lands of the Liard were largely ice and water free (Mathews, 1980: Figure 4A) and Laurentide meltwaters were discharging into the Fort Nelson and Liard systems. Dates from the Mackenzie indicate Glacial Lake McConnell had drained and that the river was in place by 11,000 years ago: 10,600 +/- 230 (GSC-2328) on the Great Bear River exit into the Mackenzie, 11,200 +/- 220 (GSC-1573) at Sans Saulte Rapids (Lowdon and Blake, 1979), and 11,140 +/- 160 (I-3913), 11,530 +/- 170 (I-3734) from similar sections near Fort Good Hope (Mackey and Matthews, 1973). Initial post-glacial steppe tundra communities are present in the central Mackenzie before 10,700 +/- 230 years (Slater, 1978: 176; Lowden and Blake, 1979:36). (This particular profile from Eildun Lake has a date of >29,000 [GSC-2695] from its base).

Summary

The only physical "barrier" in Late Wisconsin times was water. The rivers flowing from the Rocky Mountains discharged first into the large proglacial lakes, which in turn flowed through a series of lakes and proglacial channels into the Saskatchewan and Mackenzie rivers. These water systems would not pose any particular difficulty to the interior adapted peoples of Beringia who, like other peoples, would of necessity have the technology required to cross streams and rivers.

While ice or water barriers are not significant factors, the environment may have been. Popular views of the corridor environment at the maximum glaciation range from scenarios of vast, and perpetually frozen lands of ice, snow and barren rock, swept by howling winds, to more pleasant climes. I prefer the latter interpretation, for the pollen profiles in the southern Alberta foothills previously noted, and other unpublished profiles from the central Alberta foothills (Hapgood: personal communication, 1981), suggest an open cold steppe tundra grassland during Late Wisconsin times. Coniferous components were confined to the southern portion.

The profiles, while open to alternate interpretation as to the steppe/tundra plant community ratios (Ritchie, 1980), suggest to me that a cold open steppe climate characterized the higher drier foothills, plateaus and plains along the eastern slopes. The vegetation community reflects the cold, dry glacial climate, partially the result of the Cordilleran ice dome to the west, which both trapped moisture normally falling on the eastern slopes and increased the drying effect of the Chinook winds. The Peace River grasslands, I would also note, are composed in part of southerly species. These most probably spread north during the cold dry Late Wisconsin or earlier glacial times.

If the above scenario is reasonably correct, the Eastern Slopes would have supported grazers, comparable to those of Late Glacial times recorded on the plains at Empress at 14,500 B.P. (Lowdon and Blake, 1975: 16), in the foothills at Cochrane west of Calgary ca. 10,500 B.P. (Stalker, 1968) and in the Peace at ca. 10,000 years ago (Churcher and Wilson, 1979). These diverse Pleistocene fauna are dominated by bison, followed by horse and mammoth.

While the terrestrial grazers would be a significant food source for early peoples, lakes such as Glacial Lake Peace, would have supported a variety of fish including lake trout, white fish, pike and pickeral. Dispersal of these species into their present lake habitats behind the Late Wisconsin maxima was controlled by the

sequence of deglaciation.   Fish lakes are a focal point for
settlement and subsistance for Native Peoples throughout Holocene
times in northern Alberta.   As well as fish, the proglacial and
other lakes would serve as major nesting habitats for migratory
water fowl, by those birds which today, and presumably then,
utilized the Rocky Mountain Fly-way (Fladmark, 1981).

In sum, the Late Wisconsin Ice Free Corridor rather than a
barren wasteland was a steppe tundra/grassland throughout its
length with productive terrestrial and aquatic habitats exploitable
by man.   Conditions, while rigorous, were not adverse, and no
significant environmental barriers appear to have existed to
prevent movement within or along the corridor, between the Yukon
Refugium and the continental interior below 48 degrees north.

MID-WISCONSIN

The Mid-Wisconsin in Western Canada, dating in the Interior Plains
from 20,000 years B.P. to greater than 54,000 years B.P. and in the
Cordillera and Coastal Region from greater than 58,000 to 22,000
years ago, can best be conceptualized as an analogue of the
Holocene, characterized by a three-fold climatic and
environmental sequence.   Coastal, Interior Plateau, Eastern Slope
and Plains environments were analagous to today's, supporting in
the interior a diverse Rancholabrean fauna (Stalker and Churcher,
1970), dominated by bison in southern Alberta (Stalker and
Churcher, 1970).

The Mid-Wisconsin, a "window" some 30,000 years long, extended
over the entire area of former and later glaciated terrain.   It was
of sufficient duration for peopling the New World as people were
present in the Yukon at that time (Jopling et al., 1981; Morlan,
1981).   One factor, however, which might be significant for initial
movement south at this time would be the extent of the Western
Boreal Forest.   If the Mid-Wisconsin forest was analogous to
today's forest characterized by low productivity, it would have
been an initial barrier to people with focal hunting economies
moving south from Beringia.   While a barrier of sorts from the
Peace River north, it would not be significant given the millennia
available.

In contrast to the forest, the interior plateaus with their
diversified habitats and terrestrial and aquatic resources -
including annual salmon runs which would have existed in
Mid-Wisconsin times - form a continuous and easily traversed
landscape - from the lake district of the Southern Yukon to the
grasslands of the Columbia Plateau.   Similarly, the Northwest
Coast would be particularly attractive to coastal littorally-adapted
people, who with or without water-craft could populate the
coastal region of the Western Hemisphere in a matter of a few
thousand years.

In summary, given these most positive conditions, during Mid-Wisconsin times, Late Wisconsin "windows" are not particularly relevant for first peopling. However, the latter windows are a concern for later movement and contact between, as well as "cultural" isolation of, Beringia and the unglaciated areas of coastal and continental North America.

PRE-MID-WISCONSIN "WINDOWS"

The increasing number of well documented early Late Wisconsin archaeological sites such as Meadowcroft (Adovasio et al., this volume), Wilson Butte (Gruhn, 1965), Ayacucho (MacNeish, 1971), to mention a few, as well as earlier Mid-Wisconsin sites: Basalt Ridge (Davis et al., 1981), El Cedral, (Lorenzo and Mirombell, 1981), and Taber Child (Stalker, 1969b), point to man's entry in Mid-Wisconsin if not earlier times, as suggested by earlier and controversial sites Calico (Schuiling, 1981), Valsequillo (Steen-McIntyre et al., 1981), Wooley Mammoth (Berger, 1981), dating to Sangamon or Illinoian times.

The presence of man in Beringia in Sangamon (Jopling et al., 1981; Morlan, 1981) and possibly Late Illinoian times presents the possibility of much earlier movement south, necessitating examination of the earlier windows beyond the limits of radiocarbon dating. Pre Mid-Wisconsin glacial and non-glacial events are represented by tills and non-glacial deposits in the Coastal, Cordilleran, Rocky Mountain, and Interior Plains areas. Correlations between these areas are difficult at best.

The Western Cordilleran Coastal glaciation preceding the Mid-Wisconsin is the Salmon Springs, greater than 57,000 years in age (Clague, 1980). Underlying the Salmon Springs are non-glacial deposits which, if the Salmon Springs is Early Wisconsin are Sangamon in age. Alternatively Salmon Springs may be Illinoian. This glacial event, the maximum Late Pleistocene glaciation, markedly reduced available unglaciated land along the shelf, probably precluding the movement by peoples along the coast at this time.

The Pre-Mid-Wisconsin sequence on the eastern slopes and interior plains is complex. In southern Alberta, the Laurentide sequence is best defined at Medicine Hat (Stalker, 1969a). Here it consists of an Early Wisconsin till underlain by Sangamon non-glacial deposits, containing a Rancholabrean fauna. These in turn are underlain by two Illinoian tills. Problems exist in both the correlation and dating of the Medicine Hat sections (Stalker, 1969a, 1975, 1980; Szabo and Stalker, 1973). The Sangamon deposits (Mitchell Bluff Section) are dated by Uranium/Thorium to 72,000 +/- 6,000 (ibid. 1973). Stalker does not accept this date on the basis of geological and paleontological correlations. Grazers, particularly bison, dominate the assemblage. Horse, mammoth, camel, elk, deer, llama, sheep, caribou, antelope, and others are present. The Medicine Hat Sangamon section correlates with others to the east in Saskatchewan indicating a major non-glacial interval existed across the Western Interior during this time. Environmental conditions were analogous to those during the Mid-Wisconsin and Holocene.

The westward extent of Early Wisconsin Ice overlying these Sangamon deposits depends on the correlated end morainal position. It probably correlates with an easterly ice front position, back from the foothills front as the Early Wisconsin appears to be a weakly expressed glacial event if not absent in the Western interior. For example, it is not represented in the Old Crow Glacial Lake sequence by glacial lacustrine sediments, (Jopling *et al.*, 1981; Morlan, 1980) suggesting that Laurentide ice did not penetrate the MacKenzies or Richardsons, in contrast to Late Wisconsin and Illinoian times. The earlier pre-Sangamon till would then represent the Illinoian maximal ice frontal position and Foothills Erratic Train Glaciation. This glaciation resulted in coalescence of Rocky Mountain and Laurentide Ice at a few locations along the Ice Free Corridor (Fig. 3). Much of the area, while ice free, however, was occupied by proglacial lakes and channels.

Most Rocky Mountain glaciers, during the Erratic Train Glaciation consisted of valley glaciers and piedmont lobes terminating at or just outside the mountain front. Only a few Rocky Mountain glaciers, whose flows were augmented by ice flowing across the continental divide from the Cordilleran-Salmon Springs Glaciation, coalesced with Laurentide ice; definite evidence of which in Late Pleistocene times occurs only at the Athabasca (Roed, 1975). Here the Laurentide ice advanced southwest. It had not been previously deflected to the northeast suggesting no closure in the Peace. In the Peace this event would correlate with the Early Portage Mountain advance (Rutter, 1977), predating the Late Portage Mountain Advance and Glacial Lake Besaborough (Mathews, 1980).

Environmental conditions in the narrow "Ice Free Corridor" during the Foothills Erratic Train Glaciation are very poorly known. Palynological analysis from a proglacial lake in southwestern Alberta suggest barren periglacial conditions existed (Alley, 1972). Glacial lakes and proglacial channels would be prominent features in the landscape at this time, which combined with the apparent adverse environmental conditions along the corridor would effectively preclude utilization of it by mammals and people at the height of Illinoian glaciation.

In summary, the Foothills Erratic Train appears to be the maximum Late Pleistocene glaciation in the Western Interior. The Early Wisconsin is a more limited event, lying somewhat east of the Foothills Front, perhaps in Southern Alberta, represented by

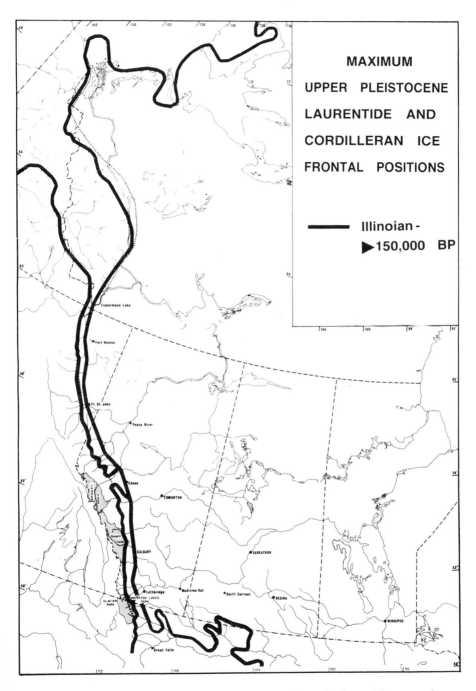

FIG. 3. *Ice front positions calculated for the maximum glacial extent in the Illinoian.*

the Lethbridge End Moraine. Conditions in the Ice Free Corridor west of this front would during Early Wisconsin times be intermediate between those projected for the Late Wisconsin and Illinoian.

FIRST ENTRIES - A QUESTION OF TIMING?

The data summarized above and the models proposed suggest that during the inter-glacial Sangamon and Mid-Wisconsin intervals environmental conditions in Western Canada were essentially analogous to today's. Man, whose presence in Beringia may date to Sangamon and possibly Late Illinoian times, had more than adequate time to move gradually south during these non-glacial times.

Later during the height of Late Wisconsin glaciation *ca*. 20,000 years ago, conditions in the Late Wisconsin Ice Free Corridor were not sufficiently adverse to prohibit native occupation of or movement within it. A similar case applied to the Coastal Corridor.

Earlier "corridors", however, were much more limiting, particularly those during the maximum Late Pleistocene glaciation, during Illinoian times, some 150,000 years ago. These probably precluded utilization by man and mammals of the corridor at the height of glaciation. Coastal movement was also not possible at this time.

Evidence from Old Crow suggests man was present in Late Illinoian time - the time most ecologically favorable for dispersal of the Rancholabrean grazers particularly bison, sheep, and the wooly mammoth (*M. primigenius*) to the continental interior, prior to the onset of full non-glacial conditions and establishment of the Western and Northern Boreal Forests.

The Rancholabrean fauna have, in my opinion, important implications for the first peopling of the interior of North America. The grazers would have gradually moved south along the eastern slopes and interior plateaus, following the cold steppe/tundra vegetation which appeared as pioneer communities in the freshly deglaciated and dewatered lands along the Ice Free Corridor. Bighorn sheep, today for example, will not move through closed forests to reach isolated grasslands, suggesting their original southern movement occurred at a time when continuous open grassland/tundra habitat existed in the Cordillera, Rocky Mountains and Eastern foothills. Such a time would be during the Late Illinoian. Early people then present in Eastern Beringia would follow the southward expansion of the Paleoarctic Rancholabrean grazers and browsers - bison, caribou, elk, sheep, goat, mammoth and muskoxen - into previously unoccupied terrain or ecological niches along the opening corridors eventually reaching the unglaciated plains, mountains and plateaus far to the south.

This hypothesis is both economical and attractive, and I suggest, worthy of serious consideration. Man had the cultural capability to live effectively in the harsh Arctic conditions in Beringia at that time. The Rancholabrean faunal expansion east from Eurasia through Beringia and into the continental interior of North America in Late Illinoian times provides both a causal mechanism and sufficient explanation for the inital peopling of the New World. [W.N. Irving (personal communication, 1981) has independantly arrived at the same hypothesis as I for the relationship of Rancholabrean Fauna and Man in the New World.] There is no need to invoke pulsating glaciers, over-population, extremely advanced technologies, and similar *deus ex machina* explanations to move people around.

Similarly, litorally adapted Late Pleistocene people from the East Asian Pacific Rim almost certainly moved down the west coast in Sangamon times. They probably brought with them a simple cobble core/unifacial flake technology, represented at sites such as Woolly Mammoth (Berger, 1981) on Santa Rosa and the Texas Street type sites in San Diego (Carter, 1957; Reeves, 1981).

In closing, I would suggest there were by *ca*. 100,000 years ago, three basic cultural patterns in western North America - an interior plains hunting pattern, a mountain hunting, fishing, fowling pattern, and a coastal, littorally adapted pattern. The principal role the "corridors" played in initial peopling was during Late Illinoian times. Subsequent non-glacial windows of Sangamon and Mid-Wisconsin times were sufficiently broad to permit later movements and exchange between Beringia and below the forty-ninth parallel. The Late Wisconsin corridors' roles were to limit rather than physically restrict these exchanges.

Justification for much of this scenario, of course, depends on finding *bona fide* sites. Radiometric dating of glacial events is bound to change, as well as the correlation of these to the land mammal ages (Kurten and Anderson, 1980). Significant advances can be expected in the next decade, which will allow for a third and better approximation to be made of the nature and extent of the Late Pleistocene Ice Free Corridors in the Western Interior of North America (Reeves, 1973).

REFERENCES

Adovasio, J.M., Donahue, J., Giulday, J.E., Stukenrath, R., Garr, J.D. and Johnson, W.C. (1983). Meadowcroft rockshelter and the peopling of the New World. Paper presented at the Quaternary Land Sea Migration Bridges and Human Occupation of Submerged Coastline Symposium, Scripps Institute of Oceanography, La Jolla, California. This volume.

Alley, N.F. (1972). Glacial history of the Rocky Mountain Front Ranges, Foothills, Plains and Porcupine Hills region of southwestern Alberta. Unpublished Ph.D. dissertation, Department of Geography, University of Calgary.

Alley, N.F. (1973). Glacial stratigraphy and the limits of Rocky Mountain and Laurentide ice sheets in southwestern Alberta, Canada. *Bulletin of Canadian Petroleum Geology* 21, 153-177.

Alley, N.F. and Harris, S.A. (1974). Pleistocene glacial lake sequences in the foothills, southwestern Alberta, Canada. *Canadian Journal of Earth Sciences* 11, 1220-1235.

Berger, Rainer (1981). Early man on the California Channel Islands. Paper presented at the X Congress, International Union of Prehistoric and Protohistoric Science, October 1981, Mexico City.

Boydell, A.N. (1978). Multiple glaciations in the Foothills, Rocky Mountain House area, Alberta. *Alberta Research Council Bulletin* 36.

Bretz, J.H. (1943). Keewatin end moraines in Alberta, Canada. *Bulletin of the American Geological Society* 53, 31-51.

Carter, George F. (1957). *Pleistocene Man at San Diego.* John Hopkins Press, Baltimore.

Christiansen, E.A. (1979). The Wisconsinan deglaciation of southern Saskatchewan and adjacent areas. *Canadian Journal of Earth Sciences* 16, 913-938.

Christiansen, E.A. (1980). The Wisconsinan deglaciation of southern Saskatchewan adjacent areas: Reply to Teller *et al. Canadian Journal of Earth Sciences* 17, 541.

Churcher, C.S. and Wilson, M. (1979). Quaternary mammals from the eastern Peace River District, Alberta. *Journal of Paleontology* 53, 71-76.

Clague, John J. (1980). Late Quaternary geology and geochronology of British Columbia. Part 1: Radiocarbon dates. Geological Survey of Canada Paper 80-3.

Clague, John J. (1981). Late Quaternary geology and geochronology of British Columbia, Part 2: Summary and discussion of radiocarbon-dated Quaternary history. Geological Survey of Canada Paper 80-35.

Davis, E.L. Jefferson, G. and McKinney, C. (1981). Notes on a Mid-Wisconsinan date for man and mammoth, China Lake, California. Paper presented at the X Congress, International Union of Prehistoric and Protohistoric Sciences, October 1981, Mexico City.

Ferguson, A.J. (1978). Late Quaternary geology of the Upper Elk Valley, British Columbia. Unpublished M.Sc. thesis, Department of Geology, University of Calgary.

Ferguson, A.J. and Osborn, G.A. (n.d.) Minimum age of deglaciation of the Upper Elk Valley, British Columbia. *Canadian Journal of Earth Sciences*. In press.

Fladmark, R.K. (1979). Routes: alternate migration corridors for Early Man in North America. *American Antiquity* 44, 55-69.

Fladmark, R.K. (1981) Times and places: environmental correlates of initial human population expansion in North America. Paper presented at the 40th Annual Meeting, Society for American Archaeology, April 1981, San Diego.

Goodman, G. (1981). *American Genesis*. Summit Books, New York.

Gruhn, R. (1965). Early radiocarbon dates from the lower levels of Wilson Butte Cove, South Central Idaho. *Tebiwa* 8, 57.

Harrison, J.E. (1976). Dated organic material below the Mazama (?) tephra, Elk Valley, British Columbia. *Geological Survey of Canada Paper* 76-1C, 169-170.

Holloway, R.G. (1978). Absolute pollen analysis of Lake Wabamun, Alberta, Canada. *Abstracts of Fifth Biannual Meeting, AMQUA Edmonton* 213.

Irwin-Williams, Cynthia (1981). Commentary on Geologic Evidence for age of deposits at Hueyatlaco archaeological site, Valsequillo, Mexico. *Quaternary Research* 16, 258.

Jackson, L.E. Jr. (1979) New evidence for the existence of an ice-free corridor in the Rocky Mountain foothills near Calgary, Alberta, during Late Wisconsin times. *Geological Survey of Canada Paper* 79-1A.

Jackson, L.E. Jr. (1980a). Glacial history and stratigraphy of the Alberta portion of the Kannanaskis Lakes map area. *Canadian Journal of Earth Sciences* 17, 459-477.

Jackson, L.E. Jr. (1980b). Quaternary stratigraphy and history of the Alberta portion of the Kananaskis Lake map area (82 -J) and its implications for the existence of an ice-free corridor during Wisconsin times. In the Ice-Free Corridor and Peopling of the New World. *Canadian Journal of Anthropology* 1, 9-10.

Jackson, L.E. Jr., Wilson, M. and MacDonald, G.M. (1981). Paraglacial and non-glacial fluvial origins for river terraces and terrace sediments in the Bow River valley, Alberta, Canada. Paper presented at the 2nd International Fluvial Sedimentology Conference, September 1981, Keele, England.

Jopling, A.V., Irving, W.N. and Beebe, B.F. (1981). Stratigraphic, sedimentological and faunal evidence for the occurrence of Pre-Sangamonian artifacts in norther Yukon. *Arctic Anthropology* 34, 3-33.

Klassen, R.W. (1978). A unique stratigraphic record of Late Tertiary-Quaternary events in southeastern Yukon. *Canadian Journal of Earth Sciences* 15, 1884-1886.

Kostaschuk, R.A. (1980). Late Quaternary history of the Bow River valley near Banff, Alberta. Unpublished M.Sc. thesis, Department of Geography, University of Calgary.

Kurten, Bjorn and Anderson, E. (1980). *Pleistocene Mammals of North America.* Columbia University Press, New York.

Lorenzo, Jose Luis and Mirombell, L., (1981). El Cedral, S.L.P. Mexico: Un ditio con presoncia humana de mas cie 30,000 anos. Paper presented at X Congress International Union Prehistoric and Protohistoric Sciences Mexico City.

Lowden, J.A. and Blake, Jr. W. (1975). Geological Survey of Canada radiocarbon dates XV. *Geological Survey of Canada Paper* 75-7.

Lowden, J.A., and Blake, Jr. W. (1979). Geological Survey of Canada radiocarbon dates XIX. *Geological Survey of Canada Paper* 79-7.

Luckman, B.H. and Kearny, M.S. (1978). Analysis and interpretations of a Holocene deposit from Castleguard Meadows, Banff National Park, Alberta. Report to Environmental Canada, Contract KL229-7-2083.

MacDonald, G.M. (1980). The post-glacial paleoecology of the Morley Flats and Kananaskis Valley region, southwestern Alberta. Unpublished M.Sc. thesis, Department of Geography, University of Calgary.

Mackay, J.R. and Mathews, W.H. (1973). Geomorphological and Quaternary history of the Mackenzie River valley near Fort Good Hope. *Canadian Journal of Earth Sciences* 10, 26-41.

MacNeish, Richard S. (1971). Early Man in the Andes. *Scientific American* 64, 316-327.

Mathews, W.H. (1978). Quaternary stratigraphy and geomorphology of Charlie Lake (94A) map area, British Columbia. *Geological Survey of Canada Paper* 76-20.

Mathews, W.H. (1980). Retreat of the last ice sheets in northeastern British Columbia and adjacent Alberta. *Geological Survey of Canada Bulletin* 331.

McCallum, K.J., and Wittenberg, J. (1968). University of Saskatchewan radiocarbon measurements V. *Radiocarbon* 10, 365-378.

Morlan, R.E. (1980). Taphonomy and archaeology in the Upper Pleistocene of the Northern Yukon Territory: A glimpse of peopling of the New World. *National Museum of Man Mercury Series* No. 94.

Morlan, R.E. (1981). Big bones and tiny stones. Early evidence from the Northern Yukon Territory. Paper presented at the International Union of Prehistoric and Protohistoric Sciences, October 1981, Mexico City.

Mott, R.A. and Christiansen, E.A. (1981). Palynological study of slough sediments from central Saskatchewan. *Geological Survey of Canada Current Research Part B Paper* 81, (18) 131-133.

Reeves, B.O.K. (1973). The nature and age of the contact between the Laurentide and Cordilleran ice sheets in the Western Interior of North America. *Arctic and Alpine Research* 5, 1-16.

Reeves, B.O.K. (1981). Mission River and the Texas Street question. Paper read at the X Congress, International Union of Prehistoric and Protohistoric Sciences, October 1981, Mexico City.

Ritchie, J.C. (1980). Towards a Late-Quaternary paleoecology of the ice-free corridor. In the Ice-Free Corridor and peopling of the New World. *Canadian Journal of Anthropology* 1, 15-28.

Roed, M.A. (1975). Cordilleran and Laurentide multiple glaciation west-central Alberta, Canada. *Canadian Journal of Earth Sciences* 12, 1493-1515.

Rutter, N.W. (1972). Geomorphology and multiple glaciation in the area of Banff, Alberta. *Geological Survey of Canada Bulletin* 206.

Rutter, N.W. (1977). Multiple glaciation in the area of Williston Lake, British Columbia. *Geological Survey of Canada Bulletin* 273.

Rutter, N.W. (1980). Late Pleistocene history of the western Canadian ice-free corridor. In the Ice-Free Corridor and Peopling of the New World. *Canadian Journal of Anthropology* 1, 1-8.

Schuiling, W.C. (1979). *Pleistocene Man at Calico*. San Bernadino County Museum.

Simpson, R.D., Patterson, L.W., and Singer, Clay A., (1981). Early lithic technology of the Calico site, southern California. Paper read at the X Congress, International Union of Prehistoric and Protohistoric Sciences, October 1981, Mexico City.

Slater, D.S. (1978). Late Quaternary pollen program from Central Mackenzie Corridor area. *Abstracts, of the Fifth Bi-annual Meeting*, AMQUA Edmonton, 176.

Stalker, A. MacS. (1968). Geology of the terraces of Cochrane, Alberta. *Canadian Journal of Earth Sciences* 5, 1455-1466.

Stalker, A. MacS. (1969a). Quaternary stratigraphy in southern Alberta. Report 11: sections near Medicine Hat. *Geological Survey of Canada Paper* 69-26.

Stalker, A. Macs. (1969b). Geology and age of the Early Man site at Taber, Alberta. *American Antiquity* 34, 424-429.

Stalker, A. MacS. (1975). The probable extent of classical Wisconsin ice in southern and central Alberta. *Canadian Journal of Earth Sciences* 14, 2614-2619.

Stalker, A. MacS. (1980). The geology of the ice-free corridor: the southern half. In the Ice-Free Corridor and Peopling of the New World. *Canadian Journal of Anthropology* 1, 11-14.

Stalker, A. MacS., and Churcher, C.S. (1970). Deposits near Medicine Hat, Alberta, Canada: composite section of successive faunas. *Geological Survey of Canada Map.*

Stalker, A. MacS., and Harrison, J.E. (1977). Quaternary glaciation of the Waterton-Castle River region, Alberta. *Bulletin of Canadian Petroleum Geology* 25, 887-906.

Steen-McIntyre, V., Fryxell, R., and Malde, R.H.F. (1981). Geologic evidence for age of deposits at Hueyatlaco archaeological site, Valsequillo, Mexico. *Quaternary Research Bulletin* 16, 1-7.

St. Onge, D. (1972). Sequence of glacial lakes in north-central Alberta. *Geological Survey of Alberta Bulletin* 213.

St. Onge, D. (1980). The Wisconsin deglaciation of southern Saskatchewan and adjacent areas: discussion. *Canadian Journal of Earth Sciences* 17, 287-288.

Szabo, B.J., and Stalker, A. MacS. (1973). Uranium-series ages of some Quaternary deposits near Medicine Hat, Alberta. *Canadian Journal of Earth Sciences* 10, 1464-1469.

Westgate, J.A., Fritz, P., Matthews, J.V., Jr., Kalas, L., Delorme, L.D., Green, R. and Aario, R. (1972). Geochronology and paleoecology of Mid-Wisconsin sediments in west-central Alberta. *Abstracts: International Geological Congress, 24th Session,* Montreal.

White, J.M., Mathews, R.W. and Mathews, W.H. (1979). Radiocarbon dates from Boone Lake and their relation to the ice free corridor in the Peace River district of Alberta, Canada. *Canadian Journal of Earth Science* 16, 1870-1874.

MEADOWCROFT ROCKSHELTER AND THE PEOPLING OF THE NEW WORLD

J. M. Adovasio*, J. Donahue [1], J.E. Guilday [2],
R. Stuckenrath [3], J.D. Gunn [4] and W.C. Johnson*

Departments of Anthropology and Geology,
and Planetary Sciences [1], University of Pittsburgh,
Pittsburgh, Pennsylvania 15260, USA.
[2]Carnegie Museum of Natural History,
Pittsburgh, Pennsylvania 15213, USA.
[3]Radiation Biology Laboratory, Smithsonian Institution,
Rockville, Maryland 20852, USA.
[4]Division of Social Sciences,
University of Texas at San Antonio,
San Antonio, Texas 78285, USA.*

ABSTRACT

Meadowcroft Rockshelter is a deeply stratified multicomponent site in Washington County, southwestern Pennsylvania. The 11 well-defined stratigraphic units identified at the site span at least 16,000 years and perhaps 19,000 years of intermittent occupation by groups representing all of the major prehistoric cultural stages/periods now recognized in northeastern North America. Throughout the sequence, the site served as a locus for hunting, collecting and food-processing activities which involved the seasonal exploitation of the adjacent Cross Creek Valley and contiguous uplands. Meadowcroft Rockshelter represents the longest occupational sequence in the Western Hemisphere. Dates for the earliest units imply migrations across Beringia into the New World in the range of 20-25,000 years ago.

INTRODUCTION

Meadowcroft Rockshelter (36WH297) is a stratified,

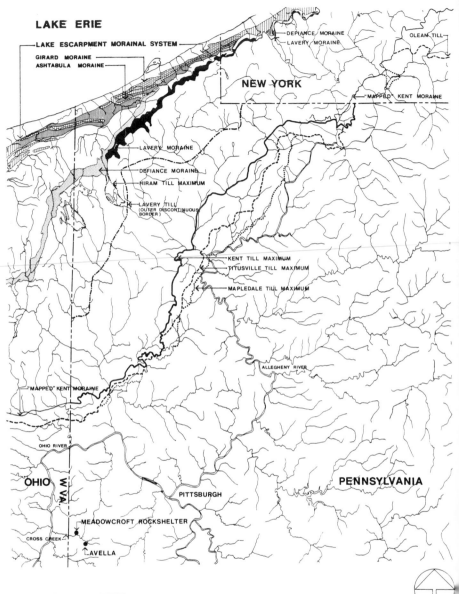

FIG. 1. *Location of Meadowcroft Rockshelter on Cross Creek in the Upper Ohio Valley of southwestern Pennsylvania. The site is depicted in relation to Pleistocene glacial deposits in northwestern Pennsylvania and adjacent states. (Glacial mapping is abstracted from information in Calkin and Miller, 1977, p. 298, Fig. 1; Goldthwait et al., 1967; Muller, 1963, Plate 1, insert; Schooler, 1974, Plate 1b, insert; Shepps et al., 1959, Plate 1 insert; Tesmer, 1975, p. 13, Plate 2; White et al., 1969, p. 10, Fig. 2. This is a revised version of that presented in Johnson, 1981, Fig. 6.)*

multicomponent site 79 km via road southwest of Pittsburgh and 4.0 km northwest of Avella in Washington County, Pennsylvania (Fig. 1). The site is on the north bank of Cross Creek, a small tributary of the Ohio, ca. 12.16 km to the west. The location of the site is 40°17'12" N, 80°29'0" W.

Meadowcroft Rockshelter is oriented roughly east-west; it has a southern exposure and stand ca. 15.06 m above Cross Creek and 260 m above sea level. The area protected by the extant overhang is ca. 62 m², the overhang itself is some 13 m above the modern surface of the site. In addition to the water available in Cross Creek, springs are abundant in the immediate vicinity of the shelter. The prevailing wind is west to east across the mouth of the shelter providing ventilation and egress for smoke and insects.

Geologically, Meadowcroft is in the unglaciated portion of the Appalachian or Allegheny Plateau, west of the Valley and Ridge Province of the Appalachian Mountains and on the northwest margin of the Appalachian Basin. The area is unaffected by glacial ice since the terminal Wisconsinan till (see Fig. 1) extends south only to northern Beaver County (ca. 48.5 km north of the site).

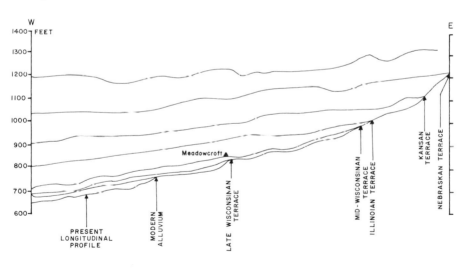

FIG. 2. *Longitudinal profile for Cross Creek from its confluence with the Ohio River on the west to its headwaters on the east. Uppermost line shows the elevation of uplands in the region, indicating that Cross Creek had ca. 170' of relief in Nebraskan time. Five discontinuous terraces, Nebraskan, Kansan, Illinoian, early Middle Wisconsinan and Late Wisconsinan in age, are indicated (after Beynon, n.d.).*

416   J.M. Adovasio *et al.*

The construction of a longitudinal profile along Cross Creek from 7.5' topographic maps demonstrates the presence of five discontinuous terraces (Beynon, n.d.). The terraces can be correlated with similar features on the Ohio River and are Nebraskan, Kansan, Illinoian, early Middle Wisconsinan and Late Wisconsinan in age (Fig. 2). These terraces are critical for understanding the development of Meadowcroft Rockshelter. Cross Creek apparently has been present since pre-Pleistocene time as a tributary to the ancestral northern Ohio River (Leverett, 1902). However, until Wisconsinan time, Cross Creek's valley had not been downcut to the level of Meadowcroft Rockshelter. The early Middle Wisconsinan terrace (Fig. 3) is at an elevation coincident with the base of the depositional sequence at Meadowcroft and is well-developed on the south side of Cross Creek. Therefore,

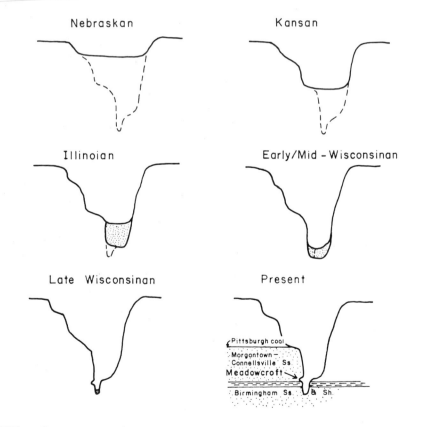

FIG. 3. *Sequential cross sections of Cross Creek at Meadowcroft Rockshelter. Progressive deposition and downcutting through Pleistocene terraces are illustrated (after Beynon n.d.).*

undercutting and development of the shelter was accomplished by
about 40,000 years B.P. The Late Wisconsinan terrace (21,000
years B.P.) is present at an elevation 3 to 9 m above Cross Creek
and well below the cultural deposits at the site. The terraces
along Cross Creek thus articulate quite well with and support the
radiocarbon chronology established at Meadowcroft Rockshelter.

Meadowcroft Rockshelter contains colluvial sediments emplaced
by rock fall and grain-by-grain attrition from the overhanging
sandstone cliff and by sheet wash from the upland surface. The
term "colluvium" as used here does not imply mass movement or
wasting of sediments at Meadowcroft. The only clear indication of
postdepositional movement is deformation caused by large rock
falls that have pushed through sediments at points of impact.
Colluvium is thus used here only to indicate sediments
accumulating by rock fall, attrition and sheet wash. The
radiocarbon chronology reported here indicates that the colluvial
sediments at Meadowcroft were being deposited by at least late
Wisconsinan times.

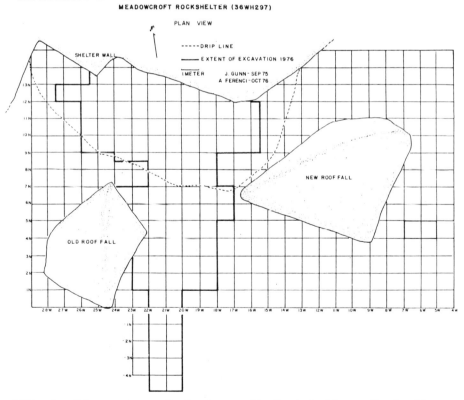

MEADOWCROFT ROCKSHELTER (36WH297)

FIG. 4. *Plan view of Meadowcroft Rockshelter. Dark lines
indicate limits of excavation.*

418   J.M. Adovasio *et al.*

EXCAVATION PROCEDURES

The excavation procedures employed at Meadowcroft Rockshelter are detailed in Adovasio *et al.* (1975, 1977a,b, 1978,a,b, 1979-80a,b, 1980) and Adovasio and Johnson (1981). During the 466 working days of the 1973-1978 projects, *ca.* 60.5 m² of surface area inside the drip line and *ca.* 46.6 m² outside the drip line were excavated (Fig. 4). This resulted in the removal of over 230 m³ of fill. Because of the inordinate amount of rock fall in the fill of the site, nearly all of the excavation was conducted with trowels or smaller instruments.

GEOLOGY OF SITE

Meadowcroft Rockshelter is formed beneath a cliff of Morgantown-Connellsville sandstone; this is a thick, fluvial or channel sandstone within the Casselman Formation (Flint, 1955) of the Pennsylvanian Period. The cliff above the rockshelter is 22 m high (Fig. 5). The sandstone was deposited as two superimposed point-bar or sand bar sequences ranging from cross-bedded, coarse-grained sandstone to laminated, fine-grained sandstone. The

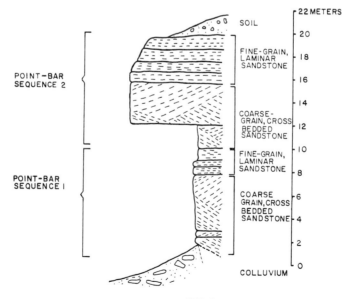

FIG. 5. *Diagrammatic sketch of Morgantown-Connellsville sandstone at Meadowcroft Rockshelter showing change in sedimentary structure and grain size through the two point-bar sequences.*

rock unit immediately underlying the Morgantown-Connellsville sandstone, exposed during the 1975-1978 field seasons, consists of less resistant shale which permitted the development of a rockshelter beneath the sandstone cliff.

The ceiling of this re-entrant is gradually migrating upward and cliffward as erosion occurs both on the rockshelter ceiling and the cliff face. In the rockshelter excavation, the recession of the drip line, representing the cliff edge position, can be seen plainly and can be traced from its maximum extent to its present position.

Eleven natural strata have been distinguished in Meadowcroft Rockshelter. These have been assigned Roman numerals beginning with the earliest stratum (I) and proceeding to the latest (XI). Details of the stratigraphy are available in Adovasio *et al.* (1977a, 1980) and Donahue *et al.* (1978).

Sediment in excess of 3 m thick at Meadowcroft Rockshelter is the result of weathering and downslope movement of boulder-sized to clay-sized sediment grains, both from the upland surface and the sandstone cliff. Rock fall provides larger grained rock fragments ranging in size from granules (less than 2 mm) to large boulders. A second sediment source is grain-by-grain attrition from the sandstone cliff. The sediments derived from this source consist of individual sand grains and small rock fragments (generally less than 4 mm in size). The third sediment source is rain-carried sheet wash from the upland surface. It is apparently the only source for clay-sized material, a relatively common grain size within the colluvial pile.

Stratification in the excavation profiles consists essentially of thick, poorly sorted units. Sandstone blocks that have fallen from the Morgantown-Connellsville cliff are scattered throughout the sediment, occasionally in large concentrations indicative of major roof fall episodes. The existence of a distinct drip line shows that sediment was not transported after falling from the cliff and upland region. If the sediments had been reworked by stream or lake currents, a finer stratification could be expected, and any indication of a drip line would have been erased.

Size analyses are now complete for a long series of microstrata from the east face of the excavation, and these provide a good picture of changes in sedimentation from the top of Stratum IIb upward to Stratum XI.

In both mean grain size and sorting changes within the microstrata column, three distinct zones are obvious. From Stratum IIb to the top of Stratum V, mean grain size ranges from 0.25 to 0.1 mm while sorting fluctuates at *ca.* 1.75. In Stratum VI, the time of the New Roof Fall, mean grain size increases to *ca.* 0.5 mm, and sorting becomes poorer with values of *ca.* 3.25 (very poorly sorted sediment). Finally, from Stratum VII to Stratum XI, mean grain size shows a gradual decrease from 0.25 mm to 0.125 mm while sorting gradually improves from 3.25 to values of *ca.* 2.0.

The sequence suggests the following depositional history. From upper Stratum IIb through Stratum V times, attrition was a dominant sediment source. During Stratum VI times, with dislodgment of the New Roof Fall, rock fall became a more important sediment source. This is reflected by the increase in mean grain size and a shift to more poorly sorted sediments. Finally, from Stratum VII through Stratum XI times, attrition and especially sheet wash were important sediment sources. After the time of the New Roof Fall, a re-entrant opened on the east side of the rockshelter and allowed access to sheet wash from the upland surface. Although incompletely analysed, grain size analysis from lower and middle Stratum IIa suggests that attrition was the primary source of sediment at the beginning of the Meadowcroft depositional sequence.

The construction of paleotopographic maps for the site (Donahue et al., 1979) reveals a very similar picture. By utilizing excavation levels it has been possible to construct topographic maps for the top of each stratum. Maps were constructed for time intervals prior to and after the Old Roof Fall (ca. 10,000 B.C.) and after the New Roof Fall (ca. A.D. 300-600). A hummocky terrain existed prior to the Old Roof Fall, and attrition from the roof of the rockshelter was the primary sediment source. After the collapse that is termed the Old Roof Fall, a sediment slope (inclined from the west) was able to accumulate. This accumulation reflects sheet wash from a source west of the rockshelter and an increased rate of sedimentation. Finally, there was a pronounced change in topography after the New Roof Fall in which a sheet wash cone rapidly took shape behind the New Roof Fall on the eastern margin of the site. In summary, it appears that type and rate of sedimentation were influenced primarily by changes in the configuration of the rockshelter through time, with some influence from paleoclimatic fluctuations.

SUMMARY OF CULTURAL FEATURES

The most common cultural features encountered during the 1973-1978 field seasons at Meadowcroft Rockshelter are firepits of a variety of configurations (147), ash and charcoal lenses (52), large, burned areas designated as firefloors (33) and refuse/storage pits (21). Also encountered were concentrations of lithics, ceramics and bone that suggest the presence of specialized activity areas (16), roasting pits (5) and possible human (1) and animal (1) interments.

The frequency of cultural features through time at Meadowcroft is a reflection not only of the changing intensity of human occupation at the rockshelter but also of changing depositional conditions within the site. Cultural features are most numerous before the cataclysmic New Roof Fall episode associated with

Stratum VI and trail off markedly thereafter. The New Roof Fall collapsed over the epicenter of Archaic occupation at Meadowcroft forcing all later occupants to utilize the western and west central portions of the site. The eastern segment of the site essentially was unused after *ca.* A.D. 600 as this was a locus for rapid sheet wash deposition. Further particulars on the cultural features at Meadowcroft Rockshelter are available in Adovasio *et al.* (1975, 1977a,b, 1978a, 1979-81a,b, 1980).

RADIOCARBON CHRONOLOGY

One hundred samples were submitted for radiocarbon assay to the Radiation Biology Laboratory of the Smithsonian Institution. In all but two cases the charcoal was derived from firepits, firefloors or charcoal lenses within the deposits. The exceptions represent portions of completely carbonized simple plaited basketry fragments (see Adovasio *et al.*, 1977a). To date, 69 of the samples have been processed. Twenty-two samples were too small to count. The results of the other assays are presented in absolute stratigraphic order in the accompanying table. As indicated there, the initial occupation of the rockshelter is positively ascribable to the fifteenth millennium B.C. while the latest radiocarbon assay on purely aboriginal occupation materials is A.D. 1265 ± 80 (SI-2363). The deepest microstrata within Stratum IIa have produced two radiocarbon dates in excess of 17,000 B.C. suggesting an even earlier initial occupation. Cross-dated lithics and ceramic remains from Strata VIII-XI indicate continuing occupation or utilization of the rockshelter through the Historic period as attested to by the radiocarbon date of A.D. 1775 ± 50 (SI-3013) and historical research (Carlisle, n.d.).

The radiocarbon sequence is consistent with the observed stratigraphy and currently represents not only the longest occupational sequence in eastern North America but also one of the longest in this hemisphere.

Questions have been raised regarding the pre-10,000 B.C. radiocarbon dates from Meadowcroft (e.g. Haynes, 1977, 1980; Mead, 1980; Dincauze, 1981). For reasons fully explained in other publications, however, evidence for particulate (Adovasio *et al.*, 1978a) or non-particulate (Adovasio *et al.*, 1980, 1981) contamination of the Stratum IIa samples is nil.

The Stratum IIa dates and associated stratigraphy have great significance for understanding the prehistory of the Upper Ohio Valley and the northeastern United States, as well as the problem of the peopling of North America. For this reason, essential portions of an earlier discussion (Adovasio *et al.* 1980: 588-589) concerning the specific dating of this depositional unit are reiterated below with certain modifications.

Stratum IIa is the deepest and oldest culture-bearing depositional

TABLE 1

Radiocarbon Chronology from Meadowcroft Rockshelter as per March, 1979
NOTE: All dates are uncorrected in absolute stratigraphic order

Stratum (Field Designation)	Provenience/Description	Lab Designation	Date	Cultural Period
XI (F-3)	Charcoal from firepit/ middle 1/3 of unit	SI-3013	A.D. 1775± 50	Late Woodland/Historic
X (F-25)	Charcoal from firepits	Too small to process		Late Woodland
IX (F-9)	Charcoal from firepit/ upper 1/3 of unit	SI-2363	A.D. 1265± 80	Late Woodland
VIII (F-12)	Charcoal from firepit	SI-3023	A.D. 1320±100	Late Woodland
VII (F-13)	Charcoal from firepits/ middle 1/3 of unit	SI-2047 SI-3026	A.D. 1025± 65 A.D. 660± 60	Late Woodland
VI (F-63)	Charcoal from firepits and lenses	Too small to process		Middle/Early Woodland
V (F-14)	Charcoal from firepits/ upper 1/3 of unit	SI-3024 SI-3027 SI-3022 SI-2362 SI-2487	A.D. 285± 65 A.D. 160± 60 A.D. 70± 65 125±125 B.C. 205± 65 B.C.	Middle/Early Woodland
IV (F-16)	Charcoal from firepits/ upper 1/3 of unit	SI-2051 SI-1674 SI-2359 SI-3031	340± 90 B.C. 375± 75 B.C. 535±350 B.C. 705±120 B.C.	
	Charcoal from firefloor/ middle 1/3 of unit	SI-1665	865± 80 B.C.	Early Woodland/Transitional
	Charcoal from firepits/ middle 1/3 of unit	SI-1668	870± 75 B.C.	
	Charcoal from firepit/ firefloors lower 1/3 of unit	SI-1660 SI-2049	910± 80 B.C. 1100± 85 B.C.	
III (F-18)	Charcoal from firepits/ upper 1/3 of unit	SI-2066 SI-1664 SI-2053 SI-3030 SI-2046	980± 80 B.C. 1115± 80 B.C. 1140±115 B.C. 1150± 90 B.C. 1165± 70 B.C.	Transitional (Broadspear Tradition)/Archaic
	Charcoal from firepit/ middle 1/3 of unit	SI-1679	1305±115 B.C.	

Stratum	Provenience	Sample number	Date	Cultural association
IIb (F-46 Upper)	Charcoal from firepits/firefloors lower 1/3 of unit	Too small to process		
	Charcoal from firepit/upper 1/3 of unit	SI-1681	1260 ± 95 B.C.	
	Carbonized basketry fragment/upper 1/3 of unit	SI-1680	1820 ± 90 B.C.	
	Charcoal from firepits/middle of 1/3 of unit	SI-2063	2000 ± 240 B.C.	
		SI-2058	2020 ± 85 B.C.	
		SI-2054	2055 ± 85 B.C.	
		SI-2356	2430 ± 500 B.C.	Archaic
		SI-1685	2870 ± 85 B.C.	
		SI-2358	4340 ± 355 B.C.	
	Charcoal from firefloor/lower 1/3 of unit	SI-2055	4720 ± 140 B.C.	
	Charcoal from firepit/lower 1/3 of unit	SI-2056	3355 ± 130 B.C.	
IIa (F-46 Lower)	Charcoal from firepits/firefloors lower 1/3 of unit	Too small to process		
	Charcoal from firepits/upper 1/3 of unit*	SI-2064	6060 ± 110 B.C.	
		SI-2061	7405 ± 115 B.C.	
	Charcoal from firepit/firefloor middle 1/3 of unit	SI-2491	9350 ± 700 B.C.	
	Charcoal from firepits/lower 1/3 of unit	SI-2489	10,850 ± 870 B.C.	
		+SI-2065	11,290 ±1010 B.C.	
		SI-2488	11,320 ± 340 B.C.	Paleo-Indian
		+SI-1872	12,575 ± 620 B.C.	
		SI-1686	13,170 ± 165 B.C.	
		SI-2354	14,225 ± 975 B.C.	
	Charcoal concentration/deepest level within unit	SI-2062	17,150 ± 810 B.C.	
	Carbonized fragment of cut bark-like material/possible basketry fragment/deepest level within unit	SI-2060	17,650 ±2400 B.C.	
I/IIa Interface	Charcoal from lenses at the interface	SI-2121	19,430 ± 800 B.C.	No cultural assocations
		SI-1687	28,760 ±1140 B.C.	
I (F-85) (Omega Unit)	No Samples	No dates		No cultural associations

* Provenience originally listed incorrectly in Adovasio et al. 1975
+ Data originally listed incorrectly in Adovasio et al. 1975

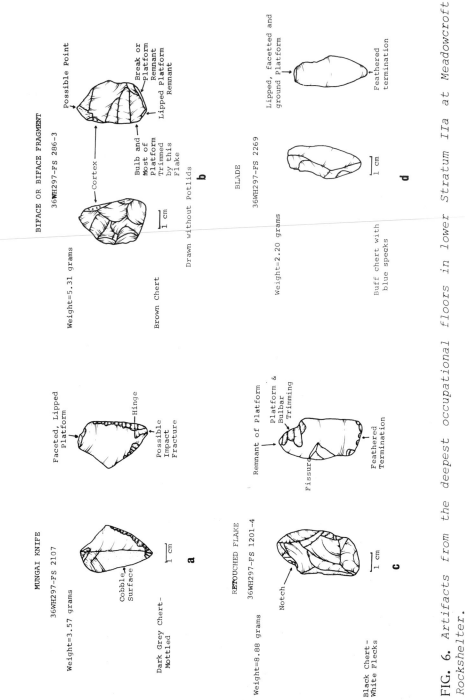

MUNGAI KNIFE

36WH297-FS 2107

Weight=3.57 grams

Faceted, Lipped Platform

Hinge

Possible Impact Fracture

Cobble Surface

Dark Grey Chert-Mottled

a

RETOUCHED FLAKE

36WH297-FS 1201-4

Weight=8.88 grams

Remnant of Platform

Platform & Bulbar Trimming

Fissure

Feathered Termination

Notch

Black Chert-White Flecks

c

BIFACE OR BIFACE FRAGMENT

36WH297-Fs 286-3

Possible Point

Break or Platform Remnant

Lipped Platform Remnant

Cortex

Bulb and Most of Platform Trimmed by this Flake

Weight=5.31 grams

Brown Chert

Drawn without Potlids

b

BLADE

36WH297-FS 2269

Weight=2.20 grams

Lipped, faceted and ground Platform

Feathered termination

Buff chert with blue specks

d

FIG. 6. *Artifacts from the deepest occupational floors in lower Stratum IIa at Meadowcroft Rockshelter.*

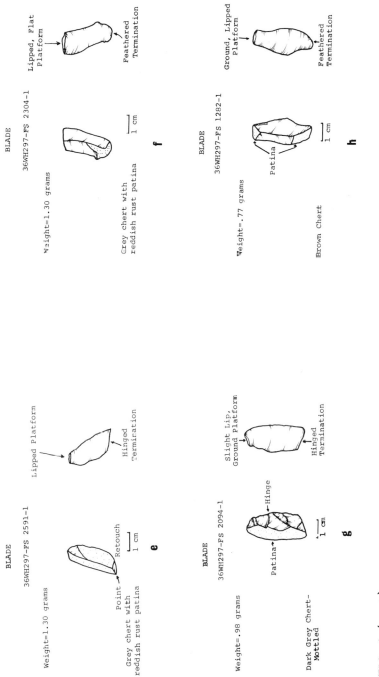

BLADE

36WH297-FS 2591-1

Lipped Platform

Hinged Termination

Weight=1.30 grams

Point Retouch

1 cm

Grey chert with reddish rust patina

e

BLADE

36WH297-FS 2094-1

Slight Lip, Ground platform

Hinged Termination

Weight=.98 grams

Patina Hinge

1 cm

Dark Grey Chert-Mottled

g

BLADE

36WH297-FS 2304-1

Lipped, Flat Platform

Feathered Termination

Weight=1.30 grams

1 cm

Grey chert with reddish rust patina

f

BLADE

36WH297-FS 1282-1

Ground, Lipped Platform

Feathered Termination

Weight=.77 grams

Patina

1 cm

Brown Chert

h

FIG. 6. (cont.)

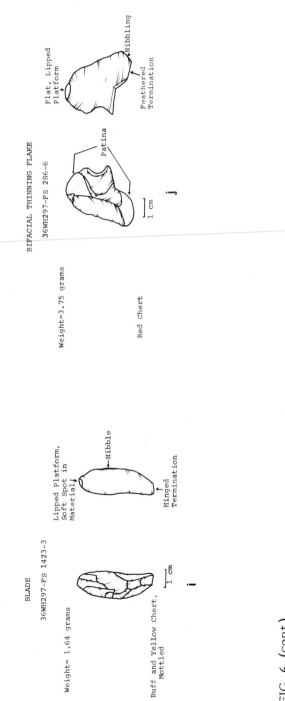

BLADE

36WH297-FS 1423-3

Weight= 1.64 grams

Lipped Platform,
Soft Spot in
Material

Nibble

Hinged
Termination

Buff and Yellow Chert,
Mottled

1 cm

i

BIFACIAL THINNING FLAKE

36WH297-FS 286-6

Weight=3.75 grams

Red Chert

Flat, Lipped
Platform

Nibbling

Feathered
Termination

Patina

1 cm

j

FIG. 6. (cont.)

unit at Meadowcroft Rockshelter. This unit lies conformably beneath and is uniformly separated by a roof spalling event from Stratum IIb in all excavated units at the rockshelter both inside and outside the extant drip line. Stratum IIa, consists essentially of sand-sized and finer material derived principally through grain-by-grain erosion from the roof and walls of the rockshelter. Stratum IIa is subdivided into three subunits of unequal thickness that are labeled upper, middle and lower Stratum IIa. Each of these units is bracketed by major roof spalling episodes, and each is welldated by radiocarbon assay (see Table 1).

Upper Stratum IIa has a terminal date of 6060 ± 110 B.C. from the uppermost living or occupation floor within this subunit and a date of 7165 ± 115 B.C. from a slightly deeper occupational surface within the unit. An assay of 9350 ± 700 B.C. is available from directly beneath the roof spalling event that separates upper from middle Stratum IIa. Hence, upper Stratum IIa dates ca. 9,000 to 6,000 B.C. and is of Holocene age.

Middle Stratum IIa also is terminated by a roof spalling episode. Directly beneath the latter roof spall is a date of 10,850 ± 870 B.C. Middle Stratum IIa is therefore bracketed by dates ranging ca. 9,000 to 11,000 B.C.; it is of terminal Pleistocene age.

Lower Stratum IIa has seven additional radiocarbon dates ranging from 11,290 ± 1,010 B.C. to 17,650 ± 2,400 B.C. The eighteenth millennium B.C. date constitutes the deepest date from the rockshelter that is associated with materials of indisputable human manufacture and also marks the onset of human utilization of this locality.

The maximum excavated depth of Stratum IIa varies between 70 and 90 cm in different portions of the rockshelter. At the interface between lower Stratum IIa and Stratum I are several lenses of charcoal that have produced radiocarbon dates in the twentieth and twenty-ninth millennia B.C. range. These dates are not associated with any cultural materials. Furthermore, they are separated from the deepest occupational floors within Stratum IIa by a considerable thickness of sterile deposits.

ARTIFACTUAL REMAINS

Seven classes or artifactual remains have been recovered from Meadowcroft Rockshelter. These include lithic, bone, wood, shell, basketry, cordage and ceramic materials. The earliest flaked stone assemblage from Meadowcroft Rockshelter is associated with the deepest occupational floors within middle and lower Stratum IIa. This assemblage currently includes some 13 tools and 104 pieces of flaking debitage recovered during the 1973-1976 excavations and an additional 300+ specimens recovered in 1976-1978. The 400-odd items are directly associated with the radiocarbon-dated fire features from middle and lower Stratum IIa and represent not only

428   J.M. Adovasio *et al.*

the earliest securely dated collection of lithic tools in eastern
North America but also one of the earliest reliably dated
assemblages recovered anywhere in the Western Hemisphere. It
should be stressed that all of the aforementioned artifacts were
recovered from units sealed beneath the rock fall associated with
the onset of the deposition of middle Stratum IIa. Representative
artifacts and flaking debitage recovered from middle and lower
Stratum IIa during the 1973-1975 excavations are illustrated in
Figs 6 and 7b.

   Among the 300+ flaked stone artifacts recovered during the
1976-1978 excavation seasons are ca. 30 items found in 1976 on a
single occupation floor directly beneath the rock fall which marks
the middle and upper Stratum IIa interface. These artifacts
potentially represent the terminal Pleistocene occupation at the
shelter. Further, this group of tools includes the first definite
projectile point recovered from the deeper levels at the site. A
sample of these materials is illustrated in Figs 7a, 8 and 9.

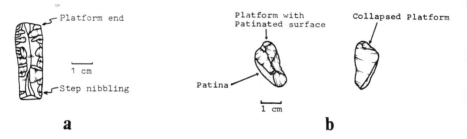

FIG. 7. *Artifacts from lower and middle Stratum IIa at
Meadowcroft Rockshelter. (a) blade located on floor directly
beneath the ca. 10,000 B.C. rock spalling event associated
with the Old Roof Fall; (b) bifacial thinning flake from
deep occupational floor.*

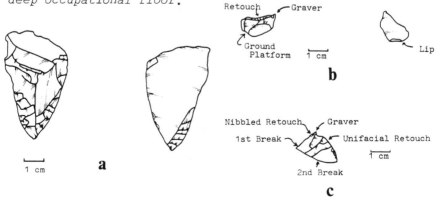

FIG. 8. *Artifacts from surface of middle Stratum IIa at
Meadowcroft Rockshelter. Note: All specimens were located on
the same occupational floor directly beneath the ca. 10,000
B.C. rock spalling event associated with the Old Roof Fall.*

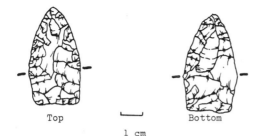

Terminology for bifaces found in situ and cross section of
                    Biface 4471.

Top Left ⊂⎯⎯⎯⎯⎯⊃ Top Right
Bottom Left   Bottom Right
          Occupation Floor

Sequence of Manufacture

1. Bifacial trimming and shaping
2. Basal thinning
3. Grinding of basal portion of lateral edges
4. Tip broken by impact fracture, scar remnant
   on Bottom face, see illustration
5. Reshaping and resharpening
   a. Top resharpened
   b. Bottom resharpened
   c. direction of movement during resharpening
      is undetermined because of alternating flake
      pattern

                    J. Gunn 3AUG76

FIG. 9. *Lanceolate projectile point, surface of middle
Stratum IIa at Meadowcroft Rockshelter. This specimen was
located on the same occupational floor as items illustrated
in Fig. 7a and Fig. 8.*

HUMAN REMAINS

Human remains from Meadowcroft Rockshelter are relatively rare
and include only one possible interment and 32 isolated
occurrences of individual bones, bone fragments and teeth. All
human remains, with two exceptions, are confined to Stratum IIb
or above. The two exceptions include the distal one-third of a
small middle phalanx and a weathered fragment of an occipital
bone, both of which are ascribable to lower Stratum IIa. Both
specimens derive from the same occupation surface, and both are
directly associated with firepits that have produced radiocarbon
dates of 11,320 ± 340 B.C. and 11,290 ± 1,010 B.C. At present
these two specimens constitute the earliest dated human
osteological remains from the Northeast.

VERTEBRATE FAUNAL REMAINS

Vertebrate faunal remains constitute the single most commonly
encountered set of inclusions in the rockshelter. Over 115,166

bones or fragments were individually examined. Remains of at least 5,634 individual vertebrates, representing 151 taxa, are present. One hundred and forty nine have been identified to the species level: 66 birds, 44 mammals, 26 reptiles, 8 fish and 5 amphibians. (*cf.*, Adovasio *et al.*, 1979-1980b: 108-109). Over 90% of the remains are from digestive pellets regurgitated by raptorial birds, primarily owls, that formerly roosted on the cliff face of the rockshelter during the time that the deposits were building. Southern flying squirrel, the extinct passenger pigeon and toad (*Glaucomys volans, Ectopistes migratorius, Bufo* sp.) account for 68% of all identified vertebrates. Some idea of raptor activity at the site can be gathered from the fact that 44% of all individual vertebrates from the site, at least 2,503 individuals, constitute but a single species, the mouse-sized southern flying squirrel.

Approximately 7% of the bone collection is probably attributable to Indian activity; the remaining 93% is the result of either raptor activity or adventitious occurrence. The Indian refuse component is dominated by white-tailed deer (*Odocoileus virginianus*). Butchering marks were noted on elk, turkey, ruffed grouse and hooded merganser bones (*Cervus elaphus, Meleagris gallopavo, Bonasa umbellus, Lophodytes cucullatus*). Deer and turkey bone awls, deer bone beamer fragments and three partial turtle (*Terrapene carolina*) carapace cups were recovered.

Bone preservation at all levels inside the present drip line of the rockshelter is good, but remains of large and medium-sized vertebrates have been reduced to bone fragments or isolated teeth. Twenty-three per cent of all fragments are charred, a figure which increases to 93% outside the drip line. No charring patterns were noted. All species were involved in what appears to have been the result of random, accidental burning of fragments in the aboriginal hearth substrata; they were not necessarily burned as a result of aboriginal food preparation techniques.

A clear picture of a temperate "Carolinian Zone" fauna characteristic of the oak-dominant forest of southwestern Pennsylvania in early Historic times is presented from early Historic levels to as far back as 9,350 ± 700 B.C. At least 21 species, 14% of the identified taxa, no longer occur at or near the site. Fifteen of these are absent due to human-induced ecological changes, and six reptiles, whose ranges now lie somewhat south or west of the site and whose presence suggests warmer, milder conditions in at least the mid-levels of the deposit, are no longer resident in the area.

Faunal remains from older levels of the rockshelter and beyond the present drip line are too poorly preserved to furnish explicit environmental conclusions. The remains include white-tailed deer, passenger pigeon, southern flying squirrel and chipmunk (*Tamias striatus*). These four species ranged in Historic times marginally into Canadian Zone situations but are more characteristic of modern Carolinian fauna of the area. However, taken in conjunction with the botanical evidence, also temperate in nature, they suggest temperate conditions as far back as 17,150 ± 110 years B.C. This conclusion is at variance with other studies that suggest boreal woodlands and associated boreal vertebrates in the eastern periglacial prior to *ca*. 11,000 years B.P.

INVERTEBRATE FAUNAL REMAINS

A modest assemblage of invertebrate faunal remains was recovered from Meadowcroft Rockshelter including terrestrial and aquatic snails as well as naiads, crayfish and insects. This assemblage is summarized in a preliminary fashion in Adovasio *et al*. (1977a) and Adovasio *et al*. (1979-1980b). With the notable exception of naiads, which were extensively exploited during Strata IV and V times, invertebrates do not seem to have contributed extensively to the diet of the subsequent Meadowcroft human populations.

FLORAL REMAINS

Floral remains constitute the second most abundant class of material recovered from Meadowcroft Rockshelter. These remains range from moderately large sections of tree trunks and limbs, with and without bark, to minute seeds and seed coats and small amounts of pollen. Intensive scrutiny of the 1973-1978 floral material from both the 1/4 inch screens and the *ca*. 3,600 pints of flotation samples, indicates that some vegetal remains have been recovered from all occupational levels, including Stratum IIa.

Like the Meadowcroft fauna, the vast bulk of the floral assemblage (over 97%) was recovered from upper Stratum IIa and above, and it too is therefore of Holocene or modern aspect. Portions of this larger assemblage are discussed in Adovasio *et al*. (1977a) and Adovasio *et al*. (1979-1980b). A moderate amount of floral material, usually charred, was recovered from middle and lower Stratum IIa and does include small quantities of deciduous forest elements.

Palynological analyses are thus far incomplete, and discussion is restricted here to macrobotanical remains. Preliminary investigations indicate that several taxa are represented in levels dating prior to 9,000 B.C. These include modest to meager amounts of walnut (*Juglans* sp.), hackberry (*Celtis* sp.), oak (*Quercus* sp.), hornbeam (*Carpinus* sp.), sycamore (*Platanus* sp.), maple (*Acer* sp.), black cherry (*Prunus* sp.), hickory (*Carya* sp.), hemlock (*Tsuga* sp.), blackgum (*Nyssa* sp.), beech (*Fagus* sp.) and pine (*Pinus* sp.). It should be stressed, however, that these floral elements have been subjected not only to the capriciousness of depositional conditions, but also to the fickleness of human selectivity. Macrobotanical material, in some cases, may be more indicative of local microhabitats than are palynological data, but it is biased in that its presence at the site is due most probably to human transport. Taxa not represented in the Meadowcroft cultural assemblage may not necessarily have been absent from the local floral assemblage. Lack of preservation or lack or collection by site inhabitants would serve to exclude various species from paleobotanical posterity.

Minimally, the floral data recovered from lower and middle Stratum IIa indicate that deciduous forest elements were available if only in extremely low frequency to the earliest human occupants of the site.

The data currently at hand suggest that the principal wild plant materials exploited for consumption at Meadowcroft were hackberry, chenopods and to a somewhat lesser extent, nuts and other berries.

Domesticates recovered at the site are summarized in Adovasio and Johnson (1981).

OVERVIEW

As stressed in virtually every earlier Meadowcroft publication, all of the recovered data suggest that throughout its history, the site served primarily as a locus or station for hunting, collecting and food processing activities. The predominance of projectile points, knives and scrapers in the lithic assemblage, the abundance of food bone and the remains of edible plants as well as the general absence of evidence for extensive *in situ* manufacture of lithic, ceramic or shell artifacts strongly support this conclusion.

The lower Stratum IIa assemblage, which currently represents the earliest well-dated evidence of human occupation of the southwest margin of the Northeast, also constitutes the best evidence to date of the pre-Clovis occupation anywhere in the hemisphere. While MacNeish (1976), Bryan (1969) and Krieger (1964) enumerate a host of localities in North, Middle and South America where putatively early materials occur, the simple fact remains that few, if any, of these localities fulfill the minimal standards of evidence necessary for "proof positive".

It is the contention of this paper, following Wendorf (1966) and Haynes (1969), that poorly substantiated data will not suffice to document pre-Clovis occupation in this hemisphere. Further, proper documentation must include excellent stratigraphy coupled with multiple radiocarbon determinations of artifacts of indisputable human manufacture in direct association. When these criteria are applied to the vast majority of allegedly pre-Clovis sites, one or another deficiency is inevitably apparent. Specifically, most of these sites possess either questionable or nonexistent stratigraphy, few (1-3) or no radiocarbon dates, "artifacts" of doubtful origin, poor associations or any combination of the foregoing. These observations are not offered to disprove or deride the putative antiquity of other pre-Clovis localities but rather to stress the inherent difficulty in effectively comparing the early Meadowcroft materials to early assemblages from elsewhere. Given this condition, the following comments remain pertinent.

The lower Stratum IIa assemblage does share a number of technological and morphological features with other, possibly related assemblages in both eastern and western North America. Though fluted points are absent, the bifacial lanceolate point from the surface of middle Stratum IIa is morphologically similar to points recovered in the basal strata of Fort Rock Cave, Oregon (Bedwell, 1973), Ventana Cave, Arizona (Haury, 1950), Levi, Texas (Alexander, 1963) and Bonfire Shelter, Texas (Dibble and Lorrain, 1968). In general, the point is also superficially similar to the Plainview and Milnesand types of the Great Plains region. The Plenge site in New Jersey (Kraft, 1973), the St. Albans site in West Virginia (Broyles, 1971) and numerous surface finds attest to the presence of unfluted lanceolate points in the eastern United States. However, the lanceolate point from Meadowcroft appears to antedate all of these specimens and may, in fact, represent the ancestral form for both fluted and unfluted Plano-like points. Tools similar to the Mungai "knives" from Meadowcroft appear at the Shoop site in eastern Pennsylvania (Witthoft, 1971, p. 29, Plate 4.3), Kellogg Farm, western Pennsylvania (McConaughy et al., 1977) and Lindenmeier, Colorado (Wilmsen, 1974, p. 64, Fig. 5.1g). The blades, bifaces, graver and retouched flakes are more-or-less duplicated at Shoop (Witthoft, 1952, 1971), Debert, Nova Scotia (MacDonald, 1968), Williamson, Virginia (McCary, 1951), Blackwater Draw, New Mexico (Hester, 1972), Lindenmeier (Wilmsen, 1974) and many other fluted point localities. Moreover, some general resemblances can be seen both to the unfortunately scant basal assemblages from Fort Rock Cave, Oregon (Bedwell, 1973) and Wilson Butte Cave, Idaho (Gruhn, 1961) and to the extensive, though undated lithic materials from Wells Creek, Tennessee (Dragoo, 1973).

Given the fact that the Stratum IIa assemblage clearly combines bifacial thinning techniques with blade tool manufacture, it may well prove that industries like this provided the genesis for or represent the substratum of the widely dispersed fluted point industries of North America. In this regard, another site in the Cross Creek drainage, 36WH351, recently has produced morphological duplicates (except for unifacial fluting) of the unfluted lanceolate point from Meadowcroft as well as microblade cores and microblades strongly reminiscent of those from middle and lower Stratum IIa at the rockshelter. While the dating of these recent materials remains to be established, they do indicate that the basal Stratum IIa diagnostic lithics are neither unique nor unrelated to the much more widespread fluted point industries of North America.

While a number of general resemblances to Upper Paleolithic complexes in Siberia, Japan and the North Pacific littoral can be seen, it is too early to specify the nature or intensity of any connections to these complexes.

The evidence from the Meadowcroft/Cross Creek project strongly indicates the presence of pre-fluted projectile point-using populations in the New World. As such, this information casts severe doubt on the "late entry" hypothesis as advanced and championed by Haynes, Martin and other scholars. Put succinctly, the data from Meadowcroft appear to confirm at least a "middle entry" date range for the peopling of the New World and place the initial crossing of the Bering Straits no later than 20,000-25,000 years B.P.

ACKNOWLEDGEMENTS

The excavations at Meadowcroft Rockshelter were conducted under the auspices of the Archaeological Research Program (now the Cultural Resource Management Program) of the Department of Anthropology, University of Pittsburgh, with financial and logistic support provided by the University of Pittsburgh, the Meadowcroft Foundation, the Alcoa Foundation, the Buhl Foundation, the Leon Falk Family Trust, the National Science Foundation, the National Geographic Society and Mr John Boyle of Oil City, Pennsylvania. Line drawings were drafted by K. and F. Adkins, R. L. Andrews, A. Ferenci and J. D. Gunn. This manuscript was edited by R. C. Carlisle, Editor, Cultural Resource Management Program and Assistant to the Chairman and was typed by G. Placone.

This report is an overview of a small segment of the work done at Meadowcroft. It is expected that a portion of the data presented here will be modified by further analyses. The final report on the Meadowcroft Project will be published by the University of Pittsburgh Press.

REFERENCES

Adovasio, J.M. (n.d.) Multidisciplinary Research in the Northeast: One View from Meadowcroft Rockshelter, *Pennslyvania Archaeologist* (in press).

Adovasio, J.M. and Johnson, W.C. (1981). The Appearance of Cultigens in the Upper Ohio Valley: A View from Meadowcroft Rockshelter. *Pennsylvania Archaeologist* 51(1-2), 63-80.

Adovasio, J.M., Donahue, J., Stuckenrath, R. and Gunn, J.D. (1981).
The Meadowcroft Papers: A Response to Dincauze. *Quarterly
Review of Archaeology* 2(3), 14-15.

Adovasio, J.M., Gunn, J.D., Donahue, J. and Stuckenrath, R. (1975).
Excavations at Meadowcroft Rockshelter, 1973-1974: A Progress
Report. *Pennsylvania Archaeologist* 45(3), 1-30.

Adovasio, J.M., Gunn, J.D., Donahue, J. and Stuckenrath, R. (1977a).
Meadowcroft Rockshelter: Retrospect 1976. *Pennsylvania
Archaeologist* 47(2-3), 1-93.

Adovasio, J.M., Gunn, J.D., Donahue, J. and Stuckenrath, R. (1977b).
Progress Report on the Meadowcroft Rockshelter - A 16,000
Year Chronicle. In Amerinds and Their Paleoenvironments in
Northeastern North America, edited by W.S. Newman and B.
Salwen, pp. 137-159. *Annals of the New York Academy of
Sciences* 228.

Adovasio, J.M., Gunn, J.D., Donahue, J. and Stuckenrath, R. (1978a).
Meadowcroft Rockshelter, 1977: An Overview. *American
Antiquity* 43(4), 632-651.

Adovasio, J.M., Gunn, J.D., Donahue, J., Stuckenrath, R., Guilday,
J., and Lord, K. (1978b.) Meadowcroft Rockshelter. In Early Man
in America from a Circum-Pacific Perspective, edited by A.L.
Bryan, pp. 140-180. *Occasional Papers of the Department of
Anthropology, University of Alberta 1.*

Adovasio, J.M., Gunn, J.D., Donahue, J., Stuckenrath, R., Guilday,
J., and Lord, K. (1979-1980a). Meadowcroft Rockshelter -
Retrospect 1977 (Part 1). *North American Archaeologist* 1(1),
3-44.

Adovasio, J.M., Gunn, J.D., Donahue, J., Stuckenrath, R., Guilday,
J., and Lord, K. (1979-1980b). Meadowcroft Rockshelter -
Retrospect 1977 (Part 2). *North American Archaeologist* 1(2),
99-137.

Adovasio, J.M., Gunn, J.D., Donahue, J., Stuckenrath, R., Guilday,
J.E. and Volman, K. (1980). Yes Virginia, It Really Is That Old:
A Reply to Haynes and Mead. *American Antiquity* 45(3),
588-595.

Adovasio, J.M. *et al.* (n.d) (ordering of other authors not yet
determined). *Meadowcroft Rockshelter and the Archaeology
of the Cross Creek Drainage.* University of Pittsburgh Press,
Pittsburgh (in preparation).

Alexander, H.L., Jr. (1963). The Levi Site: A Paleo-Indian Campsite in Central Texas. *American Antiquity* 28(4), 510-528.

Bedwell, S.F. (1973). *Fort Rock Basin: Prehistory and Environment*. University of Oregon Books, Eugene.

Beynon, D.E. (n.d.). Geoarchaeology of Meadowcroft Rockshelter and the Cross Creek Drainage. In *Meadowcroft Rockshelter and the Archaeology of the Cross Creek Drainage*, by J.M. Adovasio *et al.* (in preparation).

Broyles, B. (1971). The St. Albans Site, Kanawha County, West Virginia: Second Preliminary Report. *West Virginia Geological and Economic Survey*.

Bryan, A.L. (1969). Early Man in America and the Late Pleistocene Chronology of Western Canada and Alaska. *Current Anthropology* 10(4), 339-365.

Calkin, P.E. and Miller, K.E. (1977). Late Quaternary Environment and Man in Western New York. In Amerinds and Their Paleoenvironments in Northeastern North America, edited by W.S. Newman and B. Salwen, pp. 297-315. *Annals of the New York Academy of Sciences* 228.

Carlisle, R.C. (n.d.). The Cross Creek Drainage in the Historic Time Period (tentative title). In *Meadowcroft Rockshelter and the Archaeology of the Cross Creek Drainage*, by J.M. Adovasio *et al.* University of Pittsburgh Press, Pittsburgh (in preparation).

Dibble, D.S. and Lorrain, D. (1968). Bonfire Shelter: A Stratified Bison Kill Site, Val Verde County, Texas. *Texas Memorial Museum Miscellaneous Papers* 1.

Dincauze, D. (1981). The Meadowcroft Papers. *Quarterly Review of Archaeology* 2, 3-5.

Donahue, J., Adovasio, J.M. and Beynon, D.E. (1979). *Geological Investigations at Meadowcroft Rockshelter*. A Paper Prepared for the 44th Annual Meeting of the Society for American Archaeology, Vancouver, B.C.

Donahue, J., Storck, P.L., Adovasio, J.M., Gunn, J.D. and Stuckenrath, R. (1978). Archaeological Sites: Pittsburgh to Toronto. *Toronto '78: Field Trips Guidebook* (A.L. Currie and W.O. Mackasey, eds). pp. 65-72. Geological Association of Canada.

Dragoo, D.W. (1973). Wells Creek: An Early Man Site in Stewart County, Tennessee. *Archaeology of Eastern North America* 1(1), 1-55.

Flint, N.K. (1955). Geology and Mineral Resources of Somerset County, Pennsylvania. *Pennsylvania Geological Survey County Report* C56A.

Goldthwait, R.P., White, G.W. and Forsythe, J.L. (1967). Glacial Map of Ohio, Revised. *U.S. Department of the Interior, United States Geological Survey, Miscellaneous Geologic Investigations Map* 1-316. Washington, D.C.

Gruhn, R. (1961). The Archaeology of Wilson Butte Cave, South-Central Idaho. *Occasional Papers of the Idaho State College Museum* 6.

Haury, E.W. (1950). *The Stratigraphy and Archaeology of Ventana Cave, Arizona.* The University of New Mexico and University of Arizona Presses, Albuquerque and Tucson.

Haynes, C.V. (1969). Comment on Early Man in America and the Late Pleistocene Chronology of Western Canada and Alaska, by A.L. Bryan. *Current Anthropology* 10(4), 353-354.

Haynes, C.V. (1977). When and From Where Did Man Arrive in Northeastern North America: A Discussion. In Amerinds and Their Paleoenvironments in Northeastern North America, edited by W.S. Newman and B. Salwen, pp. 165-166. *Annals of the New York Academy of Sciences* 228.

Haynes, C.V. (1980). Paleoindian Charcoal from Meadowcroft Rockshelter: Is Contamination a Problem? *American Antiquity* 45(3), 582-587.

Hester, J.J. (1972). Blackwater, Locality No. 1. *Publications of the Fort Burgwin Research Centre* 8.

Johnson, W.C. (1981). *Archaeological Review Activities in Survey Region IV, Northwestern Pannsylvania: Year End Report of the Regional Archaeologist for the Period September 1979 through August 1980.* A Report Prepared for the Pennsylvania Historical and Museum Commission by the Cultural Resource Management Program, University of Pittsburgh, Pittsburgh, Pennsylvania, Under the Supervision of Dr J.M. Adovasio, Ph.D., in Accordance with the Provisions of Service Purchase Contract 645987.

Kraft, H.C. (1973). The Plenge Site: A Paleo-Indian Occupation
Site in New Jersey. *Archaeology of Eastern North America*
1(1), 56-117.

Krieger, A.D. (1964). Early Man in the New World. In *Prehistoric
Man in the New World,* edited by J.D. Jennings and E. Norbeck,
pp. 28-81. University of Chicago Press, Chicago.

Leverett, F. (1902). Glacial Formations and Drainage Features of
the Erie and Ohio Basins. *U.S. Geological Survey Monograph*
41.

Lord, K. (n.d.). Molluscan Fauna from Meadowcroft Rockshelter and
the Cross Creek Drainage (tentative title). In *Meadowcroft
Rockshelter and the Archaeology of the Cross Creek
Drainage,* by J.M. Adovasio et al. University of Pittsburgh
Press, Pittsburgh (in preparation).

MacDonald, G.F. (1968). Debert: A Paleo-Indian Site in Central
Nova Scotia. *National Museum of Canada Anthropological
Papers* 16.

MacNeish, R.S. (1976). Early Man in the New World. *American
Scientist* 63(3), 316-317.

McGary, B.C. (1976) A Workshop of Early Man in Dinwiddie County,
Virginia. *American Antiquity* 17(1), 9-17.

McConaughy, M.A., Applegarth, J.D. and Faignaert, D.F. (1977).
Fluted Points from Slippery Rock, Pennsylvania, *Pennsylvania
Archaeologist* 47(4), 30-36.

Mead, J.I. (1980). Is It Really That Old? A Comment About the
Meadowcroft Rockshelter "Overview." *American Antiquity*
45(3), 579-582.

Muller, E.H. (1963). Geology of Chautauqua County, New York,
Part II, Pleistocene Geology. *New York State Museum and
Science Service Bulletin* 392.

Pettijohn, F.J. (1975). *Sedimentary Rocks.* Harper and Row, New
York.

Schooler, E.E. (1974). Pleistocene Beach Ridges of Northwestern
Pennsylvania. *Pennsylvania Geological Survey, Fourth
Series, General Geology Report* 64.

Shepps, V.C., White, G.W., Droste, J.B., and Sitler, R.F. (1959). Glacial Geology of Northwestern Pennsylvania. *Pennsylvania Geological Survey, Fourth Series, Bulletin* G-32.

Tesmer, I.H. (1975). Geology of Cattaraugus County, New York. *Buffalo Society of Natural Sciences Bulletin* 27.

Wendorf, F. (1966). Early Man in the New World: Problems of Migration. *American Naturalist* 100(912), 253-270.

White, G.W., Totten, S.M. and Gross, D.L. (1969). Pleistocene Stratigraphy of Northwestern Pennsylvania. *Pennsylvania Geological Survey, Fourth Series, General Geology Report* G-55.

Wilmsen, E.N. (1974). *Lindenmeier: A Pleistocene Hunting Society.* Harper and Row, New York, Evanston, San Francisco.

Witthoft, J. (1952). A Paleo-Indian Site in Eastern Pennsylvania: An Early Hunting Culture. *Proceedings of the American Philosophical Society* 96, 464-495.

Witthoft, J. (1971). A Paleo-Indian Site in Eastern Pennsylvania. In *Foundations of Pennsylvania Prehistory* (B.C. Kent, I.F. Smith, III and C. McCann, eds). pp. 13-64. The Pennsylvania Historical and Museum Commission, Harrisburg.

EARLY MAN IN THE NEW WORLD

Clement W. Meighan

*Department of Anthropology,
University of California Los Angeles,
Los Angeles, California 90024, USA*

ABSTRACT

The debate about man's earliest entry into the New World concerns the time frame suggested by the claims for great antiquity of humans in the New World. While all evidence indicates that man did not originate in the New World, there are major disagreements as to the time of man's entry via the Bering Straits region. When this crossing was believed to be within the past few thousand years, it was clear that the major geological events of the Pleistocene were not relevant to human history in the New World. But as evidence for human remains showed ever greater antiquity, culminating in the discovery of human remains associated with extinct bison (the Folsom discovery of over 50 years ago), it became apparent that the Pleistocene lowering of sea levels and the consequent emergence of Beringia was a factor of major importance in explaining New World archaeology. Further, many other effects of the glacial period, including terrace-building, silting in of lagoons, fluctuations in lake levels, and transient barriers to human travel, also had to be recognized and taken into account. The present discussion reviews the debate about human settlement in the New World, with some comment about the Pleistocene phenomena affecting that settlement.

WHAT IS EARLY MAN?

The definition of "early" changes as older and older finds are made. What was thought of as "early man" when I was a student is now well established to represent a relatively late time period in human history. "Early" also depends upon one's geographic area of interest - nothing in the New World looks very early to people concerned with origins of human tool use in the Old World. Martin (1973, p. 73), recognizing that the big-game hunters of 11,000 years ago were no longer to be considered "early man" finds, tried to deal with this problem by referring to "early-early" man sites. For present purposes, I will consider as "early man" the various finds purported to deal with the earliest entry of man into the New World, which are variously dated (depending on one's point of view) as little as 15,000 years ago (Martin, 1973) and as long as about 100,000 years ago, (Carter, 1980). There seems reasonable agreement on the sites less than 15,000 years old, but massive controversy on everything in the 85,000 years between 15-100,000 years ago (Taylor and Meighan, 1978).

My discussion will concentrate on the archaeological viewpoint of early man and will say little about areas of expertise to which other scholars must direct their attention (geological evidence, problems in dating methods, etc.). I will also say most about California material where I have some familiarity with most of the sites and collections. I am less able to evaluate claimed early sites at a distance, although a review of the literature shows them to be subject to all the same kinds of arguments (pro and con) as the California sites.

SUBMERGED COASTLINES AND MIGRATION BRIDGES

So long as the time span of humans in the New World was believed to be very short, the question of changing sea levels and shorelines was not of much importance to New World archaeology. As the time of human occupation in the New World was shown to be greater and greater, and was demonstrated to be old enough to reach the period of Pleistocene megafauna, it became apparent that serious attention must be paid to geological and climatic events and to the fact that past human environments were quite different in size and quality from present environments. However, in the New World such researches are still in the beginning stages so far as archaeological correlations are concerned. The greatest attention has been paid to the termination of the glacial period (Beringia and the presence of ice-free corridors) which allows man's passage from Asia to North America. (Scientific American, 1973). This literature is not reviewed here except to comment that many arguments still exist, particularly with respect to the existence of ice-free corridors at various time periods (see Reeves, 1983, this volume).

Once into the New World, the issue of migration bridges, or geographic barriers to expansion, is a matter of local significance only. While there were undoubted barriers that must have affected routes of travel (deserts, mountains, rivers, and on a smaller scale lakes and glacier remnants), early man seems to have been able to find his way over or around all of the barriers and to spread through the New World in a surprisingly rapid way. This is best shown by sites in the area of Patagonia, which are dated by radiocarbon as having occupation 12,600 years ago (Los Toldos site, Level 11; (see Gradin, n.d.), also the site of Tagua Tagua in central Chile, with a published radiocarbon date of 11,380 B.P. (Nuñez, n.d.) and a reported but unpublished date of slightly over 12,000 years ago). These are remarkably old dates considering that the sites in question are at the greatest possible distance from the Bering Straits. These ages are as old or older than comparable finds in North America. I conclude that migration bridges within the New World were abundant and easy to follow, and that barriers to expansion which may have had a large effect on plants and animals did not have much of an effect on *Homo sapiens*. [There are, of course, proposed finds much older than 12-13,000 years in North America, as there are in South America; some of these are discussed below but these controversial dates do not change the conclusion because those who accept them also accept the equivalent dates in South America. Hence, whether or not one rules out part of the dating evidence, whatever frame of reference is used leads to the conclusion that man got to South America with minimal delay once the Bering Straits were crossed.]

As for submerged coastlines, the important question for achaeology is not whether submerged sites exist, for of course they do. The key query is whether the submergence of early sites might have removed from the archaeological record *all* the evidence of very early humans in the New World, leaving only a partial picture from which the earliest evidences have been removed by rising sea levels since the end of Pleistocene. This conclusion has sometimes been implied as a way of asserting that very early New World sites exist even though they have not been found. Aside from the difficulties of arguing from negative evidence, always hazardous in archaeology, it seems to me very unlikely that submerged coastlines can be used in the early man argument. In the first place, direct evidence is very limited, but what evidence we have of submerged sites does not include any truly ancient site - they may exist but the submerged sites of the New World are so far all within the past few thousand years.

Other reasons for doubting the value of submerged sites as the source of information on the earliest humans in the New World may be briefly enumerated:

1) By definition, all truly coastal sites in the USA earlier than about 5,000 B.P. must now be below sea level. Midden and habitation sites immediately adjacent to coasts earlier than

5,000 B.P. are submerged, and we would not expect to find them above present sea level. Nevertheless, coastal peoples often carried shellfish several km before consuming them and discarding the shells (see Bailey, 1983, this volume). Also, some peoples alternated shellfish gathering and animal hunting according to season. Thus, it would be reasonable to find evidence of shellfish consumption above present sea level at least as old as 8-10,000 years. On steep coasts, even older marine oriented sites might be found.

All the evidence for early humans found on land in the New World indicates that they were land-oriented hunters and gatherers, primarily dependent upon land resources and hence *not* oriented to coastal living. The oldest shell mounds appear to be fairly recent and dated New World shell mounds are no more than 10,000 years old; the vast majority are in the past 8,000 years. Evidence of fishing is also quite late in the archaeological record. The early sites associated with terminal Pleistocene animals, in both North and South America, are not in coastal areas but inland a considerable distance. Hence even the earliest peoples into the New World were widely dispersed into areas which would not be affected directly by sea level changes.

2. There are numerous counterbalancing changes accompanying sea-level rise; these have the effects of isolating some early sites from the water rather than submerging them. Some of the things which act to preserve sites from disappearing beneath the rising sea:

a) Behaviour of humans in coastal areas. People *may* establish settlements directly on the beach or near marshes but very frequently select locations having considerable elevation above the beach (commonly 50-150 meters along the California coast), for cultural reasons having to do with defense, desire for a wide view of the ocean, etc. Sea level changes have to be of a large magnitude to have any effect on such archaeological sites.

b) Tectonic changes and rising land surfaces. Extensive areas of the Southern California coast (Santa Monica Mountains and areas inland from Santa Barbara) have risen 400-600 meters during the Pleistocene. The total uplift during the Holocene could be 4-6 meters.

c) Alluviation and silting-in as sea level rises and rivers deposit sediments in bays, estuaries, and lagoons. In some areas, this has the effect of leaving archaeological sites which were once on the shore now a distance of several km inland.

d) Changing river courses, related to (b) and (c) above, may isolate archaeological sites many km. from their former riverine locations on a watercourse.

e)   Drying of lakes; in the Great Basin, most of the major Pleistocene lakes declined in size as the sea level was rising. Hence, at the same time the coastal sites were being submerged, inland sites on lake shores were on receding beach lines and exist today on the margins of dry lakes.

These observations do not diminish the value of archaeological remains found offshore, but they do argue strongly that it is unlikely for all of the archaeological remains of any period of New World prehistory to be entirely preserved in underwater sites. Of course, this is from a continental perspective, and in local areas it is well known that much of the archaeology of even a few thousand years ago has been submerged by rising sea level.

REVIEW OF EARLY MAN SITES IN THE NEW WORLD

The early man material has been reviewed many times by many writers, among them Davis, Brown, and Nichols (1981), Glennan (n.d.), Berger (1971), Carter (1980), Heizer (1952, 1964), Haynes (1969), Meighan (1965, 1978), and Taylor and Payen (1979). In addition, all writers of general texts have been forced to deal with this issue; finally, there are many symposium volumes (Bryan, 1978; Rogers *et al*, 1966; see also the collected papers in Scientific American, 1973). This literature deals with many regions from Alaska to Tierra del Fuego. The archaeological finds range from single isolated discoveries of artifacts to extensive excavations of caves, settlements, and hunting or kill sites used by ancient man. It is impossible to review all of the discussion in a brief article, and I use California as my example and case history for the general early man issue. My review of the evidence convinces me that no region has any better evidence than the California workers have provided, and California has more claims for early man sites than any other comparable region, as well as the benefit of a large number of investigators over a long period of time.

As a general comment, the literature on Early Man has many documents which show advocacy of one set of interpretations. These often go beyond mere conviction that one's evidence is sound and pursue the questionable path of selecting evidence and citations so that contrary evidence is not cited or discussed. There tends to be, therefore, two sets of literature on early man in the New World, each of which works internally without much reference to other viewpoints, or the careful examination of other evidence. It is difficult to avoid this problem, and even my own list of references above, which I consider to represent the full spectrum of opinion, is seen as somewhat selective by George Carter who discussed this with me. I admit that it is selective, partly for reasons of space. More important, I think the divisions in the literature have to do with some fundamental disagreements about the nature of archaeological evidence itself; the selectivity in many of the early man bibliographies results from the feelings of individual researchers that some publications are non-evidence and therefore need not be taken seriously.

For western North America, I am impressed by the longevity of the arguments about several of the key sites proposed as early man locations. Texas Street and the Scripps Fan locations were originally published in the 1950s; over 20 years later the original arguments about the validity of these sites are still unresolved and there is little new in current discussion. Carter (1957) does not differ much from Carter (1980) nor do the comments of his critics during that period of time (Krieger, 1964; Martin, 1973). Similarly, the preliminary report on Calico appeared 13 years ago (Leakey, Simpson and Clements, 1968), and subsequent work does not seem to have changed anyone's evaluation of this site, (Dixon, 1970; Schuiling, 1972). For example, there are at least four discussions of the assemblage from Calico which apply statistical methods to verify human workmanship of the broken stones at that site. Two of these studies conclude that the assemblage is indistinguishable from naturally-fractured rock; two of them conclude that human agency is demonstrated in the assemblage (Taylor and Payen, 1979, p.263-273, review this argument; see also Haynes, 1973; Singer, n.d.; and Duvall and Venner, n.d.).

The key contribution to studies of early man on the west coast in the past 20 years can be briefly summarized:

Extensive efforts have been made at improved dating, particularly applied to human skeletal remains, by Bada using amino acid racemization and by Berger and others using radiocarbon dating (see Bada and Finkel, this volume; and Berger, this volume). Several finds of human skeletons are stated to have ages from 17,000 to 50,000 years. These finds, including such parts of skulls and skeletons as Los Angeles Man, Laguna, Del Mar, and Yuha, are viewed by most archaeologists with considerable reservation, partly because they cannot be linked to any archaeological or cultural evidence. All have been challenged by critics presenting opinions that the finds are more recent than claimed, most recently in the case of Del Mar man (Bischoff and Rosenbauer, 1981).

Interesting and potentially promising explorations are being carried out by Riddell in the San Joaquin Valley, Davis in the Panamint Ranges, Moriarty in San Diego County, Kaufman in the North Coast Ranges, and Berger on Santa Rosa Island. Some of these look like good possibilities for early man locations, particularly the site recently described in an article by Berger (1980). However, it must be agreed that all of these sites are still published only as preliminary reports and journalistic accounts, and that they may or may not prove to be what they appear to be when all the evidence is in.

Some of the contenders for early man status have been removed from the list as more thorough investigations have been completed. Tule Springs, Nevada, is a good example. Formerly proclaimed to be over 23,000 years old, it seems to be no more than 11-12,000 years in age, hence an important but not earth-shaking discovery.

Those not immersed in the controversies about early man in the New World may see all this as a pedantic issue about which it is hard to get excited. After all, proving the presence of man in the New World at ever earlier ages may push the time scale back a little, but it does not alter fundamentally our notions about human cultural development. Probably the most significant question concerns the level of knowledge carried by the first people into the New World. Were they relatively advanced and specialized Upper Paleolithic hunters, or were they much simpler peoples, with only a crude technology and a Middle Paleolithic or even Lower Paleolithic stage of development? So far as New World culture history goes, this is a very important question, for it defines the cultural base on which all New World developments took place. Many issues of cultural process and change, of human inventiveness and parallel developments, depend upon understanding what knowledge came to the New World with the first Americans, and what knowledge was developed by those people after they were cut off from their Old World origins. It is not merely a matter of historical interest, but also of theoretical importance, to discover the earliest cultural remains in the New World.

Unfortunately, these intellectual problems are often not the driving force in early man explorations. Russell Kaldenberg, in introducing a recent symposium on early man in California, said: "Anything old is of interest, anything that is older than everything else is of greater public interest, and the absolute oldest is of the greatest public interest." This universal public interest in "ancient, more ancient, most ancient" has lead to many of the negative aspects of early man studies: the rush to press releases with claims of great new discoveries, the premature publication of poorly defined and analysed sites and collections, the use of unassimilated and often dubious evidence to promote large grants, and even the maintenance of the Calico site as a tourist attraction at the taxpayers' expense. Trained archaeologists do not believe that the primary purpose of their studies is to find remains that are more ancient than those previously reported, but it is true that the public has this perception (as do many scholars in fields outside of archaeology). A certain amount of the negative feeling of many archaeologists toward each new early man claim arises from a long history of slovenly scholarship and the discrediting of claim after claim dating back to Calaveras Man over 100 years ago.

PRESENT ARCHAEOLOGICAL ATTITUDES TOWARD EARLY MAN CLAIMS

There is a wide spectrum of belief (or disbelief) among archaeological scholars concerning the early man finds so far reported. Reviewing what the professionals have to say (omitting enthusiasts and non-scholars), there seems to be three main strands of opinion, each of which has strong supporters. These include:

1) The believers. The outstanding exponent of this group is George Carter, whose recent book (1980) opens with the sentence: "It has long been my contention that man entered America with a Lower Paleolithic culture about 100,000 years ago". This is a minority point of view, and few of those who share it are PhDs whose career has been in archaeology. This has led some of the believers to the position that a PhD is a positive deterrent to clear thinking and recognition of evidence, a position we can all share in moments of frustration but hardly a guide to evaluating archaeological evidence.

Although the believers have no doubt that early man came to the New World at a far earlier time than most archaeologists accept, their minority view is worth careful thought. George Carter, Ruth Simpson, and a few others I would put in the "believer" class, have made an important contribution to American archaeology. They have investigated issues few other archaeologists were actively concerned with, they have goaded the establishment into entertaining new kinds of possibilities for interpretation, and they have diligently devoted years of effort to their studies. They have certainly earned the right to be heard, and even if it turns out that their early man claims are totally invalid, their investigations were still worth doing and still mark an important chapter in New World archaeological studies.

The believers are not subject to the same doubts as the groups discussed below. Nor only do the believers recognize the certainty of early man sites of great antiquity, but they also believe that they have the evidence; they cannot understand why everyone else is still looking for it.

Some of the observations that cheer on the believers include such historical facts as the more or less continuous pushing back of age estimates for human activity. It is certainly true that archaeological finds of greater and greater age have been made in both the Old World and the New; when I was an undergraduate student the oldest sites we felt sure of in California were only a few thousand years old; today the most conservative of the establishment archaeologists would accept an age of 11-12,000 years for man's presence in California. So in 30 years we have doubled or tripled the age of archaeological remains with evidence acceptable to everyone. The early man believers expect that it is just a matter of time until the establishment scholars get their understanding back to 100,000 years, and they may be right. On the other hand, common sense indicates that man's history in California does not extend back to infinity, and sooner or later we will come to a limit beyond which there is no human occupation. I doubt that anyone believes that we have found the oldest archaeological site in California. However, as time goes by and the search continues, the point will be reached where we will have a reasonably good fix on the age of man in California, and changes in this estimate will be smaller and smaller as time goes by.

The believers also point to the many cases in the history of science where the minority view has proven correct and the establishment view has been overthrown by ideas not acceptable when first put forward. I agree with the believers that the early man issue is not a popularity contest and cannot be decided by taking a vote on it; the issue can only be resolved by the presentation of convincing scholarly evidence.

Finally, the believers are not daunted by the discrediting of individual finds, for they believe that there are many sites of the most ancient age. Where there is so much smoke there must be fire, and the assemblage of many finds (in both North and South America) carries enough weight to overcome the uncertainties about any single one of these finds. One student who began with this idea believed that he could examine a series of early man finds in Southern California and sort out which were "smoke" and which were "fire" (Glennan, n.d.). After a one-by-one scrutiny of the finds, he slipped from the ranks of believers and became a member of the second community:

2) The agnostics. The agnostics are willing to be converted, but they want to be convinced by scholarly evidence of specific kinds (discussed below). These people sort out what they think is likely to be the case from what they *know* based on archaeological evidence. A good brief statement of this viewpoint is that of Willey (1966) in his textbook on North American archaeology:

> First, I think it likely that the "pre-projectile point horizon" is a reality and that man first crossed into America as far back as 40,000 to 20,000 B.C. . . . I wish again to make it explicit that I do not believe that present evidence is adequate to support it beyond reasonable doubt.

This is the "establishment view" of professional archaeology, shared by many of the archaeologists in the U.S. in varying degrees. It is first of all not nearly so doctrinaire and rigid as the believers claim in their complaints about persecution from the establishment. On the other hand, it is a statement that solid scholarly evidence is needed to tip this group into the ranks of the believers - they want to be shown. Furthermore, as archaeologists, they want to be shown with archaeological evidence. If information generated by other disciplines such as geology, soil science, or geochemistry suggests a particular antiquity, then this information must eventually be substantiated by an archaeological record.

A more serious criticism might be that statements like Willey's are an evasion - a way of sitting on the fence without making any decisions and perhaps a way of sidestepping the whole issue. There is some truth in such a criticism. Most archaeologists are not dealing first-hand with early man sites, and most of them cannot deal directly with the evidence but must rely on publications. Furthermore, since the evidence often requires considerable knowledge of disciplines external to archaeology (such as paleontology, geology, soil science, paleoecology, not to mention land bridges and sea level changes), this can be a frustrating body of literature for the average archaeologist. Even if he invests the time to understand the local situation, he may be ill-equipped to examine the evidence for an early man site on the other side of the continent. So it is easy for the archaeologist to follow the prudent man's rule: when the expers are disagreed, the non-expert is well-advised to withhold judgement until more evidence is available. However faint-hearted such a position may appear, it is reasonable to ask for evidence that conforms to the ordinary rules of scientific inquiry before coming to a conclusion.

The spectrum of archaeological opinion about early man claims includes another polar position:
3) The Sceptics. Paul Martin (1973) and his followers are the clearest exponents of this position. Based on abundant evidence of early hunters at about 12,000 years ago, this group sees the entry of man into the New World at about that time (or perhaps 15,000 years ago depending on how much time is allowed for the spread of humans throughout the continents of North and South America). This entry of skilled hunters into a virgin territory that had not previously experienced human hunters presumably led to the extinction of the Pleistocene megafauna. Acceptance of this viewpoint does not allow for a "pre-projectile point horizon" nor a very long time of human occupation in the New World. As Martin says (*ibid*., p. 973): "I can envision only one circumstance under which an ephemeral discovery of America might have occurred. It is that sometime before 12,000 years ago, the earliest early man came over the Bering Straits without early woman."

This group has in its support a large and growing body of solid evidence for the Early Hunter tradition, contrasted with much thinner and more arguable claims for anything prior to that tradition. (i.e. prior to 12,000 years ago). However, in its most extreme form, the position of the sceptics is certainly not the majority view of archaeologists today (contrary to the claims of the believers, who like to cast themselves in polar opposition to a viewpoint that man in the New World has an antiquity of only 12,000 years). Most archaeologists are fearful, and rightly so, of negative evidence. They do not want to get into a position of arguing that since something has not yet been found, it will *never* be found; there have been too many surprises in archaeological research for that to be a comfortable position. On the other hand, how many thousand man-years of archaeological investigation are needed before one can be reasonably sure that he has the basic facts? The incredible expansion of archaeological study since World War II has had thousands of archaeologists poking into every nook and cranny of North America, and while there are no doubt many new discoveries to be made, the odds against clinching the argument with a site 100,000 years old are growing with every passing year. Eventually one may reach the conclusion that we have not found an early man site because it is not there - a conclusion held by the present group of sceptics.

All scholars reserve the right to change their opinion as new evidence comes forward. The sceptics may all become believers, as indeed happened to the sceptics of 50 years ago when fluted points were found with the bones of extinct bison. Similarly, some believers may weaken in their faith and become agnostics, and a few will find that they spend some of their career time in all three of the camps: believers, agnostics, and sceptics. It is important to recognize that these broad differences in opinion about ancient sites do not indicate a total confusion or lack of scholarly ability on the part of archaeologists. Believers, agnostics, and sceptics can be found in all fields where the evidence is difficult to obtain, often difficult to interpret, and subject to valid differences of opinion. We need only think of theories of biological evolution, or of continental drift, to find parallel situations in disciplines other than archaeology. So in archaeology it is not useful to tally up votes, invoke authority figures, or descend to name-calling. All we can do it to recognize two facts:

1) The experts are disagreed.
2) More work is needed.

ARCHAEOLOGICAL EVIDENCE AND ITS EVALUATION

One of the benefits of the long period of controversy and inquiry into early man finds is the gradual crystallization of some basic principles which are referred to by many writers dealing with archaeological finds. These basic principles apply to the validation of *all* archaeological finds, regardless of age, but they seldom become controversial in recent sites, partly because the evidence can be overwhelming and partly because misinterpretations of recent sites are not errors of the significance associated with early man sites. To accept a site as 50,000 years older than any other known location is to make a major revision in one's view of culture history; errors in recent sites seldom require such readjustment of basic concepts.

The three things needed to validate any site are knowledge that man was present, knowledge of the age of the find, and knowledge that the associations (with stratigraphy or other finds) are what they appear to be. These are discussed individually below.

The problem of whether or not man was present (i.e. the site is in fact the product of human activity and not merely a natural feature) rarely exists for recent sites because of the large number of unquestionable artifacts present. For some claimed very early locations, however, the evidence is so amorphous that it is difficult to decide whether it was produced by nature or by the hand of man. This is the "eolith controversy", still very much of a live issue in the earliest archaeological sites in both Old and New World. Many of the claimed early sites in California, including Texas Street and Calico, are dismissed by critics on the grounds that the broken rocks collected as "artifacts" are merely naturally broken rock, (see Taylor and Payen, 1979; Haynes, 1973). This problem is recognized and responded to by the discoverers of such sites (cf. Carter, 1967), and there exists a considerable literature dealing with scholarly methods for discriminating man-made stone tools, however crude, from rocks broken in a creek-bed or gravel terraces. The lines of approach vary from actual experimental studies to record and measure such things as the effects of fire in fracturing rock to the replication of stone tools in the laboratory. In addition, there is an increasing number of statistical studies comparing naturally-fractured rock with man-made stone tools, seeking some diagnostic feature that will discriminate man-made from natural assemblages. (Taylor and Payen, 1979; Barnes, 1939; Ascher and Ascher, 1965). Unfortunately, as in all such studies biases of the investigator can lead to quite different conclusions. I agree with Carter (*ibid*) that a statistical measure that is a reliable discriminator of man-made tools in one kind of assemblage may not be a reliable discriminator with another and quite different kind of tool assemblage. Conclusion: with very crudely fractured stones, it is not always possible to decide from objective evidence whether the assemblage consists of "tools" or just busted rocks. The decision tends to be based on other considerations, such as the context in which the finds were made (a gravel terrace full of broken rock is not the same thing as a sand dune with some broken rocks in it), or by confirming evidence from other finds.

The most often-used "confirming evidence" brought forward is the claim that the location of the stone tools also has present "hearths" or man-made fireplaces or cooking areas. Since a hearth is by definition a man-made object, the use of this term (rather than a more neutral term like "burned area") tends to build in a conclusion of human activity. Hearths are claimed to be present at Calico, Texas Street, on Santa Rosa Island, and in fact in most of the early man locations where stone "tools" are found. (Taylor and Payen, 1979). It has been pointed out in some detail (Johnson and Miller, 1958) that burned areas or evidence of fire in the past need not be interpreted as "hearths" since such features can also occur naturally.

Without pursuing this discussion in detail, it is easy to see how one observer can be a "believer", seeing a large number of stone tools and fireplaces, and another observer can be a "sceptic" arguing that man was not present at all and that the observed material is all naturally produced.

The one unquestionable evidence that man was present in an early site is the finding of the bones of the man himself. One cannot argue against the physical remains of human beings; hence the effort in recent years to obtain reliable dates on many claimed early skeletons. Here the argument cannot be whether man was present, but must fall in one of the other problem areas.

The second area in which we must have secure information to interpret any site, new or old, is that of chronology - we must *know* the age of the site. This requires little discussion; merely the reminder that guessing at the age is not sufficient. It is also worth noting the many instances in which erroneous attributions of age are made, based on misinterpretations of geological or other evidence, or sometimes confusions and problems in the dating laboratory. There is no dating method that cannot on occasion yield an incorrect answer, and there is substantial misuse of dating information on the part of archaeologists. Radiocarbon specialists and archaeologists equally recognise that obtaining a single date for a site is inadequate methodology (Taylor, 1978).

Much of the misuse and misinterpretation of chronological evidence is linked to problems in the third prerequisite for archaeological validation: knowing that the associations are valid. Hunters and gatherers do a lot of digging - for fireplaces, house floors, offerings, caches of things to be stored and hidden, and most of all graves. Large numbers of things found in archaeological contexts do not belong in time with the level where they are found. Since archaeological dating depends heavily upon dating the stratigraphic level and transferring that date to the human remains in that level, the possibility for error is evident. When dealing with graves, the problem may be even more serious since human bones may be several feet below the occupation layer. With the development of reliable dating methods for human bones, this problem can be avoided if the bones are dated directly.

A few other problems in association, commonly known to field archaeologists, may be briefly mentioned to show how common this difficulty is, and why it has to be examined with care in all archaeological sites:

1) Fairly recent man can decide to inhabit a paleontological site and dispose of his dead in it, thereby creating a very good physical association between human remains and ancient contexts. Examples are Gypsum Cave, Nevada (sloth dung dated at over 10,000 years, associated artifacts at only about 3,000 years); the La Brea tar pits (up to 40,000 years of Pleistocene fauna, accompanied by a human skeleton about 9,000 years old and wooden foreshafts only 4,000 years old by radiocarbon date); and the Tranquility Site in Fresno County (human burials accompanied by Pleistocene fauna including camels; dates of the human material only about 3,000 years). All of these associations looked like valid "early man" contexts when they were first discovered, (Hewes, 1943; Heizer, 1952; Krieger, 1964), and all of the human remains were believed to be much older than they are for many years until detailed dating studies were done (Meighan, 1965; 1978).

2) Humans of the past often brought into their recent sites materials of greater age. Indians picked up ancient points which find their way into association with vastly more recent artifacts. In the Southwest, tree-ring dating can be misinterpreted because the Indians dragged an ancient log into a building and used it as a beam. In a site I dug in Chile, there is much fossil wood in a very dry desert region; the ancient Indians dug this out and used it for fuel, so that wood 5,000 years old appears in a site only 2,000 years old (and this practice is still going on so some of this wood is being used in contemporary fires).

3) Archaeologists can also be misled by associations between human remains and correlated stratigraphic features apparently of considerable age. Brooks, Conrey, and Dixon (1965) report a find of a human skull in old marine deposits, 16 feet below the present sea level and 32 feet below the present ground surface. The radiocarbon age of the skull is less than 1,000 years (UCLA 119: 980 ± 80 years B.P.). A site in Monterey County at Willow Beach poses a similar problem. Here there is a shell midden seven feet thick overlain by 10 feet of banded, waterlaid gravels. Above this is another shell midden 6 feet thick, forming a stratigraphic column with a height of 23 feet. Furthermore, the lower midden rests on an old rocky beach which is buried over 3 feet beneath the present beach at this location, indicating a sea level change (or land subsidence) at this location. The radiocarbon dates on the bottom of the lower midden, on a buried beach and 23 feet below the present ground surface: C628: 1879 ± 250 years B.P.; C695: 1840 ± 400 years B.P. (Pohorecky, 1976, p. 97). Here there is no question about human presence, the age is known, but the apparent association with an ancient geological event is misleading.

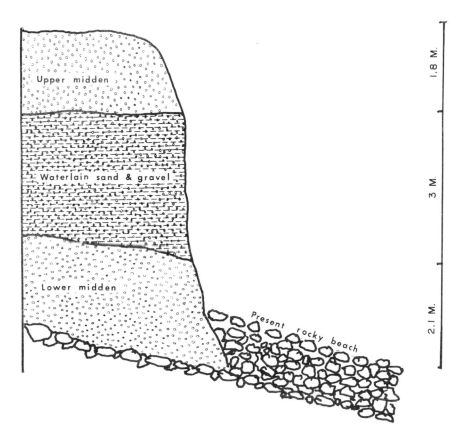

Upper midden

Waterlain sand & gravel

Lower midden

Present rocky beach

1.8 M.

3 M.

2.1 M.

FIG. 1. *Willow Creek, Monterey County, California.*

These examples indicate the serious difficulties of relating archaeological sites to the major events of the early Holocene or late Pleistocene. It is abundantly clear that past human populations responded to local idiosyncratic conditions very rapidly. The individual sites we see are mostly to be related to transient events - short-term fluctuations in climate and water supply, local tectonic events affecting very small areas, and minor relative changes in sea level. Most sites, therefore, do not reflect major glacial or interglacial events, but rather short-term responses to local conditions which have varied throughout the Pleistocene.

In order to validate archaeological finds, it is necessary to have solid evidence that man was present, that the age is known, and that the associations are valid - all three of these conditions need to be met. It is not sufficient to have one part of the evidence. This is far from an easy task; hence the fact that some of the claimed sites may be valid but are held in limbo because one or more of the key pieces of evidence cannot be obtained.

Hence also the agnostic position of most professional archaeologists, who like Willey (*op. cit.*) may have the feeling that early man sites exist, but that the present evidence is not adequate to sustain this conclusion beyond reasonable doubt.

If the existing claims for early man sites in California are tested against the three lines of evidence needed, it is regrettably true that not a single one of them can meet the test. This does not mean that some of these sites may not prove to be valid as future work is done, nor does it mean that there can be no early man sites to be found in the future. It does mean that there are serious challenges to our techniques, our data-gathering procedures, and our methodology, and that a great deal of additional effort will be needed before the exciting and important question of human origins in the New World is fully answered.

SOME TROUBLESOME QUESTIONS

Finally, I suggest some questions for future research. I do not know the answers to these questions, and they probably are not answerable from archaeological evidence alone, but will depend on studies from other kinds of scholars. Yet the answers will be relevant to conclusions about the antiquity of man in the New World, and to the effects of sea level and other changes on his settlement pattern in the past.

Why does early man seem to be absent from the La Brea tar pits? This is an ideal location for evidence of hunting and butchering practices from 15,000 to 40,000 years ago. It is environmentally ideal, has excellent dating evidence, extensive excavation over many years, and some two *million* cataloged finds. The absolute size of the excavation sample (in cubic meters dug and studied) is greater than the total digging in all of the other claimed early man sites in California put together. Yet the rather considerable amount of human material associated with this site is all in the past 9,000 years or so (human skeleton and many artifacts as well as chipping waste and other evidence of human activity). With this apparent absence of early man at La Brea, it troubles me to believe that man was systematically hunting and cooking mammoth on Santa Rosa Island 30,000 or more years ago (Orr, 1968; Berger, 1980). Is it possible for man to be a predator of mammoth on an island of limited size for more than 20,000 years? The most recent of the mammoth on Santa Rosa Island is dated at only 8,000 years ago. (Berger, 1971; 1980).

If man was in the New World 50,000 years ago, where are all the artifacts? One can argue that there was a minute population for a long time, and that the explosion of artifactual evidence at about 12,000 years ago simply goes with an increase in population.

However, it takes very few people to produce great quantities of stone artifacts if the people are present for thousands of years. Haynes (1966, p. 52) estimated the production rate for Clovis points, starting with a band of only 30 mammoth-hunters as the original population. He believes that in only 500 years this band and its multiple descendants will have made between 2 and 14 million Clovis points. There should therefore be many millions of stone tools dating from 100,000 to 12,000 years ago if man was in the New World at that time. There is certainly no difficulty in finding them and recognizing them in the Old World during this time period; why do we have in the New World only uncertain "eoliths" to represent the cultural production of the same period? The beginnings of an answer to this question may be developing in the reported early man sites from the Arctic (Irving and Harington, 1973; Bryan, 1978) where clearly defined technological assemblages are present, but for the California sites there is nothing like this reported, and I cannot evaluate the Arctic sites from first-hand experience.

I am puzzled by the number of presumed ancient skeletons unaccompanied by any cultural evidence, and the virtual absence of such human remains from the big-game hunter traditions of 10,000-12,000 years ago, where there are abundant cultural remains but almost no human remains. Maybe it is just the luck of the draw that we can have several California skeletons claimed to be over 17,000 years old and none in the period 9,000-17,000 years ago; is any other explanation possible?

Perhaps the lack of convincing answers to all these questions is merely a function of the limited study that has been done, and the questions will be answered (or shown to be irrelevant) in future. These queries do raise some problems for the proponents of early man claims in California, however. They also show clearly that the search for early man is very much a multi-disciplinary study, and that multiple lines of evidence will have to be co-ordinated and interwoven before general conclusions about early man can be firmly established.

Finally, whilst I believe that it is unlikely that material below sea level will turn out to be older than that found on land, it is worth studying submerged remains, as stated earlier in this paper, in order to reveal the full range of cultural variation in the Americas during the last 10-15,000 years.

REFERENCES

Ascher, R., and Ascher, M. (1965). Recognizing the Emergence of Man. *Science* 147, 243-50.

Barnes, A.S. (1939). The Differences between Natural and Human Flaking on Prehistoric Flint Implements. *American Anthropologist* 41, 99-112.

Berger, Rainer, (1971). New Radiocarbon Dates Based on Bone Collagen of California Paleoindians. University of California Archaeological Research Facility, Contributions, Np. 12, pp. 43-49. Berkeley.

Berger, Rainer, (1980). Early Man on Santa Rosa Island. In: *The California Islands, Proceedings of a Multidisciplinary Symposium*, pp. 73-78. Santa Barbara Museum of Natural History, Santa Barbara.

Bischoff, James L. and Rosenbauer, Robert J. (1981). Uranium Series Dating of Human Skeletal Remains from the Del Mar and Sunnyvale Sites, California. *Science* 213, 1003-1005.

Brooks, Sheilagh T., Conrey, Bert L. and Dixon, Keith A. (1965). A Deeply-Buried Human Skull and Recent Stratigraphy at the Present Mouth of the San Gabriel River, Seal Beach, California. *Bulletin of the Southern California Academy of Sciences* 64 (4), 229-241.

Bryan, Alan L. (Ed.) (1978). Early Man in America from a Circum-Pacific Perspective. Occasional Papers No. 1, Dept. of Anthropology, University of Alberta. Archaeological Researches International, Edmonton.

Carter, George F. (1957). *Pleistocene Man at San Diego*. Johns Hopkins Press, Baltimore.

Carter, George F. (1967). Artifacts and Naturifacts. *Anthropological Journal of Canada* 5, (1), 2-5.

Carter, George F. (1980). *Earlier Than You Think*. Texas A & M University Press, College Station, Texas.

Davis, Emma Lou, Brown, Kathryn H. and Nichols, Jacqueline (1981). *Evaluation of Early Human Activities and Remains in the California Desert*. Bureau of Land Management, California Desert District.

Dixon, K.A. (1970). Archeology and Geology in the Calico Mountains: Results of the International Conference on the Calico Project. Anthropology Department, California State University, Long Beach.

Duvall, J.G. and Venner, W.T. (n.d.). A Statistical Analysis of the Lithics from the Calico Site (SBCM 1500A). Unpublished manuscript.

Glennan, William S. (n.d.). The Hypothesis of an Ancient, Pre-Projectile Point Stage in American Prehistory: Its Application and Validity in Southern California. PhD Dissertation, UCLA [1972].

Gradin, Carlos A. (n.d.). A Plan of Cultural Chronology for the Southern Part of Argentine Patagonia. Ms. [1981].

Haynes, C. V., Jr. (1966). Elephant Hunting in North America. Scientific American, June, 1966. Reprinted in Early Man in America (*Scientific American*, 1973, pp. 44-52).

Haynes, C. Vance, Jr. (1969). The Earliest Americans. *Science* 166, 709-715.

Haynes, C. V. Jr. (1973). The Calico Site: Artifacts or Geofacts? *Science* 181, 305-309.

Heizer, Robert F. (1952). Observations on Early Man in California. University of California Archaeological Survey, Reports No. 7, pp. 5-9. Berkeley.

Heizer, Robert F. (1964). The Western Coast of North America. In: *Prehistoric Man in the New World* (J.D. Jennings and E. Norbeck, eds), pp. 117-148. University of Chicago Press, Chicago.

Hewes, G.W. (1943). Camel, Horse, and Bison Associated with Human Burials and Artifacts near Fresno, California. *Science* 97, 328-329.

Irving, W.N. and Harington, C.R. (1973). Upper Pleistocene Radiocarbon-Dated Artefacts from the Northern Yukon. *Science* 179, 335-340.

Johnson, Frederick and Miller, John P. (1958). Review of Pleistocene Man at San Diego (see Carter, 1957). *American Antiquity* 24, 206-210.

Krieger, Alex D. (1959). Additional Comments. In: *Man, Time, and Space in Southern California* (Wm. L. Thomas, Jr., ed.). *Annals of the Association of American Geographers* 49, Part 2, p. 33.

Krieger, Alex D. (1964). Early Man in the New World. In: *Prehistoric Man in the New World* (J.D. Jennings and H. Norbeck, eds), pp. 23-81. University of Chicago Press, Chicago.

460 C.W. Meighan

Leakey, L.S.B., Simpson, Ruth D. and Clements Thomas (1968). Archaeological Excavations in the Calico Mountains, California: Preliminary Report. *Science* 160, 1022-1023.

Martin, Paul S. (1973). The Discovery of America. *Science* 179, 969-974.

Meighan, Clement W. (1965). Pacific Coast Archaeology. In: *The Quaternary of the United States* (H.E. Wright and David Frey, eds), pp. 709-720. Princeton University Press.

Meighan, Clement W. (1978). California. In: *Chronologies in New World Archaeology* (R.E. Taylor and C. Meighan, eds), pp. 122-139. Academic Press, New York.

Nunez A., Lautaro (n.d.). Arqueologia Cronologica de Chile Septentrional y Relaciones Limitrofes, Manuscript (1981).

Orr, Phil C. (1968). Prehistory of Santa Rosa Island. Santa Barbara Museum of Natural History, Santa Barbara.

Pohorecky, Zenon Stephen (1976). Archaeology of the South Coast Ranges of California. Contributions of the University of California Archaeological Research Facility, No. 34. Berkeley.

Rogers, Malcolm J., Wormington, H.M., Davis, E.L. and Brott, Clark W. (1966). *Ancient Hunters of the Far West*. Union-Tribune Publishing Co., San Diego.

Schuiling, Walter C. (ed.) (1972) *Pleistocene Man at Calico*. San Bernardino County Museum Association, San Bernardino.

Scientific American (1973). Early Man in America. Readings from *Scientific American,* with an Introduction by Richard S. MacNeish. W.H. Freeman & Co., San Francisco.

Singer, Clay A. (n.d.). Short Report on the Analysis of Calico Lithics. Unpublished manuscript. Dept. of Anthropology, University of California, Los Angeles (1977).

Taylor, R.E. (1978). Radiocarbon dating: an archaeological perspective. In *Archaeological Chemistry II* Advances in Chemistry Series 171, American Chemical Society, Washington, D.C. (G.F. Carter, ed.), pp. 33-69.

Taylor, R.E. and Payen, Louis A. (1979). The Role of Archaeometry in American Archaeology: Approaches to the Evaluation of the Antiquity of *Homo sapiens* in California. *Advances in Archaeological Methods and Theory,* Vol. 2, pp. 239-283. Academic Press, New York.

Taylor, R.E. and C.W. Meighan (eds) (1978). *Chronologies in New World Archaeology.* Academic Press, New York.

Willey, Gordon R. (1966). *An Introduction to American Archaeology,* Vol. I, North and Middle America. Prentice Hall, Englewood Cliffs, N.J.

THE UPPER PLEISTOCENE PEOPLING
OF THE NEW WORLD:
EVIDENCE DERIVED FROM RADIOCARBON,
AMINO ACID RACEMIZATION AND
URANIUM SERIES DATING

Jeffrey L. Bada and Robert Finkel

*Scripps Institution of Oceanography,
University of California, San Diego,
La Jolla, California 92093, USA*

ABSTRACT

Three geochronometers, radiocarbon, amino acid racemization, and uranium series dating, have been used to estimate the ages of several human skeletal remains from California. Both the radiocarbon and aspartic acid racemization ages of one of these skeletons, Los Angeles Man, indicate that human beings were present in the Americas by ~26,000 years ago. The aspartic acid racemization and uranium series ages of another paleoindian skeleton, Del Mar Man, suggest that the initial migration into the New World probably occurred sometime during the middle part of the Upper Pleistocene. The anticipated radiocarbon dating of several of the skeletons using particle accelerators should help determine a more precise time for the first human migrations into the New World.

INTRODUCTION

The time when human beings first migrated to the Americas continues to be an area of intense debate. Although it is generally agreed that the migration route was through Beringia during a period of depressed sea level, the precise time of the first migration is still uncertain. The ages of several human

TABLE 1.

Geochronometers used in Dating Upper Pleistocene Fossils

Method and Bases	Dating Range (yrs)	Limitations.
1) C-14 measures radiocarbon activity in carbon component	Few hundred to 40,000[a]	i) Subject to secondary carbon contamination ii) Large sample requirements
2) Amino acid method-based on the extent of racemization of amino acids in sample	Few thousand to 1×10^6 (range dependent on temperature of study area	i) Requires "calibration" of racemization rate using sample dated by another method ii) Reaction rate highly temperature dependent
3) Uranium series dating-measures activity of daughter isotopes in the uranium decay scheme	Th-230-Few thousand to ∿300,000 Pa-231-Few thousand to ∿130,000	i) Uranium accumulation mechanism complex and poorly understood ii) Gives integrated age of uranium accumulation which is always younger than burial age.

[a]Range may be extended by direct counting methods using particle accelerators.

skeletons from California provide some of the best evidence for an Upper Pleistocene migration into the New World. However, because of uncertainties about the accuracy of some of the geochronometers used to date these skeletal remains, their ages are quite controversial.

The three geochronometers which have been used to date fossil bones of Upper Pleistocene age are listed in Table 1. Each method has its advantages and limitations (see Table 1) which in turn affect the accuracy of the derived age. In this paper, we discuss the bases of the various Upper Pleistocene geochronometers and their use in dating human skeletal materials from California.

UPPER PLEISTOCENE GEOCHRONOMETERS

Radiocarbon Dating

The well known radiocarbon dating method is based on the measured C-14 activity of an organic component isolated from a fossil. The radiocarbon dating range is from a few hundred to $\sim$40,000 years, using conventional methods and possibly up to 70,000 to 80,000 years using direct counting, particle accelerator methods now being tested in various laboratories (Hedges, 1981). Since the Upper Pleistocene time interval ranges from 10,000 to $\sim$120,000 years, the C-14 method can be used to date only the latter half or so of this epoch.

Although the radiocarbon method yields reliable ages for carbon-rich materials such as wood or charcoal, the radiocarbon dating of bones continues to be problematic, since the organic material in bones tends to degrade rapidly, especially in temperate and tropical environments. Collagen is the most abundant and well characterized organic material present in modern bone. Thus, it has been assumed that collagen isolated from fossil bones should be an indigenous constituent, and should therefore provide a highly reliable age. However, many fossil bones contain only trace amounts of collagen. It has been found that collagen based radiocarbon dates are sometimes too young, probably because the material isolated for radiocarbon dating was not pure collagen but rather was contaminated to some extent with organic compounds of more recent origin (Bada, 1981; Delibrias, 1981).

An additional problem is that the collagen based radiocarbon dating of fossil bones using conventional counting methods requires large sample sizes, typically on the order of kilogram quantities of bone. This presents a severe limitation in attempting to date human remains since anthropologists, archaeologists and museum curators are reluctant to sacrifice an entire skeleton for radiocarbon analysis. Using particle accelerators, it will be possible to date as little as 1 mg of carbon. This will simultaneously reduce the amount of bone required for C-14 dating and help to minimize contamination problems by making it more feasible to isolate and date the small quantities of indigenous organic material which remain in fossil bones. However, the accelerator methods are not yet operational, and the exact sample requirements have yet to be established.

Amino Acid Dating

Some 20 different amino acids are present in the proteinaceous material of all living organisms. Each of these amino acids, with the exception of glycine, can exist in two different isomeric forms called the D- and L- enantiomers. The physical and chemical properties of these D- and L- enantiomers are essentially equivalent and, as a result, under conditions of chemical equilibrium both enantiomers are present in equal amounts. However, in living organisms only the L- enantiomers are present, a fact which was discovered around 1850 by Pasteur.

Living organisms maintain a disequilibrium state with respect to the amino acid enantiomers. This is accomplished by enzymes which are highly stereoselective, and function using only the L- enantiomers. However, once an organism dies, the amino acids which are present in the skeletal parts are isolated from these stereospecific biochemical reactions and a chemical reaction called racemization begins. The racemization reaction reversibly converts the L- amino acids into the D- amino acids, ultimately leading to an equilibrium mixture of the D- and L- enantiomers (see Bada, in press and references therein for a review of the racemization reaction). This reaction forms the basis of the amino acid dating method. Although in a modern bone the D/L amino acid ratio is close to 0, with increasing time racemization slowly converts this optically active mixture to an optically inactive racemic mixture (i.e. D/L = 1.0).

The amino acid racemization reaction can be written as

$$\text{L-amino acid} \underset{k_i}{\overset{k_i}{\rightleftharpoons}} \text{D-amino acid} \qquad (1)$$

where k_i is the rate constant for the interconversion of the enantiomers. The kinetic equation for the racemization reaction is (taken from Bada, in press)

$$\ln \frac{(1 + D/L)}{(1 - D/L)} - \ln \frac{(1 + D/L)}{(1 - D/L)}_{t=0} = 2k_i t \qquad (2)$$

Each amino acid has a specific interconversion rate (i.e. k_i value). The rate of racemization of an amino acid is equal to 2 k_i. Aspartic acid has one of the fastest rates with a racemization half life for free aspartic acid at pH 7.6 and 25°C of ~3,500 years. Isoleucine, on the other hand, has one of the slowest racemization rates with a half life at 25°C, pH 7.6 of ~50,000 years. [Since isoleucine is a diastereomeric amino acid, the reaction of this amino acid is more properly termed epimerization but for simplicity the reaction will be referred to here as racemization.]

As can be seen from Equation (2) there are two parameters which affect the extent of racemization (i.e. the D/L amino acid ratio) in a fossil. One of these is time: the older the sample, the higher the D/L ratio. The other parameter is the value of k_i, which is the rate at which the racemization reaction takes place. Since racemization is a chemical reaction the value of k_i is a function of temperature; the higher the temperature, the faster the rate of racemization. Parameters such as pH, humidity, etc., also influence racemization rates, especially in aqueous solution, but in fossils, these factors apparently have only minor effects on rates (Bada and Helfman, 1975; Bada, in press and references therein).

In order to use racemization as a dating tool a value of k_i for a particular site must be determined. The value of k_i can be estimated using a "calibration" procedure wherein a sample of known age from the study site is analysed for its extent of racemization (Bada and Protsch, 1973; Bada et al., 1979). The D/L amino acid ratio in this known age sample is then substituted into Equation (2) along with the sample's age and an in situ value of k_i is obtained. This k_i value is the rate of interconversion of the amino acid enantiomers at that particular site integrated over the time interval represented by the age of the "calibration" sample. Once the value of k_i has been determined for a particular site, it can be used with certain limitations to date other samples from the immediate area (Bada et al., 1979; Bada, 1981) provided the sample which is being dated has had an exposure temperature history similar to that of the "calibration" sample.

One advantage of the amino acid method in comparison to radiocarbon is that very small amounts of material are required, on the order of a few grams of bone. Moreover, since the racemization rates of amino acids in bones in most geological environments are substantially slower than the decay rate of radiocarbon (Bada and Helfman, 1975), the amino acid method has the potential of dating samples which are too old to be dated by the radiocarbon method (Bada and Deems, 1975) provided a suitable "calibration" sample is available.

The accuracy of racemization ages deduced using the "calibration" procedure has been cross-checked at numerous sites throughout the world by various laboratories (Bada et al., 1979; Hare, Turnbull and Taylor, 1978; Bada, 1981; Belluomini, 1981). Probably the most extensive study of the accuracy and reliability of racemization deduced ages has been carried out in the Olduvai

Gorge region of Tanzania, East Africa (Hare, Turnbull and Taylor, 1978; Bada, 1981). In these studies it was found that racemization of aspartic acid could be used to date Holocene and Upper Pleistocene fossils but for older fossils, extensive aspartic acid contamination resulted in unreliable age estimates. However, hydrophobic amino acids such as isoleucine and leucine are apparently less affected by contamination and thus the racemization reaction of these amino acids could be used to date even the Middle and Lower Pleistocene samples in the Olduvai Gorge region. The reason hydrophobic amino acids may be less susceptible to contamination that aspartic acid is probably related to the fact that peptide bonds which contain these amino acids are more stable to hydrolysis than are peptide bonds which contain aspartic acid. Thus aspartic acid in the proteins originally present in bones is probably hydrolysed more rapidly than hydrophobic amino acids.

The Olduvai Gorge results demonstrate that racemization provides a potential method for dating samples which have ages in the range of a few thousand to several million years.

Uranium Series Dating

U-238 and U-235 decay through a series of daughter radioisotopes eventually producing the stable isotopes Pb-206 and Pb-207, respectively (Ku, 1976). U-238 decays to U-234 (t_1 = 248,000 years) which then decays to Th-230 (t_1 = 75,200 years). U-235 decays to Pa-231 (t_1 = 32,500 years). Their half lives make both Th-230 and Pa-231 potentially useful clocks for dating Upper Pleistocene events.

The uranium decay series dating of fossils has been investigated since the late 1950s and early 1960s. It is now generally agreed that corals are suitable materials for dating by this method, whereas shells and especially bones yield results which must be interpreted with caution (Ku, 1976). Problems in applying the uranium decay series method to fossil bones arise from the mode of uranium acquisition by bones. Modern bones contain only trace quantities of uranium (Fleming, 1977 and references therein). However, fossil bones assimilate uranium during their depositional history. [This was one of the three methods used to demonstrate that the famous Piltdown Man was a hoax and actually was composed of both modern and fossil components (Fleming, 1977).] The uranium in a fossil bone is therefore secondary. A uranium series age is thus the average integrated age of uranium incorporation into a bone. This age is often significantly less than the bone's burial age (Szabo, 1980).

The processes by which bones acquire uranium are complex, possibly episodic, and poorly understood (Labeyrie and Lalou, in press). As a result the rate of uranium incorporation into any

TABLE 2.

Comparison of Uranium Series Ages[a] of fossil bones with radiocarbon and racemization derived ages

Sample and Site Locality	Age (yrs) by various methods			
	Th-230	Pa-231	Collagen based radiocarbon[b]	Aspartic acid racemization
San Deigo County, near La Jolla W-12, SDi 4669 human burial, SDM 16709	$3,000^{+300}_{-200}$	$3,700^{+600}_{-500}$	$8,360 \pm 75$ (Pta 1725)	$8,000^c$
Grotta di Castelcivita, near Salerno, Italy Layer 14	$20,800^{+1,000}_{-900}$	$24,000^{+1,900}_{-1,800}$	$33,320 \pm 780$ (R-100)	--
Külna Cave, near Brno, Czechoslovakia 3.8–4.0 m (layer 7A)	--	--	$45,630^{+2,850}_{-2,200}$ (GrN 6060)	$50,000^d$
4.6–5.6 m (layer 8A)	$22,100^{+1,800}_{-1,600}$	$23,600^{+4,300}_{-3,600}$	--	$\sim 80,000^e$

[a] Th-230 and U-238,234 concentrations were determined by α particle spectrometry of purified Th and U fractions for 5-15 g bone samples. Pa-231 concentrations were determined by measuring the Th-227 daughter. Ages were calculated using the half-lives given in the text and the equations given in Ku (1976).

[b] Radiocarbon laboratory number is in parentheses.

[c] Taken from Ike et al. 1979.

[e] Calculated based on a measured D/L aspartic acid ratio of 0.1 (4 hour hydrolysis) and the k_{asp} value given in Masters and Bada, 1978.

particular bone is impossible to evaluate. Attempts to circumvent this uranium accumulation problem have been made. Recently Bischoff and Rosenbauer (1981), for example, suggested that there is an initial period in which uranium is rapidly incorporated into bones after which they become a closed system with respect to migration of uranium and its daughter isotopes. They further suggest that internal concordancy betwen the independent U-238 and U-235 decay scheme ages provides a test of the validity of the proposed uranium accumulation model for any single fossil bone sample. A close examination of the Th-230-U-234 and Pa-231-U-235 concordia diagram, however, shows that, for fossils with ages of several tens of thousands of years or less, concordancy is a very insensitive test for the validity of the rapid uranium uptake model. For samples at the young end of the concordia curve, late uranium uptake can decrease apparent radiometric ages without disturbing the Th-230-Pa-231 concordancy beyond the range of experimental uncertainty.

In general even concordant Th-230 and Pa-231 ages for fossil bones appear to be too young (Szabo, 1980) and as a result a uranium series age sets the lower limit for the age of a fossil bone. Judging just how much too young any particular uranium series age actually is remains a serious problem. According to Szabo (1980), concordant uranium series ages may be possibly too young by as much as many tens of thousands of years. To investigate this possibility we have recently determined the uranium series ages of several radiocarbon-dated fossil bones; these results are shown in Table 2. In the case of the Holocene burial from San Diego the concordant Th-230-Pa-231 ages are too young by 4,000-5,000 years, while for the sample from Czechoslovakia the concordant ages are as much as ∿50,000 years too young. These results are similar to those obtained by Szabo (1980).

THE DATING OF HUMAN SKELETAL MATERIAL FROM CALIFORNIA

Each of the various geochronometers which have been discussed has been used to date various human skeletons from localities in California. The ages which have been determined for these skeletons are listed in Table 3, along with a description of the localities where the skeletons were found, and their time of discovery.

Laguna Woman

The collagen-based radiocarbon date of 17,150 ± 1,470 years clearly places the age of the Laguna Woman in the Upper Pleistocene. Although the accuracy of the C-14 date itself has not been challenged, it has been questioned whether the skeleton that was dated at UCLA in the 1970s was actually the skeleton that was discovered in 1933. The Laguna skeleton had a rather peripatetic post-excavation history (Berger et al., 1971). It went to Europe where it was analyzed by a series of investigators. It then traveled to East Africa where it was studied by L.S.B. Leakey, who in fact actually submitted the material for radiocarbon dating (Berger and Libby, 1969). The question later arose as to whether the material that was dated at UCLA was indeed the original, or whether some African or European skeleton had been accidentally substituted in its place. Although comparison (Berger et al., 1971) of the dated material with photographs taken at the time the Laguna skeleton was discovered in 1933 suggested the dated sample was the original, this uncertainty has persisted (Gerow, 1981).

Amino acid racemization analysis of the Laguna skeleton yielded a D/L aspartic acid ratio of 0.25 (Bada, Schroeder and Carter, 1974). Using Equation (2) and the radiocarbon age determined by UCLA it is possible to calculate a value for k_{asp}, the first order rate constant for inverconversion for D- and L- enantiomers of aspartic acid. The calculated value is 1.1×10^{-5} yr^{-1}. This k_{asp} value is the average integrated value over the 17,000 year age of the Laguna sample. If we use this k_{asp} value to estimate the average exposure temperature of the Laguna sample, a value of $\sim 14^{\circ}C$ is obtained (procedures used given in Bada et al., 1979). The present day yearly temperature at Laguna Beach is $\sim 16^{\circ}C$ (Felton, 1965). Because the Laguna sample is of Upper Pleistocene age the average temperature to which it has been exposed is expected to be less than the present day temperature by a few degrees celsius (Kahn, Oba and Ku, 1981). The racemization deduced temperature is thus consistent with the predicted temperature history of the Laguna material. If the skeletal remains dated by the UCLA Laboratory actually came from Africa or elsewhere, the temperature calculated from racemization would likely not be consistent with the exposure temperature estimated for the Laguna skeleton. Racemization analyses suggest that the radiocarbon dated material was authentic.

Los Angeles Man

The collagen based radiocarbon age of the Los Angeles Man skeleton is >23,600 years. Because of the low collagen content of the skeleton it was not possible to isolate sufficient material to determine an absolute age by radiocarbon. The amino acid racemization age of the Los Angeles Man skeleton is 26,000 years, which is consistent with the radiocarbon age determined for the skeleton (Bada, Schroeder and Carter, 1974). The racemization age was determined using the Laguna-based k_{asp} value. The use of the Laguna based k_{asp} value seems justified since it is probable that the exposure temperature histories of the two skeletons are similar.

Both the radiocarbon and amino acid ages of this skeleton indicate that it is Upper Pleistocene in age.

Del Mar Man Skeleton

There have been no direct radiocarbon dates of the Del Mar skeleton, although there are some radiocarbon dates for shell from a midden which apparently overlaid the skeletal material (Masters and Bada, 1977). These ages range from 6,000 to 9,000 years but these dates must be considered of questionable reliability since they are not stratigraphically consistent; the oldest radiocarbon dates came from the top of the deposit while ages at the base were the youngest.

The racemization age of 45,000 years makes the Del Mar skeleton the oldest dated human remains in North America. The racemization age was calculated using the Laguna-based k_{asp} value. As was the case of the Los Angeles Man skeleton, this seems justified since the locality where the Del Mar Man skeleton was found should have had an exposure temperature history similar to that of the Laguna locality.

The Del Mar Man racemization age is consistent with the fact that Holocene radiocarbon dated human skeletons in the immediate vicinity all have low D/L aspartic acid ratios (Bada and Masters, 1978). Moreover, an Upper Pleistocene horse eroding from strata dated >38,000 years old by C-14 has yielded a D/L aspartic acid ratio of ∿0.5 which is equivalent to that determined for Del Mar skeleton (Masters and Bada, 1978). Thus both the Holocene burials and Upper Pleistocene horse racemization analyses support an Upper Pleistocene age for the Del Mar skeleton.

Uranium series ages of the Del Mar skeleton have been recently determined (Bischoff and Rosenbauer, 1981); the resulting concordant Th-230-Pa-231 age is ∿11,000 years old. However, as has been discussed above, since uranium in bones is secondary, this is a minimum age with the actual burial age being older. Based on the results of Szabo (1980) and those given in Table 2, the uranium series results for the Del Mar skeleton suggest that its actual burial age could be on the order of several tens of thousands of years which is not inconsistent with the 45,000 year racemization age determined for this skeleton.

Both the uranium series age and the racemization age for the Del Mar skeleton indicate that it is Upper Pleistocene in age. However, considerable controversy remains concerning the precise age of this skeleton. The anticipated radiocarbon dating of this skeleton using the particle accelerator method should help clarify the age of this important human skeletal material.

Dates Determined for Several Possibly Upper Pleistocene Age Human Skeletons from California

Skeletal name, and locality and time of discovery		C-14[a]	Age (years) by various methods	
			Aspartic acid racemization[e]	Uranium decay series
Laguna Woman	Discovered in Laguna Beach in 1933	17,150±1,470 (UCLA 123A)[b]	$k_{asp}=1.1 \times 10^{-5} yr^{-1}$ (0.25)[f]	—
Los Angeles Man	Found in Baldwin Hills near Los Angeles, 1936	>23,600 (UCLA 1430)[b]	26,000 (0.35)[f]	—
Del Mar Man	Found at SDM Site W-34A (Lower Midden) near Del Mar, 1929	—	45,000[f] (0.51)	11,200[i]
Sunnyvale Skeleton	Excavated (early 1970s) from Sunnyvale East Drainage Channel, near San Jose	3,390±150[c] (UCR 1437A)	~70,000[f]	8,700[i]
Yuha Skeleton	Cairn burial (burial depth ~40-56 cm below (surface) excavated 1971 in desert area of southeastern Imperial County	22,000[d] (GX 2674)	23,600[g] ~5,000[h]	19,000±3,000[d,j]

[a] Radiocarbon laboratory number is in parentheses.
[b] "Collagen" fraction.
[c] 0.5 to 1 N HCl soluble fraction.
[d] Age of a caliche encrustation on the skeletal bones.
[e] The D/L aspartic acid ratios are in parentheses. The ages were calculated from Eq. (2) using the Laguna sample for "calibration", i.e., k_{asp} determination.
[f] Taken from Bada, Schroeder and Carter, 1974 and Bada and Helfman, 1975.
[g] Taken from Bischoff and Childers, 1979, and based on the estimated exposure temperature of the Yuha skeleton.
[h] See text for a discussion of this age estimate.
[i] The average concordant Th-230-Pa-231 age, taken from Bischoff and Rosenbauer, 1981.
[j] Th-230 age, taken from Bischoff et al., 1976.

Sunnyvale

Conflicting ages ranging from 3,000 to 70,000 years have been determined for the Sunnyvale skeleton, but these determinations are not equally reliable.

As can be seen in Table 3 the radiocarbon age of the Sunnyvale skeleton is younger than the uranium series age. Since uranium series ages are minimum ages, it seems unlikely that the C-14 age determined for this skeleton is reliable. The radiocarbon age was determined on the HCl soluble fraction isolated from the bone (R.E Taylor, personal communication). Since numerous soil organic constitutents, e.f., fulvic acid, etc., are soluble in HCl, it is likely that the young C-14 age determined for the Sunnyvale skeleton is actually the age of some secondary organic component. Support for this possibility is provided by the fact that the δ C-13 value of -25 % (R.E. Taylor, personal communication) for the fraction dated by radiocarbon is not within the range of proteinaceous material, but is more compatible with that of humic acids (Degens, 1969).

The same analysis used for interpreting the uranium series age of the Del Mar skeleton implies that the uranium series age of Sunnyvale does not rule out the possibility that this skeleton has an age of many tens of thousands of years. However, even if this is the case, the racemization age of $\sim$ 70,000 years seems unreasonably old. The racemization age determined for the Sunnyvale skeleton, however, should be considered only a rough estimate since it was calculated by adjusting the Laguna k_{asp} value to the estimated temperature of the Sunnyvale site (Bada and Helfman, 1975). As was emphasized previously by Bada and Helfman, this adjustment could give rise to substantial errors. Holocene radiocarbon dated human burials from the vicinity where the Sunnyvale skeleton was found all have low D/L aspartic acid ratios as does a $\sim$20,000 year old camelops bone (Lajoie, Peterson and Gerow, 1980; Bada and Masters, 1978; Gerow, 1980). Although these results all suggest that the Sunnyvale skeleton is likely Upper Pleistocene in age, its absolute age remains uncertain. As was the case for the Del Mar skeleton radiocarbon dating using the particle accelerator should help fix the age of this human skeleton.

Yuha

Both the radiocarbon and Th-230 ages determined for the Yuha skeleton are $\sim$ 20,000 years. However, both of these age determinations are for a caliche deposit which coated the bone. The C-14 and uranium series ages are thus for a secondary component. Since the geochemistry of caliche formation is not well understood, especially with regard to the sources of both the carbonate and uranium in the caliche, the agreement between radiocarbon and uranium series ages of the caliche may be fortuitous.

A racemization age estimate of $\sim$ 20,000 years has been determined. This estimate was not derived, however, using the calibration procedure but rather was estimated using an assumed exposure temperature history of the skeleton (Bischoff and Childers, 1979). As was the case with the Sunnyvale skeleton, the estimated exposure temperature is fairly uncertain, and the resulting racemization age should be considered only a rough estimate of the Yuha skeleton's age.

It may be possible to determine a calibration value which can be used to calculate a racemization age for the Yuha skeleton. The Truckhaven human burial was discovered in the desert region of southeastern California, at a site $\sim$ 75 km away from the Yuha burial locality. The radiocarbon age determined on the carbonate apatite fraction from this skeleton is $4,990 \pm 250$ years (GX 2342). Although the carbonate apatite fraction has been shown to provide reasonable ages in some instances (Haynes, 1968), the ages determined using this fraction are not as reliable as those determined using the collagen fraction. Nevertheless, this age provides at least a potential basis for calibrating the racemization reaction in the desert region of southeastern California. The measured D/L aspartic acid ratio of the Truckhaven skeleton was 0.52 (J.L. Bada, unpublished results), essentially the same as that determined for the Yuha skeleton. Assuming the two burials have had similar exposure temperature histories, then the racemization results suggest that the Truckhaven and Yuha burials are approximately the same age. The racemization results indicate that either the Yuha skeleton is only $\sim$5,000 years old or that the Truckhaven C-14 age of 5,000 years is too young. Until a suitable "calibration" sample becomes available, the racemization age of the Yuha skeleton must be considered uncertain.

The absolute age of the Yuha skeleton is not well established and will apparently remain so; this skeleton was stolen in the latter part of 1980 and its present whereabouts remain a mystery.

CONCLUSION

Radiocarbon, amino acid racemization and uranium series geochronometers are all applicable to dating fossil bones of Upper Pleistocene age. If sufficient material is available (i.e., a few kilograms of bone) to allow the separation of several grams of pure collagen fraction, C-14 dating provides the most accurate ages. In the absence of such large amounts of fossil material, amino acid racemization and uranium series dating, which require only gram sized quantities of bone, can give useful information, provided the ages are interpreted with the appropriate caution.

Because of sampling problems, none of the human skeletons from

California discussed have been accurately dated by rdiocarbon, with the exception of the Laguna Woman. The 17,150 ± 1,470 year age of this skeleton has been used to "calibrate" the aspartic acid racemization rate for southern coastal California localities. This "calibration" value was used to calculate the racemization ages for the Los Angeles Man, Del Mar Man and the Sunnyvale skeletons. The Los Angeles Man results are probably the least ambiguous; both the radiocarbon and racemization ages of this skeleton indicate it is ∿ 26,000 years old, which demonstrates that human beings were present in the New World during the latter part of the Upper Pleistocene. The Del Mar Man racemization age suggests that the inital human migration into California and thus the Americas, may have occurred at least 45,000 years ago. We emphasize that this estimate relies strongly on the accuracy of the C-14 age for the Laguna Woman and on the extrapolation of the temperature history of the Laguna burial site to the Del Mar site. The Sunnyvale racemization age suggests this skeleton is also Upper Pleistocene in age, but this result is less reliable than those for the Los Angeles and Del Mar Man skeletons due to the lack of a suitable local racemization calibration sample for the Sunnyvale region.

Uranium series dating gives concordant Th-230 and Pa-231 ages for the Del Mar and Sunnyvale skeletons which are younger than the racemization ages of these skeletons. However, uranium series ages should be considered minimum ages and as a result the younger uranium series ages for these skeletons are not necessarily in conflict with the significantly older racemization ages

It is hoped that the expected advances in accelerator-based C-14 detection by direct atom counting will, in the near future, allow the C-14 dating of gram sized bone fragments. This will help both to resolve the question of the time of migration of human beings into the Americas and will provide important calibration information for improving the accuracy of the racemization and uranium series geochronometers.

REFERENCES

Bada, J.L. (1981). Racemization of amino acids in fossil bones and teeth from the Olduvai Gorge region, Tanzania, East Africa. *Earth and Planetary Science Letters* **55**, 292-298.

Bada, J.L. (in press). Racemization of amino acids in nature. *Interdisciplinary Science Revue*.

Bada, J.L. and Deems, L. (1975). Accuracy of dates beyond the C-14 dating limit using the aspartic acid racemization reaction. *Nature* **255**, 218-219.

Bada, J.L. and Helfman, P.M. (1975). Amino acid racemization dating of fossil bones. *World Archaeology* 7, 160-173.

Bada, J.L. and Masters, P.M. (1978). The antiquity of human beings in the Americas; evidence derived from amino acid racemization dating of paleoindian skeletons. *Society California Archaeology Occasional Papers Method Theory* No. 2, 16-24.

Bada, J.L. and Protsch, R. (1973). Racemization reaction of aspartic acid and its use in dating fossil bones. *Proceedings National Academy of Science USA* 70, 1331-1334.

Bada, J.L., Schroeder, R.A. and Carter, G. (1974). New evidence for the antiquity of man in North America deduced from aspartic acid racemization. *Science* 184, 791-793.

Bada, J.L., Masters, P.M., Hoopes, E. and Darling, D. (1979). The dating of fossil bones using amino acid racemization. In: *Radiocarbon Dating* (Berger, R. and Suess, H.E., eds) University of California Press, Berkeley and Los Angeles, California, pp. 740-756.

Belluomini, G. (1981). Direct aspartic acid racemization dating of human bones from archaeological sites of Central Southern Italy. *Archaeometry* 23, 125-137.

Berger, R. and Libby, W.F. (1969). UCLA radiocarbon dates IX. *Radio Carbon* 11, 194-209.

Berger, R., Protsch, R., Reynolds, R., Rozaire, C. and Sackett, J.R. (1971). New radiocarbon dates based on bone collagen of California paleoindians. In: *The Application of the Physical Sciences to Archaeology* (Stross, F.H., ed.). Contributions of the University of California Archaeological Research Facility 12, pp. 43-50.

Bischoff, J.L. and Childers, W.M. (1979). Temperature calibration of amino acid racemization: age implications for the Yuha skeleton. *Earth and Planetary Science Letters* 45, 172-180.

Bischoff, J.L. and Rosenbauer, R.J. (1981). Uranium series dating of human skeletal remains from the Del Mar and Sunnyvale sites, California. *Science* 213, 1003-1005.

Bischoff, J.L., Merriam, R., Childers, W.M. and Protsch, R. (1976). Antiquity of man in America indicated by radiometric dates on the Yuha burial site. *Nature* 261, 128-129.

Degens, E.T. (1969). Biogeochemistry of stable carbon isotopes. In: *Organic Geochemistry: Methods and Results* (Eglinton, G., and Murphy, N.T.J., eds.) Springer-Verlag, Berlin-Heidelberg, pp. 304-329.

Delibrias, G. (1981). La datation par le carbone 14 des assements du gisement paleolithique de la Ferrassie. In: *Union Internacional de Ciencias Prehistoricas y Protohistoricas, X Congress; Coloquia, Tecnicos de Datacion en el Paleolitica*, Mexico City, pp. 89-98.

Felton, E.E. (1965). *California's Many Claimates*. Pacific Books, Palo Alto, California, pp. 62-69 and p. 74.

Fleming, S. (1977). *Dating in Archaeology*. St. Martin's Press, New York, p. 106 and pp. 191-193.

Gerow, B.A. (1981). Amino acid dating and early man in the new world: a rebuttal. *Society California Archaeology Occasional Papers Method Theory*, No. 3, 1-12.

Hare, P.E., Turnbull, H.F. and Taylor, R.E. (1978). Amino acid dating of Pleistocene fossil materials; Olduvai Gorge, Tanzania. In: *View of the Past; Essays in Old World Prehistory and Paleoanthropology* (Freeman, L.G., ed.) Mouton Publishers, The Hague, pp. 7-12.

Haynes, C.V. (1968). Radiocarbon analysis of inorganic carbon from fossil bones and enamel. *Science* 161, 687-688.

Hedges, R.E.M. (1981). Radiocarbon dating with an accelerator; review and preview. *Archaeometry* 23, 3-18.

Ike, D., Master, P.M., Bada, J.L., Dennedy, G. and Vogel, J.C. (1979). Aspartic acid racemization and radiocarbon dating of an early milling stone horizon burial in California. *American Antiquity* 44, 524-530.

Kahn, M.I., Oba, T. and Ku, T.-L. (1981). Paleotemperatures and the glacially induced changes in the oxygen-isotope composition of sea water during the late Pleistocene and Holocene time in Tanner Basin, California. *Geology* 9, 485-490.

Ku, T.-L. (1976). The uranium series methods of age determination. *Annual Review Earth and Planetary Science* 4, 347-379.

Labeyrie, J., and Lalou, C. (in press). Limites et éspoirs de la methode uranium-ionium (Th-230). In: *Absolute Dating and Isotopic Analyses in Prehistory; Method and Limits - Dating the Cave Deposit of the Caune de L'Arago at Tautavel* (de Lumley, H. and Labeyrie, J., eds), Centre National de la Recherche Scientifique, Paris.

Lajoie, K.R., Peterson, E. and Gerow, B.A. (1980). Amino acid bone dating: a feasibility study, South San Francisco Bay Region, California. In: *Biogeochemistry of the Amino Acids* (Hare, P.E., Hoering, T.C., and King, K., eds), John Wiley, New York, pp. 477-489.

Masters, P.M. and Bada, J.L., (1977). Racemization of isoleucine in fossil molluscs from Indian middens and interglacial terraces in Southern California. *Earth and Planetary Science Letters* **37**, 173-183.

Masters, P.M. and Bada, J.L., (1978). Amino acid racemization dating of bone and shell. In: *Archaeological Chemistry II* (Carter, G.F., ed.) *Advances in Chemistry Series* **171**, American Chemical Society, pp. 117-138.

Szabo, B.J. (1980). Results and assessment of uranium series dating of vertebrate fossils from Quaternary alluviums in Colorado. *Arctic Alpine Research* **12**, 95-100.

THE CALIFORNIA CONTINENTAL BORDERLAND: LANDBRIDGES, WATERGAPS AND BIOTIC DISPERSALS

Donald Lee Johnson

*Department of Geography, University of Illinois,
Urbana, IL 61801, USA, and
Research Associate, Santa Barbara Museum of Natural History
Santa Barbara, CA 93105, USA*

ABSTRACT

The purpose of this essay is to assess evidence that illuminates the changing character of the late Quaternary environment of the California Borderland in general terms of its climate and vegetation, and in more specific terms of its faunal and human dispersals, migrations, and occupations. Emphasis is placed on changing subaerial Borderland environment, ecospace, and watergaps and landbridges *vis-a-vis* sea level during the past 128,000 years as reflected by the recently established oxygen isotope sea level curve correlated with dated marine terraces in New Guinea, Barbados, Haiti, and Bermuda. While firm, unequivocal evidence of humans in the Borderland covers only the last 8,000 or so years, the late Quaternary coverage (i.e., the last 128,000 years) presented here provide a broader context in the event that recent suggestive evidence for an earlier human presence in California is unequivocally confirmed (Bada *et al.*, 1974; Berger. 1980; Carter, 1956, 1959, 1980: Davis *et al.*, 1981; Johnson, 1979a, 1981; Orr 1968 and Berger, 1966; Bryan, 1975; and see Bischoff and Rosenbauer, 1981, and Meighan, this volume)

INTRODUCTION

The offshore area of North America known as the California Continental Borderland stretches nearly 1000 km from Point

QUATERNARY COASTLINES
ISBN 0 12 479250 2

Arguello south to Cedros Island, well beyond the Mexican-US border (Vedder, 1976). This study encompasses that portion of the California Continental Borderland north of latitude $32^{\circ}N$ (Fig. 1). It includes all the offshore islands of southern California and northwestern Baja California and the now submerged islands and associated formerly exposed shelves. Henceforth it will generally be referred to as the California Borderland, or just the Borderland.

California is a Mediterranean ecological enclave unique in North America. Though it has been aptly referred to as a "biogeographical island" (Bakker, 1971), it nevertheless possesses an amazing diversity of rock types, landforms, soils, plant communities, and habitats for humans and other fauna. Not surprisingly, the coast region produced abundant game and plant resources for historic aboriginal groups (Heizer and Elsasser, 1980). Indeed, the combination of juxtaposed ocean and land food resources in a year-round equable environment was a living advantage enjoyed by few Indian groups in the New World. Prehistoric aboriginal densities and cultural diversity in California were among the greatest in North America. For humans, both recent aborigines and historic settlers, the California region in general, and the coastal area in particular, is and, as we shall see, has long been an optimal living environment. By the same token, it has not escaped environmental change.

QUATERNARY ENVIRONMENTAL CHANGES OF CLIMATE AND VEGETATION

During late Quaternary time (defined here as the last 128,000 years) the Borderland experienced many environmental changes, some modest, some drastic. Regarding the modest changes, in several earlier papers (Johnson, 1972, 1977a,b) this writer reviewed eclectic lines of paleoenvironment evidence which indicated that though fluctuations in precipitation and temperatures occurred, with local and regional vegetation communities accordingly restructured, the late Quaternary climate of coastal California remained equable and basically Mediterranean in character. A similar conclusion was recently reached by Sims and others (1981) and Adam and others (1979, 1981). Dry, fire-prone summers that were cooler than at present followed winters that were wetter.

Glaciation occurred in the higher California mountains. Both the high Sierra Nevada and Cascade Ranges of California had some rather extensive alpine ice fields with glacial tongues extending down valleys to lower elevations, in several places as low as 600 to 1000 m (2,000-3,000 feet) (Hilton and Lydon, 1976). Smaller valley glaciers, cirque glaciers, and glacierets occurred in the northern Coast Ranges, Klamath Mountains, Warner Mountains, San Bernardino Mountains and in the White Mountains of California

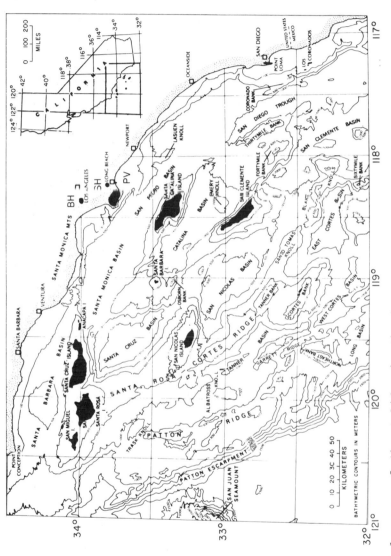

FIG. 1. Index map of the California Continental Borderland (modified from Vedder and Howell, 1980). Palos Verdes Hills, Signal Hill, and Baldwin Hills, mentioned in the text, are indicated respectively as PV, SH, and BH.

(Woods, 1976). With the exception of the higher elevation areas of the north Coast Ranges in northern California, most of the area westward of the High Sierra, including the entire coastal zone, escaped the climatic extremes (ice and cold) that visited the higher Alpine zones of California and other parts of North America.

This paleoecological picture is augmented by: (1) pollen, oxygen isotope and other data from marine sediment cores taken from off Oregon and northern California, and from California Borderland basins (Dunbar, 1981; Gorsline and Barnes, 1970, 1972; Gorsline and Prensky, 1975; Heusser, 1978; Heusser and Shackleton, 1979; Heusser *et al.*, 1981; Kahn *et al.*, 1981; Pisias, 1978, 1979; Pisias *et al.*, 1981; Soutar and Isaacs, 1975; Soutar and Crill, 1977); (2) terrestrial sediment cores from Lagunda de las Trancas and Clear Lake on the California mainland (Adam *et al.*, 1979, 1981; Sims *et al.*, 1981); (3) climatic modelling research (CLIMAP, 1976; Gates, 1976, and personal communication, 1982); (4) the land vertebrate faunal record (Brattstrom, 1953a, 1953b, 1955; Miller, 1971); (5) the marine vertebrate faunal record (P. Walker, personal communication, 1980); (6) and the geologic-pedologic record (Birkeland and Janda, 1971; Borchardt *et al.*, 1978; Glassow *et al.*, n.d.; Harden and Marchand, 1979, p. 7; Janda and Croft, 1967; Keller *et al.*, 1981; McFadden and Bull, 1981; McFadden *et al.*, 1981; Stout, 1969, 1975, 1977; Swan *et al.*, 1977), and by other data (Johnson, 1981; Johnson *et al.*, 1980, 1980c, 1982; n.d.; King and Johnson, n.d.; Liu and Coleman, 1981; Van Devender and Spaulding, 1979).

Probably the most compelling of these paleocologic data, at least in terms of reconstructing the late Quaternary coastal environment of southern California, are the fossil floras, and the pollen and oxygen isotope records. Figure 2 shows the location of the floras and where the principal pollen-oxygen isotope sediment cores have been taken to date. Figure 3 shows the pollen frequency curve obtained from a 114 m core taken from Clear Lake (Sims *et al.*, 1981). On this curve, the shift from low to high oak frequencies, such as occurred about 8,000 years ago, indicates a change to a warmer, drier climate. Although Clear Lake is some 600 km north of the Borderland, and the late Quaternary pollen curve reflects changes in vegetation composition for that particular area, the shift at *ca.* 8,000 years ago between the oak-conifer assemblages is also seen in the pollen profile from a Santa Barbara Basin core (Heusser, 1978). From a cosmopolitan perspective, the Clear Lake pollen record is amazingly compatible with pollen records of long cores pulled in the northeastern Pacific Ocean off California and Oregon (Heusser and Shackleton, 1979; Heusser *et al.*, 1981) and the Grande Pile in northeastern France (Woillard and Mook, 1981).

The data of Fig 3 are also compatible with the other data from the central and southern California coast (see especially Adam

FIG. 2. *Map showing locations of pollen cores (Osgood Swamp, OS; Clear Lake, CL; deep sea, Y72-11-1; Santa Barbara Basin, Y71-10-117P), oxygen isotope cores (deep sea, Y72-11-1 and 6910-2; Tanner Basin, AHF10614), and plant macrofossil localities (from Johnson, 1977b); (1) Bull Creek; (2) Tomales; (3a) San Bruno; (3b) Mountain View Dump; (3c) Lagunas de las Trancas; (4) Little Sur; (5) McKittrick; (6) Point Sal Ridge; (7) Carpinteria; (8) San Miguel Island; (9) Santa Rosa Island; (10) Willow Creek; and (11) Rancho La Brea. While these are the principle localities, pollen studies have been conducted at several other localities in California (D. Adam, personal communication, 1982).*

et al., 1979; Gorsline and Prensky, 1975; Johnson et al., 1982d, n.d.; Kahn et al., 1981; and Stout, 1977), which suggest that Borderland winters were cooler and wetter than now during most of oxygen isotope stage 5 through 2, at times probably markedly wetter. Summers were probably foggier and cooler. Conifers were more widely distributed over the northern Borderland during this time. As indicated by Fig 3, this wetter, more mesic period began in moderate but fluctuating expression about 120,000 B.P. (before present), became near-optimally expressed after about 75,000 B.P.,

D.L. Johnson

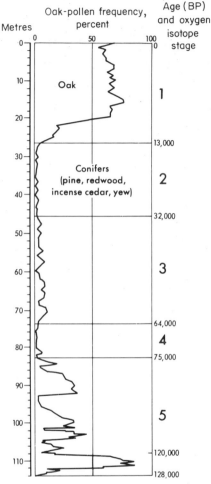

FIG. 3. *Clear Lake pollen frequency diagram calibrated by radiocarbon dates (upper portion) and correlated with the oxygen isotope record of east equatorial Pacific core V28-238 (lower portion) (diagram modified from Sims et al., 1981).*

especially through the classic maximum Wisconsin glaciation of 24,000-14,000 B.P., then rapidly waned and became drier at the onset of the xerothermic period about 8,000 years ago. This more mesic period includes 112,000 (or nearly 90 per cent) of the last 128,000 years. Interestingly, the duration of the Sangamon interglaciation as given in most geochronological schemes includes essentially all of oxygen isotope stage 5, from about 128,000 to about 75,000 B.P., some 53,000 years of time. However, as indicated by Fig 3, the "true" interglaciation, at least in terms of close similarity to today's climate as expressed by vegetation, may have been exceedingly brief in California, perhaps lasting a mere 5,000 years or less.

These paleoecological data indicate that during the past 128,000 years the Borderland and the adjacent mainland coast was an optimal Mediterranean living environment for prehistoric man and other animals. In fact, for most of this long span of time, they indicate an environment resembling the central California coast between Monterey and Point Reyes.

In regard to the more drastic environment changes, it has been suggested by several writers that significant changes in total subaerial ecospace of the littoral zone took place in the late Quaternary, ecospace being maximal during times of glacially withdrawn ocean water and attendant low sea levels, and minimal during interglaciations as at present (Berger and Orr, 1966; Carter, 1959; Johnson, 1972, 1978; Orr, 1968; Vedder and Howell, 1980). Further, these and other authors have cited evidence for and against the creation and destruction of watergaps and landbridges to and among the offshore islands of the Borderland (see review in Wenner and Johnson, 1980). The changing character of landbridges and watergaps, the fluctuations in total ecospace, and changes in precipitation, temperature, vegetation and other environmental elements should seemingly have played collectively significant roles in interisland and mainland-to-island biotic dispersals and migrations, and in the adaptive strategies of land animals, including prehistoric man.

THE OXYGEN ISOTOPE RECORD, SEA LEVEL CURVES, AND MARINE TERRACE STUDIES

A wealth of information on sea level changes and on the causal role of glaciation and hydro-isostasy (and, ultimately, astronomical changes) to sea level changes, has appeared in the literature over the past four decades (see Bowen, 1980; Broecker et al., 1968; Hays et al., 1976; Mörner, 1980; Shackleton, 1977; and Shackleton and Matthews, 1977). The principal bases of this work are three-fold: (1) the development of several rival glacioeustatic sea level curves, (2) analyses of the ages and sea level correlation of raised marine terraces in tectonically unstable areas; and (3) oxygen isotope studies. Pioneer work by Emiliani (1955,1966) produced an oxygen isotope record through analysis of deep sea sediment cores from the Caribbean and elswhere. The record was refined and and extended in work by Shackleton and Opdyke (1973, 1976) and many others on the oxygen isotope and magnetic stratigraphies of deep sea cores. Particularly useful are cores V28-238 and V28-239 because they were taken in the west-equatorial Pacific, an ideal location far from the glaciated middle and high latitudes and minimally influenced by terrigenous sediments (see reviews in Shackleton, 1977, and Berggren et al.,

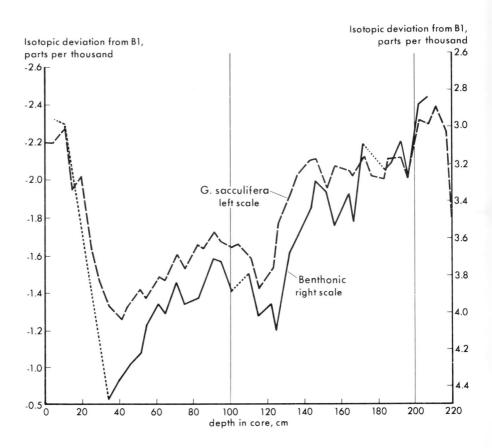

FIG. 4. *Comparison of planktonic and benthonic oxygen isotope record of west equatorial Pacific core V28-238 (modified from Shackleton and Opdyke, 1973; their Fig. 6). The two sequences are plotted to the same scale of isotopic change, but with scale zero-points differing by 5.3 parts/thousand (the present day planktonic difference).*

1980). Core V28-238 yielded an oxygen isotope record based on the combined analysis of planktonic and benthonic foraminiferal species, shown in Fig 4. Most of the planktonic oxygen isotope record (dashed curve of Fig. 4), and part of the benthonic were displayed as a smoothed generalized glacio-eustatic sea level curve to which were added Emiliani's modified stages and age boundaries, as shown in Fig. 5 (Fig. 7 of Shackleton and Opdyke, 1973). (Though Hayes *et al.,* (1976) suggested slight age boundary revisions, I have retained Shackleton and Opdyke's (1973) age boundaries for Fig. 5, with one modification explained below).

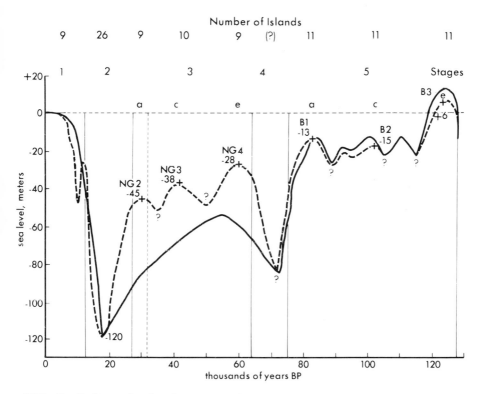

FIG. 5. *Inferred glacio-eustatic sea level curve (solid line) derived from smoothed upper oxygen isotope curve of Figure 4 calibrated with raised marine terraces, mainly from Barbados (B1, B2, B3) (from Shackleton and Opdyke, 1973; their Fig. 7). Synthetic curve (dashed line) generated for this study is calibrated with the three Barbados terraces, and New Guinea terraces II, III, and IV; the upper portion of synthetic curve (last 18,000 years) is from the sea level curve of Nardin and others (1981) that is based on data from the Borderland (mainland shelf near Santa Monica). Oyxgen isotope stages (1-5) as shown in Table 1, and substages (a,c,e), are plotted above curve. The number of islands exposed in Borderland during each stage and substage of the oxygen isotope record is indicated across the top. See text for other explanations.*

This curve (solid line) is in good agreement with the oxygen isotope records of many other cores pulled in other oceans (Shackleton, 1977), and from Camp Century ice core of Greenland (Bowen, 1978, p. 196). It is, however, only a general approximation of world sea level and lacks the precision required for the present study.

Marine terrace age-correlation studies have been conducted in many areas, but those in New Guinea, Barbados, Haiti, and on Bermuda seem to be particularly well suited for correlations with the deep sea oxygen isotope record either because of their raised character (New Guinea, Barbados, Jamaica, Haiti), or their stability (Bermuda) (see Bender et al., 1979; Bloom et al., 1974; Broecker et al., 1968; Chappell, 1974; Chappell and Veeh, 1978; Dodge et al., 1981, and personal communication, 1982; Harmon et al., 1981; Land, 1973; Matthews, 1973; Shackleton and Matthews, 1977).

Sea level curves based on various lines of geologic evidence apart from the deep sea oxygen isotope record have also been formulated from many areas of the world (see Inman, this volume). These, however, appear to be valid only for the specific areas where the data were collected because of the differential glacio-eustatic and hydro-isostatic components related to unloading and loading of the ocean floor or continental shelf by water during glaciations and deglaciations (Hyvarinen, 1981; Mörner, 1980; Nardin et al., 1981; Walcott, 1972; Inman, this volume).

I have integrated the oxygen isotope (solid) curve of Fig 5 with certain aspects of the marine terrace age dating schemes of Bloom and others (1974) and Chappell (1974), and with the local southern California sea level curve of Nardin and others (1981) to produce a synthetic (dashed) curve in Fig 5. The latter is based on the assumption that during oxygen isotope stage 2, 17,000 to 18,000 years ago, sea level dropped to minus 120 m, a value considered conservative (for reasons discussed later). Table 1 gives the durations and boundary ages of the oxygen isotopic stages cf Fig 5. Odd numbered stages (5,3,1) represent times of relatively high sea level and begin midway through major sea level transgressions, and terminate midway through major regressions. Conversely, even numbered stages 4 and 2 represent low sea level periods that begin midway through regressions and end during transgressions. Based on these data it appears that the stage 3-2 boundary should probably be placed at about 27,000 B.P. as shown in Table 1 and Fig 5 rather than 32,000 as suggested by Shackleton and Opdyke (1973) or 29,000 as suggested by Hayes and others (1976).

Because the basis of much of the next section rests with the soundness of Fig 5, and its reliability as a sea level indicator for any point in time during the last 128,000 years, further discussion of its construction and the date upon which it is based is desirable. The widely cited but generalized oxygen isotope sea level curve (solid line in Fig. 5) is, as noted earlier, a smoothed version of the upper (mainly planktonic) curve of Fig. 4. During the smoothing process several small peaks of the stages 3 through 1 portion of the curve, probably thought to represent scatter,

TABLE 1

Estimates of the ages of the oxygen isotope stage boundaries (a) and stage durations (b). Except for the age boundary of stages 3-2 at 27,000 B.P., this scheme follows Shackleton and Opdyke (1973). Their stage 3-2 boundary was originally 32,000 B.P.; Hayes and others (1976) subsequently suggested 29,000 B.P. The 27,000 B.P. estimation is offered on the basis that it follows the fairly well established age of about 28,000-30,000 for the last high sea stand of stage 3 (-45 m) as recorded from Reef Complex II in New Guinea (Bloom et al., 1974; Chappell, 1974; Chappell and Veeh, 1978).

(a) Oxygen Isoptope Stage Boundary	Age (X 10³ years B.P.)	(b) Oxygen Isotopic Stage	Duration of Stage (X 10³ years B.P.)
2-1	13	1	13
3-2	27	2	14
4-3	64	3	37
5-4	75	4	11
6-5	129	5	53

were lost; peaks in the stage 5 portion of the record, however, were preserved. Presumably this was because three of the stage 5 isotope peaks are somewhat more prominent, and they correlated well with dated, raised Barbados terraces I, II, and III (and the more recently dated Haitian terraces [R.F. Dodge, personal communication, 1982]), which represent relatively high sea level stands.

Scans of various oxygen isotope curves from different oceans, however, broadly indicate the general presence of several, usually three, substage peaks in early, middle, and very late stage 3 time (Broecker and van Donk, 1970; Emiliani, 1966). These peaks, more apparent on the lower (benthonic) curve of Fig. 4 than on the upper (planktonic) one, probably are meaningful and therefore should not have been smoothed in producing the solid curve of Fig. 5. They are seen as three peaks in northeast Pacific core 6910-2 pulled from the deep ocean off northern California (Fig. 6; see Fig. 2 for location). They correlate well with dated raised New Guinea terraces, IV, III and II (Bloom *et al.,* 1974; Chappell, 1974; Chappell and Veeh, 1978) and the oxygen isotope record of the Camp Century (Greenland) ice core (Bowen, 1978, p. 196) and probably are correlative with three broadly recognized mid-Wisconsin interstadials in North America at roughly 60-50,

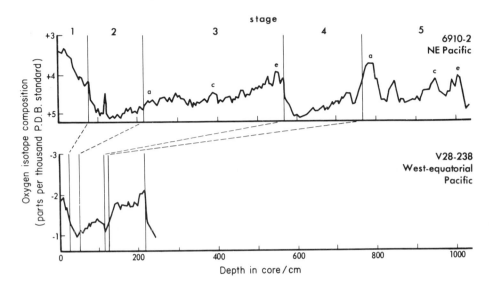

FIG. 6. *Comparison of Oxygen isotope records of cores 6910-2 and V28-238 (modified from Shackleton, 1977). The resolution of core 6910-2 is much greater because sedimentation rates off California where the core was pulled are much higher than in the equatorial western Pacific Ocean where V28-238 was pulled. The three peaks in oxygen isotope stage 3 that represent relatively high sea level stands are thus more apparent in 6910-2.*

45-40, and 30-28 thousand years ago (Port Talbot I, II, and Plum Point/Farmdalian). Because they indicate short intervals of glacial ice melting due to climatic warming, pollen records should show equivalent similar peaks of dry or warm adapted forms, and they do (Woillard and Mook, 1981; Heusser and Shackleton, 1979; Sims *et al.*, 1981).

128,000 YEARS OF FLUCTUATING SUBAERIAL ECOSPACE IN THE CALIFORNIA BORDERLAND

Drastic fluctuations in total subaerial ecospace have occurred during the past 128,000 years in the Borderland. Analysis of submarine contours of 10 m interval bathymetric maps (Coast and Geodetic Survey Bathymetric Maps 1206N-15, 16, 19 and 20) provide a close approximation of the total number of islands present and total area exposed (north of $32^\circ N$ to Point Conception) at any date. The numbers of islands thus estimated for the various oxygen isotope stages and substages are shown across the top of Fig. 5. In the following analyses, where changing island area is related to total island number and sea level position during the last 128,000 years, a tectonically static Borderland is assumed. This assumption cannot be literally valid because the contrasting altitudes of insular and mainland marine terraces of the same age indicate that some deformation occurred (see, for example, Fig. 9 of Vedder and Howell, 1980; Fig. 1 of Szabo and Vedder, 1971; Muhs and Szabo, 1982; and Inman, this volume; and references therein). Also, some hydro-isostatic adjustments must have occurred through time over the Borderland. These two elevational perturbations, while believed to be slight, require that the following analyses be viewed as a first approximation.

Stage 5: Sangamon Interglaciation

We have seen that oxygen isotope stage 5 began 128,000 years ago, lasted roughly 53,000 years, and is broadly equated to the Sangamon interglaciation. The record also shows that significant ice-volume and sea level changes occurred during this long span of time and that stage 5 is thus subdivided into five substages representing three relatively high sea level stands, 5e, 5c, and 5a, and two intervening low stands 5d, and 5b. During 5e time, which lasted only a few thousand years (roughly 125,000-120,000 years B.P.), sea level was about +6 m above the present level. All nine* present Borderland Islands were then subaerially exposed, but owing to a higher sea level they had less ecospace than at present (Table 2). Palos Verdes Hills and Point Loma (and possibly also Signal and Baldwin Hills - see Poland et al., [1956, pp. 52-55], and Woodward and Marcus [1976]), were then also islands as these two peninsulas are bounded on all sides by terraces correlated with oxygen isotope substage 5e (Kern, 1977; Muhs, personal correspondence, 1982; Woodring, et al., 1946). As indicated in the previous section and Fig. 3, stage 5e climate and vegetation were very similar to the present, in fact probably more like the present than at any time during the ensuing 120,000 years until early Holocene time.

Substages 5d through 5a saw fluctuating but generally increasing ecospace under a more mesic climate with at least 11 islands variously exposed (Table 2). During substage 5d, some 120,000 years ago a new island joined San Nicolas on that island's shelf. Nearby, towards the southwest, the island of Cortes began its lengthy late Quaternary existence. While it subsequently flucuated widely in area during stage 5, it remained continuously exposed for about 100,000 years, until the early Holocene when it was finally flooded by rising stage 1 seas.

*In this paper the three Anacapas are considered as one island, as are Los Coronados.

TABLE 2

California Borderland Islands Exposed During Oxygen Isotope Stage 5.

Islands	Substages 5e(+6m)	5c(-15m) and 5a(-13m)
Anacapa	X	X
Baldwin Hills	X?	?
Cortes	--	X [1]
Los Coronados	X	X
Palos Verdes	X	?
Point Loma	X	?
San Clemente	X	X
San Miguel	X	X
San Nicolas	X	X
Santa Barbara	X	X
Santa Catalina	X	X
Santa Cruz	X	X
Santa Rosa	X	X
Signal Hill	X?	?

[1] *Two islands at this time*

The Clear Lake pollen diagram (Fig. 3) shows that a major shift towards more mesic, less dry-adapted vegetation occurred at the onset of substage 5d, and subsequently fluctuated during the Sangamonian interglaciation for about 45,000 years between moist-cool adapted and dry-warm adapted forms.

Stage 4: First Major Wisconsin Stadial

The levels of stage 4 seas are uncertain owing to a dearth of data for that period, which spanned about 11,000 years of time (Table 1). However, judging from the oxygen isotope curve of Fig. 5, sea level probably fell to somewhere between -60 and -85 m. Assuming approximately this sea level lowering, some of the islands in the Borderland merged, some new ones appeared, and insular ecospace greatly increased. The four Northern Channel Islands were joined together into a large superisland at this time, since a drop in sea level to only minus 40 m would presently connect the 3 biggest islands of the chain. San Nicolas and Santa Barbara islands were, respectively, at least three and seven times larger than now, and Osborn, some 10 km south of Santa Barbara Island, made its late Quaternary subaerial debut. Cortes and Tanner were then three islands, collectively about as large as present day San Nicolas. Los

TABLE 3

California Borderland Islands Exposed During Oxygen Isotope Stage 3

Islands	Substages 3e(-28m)	3c(-38m)	3a(-45m)
Anacapa	X	X	--
Cortes	--	X [1]	X [1]
Los Coronados	X	X	X
Middle Pilgrim	--	X	X
San Clemente	X	X	X
San Miguel	X	--	--
San Nicolas	X	X	X
Santa Barbara	X	X	X
Santa Catalina	X	X	X
Santa Cruz	X	--	--
Santa Rosa	X	--	--
Santarosae[2]	--	X	X

[1]*Two islands*
[2]*Collectively Anacapa, San Miguel, Santa Cruz, and Santa Rosa.*

Coronados were then part of the mainland. Considerably more subaerial ecospace was present in the Borderland at this time than in preceding stage 5 time, or ensuing stage 3 time.

The Clear Lake pollen record (Fig. 3) during stage 4 time shows a definite shift in plant species composition towards wetter - cooler adapted forms, probably matched by an increase of conifers along the coast, including at least the northern Borderland.

Stage 3: Main Wisconsin Interstadial(s)

This oxygen isotope stage began roughly 64,000 years ago and represents the main mid-Wisconsin general interstadial. It lasted until about 27,000 years ago and covered about 37,000 years of time. Like stage 5, it is subdivided (in this paper) on the basis of three successively younger and lower high sea level stands, substages 3e, 3c, and 3a, interrupted by two relatively low stands, substages 3d and 3b.

The sea level rise which culminated in substage 3e at -28 m caused a marked decrease of subaerial ecospace in the Borderland. Nine islands were exposed at this time (Table 3). Cortes, which during the stage 4 was a large island of changing dimensions, was greatly reduced in size, ultimately becoming two islands separated by an isthmus. Sea level fell to uncertain levels during substage 3d, which led to increased ecospace, then later rose to -38 m

TABLE 4

California Borderland Islands Exposed During Oxygen Isotope Stage 2[1]' and Estimated Areas.

	Area at -120 m km²(mi²)
Barbarita Norte	0.8(0.3)
Barbarita Sur	0.8(0.3)
Cortez	337(130)
Middle Pilgrim	1(0.4)
North Pilgrim	0.4(0.2)
Diego	11(4)
Dieguito	0.4(0.2)
Forty Mile	2(1)
Garrett	0.4(0.2)
Gordita	0.4(0.2)
Juana Maria[2]	12(5)
Lausen	0.8(0.3)
Middle Dall	1(0.4)
Nidever	24(9)
North Dall	3(1)
Osborn	13(5)
Rosita	33(13)
Sixty Mile North	2(0.8)
Sixty Mile South	0.4(0.2)
South Dall	8(3)
Tanner	151(58)
Clemente	367(142)
Nicolas	864(334)
Barbara	84(32)
Catalina	378(146)
Santarosae[2]	2331(900)
Total	4626(1786)

[1] *Excludes Los Coronados (2.5 km [1 m²], which   part of the mainland.*
[2] *A small peninsula slightly above sea level connected Juana Maria to the mainland at this time, but because it was an island for a short period before and after the -120 m low sea level, it is included here.*
[3] *Collectively Anacapa, San Miguel, Santa Cruz, and Santa Rosa.*

during substage 3c time. Middle Pilgrim emerged north of a then larger Santa Barbara Island during substage 3d and remained exposed throughout stage 3 and subsequent stage 2 time.   The superisland Santarosae which comprised the Northern Channel Islands expanded during substage 3d, partially disintegrated during 3c time, then fluctuated areally through substages 3b and 3a. Los Coronados alternatively became islands or part of the mainland during stage 3 times.   Substage 3 sea level, at about -45 m, marked the approximate end of the Wisconsin interdstadial "high" sea levels.

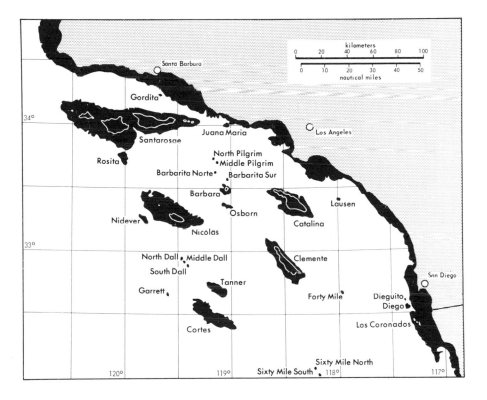

FIG. 7. *Inferred subaerially exposed portion of the California Continental Borderland during oxygen isotope stage 2, 18,000 years ago. Bathymetry taken from U.S. Coast and Geodetic Survey Bathymetric Maps 1206N-15, 16, 19, and 20.   Island names taken from existing names, Orr (1968, Santarosae); Vedder and Toth (1976), or coined wholly or partially for this paper.   Due to errors acquired in transfering areally computed data from large to small scale maps, exposed borderland area shown is approximate; reader should consult Table 5 for more accurate values of area.*

TABLE 5

Changing Area of the Eight Present California Borderland Islands[1] During Past 18,000 Years.

	Present Area km²(mi²)	Area at -120m km²(mi²)	Increase at Stage 2 Area
San Clemente	145(56)	367(142)	2.5X
San Nicolas	58(22)	864(334)	15X
Santa Barbara	2.6(1)	84(32)	32X
Santa Catalina	194(75)	378(146)	2X
Santarosae[2]	506(195)	2331(900)	4.6X
Totals	906(349)	4024(1554)	4.4X

[1]*Los Coronados are omitted.*

[2]*Collectively Anacapa, San Miguel, Santa Rosa, and Santa Cruz.*

The Clear Lake pollen diagram, though registering a slight shift towards dry-adapted plant form like oak, was still dominated by mesic elements during stage 3. As in stage 4, conifers were likely well represented in Borderland vegetation during stage 3, especially in its northern portion.

Stage 2: Final Major (Maximum) Wisconsin Stadial

About 28,000 years ago sea level began dropping very rapidly, reaching about -120 m 17,000 to 18,000 B.P., marking its lowest level in late Quaternary times. A great archipelago of 26 islands was scattered over a wide area of the Borderland (Fig. 7; Table 4). Ecospace increased to well over 4600 km² (1780 mi²) compared to 906 km² (349 mi²) for the present islands. This amounted to 18 more islands than at present and a five-fold increase in insular ecospace. The present 9 Borderland islands were reduced in number to 5 by the joining of Los Coronados to the mainland, and by the coalescence of the 4 northern islands into the superisland Santarosae. Nevertheless, these 5 islands were then giants compared to their present sizes (Table 5). Clearly, an impressive amount and array of insular Borderland real estate was available for animal and plant colonizations during oxygen isotope stage 2 time.

These islands may actually have been even larger. As mentioned earlier, the estimated -120 m lowering of sea level during stage 2 may be a conservative figure, and several independant lines of evidence suggest values in the neighborhood of -130 to -165 m (see Shackleton, 1977, for discussion). Close examination of the island-shelf bathymetry on the maps from which the depth-area data for Tables 2-5 were derived, for example, suggest that sea level in the Borderland conceivably may have fallen to around minus 140 m. The main shelf-slope break on several of the insular shelves occurs at about this depth (e.g., western Santarosae, Santa Rosita, and San Nicolas on Coast and Geodetic Survey Maps 1206N-15,16,19,10), and numerous depressional contours on flattish shelf surfaces at roughly this depth suggest former subaerial features (dunes?). Additionally, removal from the Borderland of overburden weight of water ranging from +6 m (substage 5e) to -120 m (stage 2) depths covering the period 120,000 to 8,000 years ago must surely have been expressed in some upward hydro-isostatic rebound. The effect would have been felt especially during the waning phases of oxygen isotope stage 2 when maximal amounts of water had been removed during the roughly 10,000 year period covering 24,000 to 14,000 B.P. Superimposed on these hydro-isostatic adjustments was, as mentioned earlier, slow tectonic uplift of variable dimensions. For these reasons, probably more land was exposed in the Borderland during stage 2 than the values of Tables 4-5 and 5-7 indicate, and these values may therefore be regarded as minimal. One should bear in mind, however, the tectonic uplift of the coast at present.

Stage 1: Present Holocene Interglaciation

Deglaciation began about 16,000-17,000 years ago and initiated the Flandrian transgression, which rapidly rose to within a few meters of the present sea level some 6,000 to 7,000 years ago (Inman, this volume). Since then, sea level has continued to rise at a slower rate to the present level.

Clear Lake and more local pollen records (Fig. 3, and Heusser, 1978), plus other data (Axelrod, 1967), indicate that the climate of the Borderland during the period from about 8,000 to 4,000 years ago coincided with a worldwide warming episode, locally called the xerothermic period. Vegetation in the Borderland then became somewhat more dry adapted than at present, and thus ecologically more closely matched the vegetation of the exceedingly brief oxygen isotope stage 5e period than at any time since.

CALIFORNIA BORDERLAND LANDBRIDGES, WATERGAPS, AND LAND FAUNA DISPERSALS

Significant changes in the precipitation, temperature and vegetation occurred in the California Borderland during late Quaternary time. These changes were within the context of a Mediterranean climate that was seasonal and probably equable. The area between Monterey and Point Reyes on the central California coast is suggested as being the closest modern analog of the

Borderland.   Land animals, including human beings, were thus
afforded an optimal mid-latitude living environment for all of the
past 128,000 years.   Drastic ecospace fluctuations occurred in the
Borderland that were principally due to glacially induced sea level
fluctuations but with slight tectonic and hydro-isostatic overprints.
Let us now assess how these ecospace fluctuations may have
influenced the late Quaternary dispersal and migration of land
fauna to and within the Borderland.   We shall accomplish this by
first listing all the known living and extinct Borderland land
animals, followed by an assessment of how they may have migrated
to and between islands via landbridges and/or watergaps.

Borderland Land Vertebrates

Native Borderland land vertebrates, including humans, have been
discussed by von Bloeker (1967), Johnson (1975) and others
(Cushing et al., n.d.; Remington, 1971; Van Gelder, 1965; Weaver.
1969; Weaver and Doerner, (1967); see updated summaries in
Glassow (1980), Johnson (1978; 1980a), Wenner and Johnson (1980),
and bibliographies of various papers in Power (1980).   Table 6 lists
all the known extant and extinct land vertebrates excluding human
domesticates (dogs, cattle, etc.) that are, or were, on the
Borderland islands during the Quaternary.   Figure 8 shows
pictorially the non-volant terrestrial vertebrates by island.
     Several patterns and facts emerge from a critical appraisal of
these data.   First, some populations of major forms are disjunct
(e.g., foxes, mice, elephant, lizards).   That is, they occur on two or
more islands.   Second, some populations are specific to one island
only (e.g., a ground squirrel and a rattlesnake on Santa Catalina).
Third, some forms are disjunct at the subspecific level (fox,
white-footed mouse, lizard), the species level (fox, elephant), and
possibly at the subgeneric level (island night lizard; Bezy et al.,
1980).   Fourth, the islands as a group are faunally impoverished
and depauperate (that is, it is almost certain that more species of
land vertebrates could live on the islands than presently do.)

Landbridges and Watergaps

With the exception of Los Coronados, at no time during the late
Quaternary did a landbridge connect any of the Borderland islands
to the mainland. (Los Coronados were intermittently connected to
the mainland, including at least a 10,000 year span during oxygen
isotope stage 2 time).   Secondly, the only existing islands that
were connected to one another were the four Northern Channel
Islands when they coalesced to form Santarosae.   Thirdly, the
southern islands of San Clemente, Santa Catalina, San Nicolas and
Santa Barbara were likewise not connected to one another, to the
mainland, nor to any of the northern islands. If mainland-to-island,

TABLE 6

Native Extinct and Living, Pre-European Non-Volant Land Vertebrates, Southern California Borderland[1]

	SMI	SRI	SCI	A	SBI	SNI	CAT	CLEM	CORO
AMPHIBIANS									
Salamanders									
Arborael salamander (*Aneides lugubris*)							X		
Pacific slender salamander (*Batrachoseps pacificus pacificus*)	X	X	X						
Gardner slender salamander (*B.p. major!*)							X		X
California slender salamander (*B. nigriventris*)						X			
Frogs									
Pacific treefrog (*Hyla regilla*)		X	X				X		
REPTILES									
Lizards									
California legless lizard (*Anniella pulchra*)									X
Western whiptail (*Cnemidophorus tigris*)									X
Western skink (*Eumeces skiltonianus*)							X		X
Southern alligator lizard (*Gerrhonotus multicariratus*)	X		X	X		X[6]	X		X
Island night lizard (*Xantusia riversiana*)					X	X		X	
Western fence lizard (*Sceloporus occidentalis*)	X	X	X	X					X
Side-blotched lizard (*Uta stansburiana*)	X	X	X	X		X[6]	X	X	X

		SMI	SRI	SCI	A	SBI	SNI	CAT	CLEM	CORO
Snakes										
Western racer	(*Coluber constrictor*)						X			
Western rattlesnake	(*Crotalus viridis*)							X		X
Western ringneck snake	(*Diadophis punctatus*)							X		
Spotted night snake	(*Hypsiglena torquata*)			X						
Common kingsnake	(*Lampropeltis getulus*)							X		
Gopher snake	(*Pituophis melanoleucus*)	X	X				X		X	
Western aquatic garter snake	(*Thamnophis couchu*)	X					X			
MAMMALS										
Elephants										
Columbian mammoth	(*Mammuthus columbi*)	X	X	X	?					
Pygmy mammoth	(*Mammuthus exilis*)	X	X	X	?					
Fox										
Island fox	(*Urocyon littoralis catalinae*)							X		
	(*U.l. clementae*)								X	
	(*U.l. dickeyi*)						X			
	(*U.l. littoralis*)	X								
	(*U.l. santacruzae*)			X						
	(*U.l. santarosae*)		X							

	SMI	SRI	SCI	A	SBI	SNI	CAT	CLEM	CORC
Humans									
Amerindian (*Homo sapiens americanus*)	X³	X³	X³	X³	X³	X³	X³	X³	X³
Rodents									
Deermouse (*Peromyscus maniculatus assimilus*)									X
(*P.m. anacapae*)				X					
(*P.m. catalinae*)							X		
(*P.m. eiusus*)					X⁵				
(*P.m. exterus*)						X			
(*P.m. santarosae*)		X							
(*P.m. santacruzae*)			X						
(*P.m. streatori*)	X⁴								
"Giant" deermouse (*P. nesodytes*)	X²	X²							
Extinct Anacapa deermouse (*P. anayapahensis*)				X²					
Western harvest mouse (*Reithrodontomys megalotis santacruzae*)			X⁶						
(*R.m. catalinae*)							X	?	
Insectivores									
Ornate Shrew (*Sorex ornatus*)	X²?								
(*S.o. willetti*)						X			
Skunk									
Spotted Skunk (*Spilogale putorius amphiala*)	X³	X	X	?					

[1]Based on taxonomies and species lists in Hall (1981), Johnson (1972, p. 93), Laughrin (1977), Savage (1969; 1967, as modified by Wilcox [1980]), Walker (1980), Wenner and Johnson (1980), and Yanev (1980).
[2]This list does not include unequivocally known introduced forms, or domesticates (full or partial).
[3]Extinct.
[4]Locally extirpated.
[5]Also on Prince Island (von Bloeker, 1967).
[6]Also on Sutil Island (von Bloeker, 1967; Yanev, 1980).
[6]Possible historic introduction.

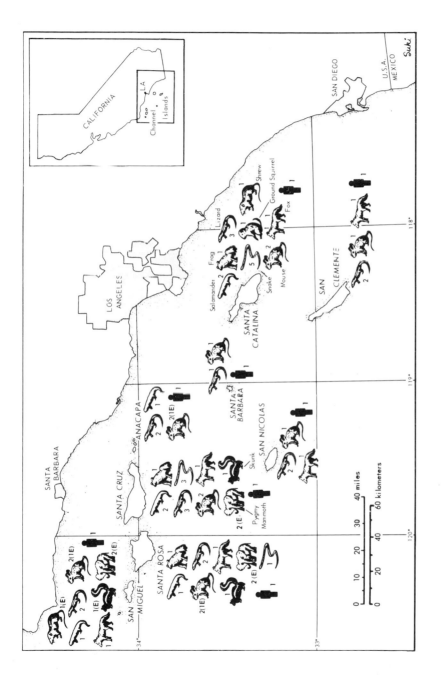

FIG. 8. Pictorial map showing present distribution of non-volant native land vertebrates on the non-landbridge Borderland islands.

or island-to-island connections existed beyond those indicated here, they either occurred in pre-late Quaternary time (i.e., before stage 5), or were tectonically induced. Evidence is lacking for either of these two hypotheses (Johnson, 1978; Junger and Johnson, 1980; Wenner and Johnson, 1980). Published oxygen isotope curves for the early and middle Quaternary (Berggren *et al.*, 1980; Gartner and Emiliani, 1976) lack persuasive evidence that pre-stage 5 sea lavels were low enough to effect such connections. Distances separating the islands from one another and the mainland, however, were then greatly reduced.

Biotic Disperals

Non-volant land vertebrates disperse to islands by one or more of three mechanisms: (1) landbridges, (2) atmospheric transport, (3) overwater dispersal. Assuming that no late Quaternary mainland-to-island and island-to-island landbridges existed in the Borderland other than the intermittent interconnections of Santarosae, and Los Coronados (which are on the mainland shelf), we are left with (2) and (3) as possibilities. Atmosphere transport seems totally out of the question, except for the possibility of amphibian disperal. Amphibians lay eggs in water, and while the odds are exceptionally low, one can conceive of a situation where salamander or frog eggs became stuck to the feet or feathers of a shore-bird wading in a mainland pond. A quick flight to a Santa Cruz Island, Cortes, or Catalina Island pond or stream, and - dispersal occurs. Let us admit to this mechanism as a possibility, albeit a low one, for the successful migration of amphibians to the present Borderland islands on which they occur (Table 6). To explain the origin of the remaining vertebrates we are left with mechanism (3), overwater dispersal. Overwater dispersal of land vertebrates may be effected by rafts, human watercraft, and by swimming.

Rafts. Debris and kelp rafts are distinct possibilities. Coastal California not infrequently experiences torrential winter rains where rivers become swollen, undercut their vegetation-laden banks, and carry a profusion of trees, branches, and other flotable items to the sea. The Ventura, Santa Clara, Los Angeles, Santa Ana and San Diego Rivers all have sizable drainage basins, and (prior to dams) all of them flooded fairly regularly. Savage (1967) mounted a persuasive argument for overwater dispersal to account for all the Borderland herpetofauna. Brown (1980) concurred, with equal persuasion, as did Yanev (1980).

Effectiveness of storms and rivers in providing debris to the Borderland waters is demonstrated by a late winter, 1978, report of a large quantity of fruit floating 16 km offshore in the Santa Barbara Channel. The fruit had been "knocked from trees in orchards of central Ventura County by 'fierce thunderstorms' . . . and had floated 20 miles (30 km) downriver to the sea" (Yanev, 1980, p. 543). A more literal demonstration of how rafts can deliver land animals to Borderland islands was provided in 1955. In August of that year a live but thin and weak black-tailed jack rabbit *(Lepus californicus)* was observed at sea some 60 km off the mainland coast of California on a giant free-floating kelp raft that measured 12 m by 8 m (Prescott, 1959). The raft location was about 35 km west of Santa Catalina and 24 km northwest of San Clemente Island at latitude 33° 13' N, longtitude 118° 45' W. Since jack rabbits do not occur on any of the Channel Islands, this individual had to have come from the mainland and somehow had gotten sea-borne. Oceanic rafts of kelp, terrestrial debris, and other floatable items such as large ocean-going trees are actually not all that uncommon. Anybody walking along the cove beaches of the outer islands, as I have many times on San Miguel and Santa Rosa, would have to be impressed by the profusion of flotsam and jetsam that accumulates on them. These debris piles often contain a redwood or Douglas fir tree trunk or two. Much of this modern debris is probably of human origin, but in prehistoric time before commercial logging most or all of it was natural, and it also included large trees and logs (Hudson et al., 1978: 47).

Debris rafts have been sighted in various oceans of the world. On July 1-2, 1969, a floating island was sighted about 100 km south of Guantanamo Naval Base in eastern Cuba (Smithsonian Institution Center for Short Lived Phenomena, Numbers 662, 664-666, reported in MacArthur, 1972: 84-85). By July 11 it had moved about one quarter of the distance to eastern Jamaica. It was estimated to be 6 to 12 m tall, 13 m in diameter, and consisted of 10 to 15 trees and matted understory vegetation. Unfortunately it was not examined for any contained fauna. Another raft was sighted in the Atlantic off the coast of North America in 1892 (Powers, 1911). This raft was estimated to be 30 m in diameter, contained trees 9 m high, and travelled at least 1600 km. Carlquist (1965: 19), quoting Wallace, related how a large boa constrictor once floated to the island of St Vincent (West Indies) on the trunk of a cedar tree. It is presumed to have come from mainland South America some 320 km distant. The snake had enough energy left after its long voyage to capture several sheep before it was dispatched.

That herpetofauna can disperse rather easily on rafts and logs is a point stressed by Darlington (1938, 1957: 14) and McCann (1953) in their island studies. When the volcano on Krakatoa erupted in 1883 all biota on the island except possibly an earthworm species, were extinguished (Allee and Schmidt, 1951: 68). Twenty-five years later some 262 species were present, of which 240 were arthropods, 4 were land snails, 16 were birds, and 2 were reptiles (a lizard had arrived by 1889, 6 years after the eruption). By

1920-1921 there were 573 species, including a snake (python), 26 breeding birds, and three mammals (2 bats and a rodent, *Rattus rattus*).   By 1928, 45 years after the eruption 47 species of vertebrates had colonized the island, which included 2 subspecies of rodents, *5 lizards,* (my emphasis), a crocodile, and the python. The nearest island not destroyed in the eruption was Sibesia, 19.5 km distant, so that the new migrants came at least that far.

Similarly various kinds of reptiles, including land tortoises, iguanas, iguanids, geckos, snakes, and even one mammal *(Oryzomys,* the same genus that also reached Jamaica) have also successfully dispersed to the geologically young Galapagos Islands which are oceanic and which lie nearly 1000 km off Ecuador (Darlington, 1957: 529-530).

The implications of the above rafting data with respect to the colonization of California Borderland islands by herpetofauna and other land vertebrates are profound. One may conclude that debris raft colonization of Borderland islands during late Quaternary and earlier times by land vertebrates not only is possible - it is expectable. Once an island emerges from the sea a few tens of km off California, and once habitats are established, it would only be a matter of time before colonizers arrived; that process required very little time on Krakatoa Island.

Human Watercraft.   It has been variously proposed that canoe-going Indians were probably responsible for either consciously or inadvertently introducing certain mainland land vertebrates to Borderland islands, or moving them from one island to another (Norris, 1951: 74; Orr, 1968: 16; Vedder and Norris, 1963; Walker, 1980; Wenner and Johnson, 1980; see review in Collins and Laughrin, 1979: 128, and Collins, 1982). Those forms that may have been purposely transported to the islands by human beings, or moved by them from one island to another, include foxes, skunks, some herpetofauna (including the island night lizard and rattlesnake), and possibly the ground squirrel (on Catalina) and shrew (on Catalina and San Miguel [?]). P.W. Collins, for example, in personal correspondence (1982) indicated that Gabrielino Indians practiced a rattlesnake ritual, and suggested that mainland rattlesnakes may have been imported to Santa Catalina Island for the purpose.

Those that could have been accidental stowaways on aboriginal watercraft include some herpetofauna, rodents (especially), and possibly the ground squirrel and shrew. Obviously some forms would more likely have been moved by humans than others, and the two that come immediately to mind are the fox (purposeful)and rodents (accidental).

It has been established that Borderland Indians carried diverse cargoes in their watercraft, such as grain, seeds, acorns, fish, abalone, shells, soapstone, and dogs, among other things, (Johnson, 1972; Walker, 1980; Wenner and Johnson, 1980; and references therein). If Indians carried dogs in their canoes, might they not also carry foxes? The Chumash Indians valued foxskin for shawls, and placed importance on foxes in ceremonial practices, as in the fox solstice dance on Santa Rosa Island (King, 1971). These animals make good pets (Wenner and Johnson, 1980) and as Orr (1968: 16) wrote, ". . . we can easily imagine an Indian lad taking a pet fox . . . in a canoe . . ."

The six populations of island foxes occur on the six largest Borderland islands (Table 6). These populations show little divergence from one another, but show marked divergence from the larger, longer-tailed and more brightly coloured mainland gray fox. The phenetic analysis of Collins (1982) firmly established that the island fox evolved from the larger adjacent mainland gray fox, and not the smaller Central American gray fox as suggested by others. Collins believes that the ancestral founding gray fox population initally dispersed to one of the Northern Channel Islands during the later Pleistocene where it evolved its distinctive smallish island fox characters. This general notion was originally made by Norris (1951), then Vedder and Norris (1963), and subsequently stressed by others (Johnson, 1972; Wenner and Johnson, 1980) (see reviews in Collins and Laughrin, 1979, and Collins, 1982). According to this model, after lengthy isolation and diminution the island fox subsequently dispersed south from the Northern Channel Islands to San Nicolas, Santa Catalina, and San Clemente Islands. Because the morphological differences between the island populations are slight, dispersal is presumed to have occurred in geologically recent times. In the absence of land bridges, they must surely have dispersed overwater, which points to *Homo sapiens* as the obvious dispersal vector. Collins (1982) appears to have resolved the issue through his study of fox remains in island Channel Indian archaeological sites; he found fox remains only in the uppermost levels of middens on San Nicolas, Santa Catalina and San Clemente, but in all levels of Indian occupation on the Northern Channel Islands. A fossil island fox skull, taken from the upper Pleistocene Tecolote Formation on Santa Rosa Island by Orr (1968: 42) proves the long late Quaternary residency of foxes on the Northern Channel Islands. Long thought lost, this skull was recently relocated by Collins (personal communicationm 1982). The close phenetic affinities of this specimen with present-day San Miguel and Santa Rosa Island foxes suggest that island foxes have not changed in size appreciably for the last 10,000 or so years (Collins, personal communication, 1982). Based on archaeological and phenetic analyses of island fox, Collins suggested that the fox was first transported from Santa Cruz Island to Santa Catalina Island sometime after 2500 years ago. Around 1000 years ago they were sometime after 2500 years ago. Around 1000 years ago they were transported from Santa Catalina to San Nicolas Island, and during the past 500 years were taken to San Clemente Island from either San Nicolas or Santa Catalina Island.

Besides foxes, there probably were occasional inadvertent rodent passengers aboard the aboriginal watercraft. The Chumash practice of storing idle canoes in thick tules to keep them from drying out (Hudson *et al.*, 1978: 131, 150, 157) would enhance the prospect of animal stowaways being transported to and about the islands. Canoes often contained a tangle of items (seeds, acorns, fishing gear, pelts [Hudson *et al.*, 1978; King, 1971]) that would have provided hiding places. One can imagine deer and harvest mice, shrews, and possibly some herpetofauna, all of whose habitats include estuarine tules (Bills, 1969; Walker, 1980) dispersed in this way (Collins, 1982; Collins and Laughrin, 1980; Collins *et al.*, Johnson, 1972; Wenner and Johnson, 1980). Collins (1982, and personal correspondence, 1982), for example, believes that the present confined distribution of *Reithrodontomys* on Santa Cruz Island near the mouths of two large drainages implicates Indian transport via canoes as the most likely mode of dispersal of this species to Santa Cruz Island. Further, the findings of Gill (1980) in her evolutionary genetics studies of *Peromyscus* can be largely explained by human transport of mice.

In light of the efficacy of natural rafts in transporting land vertebrates to islands, and in light of continuous Borderland trafficking by Indians over many thousands of years, it seems surprising that even more mainland vertebrates were not introduced to Borderland islands via overwater dispersal.

Swimming. For over a century the presence of mammoth bones (some of dwarfed forms) on the Northern Channel Islands has evoked debate on their origin (Anonymous, 1873; Azzaroli, 1981; Chaney and Mason, 1930; Fairbanks, 1897: 227; Goodyear, 1890; Johnson, 1973, 1974, 1978, 1980a; Leconte, 1891: 562; 1892: 393; Madden, 1981; Orr. 1967, 1968; Stock, 1935, 1943; Valentine and Lipps, 1967). Serious arguments now centre about two positions: (1) The ancestral mammoths either were present when these islands formed part of a mainland mega-peninsula and became stranded when the isthmus submerged, or (2) no peninsular existed, which requires that they swam. The first position has several unsatisfying aspects. For example, what happed to the Pleistocene supporting cast? (i.e., the aggregate of large extinct but formerly abundant mainland Rancholabrean forms that must have co-existed with mammoths on this supposed mainland arm). Why did only one, the elephant (which swims well) become stranded, and why are its remains in such surprising abundance if the others, who left not a trace, once lived there too? In fact, the abundance of diverse Rancholabrean forms in mainland deposits, and their total absence in the Quaternary geologic sections on the Northern Channel Islands strongly suggests that they were never there, probably because they could not get there (i.e., no peninsula existed).

The second position, that the elephants swam, fits the evidence. Elephants do swim well (Johnson, 1972, 1978, 1980a), and the periodic narrowing of the Santa Barbara Channel to as little as 6 km during low sea level episodes of the middle and late Pleistocene should have increased the likelihood of proboscidean crossings. A total of 8 glacial cycles during the past 700,000 years alone (Berggren *et al.*, 1980) afforded water-loving proboscideans many opportunities for swimming distances that were entirely within their capacities. Successive phases of arrival, coupled with rapid (punctuated) evolution of elephants to small size (for reasons given in Johnson, 1978), may have resulted in pene-contemporaneously existing populations showing wide size ranges. Multiple arrivals may also have served to cause multiple phases of extinction.

CHANGING BORDERLAND ECOSPACE, BIOTIC ISLAND COLONIZATIONS, AND EXTINCTION IMPLICATIONS

Important paleoecological conclusions may be drawn from the foregoing analysis. The synthetic sea level curve of Fig. 5 shows that sea level has been constantly fluctuating and has remained stable for only short periods. Borderland ecospace available for subaerial biological use has thus experienced wide fluctuations. It was minimal during substage 5e, and now, 125,000 years later, it is again close to that minimum. As Borderland ecospace expanded following substage 5a, the probability of successful overwater dispersal via rafting increased because the islands became bigger targets while the overwater distances decreased. Moreover, as ecospace increases, so generally does habitat diversity and ecological opportunity, which would increase the possibility of an "ecological take" once a dispersing "waif" lands on an island. These conditions waxed during the onset of stage 4 low sea levels, and waned some 11 millenia later when sea level began rising to substage 3e. Though sea level fluctuated, the general trend during stage 3 was of gradually increasing Borderland ecospace, which ultimately culminated during stage 2 time (Fig. 7). Possible and probable scenarios abound: multiple rafting and swimming events, island colonizations, changing ecospace and habitat diversity, endemic evolution and punctuated (allopatric) speciations, and extinctions, occurring at different times on different islands, many of which are now submerged. How many land vertebrates were present on the islands of Cortes and Tanner (in stage 2 times larger than present day Santa Catalina and San Clemente) we will, alas, never know. Neither will we ever know how many forms suffered extinction as a consequence of ecospace reductions owing to the Flandrian transgression, which flooded over 78 percent of stage 2 Borderland ecospace. Did that event, perhaps preceded by a stage 2 influx of *M. columbi* genes from the mainland coupled with post glacial climatic change, bring about the demise of the island elephants? or was man the culprit?

HOMO SAPIENS IN THE BORDERLAND

We do not know when people first arrived on the Channel Islands, but it is probably safe to assume that once they arrived in coastal California they reached the Borderland islands shortly thereafter. Similarly, arrival of man in California probably closely followed his arrival in the New World. When people first entered the New World, presumably from the Bering area, is not known but it was at least by about 11,500 years ago (Haynes, 1976). Whereas arguments for an earlier entry have been advanced by some investigators (e.g., Bryan, 1978; Davis, 1978; Orr, 1968, *inter alia;* see Dikov; Adovasio *et al.,* Reeves; and Meighan, this volume), others believe that evidence for such claims is either uncertain or in unclear context (M.A. Glassow, C.V. Hayes, personal communications, 1982). Radiocarbon dated shell middens place man on San Clemente, Santa Cruz, and San Miguel Islands by about 7,500 to 8,000 years ago (Glassow, 1980; Johnson, 1972: 206-208; 1980b). On Santa Rosa Island the earliest known shell midden dates were inferred by Glassow (1980) to be in this range, whereas Orr (1968: 54) claimed that the earliest middens are in the range of 11,900 to 12,600 B.P.

Unfortunately, as in all coastal areas, most of the earliest (pre-stage 1) sites of Indians that had ocean-oriented economies must now be submerged (see Inman, and Masters, this volume). Thus it is not suprising that most early mainland and island shell middens lie within the range of about 7,500 to 9,000 B.P. when the Flandrian transgression was nearly complete (Johnson, 1980b: 118). Tantalizing but admittedly as yet uncertain and equivocal evidence hints that people may have hunted island mammoths. The evidence is principally on Santa Rosa and San Miguel Islands where many burned and calcined mammoth bones have been found, in a few instances associated with oxidized hearth-like features in late Quaternary alluvium that some investigators have asserted are aboriginal barbecue pits (Orr, 1968: 76; Orr and Berger, 1966; Carter, 1956; Berger, 1980). Artifacts or artifact-like materials have been found but in uncertain contexts. Radiocarbon dates on four of these mammoth-bearing "fire areas" have yielded ages of about 12,500±250 (L-290T, a solid carbon date), 15,630±460 (ISGS-525) and 16,500±150 (ISGS-518), 29,700±3000 (L-290R, another solid carbon date), and greater than 40,000 (UCLA-2100A-D) radiocarbon years before present (Berger, 1980; Johnson, 1981; Orr, 1968: 73-74). Such a range of ages poses a severe problem, for it seems most unlikely that human beings and elephants would have co-existed on the Northern Channel Islands for tens of thousands of years (Meighan, this volume). Once people arrived on the islands the quick demise of the island mammoths would be expected because these beasts, once isolated, would lose defense behaviorisms toward predators, including the most effective predator of all - *Homo sapiens*. Therefore, if all four of the above radiocarbon measurements reliably date their geologic contexts, then several of these dates are either from non-anthropic contexts, or multiple proboscidean founder-human predator-extinction events occurred. On the other hand the dates may be flawed. Resolution of these problems must await more island research.

Finally, in this paper, I assume that the first people to arrive on Borderland islands did so prior to about 8,000 or 9,000 years ago. They experienced a comparatively benign Mediterranean climate, one that was somewhat cooler and wetter than at present. *If* their arrival in California was prior to the onset of the Flandrian transgression during oxygen isotope stage 2 times (evidence for this being equivocal), they would have faced three times as many islands, and far bigger ones, than are present today. Two of them (Catalina and Santarosae) loomed exceedingly large and were much closer to the mainland than any island is at present. Clearly, if necessity and desire are (and were) the twin mothers of invention, and *if* humans were present, the Borderland environment during oxygen isotope stage 2 time would have been optimal for encouraging the early design and production of watercraft by *Homo sapiens* in southern California, and for early colonization of Borderland islands.

ACKNOWLEDGEMENTS

I thank C.S. Alexander, A.L. Bloom, P.W. Collins, J.E. Cushing, G.R. Dembroff, M.A. Glassow, D.N. Johnson, E.A. Keller, K. LaJoie, S. Miller, D.R. Muhs, D.M. Power, T.K. Rockwell, S.E. Stegner, J.G. Vedder, P.L. Walker, W. Wendland, D. Watson-Stegner, A.M. Wenner, and the editors for critically reviewing this manuscript, B. Bonnell for typing, and J.A. Bier for cartography. I alone am responsible for any errors of omission or commission.

REFERENCES

Adam, D.P., Bryne, R. and Luther, E. (1979). A late Pleistocene and Holocene pollen record from Laguna de las Trancas, northern coastal Santa Cruz County, California. U.S. Geological Survey Open File Report No. 79-545, 29p.

Adam, D.P., Sims, J.D. and Throckmorton, C.K. (1981). 130,000-yr continuous pollen record from Clear Lake, Lake County, California. *Geology* 9, 373-377.

Allee, W.C. and Schmidt, K.P. (1951). *Ecological Animal Geography*, 2nd edn. New York: John Wiley & Sons, Inc. 715 pp.

Anon. (1873). *Proceedings of the California Academy of Science* 5, 152.

Axelrod, D.I. (1967). Geologic history of the California insular flora. In: *Proceedings of the Symposium on the Biology of the California Islands* (R.N. Philbrick,, ed.). Santa Barbara: Santa Barbara Botanic Garden, pp. 267-315.

Azzaroli, A. (1981). About pygmy mammoths of the Northern Channel Islands and other island faunas. *Quaternary Research* 16, 423-425.

Bada, J.L., Schroeder, R.A. and Carter, G.F. (1974). New evidence for the antiquity of man in North America deduced from aspartic acid racemization. *Science* 184, 791-793.

Bakker, E. (1971). *An Island Called California*. Berkeley: The University of California Press.

Bender, M.L., Fairbanks, R.G. Taylor, F.W. Matthews, Goddard, J.G. and Broecker, W.S. (1979). Uranium-series dating of the Pleistocene reef tracts of Barbados, West Indies. *Geological Society America Bulletin* 90, 5577-5594.

Berger, R. (1980). Early man on Santa Rosa Island. In: *The California Islands: Proceedings of a Multidisciplinary Symposium* (D.M. Power, ed.). Santa Barbara: Santa Barbara Museum of Natural History, pp. 73-78.

Berger, R. and Orr, P.C. (1966). The fire areas on Santa Rosa Island, California, II. *Proceedings, National Academy of Sciences* 56, 1678-1682.

Berggren, W.A., Burckle, L.H., Cita, M.B., Cooke, H.B.S., Funnell, B.M., Gartner, S., Hayes, J.D., Kennett, J.P., Opdyke, N.D., Pastouret, L., Shackleton, N.J. and Takayaragi, Y. (1980). Towards a Quaternary time scale. *Quaternary Research* 13, 277-392.

Bezy, R.L., Gorman, G.C., Adest, G.A. and Kim, Y.J. (1980). Divergence in the island night lizard *Xantusia riversiana* (Souria: Xantusiidae). In: *The California Islands: Proceedings of a Multidisciplinary Symposium* (D.M. Power, ed.). Santa Barbara: Santa Barbara Museum of Natural History, pp. 565-583.

Bills, A.R. (1969). A study of the distribution and morphology of the mice of Santa Cruz Island: an example of divergence. M.A. thesis, University of California, Santa Barbara.

Birkeland, P.J. and Janda, R. (1971). Clay mineralogy of soils developed from Quaternary deposits of the eastern Sierra Nevada, California. *Geological Society America Bulletin* **82**, 2495-2514.

Bischoff, J.L. and Rosenbauer (1981). Uranium series dating of human skeletal remains from the Del Mar and Sunnyvale Sites, California. *Science* **213**, 1003-1005.

Bloom, A.L., Broecker, W.S., Chappell, J.M.A., Matthews, R.K. and Mesolella, K.J. (1974). Quaternary sea level fluctuations on a tectonic coast: new Th-230/U-234 dates from the Huon Peninsula, New Guinea. *Quaternary Research* **4**, 185-205.

Borchardt, G., Rice, S. and Taylor, G. (1978). Paleosols overlying the Foothills Fault system near Auburn, California. California Division of Mines and Geology Open File Report 78-16 SF, 125 pp.

Bowen, D.Q. (1978). *Quaternary Geology: A stratigraphic framework for multidisciplinary work.* Oxford. Pergamon Press, 221pp.

Bowen, D.Q. (1980). Antarctic ice surges and theories of glaciation. *Nature* **283**, 619-620.

Brattstrom, B.H. (1953a). The amphibians and reptiles from Rancho La Brea. *Transactions of the San Diego Society of Natural History* **11**, 365-392.

Brattstrom, B.H. (1953b). Records of Pleistocene reptiles from California. *Copeia* No.3, 174-179.

Brattstrom, B.H. (1955). Small herpetofauna from the Pleistocene of Carpinteria, California. *Copeia* No.2, 138-139.

Broecker, W.S., Thurber, D.I., Goddard, J., Ku, T.L., Matthews, R.K. and Mesolella, K.J. (1968). Milankovitch hypothesis supported by precise dating of coral reefs and deep sea sediments. *Science* **159**, 297-300.

Broecker, W.S. and van Donk, J. (1970). Insolation changes, ice volumes, and the record in deep-sea cores. *Reviews of Geophysics and Space Physics* **8**, 169-198.

516 D.L. Johnson

Brown, T.W. (1980). The present status of the garter snake on Santa Catalina Island, California. In: *The California Islands: Proceedings of a Multidisciplinary Symposian* (D.M. Power, ed.). Santa Barbara: Santa Barbara Museum of Natural History, pp. 585-595.

Bryan, A.L. (1975). Palaeoenvironments and cultural diversity in late Pleistocene South America: a rejoinder to Vance Haynes and a reply to Thomas Lynch. *Quaternary Research* **5**, 151-159.

Bryan, A.L. (ed.) (1978). *Early man in America, From a Circum-Pacific Perspective*. Occasional Papers No. 1, Department of Anthropology, University of Alberta. Edmonton: Archaeological Researches International, 327pp.

Carlquist, S. (1965). *Island Life: A Natural History of the Islands of the World*. New York: The Natural History Press, 451pp.

Carter, G.F. (1956). Roast elephant, 27,000 B.C. *Scientific American* **194,68**.

Carter, G.F. (1957). *Pleistocene Man at San Diego*. Baltimore: The Johns Hopkins Press, 400pp.

Carter, G.F.(1959). Man, time, and change in the far Southwest. *Annals, Association of American Geographers* **49**, 8-30.

Carter, G.F. (1980). *Earlier Than You Think: A Personal View of Man in America*. College Station: Texas A & M University Press.

Chaney, R.W. and Mason. H.L. (1930). A Pleistocene flora from Santa Cruz Island, California. *Carnegie Institution of Washington Publication* **415**, 1-24.

Chappell, J. (1974). Geology of coral terraces, Huon Peninsula, New Guinea: a study of Quaternary tectonic movements and sea-level changes. *Geological Society of America Bulletin* **85**, 553-570.

Chappell, J. and Veeh, H.H. (1978). Th-230/U-234 age support of an interstadial sea level of -40 m at 30,000 yr B.P. *Nature* **276**, 602-603.

CLIMAP (1976). The surface of the ice-age Earth. *Science* **191**, 1131-1137.

Collins, P.W. (1982). Origin and Differentiation of the Island Fox: A Study of Evolution in Insular Populations. Unpublished M.A. Thesis, University of California, Santa Barbara, CA.

Collins, P.W. and Laughrin, L.H. (1979). Vertebrate zoology: the island fox on San Miguel Island. In: *Natural Resources Study of the Channel Islands National Monument, California* (D.M. Power, ed.). Santa Barbara: Santa Barbara Museum of Natural History, pp. 12.1-12.47.

Collins, P.W., Storrer, J. and Rindlaub, K. (1979). Vertebrate zoology: the biology of the deer mouse. In: *Natural Resources Study of the Channel Islands National Monument, California* (D.M. Power, ed.). Santa Barbara: Santa Barbara Museum of Natural History, pp. 11.1-11.63.

Cushing, J.E., Daily, M. Noble, E.R. Roth, L.V, and Wenner, A.M. (n.d.). Mammoth fossils found on Santa Cruz Island, California.

Darlington, P.J. (1938). The origin of the fauna of the Greater Antilles, with discussion of dispersal over water and through the air. *Quaternary Review of Biology* 13, 274-300.

Darlington, P.J. (1957). *Zoogeography: The Geographical Distribution of Animals*. New York: John Wiley and Sons, Inc. 675pp.

Davis, E.L., (ed.). (1978). *The Ancient Californians: Rancholabrean Hunters of the Mojave Lakes County*. Los Angeles County Museum of Natural History Science Series 29, 193 pp.

Davis, E.L., Jefferson, G. and McKinney, C. (1981). Man-made flakes with a dated mammoth tooth at China Lake, California. *Anthropological Journal of Canada* 19, 2-7.

Dodge, R.E., Fairbanks, R.G. Benninger, L.K. and Maurrasse, F. (1981). Elevated Pleistocene coral reefs of Haiti: uranium series dating. *Geological Society of America Abstracts with Programs* 13, 440.

Dunbar, R.B. (1981). The glacial-Holocene transition: a detailed isotopic record of surface and bottom water events from San Clemente Basin (California). *Geological Society of America Abstracts with Programs* 13, 443.

Emiliani, C. (1955). Pleistocene temperatures. *Journal of Geology* 63, 538-578.

Emiliani, C. (1966). Palaeotemperature analysis of Caribbean cores P6304-8 and P6304-9 and a generalized temperature curve for the past 425,000 years. *Journal of Geology* 74, 109-126.

Fairbanks, H.W. (1897). Oscillations of the coast of California during the Pliocene and Pleistocene. *American Geologist* 20, 213-245.

Gates, W.L. (1976). Modeling the Ice-Age climate. *Science* 191, 1138-1144.

Gartner, S. and Emiliani, C. (1976). Nannofossil biostratigraphy and climatic stages of Pleistocene. *American Association of Petroleum Geologists Bulletin* 60, 1562-1564.

Gill, A. (1980). Evolutionary genetics of California Islands *Peromyscus*. In: *The California Islands: Proceedings of a Multidisciplinary Symposium* (D.M. Power, ed.). Santa Barbara Museum of Natural History, pp. 719-743.

Glassow, M.A. (1980). Recent developments in the archaeology of the Channel Islands. In: *The California Islands: Proceedings of a Multidisciplinary Symposium* (D.W. Power, ed.). Santa Barbara: Santa Barbara Museum of Natural History, pp. 79-99.

Glassow, M.A., Johnson, D.L. and Walker, P.L. (n.d.). Pleistocene fires, dust, and Santa Ana winds (in prep.).

Goodyear, W.A. (1890). *Santa Cruz Island*. California State Minerologist, 9th Annual Report: 155-170.

Gorsline, D.S. and Barnes, P.W. (1970). Evidence for Holocene climate changes from Tanner and Santa Cruz Basins, California Continental Borderland. *American Quaternary Association (AMQUA) Abstracts,* p. 54.

Gorsline, D.S. and Barnes, P.W. (1972). Carbonate variations as climatic indicators in contemporary California flysch basins. In: *24th International Geologic Congress, Section 6,* Montreal, pp. 270-277.

Gorsline, D.S. and Prensky, S.E. (1975). Paleoclimatic inferences for late Pleistocene and Holocene from California Continental Borderland basin sediments. In: *Quaternary Studies* (R.P. Suggat and M.M. Creswell, eds.). The Royal Society of New Zealand, Wellington, pp. 147-154.

Hall, E.R. (1981). *The Mammals of North America I,II*. New York: John Wiley and Sons, 2nd edn.

Harden, J.W. and Marchand, D.E. (1979). Quaternary stratigraphy and interpretation of soil data from the Auburn, Oroville, and Sonora areas along the Foothills Fault system, western Sierra Nevada, California. U.S. Geological Survey Open-file report 80-305.

Harmon, R.S., Land, L.S. Mitterer, R.M. Garrett, P. Schwarcz, H.P. and Larson, G.J. (1981). Bermuda sea level during the last interglacial. *Nature* 289, 481-483.

Haynes, C.V., Jr. (1976). Ecology of early man in the New World. *Geoscience and Man* 13, 71-76.

Hays, J.D., Imbrie, J. and Shackleton, N.J. (1976). Variations in the earth's orbit: pacemaker of the Ice Ages. *Science* 194, 1121-1132.

Heizer, R.E. and Elsasser. A.B. (1980). The Natural World of the California Indians. Berkeley: University of California Press, 271 pp.

Heizer, R.F. and Brooks, R.A. (1965). Lewisville-ancient campsite or wood rat houses? *Southwestern Journal of Anthropology* 21, 155-165.

Heusser, L.E. (1978). Pollen in Santa Barbara Basin, California: A 12,000-yr record. *Geological Society of America Bulletin* 89, 673-678.

Heusser, L. and Shackleton, N.J. (1979). Direct marine-continental correlation: 150,000-year oxygen isotope-pollen record from the north Pacific. *Science* 204, 837-839.

Heusser, L.E., Barron, J.A. Poore, R.Z. Gardner, J.V. and Stone, S.M. (1981). Correlation of continental and marine paleoclimatic records of central California and the adjacent slope of the Pacific Ocean. *Geological Society of America Abstracts with Programs* 13, 473.

Hilton, R.P. and Lydon, P.A. (1976). Low-elevation glaciation in northern California. *California Geology* 29, 114-116.

Hudson, T., Timbrook, J. and Rempe, M. (eds) (1978). *Chumash watercraft as described in the ethnographic notes of J.P. Harrington*. Ballena Press Anthropological Papers No.9 Socorro (N.M.): Ballena Press, 197 pp.

Hyvarien, H. (1981). Sea-level changes and their causes. *Boreas* 10, 90.

Janda, R.J. and Croft, M.G. (1967). the stratigraphic significance of a sequence of noncalcic brown soils formed on the Quaternary alluvium of the northeastern San Joaquin Valley, California. In: *Quaternary Soils* (R.B. Morrison and H.E. Wright), Jr, eds). International Association for Quaternary Research (INQUA) Proceedings Volume 9, VIII Congress, pp. 157-190. Reno: University of Nevada.

Johnson, D.L. (1972). Landscape evolution on San Miguel Island, California. Ph.D. thesis, University of Kansas, Lawrence (also "Dissertation Abstracts," University Microfilms, Inc., Ann Arbor, Mich., Order No. 73-11, 902).

Johnson, D.L. (1973). On the origin and extinction of pygmy elephants, Northern Channel Islands, California. *Geological Society of America Abstracts with Programs* 5, 683.

Johnson, D.L. (1974). Symposium: archaeological geology: New World. *Geology* 2, 77-78.

Johnson, D.L. (1975). New evidence on the origin of the fox *(Urocyon littoralis clemente)* and feral goats on San Clemente Island, California. *Journal of Mammalogy* 56, 925-928.

Johnson, D.L. (1977a). The California ice-age refugium and the Rancholabrean extinction problem. *Quaternary Research* 8, 149-153.

Johnson, D.L. (1977b). The late Quaternary climate of coastal California: evidence for an Ice-age refugium. *Quaternary Research* 8, 154-179.

Johnson, D.L. (1978). The origin of the island mammoths and the Quaternary land bridge history of the Northern Channel Islands, California. *Quaternary Research* 10, 204-225.

Johnson, D.L. (1979a). Running Springs: a late Pleistocene-Holocene fossil complex on San Miguel Island, California. Abstracts, 2nd conference on Scientific Research in the [U.S.] National Parks (National Park Service-American Institute of Biological Sciences), p. 152.

Johnson, D.L. (1980a). Problems in the land vertebrate zoogeography of certain islands and the swimming powers of elephants. *Journal of Biogeography* 7, 383-398.

Johnson, D.L. (1980b). Episodic vegetation stripping, soil erosion, and landscape modification in prehistoric and recent historic time, San Miguel Island, California. In: *The California Islands: Proceedings of a Multidisciplinary Symposium* (D.M. Power, ed.). Santa. Barbara: Santa Barbara Museum of Natural History, pp. 103-121.

Johnson, D.L. (1980c). The California coastal region: its late Pleistocene and Holocene climate and function as a Ice Age regium. In: *Early Native Americans* (D.L. Brownman, ed.), World Anthropolgy Series. The Hague: Mouton Publishers, pp. 99-117.

Johnson, D.L. (1981). More comments on the Northern Channel Islands mammoths. *Quaternary Research* 15, 105-106.

Johnson, D.L. Coleman, D.D. Glassow, M.A. Greenwood, R.S. Koeppen, R. and Walker, P.L. (1980). Late Quaternary environments and [fire] events on the California Channel Islands [and adjacent mainland] [abstr.] *Ecological Society of America Bulletin* 61, 106-107.

Johnson, D.L., Dembroff, G.R. Keller, E.A. and Rockwell, T.K. (1982). Geochronology and pedology of the Oak View terrace, western Tranverse Ranges, Ventura County, California. *Geological Society of America Abstracts with Programs* 14, 176.

Johnson, D.L., Keller E.J. Dembrogg, G.R. and Rockwell, T.K. (n.d.). The Oak View soil, its age and evidence for unusually strong and rapid pedogensis, Ventura area, California. (in prep).

Junger, A., Johnson, D.L. (1980). Was there a Quaternary land bridge to the Northern Channel Islands? In: *The Channel Islands: Proceedings of a Multidisciplinary Symposium* (D.M. Power, ed.). Santa Barbara: Santa Barbara Museum of Natural History, pp. 33-39.

Kahn, M.I. Oba, T. and Ku, T.L. (1981). Paleotemperatures and the glacially induced changes in the oxygen isotope composition of sea water during late Pleistocene and Holocene time in Tanner Basin, California. *Geology* 9, 485-490.

Keller, E.A., Johnson, D.L. Rockwell, T.K. Clark, M.N. and Dembroff, G.R. (1981). Quaternary stratigraphy, soil geomorphology, chronology and tectonics of the Ventura, Ojai, and Santa Paula Areas, western Transverse Ranges, California. Guidebook, Friends of the Pleistocene, Pacific Cell, Part I, pp. 1-125.

Kern, J.P. (1977). Origin and history of upper Pleistocene marine terrace, San Diego, California. *Geological Society of America Bulletin* 88, 1553-1566.

King, C. (1971). Chumash inter-village economic exchange. *The Indian Historian* 4, 31-43.

King, J.E. and Johnson, D.L. (n.d.). A late Pleistocene pollen record from Santa Rosa Island, California. (in prep).

Land, L. (1973). Contemporaneous dolomitization of middle Pleistocene reefs by meteoric water, North Jamaica. *Bulletin of Marine Science* 23, 64-93.

Laughrin, L.L. (1977). The Island Fox: A Field Study of its Behaviour and Ecology. Ph.D. Thesis, University of California, Santa Barbara, 83 pp.

Le Conte, J. (1891). *Elements of Geology,* 2nd edn. New York: Appleton.

Le Conte, J. (1898). *A Compendium of Geology*. Chicago: American Book Company.

Liu, C.L. and Coleman, D.D. (1981). Illinios State Geological Survey radiocarbon dates VII. *Radiocarbon* 23, 352-383.

MacArthur, R.H. (1972). *Geographical Ecology: Patterns in the Distribution of Species*. New York: Harper and Row, Publishers, 269p.

Madden, C.T. (1981). Origin(s) of mammoths from Northern Channel Islands, California. *Quaternary Research* 15, 101-104.

McCann, C. (1953). Distribution of the Gekronidae in the Pacific area. *Proceedings of the Seventh Pacific Science Congress* 4, 27-32.

McFadden, L.D. and Bull, W.B. (1981). Impact of Pleistocene-Holocene climatic change on soils genesis in the eastern Mojave Desert, California. *Geological Society of America Abstracts with Programs* 13, 95.

McFadden, L.D. Hendricks, D.M. and Tinsley, J.C. (1981. Changes in pedogenic iron oxyhydroxide with time in soils formed on lithic arkosic alluvium, southern California. *Geological Society of America Abstracts with Programs* 13, 96.

Matthews, R.K. (1973). Relative elevation of late Pleistocene high sea level stands: Barbados uplift rates and their implications. *Quaternary Research* 3, 147-153.

Miller, W.E. (1971). Pleistocene vertebrates of the Los Angeles Basin and vicinity (exclusive of Rancho La Brea). *Natural History Museum of Los Angeles County Science Bulletin* 10.

Morlan, R.E. (1980). Taphonomy and Archaeology in the upper Pleistocene of the Northern Yukon Territory: a glimpse of the peopling of the New World. National Museum of Man, Mercury Series. *Archaeological Survey of Canada Paper No. 94*; 398 pp.

Mörner, N.A. (ed.). (1980). *Earth Rheology, Isostasy and Eustasy.* John Wiley & Sons, New York, 599 pp.

Muhs, D.R. and Szabo, B.J. (1982). Uranium-series age of the Eel Point terrace, San Clemente Island, California. *Geology* 10, 23-26.

Nardin, T.R., Osborne, R.H. Bottjer, D.J. and Scheidemann, R.C. Jr. (1981). Holocene sea-level curves for Santa Monica shelf, California Continental Borderland. *Science* 213, 331-333.

Norris, R.M. (1951). Marine Geology of the San Nicolas Island Region, California. Ph.D. Thesis, Scripps Institution of Oceanography, La Jolla, California.

Orr, P.C. (1967). Geochronology of Santa Rosa Island. In: *Proceedings of the Symposium on the Biology of the California Islands* (R.N. Philbrick, ed.). Santa Barbara: Santa Barbara Botanic Garden, pp. 317-325.

Orr, P.C. (1968). *Prehistory of Santa Rosa Island.* Santa Barbara: Santa Barbara Museum of Natural History, 253 pp.

Orr, P.C. and Berger, R. (1966). The fire areas on Santa Rosa Island, California, I. *Proceedings of the National Academy of Sciences* 56, 1409-1416.

Pisias, N.G. (1978). Paleoceanography of the Santa Barbara Basin during the last 8000 years. *Quaternary Research* 10, 366-384.

Pisias, N.G. (1979). Model for paleoceanographic reconstructions of the California current during the last 8000 years. *Quaternary Research* 11, 373-386.

Pisias, N.G., Heusser, L.E. Moore, T.C. Jr., and Shackleton, N.J. (1981). Direct comparison of marine and continental climatic records. *Geological Society of America Abstracts with Programs* 13, 529.

Poland, J.F., Piper, A.M. and others. (1956). Ground-water geology of the coastal zone, Long Beach-Santa Ana area, California. *Geological Survey Water-Supply Paper* 1109, 162 pp.

Power, D.M. (ed.) (1980). *The California Channel Islands: Proceedings of a Multidisciplinary Symposium*. Santa Barbara: Santa Barbara Museum of Natural History, 787 pp.

Powers, S. (1911). Floating islands. *Popular Science Monthly* 79, 303-307.

Prescott, J.H. (1959). Rafting of jack rabbit on kelp. *Journal of Mammalogy* 40, 443-444.

Remington, C.L. (1971). Natural history and evolutionary genetics of the California Islands. *Discovery* 7, 2-18.

Savage, J.M. (1960). Evolution of a peninsular herpetofauna. *Systematic Zoology* 9, 184-212.

Savage, J.M. (1967). Evolution of insular herpetofaunas. In: *Proceedings of the Symposium on the Biology of the California Islands* (R.N. Philbrick, ed.). Santa Barbara: Santa Barbara Botanic Garden, pp. 219-228.

Shackleton, N.J. (1977). The oxygen isotope stratigraphic record of the late Pleistocene. *Philosophical Transactions of the Royal Society of London (B)* 280, 169-182.

Shackleton, N.J., and Opdyke, N.D. (1973). Oxygen isotope and paleomagnetic stratigraphy of equatorial Pacific core V28-238: oxygen isotope temperatures and ice volumes on a 10^5 and 10^6 year scale. *Quaternary Research* 3, 39-55.

Shackleton, N.J. and Opdyke, N.D. (1976). Oxygen-isotope and paleomagnetic stratigraphy of Pacific core V28-239 late Pliocene to latest Pleistocene. *Geological Society of America Memoir* 145, 449-464.

Shackleton, N.J. and Matthews, R.K. (1977). Oxygen isotope stratigraphy of late Pleistocene coral terraces in Barbados. *Nature* 268, 618-620.

Sims, J.D., Adam, D.P. and Rymer, M.J. (1981). Late Pleistocene stratigraphy and palynology of Clear Lake. In: *Research in The Geysers-Clear Lake Geothermal Area, California* (R.J. McLaughlin and J.M. Donnelly-Nolan, eds). U.S. Geological Survey Professional Paper 1141, pp. 219-229.

Soutar, A. and Isaacs, J.D. (1975). The influence of climatic conditions for California and the northern Pacific from the varved sediment record. *Pacific Science Congress, Records of Proceedings* 13 (1), 266.

Soutar, A. and Crill, P.A. (1977). Sedimentation and climatic patterns in the Santa Barbara Basin during the 19th and 20th centuries. *Geological Society of America, Bulletin* 8, 1161-1172.

Stock, C. (1935). Exiled elephant of the Channel Islands, California. *Scientific Monthly* 41, 205-214.

Stock, C. (1943). Foxes and elephants of the Channel Islands. *Los Angeles County Museum Quarterly* 3, (2,3,4), 6-9.

Stout, M.L. (1969). Radiocarbon dating of landslides in southern California and engineering geology implications. *Geological Society of America Special Paper* 123, pp. 167-179.

Stout, M.L. (1975). Age of the Blackhawk landslide, Southern California. *Geological Society of America Abstracts with Programs* 7, 378-379.

Stout, M.L. (1977). Radiocarbon dating of landslides. *California Geology* 30, 99-105.

Swan, F.H., III, Hanson, K.L. and Page, W.D. (1977). Landscape evolution and soil formation in the western Sierra Nevada foothills, California. In: *Soil Development, Geomorphology, and Cenozoic History of the Northwestern San Joaquin Valley and Adjacent Areas of California*. Guidebook for the Joint Field Session of the American Society of Agronomy and the Geological Society of America, Part XI E, p. 300-311. University of California, Davis.

Szabo, B.J. and Vedder, J.G. (1971). Uranium series dating of some Pleistocene marine deposits in southern California. *Earth and Planetary Science Letters* 11, 283-290.

Valentine, J.W., and Lipps, J.H. (1967). Late Cenozoic history of the southern California Islands. In: *Proceedings of the Symposium of the Biology of the California Islands* (R.N. Philbrick, ed.). Santa Barbara: Santa Barbara Botanic Garden, pp. 21-35.

Van Devender, T. and Spaulding, W.G. (1979). Development of vegetation and climate in the southwestern United States. *Science* 204, 701-710.

Van Gelder, R.G. (1965). Channel Island Skunk. *Natural History* 74, 30-35.

Vedder, J.G. (1976). Precursors and evolution of the name California Continental Borderland. In: *Aspects of the Geologic History of the California Continental Borderland* (D.G. Howell, ed.). Pacific Section, Association of American Petroleum Geologists, Miscellaneous Publications 24, pp. 6-11.

Vedder, J.G. and Howell, D.G. (1980). Topographic evolution of the Southern California Borderland during Late Cenozic time. In: *The California Islands: Proceedings of a Multidisciplinary Symposium* (D.M. Power, ed.). Santa Barbara: Santa Barbara Museum of Natural History, pp. 7-31.

Vedder, J.G. and Toth, M.I. (1976). Proposed new geographic names for features in the California Continental Borderland. In: *Aspects of the Geologic History of the California Continental Borderland* (D.G. Howell, ed.). Pacific Section, American Association of Petroleum Geologists, Miscellaneous Publications 24, pp. 60-79.

Vedder, J.G. and Morris, R.M. (1963). Geology of San Nicolas Island, California. *U.S. Geological Survey Professional Paper*, 369, 65 pp.

von Bloeker, J.C., Jr. (1967). The land mammals of the southern California Islands. In: *Proceedings of the Symposium on the Biology of the California Islands* (R.N. Philbrick, ed.). Santa Barbara: Santa Barbara Botanic Gardens, pp. 245-263.

Walcott, R.I. (1972). Past sea levels, eustasy and deformation of the earth. *Quaternary Research* 2, 1-14.

Walker, P.L. (1980). Archaeological evidence for the recent extinction of three terrestrial mammals on San Miguel Island. In: *The California Islands: Proceedings of a Multidisciplinary Symposium* (D.M. Powe, ed.). Santa Barbara: Santa Barbara Museum of Natural History, pp. 703-717.

Weaver, D.W. (ed.) (1969). *Geology of the Northern Channel Islands.* Special Publications, Pacific Sections, American Association Petroleum Geologists-Society of Economic Paleontologists and Mineralogists.

Weaver, D.W., and Doerner, D.P. (1967). Western Anacapia - a summary of the Cenozoic history of the Northern Channel Islands. In: *Proceedings of the Symposium on the Biology of the California Islands* (R.N. Philbrick, ed.). Santa Barbara: Santa Barbara Botanic Garden, pp. 13-20.

Wenner, A.M., and Johnson, D.L. (1980). Land vertebrates on the California Channel Islands: sweepstakes or bridges? In: *The California Islands: Proceedings of a Multidisciplinary Symposium* (D.M. Power, ed.). Santa Barbara: Santa Barbara Museum of Natural History, pp. 497-530.

Wilcox, B.A. (1980). Species number, stability and equilibrium status of reptile faunas on the California Islands. In: *The California Islands: Proceedings of a Multidisciplinary Symposium* (D.M. Power, ed.). Santa Barbara: Santa Barbara Museum of Natural History, pp. 551-564.

Woillard, G.M. and Mook, W.G. (1981). Carbon-14 dates at Grande Pile: correlation of land and sea chronologies. *Science* 215, 159-161.

Woodward G.D. and Marcus, L.F. (1976). Reliability of Pleistocene correlation using C-14 dating: Baldwin Hills-Rancho La Brea, Los Angeles, California. *Journal of Paleontology* 50, 128-132.

Woodring, W.P., Bramlette, M.N. and Kew, W.S.W. (1946). Geology and Paleontology of Palos Verdes Hills, California. *U.S. Geology Survey Professional Papers* 207, 146 pp.

Woods, M.C. (1976). Pleistocene glaciation in Canyon Creek area, Trinity Alps, California. *California Geology* 29, 109-113.

Yanev, K.P. (1980). Biogeography and distribution of three parapatric salamander species in coastal and Borderland California. In: *The California Islands: Proceedings of a Multidisciplinary Symposium* (D.M. Power, ed.). Santa Barbara: Santa Barbara Museum of Natural History, pp. 531-550.

PREHISTORY AND PALAEOECOLOGY
OF
TORRES STRAIT

A. J. Barham and D. R. Harris

*Institute of Archaeology, University of London
and Department of Geography,
University College London, London, UK*

ABSTRACT

Torres Strait, an island-studded channel that narrowly separates
Australia from New Guinea, was formed between 8,500 and 6,500
years ago when the postglacial rise of sea level flooded the Sahul
shelf. Since that time it has functioned both as a barrier and as a
bridge for the movement of plants, animals, and people. The
ethnohistorical record indicates that in pre-European times
settlement and subsistence in the islands of the Strait focused
upon the coastal zone and on offshore fringing and platform reefs.
It is precisely these environments, rather than the interiors of the
islands or the submerged shelf beneath the Strait, that offer the
best chance of reconstructing late Pleistocene-Holocene
environmental history chronostratigraphically. Little
archaeological or palaeoenvironmental research has so far been
carried out in the Strait, so it is necessary to draw on data from
adjacent areas to north and south. In the first part of the paper
the present physiography of the Strait, below and above sea level,
is described. The role of the Strait as both a biogeographical
boundary and a cultural filter is then summarized. The pattern of
pre-European settlement and subsistence, and the prehistoric
context of the Strait, is next outlined, and the paper concludes
with a discussion of changing palaeoenvironmental conditions in
the late Pleistocene, during the phase of marine transgression, and
in post-transgression, Holocene times.

QUATERNARY COASTLINES
ISBN 0 12 479250 2

INTRODUCTION

Torres Strait, as an island-studded channel narrowly separating Australia from New Guinea, offers challenging opportunities for research into prehistoric human migration, environmental change, and the dynamics of cultural contact. Its function as a frontier zone between the hunter-gatherers of Aboriginal Australia and the horticulturalists of New Guinea has attracted the attention of visiting Europeans since at least the time of Cook's passage through the Strait in 1770 (Harris, 1978, p. 206). But, in relation to the worldwide pattern of human land-sea migration routes in the Quaternary, it is less significant than Wallacea: the changing complex of islands and channels that separated the continental shelves of Sunda and Sahul and conditioned the movement of man between Southeast Asia and Greater Australia (Birdsell, 1977).

Systematic scientific observation of the Torres Strait region by Europeans dates from 1770 when the naturalists Banks and Solander accompanied Cook on board the Endeavour. Knowledge of the peoples and environments of the region increased rapidly in the 1840s as a result of the observations of Jukes (1847) and Macgillivray (1852), who accompanied the surveying voyages of the Fly and the Rattlesnake (Allen and Corris, 1977; Moore, 1979). Later in the nineteenth century the arrival of Christian missionaries added further to knowledge of the peoples of the Strait (Gill, 1876; McFarlane, 1888; Murray, 1876), as did the voyage of the Basilisk (Moresby, 1876). Then, in 1898, Haddon, who had first visited the Strait in 1888 (Haddon, 1890; Haddon et al., 1894), returned as leader of an expedition to undertake a systematic ethnographic survey of the region, the results of which were ultimately published in six volumes (Haddon 1901-35). This monumental study provides an invaluable point of reference for later work, but it should not be regarded as a portrayal of pristine, pre-European culture because Haddon's observations had been preceded by nearly three centuries of intermittent European contact with the peoples of the Strait. Haddon's work is the only comprehensive ethnographic study of the region, but during recent years many anthropologists, archaeologists, geographers, and geologists have turned their attention to the Strait (Baldwin, 1976; Barham, 1981; Beckett, 1972, 1977; Chappell, 1976; Golson, 1972; Harris, 1976, 1977, 1978, 1979; Jennings, 1972; Kirk, 1972; Laade, 1968, 1971; Lawrie, 1970; Maxwell, 1968; Moore, 1972, 1979; Nietschmann, 1977; Swan, 1979; Vanderwal, 1973; Wace, 1972; Walker, 1972; J.P. White, 1971; Whitehouse, 1973; Willmott et al., 1973; Wurm, 1972).

Our own interest in the region dates from 1974 when one of us (D.R.H.) carried out ethnoecological field work in the western islands of the Strait. Archival research into the ethnohistory of the islands followed, in Australia and Britain, and in 1980 a first season of palaeoenvironmental field work was undertaken (by A.J.B.). Our purpose in this paper is to place Torres Strait in its environmental, ethnographic, and prehistoric context, and to outline changing environmental conditions in the region in late Pleistocene and Holocene times. Our long-term aim is to reconstruct aspects of the human palaeoecology of the Strait, with particular reference to the western islands, by relating to late Pleistocene and Holocene environmental conditions what can be inferred about pre-European subsistence from ethnohistorical and archaeological evidence. It is not our intention here to present a hypothetical reconstruction of the prehistory of the Strait, such as has been attempted in outline by Golson (1972) and by Moore (1979, pp. 308-13), but an understanding of when and how human occupation of the region took place is a central objective of our longer-term research programme. In the sections that follow we first examine the present physiography of the Strait, before summarizing its role as a biogeographical boundary and cultural filter. The pre-European pattern of settlement and subsistence, and the prehistoric context of the Strait, is then outlined, before changing palaeoenvironmental conditions in the late Pleistocene, and during and after the phase of marine trangression, are discussed.

THE PRESENT PHYSIOGRAPHY OF THE STRAIT

Torres Strait is a shallow shelf, predominantly 10-15 m deep along the north-south axis of 142° 15' E which bisects the western islands, and which approximates the position of the sill that existed when the postglacial transgression breached the pre-existing land bridge in the early Holocene between 8,500 and 6,500 B.P. (see below). According to the available Admiralty charts, water deeper than 30 m does not occur within 100 km to the west of the north-south axis, and only rarely in isolated troughs 70 km to the east, beyond the natural barrier of the Bet-Dungeness-Warrior reef complex which runs nearly continuously from Waraber to the mud banks south of Bobo Island only 18 km south of the Papuan coast (Fig. 1). The northern extension of the Great Barrier Reef lies a further 90 km east of this inner-reef barrier, beyond which water depths increase rapidly east of Mer. The intervening area is characterized by patch reefs of irregular shape rising from depths of 25-30 m near Masig and Erub islands.

Tidally, the Strait forms a buffer zone between the differing regimes of two large seas: a semi-diurnal component to the east in the Coral Sea, and a diurnal regime in the Arafura Sea to the west. The tides within the Strait are predominantly diurnal, except in the eastern part at springs when semi-diurnal tidal currents with speeds up to 6 knots occur, but the pattern is

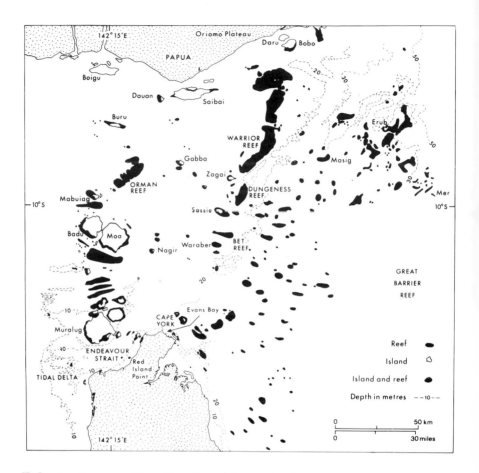

FIG. 1. *Torres Strait: location of places mentioned in the text (submarine contours from R.A.N. Hydrographic Service charts Aus. 700, 839 and 840).*

complex and highly variable seasonally (Easton, 1970, pp. 55-56, 168). Recorded tidal ranges excluding storm effects reach maxima of up to 3.5 m due to the convergence of tidal systems radiating from the Arafura, eastern New Guinea, and southern Pacific nodes, which, combined with the shallowness of the Strait and the forcing effect of platform reefs, give rise to high tidal-current velocities. Consequently, bottom topography is characterized by elongated ridges and channels and marginal sea floors of subdued relief, and the calibre of bottom sediments is a function of current velocity (Maxwell, 1968, p. 78).

Reef morphology is determined in many areas by the east-west axis of the water movements between the Arafura and Coral seas, which are dominantly westward during July and eastward during January for surface waters (Wyrtki, 1960). This is particularly true of the reefs north and south of Badu and Moa islands (Fig. 1), where topographic constraints on water movements are greatest (Whitehouse, 1973, p. 174). Reef growth is enhanced both by the high rate of water flux, and the presence throughout the dry season (March-November) of the Coral Sea water mass, the average salinity (35.6%) and temperature (21.3°C) of which favour high carbonate-ion concentrations (Maxwell, 1968, p. 16). Bottom sediments are 80-90% carbonate facies for most of the zone around 10-15 m depth, with zones of mud deposition east and west of the 142° 15' axis beyond the areas of bottom scour associated with high current velocities (Maxwell, 1968, Figs 138D, 144D), and with a major submarine delta, probably associated with turbidity currents, at the western outflow of Endeavour Strait (Fig. 1). The interaction between shore and nearshore processes is contingent on varying storm frequencies and tides, associated with the north-west monsoon of the wet season and the southeast trades of the dry season. These variables have complex relations to local site conditions, particularly the inundation of mangroves during the wet season, and they are relevant to the interpretation of facies changes and the distribution of archaeological materials within littoral habitats.

The Strait contains over 100 islands and islets which can be divided into four groups according to their location, physical make-up, and relief: an eastern group of high islands consisting of basic volcanic rocks; a central group of low sandy islands made up of coral-derived carbonate sediments; a western group of high islands of acid volcanic and granitic rocks; and a northwestern group of low islands where mangrove muds and peats overlie dead coralline platforms (Fig. 1). The western high islands, the rocks of which have been dated isotopically to the Upper Carboniferous period (Richards and Willmott, 1970), represent the drowned remnants of a pre-Mesozoic structural basement (Jennings, 1972, p. 34). They reach maximum heights above present mean sea level (MSL) of 209 m on Badu, 242 m on Dauan, 246 m on Muralug, and 399 m on Moa. On the larger islands ranges of hills are separated by broad plains of colluvial and alluvial sands derived from extensively weathered bedrock which frequently forms small tors and large isolated boulders on spurs and ridges. Hill slopes are steep and boulder-covered, with limited soil development. The northwestern low islands - Boigu and Saibai - rise only 2-3 m above MSL and contain interior depressions of brackish swamp which are flooded by spring tides during the northwest-monsoonal wet season (December-April).

The valley infills and plain deposits of the high islands such as

Badu and Moa probably date from weathering processes that have been continuous, although varying in rate, from the early Cainozoic to the present, and differentiation of Holocene and Pleistocene stratigraphy in these inorganic and highly weathered sands is problematic. There are no permanent lakes, and the only significant inland organic deposits found during the 1980 field season were in a 2.8 m deep paperbark (*Melaleuca* spp.) fringed freshwater swamp located 0.6 km inland on the southeastern tip of Badu. They are unlikely to provide a palaeoenvironmental record longer than the last 3-4,000 years. Elsewhere inland highly seasonal rainfall and runoff, and annual burning, inhibit the preservation of both organic sediments and archaeological materials. Most freshwater stream courses are ephemeral, and gullying is often extensive.

At the coast, rocky peninsulas alternate with broad shallow embayments, where carbonate sand, silica sand, or organic muds dominate the nearshore and beach facies, depending on the degree of exposure, the width of fringing reef, and proximity to colluvial and fluvial inputs of granite-weathering products. On Moa and Badu the northern, and to a lesser extent the southern, coastlines comprise 0.75-3.0 km-wide prograded mud flats, with well developed mangrove communities at the seaward edge, backed by hypersaline mud flats with irregular and poorly developed chenier ridges (Fig. 2). On more exposed coasts mangroves are largely absent, and the nearshore, reef-flat environments are dominated by calcareous sand and muds, often partially colonized by seagrasses, particularly species of *Cymodocea* and *Thalassia* (Fig. 3). The occurrence of these habitats may have palaeoecological significance because seagrasses form the staple food of the

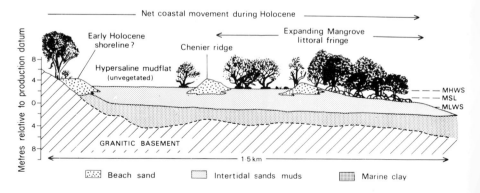

FIG. 2. *Progradational facies for a low-energy coastal environment in a north-facing embayment near Totelai Point, north Moa Island.*

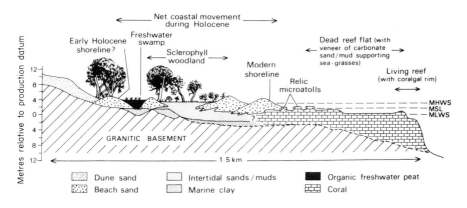

FIG. 3. *Progradational facies for a moderate-energy coastal environment in a southeast-facing embayment near Zigini Point, south Badu Island.*

dugong, a large marine mammal traditionally hunted by the islanders. The reef flats exhibit evidence of progradation at the landward margin, where modern beaches overlie relic microatolls *in situ* which are capable of providing dateable and tidally specific absolute chronologies of the rates of change of both shoreline and sea level during the Holocene (Scoffin and Stoddart, 1978). Suitable sites for such reconstruction exist on Moa, Badu, Gabba, and Nagir.

Carbonate beachrock occurs on a number of contemporary beaches on Moa and Nagir (Barham, 1981, p. 26), but only on Nagir has beachrock been located inland marking the former position of the coastline. This outcrop was first described by Macgillivray (1852, II, pp. 38-9), and shell samples within the beachrock matrix collected in 1980 have yielded a date of 3,680 ± 120 B.P. (ANU-2514). This sample suggests a seaward movement of the coastline of 150 m since deposition of the shell, but the formation of beachrock is not well understood (Russell, 1967; Scoffin, 1977), which, together with its irregular distribution within the islands, precludes its extensive use as an indicator of former shorelines. Beaches often exhibit progressively higher crest levels inland of the present shore, but although Torres Strait lies outside the area of high cyclone frequency, and has a higher tidal range than the Queensland coast farther south (Hopley and Harvey, 1978, p. 166) - which means that it is less likely to exhibit high beach-crest levels related to storm surges - such deposits offer only ambiguous data for the interpretation of Holocene coastal change. Much greater chronological and stratigraphic resolution is possible by coring and levelling the prograded hypersaline mud flats, mangrove foreshores, and adjacent coral-reef flats, and it is on these palaeoecologically significant resource zones that our research is now focused.

Comparable progradational sediments characterize the low islands of Saibai, Boigu, and Zagai. Extensive shallow coring on Saibai has demonstrated that between 2.8 and 4.2 m swamp peats overlie a highly recrystallized carbonate bedrock. As yet the calcareous facies have not been drilled, but the recrystallized nature of associated molluscs of *Pyrazus* sp. and *Terebralia* sp. already suggests that the horizon is the upper surface of a Pleistocene reef subsequently overlain by muddy foreshore deposits and colonized by mangroves. Similar progressive sedimentation on platform-reef surfaces is occurring on Zagai and Sassie reefs to the south, and is probably comparable to similar environments to the south on the Great Barrier Reef (Stoddart, 1980). Unlike the high islands, where prograding sediments derive from terrigenous and reef sources, the low islands in the north of the Strait receive sediment derived from the rivers of the south-Papuan coast.

In general, there are strong pragmatic and theoretical reasons for focusing on the coastal zone in attempting to reconstruct human occupation of the Torres Strait region in the Holocene. Transgression of the 200 km-wide shelf by the rising postglacial sea was probably completed in 2–3,000 years, during which time the shoreline migrated from positions close to -30 m at 9,000 B.P. to approximately the present configuration by 6,000 B.P. Archaeological sites on the shelf earlier than 10,000 B.P. are unlikely to have survived transgression and subsequent tidal-current scour. Inland sites will tend to be few and difficult to locate, given the ethnohistorically attested minor importance of the inland zone for resource exploitation (see below), the low probability of remains being preserved in inland environments, and the lack of good stratigraphic differentiation in those environments. By contrast, the coastal zone and regenerating reefs would have offered to human populations a rapidly expanding resource base over the last 6,000 years, and they also represent the sedimentary environments where chronostratigraphic reconstruction utilizing absolute dating techniques has the highest potential.

TORRES STRAIT AS A BIOGEOGRAPHICAL BOUNDARY

The biogeographical significance of Torres Strait derives from its location at the boundary between the Australian continent and the continental island of New Guinea, the latter backed by insular and mainland Southeast Asia; but the narrowness of the Strait from north to south (150 km at its narrowest point), and the existence of islands within it, have ensured that many floristic and faunal continuities link the Papuan and Australian mainlands. Since the postglacial rise of sea level flooded the Sahul shelf between 8,500 and 6,500 years ago, the Strait has functioned as a bridge as well as a barrier (Walker, 1972).

Floristically Torres Strait has long been regarded as marking the southern boundary of the Malesian (formerly Malaysian) floral region (Good, 1947, Pl. 4), where, according to Van Steenis (1950), 984 genera reach their southern or northern limits. Despite the sharpness of this floristic discontiniuty, many species and some genera occur both north and south of the boundary (Barlow, 1972; Burbidge, 1960, pp. 134-43; Carr, 1972; Hoogland, 1972; Wace, 1972; Webb and Tracey, 1972). These taxa consist mainly of coastal plants, such as mangroves and beach species, which have wide ranges and the capacity for dispersal in salt water. The remainder include trees of open-canopy woodlands, such as certain species of *Acacia* and *Eucalyptus,* a few rain-forest species, and a disproportionate number of plants that have been incorporated into traditional subsistence economies for food and other purposes: for example Golson (1971a, p. 207) estimates that 88.5% of the plants used for food by Aborigines in the Cape York Peninsula are of Malesian affiliation. Even allowing for the possibility that some of these plants may have been transferred by man from Malesia to Australia, this evidence confirms the existence of strong floristic links across Torres Strait. In general, the fact that continuities do exist at species level among non-coastal plants is a function of the narrowness and recency of the Strait, the proximity of equivalent habitats north and south of it, and the recurrent exposure of the Sahul shelf at times of lowered sea level during the Quaternary.

Torres Strait has not traditionally been viewed by zoogeographers as a major faunal boundary - the main division between faunas of Australian and Asian affinity is located well to the west in Wallacea - but faunal discontiniuties among species of mammals, birds, frogs, and reptiles do occur at it (Cameron *et al.,* 1978; Schodde and Calaby, 1972, pp. 265-7; Tyler, 1972, p. 241). There are, nevertheless, close faunal similarities on either side of the Strait which, like the floristic ones, correlate with equivalent habitats. The open-canopy woodlands to north and south share many species of birds and mammals, as do the rain forests, but the relative faunal poverty of the Papuan woodlands and of the rain forests of the Cape York Peninsula suggests that speciation among the woodland animals has occurred mainly in Australia whereas the rain-forest fauna has evolved chiefly in New Guinea (Schodde and Calaby, 1972). Thus Torres Strait appears to have played a relatively minor and recent role as an intermittent marine barrier between two evolving regional faunas. Its main effect has been to attenuate faunal diversity northward in woodland habitats, and southward in rain-forest habitats, rather than to create a sharp faunal boundary between Papua and the Cape York Peninsula.

TORRES STRAIT AS A CULTURAL FILTER

Just as Torres Strait has functioned both as a barrier and a bridge for plants and animals, so it has for people. Its role as a frontier zone between horticulturalists and hunter-gatherers is often emphasized, but this should not obscure the fact that close cultural connections did exist between the peoples of Papua, the Torres Strait Islands, and the Cape York Peninsula in pre-European times. These connections are apparent not only in aspects of material culture but also in languages, myths, and ceremonies. Evidence of Papuan and Islander influences on Peninsular culture is abundant (Haddon, 1935, pp. 266-73; Hale and Tindale, 1933; McConnel, 1936; Thomson, 1933, 1934), but the extent to which Australian Aboriginal culture influenced Islander and Papuan populations is less clear (Golson, 1972; Moore, 1972; Wurm, 1972). The most important shared trait of material culture was the dugout canoe equipped with mat sails and outriggers. It was presumably the principal means by which northern ideas and artefacts penetrated the Peninsula and it was made and used there as well as acquired by trade from the Strait. Other material traits of northern origin include drums, bark-strip skirts, masks, plaited armlets, pearlshell pendants, cowrie and pearlshell necklets and headbands, nautilus-shell nosepegs, wooden ear-cylinders, ornamental clubs, and possibly the bow and arrow (Haddon, 1904, p. 295; McConnel, 1936; Thomson, 1933, 1934). These objects were traded into, and copied in, the northern Peninsula, but their use was restricted to ceremonial dances and they were not objects of everyday life. Other practices shared with, and probably derived from, the Strait include the use of sleeping platforms, round bark houses, and mummification with subsequent cremation; and myths record the introduction of some songs and dances, such as those of the sea eagle, gull, and Torres Strait pigeon, into the Peninsula from Mabuiag Island and Papua.

The more limited evidence in the Strait of cultural influences from the Peninsula refers to weapons, myths, and languages. The spear and spear thrower (woomera) was the main hunting and fighting weapon of the Peninsular Aborigines and it was valued and used in the western islands as far north as Mabuiag (Moore, 1972, p. 333). The principal myth of the western islands concerned a culture hero, Kwoiam, who possessed Aboriginal physique and weapons and was said to have come from the Australian mainland and to have raided as far north as the Papuan coast (Moore, 1979, pp. 286-88). There is incontrovertible evidence that the language of the western islands, which is often referred to as Mabuiag, is structurally related to Australian rather than to Papuan languages, and there are even Australian loan words in western Papuan languages (Wurm, 1972); but it is uncertain whether this implies the prehistoric presence of a population of Aboriginal derivation whose language was subsequently adopted and modified by incoming Papuans, or whether it implies a more recent - and seemingly improbable - northward thrust of Mabuiag into the western islands (Golson, 1972, pp. 385-86). The language spoken in the eastern islands - Miriam - belongs to the Eastern Trans-Fly family of Papuan languages and shows negligible Australian influence: evidence which suggests that the eastern islands were settled from Papua (Wurm, 1972, pp. 349-64). This proposition is reinforced by early European observations that the Islanders resembled Papuans more closely than Aborigines in physical characteristic, particularly hair form; and the hypothesis of a prehistoric "Australian" population in the western islands speaking a language ancestral to Mabuiag receives some support from Haddon's anthropometric demonstration of differences between the eastern and western islands, including the presence in the western islands of a few skulls that were said to resemble Australian skulls and to be quite unlike anything found in New Guinea (Haddon, 1935, pp. 282-83; Kirk, 1972, pp. 367-68).

There is thus strong ethnographic evidence for Torres Strait having had a filtering effect on the diffusion of cultural traits between Papua and the Cape York Peninsula. The richness of the ethnohistorical record adds greatly to the potential of the region for research into the prehistory of human occupation, but it also poses severe chronological problems. It has been pointed out that the main source of ethnographic data - the Haddon *Reports* - describes a cultural pattern already altered by European contact. The difficulty of distinguishing between pre- and post-European cultural traits is accentuated by the general lack in the ethnohistorical record of a chronological framework that relates to events prior to about 1800 A.D., and there is even a problematic gap in the record between the 1840s (the voyages of the Fly and Rattlesnake) and the late-nineteenth century (the missions, the Basilisk voyage, and the Haddon expedition) just at the time when the rate of cultural change under the impact of European navigators, and especially bêche-de-mer and pearlshell fishermen (Becket, 1977; Harris, 1979, pp. 80-81), was accelerating. Any attempt to reconstruct the pre-European cultural pattern, with the hope of then "testing" the reconstruction against archaeological and palaeoenvironmental data, is therefore fraught with imterpretative difficulties (quite apart from the problems - already discussed - that are inherent in obtaining such data in the field). Nevertheless, judicious interpretation of the ethnohistorical record does permit a reconstruction, in outline at least, of the pre-European, - or, more precisely, the mid-nineteenth century - pattern of settlement and subsistence in the Islands (Harris, 1979).

PRE-EUROPEAN SETTLEMENT AND SUBSISTENCE IN THE TORRES STRAIT ISLANDS

In early historical times, before sustained European contact disrupted indigenous society, the total population of the Islands probably numbered between 4,000 and 5,000 people, divided into five or six kin-based communities, each of which occupied two or more islands. In the eastern and northwestern islands the people lived in permanently established villages and hamlets and they depended substantially on horticulture as well as on fishing and some gathering of wild-plant foods. This sedentary way of life contrasted with the more seasonally mobile life of the inhabitants of the mid-western and southwestern islands who moved within and sometimes between islands, who depended mainly on wild marine and terrestrial foods, and who practised horticulture only on a very small scale. Throughout the Islands resource exploitation focused on the coasts, reefs, and inshore waters. The basic socioeconomic unit was the clan or band, each one of which consisted of approximately 50 people and exploited its own stretch of coast. The clans belonged to larger territorial districts and communities, and a complex system of inter-island and trans-Strait trade by canoe allowed food and craft goods to be exchanged between islands and with the mainlands to north and south (Harris, 1979, pp. 84-87).

The main sources of protein and fat in the diet of the islanders were fish (trapped as well as caught by hook and line), marine molluscs, crustaceans, turtles, and the dugong which was hunted with a specialized harpoon and the capture of which conferred special prestige on the hunter (Haddon, 1912, pp. 166-71). Terrestrial animals contributed much less to the diet. Carbohydrate was derived from horticultural produce, the main crops being yams, sweet potatoes, taro, bananas and sugar cane, and also from wild plants, particularly the tubers of wild yams and the germinating embryos of certain species of mangrove (Harris, 1977, pp. 439-48). The wild plants that were exploited grew mainly in coastal habitats: in the littoral woodlands and thickets just inland of sandy beaches and along muddy, mangrove-fringed shores.

The coastal zone also yielded shellfish and gave access by canoe to the rich fishing and gathering grounds of the fringing and platform reefs. Even horticulture seems mainly to have been carried out near the coast, often on piedmont, colluvial soils on the inland side of littoral thickets and woodlands. The interiors of the larger high islands probably contributed relatively little to subsistence, but the northwestern low islands of Saibai and Boigu contain large interior swamps with rich wet-season resources of fish and waterfowl; and on Saibai there are also extensive traces of formerly cultivated mound-and-ditch field systems ("raised fields") on slightly higher ground adjacent to the swamps. In general, however, resource procurement focused heavily on the coastal zone and it is not surprising that settlements, both permanent and seasonal, were located almost exlusively at or close to the coast.

TORRES STRAIT IN PREHISTORIC CONTEXT

In order to understand how the pre-European or mid-nineteenth century pattern of settlement and subsistence came into being, and, more generally, how Torres Strait has functioned in the past in its dual role as a cultural bridge and barrier, we need archaeological and palaeoenvironmental evidence from within the region itself. At present this is almost entirely lacking, but some inferences can be drawn from the evidence now available of prehistoric human occupation of the mainlands to north and south. This demonstrates the presence of man in the New Guinea Highlands and in the Australian interior more than 25,000 years ago (Bowler and Thorne, 1976; Jones, 1973; J.P. White, 1972), well within the last glacial period when the Sahul shelf was exposed and the two land masses were united in the super-continent of Greater Australia. No archaeological sites of proven Pleistocene age have as yet been discovered within the Torres Strait region - the nearest such sites are located in the New Guinea Highlands (J.P. White, 1972), in Arnhem Land (C. White, 1971), and at Laura in the southern Cape York Peninsula (Campbell, 1980; Rosenfeld, 1975) - but the distribution of these sites both north and south of the region argues strongly for the presence of human populations on the Sahul shelf at least by the late Pleistocene.

The environmental conditions that may have prevailed on the shelf at that time are discussed in the next section, but it is evident that even if much of the region was so arid as to be saline and inhospitable, the coastal zone, any areas of freshwater swamp that existed, and perhaps the higher land of the Cape York-Oriomo ridge and of remnant, karstic reefs, are likely to have favoured human occupation. However, as is argued below, the chances of locating and investigating now-submerged occupation sites in the dynamic marine environment of the present Strait seem remote. The flaked stone artifacts recovered from Pleistocene sites in the New Guinea Highlands and Australia do not suggest particularly close links at a continental scale of comparison, but the fact that edge-ground axes have only been found in Pleistocene contexts within Australia in Arnhem Land (C. White, 1971) and the Cape York Peninsula (Wright, 1971), and that some of those from Arnhem Land are shaped for hafting like the so-called "waisted" axes of Pleistocene and later date in the New Guinea Highlands (Golson, 1971b), may imply that the Pleistocene populations of the Sahul shelf and adjacent uplands shared a common technological tradition.

The prehistory of man within the Torres Strait region cannot yet even be outlined for lack of archaeological evidence. Only two archaeological surveys have been carried out: one in 1971 and 1973 by Moore (1979, pp. 13-15), who test excavated three coastal sites, one on Muralug and two on the adjacent mainland of Cape York; and the other by Vanderwal (1973), who carried out a reconnaissance of the Strait as a whole in 1972 and only found occupation deposits that appeared worthy of excavation on Pulu islet off Mabuiag in the western, and on Mer in the eastern, islands. Vanderwal (1973, p. 180) recovered a stone scraper and two perforated shell artifacts from a test pit on Pulu (for which no date has been published) but he did not excavate on Mer. The three sites that Moore investigated yielded a few flaked stone artifacts, part of an edge-ground diorite axehead, cooking stones, and fragments of pumice, bone, and shell. Charcoal from the site on Muralug was dated to 610 ± 90 B.P. (ANU - 1364), and charcoal from the sites to the southwest (Red Island Point) and southeast (Evans Bay) of Cape York gave dates of 1120 ± 430 B.P. (ANU-1365) and 610 ± 80 B.P. (ANU - 1366) respectively. The fact that the date from Red Island Point is older than the other two has little intrinsic significance, and, according to Moore, probably relates to the greater durability of this rock-shelter site compared with the other two open sites which were located behind beaches. Nor should the low age of all three dates be taken to imply that human settlement of the Cape York area occurred only recently.

No other archaeological surveys were carried out in the Islands prior to 1980, but in 1974 one of us had noted the existence of artificial inter-swamp "canals" on Saibai (Harris, 1977, pp. 450-51) which, we now believe, afforded access to areas of raised-field cultivation adjacent to the swamps. In 1980 several archaeological sites were located on Moa in the form of rock shelters, pictographs, surface concentrations of shell, and coastal fish traps, and one of the extensive areas of raised fields on Saibai was studied on the ground and from the air (Barham, 1981, pp. 11-19). During the 1981 field season we located further rock shelters, pictographs, and fish traps on Moa and on the now unoccupied island of Nagir, as well as continuing to investigate the raised fields on Saibai. Test excavations of shell middens on Moa and Saibai were undertaken, but radiocarbon dates are not yet available from these sites. In November, 1981, M.J. Rowland visited Moa and Nagir, where he excavated selected coastal midden sites, and it is hoped that further archaeological work will be undertaken in the western islands in the near future.

It is clearly premature to attempt to synthesize the fragmentary evidence for human occupation of the Islands, but despite the general absence of good preservational environments for archaeological remains, the prospect exists of piecing together the prehistory of the Strait by combining ethnohistorical, archaeological, and palaeoenvironmental evidence. Research on the environmental history of the Islands has now proceeded sufficiently far for us to report some preliminary results and interpretations in the concluding sections of this paper. We also expect that it will in due course prove possible to relate some aspects of the detailed ethnographic record directly to archaeological evidence, particularly ethnographic descriptions of specific locations and of durable artefacts of stone, bone, and shell (Vanderwal, 1973, pp. 171-74).

LATE PLEISTOCENE ENVIRONMENTS

At present, little direct evidence exists of the palaeoenvironment of Torres Strait during the last 120,000 years. Interpretation must therefore draw on data from adjacent areas. There is general agreement that the period was one of interglacial conditions initially (oxygen-isotope stage 5), with sea level at or close to present MSL (Chappell, 1974). This was followed by a period of greater ice cover when world sea levels oscillated, but were lowered by more than 75 m relative to present MSL (Street, 1981, p. 160). The exposure of broad shelves during the greater part of the period due to eustatic lowering of sea level increased the climatic continentality of areas such as northern Australia (Nix and Kalma, 1972; Verstappen, 1975; Webster and Streten, 1972, 1978).

To the west of Torres Strait this exposure is confirmed by nodular calcrete from the Sahul shelf floor, together with pedogenic calcarenites down to the -90 m submarine contour, indicating subaerial conditions, except for the existence of a restricted marine lagoon in the Bonaparte Depression (Van Andel *et al.*, 1967, pp. 741-48), (Fig. 4). These conditions correlate with pollen evidence from the New Guinea Highlands and imply a semiarid climate over the shelf with precipitation in the range 150-550 mm (Bowler *et al.*, 1976, p. 368). The exposure of the shelf at the maximum of the last glacial down to -130 m is suggested by the occurrence at this depth of a littoral mollusc, *Chlamys senatorius*, radiocarbon dated to 16,910 ± 500 B.P. (Van Andel and Veevers, 1967, p. 105). In the Gulf of Carpentaria, a brackish lake deposit dating between 19,000 and 16,500 B.P. also suggests high evaporation from closed drainage basins, implying drier conditions than present (Phipps, 1970). Although generally cooler and more arid (Nix and Kalma, 1972), the wide floors of the basins were not devoid of fluvial activity. On the Sahul shelf, zones of high quartz concentration indicate extensive development of littoral sediments supplied by rivers (Van Andel and Veevers, 1967). At about 17,500 B.P., the present Strait formed a plateau watershed separating fluvial systems draining westward into the Arafura Sea basin, and eastward into the Coral Sea basin. Tentative drainage networks for the area have been modelled by Maxwell (1968, pp. 51-58).

Periods of increased aridity may have led to a decline in the density of forest cover, leading cumulatively to increases in sediment yields. General agreement between the pollen diagrams from the Atherton Tableland, Queensland, and oxygen-isotope

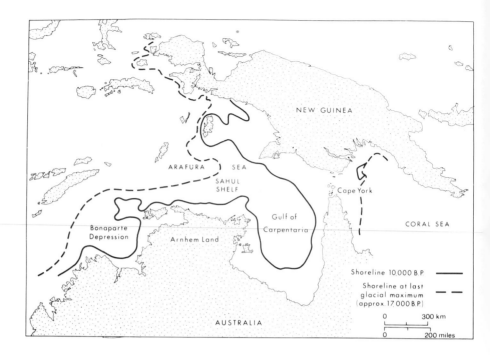

FIG. 4. *The Sahul Shelf (shorelines at 10,000 B.P. and approx. 17,000 B.P. from Chappell, 1976, Fig. 3).*

cores RC 11-120 and V23-82 tend to support the hypothesis that sea-level position and temperature changes were the major determinants of rainfall during the last glacial maximum, with a major shift to wetter conditions around 8,000 B.P. (Kershaw, 1980, pp. 398-402), which led to changes from sclerophyll to simple notophyll vine forests at both Bromfield Swamp (Kershaw, 1975) and Lake Euramoo (Kershaw, 1970). This significant change is broadly synchronous with the date put forward by Jennings (1972) for the marine transgression of the Torres Strait land bridge. There are many uncertainties in extrapolating from the upland context of the Atherton records to the low-sea-level landscape of Torres Strait, but it seems likely that, during the glacial maximum, the broad shelf formed an extensive upland plain, with remnant karstic reefs and igneous hills offering restricted and diverse habitats different from the rest of the shelf. These upland "islands" may well have been important plant, animal, and even human habitats during much of the last 120,000 years, forming a chain along which contact was maintained between floristic and faunal elements north and south of the broad shelf.

Unfortunately, without data from shallow cores and grab samples from the sea floor, the extent to which the plain, presently 10-30 m below MSL, offered a significant resource base for human populations must remain conjectural. Given the complex drainage patterns adjusting to oscillatory sea levels throughout the last 120,000 years, and the resultant changes in dominant winds and rainfall, coupled with the long lag times involved in soil and vegetation development on exposed shelf floors after regression, it is likely that no precise analogue exists for such an area. If the saline deposits of the Gulf of Carpentaria are indicative of conditions elsewhere on the shelf, even for relatively short periods of a few millennia, the combination of variable aeolian and fluvial processes, and of surface morphology and vegetation out of equilibrium with them, may have produced, for much of the late Pleistocene, a "barrier" between the Papuan coast and Cape York comparable in significance to any sea barrier. Consequently, until more data are available, the suggestions may be premature that areas on the Sahul shelf comparable to Torres Strait had a geography similar to modern Lake Chad (Webster and Streten, 1978, p. 296), or that the exposed shelf supported open forest and a greater variety of animal species than exists in the modern Australian fauna, which would have facilitated the movements and sustenance of human groups (Calaby, 1976, pp. 24-25). It is more important to stress here that the transgression to present MSL between 9,000 and 6,000 B.P. was atypical of the preceeding 60,000, and probably the last 120,000, years, and that during the late Pleistocene the modal coastline would, if we extrapolate from the eustatic curves derived from the Huon Peninsula in eastern New Guinea (Bloom *et al*., 1974; Chappell, 1974), have been between the present -30 m and -50 m bathymetric contours (Chappell, 1976, pp. 16-17), with Torres Strait persisting as a land bridge for at least the last 60,000 years. Holocene coastlines thus represent a novel configuration - when viewed in the context of the late Pleistocene as a whole - in which sediment distribution, bathymetry, and littoral processes were readjusting to a fundamentally new set of environmental conditions.

THE MARINE TRANSGRESSION

Dates for the transgression of Torres Strait, following the last glacial maximum, are currently based on the application of world sea-level curves to the bathymetry of the area, assuming tectonic stability, i.e. that the depth of the sill at -15 to -18 m (relative to present MSL) has remained geologically static in relation to varying ocean levels. At present, no data for the area suggest tectonic instability, but the proximity of deep water east and west of the shelf makes it unwise to neglect the possibility that hydro-isostatic factors may have operated (Chappell, 1974).

Variable estimates of the precise amount by which sea level was lowered in the region during the last glacial maximum (Jongsma, 1970; Veeh and Veevers, 1970) can be resolved if visco-elastic warping at shelf edges is taken into account (Chappell, 1976, p. 14), where it may alter the effective depth by up to 20 m. Given the variety of proposed global eustatic curves (Hopley, 1978, p. 160), transgression of the sill may be hypothesized for any period between 8,500 and 6,500 B.P., based on the range of the curves in relation to the 18 m bathymetric contour. There is a similar lack of agreement over the precise form of the Holocene sea-level curve for northern Queensland (Belperio, 1979; Hopley, 1974, 1978, 1980; Maclean *et al.*, 1978). Much of the uncertainty derives from attempts to correlate sequences from different locations, which neglect the possibility of recent local faulting and warping, and to use facies for radiometric dating which relate in different ways to tidal regime.

Only three (uncalibrated) radiocarbon dates relating to coastal facies in the region are available at present: the first, of 5,120 B.P., is from Maxwell (in Jones and Endean, 1973, p. 259, no site details or error given); the second, of 3,680 ± 120 B.P. (ANU-2514), is from the beachrock site on Nagir already referred to; and the third, of 5,500 B.P. (ANU-2884, error not yet available), is from a relic, *in situ* microatoll adjacent to the present sand beach overlying reef flat on the east coast of Moa. The establishment of a Holocene sea-level curve for the Strait is therefore a primary objective of our research. A programme of levelling and drilling tidally specific relic microatolls and basal mangrove peats is in progress, and a drilling project is planned in collaboration with the Australian National University and James Cook University of North Queensland. Even with the few radiocarbon dates available, it appears that transgression of the shelf had occurred well prior to *ca.* 5,500 radiocarbon years B.P., and that there have been subsequent spatial changes of coastal position, and datum changes of relative sea level, of sufficient magnitude to have important implications both for archaeological site location and for the prehistoric resource potential of the coastal zone.

POST-TRANSGRESSION ENVIRONMENTS

The initial transgression of the wide, flat shelf floor from -18 m to close to present MSL was rapid and without precedent within the last 60,000 years. It must have disrupted biotic communites and favoured taxa able to respond quickly to sudden spatial changes of habitat, particularly those capable of dispersal in salt water. Climatic changes may have been locally severe, and sediment flux rates probably increased as relic soils destabilized in the nearshore zone. The onset of deposition in the tidal delta of

Endeavour Strait may be associated with this period, between, perhaps, 7,000 and 5,000 B.P. Limited onshore aeolian sediment movement, similar to that which gave rise to the parabolic dunes around Cape Bedford and Cape Flattery in the eastern Cape York Peninsula (Whitehouse, 1963; Willmott et al., 1973), probably took place in newly exposed areas of high sediment supply, particularly intertidal foreshores, as evidenced, for example, by a dune system in southeastern Badu which is stratigraphically related to a former (early Holocene?) beach ridge 0.7 km inland (Fig. 3).

At a later stage, coastal environments must have stabilized and taken on facies characteristics commensurate with the prevailing tidal, wave-energy, and seasonal-energy patterns. The question remains problematic as to whether the progradational sequences typical of low-energy situations within the Strait (Fig. 2) have evolved at constant, irregular, or cyclical rates of seaward advance per unit of time. It is a crucial question in relation to the availability of resources for human subsistence in the mid Holocene, because, if substantial time-lags separated the transgressive rise to MSL from subsequent development of mangrove and other coastal habitats exploited by man, then resource availability may have increased irregularly as a non-linear function of facies changes in the foreshore zone. This question can only be resolved by detailed reconstruction of shorelines at a local scale.

It should be possible to obtain a comparable, and again radiometrically dateable, environmental history from the platform and finging reefs of the Strait, which constitute the other major resource zone exploited for subsistence in historical times. Reef growth resumed after transgression as soon as recolonization of suitable surfaces had taken place. Again, a small lagtime may have been involved. At present the depth of Holocene veneer on top of platform and fringing reefs is unknown. Assuming the pre-existence of reefs within the Strait during higher sea-level stands during the Pleistocene, and their subsequent exposure as karstic features during periods of low sea level, the dateable "Thurber" discontiniuty between the Pleistocene weathered surface and the Holocene regrowth that followed transgression permits reconstruction of the rate of vertical reef growth. It should also provide reasonably precise timing of the onset of transgression and of the degree of diachroneity involved in coral regrowth as sea level rose across the shelf. Calculations based on gross potential and net production rates for coral (Chave et al., 1972; Smith and Kinsey, 1976), allied to coral dating procedures (Chappell et al., 1978; Polach et al., 1978; Veeh and Green, 1977), should allow chronostratigraphic horizons related to MSL to be derived. Radiometric dating of this "Thurber" discontinuity, such as has been carried out at varying depths beneath Holocene veneer on islands of the Great Barrier Reef by drilling (Davies, 1974; Hopley *et al.*, 1978; Thom *et al.*, 1978), and by seismic refraction (Harvey, 1977, 1978), should also allow detailed reconstruction of the transgression within Torres Strait.

Spatial variability in reef regrowth, relating to muddy water conditions, and the gradual adjustment of reef morphology to tidal - and current - circulation patterns, must have been a vital factor in the subsequent human exploitation of these rich biotic habitats. During the immediate post-transgressive period, when reef growth will have been dominantly upward rather than lateral, such resources may have been minimal, and far less accessible, than later in the Holocene when reefs in shallow water probably reached equilibrium with MSL, perhaps between 4,500 and 5,500 B.P. The model proposed by Thom and Chappell (1975), where reefs on deep antecedent platforms reach modern sea level long after transgression, while reefs veneering higher platforms (such as Torres Strait) reach modern sea level soon after transgression, would predict dominantly lateral Holocene growth for most reefs in the vicinity of the western islands, standing in less than 15 m of water, and a relatively shallow depth to the Thurber discontinuity. It would also explain the lack of "blue holes" and similar features in the reefs that are located in 15-20 m of water, and the fact that they are common on the reefs in 30-50 m of water north of Mer.

CONCLUSION

As has already been emphasized, both coastal and reef environments appear to have been crucially important resource zones in the pre-European subsistence economy of the western islands. They are also the two sedimentary environments in which detailed palaeoenvironmental reconstruction over the last 7,000 years, based on radiometric chronologies, appears to be possible. Work in both these resource zones is continuing, with the object of exploring further the inter-relationships between Holocene subsistence systems and the spatially and temporally changing environments of the island shores. This paper is therefore a preliminary statement, the purpose of which has been to outline the field of enquiry and to summarize the first stage of what we hope will be a fuller investigation into the prehistory and palaeoecology of Torres Strait.

ACKNOWLEDGEMENTS

We thank the Councillors and people of the western islands for welcoming us and allowing us to carry out field work; also members of the Department of Aboriginal and Islander Advancement of the Queensland Government and of the Department of Aboriginal Affairs of the Australian Government, in

Brisbane and Thursday Island, for general assistance. We gratefully acknowledge financial support for the project from the British Social Science Research Council, the Australian Institute of Aboriginal Studies, the Archaeology Branch of the Department of Aboriginal and Islander Advancement, the Leverhulme Foundation, the Institute of Archaeology of the University of London, the Geography Department of University College London, and the Central Research Fund of the University of London. We wish also to thank the Radiocarbon Dating Laboratory of the Australian National University for assistance with radiometric dating.

REFERENCES

Allen, J. and Corris, P. (eds) (1977). *The Journal of John Sweatman*. St. Lucia: University of Queensland Press.

Baldwin, J.A. (1976). Torres Strait: barrier to agricultural diffusion. *Anthrop. J. of Canada* 14, 10-17.

Barham, A.J. (1981). Land use and environmental change in the Western Torres Strait Islands, northern Queensland, Australia. *Field-Work Report*. Department of Geography, University College London and Institute of Archaeology, University of London. Processed.

Barlow, B.A. (1972). The significance of Torres Strait in the distribution of Australasian Loranthaceae. pp. 183-196 in Walker, D. *op. cit.*

Beckett, J.R. (1972). The Torres Strait Islanders. pp. 307-326 in Walker, D. *op. cit.*

Beckett, J.R. (1977). The Torres Strait Islanders and the pearling industry: a case of internal colonialism. *Aboriginal History* 1, 77-104.

Belperio, A.P. (1979). Negative evidence for a mid-Holocene high sea level along the coastal plain of the Great Barrier Reef Province. *Marine Geology* 32, M1-M9.

Birdsell, J.B. (1977). The recalibration of a paradigm for the first peopling of Greater Australia. In: *Sunda and Sahul. Prehistoric Studies in Southeast Asia, Melanesia and Australia*, (J. Allen, J. Golson and R. Jones, eds). London: Academic Press, pp. 113-167.

Bloom, A.L., Broecker, W.S., Chappell, J.M.A., Mathews, R.K. and Mesolella, K.J. (1974). Quaternary sea level fluctuations on a tectonic coast: new Th-230/U-234 dates from the Huon Peninsula, New Guinea. *Quaternary Research* 4, 185-205.

Bowler, J.M. and Thorne, A.G. (1976). Human remains from Lake Mungo: discovery and excavation of Lake Mungo III. In: *The Origin of the Australians,* (R.L. Kirk and A.G. Thorne, eds). Canberra: Australian Institute of Aboriginal Studies pp. 127-138.

Bowler, J.M., Hope, G.S., Jennings, J.N., Singh, G. and Walker, D. (1976). Late Quaternary climates of Australia and New Guinea. *Quaternary Research* 6, 359-394.

Burbidge, N.T. (1960). The phytogeography of the Australian region. *Austr. J. Bot.* 8, 75-212.

Calaby, J.H. (1976). Some biogeographical factors relevant to the Pleistocene movement of Man in Australasia. In: *The Origin of the Australians,* (R.L. Kirk and A.G. Thorne, eds). Canberra: Australian Institute of Aboriginal Studies, pp. 23-280.

Cameron, E., Cogger, H. and Heatwole, H. (1978). A natural laboratory. *Austr. Nat. Hist.* 19, 190-197.

Campbell, J.B. (1980). Human adaptation in the Quaternary. In: *The Geology and Geophysics of Northeastern Australia,* (R.A. Henderson and P.J. Stephenson, eds). Brisbane: Geological Society of Australia, Queensland Division, pp. 402-407.

Carr, S.G.M. (1972). Problems of the geography of the tropical eucalypts. pp. 153-181 in Walker, D. *op. cit.*

Chappell, J.M.A. (1974). Late Quaternary glacio- and hydro-isostacy on a layered Earth. *Quaternary Research* 4, 429-440.

Chappell, J.M.A. (1976). Aspects of late Quaternary palaeogeography of the Australian-East Indian region. In: *The Origin of the Australians* (R.L. Kirk and A.G. Thorne, eds). Canberra: Australian Institute of Aboriginal Studies, pp. 11-220.

Chappell, J.M.A., Thom, B.G. and Polach, H.A. (1978). Radiometric dating of coral reefs. In: *Coral Reefs: Research Methods,* (D.R. Stoddart and R.E. Johannes, eds). Paris: UNESCO, pp. 81-91.

Chave, K.E., Smith, S.V. and Roy, K.J. (1972). Carbonate production by coral reefs. *Marine Geology* 12: 123-140.

Davies, P.J. (1974). Subsurface solution unconformities at Heron Island, Great Barrier Reef. *Proc. 2nd Int. Coral Reef Symp., Brisbane* 2, 573-578.

Easton, A.K. (1970). The tides of the continent of Australia. *Research Paper No. 37, Horace Lamb Centre for Oceanographical Research,* Flinders University of South Australia, Bedford Park.

Gill, W.W. (1876). *Life in the Southern Isles*. London: The Religious Tract Society.

Golson, J. (1971a). Australian Aboriginal food plants: some ecological and culture-historical implications. In: *Aboriginal Man and Environment in Australia,* (D.J. Mulvaney and J. Golson, eds). Canberra: Australian National University Press, pp. 196-238.

Golson, J. (1971b). Both sides of the Wallace Line: Australia, New Guinea and Asian prehistory. *Arch. and Phys. Anthrop. in Oceania* 6, 124-144.

Golson, J. (1972). Land connections, sea barriers and the relationship of Australian and New Guinea prehistory. pp. 375-397 in Walker, D. *op. cit.*

Good, R. (1947). *The Geography of the Flowering Plants.* London: Longmans.

Haddon, A.C. (1890). The ethnography of the western tribe of Torres Straits. *J.R. Anthrop. Inst.* 19, 297-442.

Haddon, A.C. (1901-35). *Reports of the Cambridge Anthropological Expedition to Torres Straits* (Vol. I, 1935, Vol. II, 1901 and 1903, Vol. III, 1907, Vol. IV, 1912, Vol. V, 1904, Vol. VI, 1908). Cambridge. Cambridge University Press.

Haddon, A.C., Solas, W.J. and Cole, G.A.J. (1894). On the geology of Torres Straits. *Trans. R. Irish Acad.* 30, 419-476.

Hale, H.M. and Tindale, N.B. (1933). Aborigines of Princess Charlotte Bay, north Queensland. *Records of the South Australian Museum* 5, 63-116.

Harris, D.R. (1976). Aboriginal use of plant foods in the Cape York Peninsula and Torres Strait Islands. *Austr. Inst. Abor. Studies Newsletter, New Series* 6, 21-22.

Harris, D.R. (1977). Subsistence strategies across Torres Strait. In: *Sunda and Sahul. Prehistoric Studies in Southeast Asia, Melanesia and Australia* (J. Allen, J. Golson and R. Jones, eds). London: Academic Press, pp. 421-63.

Harris, D.R. (1978). Gardening and gathering. *Austr. Nat. Hist.* 19, 206-209.

Harris, D.R. (1979). Foragers and farmers in the Western Torres Strait Islands: an historical analysis of economic, demographic, and spatial differentiation. In: *Social and Ecological Systems* (P.C. Burnham and R.F. Ellen, eds). London: Academic Press, pp. 75-109.

Harvey, N. (1977). The identification of subsurface solution disconformities on the Great Barrier Reef, Australia between latitudes 14°S and 17°S, using shallow seismic refraction techniques. *Proc. 3rd Int. Coral Reef Symp., Miami* 2, 46-52.

Harvey, N. (1978). Wheeler Reef: morphology and shallow reef structure. In: *Geographical studies of the Townsville area, Occasional Paper* 2, (D. Hopley, ed.). Townsville: James Cook University, Department of Geography, pp. 51-53.

Hoogland, R.D. (1972). Plant distribution patterns across Torres Strait. pp. 131-152 in Walker, D. *op. cit.*

Hopley, D. (1974). Investigations of sea level changes along the coast of the Great Barrier Reef. *Proc. 2nd Int. Coral Reef Symp., Brisbane* 2, 551-562.

Hopley, D. (1978). Sea level changes on the Great Barrier Reef: an introduction. *Phil. Trans. R. Soc. Lond. A.* 291, 159-166.

Hopley, D. (1980). Mid-Holocene high sea levels along the coastal plain of the Great Barrier Reef Province: a discussion. *Marine Geology* 35, M1-M9.

Hopley, D. and Harvey, N. (1978). Regional variation in storm surge characteristics around the Australian coast: a preliminary investigation. *Proc. Nat. Hazard Symp., Canberra* May 1976, 164-185.

Hopley, D., McLean, R.F., Marshall, J. and Smith, A.S. (1978). Holocene-Pleistocene boundary on a fringing reef: Hayman Island, North Queensland. *Search* 9, 323-325.

Jennings, J.N. (1972). Some attributes of Torres Strait. pp. 29-38 in Walker, D. *op. cit.*

Jones, R. (1973). Emerging picture of Pleistocene Australians. *Nature (Lond.)* 246, 278-281.

Jones, O.A. and Endean, R. (eds) (1973). *Biology and Geology of Coral Reefs, Vol. I, Geology I.* New York: Academic Press.

Jongsma, D. (1970). Eustatic sea level changes in the Arafura Sea. *Nature (Lond.)* 228, 150151.

Jukes, J.B. (1847). *Narrative of the Surveying Voyage of H.M.S. Fly,* 2 Vols. London: Boone.

Kershaw, A.P. (1970). A pollen diagram from Lake Euramoo, northeast Queensland, Australia. *New Phytologist* 69, 785-805.

Kershaw, A.P. (1975). Stratigraphy and pollen analysis of Bromfield Swamp, northeast Queensland, Australia. *New Phytologist* 75, 173-191.

Kershaw, A.P. (1980). Evidence for vegetation and climatic change in the Quaternary. In: *The Geology and Geophysics of Northeastern Australia,* (R.A. Henderson and P.J. Stephenson, eds). Brisbane: Geological Society of Australia, Queensland Division, pp. 398-402.

Kirk, R.L. (1972). Torres Strait - channel or barrier to human gene flow? pp. 367-374 in Walker, D. *op. cit.*

Laade, W. (1968). The Torres Strait Islanders' own traditions about their origin. *Ethnos* 33, 141-158.

Laade, W. (1971). *Oral Traditions and Written Documents on the History and Ethnography of the Northern Torres Strait Islands, Saibai-Dauan-Boigu.* Wiesbaden: Steiner.

Lawrie, M. (1970). *Myths and Legends of Torres Strait.* St. Lucia: University of Queensland Press.

Macgillivray, J. (1852). *Narrative of the Voyage of H.M.S. Rattlesnake,* 2 Vols. London: Boone.

Maclean, R.F., Stoddart, D.R., Hopley, D. and Polach, H. (1978). Sea level change in the Holocene on the northern Great Barrier Reef. *Phil. Tans. R. Soc. Lond. A.* 291, 167-186.

Maxwell, W.G.H. (1968). *Atlas of the Great Barrier Reef*. Amsterdam: Elsevier.

McConnel, U.J. (1936). Totemic hero-cults in Cape York Peninsula, north Queensland. *Oceania* 6, 452-477, 7, 69-105, 217-219.

McFarlane, S. (1888). *Among the Cannibals of New Guinea*. London: London Missionary Society.

Moore, D.R. (1972). Cape York Aborigines and Islanders of western Torres Strait. pp. 327-343 in Walker, D. *op. cit.*

Moore, D.R. (1979). *Islanders and Aborigines at Cape York*. Canberra: Australian Institute of Aboriginal Studies.

Moresby, J. (1876). *Discoveries and Surveys in New Guinea and the D'Entrecasteaux Islands*. London: Murray.

Murray, A.W. (1876). *Forty Year' Mission Work in Polynesia and New Guinea*. London: Nisbet.

Neitschmann, B. (1977). The wind caller. *Nat. Hist.* 86, 10-16.

Nix, H.A. and Kalma, J.D. (1972). Climate as a dominant control in the biogeography of northern Australia and New Guinea. pp. 61-91 in Walker, D. *op. cit.*

Phipps, C.V.G. (1970). Dating of eustatic events from cores taken in the Gulf of Carpentaria and samples from the New South Wales continental shelf. *Austr. J. Sci.* 32, 329-330.

Polach, H.A., McLean, R.F., Caldwell, J.R. and Thom, B.G. (1978). Radiocarbon ages from the northern Great Barrier Reef. *Phil. Trans. Roy. Soc. Lond. A*. 291, 139-158.

Richards, J.R. and Willmott, W.F. (1970). K-Ar age of biotites from Torres Strait. *Austr. J. Sci.* 32, 369.

Rosenfeld, A. (1975). Air to ground. *Hemisphere* 19, 21-25.

Russell, R.J. (1967). *River Plains and Sea Coasts*. Berkeley and Los Angeles: University of California Press.

Schodde, R. and Calaby, J.H. (1972). The biogeography of the Australo-Papuan bird and mammal faunas in relation to Torres Strait. pp. 257-300 in Walker, D. *op. cit.*

Scoffin, T.P. (1977). Sea level features on reefs in the northern province of the Great Barrier Reef. *Proc. 3rd Int. Coral Reef Symp., Miami* 2, 319-324.

Scoffin, T.P. and Stoddart, D.R. (1978). Nature and significance of microatolls. *Phil. Trans. R. Soc. Lond. B.* 284, 99-122.

Smith, S.V. and Kinsey, D.W. (1976). Calcium carbonate production, coral reef growth and sea-level change. *Science, N.Y.* 194, 937-939.

Stoddart, D.R. (1980). Mangroves as successional stages, inner reefs of the northern Great Barrier Reef. *J. Biogeogr.* 7, 269-284.

Street, F.A. (1981). Tropical palaeoenvironments. *Progress in Physical Geography* 5, 157-185.

Swan, B. (1979). The presence of sand dunes in a tropical low energy zone, Friday Island, Torres Strait (Australia). *Revue de Gomorphologic dynamique* 28, 61-72.

Thom, B.G. and Chappell, J. (1975). Holocene sea levels relative to Australia. *Search* 6, 90-93.

Thom, B.G., Orme, G.R. and Polach, H.A. (1978). Drilling investigations of Bewick and Stapleton Islands. *Phil. Trans. R. Soc. Lond. A.* 291, 37-54.

Thomson, D.F. (1933). The hero cult, initiation and totemism on Cape York. *J.R. Anthrop. Inst.* 63, 453-537.

Thomson, D.F. (1934). The dugong hunters of Cape York. *J.R. Anthrop. Inst.* 64, 237-262.

Tyler, M.J. (1972). An analysis of the lower vertebrate faunal relationships of Australia and New Guinea. pp. 231-256 in Walker, D. *op. cit.*

Van Andel, T.H. and Veevers, J.J. (1967). Morphology and sediments of the Timor Sea. *Bull. Bur. Miner. Resour. Geol. Geophys. Austr.* 83.

Van Andel, T.H., Heath, G.R., Moore, T.C. and McGeary, D.F.R. (1967). Late Quaternary history, climate, and oceanography of the Timor Sea, Northwestern Australia. *Amer. J. Sci.* 265, 737-758.

Vanderwal, R. (1973). The Torres Strait: protohistory and beyond. *Occasional Papers* 2, St. Lucia: Anthropology Museum, University of Queensland, pp. 157-194.

Van Steenis, C.G.G.J. (1950). The delimitation of Malaysia and its main plant geographical divisions. In: *Flora Malesiana Series 1, Spermatophyta Vol. 1.* (C.G.G.J. Van Steenis, ed.). Djarkarta: Noordhoff, pp. lxx-lxxv.

Veeh, H.H. and Green, D.C. (1977). Radiometric geochronology of coral reefs. In: *Biology and Geology of Coral Reefs, Vol IV: Geology 2* (O.A. Jones and R. Endean, eds). New York: Academic Press, pp. 183-200.

Veeh, H.H. and Veevers, J.J. (1970). Sea level at -175 m off the Great Barrier Reef 13,600 and 17,000 years ago. *Naure (Lond.)* 226, 536-537.

Verstappen, H.Th. (1975). On palaeoclimates and landform development in Malesia. In: *Modern Quaternary Research in Southeast Asia,* (G-J Bartstra and W.A. Casparie, eds). Rotterdam: Balkema, pp. 3-350.

Wace, N.M. (1972). Discussion on the plant geography around Torres Strait. pp. 197-211 in Walker, D. *op. cit.*

Walker, D. (ed.) (1972). *Bridge and Barrier: the Natural and Cultural History of Torres Strait.* Canberra: Australian National University, Department of Biogeography and Geomorphology.

Webb, L.J. and Tracey, J.G. (1972). An ecological comparison of vegetation communities on each side of Torres Strait. pp. 109-129 in Walker, D. *op. cit.*

Webster, P.J. and Streten, N.A. (1972). Aspects of late Quaternary climate in tropical Australasia. pp. 38-60 in Walker, D. *op. cit.*

Webster, P.J. and Streten, N.A. (1978). Late Quaternary Ice Age climates of tropical Australasia: interpretations and reconstructions. *Quaternary Research* 10, 279-309.

White, C. (1971). Man and environment in northwest Arnhem Land. In: *Aboriginal Man and Environment in Australia,* (D.J. Mulvaney and J. Golson, eds). Canberra: Australian National University Press, pp. 141-157.

White, J.P. (1971). New Guinea and Australian prehistory: the "Neolithic problem". In: *Aboriginal Man and Environment in Australia,* (D.J. Mulvaney and J. Golson, eds). Canberra: Australian National University Press, pp. 182-195.

White, J.P. (1972). Ol tumbuna: archaeological excavations in the eastern central highlands, Papua New Guinea. *Terra Australis* 2.

Whitehouse, F.W. (1963). The sandhills of Queensland - coastal and desert. *Proc. R. Soc. Qld.* 53, 1-22.

Whitehouse, F.W. (1973). Coral reefs of the New Guinea region. pp. 169-186 in Jones, D.A. and Endean, R., *op. cit.*

Willmott, W.F., Whitaker, W.G., Palfreyman, W.D. and Trail, D.S. (1973). Igneous and metamorphic rocks of Cape York Peninsula and Torres Strait. *Bull. Bur. Miner. Resour. Geol. Geophys. Austr.* 135.

Wright, R.V.S. (1971). Prehistory in the Cape York Peninsula. In: *Aboriginal Man and Environment in Australia* (D.J. Mulvaney and J. Golson, eds). Canberra: Australian National University Press, pp. 133-140.

Wyrtki, K. (1960). The surface circulation in the Coral and Tasman Seas. *C.S.I.R.O. Div. Fish. Oceanogr. Technical Papers* 8, 1-44.

Wurm, S.A. (1972). Torres Strait - a linguistic barrier? pp. 345-366 in Walker, D. *op. cit.*

PROBLEMS OF SITE FORMATION AND THE INTERPRETATION OF SPATIAL AND TEMPORAL DISCONTINUITIES IN THE DISTRIBUTION OF COASTAL MIDDENS

G.N. Bailey

Department of Archaeology,
University of Cambridge, Cambridge, UK

ABSTRACT

The presence or absence of shell middens, either above or below present sea level, may sometimes be used as evidence regarding human occupation of a coastal zone and the contemporary economic and cultural adaptation. Biasing factors can distort the representation of coastal occupation and subsistence by archaeologically surviving midden deposits. Gaps and discontinuities in the Pleistocene record are commonly considered in terms of post-depositional factors such as the erosion or burial of archaeological deposits. Two additional variables emphasized here are pre-depositional factors - (a) variation in the local availability and abundance of the marine molluscs that give bulk and visibility to midden deposits, and (b) shell discard behaviour. The second includes subsistence decisions related to other food resources and non-subsistence factors that may influence the location, frequency and spatial concentration of shell disposal. Two examples of geographical discontinuities in the distribution of shell middens are used to illustrate the complex interaction of these variables under specified environmental conditions. One example refers to Aboriginal shell mounds dated 1100 B.P. to 100 B.P. in a tropical estuarine environment of northern Australia, the other to Mesolithic shell middens dated 9000 B.P. to 7000 B.P. on the rocky shoreline of Cantabrian Spain. The results are used to clarify the issues of interpretation raised by apparent time trends and discontinuities, and to suggest specific lines of inquiry that may help to discriminate between competing hypotheses about temporal patterns.

QUATERNARY COASTLINES
ISBN 0 12 479250 2

INTRODUCTION

One of the major themes in human social evolution is the origins of agriculture, a development which is now widely accepted as having taken place more or less simultaneously in a number of areas throughout the world (Megaw, 1977; Reed, 1977). According to current views this was not a sudden development confined to the Holocene, but the culmination of a long process of intensification in hunter-gatherer subsistence economies extending well back into the late Pleistocene (Flannery, 1969; Higgs and Jarman, 1972; Cohen, 1977; Jarman, et al., in press). Intensification in this context is usually taken to mean a broadening of diet to include hitherto neglected food resources as well as the more intensive culling of existing food species. Developments in the late Pleistocene in their turn can be seen as the outcome of processes extending yet further back in time. These earlier processes include, above all, the expansion of hominid species from their sub-equatorial centres of origin to colonize new territories and ultimately new continents, a process which represents one of the other major themes in Pleistocene social evolution. Cohen (1977) has provided one of the most detailed expositions of the view that the whole record of Pleistocene prehistory should be seen as a coherent pattern of more or less continuous population expansion accommodated by progressive environmental and economic adaptations. The concept of late Pleistocene intensification is highly appealing, in the sense that it refers to a period that largely precedes the development of agriculture on the one side, and largely postdates or at any rate overlaps with the final stages of human colonization of the major habitable land masses on the other side. It is thus tempting to see in this set of chronological juxtapositions a series of causal relationships. However, the evidence for such a process of intensification is by no means unequivocal, while the theories by which such a process might be explained are likewise open to considerable controversy (Bailey and Sheridan, 1981). Some of the most suggestive evidence lies in the Quaternary record of coastal subsistence. The apparent evidence for progressive intensification of marine subsistence in the closing stages of the late Pleistocene (from at least as early as 20,000 B.P. onwards), followed by an "explosion" of evidence of coastal shell middens during the Holocene in many areas of the world, is well known (Bailey, 1978, in press (a); Binford, 1968; Klein, 1977; Osborn, 1977; Parkington, 1980; Perlman, 1980; Straus et al., 1980; Yesner, 1980). However, there are different ways in which this sequence can be interpreted.

According to one view, the sequence is genuine and reflects a world-wide intensification of coastal subsistence economies (part of the "broad spectrum revolution" of various authors). The sequence is accepted as a fact, and the main problem is then to find a satisfactory explanation in terms of changes in the natural environment, changes in human demographic pressure, or changes in social and economic organisation. Additional corroboration for this view might be seen in the progressive size decrease of mollusc shells in some late Pleistocene/Holocene archaeological sequences, which might indicate increased exploitation pressure (Klein, 1977; Straus *et al.*, 1980, 1981). However, it has not yet been demonstrated that these size changes could not equally well be explained as the result of environmental changes affecting the rate of shell growth (cf. Swadling, 1976, 1977).

A second view is that coastal middens of Pleistocene date, if they existed, have been obscured or destroyed by rising sea levels or other destructive agencies. Some evidence for this view may be seen in the long coastal sequences of African sites such as the Haua Fteah (McBurney, 1967) or Klasies River Mouth (Deacon, 1979). In both sites evidence of marine exploitation in the uppermost (Holocene) levels is matched by similar evidence in the basal deposits associated with a pre-glacial high sea-level stand. In the intervening period there is an absence of marine resources (at HF) or a hiatus of occupation (at KRM), which could be attributed to the lowering of sea level and the consequent removal of the shoreline to a distance beyond easy economic reach of the sites. However, the evidence at present available demonstrates only that some marine exploitation took place during the earlier period, not that it was of comparable intensity to Holocene exploitation levels, while the assumed continuity of exploitation patterns in the intervening period is necessarily speculative. Thus, on this second view, any decision about the "facts" of the situation should be deferred until exploration of submerged shorelines has been undertaken. If evidence exists, it must be submerged on the continental shelf (see Flemming, 1983, this volume).

Both the above views depend on assumptions about the relationship between human subsistence and settlement activity and the formation and preservation of the archaeologically visible remnants of that activity. The first view makes the simplistic equation that presence of coastal shell middens equals presence of intensive marine-oriented subsistence economies, absence of shell middens equals absence of such a subsistence economy. The second view makes no decision on this relationship at all.

I suggest that by looking at spatial variations and discontinuities in Holocene middens, where we have some control over the many variables involved, we can go some way towards understanding the factors that determine the location, formation and preservation of coastal middens as archaeologically visible deposits. I further suggest that this type of analysis can be used to aid in understanding occupation of submerged shorelines in the following three ways:

1)   it can provide uniformitarian projections about the general nature of Pleistocene coastal subsistence and settlement;

2)   it can give greater precision to the search for coastal middens on fossil shorelines, and perhaps help to realise one of the ultimate ideals of field archaeology, which is predictive site survey;

3)   it can provide a sharper focus on the environmental variables that are of particular importance in the resolution of archaeological problems.

As a preliminary it will be useful to group the factors that affect the formation and preservation of middens into three categories: (1) pre-depositional - since mollusc shells are the chief constituent giving bulk to midden deposits, considerations under this heading will be primarily concerned with variation in the productivity of intertidal and inshore habitats; (2) discard behaviour - this includes all the activities, both subsistence and non-subsistence, that may influence the location, frequency and spatial concentration of shell disposal; (3) post-depositional - factors of preservation, principally agencies of destruction such as erosion by wind, water, chemical action, mechanical disturbance or industrial activity, or agencies of burial such as sedimentation or marine submergence. Gaps and discontinuities in archaeological site distributions are commonly considered in terms of post-depositional factors of differential preservation or visibility. Here I want to emphasize the potential impact of pre-depositional and discard factors. The two areas examined below offer contrasting illustrations of the different ways in which the interaction of these variables can distort the spatial patterning of archaeologically surviving material. They refer to a tropical estuarine environment in northern Australia, and a temperate/cool-temperate rocky-shore environment in Europe.

THE CAPE YORK PENINSULA AUSTRALIA

General Features

About 500 shell middens have been recorded along the banks of the rivers that flow into Albatross Bay near Weipa (Fig. 1) (Bailey, 1977; Wright, 1971). The largest are steep-sided mounds up to 250 m x 50m in base area and 10 m high, easily visible on air photographs (see Plates 1 & 2). The smallest are surface scatters 3 m in diameter. Sites of many different sizes are found between these extremes. The deposits are uniformly constituted of densely packed shell amounting to a total 200,000 tonnes of material (Plate 3). About 95% by weight consists of the shells of the estuarine bivalve *Anadara granosa*. The deposits also contain ash remains of hearths, food remains of fish and terrestrial marsupials

PLATE 1. *Aerial view of Mission River estuary at Weipa. Large shell mounds are visible between the mangrove barrier and the woodlands on the left bank.*

PLATE 2. *Cluster of shell middens on the east bank of the Hey River, Weipa. Note large shell mound to left and smaller middens in the woodlands behind.*

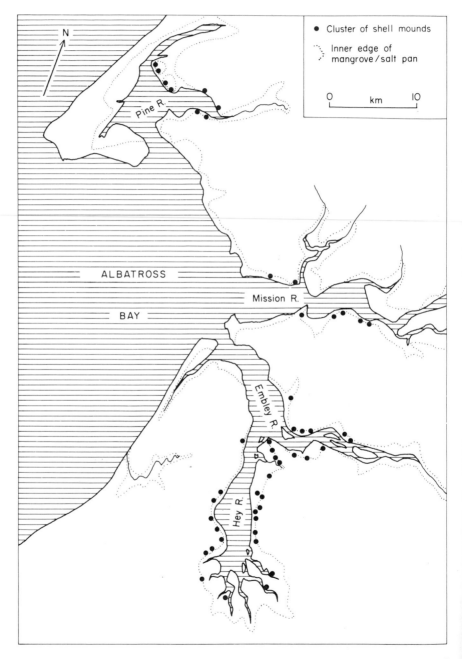

FIG. 1. *General distribution of shell middens at Weipa. Each circle represents a cluster of up to 30 individual middens.*

PLATE 3. *Close up of section through shell-midden deposit at Weipa.*

and artifacts - mainly microflakes of quartz derived from local outcrops, worked bone, and rare heavy-duty tools made on fine-grained volcanic material imported from up to 150 km away. Radiocarbon dates show that accumulation began about 1100 years ago. The sites were still in use at the time of European contact, indicating a total span of *ca.* 1000 years for the bulk of the shell accumulation. In the general features of their morphology, size, concentration and location, the Weipa mounds are comparable to those reported in other tropical areas such as the Andaman Islands (Cipriani, 1955), Brazil (Fairbridge, 1976) and Mexico (Shenkel, 1971).

In northern Australia similar shell mounds are known on parts of the Arnhem Land coast and on Milingimbi Island (Meehan, 1975; Mulvaney, 1975; Peterson, 1973), and there are recent reports of shell mounds on the east coast of Cape York Peninsula. Ground and air surveys have failed to reveal such sites elsewhere along the west coast of the Peninsula. Archaeological sites of any sort are rare. This is despite ethnographic evidence of established populations exploiting the full length of the coastline and living, as far as we can tell from imperfect sources, in comparable densities to the populations at Weipa. Shell mounds therefore appear in highly localized groupings and show a markedly discontinuous macro-geographical distribution.

Environment

The estuarine environment at Weipa is one of extensive shallow mudflats, where the *Anadara* are found, flanked by mangrove vegetation and seasonally flooded salt pans of varying width. (Plate 1). Inland is a gently sloping landscape of sand-capped laterite with an open woodland of sclerophyll or savannah type. The north-west monsoon creates a marked seasonal polarity between wet and dry conditions, with seasonally concentrated rainfall of $\geq$1000mm per annum and a mean annual temperature range of 15°C to 32°C. Some shell middens are located in the mangroves, on the salt pans or at the edge of the woodland. But the majority, and especially the large mounds, are on low-lying ground liable to seasonal flooding between the mangrove/salt pan formations and the woodland on higher ground. Some sediment has probably accumulated in the mangroves and on the salt pans since the middens were first occupied. But there is no basis for inferring from the distribution of the middens any substantial changes in the morphology of the river channels, the width of the mangrove barrier, or change in local relative mean sea level, during the past 1000 years. Although the sites are at varying distances from the present-day river banks, and some are behind mangrove barriers up to 3 km wide, all the sites would be easily accessible from the river by boat or canoe for all or most of the year, and especially during the wet season, when high tides and general flooding necessitate some form of water transport.

Subsistence

The radiocarbon dates and shell quantities give a rough measure of average annual shellfood output, which, in combination with approximate figures for local population density taken from ethnographic sources, suggests that molluscs would have supplied between about 5% and 15% of total caloric requirements. This agrees closely with Meehan's (1975, 1977) measurements of diet among modern Aborigines living in a similar environment in Arnhem Land. It is also consistent with archaeological and ethnographic evidence indicating a wide-ranging diet which included other marine foods, and terrestrial plants and animals, and which was associated with some degree of seasonal mobility. Populations probably dispersed throughout the hinterland during the dry season, forming localized aggregations around limited water supplies at the height of the dry season, and concentrated along coasts and around river estuaries during the wet season and the early part of the dry season, when marine foods would be generally abundant and easily accessible and movement in the hinterland would be restricted. The molluscs appear to have been important in this system of exploitation as a predictable day-to-day supplement and as a critical resource at the height of the wet season when other foods might be in short supply or difficult of access, because of bad weather.

Discontinuities in mound formation

Three factors are important here. The first is a preservational one. Suitable raw material for stone artifacts is scarce and the indigenous technology was strongly dependent on wood, bone and shell. Added to this is the prevalence of sandy soils, which provide a poor environment for the preservation of organic materials, including the discarded shells of food molluscs, except where the shells accumulate sufficiently rapidly or in sufficiently large and concentrated quantities to form an artificial matrix. Where the shells are deposited in small quantities or scattered as surface debris without a focus of concentration, they are more vulnerable to degradation or disappearance through physical disturbance and the chemical action of the surrounding soil.

The second factor is pre-depositional variation in the quantity of available molluscs. *Anadara granosa* is most abundant on shallow estuarine mudflats. The presence of mangroves also appears important, increasing the supply of organic nutrients that can be incorporated into the marine food chain. There is no doubt that, in terms of these features, the Weipa estuaries support a far more prolific supply of bivalves than any other river on the west coast. However, this can only be part of the explanation, since even the more limited quantities of molluscs in the smaller rivers might be expected to give rise to at least fairly substantial middens, if their shells were repeatedly deposited in the same spot. Abundant supplies of other edible and accessible molluscan species are available along the open coast, as is clear from the thick deposits of natural shell accumulations. Other marine and terrestrial resources are ample to ensure repeated human occupation along estuaries and sea shores generally.

A third factor is the particular pattern of shell discard at Weipa. The junction between terrestrial and alluvial sediments around the estuaries is an optimal zone for habitation, allowing equal access to marine and terrestrial resource zones, and is therefore likely to have served as a focus for people and their activities. There is also scope to vary the specific choice of camp-site location according to a number of micro-factors. The shell middens are often grouped in clusters, each cluster including one or more tall, substantial mounds on open ground, with smaller middens or surface scatters nearby at the edge of the woodland or on the salt pans and in the mangroves (Plate 3). This pattern is related to seasonal changes. In stormy weather during the wet season, shelter is sought amongst the trees. At other times during the wet season and especially when the rain ceases, the humidity and the affliction of insect pests cause camp sites to be shifted out onto open ground exposed to light breezes. Since the open ground is also likely to be waterlogged at this time, the ideal camp site would be on a slightly raised surface. As the ground gradually dries out during the dry season, sites may be located on a variety of surfaces in any convenient spot. Some of the biggest shell mounds are on sandy ridges forming the surface of old sand bars or beach ridges protruding through later alluvial deposits. These would have offered attractive "islands" of dry ground in the wet season, made progressively more attractive by each year's accumulations of shells. The ridges are often of limited extent, so that after a certain point the continued growth of the deposit would necessarily be upwards rather than outwards (Bailey, 1977; Peterson, 1973).

A unique combination of pre-depositional, discard and post-depositional factors have contributed to the prominence of the Weipa shell mounds. At face value the archaeologically surviving data might have been interpreted as evidence of a major concentration of prehistoric population, with an absence of occupation elsewhere along the coastline. The availability of ethnographic data as a control shows that this was clearly not the case.

CANTABRIA, SPAIN

General features

The mountainous coastline of Cantabrian Spain has yielded evidence of Palaeolithic and Mesolithic occupation from *ca.* 85 caves and rockshelters (Fig. 2), forming a composite sequence from >40,000 B.P. to <7,000 B.P. (Gonzalez Echegaray and Freeman, 1971, 1973; Straus, 1977). Remains of mollusc shells are present in varying quantity throughout this sequence. For most of the period the eustatic sea level was many tens of metres lower than at present. Species are mainly rocky shore types: limpets (*Patella spp.*), topshells (*Monodonta lineata*) and periwinkles (*Litorina littorea*). Concentrated midden deposits with dense masses of shells are not certainly present before the Holocene. At least 25 shell middens filling the mouths of caves are associated with the Asturian culture dated *ca.* 9000 B.P. to 7000 B.P. (Clark, 1971, in press; Straus, 1979). These deposits also contain bones of a variety of mammals (red deer - *Cervus elaphus* - being the most common), sea urchins, crabs and occasional fish bones, and artifacts - mainly picks, cobbles and waste flakes. The deposits were literally rubbish dumps, material being piled up to the cave roof, while the living and activity areas were elsewhere, presumably in front of the cave. Straus (1979) has plausibly argued that the Asturian artifact inventory is simply an activity

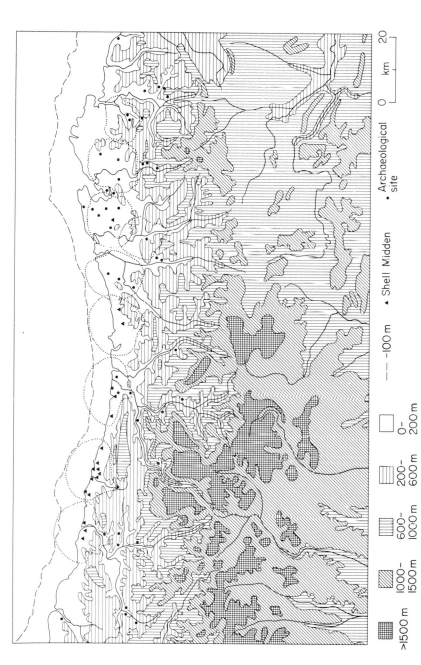

FIG. 2. *General map of the Cantabrian coastline, showing archaeological sites and topography in eastern Asturias (left) and Santander (right). Dotted boundaries around major coastal site clusters represent two-hour site exploitation territories, and indicate the maximum radius within which exploited food resources are likely to be transported in quantity back to a given site location.*

>1500 m   1000–1500 m   600–1000 m   200–600 m   0–200 m   — –100 m   ▲ Shell Midden   • Archaeological site

0   km   20

variant of the partly contemporaneous and partly preceding Azilian culture. Some shell middens are stratified above earlier deposits, notably at La Riera, where quantitative data clearly demonstrate the dramatic increase in rate of shell accumulation after 10,000 B.P. as compared with earlier periods (Straus *et al.*, 1980).

Along with the expected temporal discontinuity in the distribution of shell middens is a geographical one. The majority of the shell middens are clustered on the 60 km of narrow coastal plain in eastern Asturias. In the adjacent coastal sector of Santander, contemporaneous occupations are recorded along an equivalent length of coastline, but shell middens are largely absent, and the main focus of occupation is further inland. Sites nearer the shore line are known, but appear to have been visited infrequently or for limited and specific objectives such as the working of flint sources (Clark, 1979).

Environment

Cantabria is mainly limestone country with a coastal plain varying in width from about 5 km to 20 km, backed by a mountainous interior rising to a maximum of 2700 m only 25 km inland from the coastline in eastern Asturias. During the Asturian period the lowlands were quite heavily wooded and climatic conditions would have been similar to the present, with a mean temperature range of $8^{\circ}C$ to $21^{\circ}C$ and an evenly distributed annual precipitation of >1000 mm. During the maximum of the Last Glacial, mean temperatures were about $6^{\circ}C$ to $8^{\circ}C$ lower than the present, precipitation was about a third less, and the vegetation was open parkland or forest tundra (Butzer, 1971; Kopp, 1965). A lowered relative sea level of about 100 m would have effectively doubled the width of the coastal plain in many places. The general character of the present shoreline is one of alternating cliffs, sandy bays and narrow estuaries, and it is assumed that a similar overall pattern would have prevailed during the Last Glacial.

Subsistence and site location

In eastern Asturias the coastal plain is about 5 km wide at its widest and is backed by a steep range of coastal hills. Individual shell middens are at varying distances from the shore line, typically at least 1 km inland, but rarely further than 3 km. These locations would have been suitable for a diverse subsistence economy, with good access to the resources of the sea (molluscs, fish and crustaceans), the coastal plain (larger mammals and possibly plant foods), and the coastal hill ranges (ibex and chamois) (Clark, 1971; Straus, 1979). In addition the preferred sites - the sites used repeatedly or for long periods and with the greatest amount of remains - form clusters close to the mouths of narrow river valleys which allow easy access between the coastal plain and the intermontane valleys of the hinterland. Inland sites are known and are consistent with the hypothesis that access to hinterland resources, probably animals exploited on a seasonal basis, were an important determinant in the choice of coastal habitation sites (Bailey, 1973; Straus, 1979). This locational clustering of shell midden sites continues a pattern that was prevalent throughout the Palaeolithic occupation of the area.

In Santander the coastal plain is broader (10 km to 20 km) and coastal occupation and exploitation appears to have been generally at distances further than 5 km from the sea shore. Exploited food resources (apart from the relative rarity of marine remains) are similar to those in Asturias. There is also considerable continuity through time in faunal spectra. Slight differences in earlier periods include a shift of emphasis from bovids and equids to cervids at about 20,000 B.P., with more evidence of ibex and chamois hunting also. The relative influence of changes in environment and subsistence strategy is unclear (Bailey, in press (a), in press (b); Clark and Straus, in press).

Discontinuities in midden distributions

Neither pre-depositional nor preservational factors offer sufficient explanation in this case. Small-scale local variations in the availability and abundance of gastoropod molluscs are of course apparent. But there are no general differences between the shore lines of Asturias and Santander of sufficient magnitude to explain regional differences in midden distributions. Similarly environmental changes affecting the availability of molluscs on a scale that would account for the relative rarity of shell remains before about 10,000 B.P. are unlikely, although local variability resulting from changes in shore line morphology could have affected the representation of molluscan species at particular archaeological sites (cf. Shackleton and van Andel, 1980). Also cave sites near the sea shore are available in Santander as in Asturias and offer comparable conditions for the preservation and discovery of shell middens. An alternative explanation lies in varying patterns of shell discard in relation to factors of subsistence and site location.

In the following explanation, two assumptions are made: (1) that terrestrial rather than marine resources exercise the main "pull" (Jochim, 1976) on the location of major settlements. Preferred sites would tend to be located near the inner edge of the coastal plain with optimum access to the resources of the plain and the coastal hill ranges, and with strategic advantages for the observation and control of animal movements between coast and hinterland; (2) that frequency of shell deposition declines with increasing distance from the sea shore (regardless of the frequency

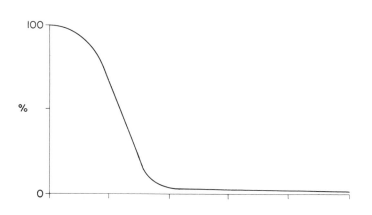

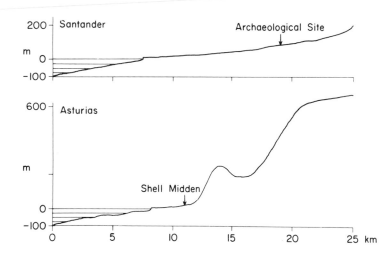

FIG. 3. *Schematic representation of site locations in relation to topography and distance from the shoreline. Upper: distance-decay curve for transportation of molluscs. Middle: the Santander coastline. Lower: the coastline in eastern Asturias.*

of shellgathering).   Theoretical considerations of the cost of carrying molluscs, combined with ethnographic observations and empirical studies of site location (Bigalke, 1974; Meehan, 1975; Bailey, 1978) suggest a fall-off curve as in Fig. 3. The curve is not precise and would vary according to the mollusc species and the method of transportation. But a sharp fall-off between about 5 km and 10 km seems widely applicable.

Figure 3 illustrates schematically the distance between the preferred sites and the sea shore in Santander and Asturias respectively. The additional variable of sea-level change is indicated by the position of the shoreline at the maximum regression ca. 18,000 B.P. (CLIMAP 1976). A figure of -100m is used here as a reasonable approximation (Bailey, in press (b)). In Santander even the modern sea shore is sufficiently far away that shellgathering, however intensive, would be unlikely to leave much impact in the form of shell debris carried back and deposited at the preferred settlements. Without the central pull of a preferred site close to the sea shore to concentrate refuse disposal, molluscs are likely to have been collected at many points along the shore line and consumed at a variety of convenient locations. Shell discard, in consequence, would have been dispersed in the form of numerous ephemeral deposits with relatively less chance of preservation or archaeological detection. Many of the discard points would now be submerged.

In eastern Asturias a similar hypothesis could apply to the period before about 10,000 B.P. when lowered sea level would have put the sea shore beyond easy economic reach of the preferred sites. Subsequent inundation of the coastal plain between 18,000 B.P. and 10,000 B.P. would have reduced the quantity of terrestrial resources accessible from the pre-existing site locations and might be expected to have caused a compensatory shift of settlement further inland, in accordance with assumption (1) above. However, such a move would have encountered the limiting effects of a steeply rising and mountainous hinterland, including a harsher winter climate and the loss of strategic control over animal movements to and from the coastal plain. Thus the pre-existing locations would have retained a relative advantage as bases for the exploitation of terrestrial resources in spite of rising sea level. The greater proximity of the shore line would have been an incidental feature, allowing an increased rate of shell discard at the preferred sites, but without necessarily implying any change in the intensity of mollusc exploitation.

The implication of the above hypothesis is that the level of mollusc collecting was essentially similar in earlier and later periods, and in eastern Asturias and Santander, in spite of apparent gaps in the surviving midden evidence. However, alternative hypotheses are possible. Straus et al. (1980,1981) have interpreted the increased rate of shell accumulation over time as evidence of resource intensification, possibly resulting from human population growth. A concomitant size decrease in Patella vulgata and an increased representation of the less easily accessible Patella intermedia, both suggestive of increased pressure on peripheral resources, are claimed in support. It is of course possible that a tendency towards intensification might have an effect on the representation of shell remains additional to that resulting from reduced distance to the sea shore with rising sea level. However, neither of the additional two indicators cited can as yet be regarded as decisive support for intensification. The interpretation of size changes in molluscs remains unproven for reasons mentioned earlier, while the increased representation of the less easily accessible limpet species might be a simple function of reduced distance or reflect minor changes in shoreline morphology. It might also be argued that the shell middens of the Holocene, being far more numerous than the sites occupied in earlier periods in the same region, provide evidence of population increase. However, this is also open to doubt since it could reflect a dispersed settlement pattern appropriate to a temperate woodland environment with diverse resources, as opposed to a nucleated settlement pattern more appropriate to hunting economies in the specialized environments of the Last Glacial period (cf. Gamble, 1978), without necessarily implying any change in population density. Finally, theoretical considerations might suggest that the inundation of the coastal plain, by reducing the availability of terrestrial resources on the coast, could have been a stress factor stimulating intensification of marine resource procurement. The hypothesis is appealing, because the coastal plain would almost certainly have been the most productive zone for mammal resources at all periods, and its areal extent is eastern Asturias would have been virtually halved between 18,000 B.P. and 10,000 B.P. However, the loss of land could have been compensated for by rising temperature and consequent opening up of the interior and a general increase in the productivity of the vegetation cover on a regional scale. Also the loss of land was a gradual process extending over 8000 years which is a long period in relation to human perceptions and demographic responses.

The evidence for intensification of marine resource exploitation then, is ambiguous in this area. Decisive evidence might most profitably be sought either in the search for coastal archaeological deposits of Last Interglacial date; or in the refinement of techniques for measuring the age-structure of mollusc shells as a guide to the intensity of their exploitation; or in the search for submerged caves or middens. For gastropods the most promising technique is the oxygen isotope analysis of seasonal growth increments, which is theoretically capable of supplying the required information, although a number of problems have yet to be resolved (Shackleton, 1973; Killingley and Berger, 1979; Killingley, 1981; Bailey *et al.*, in press (a)).

CONCLUSIONS

The implications of the above examples for our understanding of the long-term Pleistocene record can now be drawn together.

The first point to emphasize is that discontinuities in the distribution of coastal midden sites do not necessarily reflect discontinuities in subsistence or settlement. In both areas considered here a major factor in the archaeological visibility of the coastal middens is discard behaviour, and in particular the degree to which people tend to concentrate their disposal of rubbish rather than to disperse it. At Weipa I have suggested that an additional precondition is the availability of sufficient material to begin with, in the form of mollusc shells, to create a self-sustaining preservational matrix.

In the Weipa case, if we make the reasonable assumption that shell mounds would be formed wherever the appropriate pre-depositional and discard factors were operating, we should ask why shell mounds do not appear to have started accumulating before about 1100 years ago (assuming the chronology to be correct). The river estuaries were presumably present as an attractive focus for human settlement from an early period of the Holocene. One possibility is that it may have taken some thousands of years for sufficient sediment to accumulate to create the system of mudflats and mangroves that supports large quantities of bivalve molluscs today. The further implication is that in the Australian conditions described above, large shell mounds are only likely to be formed during a period of fairly stable sea level persisting for at least 5,000 to 6,000 years. Another possibility is that the fluctuations in Holocene sea level suggested by some lines of evidence (Fairbridge, oral communication) may have had an impact on the estuarine ecology and hence on the availability of bivalve molluscs. These are hypotheses, but in the Weipa area they are ones that in principle should be amenable to testing by coring and radiometric dating of the fluvial and estuarine sediments (see Kraft et al., 1983, this volume).

There is certainly no reason to suppose from the Weipa evidence that substantial shell middens would not have been accumulated on now submerged shorelines formed at earlier periods of the Pleistocene, given an appropriate coastal environment with stable estuarine conditions suitable for bivalve molluscs, easy accessibility of other marine and/or terrestrial food supplies in the near vicinity, and local surface features encouraging the repeated use of spatially restricted camp-site locations. The most recent curves of 0-18 variation in deep-sea sediment cores (Shackleton, 1977; Shackleton et al., in press) suggest that there would have been a number of relatively stable low sea-level stands of sufficient duration to provide the necessary preconditions for large shell-midden accumulations. These sea-level stands include the maximum regression (ca. 20,000 B.P. to 16,000 B.P.) as well as preceding interstadials of the last glacial period (Fig. 4). Another possibility for the discovery of early shell middens is the exploration of shorelines associated with former high sea-level stands, as for example at about 120,000 B.P. (Fig. 4). Any shell mounds of the Weipa-type formed during periods of lowered sea

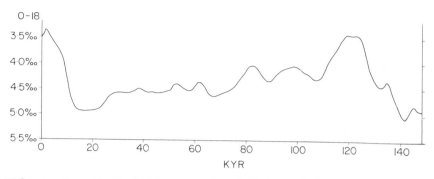

FIG. 4. *Smoothed 0-18 record of late Pleistocene deep-sea sediment from Pacific core V19-30. (After Shackleton et al., in press).*

level, by virtue of their location on the banks of river estuaries, are likely to have been protected in many cases from the full impact of wave erosion during inundation by rising sea level.

Moreover shell middens that survived initial inundation are likely to be in a state of preservation as good as if not better than their terrestrial counterparts. The latter are notoriously vulnerable to the destructive agencies of recent human activity, especially commercial and industrial digging. Identification of such submerged sites will obviously depend not only on suitable techniques of remote sensing but on detailed mapping and identification of submerged coastal environments.

In the Cantabrian case, the main conclusion is that major, repeatedly used settlement sites tend to be located in accordance with the principles of terrestrial exploitation, particularly hunting of herd animals such as red deer. In the European context this means that the large, favoured settlement sites with abundant evidence of human activity are likely to be located on the inner edge of the coastal plain, where valleys narrow as they enter more hilly or mountainous terrain. It is in these localities that people can make use of topographic restrictions to aid in the prediction and control of animal movements. In many coastal areas, as for example in northern Greece (Bailey *et al.*, in press (b)), this means that the largest sites tend to be in the hinterland, while sites nearer the coast, being in a more open and level landscape, are small and infrequently used. In other words the major archaeological settlements where people killed and consumed the animal food are asymmetrically located in relation to the major grazing territories where the animals spent most of their lives. This leads to the proposition that major shell-midden deposits would only occur where unusual topographic conditions happened to favour repeated and intensive occupation very close to the contemporaneous shoreline. It follows from this hypothesis that major sites of upper palaeolithic or last glacial date are unlikely to be found on the flat areas of the now submerged coastal plain, even though this exposed coastal plain, as a major grazing resource for herd animals, would have had an important impact on the subsistence economies of the time.

One might, however, suggest in the light of existing underwater discoveries, (Flemming, 1983, this volume) that the most suitable coastal areas to search for underwater caves and rockshelters with substantial occupation deposits would be those where steeply rising topography close to the present-day shoreline has resulted in drowned valleys, with steep valley sides plunging below the present sea level. These are areas where the postulated optimal zone for human occupation, namely at the inner junction of the coastal plain, is now submerged. Other possibilities would be to map the surface topography of the continental shelf in search of localized areas of more broken topography, with local hillocks and valleys suggesting the possibility of coralling herd animals or other features attractive to prolonged or repeated human settlement focused on terrestrial exploitation patterns.

This general conclusion would of course be subject to major modification if it were established that the general character of the shoreline during periods of lowered sea level was radically different from the steep rocky topography that prevails around much of the Mediterranean and the Iberian peninsula today. The presence of shallow coastal environments with broad river estuaries supplying abundant inshore marine resources, and capable of supporting densely populated and virtually self-sufficient coastal groups independently of the hinterland, would radically alter archaeological expectations about the potential nature of Pleistocene coastal settlement. Here, as elsewhere, mapping of submerged shoreline environments would seem to be an obvious next step in furthering an understanding of time trends in Pleistocene coastal settlement and subsistence.

ACKNOWLEDGEMENTS

I am grateful to Nic Shackleton for discussion of the 0-18 record in relation to sea-level change and for supplying the information for Fig. 4.

REFERENCES

Bailey, G.N. (1973). Concheros del norte de España: una hipótesis preliminar. *Actas del XII Congreso Nacional de Arqueologia*. 73-84.

578 G.N. Bailey

Bailey, G.N. (1977). Shell mounds, shell middens and raised beaches in the Cape York Peninsula. *Mankind* <u>11</u>, 132-143.

Bailey, G.N. (1978). Shell middens as indicators of postglacial economies: a territorial perspective. In: *The Early Postglacial Settlement of Northern Europe*. (P.A. Mellars, ed.), pp. 37-63. London: Duckworth.

Bailey, G.N. In press (a). Coasts, lakes and littorals. In: M.R. Jarman, G.N. Bailey and H.N. Jarman (eds).

Bailey, G.N. (ed.) In press (b). Economic change in late pleistocene Cantabria. In: *Hunter-Gatherer Economy in Late Pleistocene Europe* Cambridge University Press.

Bailey, G.N. and Sheridan, J.A. (1981). Ecological and social perspectives in economic archaeology. In: *Economic Archeology: towards an Integration of Ecological and Social Approaches* (J.A. Sheridan and G.N. Bailey, eds), pp. 1-13 Oxford: British Archaeological Reports, International Series, 96.

Bailey, G.N., Deith, M.R. and Shackleton, J.J. (In Press (a)). Oxygen isotope analysis and seasonality determination: limits and potential of a new technique. *American Antiquity*.

Bailey, G.N., Carter, P.L., Gamble, C.S. and Higgs, H.P. (In press (b)). Epirus revisited: seasonality and inter-site variation in the Upper Palaeolithic of north-west Greece. In: *Hunter-Gatherer Economy in Prehistory* (G.N. Bailey, ed.). Cambridge: University Press.

Biglake, E.H. (1974). The exploitation of shellfish by coastal tribesmen of the Transkei. *Annals of the Cape Provincial Museums, Natural History* <u>9</u>, 159-175.

Binford, L.R. (1968). Post-Pleistocene adaptations. In: *New Perspectives in Archeology* (S.R. Binford and L.R. Binford, eds), pp. 313-341. Chicago: Aldine.

Butzer, K. (1971). *Environmental Archeology*, 2nd edn. Chicago: Aldine.

Cipriani, L. (1955). Excavations in Andamanese Kitchen-middens. *Actes du IV Congrès International Scientifique, Anthropologique et Ethnologique* <u>2</u>, 250-253.

Clark, G.A. (1971). The Asturian of Cantabria: subsistence base and the evidence for Post-Pleistocene climatic shifts. *American Anthropologist* **73**, 1244-1257.

Clark, G.A. (1979). Liencres, an open station of Asturian affinity near Santander, Spain. *Quaternaria* **21**, 249-286, 300-304.

Clark, G.A. (In press). Boreal phase settlement/subsistence models for Cantabrian Spain. In: *Hunter-Gatherer Economy in Prehistory*. Cambridge: (G.N. Bailey, ed.). University Press.

Clark, G.A. and Straus, L.G. (In press). Late Pleistocene hunter-gatherer adaptations in Cantabrian Spain. In: *Hunter-Gatherer Economy in Prehistory*. Cambridge: (G.N. Bailey, ed.). University Press.

CLIMAP (1976). The surface of the Ice-Age Earth. *Science* **191**, 1131-1144.

Cohen, M.N. (1976). *The Food Crisis in Prehistory*. New Haven and London: Yale University Press.

Deacon, J. (1979). *Guide to Archaeological Sites in the Southern Cape*. Occasional Publications of the Department of Archaeology, University of Stellenbosch.

Fairbridge, R.W. (1976). Shellfish-eating Preceramic Indians in coastal Brazil. *Science* **191**, 353-359.

Flannery, K.V. (1969). Origins and ecological effects of early domestication in Iran and the Near East. In: *The Domestication and Exploitation of Plants and Animals* (P.J. Ucke and G.W. Dimbleby, eds), pp. 73-100. London: Duckworth.

Gamble, C.S. (1978). Resource exploitation and the spatial patterning of hunter-gatherers: a case study. In: *Social Organisation and Settlement* (D. Green *et al.*, eds), 153-185. Oxford: British Archaeological Reports, International Series (Supplementary), 47.

González Echegaray, J. and Freeman, L.G. (eds.) (1971). *Cueva Morin: Excavaciones 1966-1968*. Santander: Publicaciones del Patronato de las Cuevas de la Provincia de Santander.

González Echegaray, J. and Freeman, L.G. (eds.) (1973). *Cueva Morín: Excavaciones 1969*. Santander: Publicaciones del Patronato de las Cuevas de la Provincia de Santander.

Higgs, E.S. and Jarman, M.R. (1972). The origins of animal and plant husbandry. In: *Papers in Economic Prehistory* (E.S. Higgs, ed.), pp. 3-13. London: Cambridge University Press.

Jarman, M.R., Bailey, G.N., and Jarman, H.N. (eds) (In press). *Early European Agriculture: its Foundations and Economic Development*. Cambridge University Press.

Jochim, M.A. (1976). *Hunter-Gatherer Subsistence and Settlement*. New York: Academic Press.

Killingley, J.S. (1981). Seasonality of mollusc collecting determined from 0-18 profiles of midden shells. *American Antiquity* **46**, 152-158.

Klein, R.G. (1977). The ecology of early man in southern Africa. *Science* **197**, 115-126.

Kopp, K.O. (1965). Límite de la nieve perpétua y clima de la época glaciar Wurmiense en la Sierra de Aralar (Guipúzcoa-Navarra). *Munibe* **17**, 3-20.

McBurney, C.B.M. (1967). *The Haua Fteah (Cyrenaica) and the Stone Age of the South-east Mediterranean*. Cambridge University Press.

Meehan, B. (1977). Man does not live by calories alone: the role of shellfish in a coastal cuisine. In: *Sunda and Sahul* (J. Allen et al eds), pp. 493-531. London: Academic Press.

Megae, J.V.S. (eds) (1977). *Hunters, Gatherers and First Farmers beyond Europe*. Leicester University Press.

Mulvaney, D.J. (1975). *The Prehistory of Australia,* (revised edition). London: Penguin.

Osborn, A.J. (1977). Strandloopers, mermaids, and other fairy tales: ecological determinants of marine resource utilization - the Peruvian case. In: *For Theory Building in Archaeology* (L.R. Binford, ed.), pp. 157-205. New York: Academic Press.

Parkington, J.E. (1980). Time and place: some observations on spatial and temporal patterning in the later Stone Age sequence in southern Africa. *South African Archaeological Bulletin* **35**, 73-83.

Perlman, S.M. (1980). An optimum diet model, coastal variability and hunter-gatherer behavior. In: *Advances in Archaeological Method and Theory, Vol.3* (M.B. Schiffer, ed.), pp. 257-310. New York: Academic Press.

Peterson, N. (1973). Camp-site location among Australian hunter-gatherers: archaeological and ethnographic evidence for a key determinant. *Archaeology and Physical Anthropology in Oceania* 8, 173-193.

Reed, C.A. (ed.). (1977). *Origins of Agriculture,* The Hague: Mouton.

Shackleton, J.C., and van Andel, T.H. (1980). Prehistoric shell assemblages from Francthi Cave and evolution of the adjacent coastal zone. *Nature* 288, 357-359.

Shackleton, N.J. (1973). Oxygen isotope analysis as a means of determining season of occupation of prehistoric midden sites. *Archaeometry* 15, 133-141.

Shackleton, N.J. (1977). The oxygen isotope stratigraphic record of the late Pleistocene. *Philisophical Transactions of the Royal Society of London,* Series B, 280.

Shackleton, N.J., Imbrie, J. and Hall, M.A. (In press). Oxygen and carbon isotope record of core V19-30 implications for the formation of deep water in the Late Pleistocene North Atlantic.

Shenkel, J.R. (1971). *Cultural Adaptation to the Mollusc: a Methodological Survey of Shellmound Archaeology and a Consideration of the Shellmounds of the Marismas Nacionales, West Mexico.* Unpublished Ph.D. thesis, State University of New York at Buffalo.

Straus, L.G. (1977). Of deerslayers and mountain men: paleolithic faunal exploitation in Cantabrian Spain. In: *For Theory Building in Archaeology,* (L.R. Binford, ed.), pp. 41-76. New York: Academic Press.

Straus, L.G. (1979). Mesolithic adaptations along the coast of northern Spain. *Quaternaria* 21, 305-327.

Straus, L.G., Clark, G.A., Altuna, J. and Ortea, J.A. (1980). Ice-Age subsistence in northern Spain. *Scientific American* 242, 142-152.

Straus, L.G., Altuna, J., Clark, G.A., Gonzalez Morales, M., Laville, H., Leroi-Gourhan, Arl., Menendez de la Hoz, M. and Ortea, J.A. (1981).   Paleology at la Riera (Asturias, Spain). *Current Anthropology* 22 (6), 655-682.

Swadling, P. (1976).   Changes induced by human exploitation in prehistoric shellfish populations. *Mankind* 10, 156-162.

Swadling, P. (1977).   The implications of shellfish exploitation for New Zealand prehistory. *Mankind* 11, 11-18.

Wright, R.V.S. (1971).   Prehistory in the Cape York Peninsula.   In: *Aboriginal Man and Environment in Australia* (D.J. Mulvaney and J. Golson, eds), pp. 133-140.   Canberra: A.N.U.

Yesner, D.R. (1980).   Maritime hunter-gatherers, ecology and prehistory. *Current Anthropology* 21(6), 727-750

THE WOAKWINE TERRACE IN THE SOUTH EAST OF SOUTH AUSTRALIA AND INDICATIONS OF THE VERY EARLY PRESENCE OF MAN

Norman B. Tindale

*2314 Harvard Street, Palo Alto,
California 94306, USA; Honorary Associate in
Anthropology and Biology, South Australian Museum,
Adelaide, Australia*

ABSTRACT

First indication of the possible presence of man in South Australia in the early part of the Wisconsinan Glacial came with the excavation, by T. McCourt, at depth on the foreshore of the Woakwine Terrace, of a classic Kartan phase side-pebble chopping tool, made of transported volcanic rock (Tindale, 1968). Recently while clearing virgin land on the seaward front of the same terrace he found a further tool. This gave additional support to an early date for man's occupation of the area.

As early as 1919, implements which have come to be known as Kartan had been found at Fulham, near Adelaide, in South Australia, on an old land surface below marine deposits which can be linked with the Flandrian rise of sea level. Other sites of the Kartan culture phase have become known elsewhere, for example, at Hallett Cove and extensively on Kangaroo Island.

This paper discusses the earlier and later discoveries in the light of indications that stone implements found at Lake Mungo, in New South Wales, and dated to *ca*. 32,000 B.P., are to be identified with a culture phase considered by this author as Early Tartangan, and thus to post-date the Kartan phase.

Recent advances in the dating of the Woakwine II terrace, lying on the south eastern shore of South Australia, show clearly that the terrace shoreline lay at a level 25 feet above present day sea

584   N.B. Tindale

level, with an earlier level (Woakwine I) at 29 feet. Evidence of
the two successive stillstands is revealed in the artificial section
afforded by the drainage channel which now cuts across the
Woakwine Range west of Millicent.

Indications are thus forthcoming that the occupation of this part
of Australia may have already begun close to an Early Wisconsinan
date not far less than 100,000 years ago.

INTRODUCTION

First hint of a link between the eustatic events which led to the
formation of the Woakwine Terrace and the presence of early
aboriginal man in South Australia came with the excavation by
Tom McCourt, of Beachport, South Australia, of a classic Kartan
side-pebble chopping tool made from a basaltic rock
(Tindale, 1968) on the foreshore deposits of this terrace at a depth
of 1.5 meters. Recent clearing and ripping with a bulldozer, by
McCourt, of land being prepared for pine tree plantings, revealed
a second tool on the seaward foot of this "Range" near a dry
limestone formation which appears to have been of an old spring
such as develops at sea level in the karst country of the Southeast
of South Australia. This dead spring is on the northern boundary
of Section 180, Hundred of Symon, and situated approximately one

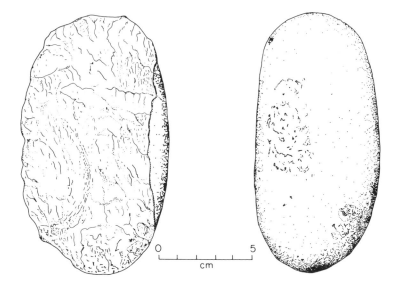

FIG. 1. *Kartan type side-pebble chopping tool with evidence
of use as a hammerstone. From excavation in foreshore
deposits of Woakwine Terrace, South Australia. Specimen is
A.55936 in the South Australian Museum, Adelaide.*

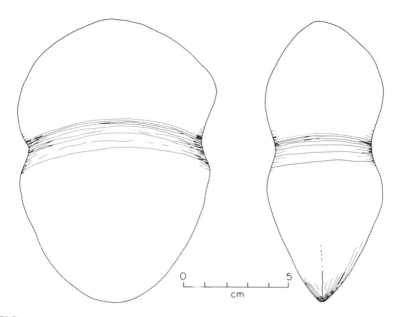

FIG. 2. *Axehead from Section 180, Hundred of Symon, South Australia. Specimen is in the T. McCourt Collection, Beachport, South Australia.*

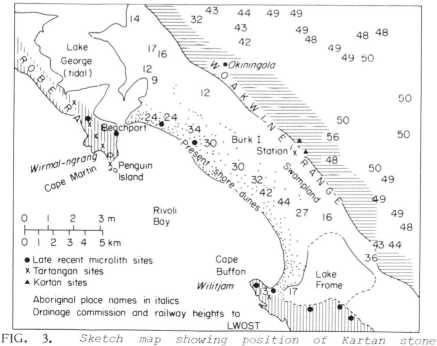

FIG. 3. *Sketch map showing position of Kartan stone implements found along the Woakwine Range, South Australia.*

kilometer away from the stockyard site at "Burk Island" Homestead where the original specimen was excavated. Unlike the side-pebble chopping tool the new find is of a grooved axe of the early type (Fig. 2) which has come to be linked with other Kartan phase implements on many sites in Australia. This specimen is in the Tom McCourt collection.

In the past fifty years considerable attention has been paid to the stratigraphic sequence of older shore line terraces preserved on the karst plateau of the South East, and more recently radiocarbon determinations have established that the latest lines of such shore dunes come within the time interval when Australian aboriginal man was present. A useful summary of recent geological work on the South East is provided by Cook *et al*. (1977). Figure 3 indicates the vicinity of the Woakwine Range and some places discussed herein.

On the Robe Range, a kilometer and more nearer to the sea than the Woakwine, *terra rossa* soils cover calcareous indurated sand dunes and reveal buried hearths containing stone implements. At Cape Martin, hearths have been dated to the earliest Recent time. This cape has, by erosion from the sea, lately become Martin Island. Many sites exist, some extending for many kilometers inland. The implements are of the Tartangan phase, widespread in the southern half of Australia from at least 32,000 to 5,000 B.P., and surviving into the ethnographic present in Tasmania. There are also recognisable elements of it still preserved in the living stone-working industries of the western part of the Great Western Desert, as among the Nakako and Pitjandjara folk as well as among people of several tribes in the north west of Western Australia (Tindale, 1964, 1965).

A persistent tool of the Tartangan phase is the sometimes relatively large discoidal flake knife, known to the Nakako and several other tribes as *tjimari*. Characteristically, when fully developed in use this tool presents a cutting edge on one side and a haft covering the opposite edge. As found archaeologically the cutting edge registers evidence that starting from a sharp, not secondarily knapped edge, it has been hammer-knapped and subjected to the removal of very fine flakes. The process may have been repeated so that in a much used knife it presents a smoothly curved margin. In strong contrast the opposite edge remains either entirely unworked or has been at most cursorily shaped, the better to accommodate the handle of resin, or in some areas among still living peoples it may be provided with a handle composed of a plastic composition of gum, often mixed with fibre, hair, or even lime sand. The basic reason for the disparity in degree of working of parts of the implement, as observed in the living culture, is that first effort in preparation is devoted to fixing a haft to cover the margin judged to be less effective in use. Only then may the sharper flake edge receive attention, sometimes if already sharp, only after some period of use. To retain the smooth cutting margin the special technique known as "rolling pressure" from a smooth hard stone is so often applied as to be a general characteristic of developed Tartangan tools (Tindale, 1982, in press).

THE KARTAN PHASE

Evidence indicates that the Tartangan phase was preceded by a highly distinctive one using a wide range of large core tools, as well as many simple flakes. These tools have come to be known as the Kartan phase of prehistoric aboriginal culture (Tindale, 1941:45). The term was derived from the Ramindjeri mainland aboriginal name, Karta, for Kangaroo Island where the first detailed study of the industry was made and an inkling gained as to its possible antiquity (Tindale and Maegraith, 1931).

As discussed in a recent summary (Tindale, 1981) surface finds of Kartan phase implements have been noted widely in all of the States of Australia and in Tasmania, and its content is being enriched as more material comes to hand. In the type area of Kangaroo Island, additional tool types await description and now more than one hundred habitation sites have been noted by field workers. Following is a list of some of the many Australian mainland and Tasmanian sites which have been recorded in the literature or are represented by series in the South Australian Museum collections. New sites are constantly being noted. On the Tasmanian mainland specimens have been noted at St. Helens (Tindale, 1937), and one at Carlton (Tindale, 1981, 77. Fig. 4), as well as on Flinders and Cape Barren Islands (Tindale, 1941) and recently on remote King Island (Jones, 1979). In New South Wales the Wellington area has many sites based on the field activities of Norman Blunden, while Tooloom has yielded a series to John Calaby. Other sites such as Rylstone, Lake Menindee, and Brewarrina, can be mentioned. A single side-pebble chopping tool was discovered in the lowest layer in the Noola Rockshelter. This layer is undated, but earlier than 11,600 B.P. (Tindale, 1981, Fig. 11).

In Queensland Bootra, Betoota, and Monamona have yielded specimens. In the Northern Territory Erldunda; in Western Australia Calligillup, Cosmo-Newbery, Laverton, Meekatharra, Moolabulla, Nicholson Station, Roebourne, Yarrie, and Flora Valley all yielded specimens on surface sites to members of the U.C.L.A. and Adelaide Universities Anthropological Expedition during 1952-54. The specimens are in the South Australian Museum collection. There is a distribution map in Tindale (1981: Fig. 3).

Some noteworthy localities in South Australia include Balcoracana, Lake Bumbunga, Mount Remarkable, Moolawatana, Port Augusta, Warnertown, Wakefield River, Islington, Noarlunga,

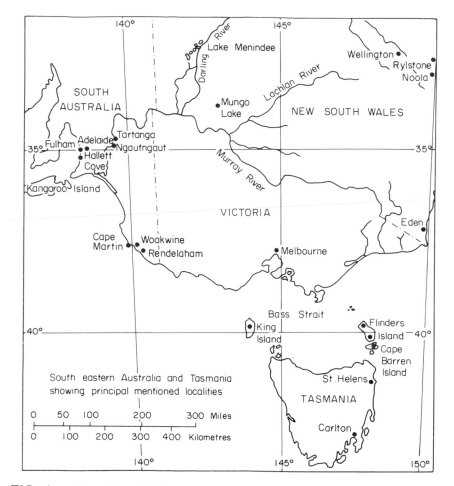

FIG. 4. *Key localities mentioned in the discussion on the Kartan and Tartangan sites of south eastern Australia and Tasmania.*

Hallett Cove, Moana, Cape Jervis, Fulham, and Woakwine Range. Figure 4 shows some of the key sites in southeastern Australia and in Tasmania.

The Fulham site was probably the first in Australia in which stone tools were discovered by excavation and found to be definitely linked with a land surface overlain with marine deposits. William White, one of South Australia's early pioneers dug an artificial lake at the Reedbeds, inland from the coastal dunes at Fulham. Marine deposits underlay the present-day surface, and below the marine sediments an older land surface was revealed and discovered to bear stone tools (White, 1919; Howchin, 1919). The suite of implements, which are in the South Australian Museum, were subsequently identified as belonging to the Kartan or earliest so-far-determined phase of Australian implement culture (Tindale, 1937, Figs 11-16).

An important work by R. Lampert (1981) has just become available, based on a decade of study and fieldwork on Kangaroo Island, South Australia. His detailed and fascinating study shows clearly that the Kartan Phase tools found so widely on the island fell out of use before the end of the Pleistocene, and the tools left by those people who remained into the Early Recent, before becoming extinct, used other and generally relatively poorly fashioned tools. Since it had not been possible to find suitable dating evidence the age of Kartan occupation was not established.

Another site of the Kartan phase which has proved of significance was discovered by Harold M. Cooper on a high sloping plateau surface at Hallett Cove, south of Adelaide and overlooking the sea. Implements similar to those from Fulham were present over an area now known to exceed 1.5 square kilometers (Tindale, 1937). Deep water immediately off shore indicates that the site had remained a potential coastal camping place during a cold phase or phases of the Last Glaciation. Considering the generally shallow shorelines surrounding most of Australia, this is perhaps a unique situation. Unfortunately, as usual with Kartan sites, associated organic occupational debris has long since disappeared.

Hindsight allows us to see that the Kartan tool suites, wherever found, had a consistency which argued for a long-time sharing of a tool tradition. From the very beginning of such finds their locations registered indications of a considerable, even Pleistocene antiquity, but efforts to be conservative with dates seem to have permitted a certain myopic attitude towards such a view. As it turns out far too little time was being allowed for the long sequence of happenings in the prehistory of Australia. Today evidence for a longer view appears increasingly significant.

SPATIAL PATTERNS AND CONTENT OF OPEN AIR SITES

It may be useful to note a few of the seeming leads which have been virtually ignored, especially during the time when only excavated sections in caves and rockshelters were being considered useful in developing an archaeological sequence in Australia. Perhaps it should have been evident from the behaviour of present-day aborigines that in their choice of living places caves are seldom used as dwellings. Caves serve only as temporary refuges when unexpected rains have washed out their fires and they are attempting to either strike new fire from their flints or generate it by friction of dry woods. Thus remains in caves would not often register the normal range of tool assemblages. Failure to evaluate the many open air sites can result in the loss of much ecological information.

Experienced students of surface sites discover that on open campsites of the near past, for example those of the last millennium or so, identified in many parts of Australia as of the so-called Murundian phase, hearths are still commonly intact, bone, even almost whole skulls of small animals killed and eaten are present and the shells often still retain their nacre, and even on occasion their hinges. In contrast in the earliest microlith tool horizon, the Pirrian of the Mid-Recent, such relics of shell food usually have been altered by time with loss of all traces of nacre, while bony remains usually are of more solid portions such as part jaw bones, often charred by fire, and teeth, along with the earliest geometric microliths. Such tools and armatures of weapons often have begun to show surface changes or patina, except those of quartzites which seemingly remain unchanged. On Late Pleistocene and Early Recent sites that are characterized by the long-lasting Tartangan phase, which had its beginning more than thirty millennia ago, remains such as hearths generally preserve only mere traces of food shells, and even charcoal often is reduced to an impalpable powder, as at Cape Martin on one dated to near 8,700 B.P. (Tindale, 1957, p. 119). Sometimes in other situations with perhaps possibilities of different past microclimates, as at Lake Menindee, a Tartangan site dated to 18,800 ± 800 B.P. (GaK -335 in Tindale, 1964) the charcoal still retained some structure.

As briefly mentioned above in the case of Hallett Cove, none of the Kartan open air sites which this author has studied show even traces of food remains, in this way perhaps registering their antiquity as beyond that of Tartangan sites.

One of my field associates, Norman Blunden, has found surface sites in western New South Wales of each of the phases which have been mentioned in this paper. Under the past local climates he has noted that the choice of camping places in many, if not in most cases, had fallen on different localities or positions. This had been particularly the case with the many and widely distributed Kartan sites. Ploughing activities have brought to the surface large numbers of buried core implements and other tools. Except in one place, which happens to be the Station on which he was brought up as a child, the Kartan sites proved to be in places not favoured by people of later culture phases. An important inference is that the Kartan phase activities must have taken place under somewhat different climatic conditions, when greater dispersal was easier than in later times when camping places tended to be placed closer to obvious water sources.

If we narrow attention down to sites near coastal areas, we find that the late N.H. Louwyck provided a useful key to the

understanding of the sequence of tool types to be found there, a
lead which may be of significance in the interpretation of the
Woakwine finds. Louwyck (personal communications) devoted much
attention in the early 1930s to studying aboriginal surface sites in
the fertile Hindmarsh Valley which runs down to the coast of
St. Vincent Gulf in the Yankalilla district of South Australia, and
found that the latest Murundian camping sites and their implement
relics were in areas well inland as well as close to the sea in the
present shore dunes. They were recognisable by their relatively
abundant food remains as well as by their crudely made, often
notched flake tools, and also pebble-end chopping tools. He also
had learned that there were other sites with well-formed
geometric microliths sometimes mixed in with the later ones when
deflation of the sand dunes had occurred but on some sites without
such. He had learned that the sites with the well-formed
geometric microliths extended no nearer to the shore than
secondary dunes situated up to about 0.5 of a kilometer inland, and
that one had to go still further inland, beyond the dunes which we
now regard as Peronian, before one could find the *pirri* projectile
points that are the marker implements of the Pirrian phase, and
thus the earliest of the microlith implement suites. The Peronian
Terraces, as defined by Fairbridge (1958), comprise in Australia a
dual series of shore dunes at three meters above present sea level
and radiocarbon dated to between about 5,000 and 3,800 B.P.

Fieldwork over half a century in the South East has revealed
sites which match the several named horizons found in the early
excavations at Tartanga and Ngautngaut (the present official name
of the Devon Downs rockshelter site) by Hale and Tindale (1930).
The earliest of these, the Tartangan, is abundantly represented by
archaeological sites throughout the South East. Extending in
favorable places far inland these sites extend no nearer to the sea
than the Robe Range, where it happens that the latest date for an
excavated site is close to 8,700 B.P. (Tindale, 1957). They are not
present anywhere seaward of the Three Meter (Peronian) Terraces
nor on the dunes which form the terrace. On the other hand the
Small Tool phase implements called Mudukian, which are later in
date, are present on seaward sites in favorable places. Further
inland they are also abundantly present, of course, and on deeply
eroded sites such as at Kongorong they form a distinct stratum
above the Tartangan horizon. Tools of the Mudukian horizon made
of the blue-black flint of MacDonnell Bay, unlike the implements
from the most recent camps, already show some chemical changes
leading to a distinctly whitish patina. The Tartangan implement
flakes and other tools in the same area have through time
undergone far greater chemical alterations and the originally black
flint appears bright yellow or almost an orange-colour which, even
in buried layers, often displays different degrees of change on the
upper and lower surfaces. Some knife flakes from the 8,700 B.P.

horizon at Cape Martin already markedly show these changes. In other sites not yet adequately studied but considered much older, the alterations have proceeded so far as to reduce all except a small part of the core to a form of chalk, without damage to the original shape of the implement. Some of these sites will almost certainly be found to date well back into the Late Pleistocene. The rise on which the Burk Island homestead is placed has a well-defined Tartangan site upon it, one determined probably by its elevation above the former marine and later lacustrine environs.

Turning now to the Kartan tools, we note that these have been recovered in association with the Woakwine Terrace in the manner noted at the beginning of this paper. No examples have been found in any situation nearer to the present shore line in the South East, where many sites have been examined over a local area which probably exceeds 200 square kilometers of Post-Woakwine terrace land surface. There is a possible terminal date for Kartan occupation sites in southeastern Australia following the last phase of the high sea interval registered by the foreshore deposits of the Woakwine II Terrace. Any possible seaward campsites have been swept away by the seas of the 25 foot terrace or are concealed below horizons upon which Tartangan deposits occur nearer to the present seashore.

If the possibility outlined above is accepted as a working hypothesis, there are recent studies which give a lead as to the time when the later Woakwine Terrace shoreline deposits may have been developed. Von der Borch *et al.* (1980) have indicated that events along this terrace occurred just before or perhaps during the earliest phase of the Last or Wisconsinan Glacial Period. Their study was made along a section through the "Range" extending inland from near Robe, and thus at a point some 40 kilometers north from Burk Island Homestead. Employing the amino acid racemization technique their Sample B yields an age of around 92,000 years for deposits linked with what appears to be a late phase of the Terrace. This perhaps can be regarded as Woakwine II. Their Sample C, obtained still further inland, may be considered to correspond in age to Woakwine I; and thus "to the maximum high-sea level stand during the last interglacial period (i.e. Stage 5e in the 0-18/0-16 palaeo-temperature curve), 125,000 B.P." (*op. cit.* p. 169.)

According to these authors there is some general support for the dates in results reported by Bloom *et al.* (1974) connected with high sea levels, in the vicinity of 85,000 and 105,000 years B.P.

Such an early Wisconsinan date for the possible presence of aboriginal man in Australia has important inferences even for South East Asia and at first sight may seem far out of line. It could indeed be far from accurate since the dating of the Early Wisconsinan is still under review. Future undersea exploration may give an answer since most of the shoreline activities of man have been hidden from us by the profound changes wrought by sea level shifts. However the evidence given above does suggest the distinct possibility of man having already made Australia his home in some phase of the earlier part of the Wisconsinan that is marked by the high sea level known as Woakwine II.

DISCUSSION

Evidence for the development of modern men points to warmer latitudes of the great Euro-Asiatic and African supercontinent of Pleistocene times as their original home. Only at a very late

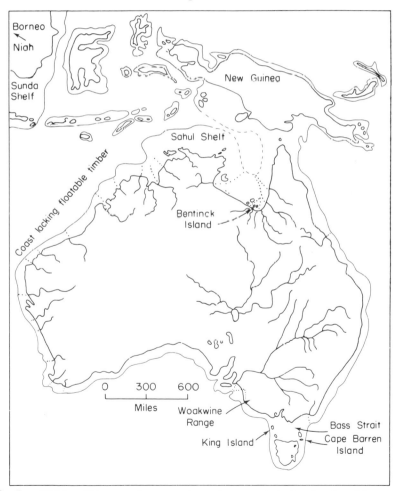

FIG. 5. *Early Wisconsinan extensions of islands leading from Asia to Australia and Tasmania.*

stage in his history was man able to extend his domain to outlying continental areas such as Australia and the Americas. Archaeologists have interest in learning at what time in the past some men developed sufficient skill to be able to cross water barriers and so began to exploit the land areas of Australia. Figure 5 suggests the extended shorelines of islands leading to Australia at a time in the early part of the Wisconsinan I period of cold.

That the Australian was a creature of the Asian tropics seems clearly indicated by the studies of W.V. Macfarlane (1976, 1980). He demonstrates that the aborigines in their physiology still reflect the characteristics of men of the tropics, although the representatives he tested are the offspring of ones who have lived in the largely desertic environment of Australia for thousands of years.

Since water gaps have always existed between Sunda and Sahul it is evident that Sunda people, perhaps shore-dwelling and foraging folk, had to have developed minimal skills, at least, before they were able to shift, island by island, across Wallacea, the Malay archipelago. It would have been much easier to do this at a time of low sea level than during warmer periods when seas were higher and water gaps were at a maximum.

Times of climatic change, perhaps bringing pressures from displaced peoples in South East Asia may have been an activating force on more than one occasion in the peopling of Australia. Data gathered both by physical anthropologists and by those interpreting the succession of material culture relics present in Australia, have encouraged views that people made that crossing more than once. The first occasion may well have been in an early part of the Wisconsinan Glaciation. The earlier and the later intensely cold glacial maxima both were possible times.

According to Birdsell (1941) there may have been three such appearances successively involving a Barrinean negritoid, a Murrayian Australoid, and a later-coming Carpentarian folk. Although some have questioned his theory, it is now known that a gracile type, as at Lake Mungo, similar to the type represented by the adult negritoid woman of Niah Cave in Borneo (Tindale, 1981), was present in Australia before 32,000 B.P. The Niah woman lived around 38,000 B.P. but as this may have been a time when the sea was at a very high level in an interstadial (Shutler, 1965), it seems likely Mungo people must have arrived at least some millennia before that date. A much more robust type which may have been a cognate group of the Murrayian Australoids has been studied at Kow Swamp. Dating evidence places the Kow Swamp people many years later than the Mungo folk.

The result of sixty years of collection and analysis of material culture remains of the aborigines confirms me in the idea that there was a long-time presence of people using Kartan phase implements and that later on there were arrivals of new ways of tool-making at least twice. The latest change, the coming of the small tool phase, was a major one, which arrived full-fledged from the direction of Asia in Mid-Recent time or somewhat earlier.

The tradition in tool-making which replaced the Kartan was the Tartangan at least 32,000 years ago, and perhaps far back beyond that date. It remained with little real change down to near 5,000 years ago in southern Australia, as has been recognised by Mulvaney (1975).

It was in a relatively late time in the Flandrian Transgression, although the exact date is still not known, that newcomers introduced such disparate elements as the dingo dog and the then up-to-date aggregate of specialist stone tools, and microliths. This small tools complex is so widespread over the Old World in the Mid-Recent that it is difficult to distinguish ones from the Upper Nile from those which were lying on the spot where Captain Cook first trod the soil of Australia at Botany Bay two centuries ago.

Mid-Recent time, with its high world temperatures leading to high sea levels, must have been an era of population pressures and change as climates shifted. It may be assumed that even before this time the skills of Southeast Asian peoples had developed superior craft which enabled them to travel more freely over the waters between the islands of their eastern archipelago, a facility which had not been attained by earlier Pleistocene peoples.

It seems clear that the Sahul shelf had already become Sahul Sea when the dingo first appeared and that Torres Strait already had been established. Thus the dingo failed to spread to New Guinea and it was another race of dog, *Canis d. hallstromi,* that was separately introduced there.

Although it is evident that all early newcomers to Australia must have entered across the Sahul Shelf we still have few tangible indications of its prehistory. Some indications of the conditions on this vast Ice Age semi-arid lowland may be deduced from study of the isolated Kaiadilt shore-dwellers of Bentinck Island (see Fig. 5) at the southern end of the Gulf of Carpentaria (Tindale, 1977). These folk seem to have preserved up to the present day the ways of life and some of the very primitive tools of early modern man of the shorelines and mangrove-laced lowland estuaries of the eastern tropics. Serologically and in other aspects of physical type they are a distinctive people. One of their normal stone tools is a bifacially knapped fist axe. Another is a large discoidal knife fashioned by hammering a large discoidal piece from a *Melo diadema* shell, roughly shaping it to ovate form, and then applying pressure-trimming unifacially along its intended cutting edge by biting with the teeth. The maker interposes a folded strip of bark over the edge to prevent jarring his teeth. The same strip of cotton tree bark may then become a handle by being wrapped around one end of the completed tool. This highly characteristic knife, used with a thrusting motion away from the user, has been found in a Late Pleistocene context, but apparently not dated, in the Niah area of Borneo. When reported there its function and its mode of trimming was not understood.

In Southern Australia field work relevant to the Bass Shelf consists of theoretical deductions and the discovery of stone tools and indications from a few old camping sites which appear on the islands which once were the higher lands of the Ice Age plains (Jones, 1977). Workers are now clear that man went across to Tasmania by way of the Bass Strait of today but are still uncertain whether he walked or whether he used the simple raft-like watercraft he had when first seen there. Until recently there were endeavours figuratively to fetch him by raft or simple canoe from as far away as the New Hebrides over more than a thousand kilometers of open ocean (Macintosh, 1949). Records of the high mortality rate which may accompany voyages of even less than fifteen kilometers, such as have been experienced by the Bentinck Islanders (Tindale, 1977: 267), during attempts to shift from one part of their domain to another "remote" one, may have had some influence in changing opinions about long voyages on readily waterlogged rafts.

Until recently there was a reluctance to recognise that the Kartan phase implements were present on the mainland of Tasmania, although finds of core implements of their type had been reported by this author on more than one of the islands in Bass Strait. Now Jones (1979) has evidence for their presence even on the remote King Island.

One important aspect of the rise of sea level inherent in the warming after the colder phases of the Wisconsinan was the severance of inward migration of land mammals. This may have had a significant bearing on the extinctions of populations of man on several islands. Kangaroo Island soils are severely deficient in more than one trace element essential to animal wellbeing. Cobalt and zinc are so critically absent on the Island that the rearing of sheep, for example was not possible until, within the last fifty years, these missing elements were supplied.

It seems very possible that once the supply of these important elements fetched in by animals migrating from the mainland was cut off by sea level rise the depletion may have had drastic effects on the viability of the human population as the pool of such elements became exhausted

The Woakwine implement occurrences suggest Kartan tool users may have been in southern Australia from near the beginning of the Wisconsinan but as yet we have no real indication of a terminal date or rather an indication when their tool using ways began to be replaced by Tartangan ones. Both phases appear to have been ones of long duration. Clearly the change came at some time after the beginning of the last major cold phase but earlier than the 32,000 B.P. indicated by finds at Mungo Lake.

For Tasmania the picture indeed is changing so rapidly that this author is encouraged to speculate on the possibility that there may have been more than one incursion to Tasmania. First may have been a people using Kartan tools, venturing south perhaps as the climate became warmer at the beginning of the warm-up foreshadowing the Wisconsinan Interstadial, but before the greater mass of land-locked ice had had time to flood Bass Shelf. It will be of interest to learn whether such an early population was maintained through the second cold phase of the Wisconsinan, or retreated northward. A second postulated people may have entered the area later possessing the tool kit of the Tartangan folk. A favorable time for their incursion may have been the period, at the beginning of the amelioration of the climate after the cold of Wisconsinan II, but again before the reflooding of Bass Strait by the Flandrian rise of sea level to its modern level.

Because of the cold which must have prevailed during the height of each glacial episode of the Wisconsinan it is possible that the hypothetical first and Kartan-tool-using folk went south to Tasmania at a time when the warmth of the major Wisconsinan Interstadial had begun. Perhaps the relative scarcity of sites so far reported from Tasmania itself may indicate that either the earlier visitors did not survive when colder times came again, or they retreated north. In such a case the King Islanders must have found themselves in a cul-de-sac. It will be of interest to test whether tools of the suggested second phase ever reached that island. We also may be able to establish whether the Tartangan-like tool phase was carried dryshod over the Bassian lowlands at a time near the beginning of the Flandrian Transgression when warmer conditions had just begun, or still earlier, during the last full glacial period.

REFERENCES

Birdsell, J.B. (1941). A preliminary report on the trihybrid origin of the Australian aborigines. *American Journal of Physical Anthropology*. 28, 6.

Birdsell, J.B. (1949). The racial origin of the extinct Tasmanians. *Records of Queen Victoria Museum (Launceston)* 2, 105-122.

Bloom, A.L., Broecker, W.S., Chappell, J.M.A., Matthews, R.K. and Mesolella, K.J. (1974). Quaternary sea level fluctuations on a tectonic coast: New Th-230/U-234 dates from the Huon Peninsula, New Guinea. *Quaternary Research* 4, 185-205.

Cook, P.J., Colwell, J.B., Firman, J.B., Lindsay, J.M., Schwebel, D.A. and von der Borch, C.C. (1977). The late Cainozoic sequence of southeast South Australia and Pleistocene sea-level changes. *BMR Journal of Australian Geology and Geophysics* 2, 81-88.

Cooper, H.M. (1959). Large archaeological stone implements from Hallett Cove, South Australia. *Transactions of the Royal Society of South Australia*. 82, 55.

Fairbridge, R.W. (1958). Dating the latest movements of the Quaternary sea level. *Transactions of the New York Academy of Science*. Series II, 20 (6), 471-482.

Hale, H.M. and Tindale, N.B. (1930). Notes on some human remains in the Lower Murray Valley, South Australia. *Records of the South Australian Museum (Adelaide)* 4 (2), 145-218.

Howchin, W. (1919). Supplementary notes on the occurrence of aboriginal remains discovered by Captain S.A. White at Fulham with remarks on the geological section. *Transactions of the Royal Society of South Australia* 43, 81-84.

Jones, R. (1977). Man as an element of a continental fauna: the case of the sundering of the Bassian Bridge. In *Sunda and Sahul*, Allen, J., Golson, J., and Jones, R., eds. Academic Press, London. pp. 317-386.

Jones, R. (1979). A note on the discovery of stone tools and a stratified prehistoric site on King Island, Bass Strait. *Australian Archaeology*.

Lampert, R. (1981). The great Kartan mystery. *Terra Australis* 5, 1-210.

Macfarlane, W.V. (1978). Determinants of tolerance in animals and man. In: *Biology and Quaternary Environments* (Walker, D., and Guppy, J.C., eds). *Sydney: Australian Academy of Science* pp. 147-149.

Macfarlane, W.V. (1980). From dump cave to desert; ecophysiology of the "milieu interieur". La transmission neuromusculaire les mediateurs et le "milieu interieur". Paris: Masson. pp. 289-309.

Macintosh, N.W.G. (1949). A survey of possible sea routes available to the Tasmanian aborigenes. *Record of Queen Victoria Museum* 7, 123-144.

Mulvaney, D.J. (1975). *The Prehistory of Australia*. Revised edition. pp. 1-327.

Shutler, R. Jr (1965). Proceedings of the Sixth International Conference on Radiocarbon and Tritium Dating. Washington State University, pp. 264-276.

Tindale, N.B. (1937). Relationship of the extinct Kangaroo Island culture with cultures of Australia, Tasmania and Malaya. *Records of the South Australian Museum. (Adelaide)* 6 (1), 39-60.

Tindale, N.B. (1941). The antiquity of man in Australia. *Australian Journal of Science* 3 (6), 144-147.

Tindale, N.B. (1957a). A dated Tartangan implement site from Cape Martin, South-East of South Australia. *Transactions of the Royal Society of South Australia* 80, 109-123.

Tindale, N.B. (1957b). Culture succession in south eastern Australia from Late Pleistocene to the Present. *Records of the South Australian Museum (Adelaide)* 13 (1), 1-49.

Tindale, N.B. (1964). Radiocarbon dates of interest to Australian archaeologists. *Australian Journal of Science* 27 (1), 24.

Tindale, N.B. (1965). Stone implement making among the Nakako, Ngadadjara and Pitjandjara of the Great Western Desert. *Records of the South Australian Museum (Adelaide)* 15 (1), 131-164.

Tindale, N.B. (1968). Nomenclature of archaeological cultures and associated implements in Australia. *Records of the South Australian Museum (Adelaide)* 15(4), 615-640.

Tindale, N.B. (1977a). Further report on the Kaiadilt people of Bentinck Island, Gulf of Carpentaria, Queensland. In: *Sunda and Sahul* (Allen, J., Golson, J., Jones, R. eds). Academic Press. London. pp. 247-273.

Tindale, N.B. (1977b). Adaptive significance of the Panara or grass seed culture of Australia. In: *Stone Tools as Cultural Markers: Change, Evolution and Complexity*. (Wright, R.V.S., eds. Australian Institute of Aboriginal Studies, Canberra, pp. 345-349.

Tindale, N.B. (1981). Prehistory of the aborigines. Some interesting considerations. Ecological biogeography of Australia. (Keast, A. editor). *Monographiae Biologicae*. Junk, The Hague. 41 (7), chapter 63.

Tindale, N.B. (In press). Australian aboriginal techniques of pressure-flaking stone implements. Essays in Honor of Don E. Crabtree. Idaho State University.

Tindale, N.B. and Maegraith, B.G. (1931). Traces of an extinct aboriginal population on Kangaroo Island. *Records of the South Australian Museum* 4 (3), 275-289.

von der Borch, C.C., Bada, J.L. and Schwebel, D.L. (1980). Amino acid racemization dating of Late Quaternary strandline events of the coastal plain sequence near Robe, southeastern South Australia. *Transactions of the Royal Society of South Australia* 104 (5 and 6), 167-170.

White, S.A. (1919). Notes on the occurrence of aboriginal remains below marine deposits at Reedbeds, Fulham, near Adelaide. *Transactions of the Royal Society of South Australia* 43, 77-80.

SUMMARY AND CONCLUSIONS

Patricia M. Masters and N.C. Flemming

INTRODUCTION

The original goal defined for this Symposium was to examine the potential for field studies on the submerged migration* corridors (Sunda, Sahul, Bass and Beringia). The data from the field surveys of drowned prehistoric sites from diverse continental shelf areas were intended as means of formulating strategies for land-bridge investigations. But the submerged site studies have created a wider perspective on the prehistory of the shelves. Because cultural habits are inseparably tied to geographical terrain, the study of marine-oriented economies in the early Holocene leads inevitably to questions about coastal environments and resources. The environments and resources are in turn strongly dependent upon fluctuating sea levels, the physiographic evolution of coastlines, and the ecology of the coastal lands, shore, intertidal zone, and nearshore waters.

This summary attempts only to present the views of its authors, and we do not wish to suggest that all those people attending the meeting reached some kind of consensus. The discussion was always lively and constructive but the papers presented do not, and could not, create a totally consistent and uniform picture. There is contradictory evidence in some areas, and difference of opinion in others. The contributors to this volume met, and discussed the papers, and revised them in the light of that

---

*The term "migration" is used frequently here and elsewhere in the volume. By migrations, we do not mean a purposeful, mass movement from one area or continent to another. In our usage, it is understood to mean movements of peoples or animals from one locality to another without teleological implications.

QUATERNARY COASTLINES
ISBN 0 12 479250 2

discussion, and differences still remain. We are dealing with a new subject, or at least a new approach to a subject, and the quantity of reliable and accepted data is very limited. It is inevitable that the facts are insufficient to answer all the questions posed, or to substantiate all the hypotheses constructed. There are differences of opinion as to the probability of survival of lithic sites offshore; there are differences as to the best ways to search for them; and differences as to the probable earliest occupation of the Americas and Australia.

Several topics recurred throughout the meeting, in the oral presentation of papers, in the discussion after each paper, and in the final open discussion session. These can be summarized briefly as follows. Why should we study continental shelf archaeology at all? It is difficult, unpredictable, and expensive, and the effort might better be devoted to other areas. Frequent reference was made to the uncertainty of the data on relative sea levels, locally, regionally, or globally. The problem of the survivability of submerged material, the sequence of burial, taphonomy, and re-exposure, either on the shore, or underwater, came up in many papers. Reference was made occasionally to predictive models, that is, assessments of regions of the continental shelf and the theoretical probability of archaeological deposits being discoverable upon them in type locations. This leads logically to the concept of a stategy for searching, and for site selection, assuming that one has defined what sites are potentially worth searching for. This in turn leads to the attempt to produce a methodology for site location, survey, and excavation. In this context there was some discussion of the federal cultural resources management on the Outer Continental Shelf of the United States. After discussion of continental shelf sites in general, there was a more specific discussion of the principal land and sea bridge migration routes, and the problems of discovering submerged sites in the bridge areas. Two ecological factors emerged as very important, but as yet almost totally unquantified; these are the response of terrestrial and shoreline marine species to geologically rapid fluctuations of sea level, and the human response to both fluctuations of sea level and ecology. Finally, the meeting tried to estimate the most fruitful lines of development in the near future.

CHANGES OF SEA LEVEL

For the purposes of this Symposium the temporal and spatial variable connecting oceanography and archaeology is the position of the sea level relative to the adjacent landmass at each time in the past. The papers by Marcus and Newman*, by Berger, and

*References without dates are to chapters in the present volume.

Inman, make it clear that even with the most complete data sets available, the variation in apparent sea level from place to place on the globe at the same time is sufficient to cast doubt upon our present understanding of the processes at work. An oral presentation by Bloom referred to the data base assembled during the International Geological Correlation Programme Project 61, which is devoted to the sea level measurements of the last 15,000 years. These data have also produced a great scatter in contemporary sea level estimates relative to the adjacent land mass, but the apparent discrepancies from place to place on the globe have been at least partially explained by the models put forward by Clark *et al.* (1978).

This regional variation in apparent sea level is attributable to factors which cause variations in level of the land relative to the centre of mass of the earth, and others which cause the sea surface to depart from parallelism to the present marine geoid. Most of these factors were outlined by Fairbridge (1961) who anticipated in qualitative terms much of the quantitative research which followed in the next two decades, and continues today. Research is progressing along several parallel paths: for example, palaeoclimatic models based on the interaction of presumed ice volumes, sea level, variations in albedo, etc.; glacial-rheological models based on ice volumes, crustal strength, stress-strain relationships for the earth's crust, and gravitational interactions of ice, earth, and water, (Clark *et al.*, 1978; numerous papers in the volume edited by Mörner, 1980) accumulation of relative land-sea level data from as many regions as possible, and the construction of models of coastal land deformation and eustatic sea level change (Bloom, 1977; Tooley, 1982; Newman *et al.*, 1980); and the effects of motions of the earth's plates.

From the point of view of the present volume, it can only be said that the precise relative position of land and sea at any locality at a specified date cannot yet be predicted accurately on the basis of a general or eustatic model. Interpretations of palaeocoastal physiography and environmental conditions do not usually depend on knowing the absolute sea level to within an accuracy of a few metres. Archaeological interpretation or prediction, on the other hand, typically requires accuracy of the order of 1.0 m. To obtain this resolution each site area must be studied specifically to determine the local sea level-time relationship.

EVOLUTION OF COASTLINES AND COASTAL ECOZONES

The paper by Inman introduced stimulating considerations of the processes involved in coastlines' responses to transgressing seas. The changing relationship of sea level relative to terrestrial drainage systems provides the driving force for the evolution of different types of beaches, of estuaries and lagoons, and of certain features of coastal plains. Taking for example the shorelines of the Southern California Bight, one is impressed by the implication of both Inman and Johnson that the major changes taking place from the late Pleistocene through the Holocene were probably not climatic (in the sense of temperature or precipitation changes) but rather physiographic in nature. Evolving coastline features (Inman) as well as increases in littoral "ecospace" (Johnson) suggest an interesting perspective on other warm temperate coasts such as the Mediterranean during Flandrian times.

A number of participants (Bailey, Barham and Harris, Dikov, Hopkins) expressed the need to understand more about the responses of plant and animal communities to sea level and coastline adjustments. The kinetics of sea level change directly influence the physiographic features of shorelines and their degree of stabilization. As much as temperature, precipitation, and other climatic factors, the rate of sea level change may thus determine the diversity and numbers of littoral biota existing at any point in time during sea level flux. Both sea level curves and the oxygen isotope curves indicate that transgressions occur more rapidly than regressions. Thus sea level kinetics can be more of a limiting factor for biotic communities during transgressions. In periods of very rapid rise, such as 16,000-6,000 B.P., what were the implications for recruitment, establishment, and diversity of plant and animal species? Could the rapidly (on the geological time scale) encroaching and reforming coasts have supported a rich littoral biota, one that could have provided resources for human populations? Masters mentions cultural changes along the southern California coast which coincide with Inman's reconstruction of shoreline changes. But the intermediate stage in the reaction sequence:

coastal stablization ⟶ biotic recruitment ⟶ cultural exploitation

is as yet almost totally unknown.

THE SIGNIFICANCE OF ARCHAEOLOGY OF THE CONTINENTAL SHELF

To provide a perspective on the influence of sea level changes in human prehistory, we can consider the last 120,000 years. Over nearly all of this time span, sea level around the world was lower than at present, on occasion by as much as 150 m. World-wide, successions of coastlines and coastal plains evolved, stabilized, and were submerged again with the Flandrian transgressions. Land areas exposed along mainland coasts and in archipelagoes increased available habitats and opportunities for gene flow for terrestrial organisms including humans. The California Channel Islands for example expanded 5-fold in land area at one point (Johnson). Land bridges emerged to connect continents and facilitate dispersal of terrestrial populations.

During this time, significant evolutionary developments were taking place both in human biology and culture. The Neandertals of Europe and southwest Asia were succeeded by anatomically modern humans. The pace of cultural development tremendously accelerated - passing from the Middle Palaeolithic to the numerous Upper Palaeolithic cultures of Europe and the Middle East, then through the Mesolithic, Neolithic, and into the origins of our modern civilisations. Of primary interest to this Symposium, the colonizations of the Americas and greater Australia took place during the past 120,000, facilitated by marine regressions. Recently Boaz *et al.* (1982) have implicated the expanding littoral zone of the Mediterranean and emergent Dardanelles land bridge during oxygen isotope stages 3 and 2 in the evolution of Neandertals and their subsequent replacement by *Homo sapiens sapiens*.

We know from the developments in marine sciences over the past four decades that submerged in the sediments on the continental shelves are records of past landscapes, environments, and climates. The information reported in this volume and elsewhere indicates that the nearshore shelves also are divulging evidence of human cultural activities. With a constructive but guarded optimism, the contributors to this volume reached some consensus as to the importance of archaeological investigation of the continental shelves. Clearly, the events leading to the colonization of Australia and the Americas are significant problems in prehistory, and they are events localised to specific continental shelf areas. Also, the contributors agreed that it is important to understand the interaction between coastal environments of the last *ca.* 100,000 years and cultures of the Palaeolithic through Neolithic, evidence of which now can be found only in the form of submerged artifact sites.

DOES THE SIGNIFICANCE MERIT THE EFFORT?

The land areas, the habitats, the plant, animal and water resources, and the migration routes contributed by the shelves have in the past been treated only speculatively, if at all, due to the technological and logistic difficulties of studying them directly. There was considerable discussion of the high costs of working offshore, the inevitable costs of ship time and modern technology, as contrasted with the comparative cheapness of excavation on land. Notwithstanding the apparent simplicity of this assumption, there are several paradoxes here. The presumed high cost of archaelogical site survey offshore derives at least in part from the large sums of money, amounting to millions of dollars, spent under the requirements of the National Historic Preservation Act of 1966 for the protection of the Outer Continental Shelf (OCS) of the USA, (Le Blanc and Rogers, 1980; Stright, 1980; Patterson, 1981; and Flemming, 1981). The Outer Continental Shelf Lands Act Amendments of 1978 state in section 206 (g) (3) . . . "such exploration (oil and gas) will not . . . disturb any site, structure, or object of historical or archaeological significance". As a result, remote sensing surveys for the detection of possible archaeological materials are required prior to lease development. As far as is known to the present authors, or to any participant at the Symposium, no prehistoric archaeological materials have ever been found during the surveys carried out of legal necessity under this legislation, although a few shipwrecks have been located. This situation was directly attacked by Patterson (1981) as expensive and unrewarding.

Another of the paradoxes involved here is the fact that the required surface mapping and seismic reflectance surveys have benefitted the industries by locating geological features hazardous to drilling platforms or other planned structures. Discoveries of ancient channel fills, shallow pockets of gas, and small faults have permitted safer placement of offshore structures. The major difference between the requirements of a cultural resource survey and what is now becoming the prescribed geological hazards survey is the spacing of the transects used for towed instruments: 300 m for the geological and 150 m for the archaeological survey.

Stright (1980) makes the case that remote sensing methods correctly applied do develop an inventory of offshore topographic and sub-bottom features which provide the basis for subsequent archaeological research. Marine archaeologists could use the legally necessary surveys as the basis for further research, joining up surveyed areas by interspersed surveys or linking traverses, and examining directly the sites predicted as being most archaeologically prospective. However, the lessee of an offshore tract is only obliged to prove that there are no archaeological materials which might be damaged in the course of drilling and exploitation. The lessee is not required to search in the areas most likely to produce archaeological finds and in fact is given the option either to avoid or to survey areas delineated as archaeologically sensitive (shipwreck or remnant topography indicative of prehistoric setlement based on the known onshore pattern). Almost invariably the industry opts for avoidance, and therefore the chance of discovery of sites directly resulting from OCS surveys is minimal.

Nevertheless, the failure to find prehistoric sites on the OCS, combined with the uncertainty of predictive models which have not been verified by the discovery of sites, lead some to suggest that the only choice is between pouring more money and technology at

TABLE 1

Distribution by depth and age of the field studies

Locality	Depth (m)	Culture	Dates B.P.
Strait of Öresund	5-8	Mesolithic	9000-8000
Normandy	0-7	Neolithic	6000-4000
	0-3	Bronze Age	4000-3000
	2-5	Iron Age (Salt Works)	3000-2000
Leucate	3-5(?)	Neolithic	7000-6000
Koiladha Bay	10	Neolithic	7000-6000
Kyra Panagia	0-10	Neolithic-Bronze Age	7000-3000
Israel	0-5	Pre-Pottery Neolithic-Chalcolithic	8000-5000
	0-2	Neolithic	8000-7000
California	3-5	La Jollan	8000-5000

the problem or abandoning the search altogether.

The ten site areas described in the present Symposium (Table 1) suggest that, at least from an academic point of view, there is an alternative strategy. Two of the survey/excavations were conducted on extremely small budgets (Koiladha, Gifford; Aghios Petros, Flemming,). In both cases the largest boat used was a rowing boat on the order of 4 m. Most of the work described by Raban and Wreschner for the coast of Israel was also conducted with a minimum of technology and logistic backing. The survey of the San Diego County Coast by Masters utilized divers and motor launches, but nothing comparable to the technology routinely deployed for the OCS surveys. In all cases the sites were in water less than 20 m deep, which explains the simplicity of the projects. However, this shallowness and simplicity should not be dismissed as trivial.

The blunt fact is that diving teams equipped with simple equipment and small budgets are at present revealing a steady flow of information about submarine prehistoric archaeology: no other technique is producing prehistoric archaeological data from any parts of the continental shelf. This observation is important when we come to consider search strategies later in this chapter. The present successful shallow water surveys do indicate that materials can survive transgression, and they do suggest how sites may be related to submerged coastal topography in deeper water. Inevitably the cost of survey and excavation will increase progressively as water depth increases, but at every stage we would be planning to spend a reasonable increment of money on a venture which was a logical and small extension of previously successful excavation.

The OCS deep water surveys are preparing the background for future archaeological excavations. As shallow water sites are discovered and excavated in greater numbers, and in deep water, there will be a progressively greater need for the background data obtained by remote sensing instruments. The two approaches are therefore convergent through time.

THE FIELD STUDIES

In this summary chapter we think it important to stress the concrete and definitive nature of the submarine lithic sites known in detail from the ten study areas as well as previous publications before embarking on more discursive analysis. Too much speculation has already been published on this subject, and we wish to base the following discussion on the facts presented in the field studies.

The papers presented describe the survey and/or excavation of seven submarine prehistoric site areas where remains have been preserved:

1)   Strait of Öresund between Denmark and Sweden, 2+ sites
      (Larsson)
2)   Koiladha Bay, Greece (Gifford)
3)   Nearshore shelf off San Diego County, California, 34 sites
      (Masters)
4)   Mediterranean coast of Israel, 9 sites (Raban, Wreschner,
      Ronen)
5)   Normandy and Brittany coasts of France, 10+ sites (Prigent
      et al.)
6)   Mediterranean coast of France (Geddes et al.)
7)   Bay of island of Kyra Panagia, Greece (Flemming (b))

In addition, the review by Flemming (a) mentions submarine sites
off the Danish island of Fune; further sites off the coast of
Normandy, France; submerged middens off the Gulf coast of
Florida; and refers to archaeological sites in karst below sea level
in Florida. Dikov refers to poorly documented reports of retrieval
of lithic artifacts off the coast of Siberia, and Hopkins (personal
communication during the Symposium) described a lithic tool of
granite which had been dredged up in the Bering Straits.
The value of these field studies derives from the in situ
occurrence of the cultural remains. Secondary depositions cannot
provide answers to the questions we are asking. In our series of
field studies, the evidence ranges from good to excellent that we
are indeed looking at in situ occurrences. The ten
well-documented studies demonstrate beyond doubt that lithic
artifacts and contemporary objects in wood and other organic
materials can survive marine transgression. We are specifically
interested in the nature of the cultural activities represented by
these remains, and what these examples demonstrate about site
distribution. We are also concerned with preservational conditions,
the manner of site discovery, and the techniques used to carry out
surveys, excavations, and analyses. Under circumstances
favourable both to preservation and to discovery, archaeological
sites have been located, surveyed, and excavated under the sea to
depths of 10-20 m, and dating from periods as old as 8,000 B.P.
(see Table 1). Field experience from these known sites indicates
the methods for advancing into deeper water, and how we should
attempt to discover and understand the archaeological remains on
the continental shelf from the whole period since 120,000 B.P.

Types and Distribution of Sites

The types of human activities reported for these sites range from
extensive permanent occupations to specialized activity locales. Of
the 11 clearly recognizable settlements, 8 are Neolithic and
Chalcolithic villages from the Mediterranean coast of Israel
(Raban; Wreschner), 2 are Neolithic and Bronze Age sites from
Normandy (Prigent et al.), and the last is the late Neolithic to

Bronze Age Kyra Panagia (Flemming,b). Possible settlements or
encampments are in Koiladha Bay (Gifford), Öresund (Larsson), and
Leucate (Geddes *et al.*). Ten of these sites are located at the
junctions of major fresh water sources with the contemporaneous
coastlines. They are found on submerged river banks (Öresund,
Koiladha Bay, and extending below waterline at the River Poleg
site of Raban and la Roussellerie of Prigent *et al.*), in river
marshlands (la Butte aux Pierres, Normandy), and along
embayments (Kyra Panagia, Atlit in Israel), estuaries (Newe Yam
and Tantura, Israel), and lagoons (Leucate). Three additional sites
in Israel are extensions of onshore villages (Tel Qatifa, Tel Harez,
Yavneh Yam) with fresh water sources unspecified.
    Other types of sites are monuments of the Neolithic (Normandy)
and Chalcolithic (Israel) and megalithic tombs (Normandy). Iron
Age salt processing works are found at -2 to 5 m (below mean high
water of spring tides) in Normandy. Two stone mortar factory
sites (California) are associated with large onshore middens and
ancient lagoons. Five potential shell fishing stations also from
southern California are situated in submerged reefs.

Preservational Conditions

The best evidence for well-preserved, inundated sites comes from
the eastern Mediterranean. As summarized above, in the range of
7,000-6,000 B.P., late Neolithic settlements flourished along
shorelines 10-15 metres below present. Through the local
Chalcolithic (*ca.* 6,000 B.P.), numerous communities clustered
around estuaries newly formed by the transgression and are now
drowned (see Raban; Wreschner; Ronen). Wreschner and Raban
describe hearths. charcoal, burned twigs, tree trunks, house floors,
pottery, bones and seeds frequently associated with brown to black
loams.   The reasons cited for such extraordinary preservation
(particularly of organics) are the protection of offshore structures
such as islets and the kurkar ridges, the location of headlands and
other types of barriers forming embayments, and very importantly,
subaerial deposition of sediment preceding transgression.   Even
though these submerged sites lie within the zone of
storm-generated waves, the sediment cover has protected them
over the past 3,000 years of near stillstand.
    The mechanisms influencing evolution of coastal forms as
explained by Inman give us a rationale for the prevalence of
underwater sites off Israel. A constant and prolific supply of fine
sediment from the Nile River to the south west, the major
sediment source for this littoral cell, has probably been available
for at least 6,000-7,000 years due to the size and seasonal
flooding regime of the Nile. Onshore movement of the sands by
waves and dune migration in response to prevailing winds could
have created an early to mid-Holocene process of subaerial

deposition followed by marine transgression - a seemingly ideal scenario for site preservation.

The exaggerated intertidal zone of the Normandy coast periodically submerges Epipalaeolithic through Iron Age remains as summarized above by Prigent *et al.* Preservational state varies, with the sea cliff sites most vulnerable to erosion. Sites of the intertidal zone may be protected by the massiveness of the monument itself or by sediment cover such as peat or sand. The discovery of these sites is in turn dependent on the movements of the beach sand. The best preservation occurs with sites in the estuaries and marshlands where peat, mud, or sand embed the remains.

Turning again to Israel, the effects of frequent exposure by winter storms (Israel's western coast is subject to the longest fetch in the Mediterranean) can be seen at Atlit. Raban describes eroded stone tools, broken pottery and scattered floor slabs. In contrast, reconnaissance of a newly opened component at Tel Harez, 40 m south of the main site, revealed hearths with charred twigs, branches, and bone *in situ.*

Both Gifford's Koiladha Bay site and Kyra Panagia (Flemming, b) demonstrate the survival of cultural materials along the generally unpromising rocky coastlines of the Aegean. In each case sheltered embayments helped. Kyra Panagia is situated in an excellent natural habour. The Koiladha Bay site had Koronis Island and the sill of the bay to block the fetch and storms.

The southern California sites exist today despite the open Pacific and a medium to high energy coastline because of the La Jolla headland, the submarine canyons, and catchment features of the reefs. A seasonal sediment cover and the relatively large, heavy nature of the artifacts have also contributed to preservation.

How Underwater Sites are Found

The lesson from the field studies in this volume is that most submarine artifacts are located unintentionally by sport divers or during offshore construction activities. All of the underwater localities known from the Southern California Bight were found by people diving for recreational or commercial fishing purposes. Hence the importance of contacting and educating local divers with regard to submerged archaeological materials. Israel's Underwater Exploration Society (Raban) shows admirably how volunteer divers can be trained and used for submarine surveying. The importance of fielding divers or surveyors immediately after seasonal sediment transport by storms, for example, is illustrated in the Israeli experience, as well as in Normandy and in southern California. Purposeful surveying offshore of extensive Neolithic and Chalcolithic settlements has yielded results at three localities south of Tel Aviv (Raban) as well as at Kyra Panagia (Flemming, b).

Dredges used in coastal construction projects have contributed some finds (Geddes *et al.*, Larsson; see also Kraft *et al.*,) Coring from ships was also suggested as a useful technique for the future by Kraft *et al.*, and Gifford reports the successful location of artifacts using a diver-held coring device in a purposefully designed search. In another planned search, two sites on submerged river banks were located by Larsson using shipboard dredge sampling, followed by diving reconnaissance.

To date, all submarine archaeological finds of prehistoric materials have been well within the maximum air diving depth, about 50 metres, Thus non-professional divers and teams of students, or archaeologists who have limited diving experience, can continue to progress research for some years to come. One can envisage prehistoric sites in 0-20 m depth being found in considerable numbers in the near future, whilst a small number will be found in depths of 20-50 m. At 50 m depth the technology required again converges on the systems used to fulfill the requirements of the USA OCS legislation. That is to say, assuming that a prospective site had been located, or restricted to a small area, by remote sensing methods, diving would have to be conducted using mixed gases and saturation, or with the aid of submersibles.

Site prediction is an entirely different matter. One conclusion from the field studies is that the existence of prehistoric underwater sites cannot be ruled out even under the least likely conditions for survival. While Kraft *et al.* considered the rocky, precipitous, and eroding coasts of the Aegean unlikely for submergence and survival, Flemming (b) was able to show that under the right combination of sheltered local conditions, artifacts and organic materials can and do survive, if not in stratigraphic relationship at least in assemblage.

Techniques of Analysis

Several analytical approaches used in field studies reported here are fine examples of methods requiring minimal technological sophistication (and investment) yet yielding important information on submerged sites. Gifford employed sediment grain size analysis to identify the submerged landscape in Koiladha Bay and to evaluate the *in situ* occurrence of the pottery sherds. Sub-bottom profiling, although not a technique readily available to every archaeologist interested in submarine sites, also aided Gifford in designing the coring strategy by indicating the submerged river channel. Taphonomic analyses described by Geddes *et al.* provided the most convincing evidence of an *in situ* Neolithic occupation off Leucate, southern France. Taphonomic analysis should prove especially useful in evaluating marine sites where transport and secondary deposition can be very troublesome.

Other standard techniques which have been applied to underwater prehistoric sites include C-14 analysis (Clausen et al., 1979), analysis of species, age, and sex structure of food animals on the basis of bone fragments (Schwartz, personal written communication, (N.C. Flemming), for Aghios Petros). Gifford plans to use pollen analysis on sediment cores, and suggests phytolith analysis in addition. In short, the analytical methods available to land archaeologists can be, and are, used for the materials found in underwater sites.

The techniques of working underwater were only discussed briefly during the Symposium, since there are many published reports on the subject, and many conferences have been held, (see for example Bass, 1972; Muckelroy 1978, 1980; Barto Arnold, 1980). Work is inevitably slower underwater than it is on land, but, given a task which warrants time and expenditure, there is no reason why accuracy should be sacrificed. Surveying, recording, photography, coring, trenching and stratigraphic control can all be achieved underwater, given a team of well trained divers.

INTERACTIONS OF HUMAN CULTURES WITH THE LITTORAL ZONE

The movements of biota and humans onto emergent continental shelves are undoubtedly related phenomena. Bailey makes the distinction between human groups with land-based economies simply expanding onto the new coastal plains, and cultures dependent on littoral gathering, hunting, or fishing. His site analyses on the Cantabrian coast also illustrate the importance of coast and shelf morphology to interpretation of subsistence and settlement patterns.

Bailey concurs with other scholars in that coastal subsistence economies of the Holocene probably had their roots in trends developing much earlier in cultural evolution. Terra Amata, a Lower Palaeolithic site at Nice, France, has yielded some shells of oysters, mussels and limpets from cultural layers (de Lumley, 1969). The age of Terra Amata is placed by de Lumley (1975) at ca. 400,000 or certainly at an interglacial due to its warm climate land fauna. Thermal luminescence dating of burned flints indicates a second to last interglacial (oxygen isotope stage 7) age, ca. 235,000 B.P. (Wintle and Aitken, 1977). At either date, Terra Amata represents the earliest known evidence of littoral gathering. The number of sites containing marine mollusc food refuse increases greatly by Middle Palaeolithic times. The cave at Lazaret, ca. 130,000 B.P., has shown indications of seaweed gathering, its use interpreted as bedding material. Other last interglacial (oxygen isotope stage 5) peoples inhabiting the

Ligurian coast of Italy at Arene Candide and the North African coast at Haua Fteah (Libya) relied extensively on marine molluscs (Emiliani *et al.*, 1964). The Klasies River Mouth Cave, among others along the South African coast, has yielded evidence of marine mammal hunting as well as mollusc collecting (Klein, 1974), and the oldest marine food refuse levels date to 110,000 B.P. (Bada and Deems, 1975).

There is little doubt, then, that prehistoric peoples were moving about on the emergent shelves during periods of lowered sea level in response to availability of littoral resources as well as resources of continental origin. Emerging from the papers is the concept that stability of landforms and littoral biota during stillstands could be providing the stimulus for the appearance of littoral economies. Understanding the interglacial or interstadial origin of cultures dependent on or exploiting littoral resources and the nature of their development through the last glacial period is a significant problem in prehistory. Yet the problem can be investigated only on the continental shelf.

Bailey expressed the opinion, in discussion, that the economic prehistory of the pre-Holocene period, and the origin of terrestrial agriculture, must be bound up with the origins of marine exploitation, especially the use of estuarine resources. Taking this view, he suggested that the aim of submarine archaeological research must be to reach the outer edge of the shelf as soon as possible, and to discover sites at depths of 100 m or more, where artifacts might be relatively free of sediment cover. By making an imaginative leap to the study of such sites, we might provide the basis for greater understanding of the Holocene events, both natural and human.

Harris pointed out that the interaction between humans and the coastal zone was a two-way process. People adapted to the coastal environment and the exploitation of its resources, but in so doing they could alter that environment. This interaction was so poorly understood that it was more important to start in the modern coastal zone and work slowly seawards, learning as we progressed into deeper water. This difference of approach was not resolved on any theoretical basis, but it seems inevitable, on grounds of expense, technical difficulties, and the need for progressive experience, that successive projects will develop from shallower to deeper water.

Bloom said that the assumed occupation of the shelf areas implied the possiblity of along-shelf migration, one effect of which would be to produce anomalies in human distributions when viewed solely from the perspective of present land masses. This too could only be understood from submarine archaeological evidence, but would be a late topic of study since any rational hypothesis would have to depend on the data from many submarine sites. However along-shelf migration is an important concept which has been used previously by Bowdler (1977) for Australia and Fladmark (1979) for North America.

Bowdler (1977) suggested that the colonisation pattern in Australia can be explained by a model of along-shelf migration. The earliest entrants logically would have come from the Indonesian island chain and had cultural adaptions to island coast and littoral environments. Rather than move into the arid interior of Australia, population expansions would have occurred along the coastal zone, much of which is now submerged shelf, and up the river drainage (e.g. Mungo and Keilor).

Fladmark (1979) discussed a Pacific shelf route into North America from Beringia which also assumes a littoral hunting and gathering adaption for the early cultures. This route south along the coasts of Alaska and British Columbia during marine regression would have avoided the cold, dry interior and problems of when the "ice-free corridor" (see Reeves, this volume) was indeed ice-free.

THE LAND-SEA BRIDGES

The crossings by land routes to the Americas had to take place before 14,000B.P. To Australia, the most opportune times would appear to be during the regressions of oxygen isotope stages 4 and 2. In the Australian case, mid-Wisconsinan migration cannot be ruled out, but the relatively higher interstadial sea levels of ca. 30,000-40,000 B.P. would have created wider water gaps to cross. Such crossings would not have been impossible, but operationally (cf. Barham and Harris), a strait implies a biogeographical boundary, a genetic bottleneck, and for humans a cultural filter. With the proper motivation, the existence of a strait can also provide technological stimulus to peoples wishing to bridge it. The driving forces for such movement could be forest fires (as described in an oral presentation by Rhys Jones for the Arnhem Land), game routes (water gaps do not stop elephants, nor presumably mammoths, according to Johnson), or in the longer run climate (more mesic environment of the Beringian coastal plains, as described by Hopkins). Fairbridge (oral presentation) suggested that rising sea levels in Indonesia could have provided impetus for the migration to Australia; or at least contributed to it. Such driving forces also apply to emergent land-bridges.

In both the Sahul and Beringia cases, submarine sites could add a great deal of useful knowledge to the existing data base, but, so far, no submarine sites have been located. Both zones are in relatively inaccessible areas in terms of distance from large modern population centres, universities, and marine laboratories, and both have therefore been relatively little studied. (As with most subjects in the environmental sciences, the distribution of data is closely related to the geographical distribution of research

establishments, and the pleasantness of environmental conditions.)
Of the two zones, the Sunda-Sahul crossing is much the more
tractable, being situated in tropical seas with clear water and low
sediment rates. Nevertheless, data presented by McManus showed
that the information required to develop a logical search for
submarine sites in the Bering Straits and Chuckchi Sea is steadily
being acquired. These two principal migration zones will be
further discussed later, but it was clear from the discussion that
all participants agreed on the primary importance of submarine
data in explaining the processes of migration. Obviously the
discovery of dated artifacts or human remains on the downstream
side of a migration route indicates that migration must have taken
place before that date. Also that date suggests the depths at
which contempory shorelines existed. But only data from the
shorelines at the time of migration can indicate how the migration
was accomplished, by whom, and when.

Submarine data are also relevant to explaining the processes of
migration into Britain, Japan, the Caribbean Islands, the California
Channel Islands, across the Straits of Gibraltar, from Tunisia to
Sicily and across the Red Sea. Whilst these migrations did not of
themselves radically alter the distribution of human populations on
the globe, they did result in the colonization of important areas. In
addition, the evolution of prehistoric cultural traditions in Europe
and North Africa is interpreted in quite a different light if one
considers that there was, in some periods, relatively easy contact
across the Mediterranean, rather than all contact being
transmitted through the Middle East, via the Dardanelles, or north
of the Black Sea.

The two land-sea bridge zones considered in most detail were
the Asia-Australia region and the Siberia-Alaska bridge. It is
appropriate to consider each region separately: tropical migrations
(Fairbridge, oral presentation) are one phenomenon, high latitude
movements of populations are another.

Considering Siberia, Dikov and Hopkins emphasize hunting
cultures specializing in the Pleistocene tundra-steppes megafauna.
Most archaeologists in the U.S. (cf. Meighan) and Canada (Reeves)
also associate the earliest entrants with large land mammal
hunting economies. Although acknowledging the possibility that
Dyuktai-type mammoth hunters may have been the ancestral
palaeo-Indians, Dikov prefers the hypothesis that predecessors of
the Early Ushki peoples followed the Bering shelf littoral zone
into North America. These hunters, using stemmed bifacial points
would have relied, Dikov believes, on diversified marine gathering
as well as bison hunting. However, the Early Ushki sites, known
only from Kamchatka and dating to 13,000-14,000 B.P. suggest but
do not define who came before them to Beringia. Does the shift
in prey emphasis from mammoth hunting represented by the sites
of Dyuktai and Berelek (referred to by Hopkins) to bison, caribou,

and diversified gathering as seen in the Early Ushki sites actually signify in cultural adaptions the environmental shift at *ca*. 14,000 that Hopkins names the "birch period"?

The climatic reconstruction that Hopkins sketches for Beringia depicts a very dry continental environment for central Beringia at 25,000-14,000 B.P. The extreme dryness may have been as much a limiting factor for the biota as was the cold. The emerged shelves of the Bering and Chukchi Seas would have provided more mesic and hence more productive environments than the interior. If the peoples moving about Beringia prior to 14,000 were land mammal hunters, they may be expected to have migrated with the game herds. The most probable type of cultural remains would then be open-air kill sites. Both Dikov and Hopkins point out that river terraces contained concentrations of living sites for Early Ushki and other late Palaeolithic peoples. Coastal occupations were confined to the Bering Coast, in Hopkins' opinion, and probably centered around river mouths and headlands now represented by the Pribilof Islands (Dixon *et al.*, 1976).

The coring and sedimentological analyses described by McManus *et al.* are providing important sea level chronology for the Bering region. Their dated cores also are revealing the succession of coastlines, landbridge topography, and sedimentary environments during the Flandrian trangression. The wider unglaciated Chukchi Valley, which existed during the Wisconsinan maximum low sea stand, had tributaries entering it from Kotzebue Sound, Bering Strait and Siberia. Laminated silty clays of the stream valley contain abundant pollen indicative of steppe tundra vegetation. Thus the Chukchi Valley prior to the Flandrian transgression is characterized by the types of environment and topography attractive to both the large land mammals and their hunters.

A search strategy for Beringia ought to include well-planned coring operations of the Chukchi Valley stream terraces as well as terraces and outlets of the large pro-glacial lake on the southern Beringian shelf east of the Chukotka Peninsula.

Turning to Australia, any investigation is faced with the absence of a direct route land bridge. There is a much broader front for migrational events and possibly a longer time span during which migrations may have taken place. Birdsell (1977) has theorized about the potential routes, all involving lesser or greater gaps of water to cross. Tindale summarizes here intriguing, if incomplete, data which may imply an early Wisconsinan or even pre-last interglacial entry for humans into Australia. Pending verification by dating methods that the Kartan culture is indeed earlier, the Mungo population still points to a minimum entry date during oxygen isotope stage 3-2 boundary times.

Barham and Harris proficiently outline the field of enquiry regarding human settlement of a tropical emergent shelf. Although the Torres Strait lands were probably not a significantly early entry route to Australia, the research approaches and preliminary findings there of Barham and Harris will aid in formulating studies of other areas of the Sahul and Sunda shelves. The two authors raise highly relevant questions concerning the relative kinetics of sea level change and the establishment of flora and fauna on newly exposed shelf or new coastal zone. The timing of human colonization is linked to the stabilization of coastal environments and their potential resources. Future detailed studies of local shorelines during the final stages of the mid-Holocene transgression should be able to quantify the time lags between successive rises in sea level and resultant establishment of mangroves and other littoral habitats exploitable by human groups.

While Barham and Harris do not place a high probability on eventual discovery of sites underwater due to the Torres Strait's strong current regime and rapid coral growth, they discuss ethnohistorical data on settlement and subsistence patterns which point almost exclusively to coastal zones, reefs and freshwater swamps. These, they suggest, would be the submerged remnant features on which to concentrate underwater searches.

Island, archipelago and reef topography appear to provide a much simpler set of subsistence and settlement choices than continental coastlines and coastal plains. Bailey discusses spatial distributions for late prehistoric middens on the Cape York Peninsula, Australia, as well as Mesolithic middens on the Cantabrian coast of Spain. He cautions first that discontinuities in coastal midden distributions may reflect changes in discard behaviour rather than changes in subsistence or settlement. However, the peculiarly late dates for the Weipa shell mounds on the Cape York Peninsular (after 1,100 B.P.) do raise the question, among, others, of lag time in the establishment of mangrove environments favourable to dense mollusc populations. Are 5,000-6,000 years necessary for coastline and ecological stabilization? Analysis and dating of cores from estuarine sediments there (cf. Kraft et al.) may resolve the question and contribute to related investigations initiated by Barham and Harris in Torres Strait to the North.

The Mesolithic sites of Cantabria offer several important lessons regarding archaeological evidence of human subsistence activities on continental coastal plains, regions of intense interest from the perspective of emergent continental shelf and land bridges. Bailey's comments are based (a) on an understanding of subsistence patterns visible archaeologically on the present-day coastal plain of Cantabria and (b) on a submerged topography characterized by a steeply sloping rocky shelf common to most of the Iberian Peninsula and the Mediterranean. His main conclusion is that prominent sites are situated for convenience of land mammal hunting rather than marine resource exploitation. Sites are found at the inner edge of the coastal plain at the mouths of valleys where herd animal movements can be predicted or managed.

Coastal sites on open and level plain, as in northern Greece, tend to be small and of infrequent occupation. Although the coastal plains themselves provided essential grazing for the herd mammals, the actual living sites of their hunters were to be found inland.

As to archaeological sites on a submerged, steep and unsedimented shelf, one should look for drowned valleys near the present shoreline. These would have been at the interface between the coastal plain and the uplands during the Flandrian transgression. Similarly, Bailey suggests coastal sites may be sought in localized areas of small hills and valleys near the contemporaneous shoreline since these topographic features would have been conducive to animal herding or hunting. Where reconstruction of palaeocoastlines reveals gently sloping shelf with large rivers and shallow estuaries, the above strategy must be revised to focus on dense coastal sites oriented primarily to marine resources. Again the need is seen for detailed mapping of the nearshore shelf.

STRATEGY FOR THE IMMEDIATE FUTURE

The editors have compiled the following set of strategy points for pursuing investigations of the prehistory of the continental shelves and land-sea bridges. Since all of the concepts involved here have been treated in greater detail in the papers or earlier in this chapter, we feel that brevity is the best emphasis for what we consider the final goal of our Symposium.

Targets

Evidence from a few land sites associated with previous interglacial shorelines (Terra Amata, Lazaret, Arene Candide, Haua Fteah, Klasies River) indicates that exploitation of marine resources started at least 120,000 B.P., and possibly 400,000 B.P. The development of this exploitation, and the skills and artifacts associated with it, can be studied by obtaining field evidence which is now almost exclusively restricted to the submerged area of the continental shelf.

Submarine prehistoric sites contribute uniquely to a knowledge of the economic and technological development of the period 100,000 to 5,000 B.P. They should be sought for and investigated in order to resolve problems of Palaeolithic and Neolithic development, probably on a regional basis.

Land bridges of primary importance are Beringia and Sunda-Sahul. There is a group of secondary land/sea bridges with critical influence on the interpretation of prehistoric cultural contacts between Africa and Eurasia.

These are Gibraltar, Sicily/Tunisia, the Dardanelles-Aegean complex, and Bab-el-Mandab. Of tertiary archaeological

importance, taking a world view, are the island and archipelago
migrations, for example, into Britain, Ireland, Cyprus, Ceylon,
Japan, the Caribbean, Tasmania, the California Channel Islands,
etc. The tractability of the problems is probably in inverse order,
partly for reasons of scale, and partly the luck of geographical
accessibility. For this reason, it is logical to concentrate for the
next 5 years or so on the submarine investigation of sites such as
the California Channel Islands, following the existing work of
Johnson and Masters; or the occupation of the Mediterranean
islands (Cherry, 1981) and (Flemming, b); or Tasmania (Jones,
1977).

Along-shelf migration by peoples exploiting coastal resources, or
merely continental shelf terrestrial resources, cannot be excluded.
Such migration, if supported by field evidence, might help to
explain the colonization pattern of Australia (Bowdler, 1977) and
the evolution and distribution of European Neandertals (Boaz
et al., 1982).

The remains of plant, bone, and wood refuse or artifacts can be
found where submerged sites are preserved whereas these clues to
subsistence patterns, environments, and technologies, are rarely
preserved in the terrestrial sites. The phenomenon of differential
preservation has been demonstrated at a number of underwater
sites in both marine and fresh water contexts (Tybrind Vig,
Anderson, 1980; Aghios Petros, Flemming, b; Little Salt Spring,
Clausen et al., 1979) and indicates the potential for highly
productive palaeoclimate studies.

Related Questions

Climatic models have been developed which give general
indications of air and sea temperatures at different times in the
past. In order to understand the palaeo-coastal environment,
models or analyses at a much smaller scale are needed, taking into
account oceanic currents, palaeo-tidal analysis, onshore and
offshore winds, and the effects of the local land topography on
winds, precipitation, etc.

Research is needed into the rate of adaption of both marine and
coastal terrestrial species to the change of sea level, and to the
rate of change. How long does it take terrestrial and coastal
species to colonize different types of sea floor as the sea
retreats? How long does it take coastal algae, mollusca and
crustacea to adapt to regression or transgression? Parts of the
rocky shore of western Crete have been elevated by 5-10 m during
the last 2,000 years (Flemming, 1978; Pirazzoli and Flemming,
1981) and the steep rocky foreshore still looks quite different from
the adjacent scrub above the original shoreline. The rate of
adaptation might be very different for sandy, muddy, or clayey
deposits with organic sediments.

The human response to transgression and regression is also completely unknown, both on the local (1-10 km) and on the regional (10-1,000 km) scale. The response pattern probably varied with the technological development and changes of hunting and agricultural patterns during the last 120,000 years. Did the addition of thousands of square km of new land make a significant difference to hunter gatherers who may not have been hunting to the limit of the terrain? Or was it literally a marginal addition? Or did significant numbers of people follow the retreating shoreline in order to avail themselves of the coastal biota? If so, to what extent was their adaptation to the shore hindered by the fact that the new land had recently been impregnated by salt water? It would be useful to study land areas in Scandinavia and Canada which have recently been uplifted by glacio-eustatic recovery in order to find models for marine regression. (The well-documented uplift of the Baltic coast of Sweden is of course not relevant, because of the extremely low salinity of the Baltic.) Comparison with the drainage of polders in the Netherlands could be valuable.

Study of the adaptation to transgression is also important. During the Neolithic a transgression would actually destroy artifactual resources and property, such as houses and fields, and in the Palaeolithic would eliminate hunting areas and separate occupiable ground areas one from another. In addition, if the rate of sea level rise was such as to reduce the productivity of the coastal marine biota, then the attractiveness of the shoreline would have been reduced. Data on this form of adaptation for different kinds of shoreline could be obtained by investigation of areas which have recently been submerged either by tectonism or isostatic subsidence.

The Present State of Investigations

Location, survival, and detection of sites are intensely dependent on the contemporary coastal geomorphology and the subsequent erosional and depositional events on a spatial scale of less than 1 km. Generalisations based on models of the shelf with broad resolution will tend to produce predictions which will deny the existence of sites when they could indeed exist and survive. The alternative error of predicting generalized survival incorrectly is less probable, but it could nevertheless prove expensive to falsify.

Sites have so far been found in general near centres of modern population where there are many sports divers and marine research institutes or universities with archaeology departments. There is no reason to suppose that Neolithic and Palaeolithic continental shelf sites are actually concentrated in these areas. It is reasonable to suppose, conditions being equivalent, that the same number of prehistoric sites could be found in the remote areas where the critical land bridges occur.

The present trend of site discovery arising from sports divers and institutes conducting compressed air scuba diving will continue to generate further discoveries down to a depth of about 50 m, and with a preponderance of discoveries in the Mediterrean, Europe, and the United States. Work in progress in Australia (Thom, Jones, Chappell, and Flemming, oral communication) suggests that submerged aboriginal sites may soon be discovered there. However, as diving archaeologists seek to discover prehistoric artifacts in deeper water, or in more remote locations, costs will inevitably mount. Beyond the depth of 50 m, submarine excavation will require either saturation diving methods or small submersibles. The costs for such projects would be on the order of many thousands of dollars per day.

It follows that the precision of site prediction must be increased for deeper water, since the costs of unsuccessful operations would be unacceptable.

Predictive models for site location have usually been developed for deeper water, 20 m plus, than that in which sites have actually been found so far. Thus there is no empirical verification of the value of the models. It is essential for the successful archaeological surveying of the outer shelf that predictive models be used, since random finds are almost inconceivable, and we cannot survey the whole area at adequate intensity. But, if predictive models are to have any "ground-truth" testing, either they must be developed for 0-20 m water depth and validated by the present generation of finds, or we must wait until finds are made in deeper water. In either case, it is probable that progress will be made by an iterative process of reliance alternately on empirical extension from known sites, and theoretical or predictive models indicating possible locations of sites in deeper water.

The existing programme of remote sensed surveys conducted under the OCS legislation can be considered a long term investment for the prehistoric submarine archaeology of the USA. Whilst these surveys have not resulted in prehistoric site discoveries so far, they are providing archaeologists with the background information which may lead to discoveries in the future. As the experience of shallow water site investigations accumulates, and work is conducted in deeper water, these surveys should eventually prove to be extremely valuable.

Site Prediction

Site discovery depends on the physical preservation of the site material, combined with ease of detection. Factors favouring preservation are as follows:

1)   A sheltered low energy environment, protected from waves and currents, e.g. within an estuary or sheltered bay, in the

lee of islands or headlands, within a karstic cave, or at the head of a submarine canyon.

2) Environments which, although exposed to high energy (waves or currents) are protected by adequate sediment cover, (e.g. equilibrium beaches, marshes, wind blown sand).

3) A sequence of events which first buries the site in sediment, and then exhumes it gradually, e.g. covering by terrestrial sediment, followed by submergence, followed by slight wave or current action.

Factors favouring detection are as follows:

1) Minimal or total absence of sediment cover at the time of search.

2) Clear water and calm sea conditions.

3) Proximity to a technically developed population involved with sports and research scuba diving.

4) Shallow water depth relative to present sea level.

5) Large recognizable features such as shell middens, menhirs, large stone tools, dug-out canoes, etc.

The probability of site occurrence in terms of the contemporary coastal configuration is related to the following requirements:

1) Availability of fresh water.

2) Availability of food resources, terrestrial, marine, or both.

3) The availability of shelter from sun, rain, snow, wind, or insects.

4) Protection from sea conditions;

and to the following specific conditions:

1) Subsistence pattern: terrestrial resource "pull" vs. littoral resource "pull"

2) Topography of shelf and coastal plain: local scale relief, presence of estuaries and embayments, etc.

The Next Steps

It is important to note how much the existence and survival of prehistoric sites depends on small-scale topography. This is true of all the sites described in this book. The first step in any survey is therefore extremely accurate topographic sea floor mapping, either by echo-sounding and side-scan sonar in low relief areas, or by diving in steep or near-vertical conditions. In order to detect beach ridges, terraces, lagoonal features, re-entrant bays, headlands, etc., soundings should be accurate to 1 m, and corrected for tide. To obtain physiographic plan-view data, sounding line spacing should be not more than 100-150 m.

Surface topography may be inadequate to indicate river valleys, shorelines, etc., when the sea floor is cloaked by recent sediments.

Shallow seismic penetration reveals the sub bottom profile, and these data may be essential for the location of diagnostic features. The point to stress is that the survey so far can only indicate the most probable environments within which sites might either occur, be preserved, or be detectable. Neither echo-sounding, sidescan, nor sub-bottom profiling has any chance of proving the existence of prehistoric materials. What these techniques can do is to locate river valleys, shorelines, and the intersections of these features.

Demonstration that submarine prehistoric materials survive *in situ* in water depths greater than 1-2 m has so far only been achieved by direct intervention with divers. Remote coring without the visual or manipulative control of divers has so far not produced data. On this evidence, the remote sensing techniques used in most OCS mandatory surveys never could have demonstrated the positive existence of submerged prehistoric cultural remains. In view of the lithic and organic nature of most target materials, it is extremely doubtful whether any conventional survey methods, based on magnetic or electrical field detection, could locate the targets. Visual or physical sampling is essential.

Assuming that a highly prospective river-shoreline intersection has been located in a sheltered bay or estuary, with positive indicator features suggestive of beach ridges, lagoonal deposits, or cliffs, etc., it would be reasonable to conduct a systematic core or dredge survey in order to map the surface and shallow subbottom sediment characteristics. It would also be suitable in some terrains, e.g., karstic, to search for submarine springs.

There is a small chance that sampling at this stage may produce data suggestive of shell midden or tool flakes. In any case, pollen data and other sedimentary evidence should give indications of climatic and hydrological conditions.

The amount of time air divers can spend at depths of 20 m or more is severely limited, and therefore the transition from the 100 m- 10 km scale of remote sensed surveys to the 1 m-100 m scale of diving surveys is difficult to achieve. There are various techniques for extended systematic searches by divers, but they are both labour and time intensive. In clear water conditions this phase of search can be greatly speeded by towed video cameras. Cameras are available with a wider angle of vision than the human eye, and greater sensitivity in poor light conditions. The transmission from such a camera can be observed by several experts simultaneously, can be recorded on tape as required, and the TV camera can be coupled with a flash-gun and still camera so as to record high quality images.

The data obtained through the video search provides the high resolution data needed to chose the optimum dive sites. The precise nature of the work by the divers will depend critically on the type of environment, but it is not difficult to anticipate sequences of tests, probes, samples, photographis, etc., which would be suitable for varying conditions.

The above sequence of steps has never been tried with success in a totally unsurveyed area for various reasons. Firstly, it is by definition highly speculative, and expensive. Secondly, all prehistoric sites found so far have been found in well surveyed areas by a combination of chance and experience based on nearby land sites. Thirdly, the areas where such surveys might have been successful, namely those subject to the requirements of the USA OCS regulations, are generally not surveyed because the lessee is given the option to conduct the remote sensing surveys for cultural resources (at 150 m spacings) or to avoid the prospective site area altogether. Seismic reflectance, sub-bottom profiler, side scan sonar, and grab coring surveys are conducted in planned platform sites for safety reasons, but the required spacing is 300 m. However, the most archaeologically promising areas may have been eliminated from consideration, it being more economical to run half the transects.

The recommended search sequence has recently been initiated by Flemming in a series of staged searches off the north coast of Australia, but it is too soon to say yet whether the programme will reveal prehistoric sites or materials. In inshore areas with good bathymetric charts the early stages of search recommended above can be ignored, and work could commence with sub-bottom profiling, video,or diver intervention. In the poorly surveyed areas such as the Sunda-Sahul shelf the whole range of techniques is required. The bathymetry and coring reported by McManus provides an excellent basis for planning higher resolution surveys in Beringia.

For reasons of cost, technical limitations, and archaeological uncertainty, it is preferable to continue to develop the general search for sites within the compressed air limit of 50-60 m. At the present date it would be a speculative exercise to search for sites at a depth of 100 m using divers and submersibles, even if the financial support were available. We would be looking for shelf sites of 18,000 B.P., in an environment which was very poorly defined, and with poor knowledge of the cultural adaptations and subsistence and settlement patterns which might have existed. Such investigation would only be justified where there was a very strong reason to suppose that there had been occupation of the continental shelf within a limited area. Just such an argument does apply to the submerged land bridges of Beringia and Sunda-Sahul.

The study of Mediterranean land-sea bridges is compatible with all the suggested requirements for success. Proximity to large numbers of divers and research institutes, ideal sea conditions (moderate temperatures, minimal tide, moderate currents, high underwater visibility, low sedimentation, moderate storminess), and reasonably well-known history of eustatic sea level changes and coastal tectonism.   The two important crossings are of course Gibraltar and Tunisia-Sicily, but so far as is known to the present authors no attempt at all has been to investigate the submarine evidence for prehistoric occupation of these areas.   Waechter and Flemming (1962) reported submerged caves off the southern coast of Gibraltar which could have been habitation sites, but the caves were not investigated further, and the original work was done without consideration of the possibility of cross channel migration.

Theocharis (1970) emphasized the importance of the coalescence of the Aegean islands during the Palaeolithic and Neolithic, and the fact that this would increase contact between Anatolia and Greece.   Such an improved link would not permit migrations or contacts which were otherwise impossible, but would tend to increase the contact between East Africa and the Middle East with Greece and Europe.   The study of such an area would improve our knowledge of the mechanisms of response to changes of sea level, and provide further data on site preservation.

Bab el Mandab, at the southern end of the Red Sea, was probably never dry during the Pleistocene, but the entrance strait would have been reduced at times to an extremely narrow river-like channel, comparable with the present Bosphorus.   The rich growth of coral along most of the Red Sea coast probably reduces the chances of submarine prehistoric finds.   Exploration below the depth of present coral growth may reveal previous terrestrial and shoreline features devoid of coral.

A PROSPECTUS

The actual trend of investigations into the prehistory of the continental shelves cannot of course be predicted. We have drawn from previous experience of our Symposium participants and others to suggest the next reasonable approaches. A major technological advance in sea floor imagery or a chance find could revolutionize and redirect all that we have envisioned. However chance favours the prepared mind, and we feel that the cross-stimulation, contacts and planned collaborations deriving from the Symposium will advance this new field of research. In addition, this volume will bring the questions of continental shelf archaeology to the attention of a diversity of scholars. Human history, both in the terrestrial and submarine record, will always be of interest to ourselves.

REFERENCES

Andersen, A.S.H. (1980) Tybrind Vig, a preliminary report on a submerged Ertebolle settlement in the litle Belt *Antikvariske Studier* 4, 7-22.

Bada, J.L. and Deems, L. (1975). Accuracy of dates beyond the C-14 dating limit using aspartic acid recemization reaction *Nature* **255**, 218-219.

Barto Arnold, J. (ed.) (1978). *Beneath the Waters of Time.* Proceedings of the 9th Conference on Underwater Archaeology. Texas Antiquities Committee, Publication 6.

Bass, G.F. (ed.) (1972). *A History of Seafaring Based on Underwater Exploration.* Thames and Hudson, London, 320pp.

Birdsell, J.B. (1977). The recalibration of a paradigm for the first peopling of Greater Australia. In *Sunda and Sahul* (J. Allen, J. Golson, and R. Jones, eds). Academic Press, London. pp. 647.

Bloom, A.L. (1977). Atlas of sea level curves. International Geological Correlation Programme, Project - 61. Cornell University, Ithaca, New York. 113pp.

Boaz, N.T., Ninkovich, D., and Rossignol-Strick, M. (1982). Paleoclimatic setting for *Homo sapiens neanderthalensis.* *Naturwissenchaften* **69**, 29-33.

Bowdler, S. (1977). The coastal colonisation of Australia. In *Sunda and Sahul* (Allen, J., Golson, J., and Jones, R., eds). pp. 205-246. Academic Press, London. 647 pp.

Cherry, J.F. (1981). Pattern and process in the earliest colonization of the Mediterranean islands. *Proceedings of the Prehistory Society* **47**, 41-68.

Clark, A., Farrell, W.E, and Peltier, E.R. (1978). Global changes in post-glacial sea level: a numerical calculation. *Quaternary Research* **9**, 265-287.

Clausen, C.J., Cohen, A.D., Emiliani, C., Holman, J.A., and Stripp, J.J. (1979). Little Salt Spring, Florida: a unique underwater site. *Science* **203**, 609-614.

de Lumley, H. (1969). A paleolithic camp at Nice. *Scientific American* **220**, 42-50.

de Lumley, H. (1975). Cultural evolution in France in its paleoecological setting. In *After the Australopithecines* (Butzer, K.W. and Isaac, G. L., eds). In *World Anthropology* Series, Mouton publishers, pp. 1-24.

628 P.M. Masters and N.C. Flemming

Dixon, E.J., Sharma, G.D., Guthrie, R.D., and Stoker, S.W. (1976). Unpublished report to the US Department of Interior, Bureau of Land Management, Contract 08550-CTS-45.

Emiliani, C., Cardini, L., Mayeda, T., McBurney, C.B.M., and Tongiorgi, E. (1964). Paleotemperature analysis of fossil shells of marine mollusks (food refuse) from the Arene Candide Cave, Italy, and Haua Fteah Cave, Cyrenaica. In *Isotopic and Cosmic Chemistry* (Craig, H., Miller, S.L., and Wasserburg, G.J., eds) pp. 133-156. North-Holland Publishing Company, Amsterdam.

Fairbridge, R.W. (1961). Eustatic changes in sea level. In *Physics and Chemistry of the Earth,* Vol.14, pp. 99-185, Pergamon Press, Oxford.

Fladmark, K.R. (1979). Routes: alternative migration corridors for early man in North America. *America Antiquity* 44, 55-69.

Flemming, N.C. (1978). Holocene eustatic changes and coastal tectonics in the northeast Mediterranean: implications for models of crustal consumption. *Philosophical Transactions of the Royal Society of London (A)* 289, No. 1362,405-458.

Flemming, N.C. (1981). More on the Outer Continental Shelf: Preservation and Rescue. *Journal of Field Archaeology* 8, No.4, 505.

Flemming, N.C. and Pirazzoli, P. (1981). Archéologie des côtes de la Crête. *Histoire et Archéologie* 50, 66-81.

Hopkins, D.M. (1979). Landscape and climate of Beringia during the Late Pleistocene and Holocene Time. In *The First American: Origins, Affinities, and Adaptations* (Laughlin, W.S. and Harper, A.B., eds) pp. 15-41. Gustav Fischer, New York.

Jones, R. (1977). Man as an element of a continental fauna: the case of the sundering of the Bassian Bridge. In *Sunda and Sahul,* (Allen, J., Golson, J., and Jones, R., eds) pp. 317-386. Academic Press, London, pp 647.

Klein, R.G., (1974). Environment and subsistence of prehistoric man in the Southern Cape Province, South Africa. *World Archaeology* 5, 249-284.

Le Blanc, J.U. and Rogers, R.M. (eds) (1980). Proceedings of Gulf of Mexico Information Transfer Meeting. Texas A & M University, Department of Oceanography Technical Report 80-T-11.

Mörner, N-A.(ed.) (1980). *Earth Rheology, Isostasy and Eustasy*. Wiley, New York, 599pp.

Muckelroy, K. (1978). *Maritime Archaeology*. Cambridge University Press, Cambridge, 270 pp.

Muckelroy, K. (1980). *Archaeology Underwater, an Atlas of the World's Underwater Sites*. McGraw Hill Book Company, London and New York, pp. 192.

Newman, W.S., Marcus, L., Pardi, R.R., Paccione, J.A., and Tomecek, S.M. (1980). Eustasy and deformation of the Geoid: 1000-6000 Radiocarbon years B.P. In *Earth Rheology, Isostasy, and Eustasy* (Mörner, N-A., ed.) pp. 555-567. Wiley, New York, 599 pp.

Patterson, L. (1981). Outer Continental Shelf: Preservation and Rescue. *Journal of Field Archaeology* 8, No.2, 231-232.

Stright, M. (1980). Federal cultural resources management on the OCS: Problems and potential. Report of U.S. Department of Interior, Bureau of Land Management, New Orleans Outer Continental Shelf Office, presented at: *11th Annual Conference of Underwater Archaeology*, New Mexico, 1980.

Theocharis, D.R. (1970). Excavation on the island of Aghios Petros (Kyra Panagia). *Archeologikon Deltion*, Chronica. Thessaly, Museum of Volos 25, 271.

Tooley, M.J. (ed.) (1982). IGCP Project 61, Sea-level movements during the last deglacial hemicycle (about 15,000 years). Final report of the UK Working Group. *Proceedings of the Geologists' Association* 93, 125 pp.

Waechter, J.D'A. and Flemming, N.C. (1962). Underwater caves of Gibraltar. The Undersea Challenge, pp. 98-106. *Proceedings of the Second World Congress of Underwater Activities*. BSAC, London, 182 pp.

Wintle, A.G. and Aitken, M.J. (1977). Thermoluminescence dating of burnt flint: Application to a lower palaeolithic site, Terra Amata. *Archaeometry* 19, 111-130.

SUBJECT INDEX

Abalone, 203
Aborigines, 530, 538, 566, 584, 589
Abrasion, 31, 254, 276, 332
Accelerators, 58, 465, 472, 474
Acheulian Flint Tool, 160
Acropolis, 104
Adriatic, 335, 336
Adzes, 149
Aegean, 88, 91, 93-99, 116,
    233-266
Aerø, 143
Afar, 160
Aghios Ilios, 97
Aghios Petros, 158, 233, 236,
    248, 262
Agriculture
  origins of, 560
  spread of, 176
Alaska, 77, 158, 345, 347, 351,
    356
Alaskan Coastal Water, 366
Alder, 314, 346
Alluvial Coast, 98, 138, 141,
    161, 444
Alonnisos, 241
Amber, 298
America, 137, 347, 413
American Indian, 108, 349
Amino Acid Dating, 466
Amphibians, 430, 501
Anadara Granosa, 562
Anadyr Gulf, 378
Anadyr Strait, 379
Anchorage, 263
Antiparos, 157
Antler, 143, 155, 285
Arafura Sea, 533
Archaeological Remains, 92

Archaeological Sites, 95, 96, 102,
    105, 110
Archaeological Surveys, 542
Archipelago, 138, 157, 158, 167,
    498
Arctic, 167, 365
Arctic Assemblages, 384
Aridity, 543
Arnhem Land, 565
Arrowheads, 355
Artifact(s), 135, 141, 145, 152, 166,
    189, 202, 259, 339, 427, 428, 452,
    456, 541
Ash, 562
Ashdod, 146
Ashkelon, 146
Asia, 137, 347
Aspartic Acid, 466
Asphalt, 202
Assos, 98, 104
Asturian Culture, 568
Atlit, 122, 150
Atlantic Coast, 93
Atmospheric Circulation, 379
Attrition, 420
Aude Valley, 183
Aurochs, 181
Australia, 82, 136, 137, 139, 157,
    158, 160, 166, 529, 530, 583-597
Australoid, 594
Awls, 430
Axes, 361, 541

Backed-Blade, 340
Bahamas, 145, 155
Baja California, 192, 482
Baltic Sea, 77
Baltimore Canyon Trough, 105, 106